THE REPUBLICANS

A HISTORY OF THEIR PARTY

by MALCOLM MOOS

In this comprehensive book—the first history of the Republican Party to be published in more than thirty years — a lifelong Republican covers the first century of the G.O.P., from its humble origins to its revived modern status under the Presidency of Dwight D. Eisenhower.

Through these pages move the great leaders of the party—Abraham Lincoln, John C. Frémont, Mark Hanna, Will Hays, Theodore Roosevelt, Charles Evans Hughes, Herbert Hoover, Wendell Willkie, Arthur Vandenberg, Robert A. Taft and all the others. Here, too, are the great conventions, filled with suspense and backstage cigar smoke; the changing policies; the vital legislation; the colorful and courageous campaigns; the memorable successes and failures of the people and the politicians.

Origins, growth, ideology, character—this lively history examines them all, and much more besides. Reading this book is like having a front-row seat at every party assemblage, from smoke-filled back room to convention hall. As exciting as a political rally, as perceptive as a party boss's estimate of voting returns, as thorough as a saturation campaign, this portrait of one of America's two great parties will entice and inform everyone interested in the past, present and future of the United States.

THE REPUBLICANS

BOOKS BY MALCOLM MOOS

The Republicans

Politics, Presidents and Coattails

with Wilfred E. Binkley:
A Grammar of American Politics

with Thomas I. Cook:
Power through Purpose

with Paul T. David and Ralph Goldman (co-editors):
Presidential Nominating Politics in 1952

THE REPUBLICANS

A History of Their Party

by

MALCOLM MOOS

RANDOM HOUSE

NEW YORK

FOR OLIVER

Contents

Preface

Several factors prompted the decision to write this book. An obvious one was that no Republican party history had appeared for almost thirty years. But the real justification lies deeper.

Party beliefs in American politics, by and large, have not been confined within rigorous lines. Yet the continuity of party loyalty is a persistent fact of American life—for, by common estimate, about one-half of those who vote today identify themselves with one or the other of our major parties on the basis of hereditary allegiance.

These loyalties, however formed, are not to be taken lightly. And the political party is still the one best hope of reaching an intelligent compromise in the face of the clamor of competing pressure groups in American society. It is still the best way we have of bringing together the beliefs, policies, and leaders of those with similar outlook.

That our parties played a crucial role in the development of a young nation requires no demonstration. But the ensuing years worked many changes in American politics. The true condition of our parties has become befogged by many factors. So the purpose of this book—simply—is to take a good long look at one of our major parties, to see what it has tried to do, what it has been able to accomplish, and to try to guess where it is likely to go in the future.

Throughout the preparation of this book I have had the unfailing support and help of many friends and advisors. Initially the work was encouraged by a grant from the American Philosophical Society. I am also indebted to P. Stewart Macaulay, Provost of the Johns Hopkins University, for his help in providing funds for typing assistance. Professors Arthur N. Holcombe of Harvard University and Wilfred E. Binkley of Ohio Northern University read the entire manuscript, and to each goes my sincere appreciation for their many suggestions.

From my colleagues in the Department of Political Science at Johns Hopkins I have taken much in time and ideas. Carl Swisher, Tommy Cook, Robert Tucker, and Francis Rourke have all patiently endured me, if not my politics, and have provided countless rich suggestions.

I wish to thank my friends at the Brookings Institution for a strong assist. Ralph Goldman, immovably a Democrat, read all of the manuscript and caught many slips. And my research association with Paul David over the past few years has been particularly fruitful.

For stenographic feats far beyond the call of duty, and for a watchful eye, I owe much to Mrs. Edna L. Fulton of Johns Hopkins. Kathleen Schelhause of the Board of Election Supervisors of Baltimore City also performed strenuously in speeding the typing schedule under very trying circumstances.

My thanks go to many of my students. Stephen Hess, now on the staff of the Republican Congressional Campaign Committee, was in on the study from beginning to end. Eugene Sekulow, Instructor at Johns Hopkins, Stanley Kelley of the Brookings Institution, and W. Dean Burnham all helped in various capacities while the work was in progress.

Several persons extended courtesies, the generosity of which I have no adequate way of acknowledging. Foremost were two old friends, Lillian and J. A. Mull of Minneapolis, in whose cabin on Ten Mile Lake it was possible to write the major part of the manuscript far from the telephone's jangle. Professor James K. Pollock, Chairman of the Department of Political Science at the University of Michigan, arranged for a stimulating and rewarding term of teaching at Ann Arbor.

To the members of the press my debt is indescribably large. As the reader will see I have drawn upon Arthur Krock, Walter Lippmann, James Reston, William S. White, Roscoe Drummond, David Lawrence, Joseph and Stewart Alsop, and many others. Over the years I have also had invaluable assistance from some members of the working press who have been constantly on the wing—the late Dewey Flemming of the Baltimore *Sun* and Tom O'Neill, also of the *Sunpapers.*

Finally my gratitude is deep for a number of friends—politicians, scholars, and newspapermen—who have influenced the pages in a variety of ways. V. O. Key of Harvard University, the Honorable Simon E. Sobeloff, Solicitor General of the United States, E. W. Kenworthy of the New York *Times,* Charles A. Darsey, President of the Board of Election Supervisors of Baltimore City, Bernard Lamb, Director of Field Operations of the Republican Congressional Campaign Committee, J. Harvey Wheeler of Washington and Lee University, and my colleagues from whom I have learned much on the Republican State Central Committee for Baltimore City.

For permission to use certain material from *Presidential Nominating Politics in 1952,* I wish to record my thanks to Harold Ingle, Director of the Johns Hopkins Press.

At closer range I must record the affectionate assistance I have had from my father, Charles Moos, and my wife Tracy. From the former I have drawn upon a storage bin of Republican politics that began building when he was executive secretary to a Minnesota governor at the age of nineteen and has burgeoned continuously to this day. To my wife, the obligation is of a dual nature, first for her hard-headed criticism of the manuscript and second for keeping away three small fry while her husband was tending the typewriter.

1
Ripon Republicans

🐘

"The duty of the Board of Regents is plain," cried the Detroit *Free Press* three days after Professor Erastus Haven delivered a principal address at the first Republican state convention "under the oaks" at Jackson, Michigan. "It is promptly to remove him" for his participation in this radical "disunion convention" of "fanaticism and political charlatanry." Heated words for the take-off of a new party; yet such was the reception of the first attempt at Republican slate-making a century ago.

The paternity of the Republican party is an uncommonly complex matter. Establishing it is almost as difficult as trying to nail currant jelly onto a wall, as the Republican Roosevelt once remarked in another context. Equally complicated is the business of determining where the party was born.

Seedtime for the Republican party embraces a tumultuous period in American politics. Between the planting and the harvest so great was the disruption of our political system that the very lifeline of the Republic became imperiled.

Where was the Republican party born? Ask the man far out in Fond du Lac county, and he will tell you the place was the little village of Ripon, Wisconsin, named for the English cathedral town. There on the evening of March 20, 1854, a resolution was adopted by a group of dissident Democrats, Whigs, Free Soilers, and others. Its terms were simple: If the measure known as the Kansas-Nebraska bill, which had been introduced into the United States Senate on January 4, should pass, thus permitting Kansas and Nebraska to come into the Union with or without slavery as their constitutions might ordain, party lines were to be henceforth declared down. A new party was to be founded and organized, known as the Republican party.

Basically double-barreled in design, the Kansas-Nebraska bill proposed to repeal the Missouri Compromise of 1820 and the Compromise of 1850 which had excluded slavery from the Northwest

Territory. Thereafter the doctrine of "squatter sovereignty" was to be applied to settle the question of slavery within these territories until they entered the union as states—with or without slavery, as their respective constitutions might decide.

Few legislative measures have become more incandescent. Its passage in the Senate on March 3, 1854, slivered party lines like a stone striking a sheet of shatterproof glass.

Well beforehand, however, sentiment for a new political organization was steadily rising, and more than a few men had been casting about in search of a new party. One who figured pre-eminently in the take-off was Allan Earle Bovay, a Whig, lawyer, and old-time friend and political adjutant of the renowned editor of the New York *Tribune,* Horace Greeley.

Something of the dragon-slayer type of reformist who yearns for one long swish of the club against his opponents, Bovay associated himself with political and social movements at an early age. Land monopoly and real estate speculation in upstate New York so enraged his conscience that he became an officer of the New York Anti-Rent Association in the early 1850's. Later, on some of his frequent visits to Greeley's *Tribune* office, he apparently became enchanted with the "perfect Western Paradise," a Fourierist community, described in Warren Chase's letters, which was established in Ripon, Wisconsin, in 1844.

Bovay arrived in Ripon on October 5, 1850, looking for a home after tramping seventy-five miles from Milwaukee, where he had left his family. It was no time at all before the anti-rent barnstormer became a social and political force in this community. Early in February of 1854 he called on his old-time friend Jehdiah Bowen— a lifelong Democrat but unalterably opposed to slavery—and asked him to forsake his party. Together the two of them rode out to see Amos Loper and enlisted his support for a drive to crystallize antislavery sentiment in Ripon. Not long afterward (March 1, 1854), the three tipped their hand about what they proposed to do with a brief announcement in the Ripon *Herald*—a Democratic paper.[1] Tucked in among the advertisements was the following message:

> NEBRASKA. A meeting will be held at 6½ o'clock this [Wednesday] evening in the Congregational Church in the village of Ripon to remonstrate against the Nebraska swindle. Signed
>
> MANY CITIZENS[2]

The week following Bovay's meeting the Ripon *Herald* published, without comment, the resolutions that had been passed at the gathering. Most suggestive of the meeting's overtones was the following:

"The passage of this bill, if pass it should, will be the call to arms of a great Northern Party, such a one as the country has not hitherto seen, composed of Democrats, and Free Soilers; every man with a heart in him united under the single banner of Repeal! Repeal!"

Thereafter, the *Herald* published one additional item signed by J. Loper, T. L. Reynolds, A. E. Bovay and five others calling for a meeting of "all citizens of all parties" on March 20 to protest the Senate passage of the Nebraska bill—the "nefarious scheme," as the aroused townsmen chose to call it.

The second meeting took place in a little wooden schoolhouse which now stands on the campus of Ripon College. There on the frosty night of March 20 in a room lighted by tallow candles fifty-three men declared that they would cut loose from existing party organizations, that they would unite in opposing extension of slavery to free territory, and that henceforth they would prefer to be known as Republicans.

Bovay makes it perfectly clear that his main purpose was to persuade his fellow townsmen to the necessity of casting aside old party ties. "I set to work in the most systematic way that I could contrive, to dissolve the Whig party and all other parties opposed to the slave power, and to organize the Republican party right here in Ripon, because I was fully convinced that sooner or later others would take similar steps elsewhere, and that in a few months we should have a great irresistible Northern party, organized on the single issue of the non-extension of Slavery." And so, as Bovay has it, "we went into the little meeting Whigs, Free Soilers, and Democrats. We came out Republicans."

While Ripon has strong claim to the honor of holding the first Republican meeting, the evidence marshaled to support the homestead rights of other hamlets is also impressive. A. J. Turner suggests several, and places the first Republican meeting at Exeter, New Hampshire, on the anniversary of Columbus's discovery, October 12, 1853.[3] Turner attached little importance to the meeting at Exeter, because of the Know-Knothing (a party also known as the American party, which was anti-Catholic and anti-immigration) wave that swept over New Hampshire soon after this meeting, attracting thousands of followers. But Turner also shows, with rather convincing evidence, that there were many meetings held throughout the North both before and after passage of the Kansas-Nebraska bill, suggesting at the very least that there are many communities entitled to enter the lists as contestants for the birthplace of the Republican party.

By far the most important of the meetings held in the North, in

Turner's judgment, was that at Grand Rapids, Michigan, in March of 1854, where a city campaign ticket was nominated under the aggressive leadership of A. B. Turner, editor of the Grand Rapids *Eagle,* with Wilder D. Foster, a Free-Soil Democrat, as the candidate for mayor, and the remainder of the ticket being completed with Whigs, Free Democrats, and Free Soilers. This ticket, designated as the "Anti-Nebraska Ticket," was triumphantly elected on April 3, 1854, immediately giving strong impetus to a movement that aimed to organize an independent party in the state of Michigan.

But despite the fifty-year-long dispute over the actual place of the first Republican meeting, Ripon still appears the most likely possibility.[4]

The naming of the Republican party, like the story of its origin, is also a matter of sharp controversy.[5] Allan Bovay is generally credited with suggesting the name to Horace Greeley in a letter of February 26, 1854, in which he expressed the opinion that the new political organization ought to be called the Republican party. But some believe that since the first paper to suggest the name "Republican" was the *Daily Forest City,* published at Cleveland, Ohio, and edited by Joseph Medill, the editor of the Chicago *Tribune,* the credit ought to go to Medill.

In his celebrated editorial piece of June 16, "Party Names and Public Duty," Greeley urged the title that Jefferson had given to his followers in 1800 and that the party of Henry Clay had taken in 1831—the National Republicans.[6]

Unquestionably the name of Jefferson struck a highly responsive chord with these neophyte Republicans of the early '50's. After the slaveholders captured the Democratic party in 1844, mention of the author of the Declaration of Independence began to be soft-pedaled by the Democrats. And it was really not until 1896, when the Democratic platform reactivated the Jeffersonian tradition under the leadership of William Jennings Bryan, that the sage of Monticello was again championed with great vigor. But in the '50's Jefferson's name was the symbol of Republican hopes and aspirations, particularly since he was thought of as an original "Free Soiler," because his formula for restricting slavery by excluding it from the territories had actually been incorporated into the Northwest Ordinance. The names of both Jefferson and Washington appeared in the first Republican platform of 1856, and on the eve of the presidential election year 1860, Abraham Lincoln declared that "the principles of Jefferson are the definitions and axioms of free society."

Eight years before Horace Greeley called for a "simple name like Republican," the veteran insurgent George Henry Evans had predicted there would be a Republican party. Evans foresaw "but two parties, the Great Republican Party of Progress and the Little Tory Party of Holdbacks." But Greeley, while dreaming of a new party, had, as one writer puts it, "remained safely a Whig." [7] When his old anti-rent friend Bovay approached him early in February about his plans to organize a party out west, Greeley dodged his request for support, saying: "I am a beaten, broken-down, used-up politician, and have the soreness of many defeats in my bones. However, I am ready to follow any lead that promises to hasten the day of Northern emancipation. Your plan is all right if the people are ripe for it. . . . But remember, editors can only follow where the people's heart is already prepared to go with them."

By his own testimony, Bovay first suggested the name "Republican" to Greeley in New York City in 1852. In any case he did write suggesting this name for a new party in February of 1854 and again on June 12. Interestingly, Greeley's editorial adopting the name appeared four days later—June 16—in the daily *Tribune* and in the June 24 *Weekly Tribune*. Apparently Bovay was more than a mite unhappy that Greeley made no mention of the source of this suggestion, for his wife later spoke of his keen disappointment when he first saw Greeley's editorial.[8]

Where the first whimper in the life of the Republican party was first heard, and who christened it with the name of a party once led by Jefferson, are of course matters that need not detain us long. For the exact site is a matter of small moment. It might have been Ohio, where in February of 1854 some one hundred citizens attended a meeting in response to a notice in the Columbus newspaper, the Ohio *State Journal,* or it might have been any town from the trans-Mississippi regions to Maine. Actually the party did not spring up with such amazing speed because Ripon or Jackson led the way. It was a case of spontaneous combustion among highly inflammable material lying around everywhere in the North and West.

Half a century later Maurice C. Mumaugh, who was then mayor of the village of Lafayette, Ohio, recalled his experiences of traveling all over Ohio as a clothing salesman during the hectic debate that attended the passage of the Kansas-Nebraska act in the early part of 1854. "Everywhere I struck," recalled Mumaugh, "the windows of churches and schoolhouses were ablaze each night of the week. Everywhere the story was the same: indignation meetings to condemn the Kansas-Nebraska act." [9]

Gravely picturing the future as these embattled citizens foregathered in churches and schoolhouses throughout the land, Horace Greeley was steadily swinging his pen in a wider arc. The Nebraska bill, said the *Tribune,* "inaugurates the era of a geographical division of political parties. It draws the line between North and South. It pits face to face the two opposing forces of slavery and freedom in the national legislature, and gives birth to the most embittered sectional strife the country has yet seen." [10]

As the paper mounted its attack against the Kansas-Nebraska bill, the *Tribune* circulation spiraled ahead during the first six months of 1854, the *Weekly* jumping from 75,000 to 112,000 while the aggregate of all its editions "vaulted from 115,000 to 157,500. . . ." [11]

Far out in Wisconsin people on the frontier were reading the *Tribune,* and here as elsewhere began emitting noises that signified a rebellious mood—an executive mood that gradually suggested the emergence of a new party. "Its members came together by a magic attraction," wrote John R. Commons, "as crystals appear in a chilled solution, not one man or one set of men formed the party, though there were many claimants for the honor of first suggesting the name or calling the first meeting that used the name. The fluid solution was there, and when the chill came the crystals formed." [12]

On the very morning after the House of Representatives took up the Kansas-Nebraska bill in March, and about the time of the second mass meeting at Ripon, Wisconsin, thirty-one members held a hastily called conference. And there they decided that the only way the spread of slave power could be checked was through the formation of a political party whose major aim was to oppose the extension of slavery. Having passed the Senate on March 3, the Kansas-Nebraska bill won approval in the House on May 22 and was signed by President Pierce on May 30. Meanwhile the spadework which was to bring the new party into being was moving ahead with incredible swiftness.

While the major focus of the attack centered on the Kansas-Nebraska bill itself, criticism of Stephen A. Douglas, the "Little Giant," a Democratic United States Senator from Illinois who was the chief architect of the bill, was thrown with great heat. Horace Greeley in particular singled out Douglas for his personal target, and kept him under fire with his editorials throughout the spring and summer of 1854.

The actual motives behind the Kansas-Nebraska bill have inspired some disagreement.[13] Behind the strategy that prompted the passage of this measure was the desire of Stephen Douglas to have the route of the transcontinental railroad then being contemplated pass through Illinois rather than through Texas and the Southwest. Jefferson Davis of Mississippi wanted the federal government to select a route for the railroad that would take it through Texas and New

Mexico on its way out to California. Douglas, of course, urged a northerly route through the unorganized Territory because it would aid the development of Chicago and Illinois. And to win this prize he indulged in a bit of log-rolling. In return for Southern support of a Northern rail route and organization of this territory, the Missouri Compromise and the Compromise of 1850 were to be repealed and the question of slavery was to be resolved through "squatter sovereignty" when the territories were ready for statehood. Meanwhile slavery was to be permitted in the Territories.

Overnight the South was accused of breaking faith with the compromises of 1820 and 1850. From the moment that the Kansas-Nebraska bill was introduced in the Senate, Douglas himself commented that he "could have travelled from Boston to Chicago by the light of his own burning effigies." Until this time it had often been estimated that violent opposition against slavery was probably not embraced in the North by more than one-fifth of its inhabitants. Lincoln himself, who was to emerge in just a few years as the greatest Republican party leader of all time, was not yet committed to the opposition of slavery, and in fact was openly critical of the tactics of the abolitionists. But out of the convulsions begun by the Kansas-Nebraska act a party was formed that would drive to national power six years later pre-eminently powered in its initial stage by the issue arising from this legislation.

Reacting swiftly, state legislatures which were in session while this bill was being debated quickly made the measure a political issue by the introduction of resolutions turning it into a test question. Nine free-state legislatures were in session at the time. Resolutions of protest were adopted by five: Maine, Massachusetts, Rhode Island, New York, and Wisconsin; with the exception of Illinois, whose legislature was the only one in a free state to endorse the Kansas-Nebraska bill, the remaining states took no conclusive action.

By the time of the summer solstice, the gathering storm that had been swirling steadily throughout winter and spring seemed about ready to break. More now was in store than a series of dust storms or wind squalls: a force of great velocity seemed ready to strike.

It broke first on July 6 at Jackson, Michigan, where some 1,500 to 5,000 citizens gathered, in response to a call to consider "the late acts of Congress on the subject of slavery and its anticipated further extension." Bronson Hall, where they first met—a place long since torn down and now the site of an industrial section—although the largest in the city, soon proved inadequate for the crowd. The convention then adjourned to a grove amidst a majestic stand of oaks situated between the village of Jackson and the county racecourse, on a tract of land then known as "Morgan's Forty." This historic grove has also bowed to the steady growth of the city of Jackson, and is now covered with homes; the plentiful stand of oaks has been reduced to a few scattered trees.

Who were the people who had gathered at Jackson on this bright and rather warm midsummer afternoon with such shining hopes that theirs was a moral cause and that they had come out of a healthy respect for the desires of "free men"? They were Whigs, Democrats, and Free Soilers, accompanied by small splinter groups from many strata of American politics. Judge Levi Baxter of Jonesville was the temporary chairman at the meeting; he was an owner of several important business enterprises who had once been a Whig and later a Free Soiler, after which he was elected to the state senate by a coalition of both Whigs and Free Soilers.

Opening the meeting at 10:30 A.M. in Bronson Hall, a small building already bulging with 200 people, Baxter appointed a committee on temporary organization by naming two from each congressional district. This accomplished, the surging throng that kept trying to crowd into the hall left the temporary chairman with no alternative but to adjourn the meeting until one P.M., with the announcement that the convention would reconvene in the oak grove at Morgan's Forty.

At the grove a temporary speaker's stand had been hastily erected and here the historic events of the afternoon took place promptly. Reverend A. St. Clair offered a prayer, following which Professor Erastus Haven of the University of Michigan called upon each member of the crowd to look upon himself as a citizen with a duty to think and act for himself regardless of political party.

For 22 of the next 28 years after the adjournment of this first Republican state convention to nominate formally a slate of candidates, the Republican party stayed in power in Michigan. And out of the Jackson convention itself came six Michigan governors, six United States Senators, nineteen Congressmen, an ambassador and three cabinet officers. An enviable record for any charter group.

From its inception the convention management in this first Republican state convention shifted gears easily and confidently. David S. Walbridge of Kalamazoo, a prominent merchant of central Michigan and a well-known Whig, was nominated and elected president of the convention, following which the large mass meeting designated representatives for the four congressional districts of Michigan to choose a committee on resolutions. The chairman of this highly important committee was Jacob M. Howard of Detroit, a well-known attorney and the first Whig Congressman from Michigan. Later he served nine years as a United States Senator, and became known as the author of the Thirteenth Amendment.

Howard was already prepared with a draft of the platform that he had written weeks before the convention convened, and the resolutions committee which met to consider this draft made only slight modifications. Interestingly, there was also little discussion over a resolution designating the new name for the party as "Republican," for by this time the term "Republican" had slipped into the political parlance of many local meetings among the schoolhouses and churches of the Middle West. Moreover, the name had now received the blessings of Mr. Horace Greeley in an extensive exchange of letters between the New York editor and Jacob Howard in the weeks preceding the Jackson meeting.

Denouncing the Kansas-Nebraska act and the Fugitive Slave law, the Jackson platform began by condemning slavery as "a great moral, social and political evil. . . ." In lashing tones the Jackson platform attacked the men in control of the national government whose plans, it said, were at variance with the desires of "free men." The repeal of the Missouri Compromise, said the resolution, was a plain departure from the policy "of the fathers of the Republic in regard to slavery." Its destruction therefore would result in admitting slavery into the territories and thus sow "the seeds of an evil which like a leprosy has descended upon their prosperity with accumulated rancor, visiting the sins of the fathers upon succeeding generations."

Having brought the indictment, the Jackson platform then laid the cornerstone for what officially became known as the birthright of the Republican party:

> Resolved, that in view of the necessity of battling for the first principles of Republican government, and against the schemes of an aristocracy, the most revolting and oppressive with which the earth was ever cursed, or man debased, we will cooperate and be known as Republicans until the contest be terminated.

The actual composition of this meeting is difficult to determine. The Democratic Detroit Free Press, certainly not a friendly paper, estimated the total number at about a thousand, of whom it said nine hundred were Free Soilers and about one hundred Whigs.[14]

Extending the warm hand of friendship and speaking more objectively, the Washtenaw Whig (July 12, 1854) admitted that while there was no telling in what proportion the old parties were represented, the best horseback opinion would seem to indicate that about one-quarter to one-third were Free Soilers, while the balance was principally Whigs, with the Free Democrats in the minority.

Highly significant in the judgment of most friendly papers was the fact that the proceedings of the convention were marked by unanimity—a broad measure of agreement hardly to have been anticipated from men who had held such sharply antagonistic political views at an earlier time.

Losing no chance to sink a barb wherever possible in the weeks following the great union under the oaks, the critical Detroit *Free Press* took separate note of the fact that among those who delivered the principal "harangues" at the "disunion convention" was a professor from the University of Michigan—Erastus Haven, and it continued to ask for his dismissal. But the *Washtenaw Whig* thought otherwise. And after the Detroit *Free Press* had continued to bark away at Professor Haven—"Truly it is a strange and fool-hardy position for one who is receiving his daily bread from the state"—the *Washtenaw Whig* (now the Ann Arbor *News*) threw its full might behind the professor and the cause of academic freedom:

> We do not speak in behalf or by authority of Professor Haven [*said the* Washtenaw Whig], but in our opinion when the regents think they have no further use for Professor Haven's services they will find him with his "knapsack slung." We have no doubt but he feels that he renders a sufficient *quid pro quo* for the "daily bread" he receives from the State, and that in accepting a salary for performing specific services, he does not thereby barter away his rights as a citizen. But we know this, that he is able to take care of himself wherever he is. He is no lick-spittle to do the work of any man or set of men. He will not become the mouth piece of a corrupt administration, the apologist or defender of slavery, or the advocate of drunkenness or debauchery for any consideration. He will do *right* according to his best judgment under all circumstances. "Strange and fool-hardy," indeed! Do you measure others by your own standard, to suppose honorable men capable of descending to the vile offices which you perform for your "daily bread"? Turn your thoughts within, you vile sink of corruption, and then if you are capable of forming an honest opinion of yourself, tell us if you are the man to teach others what is their duty.[15]

Not only did the Regents ignore this brush with the Detroit *Free Press* over Professor Haven's participation in the launching of the first Republican ticket, but some years later, in 1863, this Professor of History and English Literature, who had come to Michigan in 1852 and left in 1856 to head a Methodist paper in Boston, was brought back to Ann Arbor by the Regents to become president of the University of Michigan. There he stayed until 1869, when he resigned to take over the presidency of Northwestern University, becoming known as a champion of co-education.

Nor was the episode over professorial participation the only sour note sounded by a hostile metropolitan press toward the founding of the Republican party. Again with an air of distaste the Detroit *Free Press* gibed at the appearance of Lewis Clark, "the sable gentleman," as they called him, who played the part of George Harris in *Uncle Tom's Cabin*. It admitted, however, that among the convention rostrum performers Clark "took the palm in eloquence and argument." All papers—hostile and friendly—took a keen interest in the role of this fugitive slave at Morgan's Forty. "He is as white as most men," noted one weekly, "and has an honest open countenance, but is of slight mental cultivation. His earnest, plain, unlettered statements had a telling effect upon the company."

The story of the Jackson convention is one certain to warm the heart of any party professional. It began the same day that the Kansas-Nebraska bill passed the House and the disgusted Kinsley Bingham left his seat in Congress to hurry home to Michigan. On the very same day Charles V. Deland, the Jackson editor who ran the *American Citizen,* rushed to Detroit for a hurried conference with the Whig leader, Jacob Howard.[16] Reading of these conferences bewilderedly in Kalamazoo, David S. Walbridge then sped to Detroit for a meeting with the industrialist James F. Joy, also a Whig. Thereafter, as the news of these high-level face-to-face meetings spread through Monroe, Adrian, Jackson, Detroit, and elsewhere, the necessary conditions for an interlocking movement were quickly set up. Unsuccessful in coming together for two years, the Abolitionists under the leadership of Moses McNaughton,[17] a doctor turned capitalist, agreed to disband and join with the Free Soilers under Isaac Christiancy. Overlapping all efforts to reconcile the leading parties and splinter groups in a common cause were the newspaper editors, among them Joseph Warren of the Detroit *Tribune,* Deland of the *American Citizen,* and George A. Fitch of the Kalamazoo *Telegraph*. In short, it was a mobilization in depth and strength, propelled by conviction of a deep-smoldering variety. How deep is suggested in part by the official canvass for Jackson County in the election that fall.

The Republican slate drove in to victory, with Bingham defeating his Democratic opponent with a statewide vote of 48,652 to 38,675. Imagine today a political contest in any of our competitive two-party states with the entire slate of party nominees running neck and neck as the following did for Jackson County in 1854.

Clearly, for a slate of diverse elements coming together for the first time, the uniform support of the entire ticket from top to bottom was a major achievement.

JACKSON COUNTY OFFICIAL CANVASS, 1854[18]

Vote for Republican
Candidates

Governor	2,061
Lieutenant Governor	2,069
Secretary of State	2,059
State Treasurer	2,069
Auditor General	2,061
Attorney General	2,073

Bingham, the first Republican gubernatorial nominee, had been a tremendously popular Democratic Congressman who placed his entire political future at stake to join the Free Soilers and become their nominee for the governorship in 1854. And certainly without men like Bingham, and the head of the Free Soiler party, Isaac Christiancy, throwing the full weight of their personal followings and organizational strength into the fray, the Republican movement could not have stepped off to a victory before its first birthday.

Far from the "bitter pill" that old-line Whigs wouldn't swallow or the Detroit *Free Press* judgment that the "harmonious union anticipated is a total failure," [19] the Jackson convention moved the Republican party to higher ground. One week later, on July 13, the 68th anniversary of the Northwest Ordinance, four states—Indiana, Ohio, Wisconsin, and Vermont—held state conventions that adopted the Republican banner and placed tickets in the field pledged to fight the extension of slavery. Ohio's convention, assembled at Neil's Hall in Columbus, closed with almost riotous enthusiasm upon the receipt of a telegram from Henry S. Lane, who subsequently presided over the first Republican national convention and was then presiding over the Indiana convention. "The Indianapolis convention repudiates the Nebraska swindle," cabled Lane, "and is organized for a victorious contest." [20] His prophecy was correct.

With the advent of one convention after another, new hopes were entertained that out of the convulsive reactions to the Nebraska bill an organization would emerge with the staying power to ripen into a permanent political party. No one was more elated with the results at Jackson than Greeley, and he was determined "that New York should follow in Michigan's footsteps." [21] "The name under which the opponents of the Nebraska Iniquity have enlisted for the war," he wrote in the July 11 *Daily Tribune*, "is simply REPUBLICAN, and this, we think, will be very generally adopted." Greeley hoped to hold an anti-Nebraska-bill state convention at Saratoga, New York, on August 16, and there launch a Republican ticket after the fashion of the state conventions held in Vermont and some of the

Middle Western states. Actually he entertained some aspirations himself for the New York gubernatorial nomination. But here his plans were frustrated by two factors.

William Seward, who was then in the United States Senate, was already keeping his eye on 1856 as the year he hoped to be honored with the Whig presidential nomination—a probability already being discussed in the New York *Times*. And momentarily, at least, the course of events which had followed from the anti-Nebraska meetings of the North were working to the advantage of the antislavery faction of the New York Whigs, which Seward was leading, known as "the Woollyheads." Though the Whig party quite definitely was fading—satisfactorily, from the point of view of those who wished to replace it with a new political party—the immediate position of Seward in New York, as the leader of the anti-Whig faction, was strong. Seward was friendly with Bishop Hughes of New York, and his earlier tolerant attitude toward Catholics while he was governor strengthened him with many Catholics, who already found the party of their normal allegiance stricken with schisms.

The second force that nipped Greeley's hope of entering New York into the election lists with its own branch of the Republican movement was Thurlow Weed, leader of the Whig machine in New York city. Crafty in the domain of precinct politics after tuning up his Whig machine for many years, Weed had no intentions of relegating his organization to the scrap pile. He also considered Greeley as somewhat fuzzy and unreliable whenever the crusading editor began to think of himself in terms of public office. Weed thought it highly impolitic to launch a Republican party in New York at this time because of the tidal dimensions of Know-Nothingism. The most compelling task before them, Weed argued to Greeley, was the re-election of Seward to the United States Senate that November, which in his judgment would be an inordinately difficult task. Disliked by the Know-Nothings because he favored autonomous Catholic schools while governor of New York, and had been kindly disposed toward the foreign-born (particularly the Irish) throughout his entire career, Seward was generally not at all popular with the nativist groups. Moreover, the Democrats were doing their level best to destroy Seward in the eyes of these elements. Here was another obstacle for Republicans to surmount.

How dire the threat of Know-Nothingism was to the infancy of the Republican party, not only in New York but elsewhere, is indicated by the sweeping success of the party in the elections of 1854. Throughout the East it elected numerous local tickets, and throughout the country generally it not only elected many Congressmen but it also put nine governors into office. So it happened that Weed, by convincing Greeley that many Know-Nothings were also anti-Nebraskans and would more willingly support Seward running as an anti-slavery Whig than as the nominee of a new party, finally persuaded Greeley to abandon his idea for launching a separate Republican party at the Saratoga convention in August of 1854. Instead the convention met to condemn the extension of slavery and urged the election of anti-Nebraskans.

But if Weed for purely local reasons correctly diagnosed the need to scratch a Republican ticket in the Empire state during the midterm elections of 1854, he quickly sensed the need not only for moving over to the Republican party following the Democratic defeats in the same year, but also for straining every muscle to overtake the parade. Weed shrewdly guessed that the victorious configuration of political groups which inspired the infant Republican party would outlive the Know-Nothings, the anti-slavery or Conscience Whigs, Free Democrats, and other anti-Nebraskan groups. And he soon "began to maneuver his New York Whig machine toward the camp of the future conquerors." [22]

Signs hastening acceptance of the Republican party as something more than an ephemeral upstart were unmistakably registered at the polls in a series of successive shocks to the national leadership of the Democratic party. They began with President Pierce's own native state of New Hampshire in March of 1854. Here, despite the fact that the Whigs and Free Soilers were not joined in a coalition, an anti-Nebraska house was elected in the lower chamber of the legislature. This defeat on the President's home grounds was widely acknowledged as a serious blow to his national prestige.

In April Connecticut and Rhode Island (both Democratic in the preceding election) were captured by the Whigs, while in Vermont a fusion ticket, which has been described as "Republican in everything except its name," elected its candidate for governor. Moreover, all three Congressmen who were elected were anti-Nebraska men, and the legislature that was elected, which would fill both seats in the United States Senate, was overwhelmingly anti-administration.[23] The showing of anti-slavery strength was not so remarkable in New England, where it was generally conceded to be powerful. But in a memorable campaign that August, when Iowa turned down a Democrat to elect a governor running on a Whig ticket with Free Soil endorsement, the first straw in the wind blew from the Middle West.

Two months later the October elections gave the new opposition party in Ohio all 21 Congressmen, while in Indiana, where the convention of July 13 had refused to take on the name Republican, 7 of the 11 congressional seats went to the anti-Nebraska coalition, and the same group won control of the state legislature by a majority of 14. In both Ohio and Indiana the Know-Nothing element was significant in the coalition of political forces that brought about Democratic defeat.

Farther east, Pennsylvania, largely Democratic since the time of Andrew Jackson, saw the Democratic candidate for governor decisively defeated, and the Democrats wound up holding only 6 of 25 seats in Congress. Next month—November—the might of the Empire state also gave the political pendulum a vigorous shove in the direction of anti-Nebraska elements. There Seward's anti-slavery faction of the Whigs won an impressive victory with the endorsement of a distinct anti-Nebraska party that had organized in August and backed the Seward ticket. Seward's "Woollyheads" also elected their candidate, Myron H. Clark, as governor along with Henry J. Raymond of the New York *Times* as lieutenant governor. A majority of the state congressmen elected were anti-Nebraska men, and with the dust beginning to settle following the election the evidence seemed clear that the Seward faction of the Whig party had taken command as the champion of the anti-Nebraska cause and had also established itself as the leading opponent of Know-Nothingism. Held the same day as the New York election, the November contest in New Jersey wound up with the election to Congress of four anti-Nebraska Whigs and one Democrat.

Out in the Middle West during the same month, the Whig anti-Nebraska coalition won five of nine seats in Congress, and succeeded in winning control of the state legislature. Michigan and Wisconsin, both with slates carrying the Republican party name, turned in Republican victories in each instance, the former electing a governor and three Republican Congressmen out of five, while the latter gave the Republicans two out of three seats in Congress and placed them in control of the state legislature by a slim margin.

Massachusetts, the last of the free states to hold its election in 1854, had organized a Republican party as recently as September 7, at Worcester. Here, under the leadership of Samuel Hoar, the father of Senator George F. Hoar, an organization to be known as the Republican party was formed in 1855 and nominated Henry Wilson for governor.[24] Unlike experiences in most other free states, the results for the new party in Massachusetts were distressingly poor. Candidate Wilson was badly beaten. The Know-Nothing organization, which had enrolled 80,000 members, and in the judgment of one writer had "swept the state like a hurricane in 1854, depositing upon its shores a motley collection of self-seeking politicians, religious bigots, and ignorant enthusiasts," elected all its candidates to state office, captured all eleven of Massachusetts' congressional seats, and won most of the seats in the state legislature. While the results were a rude jolt to the first trial heat of the Republican party in the Bay state, they also made it perfectly clear that political lines were hardening against the national Democratic administration. In all likelihood the next Congress would be not only opposed to the administration but also anti-Nebraskan.

While the badly mauled Democrats were taking stock of their disastrous defeat, the compelling question of the hour was: "What party will become the dominant rival of the Democratic party?" Senator Douglas, architect of the Kansas-Nebraska bill and leading spokesman of the Democratic party in the North, preferred to ignore the Republican party as a serious contender for this honor in his speech at Chicago on November 9, 1854. Struggling to uplift the broken legions of the Democratic party, he said: "The allied forces of abolitionism, Whiggism, and Know-Nothingism, have by stratagem obtained a partial victory over the Democratic party." Yet these groups would soon divide amongst themselves over "responsibilities and spoils," he said, and he bade his followers to be of good cheer; "though the skies are partially overcast, the clouds are passing away." [25]

Weighing the results of the 1854 elections, there was little assurance that the new Republican party even had novitiate status. And early in 1855 the betting odds still favored the Know-Nothings as the coming challengers of the Democratic party. In Michigan and Wisconsin the Republican party did have an organization, and also (a somewhat spotty one) in Illinois. Elsewhere, Iowa seemed about ready for a firm implantation of the Republican party, while in Ohio and Indiana the success of a fusion experiment suggested that Republican organizations were on the way.

In New England, Massachusetts had a minor party bearing the Republican name, and Maine and Vermont had fusion parties "that were for all practical purposes Republican." [26] But the Whig party, though moribund since 1852, was still wriggling successfully in a few spots and some of its leaders, particularly in New York, hoped to stage a comeback by marketing its candidates as the real champions of anti-slavery. In the face of the Whig party, whose eclipse had not quite taken place, and the Know-Nothings, whose flamboyant appeals had mowed down its opposition almost everywhere it entered the lists, Republican prospects for a national-scale party were still a shore dimly seen.

Even amidst the uncertainty of the future and the political perils of the times, however, from the gentle sloping cornfields of Illinois a voice began to be heard late in 1854 that would in a few short years become the party's greatest asset. Not yet a Republican but still a Whig, this man had retired from politics at the end of his term in Congress in 1849 to devote himself primarily to the study and practice of law in central Illinois. Here his tall, angular figure became a familiar sight among the villages and towns in the old Eighth Judicial District. Ostensibly he had "taken the veil" as far as politics were concerned, and yet from his law partner and intimate associate and biographer, William Herndon, who knew him so well, we gain a different view. While indulging a self-imposed exile from active participation in public affairs, Abraham Lincoln was following each political thread with avid interest. He may have been "buried in the law" during all these years, as William Herndon reports, "yet he was a careful student of his time and kept abreast of the many and varied movements in politics." And he did occupy the post of Whig national committeeman from Illinois from 1852 to 1856.

Set to brooding by the great controversy arising out of the Kansas-Nebraska act, Lincoln emerged from his retirement in August of 1854 determined to oppose the Kansas-Nebraska act and assure the re-election of Richard Yates of Jacksonville, who was then the representative of the seventh Illinois congressional district. Taking the stump in late August, Lincoln began speaking for Yates, and in order to rally the Whig forces he also agreed to run for the state legislature.[27]

But Lincoln was not yet ready to be pushed into the Republican party. For him the prospect of shaking loose from old party ties was not a matter to be taken lightly, and his attitude toward his friends now turned Republican seemed to be "Don't shove!" But during this trying period when the embryonic Illinois Republican party was coiled around such anti-slavery extremism as was advocated by radicals like Owen Lovejoy and Ichabod Codding, his friends helped protect him. Herndon, his law partner and political guardian, though now a Republican himself, persuaded Lincoln to leave town until after the convention, which had been called for October 4 and 5 at Springfield. This Lincoln did under the pretext of urgent business in Tazewell County, where he remained until Codding and Lovejoy disbanded the Republican convention. But soon afterward he rebuked Codding for naming him to the newly organized state central committee, and, as Reinhard Luthin has it, "the close of 1854 still found Lincoln a Whig, and still believing a Whig could be elected as a United States senator."[28] Lincoln wanted the job, but this was not yet his time. Meanwhile he kept his own counsel, carrying on just as David C. Mearns and William Herndon agree on another perceptive point about Lincoln's behavior: "He read less and thought more than any man of his standing in America, if not in the world." [29]

That fall the man who had been meditating over the congruence of events on that dreaded day, described with foreboding by America's first great politician as the day when "a moral principle and a geographical line" might coincide, found himself in Springfield, Illinois, at the opening of the Illinois State Fair on October 3, 1854. There he delivered an address appraised by Albert Beveridge as his "first great speech." Here, in the Illinois statehouse the night after Douglas had spoken, Lincoln, in shirtsleeves and without collar or a tie, climbed to the platform in the House of Representatives chamber on October 4 to present his masterly and reasoned statement underlying his convictions for free soil and free men. With Douglas (whom Lincoln had invited to be present and to answer if he chose) in the front row, he began hesitantly in a hall already steaming from an Indian-summer heat wave.

First he reminded his listeners that the Founding Fathers of the Republic had excluded slavery from the "national domain" in furtherance of a long-range policy to drive it to extinction. Wisely, moreover, they set about to cut off the source of supply by providing for the eventual curtailment of the slave trade. Thereafter, by means of a series of compromises, the early architects of our public policy sought to preserve under freedom as much territory as possible in the new land. But the Kansas-Nebraska act, warned Lincoln, violated these sacred compacts, inflicting grievous wrongs. The repeal of the Missouri Compromise was "wrong—wrong in its direct effect, letting slavery into Nebraska and Kansas, and wrong in its prospective principle, allowing it to spread to every other part of the wide world where men can be found inclined to take it. . . .

"This declared indifference . . . for the spread of slavery I cannot but hate. I hate it because of the monstrous injustice of slavery itself. I hate it because it deprives our republican example of its just influence in the world; enables the enemies of free institutions with plausibility to taunt us as hypocrites; causes the real friends of freedom to doubt our sincerity; and especially because it forces so many good men among ourselves into an open war with the very fundamental principles of civil liberties, criticizing the Declaration of Independence, and insisting that there is no right principle of action but self-interest."

The high moral tone that Lincoln sounded carried from the inception of his speech right to the end, just as it re-echoed throughout his future utterances on the question. Showing no trait of the hate-huckster, or of violent prejudice against the Southern people, he said, "They are just what we would be in their situation," and he acknowledged that they had no more responsibility for the existence of slavery than did their Northern cousins. Reluctantly he admitted the constitutional right to own slaves, and even acknowledged that he would support legislation providing for reclaiming fugitives.

Time after time the hall rumbled with applause as Lincoln moved ahead with his speech, gradually stepping up his confidence as he left behind the jerkiness and high-pitched quality his voice had when he began.

Lincoln met the issue squarely. He directed his fire at the question of extending slavery, not at the business of answering what to do with it where it already existed. Even if he had the power, he said, he would not know exactly what to do with the institution of slavery where it already existed. Then, almost as if "he were thinking out the problem before his audience," he suggested "that some system of gradual emancipation might be adopted; but for their tardiness in this, I will not undertake to judge our brethren of the South."

Concluding, he demanded the return of the Missouri Compromise. The Whigs, Free Soilers, and Abolitionists, he said, must act together, however distasteful the alliance might seem to the old-line Whigs. "Stand with anyone that stands right," he advised in calling upon fellow Whigs to join with him in asking for the restoration of the Missouri Compromise. To desert the ground upon which one found it necessary to stand "because of any company," said Lincoln forcefully, "is to be less than a Whig—less than a man—less than American." Not until twelve days later, when Lincoln repeated this speech at Peoria, was this memorable Springfield talk of October 4 reported in its entirety. In consequence it is often known as his Peoria address.[30]

Although Lincoln did not yet wear the Republican robe, his relation to the new party at this juncture bears brief comment. For one of the distinctive features in the early rise of the Republican party was its lack of a powerful assist by an outstanding leader. And the story of the spontaneous movements springing out of the hillsides and valleys in the north central states and in parts of New England bears out this contention. Obviously the idea around which a Republican party would be organized had already begun to germinate. Seedtime for the party was already long since past by the time of Lincoln's Peoria address. It was now well on into the midsummer's growing season and the new party had secured a beachhead here and there. Yet the harvest lay a long, uncertain distance ahead. But fortunate indeed for the future of the party was the re-emergence of the man who would bring it to power six years hence. And so as the tassel-tips fluttered atop the giant cornstalks of Illinois farms in late summer, 1854—six months after the introduction of the Kansas-Nebraska act—the course of history was already shaping the joining of a party with the time, the place, and the man.

The Republican party in its infancy was "an aggregation of Free Soilers, Independent Democrats, Conscience Whigs, Know-Nothings, Barn-Burners, abolitionists, teetotallers." [31] It has been suggested that the Republicans drew four Whigs to one Democrat—an estimate augmented by the judgment that "these ex-Democrats played a part out of all proportion to their numbers because they constituted a balance whose good will had to be courted assiduously by the new party combination." [32] Of course the importance of some Democrats who came into the party, like Francis P. Blair of Maryland, who was the permanent chairman of the first Republican national convention in 1856, and Kinsley Bingham, the first Republican governor of Michigan, was considerable. So quite apart from the size of the various components that were recruited under the Republican banner, of which there can be little doubt that the disintegrating Whig party was pre-eminently the chief resource, it serves our purpose here to look briefly into the background of the leading groups that were drawn to the party in 1854.

Grinding out of opposition to the policies of Andrew Jackson's first administration, and inspired by the desires of many powerful interest groups, several elements came together in 1831 in a coalition which took the name National Republican. Highly important among the components of this combination were the banking and financial interests of the East who feared that Jackson's destruction of the United States Bank and the issuance of huge amounts of paper money by state banks would be calamitous. It also embraced many Eastern manufacturers who wanted to increase protective tariff rates, and large numbers of people who were clamoring for greater federal grants in aid of internal improvement—for roads, canals, river terminals, harbors, and other public works projects.

When the National Republicans nominated Henry Clay of Kentucky as their presidential candidate in 1831, the party platform called for "adequate protection to American industry . . . a uniform system of internal improvements sustained and supported by the general government . . . the preservation of the authority and jurisdiction" of the United States Supreme Court, and a recommendation that the Senate be maintained as "pre-eminently a conservative branch of the federal government." By and large this program conformed to the tenets of the early Federalist party, which had taken so much from the policies of Alexander Hamilton. But the life of the National Republican party was hardly more than a one-night stand, largely because it was Clay's misfortune to make "one of the major miscalculations of his career in 1832 by tying his presidential fortunes to the issue of rechartering the Bank of the United States." [33] Jackson's veto of the bill to recharter the Bank won him more friends than he lost, and Clay's support certainly did not endear him to western farmers who favored cheap money. In consequence Clay's defeat in 1832 was overwhelming.

Toward the end of 1833 a new realignment of political forces within the American party system became imminent, brought to a head this time by the conflict that developed between Andrew Jackson and South Carolina over the nullification policy of the Palmetto state. With the nullification crisis bringing the nation almost to the brink of civil war, Clay broke the stalemate between South Carolina and the Democratic administration by the introduction of his famous Compromise Tariff of 1833. This measure brought about a gradual reduction of tariff over a two-year period, and since it eased tension it won for Clay the name of The Great Compromiser. But at the same time his support of the law did alienate some of his following in New England, where protectionism was very popular. It was under these circumstances that a reshuffle of political forces took place in 1834, leading to the formation of the Whig party—its label, borrowed from English politics, in a general way signifying opposition to executive usurpation of power.

The Whig combination was a curious one. It had both a Northern and a Southern wing—the Southern wing including those who sympathized with the nullification policy of South Carolina and who had discovered a certain bond of economic unity between themselves and the residents of the Ohio Valley. Thus as the new Whig party was about to emerge there existed a very curious situation, in which one of its leaders, Clay, was working for compromise with Vice-President Calhoun and the Southern nullificationists, while another leader was rapidly rising to take Clay's place as a champion of protection—Daniel Webster.

Forsaking the National Republican label because of its bad psychological implications following the disastrous defeat of 1832, the Whig party lasted about twenty years in American politics, expiring finally after the presidential campaign of 1856. Twice it enjoyed short-lived triumphs. In 1840, without at any time making its policies clear, it succeeded in electing William Henry Harrison, a military hero. Four years later the Whigs were defeated with Clay as their candidate. Turning again to a popular hero in 1848, the Whigs elected General Zachary Taylor. But "even this design failed the Whigs the next time," comments Charles A. Beard, "for their third military hero, General Scott, was utterly routed." [34]

Basically the Whig creed stemmed from Federalist doctrine, out of which its immediate predecessors, the National Republicans, had also taken their ideas. With one exception—for a brief period surrounding the compromise of 1833, when tariff rates were lowered— the Whig party continuously espoused the cause of protectionism. Daniel Webster, who started as a Federalist, and whose father reputedly, upon being taken sick in a Democratic town, "had himself removed lest he should die in such pollution," quickly emerged to become one of the great leaders of the Whig party. But, like Clay, somehow or other he always managed to have the Presidency elude him. Unsuccessful in their attempt to re-establish the United States Bank, the Whigs were always great supporters of the federal judiciary. Commerce, another subject close to the heart of the Federalists, was also jubilantly supported by the Whigs. It was the Whigs who began subsidizing mail steamers on the high seas under the Subsidy act of March 3, 1845, and it was the Whigs who, whenever they were in power, used the facilities of our Navy and the State department to promote the sale of manufactured goods in the Far East and the Pacific. And in the domain of foreign affairs it was under the Whigs that formal diplomatic relations were established with China in 1844.

But by the '50's the lamp of Whiggery as a leadership symbol was feeble. "By habit and tradition," wrote A. D. Morse, "the party was altogether unfitted for the task under consideration. Its great achievements had been in the line of compromise. The fame of its most popular leader, Henry Clay, was based in the main on his services as an architect and promoter of the compromises of 1820, 1833, and 1850." [35]

But one should still not surmise that the Whig party was dead by 1852 and that rigor mortis had already set in. Too commonly historians have written off the Whig party before its real demise without a second long hard look at the election returns. Carrying 1,110 counties to the Whigs' 434 (the smallest number ever won by the party), the Democrats did shake the spine of Whig support savagely in all sections of the country. Even New England was lost to the Whigs this time. But percentagewise one could hardly call the election a rout. The Whigs' total of 44.1 percent of the three-party total in 1852 was only 3.3 off from 1848; 4 percent less than 1844; and 8.8 percent behind 1840 when the only Whig to win a popular majority was ever elected. In popular totals the Whig vote of 1852 topped its 1848 figure by 25,000; was 85,000 above the 1844 mark; and was 110,000 over the 1840 level.

The persistence of Whig strength, despite the serious losses, should make one mighty chary about claims that the close of 1852 ended in a political vacuum into which a rising Republicanism could easily empty. It also suggests that it was not the slavery issue alone upon which Republicans vaulted to prominence as a national party. Between 1844 and 1852 the average Whig decline was 2.85 percent, and in just six of the 26 states participating in both contests were decreases registered of 5 percent or more. Two of these were in the deep South (Alabama and Georgia) and in the other four (New Hampshire, Ohio, Massachusetts, and Rhode Island) the decline may well have been induced by disproportionate population increases or shifts among Democrats.

The fallacy of tying the Republican rise completely to the slavery issue may also be illustrated by taking a slightly different tack. Certainly in New York state the Whig party "had in no sense disintegrated up to and including November, 1854." Seward led the Whigs to victory in New York on a platform that has been described as "a flatfooted anti-slavery platform, and nothing else." If the Northern "masses," as distinct from editors, clergymen, and humanitarians, were incensed at the repeal of the Missouri Compromise, writes Lee Benson, "then in any state where the Whigs were the only party favorable to the anti-slavery 'crusade' it should have won resounding victories, or at least retained its strength." Yet this result did not follow, reminding us again of the wisdom in Tolstoy's analogy between situations on military battlefields and the realm of politics. The operations on the field of battle, he wrote, are far more complex than the accounts of generals would have us believe.

Certainly much of the bizarre ballot-behavior of the period was sharply localized—a circumstance suggesting special local conditions that make one gun-shy of generalization that tends to oversimplify. In New York, after some careful steering "toward the camp of the future conquerors," the Republican party stepped forth under the firm grasp of the same men who had dominated the Whig party. And in broad measure Whig and Republican organizations both championed similar principles and drew the bulk of their support from the same sources. Elsewhere this was not always true. Nor was the combustibility of the anti-slavery issue the same in all paths of the

Republican advance. But everywhere without exception in the fulminating fifties, men were commonly concerned with the struggle over who would be the rulers and who the ruled in the face of swift social and economic change. It was this feeling that led to the spate of splinter parties from which America has long since retreated, and it was these economic and social forces that directed the coming of a new major party.

Beyond the Whigs there were several other parties and movements from which the Republican party drew its ideas; the Abolitionists, of course, were an important source of energy. In 1831 their preeminent spokesman, William Lloyd Garrison, launched his campaign against slavery, denouncing it as sinful and immoral. Twelve years later a movement was afoot that gradually brought together a combination known as the Free Soil party. Three times the Free Soil party presented presidential candidates, with its most spirited start coming in 1848. That year its fortunes were boosted by the passage of the Wilmot Proviso "that neither slavery nor involuntary servitude" should ever exist in any territory that the United States might obtain from Mexico. Saddened by the action of the Whig national convention in voting down a resolution supporting the Wilmot Proviso, Henry Wilson of Massachusetts led a revolt of the so-called "Conscience Whigs," many of whom supported the Free Soil presidential candidate of that year, Martin Van Buren, who polled 294,-000 out of some 2,870,000 popular votes.

Attracting farmers, small merchants, mill workers, and followers generally who upheld the equalitarian ideas expressed in the Declaration of Independence, the Free Soil party appealed to many residents of New England who looked upon slavery with deep moral misgivings. The relation of this group to the nascent Republican party is best described by Binkley: "On the election map for 1848 can be perceived faintly the geographical pattern of the future Republican party in the vote for the Democratic Free Soil candidate." [36] The Free Soil party, the first third party to carry any counties since 1832, captured three in New England, seven in the Middle Atlantic states, and twenty-one in the East North Central states.

Splinter groups that never entered candidates on a national level also aided the development of America's first great third party. Two whose discontent led their followers to break with the Democratic party and subsequently take up with the Republican party in large numbers were the Barnburners and the Locofocos. The Barnburners, located largely in New York, were rural residents whose revolt against the Democratic party was primarily directed against self-seeking promoters—contractors and politicians who desired to build

canals in remote and distant communities despite a mounting indebtedness. Actually, the Barnburners organized their opposition
around a base that was larger than simply an anti-canal protest.
They were essentially reformists, and were against what they conceived to be the greed of predatory interests.

In some degree the metropolitan counterpart of the Barnburners
was another faction of the Democratic party known as the Locofocos, whose grievances, like those of their country cousins, were
directed against the controlling element of the Democratic party in
New York state. The "locofoco" was a self-lighting cigar (made
with a match composition at the end) invented about 1834. The
name of the organization is said to have sprung from a meeting in
New York city when the Tammany faction of the Democratic party
blew out the lights at a political meeting and the only light thereafter
was from cigars and locofocos.

The Locofocos were an anti-monopolist group who favored hard
money. And they bitterly resented the uncontrolled issues of paper
money which led to a sharp inflation, as a result of Jackson's policy to
shift the deposit of federal funds from the Bank of the United States
to designated state banks. Some of these, known as "pet" banks,
ultimately abused their positions as federal depositaries, and their
issuance of paper currency created an inflation which quickly aggravated the distressed economic conditions that beset New York
city in 1836 and 1837. In consequence of these inflationary policies,
and a small wheat crop, the city of New York had several serious
bread riots in those two years. And elsewhere, of course, the instability of currency and depreciation of bank notes issued by various state banks imposed a serious hardship on working men,
small shopkeepers, mechanics, and low-paid public-office holders.

Unlike that of the Barnburners, the Locofocos' influence reached
to other parts of the country, where they stepped forward with strong
organizations. In Ohio, the Locofoco faction controlled the Ohio
legislature in the late '30's. And even as late as 1851 Locofocoism
"was still strong enough to fasten into the Ohio constitution of 1851
the double liability of owners of bank stock so securely that it could
not be repealed until 1935." [37] On the ballot the Locofocos took
the name of the Equal Rights party, though they were more commonly known as Locofocos. Eventually a substantial part of the
Locofocos melted into the Democratic party, but, as Woodrow Wilson
once remarked, "it was rather because they had drawn it to themselves than because it had absorbed or defeated them." Far from
satisfied with the financial policies of the Democratic party, however, large numbers of Locofocos never did merge with the Demo-

crats again, and many were attracted to the Republican standard when it was raised aloft in 1854 and '55.

Most difficult of all to assess was the Free Democratic faction, sometimes called Free Democracy. Among dissident anti-slavery Democrats there was a small third party known as the Independent Democrats. The latter favored the Wilmot Proviso in 1846 to exclude slavery from any new territory acquired from Mexico, and it fought the Compromise of 1850. Particularly objectionable to the Independent Democrats was the Fugitive Slave act, under the Compromise of 1850, which provided for the payment of a five-dollar fee to the federal commissioner if he set a fugitive slave free, but gave him ten dollars if he returned the Negro to the claimant. Almost immediately after the introduction of the Kansas-Nebraska act in January of 1854, two anti-slavery Democratic Senators (Chase and Sumner) joined with four anti-slavery members of the lower house to publish an extremely effective denunciation of the Kansas-Nebraska bill in several newspapers. Bearing the title "Appeal of the Independent Democrats in Congress to the People of the United States," this message exhorted people to save the West from a policy that would make it into "a dreary region of despotism, inhabited by masters and slaves." It indicted the Kansas-Nebraska bill as "a gross violation of a sacred pledge; a criminal betrayal of precious rights"; and declared it to be "part and parcel of an atrocious plot to exclude from a vast unoccupied region immigrants from the old world and free laborers from our States."

The appeal to independent Democrats ignited protests among Democratic groups throughout the North. Unquestionably it was a strong influence in polarizing the political opinion that helped lift the Republican party onto the stage at Ripon, Exeter, Grand Rapids, Jackson, and elsewhere. Moreover, it also enriched the new party by bringing into the ranks Democratic leaders who were strong assets.

In the flickering firelight of the fifties, as the nation watched some of these protest movements burn out and others strive for one mighty heave to bring them to power, the rumblings of a more riotous reshuffling of political forces seemed unmistakable. In 1852 the defection of the Whig vote in the South made it clear that sectional lines of cleavage were becoming so acute it was no longer possible to have a Northern and Southern wing of the Whig party pulling together in harness. And with the defection to the Democrats of such prominent Southern Whig leaders as Stephens and Toombs of Georgia, there could no longer be any doubt that Southern loyalties were overriding party loyalties, that the Whig party would henceforth find it difficult to operate as a national party, and that it was beginning to be a truncated affair with even its Northern wing in a bad state of repair.

Meanwhile, the confused political situation of the times was revealing itself convincingly in the multiplication of political parties. Indicative of this were the Connecticut elections of 1854 and 1855, where twenty-three political parties entered candidates. Surging ahead as the most menacing challenger to the Democratic party was the Know-Nothing movement—a nativist movement based upon opposition to the foreign-born, and pledged to the exclusion from public office of all but the native-born.

While opposition to the foreign-born had proclaimed itself from time to time in the earlier course of our history, the Know-Nothing movement of the 1850's carried with it an additional ingredient— an aggressive anti-Catholicism. In some areas the Know-Nothing, or American party, as it was frequently called, started quite independently of any motivation inspired by bigotry or persecution of the foreign-born. The movement in these instances was first directed against the sinister manipulation of newly arrived immigrant voters by corrupt city bosses, and was originally designed to wrest control of some of our major metropolitan areas from the hands of those whose stewardship of public office had carried it to such low depths. But it was an easy matter to seek and find a scapegoat under the unsteady political conditions that prevailed in the 1850's, and the agitators of the Know-Nothing movement did this at every turn. Typical was the strategy employed when the Whigs became demoralized following the crushing defeat they suffered at the hands of Franklin Pierce in the landslide of 1852. Responsibility for the rout of the Whigs—so ran the Know-Nothing explanation—could be laid at the doorstep of the foreign-born. Later, the appointment of a Catholic as Postmaster General by President Pierce accentuated this feeling, and with the deaths of Clay and Webster coming at this time, just when the Whigs needed men of stature at the helm more than ever, the bolt of the Whigs to the Know-Nothing party began in earnest in many communities across the nation. (Clay died in 1852, on the day General Winfield Scott accepted the Whig presidential nomination, and Daniel Webster died that October, without saying whether he would support Scott for election.)

Graven on the face of the Republican party as it began to take shape in the early years of 1854-55-56 are the marks of these many political movements which characterized the period stretching from mid-passage of Jackson's first administration to the eve of the Civil War. Some of these movements, no doubt, hardly deserve to be digni-

fied by the term "party," yet they were not without influence in shaping the course of things to come. But, far too often in assessing the
role of these competing groups, the slavery issue has received too
great an emphasis, despite its great importance in bringing several of
these movements together. The slavery issue galvanized the party
into action, but we should be doing serious disservice to the facts if
we overlooked the significance of liberal capitalism as a cohesive
force in bringing together the elements that formed the Republican
party and giving it the staying power to last out more than one or
two political engagements.

The Republican party, to be sure, drew heavily upon the Whigs,
for both its followers and its doctrine. But while the Whigs steadily
advocated measures to stimulate business endeavor, supported tariffs
and various forms of bounties and internal improvements, and
tended to oppose the extension of government action aimed at the
regulation of business, they also divided along monopolistic and anti-
monopolistic lines. Most groups among the Whig party, says William
Carleton in his brilliant analysis of the Van Buren era, "represented
frustration." [38] Thus the National Republican wing of the Whig party
which had such a brief life span met disaster on every hand as "a
political aristocracy gave way to political democracy, and as economic monopoly gave way to economic freedom." And the Southern
Whigs—men of large agricultural holdings—"in alliance with men of
industrial property in the North, were unwittingly hastening the industrial revolution which they disliked, and were contributing to their
own ultimate ruin." Only one small faction of the Jackson-Van Buren
period was destined to emerge triumphant, and this group remained
definitely a minority element all through the period: the Seward-
Weed-Greeley-Stevens Whigs. William H. Seward, then United
States Senator from New York, had been elected governor of the
Empire state in 1838 with the active support of Thurlow Weed, a
rising political leader. Weed, who assumed the editorship of the
Albany *Evening Journal* in 1830, not only ran a newspaper that was
destined to become highly influential nationally, but also came to
head up a powerful New York political machine. Thaddeus Stevens,
of course, hailed from Pennsylvania, where he had been elected to
Congress as a Whig in 1848, and later became one of the leading
Republican Radicals of the House during the Civil War and early
Reconstruction period.

This combination—largely anti-Masonic in its origins—had wel-
comed both the political democracy and the political methods of the
Jacksonians, and had long been hostile opponents of Clay, the United
States Bank, and the economic philosophy of monopoly capitalism

espoused by the National Republican party. Welcoming and encouraging the coming of liberal capitalism and "the underlying economic forces working in its behalf," this group was joined by the liberal capitalist wing of the Democratic party in the 1850's—Preston King, William Cullen Bryant, and many others whose views were well reflected at the time by the New York *Post*. Unheralded by the prophets of a new creed, the small group making for the advance of a liberal capitalism was pushing forward its ideas in keeping with the advance of the industrial revolution. One of the dramatic consequences not yet recognized was the role of these men and ideas as a cohesive force in drawing the Republican party together. And so the small minority group of Whigs, of which the chief spokesmen were Seward, Weed, Greeley, and Stevens, along with such liberal capitalist Democrats as Preston King and William Cullen Bryant, acting as members of the Republican party in the late '50's and early '60's, "were to raise the flood tide." And what was the result? "The revolution of liberal capitalism was the opening of the West, the building of the transcontinental railroads, the passage of the Homestead Act, and the bringing of the national banks to mainstreet." [39] Within this revolution, of course, were the elements that would one day give rise to a new monopoly capitalism—but this is a matter that will engage our attention later.

That the Republican party was not simply a retreat of the old-line Whigs is also evident, though the myth dies hard, from a look at the ideas it took over at its first national convention. In its first national platform of 1856, the Republican party adopted much of the program of the Free Soilers, whose membership had embraced the Barnburners as well as the seceders from the Democratic party, and its championing of the homestead idea gave it one of its most formidable campaign weapons. "So potent was it [*the homestead idea*] in fact, that the party was even more a homestead than an anti-slavery party," writes Wilfred Binkley, while John R. Commons puts it even more strongly: "Only because slavery could not live on 160-acre farms did the Republican party come into conflict with slavery." [40]

Where did the idea of the homestead—160 acres free to every man—come from? It was inspired by an idealistic view of the public domain given expression by the vigorous editor George Henry Evans, who was editor of the *Working Man's Advocate* in 1829 and an influential thinker of the Working Man's party. Gradually, as these ideas began to shake down "into the individualistic idealism of American labor reform in 1844," agitation for a homestead law began to be spelled out in specific proposals. Thereafter the *Working*

Man's Advocate, which had now changed its name to *Young America,* started printing pamphlets called "Vote Yourself a Farm," and circulated them by the hundreds of thousands. It was at about this time—1845—that Horace Greeley began to notice the homestead clatter, and wrote an editorial speaking of the homestead scheme which said in part:

> Its objects are, the securing to every man, as nearly as may be, a chance to work for and earn a living; secondly, the discouragement of land monopoly speculation, and the creation of a universally landholding People, such as has not been since the earlier and purer days of the Israelite commonwealth. . . .[41]

While Greeley was not yet prepared to give it unqualified endorsement, noting that "the consequences of such a change must be emense [*sic*] . . . we cannot see it lightly condemned and rejected," five months later he was committed to its support and placed himself four-square on the measure by writing:

> The freedom of the public lands to actual settlers, and the limitations of future acquisitions of land to some reasonable amount, are also measures which seem to us vitally necessary to the ultimate emancipation of labor from thralldom and misery. What is mainly wanted is that each man should have an assured chance to earn, and then an assurance of the just fruits of his labors. We must achieve these results; we *can* do it.

Greeley, having felt the pinch of misery at the age of eleven, during the Panic of 1819, when his father had to abandon farming to become a day laborer, carried a passionate interest in human welfare throughout his life. Apprenticed to a printer at a tender age, he quickly became aware of the wage-earner problems in New York city. And years later, when he was editor of the New York *Tribune,* he did not hesitate to tell a convention of abolitionists, hell bent upon inciting him to riot over slavery, that he was much too aware of the wage slavery in New York at the moment to be deeply concerned with the black slavery of the South.

Greeley, of course, became not only one of the outstanding editors of the times but his *Tribune* and more particularly the weekly edition, circulated both in the East and, as we have seen, far out into the hinterlands of the West, became "pre-eminently the journalistic organ of the emerging Republican party." However distasteful it may be for some Republicans to discover today, Greeley, who so actively influenced early Republican doctrine, strained many of his ideas from his early recollections of the Working Man's party. And none of these had a greater impact on supporters who flocked to the

GOP than the homestead idea. Not unnaturally many Eastern manufacturers, who feared their labor forces might be dissipated by the
lure of free land and they would be forced into the position of
paying high wages, were uneasy or downright hostile to the emerging
Republican party. With this in mind, many manufacturers shifted
from the Whig to the conservative wing of the Democratic party,
where they prepared to wait and see what might happen as the result of the distant echoes rolling out of Ripon, Jackson, Springfield,
and other points located deep in the American heartland, as well as
from Exeter, Worcester, and other towns of rock-ribbed New England.

Greeley, taking some of his ideas from the transcendental philos-
ophers of New England, and others from his intimate experience
with the social and economic problems of the working wage-earner,
combined them and, as John R. Commons says: "In 1854 the Republican party built both into a platform." [42]

Ascending rapidly all the while as one of the balustrades of the
American economy was the western farmer, of whom the typical
representative was a member of the middle class. Indubitably "the
crowning achievement of middle class agrarianism in national politics was the Homestead Act." [43] By and large the upward surge of
the Republican party was inspired and animated by a middle-
class movement, comprising both farmers and small businessmen.
"Quite naturally the little-capitalist way of thought had taken possession of the upper Mississippi Valley employers, wage earners and
farmers alike providing a common pattern of Republican thought
and feelings from the very beginning." [44] Here the aim and objective
was to insure that each member of society should have an equal
opportunity to develop such faculties as he might possess, with only
the sky as a ceiling. Obviously a homestead act, such as the measure
passed in 1855 through the combination of the emerging Republican
groups of the East and the Republican prairie politics of the West,
could hardly be a deterrent to the unlimited opportunity to get
ahead. Here was an appeal not to be denied.

Too young yet for anyone to see what the steady upsurge of
liberal capitalism combined with the winds of protest would ultimately produce by the way of a design for a party philosophy, the
Republican party turned into the year 1855 with a proud head. But
its spokesmen were not unmindful of the perils farther down the
road, and of some immediately at hand, such as the Know-Nothing
menace, which threatened to disintegrate the party. In New England native urban working men had expressed antipathy for the incoming waves of Irish immigrants for over a generation, and in the

agrarian regions the feeling against Catholics was turned into a warm reception for Know-Nothingism. How strong the feeling was against the foreign-born in Massachusetts is well illustrated by the amendment of the state constitution in the late 1850's denying voting privileges or public-office holding to all naturalized citizens until two years after their naturalization.

Also a threat to the ballot-box fortunes of the Republican party was another movement—the Temperance Crusade. The more fanatical zealots, who rummaged around smashing whiskey kegs and decrying the sale of liquor and beer as criminal, struck a responsive chord in some sectors of New England, and worried Republican party leaders, who were fearful that it would keep the Germans of the Middle West from joining the new party. Long persuaded of the virtues and joys to be derived from the mild consumption of schnapps and beer, German settlers took a dim view of those puritanical critics who wished to prohibit the daily consumption of spirits.

But with it all—the threat of competitive movements, the difficulty of getting any new political party traveling on high dry ground, particularly in the unique absence of any outstanding party leader to take command at the formative stage—the Republican party picked its way ahead, carrying counties "wherever the census had indicated a preponderance of New England stock. . . . Persistent in establishing free schools in their communities, along with literary societies, lyceums, and libraries, these Yankees were mainly responsible for that high degree of literacy that long distinguished Republican counties." And out in many of the distant reaches of America it was Greeley's *Tribune* that "provided the political resources with which Republicans out-argued their opponents in the country church yard, the village store and the rural society."

In broad stretches of the Middle West, of course, no step-up transformers were needed to carry the voice of Republicanism. For the tone of editorial outposts here was unmistakably strident, uncompromisingly a call to action.

But curiously, there were many signs that the victors-to-be had only a dim realization that they were in possession of a new party. Rarely did the name Republican creep into the newspaper stories of the campaign, the more common reference to the ticket being "anti-Nebraska." And summing up the successful election late in 1854, the *American Citizen* made not the slightest hint that the new party should take a bow. "The verdict," said the *Citizen,* very simply, "is anti-Nebraska. The result cannot be claimed as a party victory —it is not a Whig, or Republican triumph. Whigs, the Republicans, and the Know-Nothings united their strength in the great struggle." [45]

And so the road ahead held many uncertainties as Republican enthusiasts took their battle stations early in 1855. But an asset as yet unrecognized was one that would soon be serving them in good stead. "The Republicans were born with the secret of management," writes Roy Nichols.[46] They were not long in setting up a centralized party that was ready to do business.

The Time, the Place, and the Man

Twice in one hundred years Congress has been unable to organize. In both deadlocks, Republicans were at the very heart of the storm center. The more recent stalemate was solely a family quarrel that developed in December of 1923 because an insurgent group of Republicans momentarily bucked the regular Republican organization by refusing to go along on the choice of a Speaker. But the first and more titanic struggle that tied up the House occurred in December of 1855, when the newborn Republican party began a knockdown fight to outpoint the Democrats in a bitter struggle to elect a Speaker. For nine weeks and 133 ballots the House was in labor while the nation waited for the birth of the Speaker—an event which finally took place on February 2, 1856.

When the 34th Congress convened on December 3, 1855, Democratic strength in the House had fallen from 159 to 83. Of the 154 opposition Representatives, practically all were anti-Nebraskans. Half of the anti-administration forces were called "Americans," later known as Know-Nothings, the nickname given them by Horace Greeley, while most (about 40) of the other half were Republicans, along with a number of Representatives who called themselves Independents. Know-Nothing strength embraced many shades of opinion and came largely from New England, where in Massachusetts, for example, the Americans were able to elect a governor in 1854, every state senator, and all of the state's Congressmen.

Though thoroughly trounced (except for Pennsylvania), in the recent elections, the Democrats were little downcast as the new Congress convened. Declaring themselves duty bound to defend every class in all sections of the country, they proposed for Speaker Richardson of Illinois—a protégé of Senator Douglas. Joshua Giddings of Ohio was chief spokesman for the anti-Nebraska forces.

At the outset the Democrats could only be certain of giving Richardson 74 votes out of 225, but they were reasonably confident that the inability of their opponents to agree on a nominee would play into their own hands. Then, with most of the Republicans supporting one or the other of two Know-Nothing candidates, the seesaw contest went on for 59 ballots. Finally, after Congress had struck all candidates except the two highest on December 15, and had then engaged in weary weeks of balloting, Nathaniel P. Banks, a Know-Nothing from Massachusetts, was elected with 103 votes. His election with almost the solid support of the Republican contingent signified a Republican triumph of no mean dimension. Heartened by the success of their political stratagems, which brought a Speaker of their choice to power, the Republicans moved on to Pittsburgh in a jaunty mood for their first national meeting. At last they were ready to organize machinery for a national political party.

Bearing a January 17 dateline, the call for the first national meeting was issued by the National Republican Association—a club that had grown up in Washington under the guidance of Louis Clephane. It read:

> In accordance with what appears to be the general desire of the Republican party, and at the suggestion of a large portion of the Republican press, the undersigned chairmen of the state Republican committees of Maine, Vermont, Massachusetts, New York, Pennsylvania, Ohio, Michigan, Indiana, and Wisconsin, hereby invite the Republicans of the Union to meet in informal convention at Pittsburgh on the 22nd of February, 1856, for the purpose of perfecting a national organization and providing for a national delegate convention of the Republican party at some subsequent day, to nominate candidates for the presidency and vice presidency to be supported in the election of November, 1856.
>
> *Signed*   A. P. STONE, Ohio
>   J. Z. GOODRICH, Massachusetts
>   DAVID WILMOT, Pennsylvania
>   LAWRENCE BRAINARD, Vermont
>   WILLIAM A. WHITE, Wisconsin

To Salmon P. Chase of Ohio go many laurels for making this "call" a reality. Chase's appeal to the Independent Democrats to stand up and be counted against the Kansas-Nebraska bill had come at a fortuitous time for the Republican movement in the spring of 1854. Now governor of Ohio, he was ready to provide a second lift by calling for a truly national party organization.

Brushed by presidential ambitions, Chase saw the possibilities for a new party in the very cohesion of forces that brought about his election as governor of Ohio, and his confidence surged. Writing to Governor Kinsley S. Bingham of Michigan, he advised: "The elements required for the presidential election have been harmonized by my election in Ohio, and without that harmony I could not have been elected. They would be harmonized in a much greater degree in a presidential election." [1]

Assembling at eleven o'clock in Lafayette Hall on George Washington's birthday, 1856, the first national conclave of Republicans was called together by Lawrence Brainard of Vermont. Representing sixteen Northern and eight Southern states, the convention membership was composed largely of men past middle age. Several well-known political figures apparently failed to attend because, says George Julian (a representative from Indiana who chronicled the meeting carefully), "they thought it wiser to wait upon the teaching of events." Many prominent leaders in attendance took little part in the proceedings, possibly for the same reason. But five of the nine Free Soilers who held such a strategic position of power in the House were at the convention, and they were among its most energetic workers.

High honors for the inspirational voltage that charged the meeting went to Owen Lovejoy of Illinois, who was asked to open the proceedings with a prayer. Lovejoy began by calling upon God to enlighten the mind of President Pierce and turn him from evil ways. And if this was not possible, he asked the Sovereign Disposer "to take him away" so that an honest and God-fearing man might fill his place.[2]

Warming to his task, Lovejoy, whose brother achieved martyrdom after his murder by a mob at Alton, Illinois, in 1837, for publishing an anti-slavery paper, pledged himself to avenge bleeding Kansas, threatening: "If I use Sharp's rifle, I will shoot in God's name. I am for war to the knife, and the knife to the hilt, if it must be so."

Greeley, an obvious favorite of many present, was called for again and again by the audience. But his remarks were disappointing. In temperate tones he observed that "friends" in Washington counseled caution for the Republicans. Later, explaining himself in the *Tribune* in apparent defense against criticism directed at his speech, he remarked that he did not want to antagonize many good men who had joined the Know-Nothing, or American, party. But this guarded attitude antagonized a long-time favorite among anti-slavery leaders, Joshua Giddings of Ohio, who was not at all happy with the suggestion that the convention exercise restraint. And it probably displeased a majority of the convention.

Francis P. Blair of Maryland was selected president. Backed by a career that had made him a very popular figure, he was possibly the oldest man in the convention. A distinguished journalist and political leader of national reputation, Blair had been a soldier in the war of 1812 and at one time was a close confidant of Andrew Jackson. His separation from the Democratic party came in 1848.

In his remarks to the convention Blair expressed the hope that its recommendations would be considered as the platform of his Southern friends. But apparently he misjudged the aggressive reform spirit of the convention, for his suggestion that the Compromise of 1850 (abandoning the Missouri Compromise) held the greatest hope for the slavery controversy was decidedly off-beat at the Pittsburgh meeting. George Julian remarked: "The convention was not beating a retreat to the finality of platforms of 1852, but marching in the opposite direction." [3]

Its unity rumpled a mite because of disagreement over the proper attitude to take toward the Know-Nothings, and toward the cautious course advocated by Blair, the Pittsburgh meeting was not all harmony. But threatening tension never became menacing, and uneasiness with the Know-Nothing problem was somewhat abated by a telegram from Philadelphia, where the national council of the American party was then in session. Bearing the dateline February 22, 1856, the cheering message read:

> The American party is no longer a unit. The National Council is gone to pieces. Raise the Republican banner, the North Americans are with you.
>
> *Signed* THOMAS SPOONER

This dispatch brought loud applause. The next day, following a long string of ten-minute speeches that outlined the progress of antislavery policies in various parts of the country, the convention adopted a recommendation that set up the first national machinery of the Republican party. Under it a national committee was authorized, composed of one member from each state, and E. D. Morgan of New York became the first chairman. The national committee was empowered to make additions to its own organization to fill vacancies, and to make arrangements for a national nominating convention to be held in Philadelphia on June 17. Under the rules adopted for the composition of the convention, each state was entitled to twice as many delegates as it had representation in Congress.

In its policy declarations, the Pittsburgh convention proclaimed its stand vigorously. It called for the abandonment of slavery in territories "now consecrated to freedom," and a determination to resist "by every constitutional means the existence of slavery in any of the territories of the United States." To bleeding Kansas the convention pledged its full weight in favor of the immediate admission of that Territory to the Union as a "free sovereign and independent state."

Finally the convention declared its firm intention of overthrowing the national administration, which it censured for having shown itself "to be weak and faithless. . . ."

The Pittsburgh convention gave a fresh impetus to the party by pursuing a course of radicalism rather than one of "timidity" and "hesitation." By common agreement of its participants, the convention was a success, though perhaps many questioned the validity of Mr. Greeley's remark in the *Tribune:* "Its moral and political effect will be felt for a quarter of a century."

One month later—March 27—the Republican national committee held its first meeting in Washington, together with some thirty Congressmen from both Houses, who represented many shades of the political prism—Republican, American, and those members of the American party who were described as more Republican than American.

Still threatening to demobilize the Republican movement, the Americans once again were cast in a role that had so long aggravated the political bewilderment of the times. They agreed that it was desirable to unite and make a call for a national convention, but they objected to use of the name Republican. Moreover, some Americans objected to the stand of Seward and other Republicans who favored the admission of Kansas into the Union as a free state, insisting that the repeal of the Missouri Compromise in 1854 was all they wanted at the moment. In deference to American party pressure, the call as finally issued omitted the name Republican and was addressed simply to the people of the United States without regard to past political differences or divisions. But the construction of the call also made clear that it was directed to people who favored the admission of Kansas as a free state. Each state was invited to send three delegates from every congressional district, and six delegates at large.

Pointing toward their June convention that spring, the Republicans found the campaign weather to their liking. While the Democrats attempted to divert public attention to issues beyond our borders—to Cuba, Central America, or our diplomatic relations with Great Britain—Republicans played up home affairs. And in all their efforts to make "Republican" the byword of anti-slavery opposition, fortune smiled benignly on their cause. "Time and again the new movement was saved from collapse by the imprudence of southerners."

By June the Kansas Territory was approaching a state of civil war. On several occasions men who were opponents of slavery were murdered by Southern sympathizers. Incitement to physical violence, of course, was encouraged and financed by both sides—by the abolitionists and by Southerners. But when the "border ruffians" from Missouri scampered into Kansas to stuff ballot boxes on Election Day, the Republicans were presented with a weapon of great striking force. The border warfare that followed this invasion made "Bleeding Kansas" symbolize the dastardly deeds of the slavery forces. And it was at the avenging of these wrongs that the Republican strategists fired their propaganda. At the same time, help also came from another quarter—from the operation of the Fugitive Slave law. As we might well expect, the administration of this law led to a number of incidents that tugged hard at the heartstrings of a populace that was reading *Uncle Tom's Cabin,* or witnessing its dramatization on the stage.

Meanwhile, by the time the anti-Nebraska Congressmen caucused on April 14, 1856, and resolved to bring about the immediate admission of Kansas as a free state, another pot was boiling: not over the issues in this instance, but about presidential candidates. Already several had hoisted their flags, and their advance scouts were hard at work.

Among the contestants Salmon P. Chase looked like a front-runner. His popularity was effectively demonstrated in the outstanding Ohio Republican victory in 1855 when he was elected governor. And Chase had two other assets: he was instrumental in upholding the plans for the Pittsburgh convention when the project was about to collapse, and in the jockeying for better position between the Republicans and Know-Nothings it was Chase who sustained the Republicans at the critical point. But his stature among German voters, which he himself thought high, was considerably strained by his close association with the American party.

Early in December, 1855, the pre-convention campaign to move Chase up front started in earnest, though Chase had his eyes on the Presidency well ahead of this time. By late February, when Chase's scouts reported little presidential politicking from the Pittsburgh convention of February 22, they were still hopeful that the Ohioan's nomination prospects were reasonably promising.

Commanding greater national prestige than Chase was William H. Seward, governor of New York and a man who numbered among his resources the support of the then master of New York city machine politics—Thurlow Weed. Standing in Seward's favor, as Republican strength began to overtake the earlier lead of the American party, was the fact that he was untainted by Know-Nothingism. In fact he was quite possibly its leading enemy. But his opposition to

Know-Nothingism also hurt his candidacy in New England, where sentiment in favor of the American party was strong, and the same party was disturbed by his reputation for assiduously cultivating votes among the recently naturalized citizens of New York City.

Another contender, John McLean, Associate Justice of the United States Supreme Court, was the leading candidate of the conservative forces among the anti-slavery groups. Once a Democrat and later a Whig, McLean was nudged along by his supporters with the argument that he was the strongest available candidate for carrying the all-important state of Pennsylvania. This strategy was played up increasingly after the Democrats nominated Buchanan on June 3. Since "Old Buck" hailed from the Keystone state, McLean's followers now pushed their argument with renewed vigor, insisting that the Justice was the only man who could defeat Buchanan on his own back yard. While the New York *Tribune* reported that McLean had some strength in Illinois, Maine, New Jersey, and Indiana, his candidacy never really lifted far off the ground.[4] McLean was identified widely as the most conservative candidate; his refusal to take an aggressive anti-Nebraska stand was his undoing and set him up as a target for criticism that spoke of him as "an old fogey" and a "marrowless old lawyer."[5] His candidacy was also pressed to the earth gently but firmly by Horace Greeley, who remarked that Supreme Court judges should not court presidential nominations.

Not entirely out of the running was Nathaniel P. Banks, Speaker of the House. But Banks was interested in another man, and in company with Francis P. Blair he began to promote him actively very early in the game. Their candidate was Colonel John C. Frémont—"The Pathfinder."

Explorer, soldier, and politician, Frémont was lustily hailed "as the embodiment of the spirit of the American frontier, the true emancipator of the slaves, and both as an explorer and as a conqueror of the Pacific slope."[6] A man of remarkably romantic background, Frémont had a career that sounded like a Perils of Pauline movie serial with the exploits of Wild Bill Hickok dubbed in. He had eloped with the daughter of Senator Thomas Hart Benton of Missouri, explored the craggy summits of the Rockies, and by 1850 he was a national idol.

At the close of his army career in 1848, Frémont became a candidate for the United States Senate from California, with a public announcement that he was thoroughly a Democrat "by association, feeling, principle and education," and that he adhered to the "great principles of the Democratic party." In conformity with the Senate custom when a new state is admitted to the Union, Frémont drew lots with another man elected at the same time to see who would get the long term. The Pathfinder drew the short term that expired March 4, 1851, and he was not re-elected by the California state legislature. During this period Frémont devoted himself largely to the internal problems of California.

As a candidate and a personality around whom men might rally in these times of profound social upheaval and of unpredictable economic and political change, The Pathfinder of the Rockies was eminently available. Born in Savannah, Georgia, January 21, 1813, he became a mathematics teacher, surveyor, explorer, and then a soldier in the Mexican War. Noted first for his expedition in the summer of 1842, when he was accompanied by the fabulous Kit Carson, Frémont won his early press notices by gathering information about the Oregon Trail. Springing from the narrative of his first expedition were tall tales of how he had been able to eat a dog at an Indian banquet, brave the dangers that the fearless Carson refused to face without first making a will, and how he planted the Stars and Stripes on what was presumably the highest pinnacle of the Rockies.

Frémont made two later expeditions, both of which brought him great fame. Opposed to slavery at the time he was in the Senate, Frémont became more anti-slavery in his outlook between 1851 and 1859. Because German scientists frequently accompanied him on his expeditions, Frémont enjoyed a phenomenal reputation among Germans—another factor that enhanced his availability. Admittedly he had had little training in politics. Moreover, his entire career was at least susceptible to a judgment once made by philosopher Josiah Royce, who concluded that "General Frémont possessed all the qualities of genius except ability." [7] But Frémont was undeniably a popular idol. To those seeking a winner, this mighty mountaineer who fired the imagination of young and old looked like a person peculiarly able to bring about an amalgamation of the political protest groups of his day into a concerted drive for victory.

Even by December, 1855, when preliminary plans were drafted for the Pittsburgh convention, the Frémont candidacy had already generated quite a head of steam. Blair spoke of Frémont as a possible candidate and told the group frankly that he favored The Pathfinder for the Presidency. Close by, the Baltimore *Sun* was aware of Frémont meetings in this city for at least three months before this time, and that spring several papers in other parts of the country, such as the Cleveland *Herald,* came out boldly for Frémont. On April 4 Governor Seward wrote to a friend that a majority of the Republican leaders in Washington were convinced that Frémont should be the candidate. And later the New York Republican state central committee passed resolutions endorsing him just five days before the Philadelphia convention convened.

While the Frémont managers appeared to have things well in hand, even after June 6, when Greeley finally committed the *Tribune* to The Pathfinder, one sober thought sent chills down into the dorsal regions of his followers. Ever since the March meeting of the Republican national committee, when the American Party made it perfectly clear that it had no intention of permitting itself to be swallowed up by the Republicans, Frémont's managers had worried about the possibility of a separate American party presidential ticket. To understand their feelings, it is helpful to gather up some of the slippery straws of the times.

The North American party actually began in June of 1855 when the Know-Nothings first divided along slavery lines. But it was not until the following February that the North Americans established a regular national organization—a feat accomplished just after the Southern or "National" Americans named Millard Fillmore as their candidate for the Presidency. It was the North American group, therefore, that made common cause with the Republican national committee in issuing a call to the people of the United States, but having gone this far they still determined to hold their own national convention on June 12, 1856—five days before the Republicans planned to meet.

The threat this represented to all Republican leaders, and particularly to the managers of Frémont, was a very serious one. Should the North American party nominate a candidate other than Frémont, and should the Republicans subsequently ratify this nomination, The Pathfinder would surely be lost. Yet there were hazards for Frémont if the North Americans nominated him first. For if this happened the foreign-born voters might turn against him and cause the Republicans to repudiate him.

Well aware of the disaster that might befall their candidate, Frémont's managers set about to control and manipulate the North American convention. By use of venal delegates, sometimes called "bogus Know-Nothings," Frémont men were filtered into the North American convention at New York, and a letter from S. M. Allen to Nathaniel P. Banks of June 21, 1856, tells us that $50,000 was spent in Frémont's interest.[8] Doing their own scouting at the North American convention were also Republicans like Thurlow Weed, Edwin D. Morgan, and Preston King.

In the absence of complete agreement on how to proceed, a scheme was finally hatched to nominate Banks for President, with Governor Johnston of Pennsylvania as his running mate. Then the strategy called for both men to decline the nomination at the very moment the Republicans convened in Philadelphia. Unhappily the Frémont men tarried too long, and instead of their maneuvering Banks's nomination on Friday or Saturday, when their "wire-pulling might have passed unobserved," they let the nomination go over to Monday. In consequence, the more extreme nativists, believing the convention under hostile influence, bolted and nominated a separate ticket. But Banks was nominated on Monday by the North Americans and this act quickly strengthened Frémont's hand.

One postscript to this nomination, however, requires comment. After the Republican convention nominated Frémont and Banks withdrew as presidential nominee, the North Americans reassembled and then nominated Frémont for President and Governor Johnston for Vice-President. But Johnston refused to "fade" satisfactorily and withdraw from the race. He created instead a situation where William L. Dayton was vice-presidential candidate of the Republicans and Johnston the nominee of the North Americans. Not until August was Johnston finally persuaded to withdraw in favor of Dayton. At last the way was open for overwhelming support of the Republican ticket by the anti-slavery Know-Nothings without, at the same time, alienating the foreign voters.

Meeting on the anniversary of the fight at Bunker Hill, the first Republican national convention assembled at Philadelphia on June 17, 1856. It was national committee chairman E. D. Morgan who called it to order and explained its purpose. The intent, declared Morgan, was not to determine whether the North or the South would rule this land, but whether henceforth the principles of freedom laid down by the Founding Fathers would be maintained.

The temporary chairmanship went to Robert Emmett, a former Democrat, who was the son of the Irish patriot Thomas Addis Emmett. Emmett deplored the fate of Buchanan, who he said had "allowed himself to be chained to the juggernaut of slavery."

On the second day the organization of the convention was completed, and Henry S. Lane of Indiana was made permanent chairman. An orator of uncommon ability, Lane appealed to the Democrats to unite with the Republicans on one great principle, then startled New England delegates by taking a seat and propping his feet on a table top.

On resolutions, the convention experienced few difficulties. The platform challenged the slavocracy-ridden Democratic party, and pledged the "maintenance of the principles promulgated in the Declaration of Independence." Skillfully contrived, the platform did not speak out against slavery as an institution so much as it decried the slavocracy's dominance of the government to the detriment of the small enterpriser, the working man, and the farmer. Saluting the rising political power of the West, the platform recommended a railroad to the Pacific, along with river and harbor improvements. Curiously for a party so strongly entranced by the idea of free land, no mention of homesteads appears in the first Republican platform. Apparently, with a nod to reality, the party chieftains were afraid that on their first trip before the voters in a national election they could take no chances with the Know-Nothing element. It was no secret that the latter group included many who were ever fearful that free farms on the prairies would fill the West with aliens.

The preliminaries behind it, the convention then moved on to the primary duty of all political parties, the nomination of candidates. But a motion to begin was immediately countered with a motion to block nominations. This time it was James Webb of New York who touched off the debate. Since a momentous decision was to be made, said Webb, why not reason together as the Founding Fathers had some eighty years earlier? He admitted that he happened to oppose the candidates most members approved. But Seward, he went on, the greatest champion of Republican principles, was apparently being discarded by the convention because he could not carry Pennsylvania. Why then turn to another man whose powers at the ballot box might be equally unknown? What he wanted was a conference, and unquestionably there were quite a few delegates who were ready to go along with him.[9] But by this time the possibility of any "Stop Frémont" maneuver seemed exceedingly remote. Justice McLean's name was withdrawn, while Thaddeus Stevens unsuccessfully reopened the demand that the convention have a conference, on the ground that McLean's withdrawal meant the loss of 50,000 votes in Pennsylvania. Friends of Governor Chase became convinced that his support was so small that his name should also be withdrawn. Aware that his man's case was hopeless, a Chase delegate read a letter of withdrawal removing him from contention. Eventually McLean was nominated by Judge Spaulding, and finally the convention was ready for the supreme test.

The form in this case was an informal poll. And on this casual preference poll Frémont gathered 359 votes, McLean 170, Banks 1, Sumner 2, and Seward 1. Following a request for a unanimous vote, a formal ballot was then ordered, but 37 delegates still stuck with McLean. So, on the first presidential roll call of the first Republican national convention, with 558 delegates constituting the total membership, John C. Frémont won the nomination with 520 votes. Following the formal ballot, a unanimous vote was again requested. The convention accepted this time with a throaty roar while the Frémont supporters triumphantly broke out a banner and The Pathfinder himself strode onto the platform. Many members of the Pennsylvania delegation wept, though the following day a resolution came from the Keystone delegation asking that the nomination be made unanimous. But that fall John Allison, the Pennsylvania delegate first to protest the defeat of McLean, intoned a bitter requiem on the work of the convention. Now, he complained after The Pathfinder lost the November election, perhaps "Greeley, Weed, and Company" would be convinced "that they could not make a President, even if they could nominate one."

Several names sprouted for the Vice-Presidency. Among them was the rail-splitter Abraham Lincoln, placed in nomination by Judge Palmer of Illinois, with the happy throught that here was a man with all the proper fighting qualities of a first-class candidate. In the same relaxed manner used to name a presidential nominee, the first informal ballot on the vice-presidential nomination gave Dayton 253 votes; Banks 46; Lincoln 110; Wilmot 43; Sumner 35; and ten others a show-vote. Banks's name was withdrawn by telegram, and after several other withdrawals a final ballot was taken that gave William L. Dayton the nomination.

A strong factor underlying Dayton's nomination was his high standing in Pennsylvania (Dayton himself hailed from New Jersey). Lincoln was spared the honor of receiving the nomination for the post about which John Adams once complained: "My country has in its wisdom contrived for me the most insignificant office that ever the invention of man has contrived or his imagination conceived." The man receiving the honor, of course, never even served for a day in this office, since he went down to defeat. But knowing the inexorable course of history and what the political future usually is of those who accept vice-presidential nominations, Republicans may well rejoice in the fact that Lincoln was the convention runner-up in 1856 and not the man who finally received the nod. Dayton was formerly a Whig and long a prominent political leader in New Jersey. His selection was apparently contrived to pacify the friends of Justice McLean, for it was the latter's supporters who brought him to the fore as a candidate.

Its ticket completed, the Republican party was now beset by an additional problem. Only a hundred miles away the North American party was still marking time while waiting to hear from the Republican convention. Just before the Republican convention's nomination for the Presidency was taken up, the North Americans invited the Republicans to unite with them "as friends of freedom." A motion to accept had been tabled before Judge Spaulding nominated McLean, but now, with all nominations decided upon, the question of co-operation with the North Americans was still hanging over the rostrum. Many members of the convention favored extending the hand of friendship. But Owen Lovejoy of Illinois counseled, No! Once the Republican party tied itself in with that organized body, he insisted, that "demagog, Stephen A. Douglas, would tickle the sense of the foreign born citizens of Illinois, and Illinois would be lost." Only after hectic and useless haggling between the platform committees of the Republican and North American parties did the Republican convention finally decide to call upon all parties to co-operate. The mechanics for reaching this objective were left to a committee of three. Actually the decision to side-step fusion was to the advantage of the Republicans, for obvious reasons. They had placed their own ticket before the people without regard (ostensibly, at least) to what the North American party might do. Now they could go before the voters with the legitimate claim that they had refused to consort with the North Americans in arranging any formal kind of coalition.

Like all subsequent conventions, the first Republican meeting to nominate a presidential ticket closed gently amidst flickering disappointments for those whose candidates had been bested, and the eager expectancy of victory among those who had triumphed. Whiling away the last hours of the convention, the delegates listened to endless speeches, many by Germans who vowed that the Germans would stand fast with The Pathfinder.

Two days after the Republican adjournment, the North American party resumed its convention in New York to hear the report of the liaison committee appointed to meet with its Republican counterpart. Then the name of Banks was finally withdrawn and Frémont was accepted as a presidential nominee by acclamation on June 20. Not until several weeks later, however, was the co-ordination of the two parties on the vice-presidential candidate brought about. Even then it was achieved only after an interview between Johnston and Colonel Frémont who, without making any promises, said he would remember Johnston's friends. Thus assured, Johnston wrote a letter to the secretary of the North American party formally withdrawing his candidacy, and on August 4, when the letter was made public, Frémont and Dayton at last stood alone as the presidential and vice-presidential candidates for both the Republican and the North American parties. Unanticipated by those who insisted that the anti-slavery elements of the North could never be successfully organized, the results of the two conventions lifted hopes for the general election of November. But the months ahead were striped with many shadows.

By nominating Buchanan the Democrats made a wise move in their efforts to ease the tension of the times. A popular Pennsylvanian, "Old Buck" could be merchandised as a Northerner and at the same time could also be presented as a man of conservative leanings at an hour when the Republican party was construed by many to be a catch-basin of heresies. Moreover, Buchanan's acceptance of the party platform already approved by the Southerners would assure him support in Dixie. Sizing up the situation, one Republican said the Democrats had been "wise as serpents if not as harmless as doves."

On formal notification of his nomination, Frémont delivered an acceptance speech that laid down the general theme of his campaign. Recalling that it had been the desire of the Founding Fathers to prohibit the extension of slavery, he then despaired of the small group of slave owners in the South who were controlling the policies of the nation. Not only were they bent on defeating the principles that inspired the Revolution, he said, but it was now only too apparent that their real objective was the extension of slavery across the continent. In conclusion Frémont indicted the South for the errors that agitated such quarrelsome controversy in this happy land. It was because of misguided Southern policies that Kansas was now being raked by riotous civil disorder, he said. Moreover, the Kansas-Nebraska act was essentially a scheme designed to bar free labor from the areas that had been preserved for it by a solemn covenant. Repeated with varying modifications, this theme was hammered home throughout the campaign.

Meanwhile, Republican leaders and pitchmen of the press with Republican sympathies stirred up feelings with their own notions of how to win votes. From the outset all forms of campaign gimmicks were tried. A natural for this game was the brutal caning that Representative Preston Brooks of South Carolina gave Senator Charles Sumner of Massachusetts on the floor of the United States Senate. Sumner had delivered the third and last installment of his famed "Crime of Kansas" oration on May 26, 1856, in a slashing speech that heated up Southern tempers. That afternoon, while working at his desk, he was set upon by Congressman Brooks and beaten into insensibility with a heavy gutta-percha cane.

Reaction in the North was immediate, and the anti-slavery press screamed out against this outrage committed on the person of one of its distinguished champions. The Republicans, mindful of how this famous incident in our political history could make blood pound in the veins by mere mention of the name Sumner, built one of the favorite campaign stratagems around it. Usually it was pulled off by having the Massachusetts Senator write a letter to be read at large Republican rallies, reminding the audience that so critical were his injuries that he was not yet able to return to his beloved home. This trick always sparked a sympathetic response and was probably quite effective as such emotional devices go.

Elsewhere, the appeal for Frémont votes followed a basic pattern. It started off with a denunciation of the South, exploited the sad plight of Bleeding Kansas, and the Brooks-Sumner attack, and wound up emphasizing that the policies of the South were designed to strike at free labor by diverting from its use land which had been sacredly committed to freedom.

It was a colorful campaign, with a polluted undertow. Everywhere the idea of writing parodies on popular songs and applying them to the personalities of the campaign seemed to enjoy wide popularity. Sung to the tune of the *Marseillaise,* the following is typical:

> Behold the furious storm is rolling
> Which border fiends, Confederate rise.
> The dogs of war let loose are howling
> And lo, our infant cities blaze.
> And shall we calmly view the ruin
> While lawless force with giant stride
> Spreads desolation far and wide.
> In guiltless blood his hands imbuing?
> Arise, arise, ye brave, and let your war cry be
> Free speech—, free press—, free soil—,
>   free men—
> Frémont in victory.

Frémont's wife was the subject of another song in which the reasons for turning to Jessie's husband to save the nation were glowingly set forth.

On the polemical side, Buchanan spoke mockingly of the "Black Republican" convention at Philadelphia, while others like Howell Cobb said that in the event of Frémont's election he would return immediately to Georgia and take the stump for secession; and John Tyler insisted that a Frémont victory would end the Union. Bewildered in the face of the gathering storm, manufacturers and businessmen became seriously alarmed at the prospect of secession, and threw their support to Buchanan in great force. And so the campaign oscillated between its lighter merriments and its sterner phases.

When the Republicans boasted that they had a "mustang colt"

which they were sure could whip the "old gray hoss," the Democrats threw back the rejoinder that there was not a drop of mustang blood in the Republican colt and that it was nothing but a freak from Barnum's menagerie. If the Republicans tended to play up the dash and adventure of Frémont—"that he had conquered California with 62 men," explored the craggy peaks of the windswept Rockies, eloped with Jessie Benton, or braved the rigors of a meal with Indian savages—the Democrats caricatured him as a phony. Or they subjected him to ridicule by passing around a sample menu as representative of the meals upon which Frémont and his political friends feasted:

> Soup—mutton, sheep, lamb
> Roast—black mutton, sheep
> Boiled—sheepshead
> Fried—mutton chops (wool on), Frémont stew
> Side dishes—cold "horsemeat" (from Barnum's
>   woolly horse)
> Dessert—plucked goose, nigger hash.

If today we often think campaigns hateful, we would do well to make a careful canvass of the contest in 1856. George Julian, looking back some fifty years later, remarked that never had he encountered such a mean campaign. Frémont was accused of participating in a scheme that had purchased the Speakership of the House, and it was alleged that this same group was now bent on buying the Presidency. Few scrubby stories were overlooked that could scuff up The Pathfinder. He had been involved in a few scrimmages during his life which involved physical combat, and the Democrats trotted them out gleefully, hoping to counteract the Sumner caning. Nowhere did they hesitate to lay on the lash.

Overriding all the personal charges as a source of trouble, however, was the persistent attempt to present him as Catholic. For circumstantial evidence there were several details to suggest that Frémont was a Roman Catholic. He was French, had been educated at a Catholic school, and had been married on a United States Army post by a Catholic chaplain. Feeding these charges steadily in the hope of alienating North American support from the Republican candidate, the Democrats circulated stories that Frémont had refused to accept an Episcopal prayer book that was presented to him while visiting West Point, that he once attended a Catholic mass in St. Louis, and that Bishop Hughes and the Catholic press generally were claiming Frémont as one of their communicants. Almost defenseless against this slippery campaign, the Republi-

cans were hard pressed to rebut the charges about Frémont's religion. Seward declared that Frémont was "nearly convicted of being
a Catholic." So serious did the matter eventually become that several
delegations visited Frémont and later issued public statements re-
cording that they were authorized to say he was a Protestant, and
that they found that the baptismal records of his children and their
admission to a Protestant church were all in order.

Frémont himself maintained a strict silence on the subject—a
stand that made his advisers most unhappy. Several years later his
daughter Elizabeth explained that although her father had been a
lifelong Protestant he refused to discuss his religion on the grounds
that it would admit the subject was of political importance.

With no help from the candidate, Republican managers met the
issue as best they could. They did prove that Frémont was an Episco-
palian and that he had not been educated as a Catholic. They also
showed that all of his children had been baptized as Episcopalians.
That he was married by a Catholic priest, however, was not to be
denied, and there can be little doubt that the injection of the religious issue into the campaign was harmful to Frémont in many
areas.

Turning the tables, the Republicans also threw a few curves at
Buchanan. They reminded voters that back in 1818 when he was a
Federalist he boasted in a Fourth of July speech that "if he had one
drop of Democratic blood in his veins he would open them and let it
pour out." [10] Another favorite in the Republican campaign bag was
a statement attributed to "Old Buck" that ten cents a day was
adequate pay for mechanics. It was a common sight at parades and
rallies to see tattered banners held aloft bearing the legend: "BU-
CHANAN'S WORKSHOP: TEN CENTS A DAY."

While the campaign was heating up and the politicos of both
parties were plying the branding irons the new party, in the national sweepstakes for the first time, was having trouble with its
finances. "Not until late August were serious steps taken toward
raising money," reports historian Nichols.[11] Since the need was desperate for carrying, as a morale-builder, the state elections in Pennsylvania on October 14, the money question was all the more
critical. John G. Howard of New York City was put in charge of
collecting funds, and after a very late start he began to deliver in
September. In one week $2,000 came in from Boston, along with a
promise for an additional $5,000. By October 8 the total assets of
the national committee were approximately $15,000. Ten thousand
went for procuring the support of a dozen-odd newspapers—an

outlay which the chairman of the national committee, Morgan, thought a little steep but was resigned to accepting.

Then on October 14 the blow came that shattered hopes. The Democrats carried the state election in Pennsylvania in a victory that put a sharp crease in Republican morale. But, however saddened, Republican managers kept up the fight. In the final drive for funds to put Frémont over the top, chairman Morgan gave one party worker a letter of introduction for soliciting contributions that well expressed his own feelings: "I authorized a draft on [myself] yesterday for $5,000," he said, "and for $25,000 in the event of Frémont's election."

With the Pennsylvania election over, giving the Democrats 14 congressional seats to four the Republicans picked up under their own banner, and seven they shared under a fusion arrangement, the turning-point in the campaign was reached. From here on in the signs all blared that Frémont simply could not make the grade. In the same month the Republicans received a setback in Indiana, where the Democrats carried six congressional districts to the Republicans' five, and the Democrats also captured the governorship. By the end of October the Democrats were employing the old bandwagon psychology by claiming that they were already assured of controlling the next Congress and would pick up three more Senators in the North in addition to electing another Democratic President.

Finally electioneering pounded to an end after a campaign that included many battle casualties. In the Maryland election of October 8, violence had been severe in Baltimore. Here a virulent variety of Know-Nothingism led to a fight in which the "plug-uglies" and "rip-raps" fought the eighth ward "blackguards" and four people were killed and fifty wounded.

When the national totals were added up, Buchanan took the election in easy stride. He carried every slave state except Maryland (won by Fillmore), and in addition was victorious in such states as Pennsylvania, Illinois, California, and New Jersey. The Republicans won 33 percent of the popular vote, while the Democrats captured 45 percent—which meant, of course, that the Democrats polled only a minority of the popular vote, since the combined total of the Republican and American parties exceeded that of Buchanan. (Fillmore, the American party nominee, won 21.6 percent.) In the competition for counties, the Republicans won 362 to the Democrats' 1,067. The stellar showing of the Republicans occurred in New England, where they carried every state and all but four out of 67 counties. By taking New York, the new party also added to its laurels, and its victory in Ohio, though narrow, turned out to be a portent of better things to come. For thereafter the Buckeye state stood fast in the Republican column until 1912. All in all, for a party "not even foreseen thirty months before," the capture of one-third of the popular vote was impressive. But the keystone for an effective national party organization was not yet snugly in place. And even as the election post-mortems were written the more far-seeing leaders of the Republican movement were concerned over what to do about it.

Some critics felt that, despite his romantic appeal, Frémont's vulnerable spots had cost the Republican party dearly. But the more sober judgments inclined to view the campaign as not a defeat but very likely a Republican victory. A strong political organization had made a test run and was now ready to perfect its machinery for a successful campaign in 1860. Even the disheartened candidate could take some comfort in the remark of Rutherford B. Hayes soon after the election. "Yet, he did make a fine run, and has borne himself admirably through the trying canvass which has closed. He may not become a permanent figure among the leading men, but I think he is so likely to do so that I shall now buy his portrait to put in my parlor." [12]

Also on the brighter side was the make-up of the Thirty-fifth Congress. The Democrats were in control, but the opposition was certain to be polarized around the Republican party. Finally the North Americans bowed off the political stage, never again to be reorganized, leaving the Republicans a clear field as the only consolidated anti-slavery party.

Even in command of an opposition in the House that was more clearly Republican than before, however, the Republican movement was not out of danger. As with all fresh political movements, the prospect of the party's losing the momentum that had generated over a two-year period and finding itself suddenly headed toward political oblivion was still a definite possibility. But, two days after Buchanan's inauguration in 1857, help came from a somewhat unusual quarter—the Supreme Court of the United States. Chief Justice Taney, speaking for the majority of the Court in the famous Dred Scott decision, declared that the already repealed Missouri Compromise was unconstitutional, and held that Congress had no power to interfere with the property of a slave owner in the course of governing territory. The essence of Taney's decision was that Congress had no power over slavery in the Territories. It was the first time in over fifty years that the United States Supreme Court had declared an act of Congress unconstitutional, and it was an event that set the abolitionist propaganda mills churning overnight in a violent mood of anti-slavery agitation. Many irate Northerners immediately began calling for secession. This time it was not a Southern state like South Carolina that was shouting for nullification, but the state legislature of Wisconsin that passed a resolution supporting this principle. The Court's decision in the Dred Scott case was expressed in six separate concurring opinions and two dissents. The divergence among the many voices of the Court actually weakened rather than strengthened the position of the majority—a circumstance the Northern press made the most of. Seizing several of the more unfortunate phrases in Taney's argumentation, Republican editors and orators sought to discredit both the Court and its decision. "It is safe to say," writes Carl Swisher, "that no decision in American history has done more to injure the reputation of the Supreme Court. Skillfully used by abolitionist propagandists, it played an important part, not in postponing the conflict between the North and the South, but in bringing on the crisis." [13] Abolitionists like Garrison began crying, "No union with slaveholders," while Wendell Phillips pronounced the Union to be a curse of God— "Away with it," he said. But both Lincoln and many Republicans who criticized earlier secession talk by the South now were disturbed to have their anti-slavery friends take such an extremist position.

That summer (June 26) Lincoln replied to Douglas, who was defending the Dred Scott decision, by saying that while he did not agree with those who would resist the Dred Scott decision, the decision none the less was in error. Since the Supreme Court had reversed itself on previous occasions, he urged that Republicans look ahead with this in mind. All efforts must be directed "to have it reversed if we can, and have a new judicial rule established upon this subject." He denounced the "counterfeit logic" of Douglas's contention that the Republican party stood for absolute racial equality. Because he did not want a black woman for a slave, said Lincoln, it surely did not follow that he wanted her for a wife. "In some respects she is certainly not my equal. But in her natural right to eat the bread she earns with her own hands without asking leave of anyone else, she is my equal, and the equal of all others." It was Lincoln's only address of the year, and while it had little effect on the more extreme abolitionists, it was mighty useful logic for the Republicans in the center of the stream looking for calmer counsels.

Widening the political rift was another factor that helped bounce the Republican party up to its full fighting strength. This time it was the Panic of 1857, accompanied by business failures, unemployment, and the usual bill of particulars during hard times that always discomfits those holding power. A low tariff of 1857, which hurt the ironmasters of Pennsylvania, is said to have driven thousands of Democrats in the Keystone state into the Republican party. In 1858 every Democratic Congressman in the state was defeated at the general election. The tariff had also injured the wool growers in Ohio, and out in the Northwest President Pierce's veto of several rivers and harbors bills had embittered farmers, shippers, and those engaged in commerce throughout the Mississippi Valley region and along the Great Lakes.

A third stroke of fortune for the Republican hope chest was the pitched battle that broke out in mid-year between Douglas and President Buchanan. Despite the triumph of free-state men in winning control of Kansas, a constitution, known as the Lecompton Constitution, was hastily framed at a pro-slavery convention. Later, this document was submitted to the voters, who were given no possibility of rejecting the constitution as a whole, but only the option of accepting it with or without slavery. And when the free-state men of Kansas refused to vote in the referendum, the slavery provision of the constitution was adopted by an overwhelming vote. Outraged by this entire procedure, which he considered fraudulent and a travesty on popular sovereignty, Douglas reacted swiftly: "If this constitution is to be thrust down our throats," he admonished the Senate, ". . . I will resist it to the last. . . . I will stand on the great principle of popular sovereignty, which declares the right of all people to be left free to form and regulate their domestic institutions in their own way. I will follow that principle wherever its logical consequences may take me. . . ."

They almost took Douglas right into the Republican party, for there was a time when some thought it might be Douglas rather than Lincoln who would be running for the Senate as the Republican nominee in 1858. Indignant at the state of affairs in Kansas and miffed because Buchanan slighted him in dispensing patronage (possibly because Douglas had been Buchanan's chief rival at the Democratic convention the year before and was somewhat jealous of the latter's party influence), the Little Giant opened up with savage attacks on the President in December of 1857. So complete was the breach that some Republicans felt the Republican party should join in aiding Douglas.[14] Certainly feelers were made in that direction. In January, 1858, Lyman Trumbull told Lincoln that Senator Seward hoped for Douglas's re-election, and later a rumor spread that the Little Giant and Seward "had struck a bargain to re-elect Douglas to the Senate and make the shrewd New Yorker President in 1860." [15] Horace Greeley was another who began warming up to Douglas now.

He urged that Douglas had earned Republican support—an opinion not to be dismissed lightly in view of the wide circulation of the New York *Tribune* in Illinois. And from Boston, where he was visiting, Lincoln's law partner William H. Herndon wrote to Lincoln that Governor Banks of Massachusetts asked him: "You will support Douglas in Illinois, won't you?" To which Herndon replied: "No, never!" [16] But the Douglas boom grew, and it soon began to look as if Lincoln would be passed over.

Happily, interference by interlopers from the outside was resented in Illinois. With good reason, in light of Lincoln's availability, the Chicago *Tribune* complained that there "seems to be a considerable notion pervading the brains of the political wet nurses of the East, that the barbarians of Illinois cannot take care of themselves." At the same time the Chicago *Journal* warned Easterners to lay off, indicating that the citizens of Illinois would "deal with Senator Douglas in their own way"—a sentiment that was widely accepted among editors throughout the state.

In political semiretirement for almost ten years, the "rail-splitter" was now ready to move. That February (1858) he hurried to Chicago for consultation with Norman B. Judd, chairman of the state central committee of Illinois, and soon the state was buzzing with endorsements for Lincoln. The Chicago *Tribune* said if Douglas wanted to come out openly and join the Republican party they would be happy to give him a place in the cabinet of their next President. But under no circumstances would they yield the Senatorship. That Lincoln had earned!

By early summer 95 county conventions had endorsed Lincoln for Senator. And on June 16, when Lincoln was endorsed for the Senate by the state convention, he was ready with a speech that comes down to us today as one of his most historic orations.

> "A house divided against itself cannot stand." I believe this government cannot endure permanently half slave and half free. I do not expect the Union to be dissolved—I do not expect the house to fall—but I do expect it will cease to be divided. It will become all one thing, or all the other. Either the opponents of slavery will arrest the further spread of it, and place it where the public mind shall rest in the belief that it is in the course of ultimate extinction; or its advocates will push it forward, till it shall become alike lawful in all the states, old as well as new, North as well as South.

The speech, as some friends had the vision to realize, may not have been altogether wise, for it tended to cast Lincoln in a more radical role than he actually deserved. He was still a conservative, holding to a policy of moderation. His implication that a conspiracy

was abroad for the extension of slavery went too far in the judgment
of some of his admirers. But he was convinced at the time that
slavery was on the march, and he saw no immediate way of stopping
it.

Informed of Lincoln's nomination, Senator Douglas sounded a
note of prophecy: "I shall have my hands full. He is the strong man
of his party—full of wit, facts, dates—and the best stump speaker,
with his droll ways and his dry jokes, in the West."

Starting July 9 at Chicago, where Douglas, who made the first
speech, was followed the next night by Lincoln, there began the
famous debates that "set the prairies ablaze" and became such a
celebrated landmark in the history of the Republican party. While
Douglas traveled about in a private car, with a flatcar coupled to
his train mounting a brass cannon that was fired in a crashing salute
when the train approached the prairie towns, Lincoln often was
riding on the same train as a coach passenger. All during the seven
great encounters from August into October—at Freeport, Jonesboro,
Galesburg, Quincy, and Alton—Horace Greeley sulked and the
Tribune did not report the great debates. The reason was simple.
Greeley, along with other Eastern Republicans, wanted to reward
Douglas for his stand against Buchanan on the adoption of the
Lecompton Constitution. And however discreditable their actions appeared in light of their earlier endorsements of Lincoln's statements
on the subject, this was the stand they took. Even Douglas had the
courage to insist that he intended to remain a Democrat and did not
want "Black Republican" support.[17]

Down to the very end of the campaign Lincoln and Douglas both
despaired of the sectionalism that threatened to divide the Union,
and they both sought to quiet the agitators that were leading the
nation to the brink of disaster. But Lincoln differed from Douglas in
believing that moral strictures would one day lead men to resist
slavery, while his adversary argued that the moral objections to
slavery should be suppressed.

On a rainy Election Day that fall, Lincoln lost the decision. Interestingly, the Republican legislative candidates polled 4,000 more
votes than their opponents. Notwithstanding, the antiquated apportionment law, which worked to the advantage of Democratic southern
legislative districts, assured the re-election of Douglas by the Illinois
legislature. There, when the vote was finally taken, Douglas prevailed, 54 to 46.

Going home that night, Lincoln recounted his feelings in his own
inimitable way: "The path had been worn pigback and was slippery.
My foot slipped from under me, knocking the others out of the

way; but I recovered and said to myself, 'It's a slip and not a fall.' "

The great debates had made Lincoln a national figure. For any man who could trade blows with the Little Giant and not go down was a man certain to command wide respect. And Lincoln did it with forcefulness and vigor and yet with a gentle dignity which won favor for him that would long outlast the tensions built up in the campaign. "As I have not felt, so I have not expressed any harsh sentiments toward our Southern brethren. . . ." he summed up in his last campaign speech of 1858. "I have meant to assail the motives of no party or individual, and if I have, in any instance (of which I am not conscious) departed from my purpose, I regret it. . . ."

Though Lincoln failed to win a Senate seat that fall, the election returns elsewhere soon made it clear that the Republicans were on the march. Even as Northern Congressmen began to go home for the state elections in 1858, the peculiar pulsations that warn of an overturn were already felt. Growing industrialization in the North was leading to unhappy living conditions for the working man in many cities—so much so that Senator Hammond of South Carolina was impelled to try and expose the exploitation of white labor by employers. These unfortunates, he charged, were the "mud sills" of society, actually worse off than the Negro slaves of the South. Moreover, he went on, their pietistical and hypocritical exploiters were morally more culpable than the Southern slave owners. But while the Democrats hoped to agitate the working men against the Republicans, the attempt failed. The Panic of 1857 that brought about serious unemployment along with food riots and bread lines gave the Republicans the signal opportunity to trot out the protective tariff as an ameliorative and the chance to flay the slavocracy for stirring up class feelings in the North.

On another front the steady immigration upswing was working at this time to the advantage of the new Republican party. The lure of the more abundant life in America was bringing new potential voters by the hundred thousands. How, asks Nichols (speaking of the Democrats), "could a party which stood for laissez-faire, for limited powers to the federal government, and for states' rights, which opposed tariffs, subsidies, and free homesteads—and in effect condoned slavery—gain the support of the incoming hordes?" And "how could this hoary party, tinged with corruption and plagued with feuds stand up against youth, enthusiasm, and idealism?" [18]

The simple truth of the matter, of course, was that it could not. And all through the state elections of 1858 Republicans began to show unexpected power. Their total in the Senate climbed from 20 to 26, against 36 for the Democrats. And in the House for the first time the Republicans outnumbered the Democrats 114 to 92 (24 Americans and 7 anti-Lecompton Democrats were also elected to the House). Clearly, after the break between Douglas and other Democrats in the Buchanan administration over the issue of the Lecompton Constitution in Kansas, a fissure had opened in the Democratic ranks which now seemed beyond repair. Thereafter Buchanan directed his efforts toward a rear-guard action that rested upon Southern support for a show of authority. But no longer was there any assurance of controlling the government, at least with a steady hand, without formidable support in the North and the East, and this was now beyond Buchanan's grasp.

Before the decade between 1850 and 1860 drew to a close, two of our national parties saw their organizations ground to pieces by the challenge of events. One, the Whig party, was never to rise again. The other, the Democratic party, unhinged over the slavery question, would eventually recover, but not without a series of painful disappointments. Meanwhile, a fast-rising third party had emerged from the soil of discontent, and taken on the virile character of young manhood within four years after its founding.

It was a period of great expansion, and by and large one of prosperity. Steel ribbons stretching westward signified an expanding transportation system, and a greatly speeded-up system of commerce and trade. The Middle West and the Northwest were finally united with the East. Two new states had entered the Union, Oregon and Minnesota, and during the decade the population of the nation rose from 23 to 31 million.

Born amidst these swiftly moving changes in the economy, the Republican party inescapably came to reflect some of the hopes and the aspirations of the new era. That the new party was endangered by a number of off-beat agitators under such conditions of social upheaval and continued crises is not to be wondered at. There were those of a predatory bent anxious to convert the new party into a vehicle for protecting and promoting aggregations of wealth and commercial interests at the expense of the working classes. And there were also, beating the tom-toms wildly, the abolition extremists, many of whom wished to lay the South in ruins. In light of these tendencies, the availability of Lincoln at this critical hour of his party's history was a great stroke of fortune. Lincoln possessed a striking way of clarifying public issues, and many among his audiences went away with the feeling that he had been speaking to them individually, one at a time.

No one can say for certain what went on in Lincoln's mind—what were the inner mysteries of his own thoughts about his ambitions between 1858 and 1860. Not a few of his actions suggested an attitude once described by the English leader Cromwell: "No man rises so high as he who knows not whither he is going." But a man who knew him well felt differently. William Herndon, his law partner, has a salient comment about Lincoln's earlier experience when he was considered for a seat in the United States Senate. "That man who thinks Lincoln calmly sat down and gathered his robes about him, waiting for the people to call him," wrote Herndon, "has a very erroneous knowledge of Lincoln. He was always calculating, and always planning ahead. His ambition was a little engine that knew no rest. . . . His canvass . . . was marked by his characteristic ability and vigilance. During the anxious moments that intervened between the general election and the assembling of the legislature he slept like Napoleon, with one eye open."

Shortly after his defeat by Douglas, Lincoln complained to his campaign manager, Norman Judd, that he had been paying expenses for so long without earning anything that he was without sufficient funds for even household purposes. To his friends he said he wanted to be a private in the ranks when the 1860 elections came along, and that if he had any ambition it was to unseat Douglas in 1864. And when he was approached by Jesse Fell, who wanted to do a biography of him for wide circulation to build him up as a presidential candidate, Lincoln declined—a wise decision, whatever secret ambitions he harbored. For the man out front too early is sure to be the target for most of the arrows. Meanwhile, throughout the summer of 1859, invitations to speak all over the country poured in on Lincoln as a result of the celebrated debates the fall before. At first declining most, Lincoln stepped up the number of engagements in the fall. At the Wisconsin state fair in October, where a political speech was perhaps not altogether appropriate for the occasion, Lincoln stressed the opportunities for personal improvement that were offered under a system of free enterprise. Later, in Cincinnati, he said: "There is no permanent class of hired laborers among us. Twenty-five years ago, I was a hired laborer. The hired laborer of yesterday, labors on his own account today, and will hire others to labor for him tomorrow. Advancement—improvement in condition —is the order of things in a society of equals."

Lincoln believed deeply in a fluid society within which there were equal opportunities for all. "Under a system of individualistic enterprise, it seemed of first importance to him—indeed, it seemed sufficient—merely to keep the road to high attainment clear of inequitable obstructions, with government aid to projects of general benefit." [19]

Basically Lincoln believed that labor is superior to capital, "and deserves much higher consideration. Capital has its rights, which are as worthy of protection as any other rights. Nor is it denied that there is, and probably always will be, a relation between capital and labor producing mutual benefits. The error is in assuming that the whole labor of a community exists within that relation. . . . A large majority belongs in neither class."

Invariably, in his strategy for the Republican party during these twitching times, Lincoln followed the general theme laid down in a letter to Schuyler Colfax. His constant purpose, he wrote, was "to hedge against divisions in the Republican ranks generally, and particularly for the contest of 1860." Discussed frequently as a presidential dark horse, Lincoln was thought by many papers to be a more "available" candidate than either Seward or Chase, both of whom were being vigorously pushed to the forefront. But Lincoln seemed content to forego active politicking in this direction, other than to continue making speeches on the issues.

That fall, however, one more dramatic episode crashed into the headlines of the day to plunge Lincoln deeper into national politics. In October, John Brown of Kansas, who had once declared himself "an instrument of God sent to liberate all slaves," seized the federal arsenal in Harpers Ferry, Virginia, with eighteen deluded zealots, bent on inciting a riot to free the slaves. He was captured several days later by Colonel Robert E. Lee, and by December 2 John Brown had died at the end of a federal rope. Meanwhile the screeches of the abolitionists and the Southerners over the incident were reaching fever pitch. In the November elections the Democrats charged that the Republicans were implicated in Brown's diabolical scheme, and that the Kansas martyr had drawn his misguided inspiration from the doctrines of the Republican party. Once again Lincoln was drawn irresistibly into the tumultuous debate of the hour —this time never to be released from the shining spotlight of the national public eye.

On December 20, Lincoln dispatched to Jesse Fell the autobiographical sketch that had been requested the year before. "There is not much of it," he wrote, "for the reason, I suppose, that there is not much of me." Even at the time he sent off this sketch, however, he wrote to Lyman Trumbull that he would rather be a United States Senator than President. But his friends thought otherwise, and near the close of 1859 his former campaign manager, Norman Judd, now national committeeman for Illinois, made a shrewd move. In the midst of a sharp debate at the Republican national committee meeting in New York over a selection of a site for the presidential convention, Judd dropped a casual suggestion: Why not hold the convention in a "neutral" place like Chicago, since Illinois had no favorite son of her own? Taking this up quickly, the national committee inadvertently gave Lincoln a long stride forward toward the Presidency by locating the national convention where Lincoln could run on home ground. Already his friends were readying the track, and on February 16, 1860, the Chicago *Tribune* came out four-square for Lincoln.

"Immeasurably the Fittest of All Its Candidates"

🐘

"There are always men anxious to distinguish themselves on such occasions," wrote eyewitness Murat Halstead, reconstructing the dramatic scene when, at the end of the third roll call, the victor was just 2½ votes short of the nomination. There was a profound stillness while the totals were being footed up at the Republican Convention of 1860. "I looked to see who would be the man to give the decisive vote. In about ten ticks of a watch Cartter of Ohio was up. I had imagined Ohio would be slippery enough for the crisis; and sure enough every eye was on Cartter, and every body who understood the matter at all, knew what he was about to do." Speaking with an impediment, Cartter stuttered his way to recognition: "I rise (eh) Mr. Chairman (eh) to announce the change of four votes of Ohio from Mr. Chase to Mr. Lincoln."

"The deed was done. There was a moment's silence . . . there was a noise in the Wigwam like the rush of a great wind." [1] So the National Convention of 1860 turned over the leadership of the party to a man who was "immeasurably the fittest of all its candidates."

Few things carbonate party spirit more than a national convention. And the gathering of the clan which the party staged in 1860 was a stem-winder, unsurpassed in the annals of Republicanism. P. Orman Ray has given us a lively account of both the setting and the maneuvering of the convention, which was a national political conclave without precedent. [2]

At the southeast corner of Lake and Market streets in Chicago, early in April, construction began on the wooden structure, known as the Wigwam, that would house the second national Republican convention. Work was pushed at breakneck speed; the convention was to open on May 16. At one side of the structure was a stage to hold 465 delegates and 60 newspapermen, and around the other three sides ran a gallery that seated about 1,200 spectators. Contemporary estimates of the Wigwam's maximum capacity varied considerably, from six thousand to fifteen thousand, with every cranny jammed. The cost was a modest five or six thousand dollars, but there was the usual difficulty in raising funds: in the Chicago *Tribune* on May 8 all persons who had chairs suitable for gallery use were urged to contribute them to the cause, and at convention time there remained a $2,000 debt which had to be retired through a twenty-five-cent admission fee.

Inside, the Wigwam was left rough and unplaned; for a back it simply borrowed the wall of an adjoining store. But two days before the convention the Chicago *Daily Journal* found the stark interior being transformed by "a bevy of ladies as busy as ants, decorating, sewing, and arranging wreaths."

Formal dedication of the Wigwam was set for May 12, four days before the start of the convention. "The council fires will be lighted in the hut. Come all and put a shoulder to the wheel, for tonight the ball begins to roll and the signal guns of the approaching contest between freedom and slavery will be fired," announced the *Journal.* None of the tribes failed to do its duty.

By an early hour that night the Wigwam was jammed. The roaring crowd was addressed by Henry Lane, Republican gubernatorial nominee from Indiana, by Governor Morrill of Maine, and finally by the old gladiator of the anti-slavery cause, Joshua R. Giddings of Ohio, who mounted the rostrum "amid the most deafening applause."

The selection of Chicago as convention host complimented the young Northwest, and the city strained every muscle to return the compliment. Her 42 hotels, charging rates of $1.50 to $2.50 a day, overflowed; one reporter found 132 people using billiard tables as beds. By convention time, Chicago's population may have doubled, with between 75,000 and 125,000 visitors on hand.

Adding to the carnival spirit that unhinged normal life in Chicago were the committees known as the "Wide Awakes," formed to convoy each arriving delegation to its headquarters. Rockets, cannon, and blaring bands greeted the delegates; the streets were choked with welcoming crowds. The train bearing the New York delegation accomplished "a feat in railroad annals that will long stand unsurpassed, if indeed it is safe and desirable to repeat the performance," covering the run between Buffalo and Chicago in 15½ hours. And beneath the surface of these boisterous arrivals, parades, and vigorous frivolities, the managers and champions of the various candidates were busy at the infighting. Horace Greeley, editor of the New York *Tribune,* arrived early Saturday evening, not as a delegate from New York but as a delegate by proxy from Oregon. Greeley was hostile to the Seward-Weed machine in New York, an attitude that was lustily reciprocated, and from the moment he stepped off the train he devoted his efforts to an assault on Seward. His own personal choice for the nomination was Edward Bates of Missouri.

On Saturday the crafty Thurlow Weed, Seward's campaign manager, also moved in and established himself at the Richmond House, where the activities of his delegates came in for much comment. "The New Yorkers," noted one newspaper article, "are of a class unknown to the Western Republicans. They can drink more whiskey, swear as loud and long, sing as bad songs, and get up and howl as ferociously as any crowd of Democrats you ever heard of. They are opposed, as they say, to being 'too damned virtuous.' At night most of them who are not engaged in caucusing, are doing what ill-tutored youths call 'raising hell generally.' "

Promptly at noon on Wednesday, May 16, the convention met for its opening session. Just four years earlier, the hall at Philadelphia which seated two thousand had been comfortably adequate for the convention. Now the Wigwam was not only filled to capacity but twenty thousand people were milling around outside hoping to get in. Men were hiring schoolgirls in the streets to be their escorts in order to gain entrance to the ladies' gallery. The going wage was twenty-five cents, though one girl who was offered half a dollar for this convoy duty turned it down on the grounds that she had already taken two men in "at each of the three doors and was afraid of arrest if she carried the enterprise on any further."

An aerial view of the delegates sitting on the stage would permit us to identify many of the leading figures. "That curious-looking, spectacled old gentleman, with the hair of nondescript color and lambrequin variety of whiskers, sitting under the Oregon standard," would be Horace Greeley, "the foremost newspaper editor of his generation." The gargantuan torso under the Illinois standard is Judge David Davis, Lincoln's campaign manager, who, receiving a wire from his candidate: "MAKE NO DEALS IN MY NAME," snapped back: "Hell, we're here and he's not."

With the Indiana delegation is Caleb B. Smith, soon to become Lincoln's Secretary of the Interior, while over by the Massachusetts standard we find John A. Andrew, chairman of the Old Bay state delegation and destined to become a famous war governor. Leading the Connecticut delegation is Gideon Welles, later the very capable Secretary of the Navy in Lincoln's cabinet, and at the head of the Wisconsin delegation sits Carl Schurz, who later served his country as a United States Senator from Missouri and as Secretary of the Interior. Limping to his seat with the Pennsylvania delegation is Thaddeus Stevens, who will become the leader of the Republican Radicals during the Civil War and will play a very controversial role in Republican party history.

Now Edwin D. Morgan of New York, chairman of the national committee, is rapping for order. The time is 12:10. He seems mindful of his solemn charge, and the scene impresses at least two Chicago editorial writers (albeit somewhat differently). "The representatives personally," says the Democratic Chicago *Times,* "are perhaps as fine a looking body of men as ever assembled in the Union. No one who should see them would ever suppose they entertained the extravagant and dangerous political sentiments they pretend to believe in." But the Chicago *Daily Journal* observes unblushingly:

> The scene is such as a man beholds but once in a lifetime. Along a thousand lines of a continent's open palm, Wisdom and Patriotism have come pilgrims, and the men on two seaboards are waiting for a voice from Chicago. That voice will utter a name, and its syllables will flash along lightning's spidery web from border to border; unnumbered tongues will speak it, unnumbered pens record it; hearts will cherish it; hands will uphold it.

To the 465 delegates chairman Morgan introduced David Wilmot of Pennsylvania, author of the Wilmot Proviso of 1846, and the convention was finally under way. Wilmot delivered the keynote address. George Ashmun of Massachusetts was elected permanent chairman, and finally the convention was adjourned until Thursday morning. By way of a postscript, it might be added that the Missouri delegation was reported in the press as still singing songs in the parlor as late as 2 A.M.

Early the next morning, during the report of the credentials and resolutions committee, the convention saw its first fireworks. The call of the 1856 convention, inviting delegates from "the people of the United States without regard to past differences or political divisions," established the equality of representation for each congressional district and for the state delegates at large. It would have been impossible to follow a formula proportioned to party membership, since there had been no previous test of party strength in a presidential contest. But what was to be done in 1860 about the delegates from such states as Texas, Maryland, and Kentucky, and such territories as Kansas, Nebraska, and the District of Columbia? Should "a delegation from irrevocably slave states be admitted to a convention built upon free soil and free men?" And should they have the same voice "as a delegation sent by a Northern constituency many times as large and ready and able to do yeoman service in the cause"?[3] Even as the credentials committee was reporting, the fat was in the fire.

A motion was offered to recommit that part of the report relating to the delegation from Texas, and amendments were quickly added to include also Maryland, Virginia, and Kentucky, along with the territories of Kansas, Nebraska, and the District of Columbia. On his feet to lead the attack against the admission of delegations whose loyalties he suggested might be counterfeit was David Wilmot, who stated his case poorly:

> I cast no implication upon the gentlemen who have come here to the convention. I have full confidence in their integrity and in their earnestness and zeal with which they are listed in the cause; but sir, in another convention that may assemble here, gentlemen may come up from South Carolina, from Arkansas, and from Mississippi for the express purpose of controlling, demoralizing, and breaking up the Republican party.

So it was started, and so began the great controversy that stretched right down to the arguments at Mineral Wells, Texas, in May of 1952 and the national convention that followed. In a later day it would be called "Caretaker Republicanism," but the issue would be much the same. Should the states and districts where the party is weakest enjoy equal representation in the performance of her most solemn duty—nominating a presidential candidate?

In rebuttal Messrs. Armour and Montgomery Blair of Maryland appealed to calmer counsels. Mr. Armour said, looking a long distance ahead: "If ever we expect Republican principles to prevail all over the land, we must organize, and you who live in Northern states must fraternize with us and not despise the day of our small things." Montgomery Blair's modest words were more temperate still. And when the shooting was over, the pleas of Armour and Blair prevailed. As finally adopted, the report of both the credentials and rules committees seated all delegations duly accredited by the various states and Territories, but denied a vote to the Territories. When the roll calls were taken on the platform and candidates, however, the votes of both states and Territories were counted. But the attempt of Maryland to fill up vacancies in her delegation, and thus increase the free state vote, was beaten down.

Another unsuccessful attempt that bears mention was the effort to have a rule adopted requiring a two-thirds vote to nominate. This was decisively beaten down in favor of the majority rule which has remained the principle of all subsequent Republican conventions.

The seventeen-plank platform submitted by the resolutions committee frankly aspired to avoid extreme radicalism and idealism. Already such seasoned politicians as Thurlow Weed, William H. Seward, and others sensed the need of an effective group diplomacy to carry a party to power. And the careful construction of the 1860 platform showed that the evangelical period was over, and that moderating influences were at work to head off allegations of radicalism.

Too much stress has perhaps been laid upon slavery as the force that brought together the diverse groups that made the Republican party, not enough upon the elements of liberal capitalism. By 1860 the Republican party was beginning to edge to the right, and this is suggested in the party platform.

In its bold outline, the platform "combined the solid policies of Hamiltonian Federalism with the hopeful outlook of its namesake, the party of Jefferson." It denounced the Democratic administration for forcing the "infamous Lecompton constitution upon the protesting people of Kansas," for its "reckless extravagance," and for the "new dogma that the Constitution, of its own force, carries slavery into any or all of the territories of the United States." On the positive side, the platform called for a railroad to the Pacific Ocean, to be aided with federal land grants, and two other measures which were received with by far the most enthusiasm at the convention: a protective tariff and a free homestead law. The resolution on the tariff, which had been vigorously championed by Horace Greeley, received a great ovation from the Pennsylvania delegation, while the homestead pledge had particular appeal for the Middle West and for working men in Eastern cities. When the party platform was passed by unanimous vote, there followed fifteen minutes of deafening applause.

Now the hour was at hand to proceed with nominations, and a motion was quickly offered to this effect. Had it carried, quite a few observers felt, Seward would have been nominated that evening. But fate intervened here, this time by way of a simple announcement from the convention secretary that the tally sheets for the balloting had not arrived and would not be ready for several hours. Someone then moved an adjournment until the next morning, and the meeting broke up.

Those who despaired of defeating Seward's candidacy were discouraged. At 11:40 that night, Seward's bitter critic, Horace Greeley, looked upon the situation as hopeless and telegraphed his paper: "MY CONCLUSION FROM ALL THAT I CAN GATHER TONIGHT IS THAT THE OPPOSITION TO GOVERNOR SEWARD CANNOT CONCENTRATE ON ANY CANDIDATE AND THAT HE WILL BE NOMINATED." And over at Seward's Richmond House headquarters, observers noted that champagne flowed freely and that for most of the revelers "the battle seemed all over but the shouting." But even as they rollicked, the rug was being pulled from under their candidate.

At the time the convention convened there was little doubt that Seward was the favorite and seemed to have a majority of the delegates elected to the convention.[4] It was also generally accepted that despite the promising outlook for the Republican party because of its capture of the Congress in 1858, the party would have to carry three of the following states if it was to win the necessary combination of electoral votes for the Presidency: New Jersey, Pennsylvania, Indiana, and Illinois. Here was the combination that proved to be Seward's undoing, though not without a generous amount of foxy footwork.

On May 9, just a week before the convention, the Illinois delegation had been instructed for Lincoln at the state convention held at Decatur, partly because his ability as a vote-getter had been clearly demonstrated when he opposed Douglas in the senatorial campaign of 1858. Indiana was supporting Lincoln for two reasons. The Hoosier state still had some strong sentiments for the old American, or Know-Nothing, party, and this element found Seward objectionable because of his open hostility to that party. Moreover, in line with the coattail theory—the notion that a very strong presidential candidate helps the entire ticket—it was also felt that Henry S. Lane, the highly popular Republican gubernatorial nominee in the Hoosier state, would be defeated if Seward was the presidential nominee. Neither Pennsylvania nor New Jersey was in the Lincoln camp, but they rocked uneasily in the position they found themselves occupying at convention time. Pennsylvania, also hostile to Seward, in part because of his attitude toward the old Know-Nothing party, was largely pledged to Simon Cameron (who later joined Lincoln's cabinet). New Jersey, likewise strongly opposed to Seward, was supporting William L. Dayton as its favorite son. A factor that looked large in prompting both Pennsylvania and New Jersey, like Indiana, to support favorite sons was the steady conviction that Seward could not be elected. This argument probably kept the nomination from Seward's grasp. Ninety-two years later it was reapplied with deadly effect on another candidacy: "Bob Taft can't win!"

Actually the first in the series of events that jostled the crucial delegations into position behind Lincoln occurred on Tuesday, the day prior to the opening of the convention. And apparently the responsible parties were not knowingly working for Lincoln. The initiators in fact were New Englanders, all committed to Seward.

With John A. Andrew at its head, a committee from Massachusetts and other New England states visited the delegates from the four states deemed critical for Republican success in November—Indiana, Illinois, Pennsylvania, and New Jersey. Pulling no punches,

Andrew stated at the outset that he and the New England delegates were for Seward, but that they much preferred the success of the party to the election of any specific individual. He then said that when it was made apparent to them that Seward could not carry the doubtful states, and another candidate could, they would be willing to abandon Seward in favor of the man certain of victory. Andrew closed by underscoring the fact that as yet the doubtful states had been unable to unite, but if, he said as his parting shot, they could "unite upon some one candidate and present his name, we will give him enough votes to place him in nomination."

"Andrew's talk," wrote Thomas H. Dudley, a New Jersey delegate-at-large and member of the resolutions committee, "made a profound impression upon the delegates."[5] Most of these delegates had been elected with the understanding that they would vote for a particular candidate, and it would be painful for them to break away. Yet amidst the shaking of heads were the mixed reactions of men whose desires for the party welfare and whose hunger for a winner readied them for the jump.

With Henry S. Lane, Republican gubernatorial nominee in Indiana, Andrew Gregg Curtin, candidate of the People's party for governor of Pennsylvania, and several others doing yeoman service in the cause, the efforts to unite on a candidate who could win were finally steered to a climax Thursday noon. At this time a sub-convention of delegates from the four doubtful states met at the Cameron headquarters in the Briggs House. Here Governor Reeder of Pennsylvania presided over the unofficial four-power conference in a lengthy session that brought no results. But late in the afternoon it was agreed to appoint a committee composed of three from each state to meet in the rooms of David Wilmot at six o'clock. This subcommittee was still unable to agree at 10 P.M., when Horace Greeley poked his head in the door and went off quickly to file copy for his paper which included the quip: "Man proposes, but God disposes." The lines of resistance were softening, however, and apparently a show of hands shortly after Greeley left indicated that among the anti-Seward candidates Lincoln was the strongest, and that he would win more votes than either Cameron or Dayton. Thereafter a New Jersey delegate urged that his state withdraw its favorite son, Dayton, and support Lincoln on condition that Pennsylvania also withdraw Cameron. This proposal was finally accepted with reluctance and the committee of twelve disbanded at almost midnight. An hour later the fuse was placed to set the plan in motion.

About 1 A.M., the New Jersey delegation held a special caucus to consider the recommendation of the committee of twelve. New Jersey decided to accept the proposal and support Lincoln after giving a complimentary vote to favorite son Dayton on the first ballot. But what would Pennsylvania do?

The Keystone state held her caucus at 9 A.M. Friday morning, just an hour before nominations began. Pennsylvania, after hours of earlier wrangling, elected to follow New Jersey and withdraw Cameron. On the first caucus vote Lincoln had a majority of six votes over Bates. "Damned if we haven't got them," muttered Lincoln's manager Judge Davis. "But how?" asked an eager publisher, Joseph Medill of the Chicago *Press* and *Tribune*. "By paying their price," answered Davis. Cameron had been promised a cabinet position. Now the plan was perfected and it only remained to guard against defections. There were none.[6]

William M. Evarts of New York nominated Seward first with a speech of twenty-six words: "I take liberty to name as a candidate to be nominated by this convention for the office of President of the United States, William H. Seward." Lincoln was nominated next by Mr. Judd of Illinois, in only twenty-seven words. "I desire on behalf of the delegation from Illinois, to put in nomination as a candidate for the President of the United States, Abraham Lincoln of Illinois." No long harangues of winged words and windy oratory, just as simply as that. It was quite a few years before the tiresome bores that stretched on endlessly hit Republican conventions and routinized the style of nominating addresses. Mercifully for all, however, there has been a movement back toward the fine example of 1860: the nominating speeches of 1952 were limited by convention rule to twenty minutes.

After the nominations of Seward and Lincoln, there were several others. William L. Dayton of New Jersey was presented by Mr. Dudley of Ohio, General Simon Cameron by Mr. Reeder of Pennsylvania, Salmon P. Chase by Mr. Cartter of Ohio, Edward Bates by Mr. Blair of Missouri, and Judge John McLean by Mr. Corwin of Ohio. Seward's nomination was seconded by Messrs. Austin Blair (no relation to Frank Blair) of Michigan, Schurz of Wisconsin, and North of Minnesota, while Lincoln's nomination was seconded by Messrs. Smith of Indiana, Delano of Ohio, and Stone of Iowa.

How the nominations were received is best described by Murat Halstead: "When the candidates were put in nomination, the only names that received tremendous applause were those of Seward and Lincoln. Everybody felt that the fight was between them and yielded accordingly." Response to Lincoln's nomination, he reports, was "prodigious and rising and raging far beyond the Seward shriek." It was part of the strategy of the Lincoln managers to pack the galleries, just as they were packed at the Philadelphia convention of 1940, when thousands kept chanting, "We want Willkie." To insure an adequate supply of Lincoln noisemakers, Norman Judd, a railroad attorney as well as the Illinois state Republican chairman, prevailed upon his clients to carry Lincoln supporters to Chicago free of charge. Moreover, to clinch the matter, hundreds of duplicate admission tickets to the Wigwam were printed the night before the balloting began and then distributed to Lincoln men with instructions to be on hand early the next morning.

Once again the Seward forces rallied after a seconding speech for the New York governor with a screeching demonstration that "rocked the Wigwam." Then the Lincoln forces had another go at it and pulled out all the stops, inspired by Mr. Delano's seconding speech for Lincoln in which he declared that his candidate was "a man who can split rails and maul Democrats." After three cheers for all candidates presented to the convention—on motion of Mr. Logan of Illinois, who demanded to be heard "in order or out of order"—the balloting finally began.

On the first roll call Seward stood first with 173½ votes, Lincoln second with 102, Cameron third with 50½. On the second ballot, Seward had 184½, a gain of 11; Lincoln 181, a gain of 79; Chase, 49, a loss of 6½ votes. A mighty cheer rolled out as Lincoln's vote was announced on the second ballot.

Midway in the third roll call came the carefully engineered break to send Lincoln over the top. New Jersey was called. Then Thomas Dudley, who had been selected to start the break, sprang to his feet and said that on this ballot he would vote for Lincoln. Thereafter eight New Jersey votes swung to Lincoln, who had had none from that state on the previous ballot. Pennsylvania, polled next, gave Lincoln 52, a gain of 4, while Maryland, following the Keystone state in the balloting, gave 9 of its 11 votes to Lincoln. At the end of the third roll call Lincoln had climbed to 231½ votes, just 2½ votes shy of the nomination; Seward, losing 4½ votes, had 180. It was at this moment that Cartter of Ohio jumped to his chair to announce the shift of four Ohio votes to the man who could split rails and maul Democrats with both hands.[7]

High up on the roof of the Wigwam, the man stationed to communicate the results of the balloting to thousands that waited with bated breath outside began gesticulating wildly to know what had happened. "Fire the salute!" shouted a clerk, waving a tally sheet wildly: "Abe Lincoln is nominated!" Then, the Chicago *Tribune* tells us, "a deafening roar of stentorian applause rose from the immense multitude, such as had never before been equalled on the American continent since the day that the walls of Jericho were blown down." In swift succession other delegations leaped on the bandwagon, and at last the secretary of the convention announced that Mr. Lincoln's vote was 364; necessary to nominate, 234. It was close to noon on Friday.

Sitting dejectedly in the riotous scene that followed, the Seward supporters must have wondered how they had been outgeneraled on all scores. Thurlow Weed was particularly disconsolate. The elevation of Seward to the Presidency, he had written in 1858, was "a purpose which for 20 years [has] engrossed my thoughts and controlled my action. We were beaten by a combination of the disappointed." [8] Thurlow Weed, Governor Morgan of New York, and Henry J. Raymond of the *Times* had pleaded hard with gubernatorial nominees Curtin of Pennsylvania and Lane of Indiana to join the Seward march, but to no avail. Nor had generous offers of money for campaign purposes moved them.

Among the formidable factors in Seward's defeat were the opposition of the powerful *Tribune* and editor Greeley, and the friendly devotion of Seward to his Catholic friends. In particular an executive message which the New York Governor had sent to the state legislature urging a division of school funds between Catholics and Protestants won him the enmity of the Know-Nothing elements strong in Pennsylvania and New Jersey.[9] No doubt Seward, who had been in public life longer than Lincoln, had made far more enemies than had the rising statesman of the West North Central region. Another element not to be ignored in assessing the causes for Seward's defeat was his malodorous political machine in New York. Known to have been involved in some shifty franchise legislation at Albany for the benefit of a few street-railway magnates, the Seward machine took a bad buffeting at the convention. Not only was Seward's association with the machine bemoaned, but this story, combined with the objectionable behavior of some of his followers at the Chicago convention, left another chink in his armor to be exploited.

Perhaps the overriding consideration in Seward's defeat, however, was his own failure to ride herd on the issue that was bestirring the soul of Republicanism in 1860. Seward's leadership stemmed from his "irrepressible conflict" speech at Rochester, New York, in 1858. "Shall I tell you what this collision means?" he said, taking to task those who dismissed the controversy between the North and South as the work of "interested or fanatical agitators, and therefore ephemeral. . . . It is an irrepressible conflict between opposing and enduring forces; it means that the United States must and will, sooner or later, become entirely a slaveholding nation, or entirely a free nation." Here Seward boldly proclaimed his loyalties with the progressive and radical conscience of the hour.[10]

Having already ascended to the position where he struck perhaps a majority of Republicans as the logical candidate, he sideslipped badly, partly as a result of a Senate speech. Courageous though he was, Seward took such an extremely sober view of John Brown's raid that it upset those enthusiasts who upheld the deed as an act righteously inspired. In a Senate speech, Seward declared that Brown and his men had "committed an act of sedition and tyranny" for which they were "justly hung."

Republican leaders had without exception condemned the raid, and Lincoln himself in his Cooper Union speech defied any Southerner to link a single Republican with the episode. None the less, the very conservative speech of Seward was hardly one to refuel the Republican campfires. Like some presidential candidates, he apparently failed to distinguish the very sharp difference between winning a nomination and winning an election. Hoping to wean some of the wealthier groups of the North away from their Democratic and Whig allegiances, and also bidding for the conservative votes in the Southern strip of counties in New Jersey, Pennsylvania, Ohio, Indiana, and Illinois, Seward lost face with many Republicans because of this speech. With it also went the initiative for national leadership of the Republican party. Thus Seward fell. Like others who almost grasped it, Seward faltered before the great prize of his ambition, the Presidency.

Lincoln's nomination, in the well-turned phrase of Professor Ray, was peculiarly "the triumph of availability, of party expediency, overprominence, and personal popularity." His success also demonstrated that the corn-fed politicians of the old Northwest were better at managing delegates and galleries than the crafty leaders from the big cities of the East.

Taking a short recess between 1:30 and 5 o'clock, the convention reconvened late Friday afternoon to select a running mate for Mr. Lincoln. Writing years later, Thomas Dudley, the delegate-at-large from New Jersey who started the parade to Lincoln, tells us that the committee of twelve discussed the Vice-Presidency the night the strategy was set up to defeat Seward. After agreeing upon Lincoln, the committee selected Henry Winter Davis of Maryland for Vice-President. Lincoln's campaign manager, Judge David Davis, happened to be a cousin of Henry Davis so he was delegated to wire his cousin to see if he would accept the nomination. Mr. Davis of

Maryland wired back that he would not and that settled it. Whether he would have been the nominee had he yielded to the committee's wishes, as Dudley contends, is a matter of conjecture. What did happen was that Hannibal Hamlin was nominated on the second ballot, his chief competitors on the first roll call being Cassius Clay of Kentucky, Nathaniel P. Banks of Massachusetts, and Andrew H. Reeder and John Hickman of Pennsylvania.

Hamlin, in politics for a quarter of a century, had served in the Maine legislature as speaker, several terms in Congress, and finally in the United States Senate, always as a Democrat until 1856. In the latter year he left the Democratic party and was elected as a Republican governor of Maine. Hamlin's nomination, like Lincoln's, was made unanimous.

Evening had now settled over the Wigwam and only adjournment remained. The convention closed on the motion of one delegate "to meet at the White House on the 4th of March next." [11] Meanwhile some of the delegates were scampering out in a joyous mood, none more so than the Pennsylvania contingent, which telegraphed immediately to Decatur for the entire rail fence that Old Abe put up in 1830.

Readying its forces for the campaign, the Republican party could take some comfort in the fracture that split its Democratic rival in the spring of 1860. Meeting at Charleston, the party of Jefferson and Jackson divided on the slavery question. Had its logical candidate, Stephen A. Douglas, been nominated, he might very well have won the election, but the Buchanan administration opposed Douglas, as did the Southern Rights Democrats. In the end the cotton state delegates walked out of the convention on April 30, forcing an adjournment of the convention to Baltimore, since Douglas no longer had any chance of receiving the two-thirds vote necessary for the nomination. At Baltimore, with the aid of some fresh delegates, Douglas was made the Democratic nominee, while the seceding delegates met and nominated their own candidate for the Presidency, John C. Breckinridge, then serving as Vice-President of the United States. Breckinridge ran on a platform of slavery extension. Elsewhere another candidate was brought forward, Senator John Bell of Tennessee, who became the nominee of the newly formed National Constitutional Union party. This political party was composed of a group of conservative and truculent Whigs, "the nice exclusive sort," as Lincoln derisively spoke of them, with "no political principles other than the constitution of the country, the union of the states, and the enforcement of the laws."

With such a four-cornered race developing, there was strong promise that the Republican candidate could outdistance the field. But that old joker of the American constitutional system, the electoral college, raised the haunting possibility that the Republicans might lead in the over-all popular vote but still fail to win a majority in the electoral college. Then the House of Representatives would have to elect the President. It was upon just such a contingency that the Democrats pinned their hopes. Part of the ferocity with which the midterm congressional battle of 1858 had been contested is also to be explained by this. The Republicans won a majority of the seats, but they failed to capture a majority of the state congressional delegations. Since each state has one vote in the event that a presidential election is thrown into the House of Representatives, the Republicans could not hope to elect their man if the general election in November ended with no candidate getting a majority in the electoral college. With all of these factors in mind, the Democrats hoped that if no compromise candidate could be agreed upon in the House the Senate might then elect Breckinridge's running mate Joseph Lane as Vice-President, to accede automatically to the presidential vacancy. At this time, and up to the adoption of the twentieth amendment, a lame duck congress would elect the President under such circumstances. Not without reason, therefore, did the Republicans pound away with the warning slogan, "It's Lincoln or Lane," at almost every political rally of the campaign.

With Edwin D. Morgan in charge (he was re-elected chairman of the national committee), the Republicans drove into the battle to help Lincoln maul Democrats. Lincoln's chief rivals at the convention responded loyally, and Seward himself took the lead in stumping for the success of the Republican ticket.

As the campaign warmed up, Lincoln's superb talents, which he had previously demonstrated in jousting over the issues of the hour, served him in good stead. While Lincoln excelled in unlocking a sympathetic response in a given social situation, he also well understood the need for making all possible appeals in soliciting votes. Thus, to the striking workers of a New Haven shoe industry he had said in 1859: "I am glad to see that a system of labor exists in New England under which laborers can strike when they want to, where they are not obliged to work under all circumstances, and are not tied down and obliged to work whether you pay them or not. I like a system that lets a man quit when he wants to, and wish it might prevail everywhere. One of the reasons I am opposed to slavery is just here." And, with a gentle nod to another group, he went on in the same speech: "I don't believe in a law to prevent a man from getting rich; it would do more harm than good. So while we do not propose war on capital, we do wish to allow the humblest man an equal chance to get rich with everybody else. When one starts poor, as most do, in the race of life, free society is such that he knows he can better his condition; he knows that there is no fixed condition of labor for his whole life."

The remarkable fact of the 1860 campaign, of course, was that not once did Lincoln leave Springfield. Remaining in the Illinois capital during the entire campaign, he opened an office in the statehouse where he saw various callers daily. But nary a single time did he make a public address or write anything for publication. On May 26 he wrote a letter accepting the Republican nomination with the following statement: "The declaration of principles and sentiments which accompanies your letter meets my approval; and it shall be my care not to violate it or disregard it in any part." Beyond this, Lincoln would make no political statements for publication, notwithstanding heavy pressure to do so.

Lincoln and his managers agreed that he should not commit himself publicly, and this pact was kept without breach. Once when he wrote to disclaim authorization of a particular campaign biography he took pains to explain his noncommittal conduct: "But, in my present position, when, by the lessons of the past, and the united voice of all discreet friends, I am neither [to] write or speak a word for the public, how dare I to send forth, by my authority, a volume of hundreds of pages, for adversaries to make points upon without end. Were I to do so the convention would have a right to reassemble, and substitute another name for mine."

On another occasion he reaffirmed his reasons for remaining silent with a letter which asked: "What is it I could say to quiet alarm? Is it that no interference by the government, with the slaves and slavery within the states is intended? I have said this so often already, that a repetition of it is but mockery, bearing an appearance of weakness and cowardice, which perhaps should be avoided. Why do not uneasy men *read* what I have already said and what our *platform* says?" [12]

Clearly Lincoln took very seriously his responsibilities as candidate to work harmoniously with his party's leaders, and all efforts of political alarmists to smoke him out were politely repulsed. Thus the Republicans relied upon others for mounting the offensive by way of a speaking attack. Meanwhile, Lincoln, though benched for the duration of the campaign, did not rust in inactivity.

To Carl Schurz he wrote on June 8: "I beg you to be assured that your having supported Governor Seward, in preference to myself, in the Convention, is not even remembered by me for any practical purpose, or the slightest unpleasant feeling. I go not back to the convention to make distinctions among its members; and, to the extent of our limited acquaintance, no man stands nearer my heart than yourself." [13]

Ever mindful that in the great game of politics there is no substitute for the simple courtesies, Lincoln had an unpretentious way of making the small man feel like an emperor. On the other hand, when the would-be emperors were inclined to be sniffy to the Republican candidate, he seemed to pay it little mind. Seward, for example, though campaigning vigorously for Lincoln, never left his railroad car to greet Lincoln when he returned to Springfield after a triumphal swing through the upper Northwest. But Lincoln, nudging his way through a crowd to Seward's car, shook hands with him, after which the New York Senator made a short speech and then sat down without saying a further word to the Republican standard-bearer. Without a sign of resentment, Lincoln managed to withdraw from the awkward situation and slip back into the crowd.

The Republican objective in 1860 was the decisive labor vote. Time after time Republican orators flogged the issue that was bothering the free laborer of the North, asking: How can "the free laboring man ever get two dollars a day, when a black slave costs his master but ten cents a day to keep?" If this poser failed to shake the free Northerner, there were other ways of exploiting his fears. The New York *Tribune* ran accounts of how North Carolina laws taxed mechanics' tools "twenty times as heavily as slave property." [14] There were also such tales as that of the South Carolina mechanic who was tarred and feathered for objecting to the practice of masters who hired out their slaves in competition with free labor. And if these incidents did not give rise to uneasiness among the working men, there was still another stinger left in the bag. In one of those impassioned outbursts not uncommon for the period, Senator James H. Hammond of South Carolina struck a low blow that provided Republican orators with a natural opening. He characterized laborers as the "mudsills of society," to which Senator Henry Wilson of Massachusetts, the "Natick Cobbler," promptly issued a rejoinder that was widely circulated as a Republican campaign pamphlet. Wilson, incidentally, a former shoemaker's apprentice, stumped the East extensively to win the working classes over.

Late in the campaign the three opposition parties struck up a stratagem, born of desperation, that they hoped would stem the Republican tide. The October elections which gave Curtin a 32,000 majority for governor in Pennsylvania and Lane a 10,000 majority in Indiana gave credence to the view that, barring some form of drastic intervention, Lincoln would win. The plan conceived was to arrange for fusion tickets of presidential electors in the states of New York, New Jersey, Rhode Island, Pennsylvania, and Connecticut. All three opposition parties made common cause in this effort to thwart Lincoln's election—the Douglas Democrats, the Constitutional Unionists, and the Breckinridge Democrats.

Aware that the squeaking wheel gets the most grease, diehard conservatives among all anti-Republican groups decided to step up their efforts to pump panic into Northern businessmen. They insisted that Lincoln's election would mean immediate secession and that the businessmen of the North would lose $200,000,000 owed to them by Southern debtors. Responding generously to the appeals to bring about Lincoln's defeat by fusion tickets, businessmen threw in large sums of money in the closing weeks of the campaign. In New York, William B. Astor was reported to have contributed a million dollars for the defeat of the Republican electors, quite a tidy sum for the 1860's. Elsewhere immense sums were also spent to head off a Republican victory, but all such attempts were doomed to failure. Only in New Jersey, where because of a fusion ticket Lincoln lost three out of seven votes, did the fusion gimmick bring in a single electoral vote.

In New York, where the great mercantile interests supported the anti-Lincoln fusion ticket, many Republicans worried that the Empire state would be lost. But Thurlow Weed, the leading precinct patriarch of his day, knew he had the situation well in hand. "Some of our friends are nervous," he wrote to Lincoln. "But I have no fear of the result in this state." [15] To his well-drilled organization, he sent the following instructions on November 5, election eve. "Leave nothing for tomorrow but direct work. Pick out and station your men. Let there be an assigned place for every man, and at sunrise, let every man be in his assigned place. Don't wait until the last hour to bring up delinquents. Consider every man a delinquent who doesn't vote before 10 o'clock. At that hour begin to hunt up voters!" [16]

Election Day, Weed's men stalked the precincts from dawn to dusk searching for votes with the thoroughness of a bird dog flushing a partridge. That evening the returns came in rapidly. By midnight it was fairly obvious that Lincoln would carry New York by 50,000 votes, and here was the news that the excited mob hugging the telegraph office in Springfield was waiting for. In the hall of the state House of Representatives, where he had gathered with a few close friends—Senator Lyman Trumbull of Illinois, State Treas-

urer Jesse K. Dubois, and Edward L. Baker, a Springfield editor—
Lincoln finally heard the word. Henry McPike tells us the rest:[17]

> Dubois jumped to his feet. "Hey," he shouted and they began
> singing a campaign song, "Ain't You Glad You Jined the Repub-
> licans?"
> Lincoln got up and Trumbull and the rest of us. We were all ex-
> cited. There were hurried congratulations. Suddenly old Jesse grabbed
> the dispatch out of Ed. Baker's hands and started for the door. We
> followed . . . Lincoln last. The staircase was narrow and steep. We
> went down it still on the run. Dubois rushed across the street toward
> the meeting so out of breath that he couldn't speak plain. All he
> could say was "Speech." Lincoln, coolest of the lot, went home to
> tell his wife the news.

That Election Day the balloting ended with Lincoln winning
1,866,452 popular votes. Douglas, his nearest competitor, won
1,376,957, while the Southern Rights Democrat Breckinridge and
the Constitutional Unionist Bell trailed with 849,781 and 588,879
respectively. As Herbert Agar so well expresses it, the Election Day
of 1860 gives the picture of a nation breaking in two. With the admission of Minnesota in 1858 and Oregon in 1859, there were now
eighteen free and fifteen slave states. Lincoln carried all the free
states; in the slaveholding states he won but two counties, both in
the border state of Missouri. Breckinridge carried every slaveholding state except Missouri.

New England gave the Republicans a clean sweep. In an un-
paralleled landslide, 70.5 percent of the two-party vote went to the
Republican ticket. For the first and only time until 1896, the Republican presidential candidate carried every county in New England. Elsewhere, California joined the Republican column for the
first time, though by the hairline margin of 643 out of 119,876 votes;
and Oregon gave Lincoln a plurality of 264 out of a total of 13,-
908 cast.

Two details of the tally sheets have led would-be purists to insist
that Lincoln stole a base and slid safely home because of a divided
field. First, no candidate in the four-cornered contest garnered more
than 39.8 percent of the popular vote. Second, Lincoln's plurality
over his closest competitor was not quite half a million, and his total
vote was 978,382 shy of a majority. No matter how one tries to
juggle the results, however, the simple truth is that Lincoln's victory was clear-cut and decisive. Lincoln carried the free states and
won the election hands down. Even if the votes of all three of Lincoln's competitors had been bunched in favor of a single candidate,

which they actually were in the case of anti-Lincoln fusion tickets in five states, the Republican ticket would have won. Keeping in mind that Lincoln carried every free state but California, New Jersey, and Oregon by a larger majority than the combined opposition, it is easy to see why he still would have won if all non-Republican votes went for one candidate. In this case the total opposition, polling 2,820,454 popular votes, would have won 134 electoral votes, while Lincoln, with 1,865,543 popular votes, captured 169 electoral votes and the Presidency. The outcome, of course, which was the election of a man who won just 39.8 percent of the popular vote, is a striking commentary on the electoral system and the growing weight of the northern states in the electoral college.

Who elected Lincoln? Not the capitalists. There were, of course, industrialists who sought protection in tariff rates—the ironmasters of Pennsylvania and New Jersey, who raised money to help Lincoln—but others were openly hostile. In Connecticut many manufacturers censured the Republican ticket, while in New York and New Jersey they told their employees to vote the fusion slate against Lincoln.

Quite apart from the Democratic split, which undoubtedly blunted the driving force of a unified party, it was the labor vote that gave the Republican ticket the necessary assist to bring its first national victory. Among ethnic groups much has been made of the theory that the Germans really elected Lincoln, but here the problem of unraveling the truth becomes more complex. Many German-Americans joined the Democratic party upon attaining citizenship, but their hatred of slavery and the skillful leadership of Lincoln brought them into the Republican camp by the thousands in 1860. This was particularly true of the more recent arrivals among German immigrants, such as the "Forty-Eighters." But the older German settlers outnumbered the newer groups two to one, and were inclined to look askance at the political sentiments of the latter. That the older Germans did not overwhelmingly support the Republican presidential candidate, as is often contended, is convincingly indicated by the posthumously published study of Josef Schafer. From the factual data in the Wisconsin Domesday Book project, "a superior 'Gallup Poll' covering the time in question," Schafer concluded that five-sixths of the Germans in Wisconsin supported Douglas. The German Catholics did so, in Schafer's view, because they were fearful of the Know-Nothing nativism that had crept into the Republican party. German Lutherans supported Douglas strongly, which implied that further factual studies of other West North Central states would dispel the stubbornly held belief that it was the Germans who really elected Lincoln.

Looming larger than the slavery issue in most of the northwestern states was the question of free land. "People had gone there to make homes, not to fight the Southern tiger," a St. Cloud abolitionist said of Minnesota.[18] Both the Democratic and Republican party platforms contained homestead planks, but Buchanan's veto of the Homestead bill in June of 1860 left the Democrats short on performance. Homesteading was also a high-voltage issue in Iowa, Wisconsin, and Illinois, where the Republicans made the most of it.

Election Day of 1860 really did show a nation breaking in two. Even before the electoral college convened to elect Lincoln formally, South Carolina was making firm gestures that would lead to her famous Ordinance of Secession. Before the election, Lincoln had privately expressed the theory "that the pressure of the campaign was an external force coercing the party into unity." But what was to hold the disparate elements together after Election Day? And could Republicans be persuaded to close ranks before taking over the awesome task of their first guardianship of the Republic? These were the problems uppermost in Lincoln's mind as he entrained from Springfield for the nation's capital a fortnight before his inauguration.

A Party Divided

"Newspapers report on men in the process of *becoming* great," commented the Baltimore *Sun* on Lincoln's birthday, February 12, 1955. "Looked up later, their contemporary judgments on the great men of history sometimes make strange reading." How strange, no one will dispute.

Said the *Sun* on the day Lincoln was nominated in May, 1860:

> The nomination does not strike us as being a very *strong* one.

Six months later—the day following his election—the *Sun* spoke of the event with scarcely more than a frigid nod:

> As we cannot offer the reader of the *Sun* one word of congratulation upon so inauspicious a result, we are disposed to do no more than announce the fact. . . .

And on his inauguration—displeased at the way Lincoln slipped through Baltimore (the President-Elect passed through the city at night undetected, inside a locked coach joined to a specially prepared express freight train, acting on the advice of friends who feared a plot to assassinate him)—the *Sun* pulled on the brass knuckles:

> Had we any respect for Mr. Lincoln, official or personal, as a man or as President-Elect of the United States . . . the final escapade by which he reached the Capitol would have utterly demolished it.

Not all newspapers of the Atlantic seaboard were bearers of such a grim welcome, of course. But across the nation the climate of opinion had many dissident patches that could hardly be reassuring to an incoming President.

Lincoln, at the close of the inaugural ceremonies on March 4, 1861, found himself at the head of a party about to disunite—the chief executive of a Union about to dissolve. The condition of the nation was one of political peritonitis.

That he must first lay firm hold upon his party if he was to direct the affairs of the nation effectively, is something Lincoln seems to have grasped intuitively from the outset. Though we usually think of him as a figure standing above the party battle, Lincoln, in the parlance of the precincts, was "a party man." And he needed no cues from the wings to convince him that the modern political party was the midwife of constitutional government.

His party, in the gross understatement of a contemporary who would soon become governor of Massachusetts, was composed of "somewhat diverse antecedent fellowships and associations." [1] That it surely was, and even before his inauguration he encountered brisk opposition from influential figures within the Republican party.

Some of the scar tissue so much in evidence at the time of his nomination had now healed. The Edwin Morgan (chairman of the national committee) who now consulted with Lincoln was different from the Morgan who "made no audible reply to Lincoln's greeting" when the latter was notified of his nomination at Springfield in May, 1860.[2]

Morgan worked faithfully throughout the campaign in pulling the party together, and he became an admirer of Lincoln. But his retention as national chairman in 1860 was a move for factional representation behind Lincoln's candidacy,[3] and hardly in keeping with the accepted practice today of having the presidential nominee select a chairman from his intimate councilors. All in all it was an uneasy amalgam out of which Lincoln hoped to mold a durable party—a party destined to control the Presidency for 24 years without interruption. In the 12 congressional sessions during the same period it would hold the Senate 11 times, the House 8.

Well before his election Lincoln was swiftly becoming familiar with some of the building-blocks of our party system. "If Mr. Lincoln is elected," wrote one aspirant to a Pennsylvania Congressman, "I will be an applicant. . . . I have served my party." Elsewhere another put the matter a little more crassly: "I want a good paying office." [4]

Not all of the salivating applicants for appointment were unknown men by any means. Thus J. Lothrop Motley, a noted historian of his day, interrupted his researches momentarily to write home from the Netherlands:

> I can have no doubt, writing a week before the election, of the success of the Republican party. . . . It has become necessary for me to renew my researches in the archives of the Hague, and a protracted residence there will become almost indispensable. I have thought, therefore, that the new government might be willing to give

a literary man, who has always been a most earnest Republican, ever since that party was organized, the post of minister at the court of the Hague.[5]

Happily, Lincoln took the swarm of solicitations in stride, for despite mounting pressure he was able to look upon the spoils seekers with a sense of humor. And as he listened patiently to the principals or their emissaries who called upon him at Springfield, and one day contracted a mild dose of smallpox, it is not surprising to find him saying, half humorously, half in earnest, to his secretary: "Tell all the office seekers to come at once, for now I have something I can give to all of them." [6]

Of all the patronage problems, the most pressing, of course, was the selection of the cabinet. Eventually Lincoln would draw four members of his cabinet from men who had been his rivals at the presidential convention—William H. Seward, Edward Bates, Simon Cameron, and Salmon P. Chase. But the task of reconciling in equilibrium the representatives of varying shades of opinion within the party was of incredible dimensions.

Lincoln's efforts to appoint a politically balanced cabinet met with opposition from both the radical and conservative wings of the party.[7] Not yet up to their full fighting strength, the Radicals, as they came to be known, were becoming noisier by the hour, and more insistent upon a show of force. "Without a little blood-letting, the Union will not in my estimation be worth a rush," wrote Michigan's United States Senator, Zachariah Chandler, to his governor, Austin Blair, in February of 1861. Chandler and another Senator, "Bluff" Ben Wade of Ohio, were the most violently outspoken anti-compromise extremists during the critical winter of 1860-1 as Lincoln sought to swing his party into a harmonious column, and neither was disposed to give any quarter. Even at Chandler's death in 1879, *Harper's Weekly,* looking for his nobler side, characterized him as "a warm, if not wise leader, a true Republican of yesterday, if not of tomorrow." [8]

Wade was a firebrand who took a dim view of caution in politics. It was Bluff Ben who threw out the challenge to duel all the "fire-eaters" (the name applied to violent Southern partisans) after Robert Toombs jumped up to applaud the caning of Sumner by Brooks of South Carolina. Asked to name weapons, Wade called for squirrel rifles at twenty paces, adding the further qualification that both antagonists appear with pieces of white paper pinned to their hearts! [9]

A growing obsession with the Radicals, as Lincoln's hour for assuming the responsibilities of office drew closer, was the fear that Seward would become something of a prime minister in the new government and that his conservative views would set the tone for the new administration's policy. Shortly after his election it became well known that Lincoln favored Seward for the post of Secretary of State, and this reheated Radical tempers. Now they felt certain that conservatives like Seward, Gideon Welles, and Francis Blair would gain the upper hand in the internal power structure of the new party, and their counter-maneuvers caused Lincoln endless anxieties.

One side of the argument centered on policy disagreement. The violent anti-slavery politicians of the Radical stripe looked upon the various active secession movements[10] as little more than brush fires that could be dealt with handily. A great many Northern leaders thought the South simply wouldn't put the issue of snapping the bond of the Union to a test. This belief was one of the greatest obstacles to effective Republican action. And so, while Horace Greeley was saying on November 20, 1860, that the "great majority of Southerners did not mean to dissolve the Union," and Northerners applauded, the dangerous drift continued toward the crisis that exploded with the attack upon Fort Sumter early in the spring of 1861.[11]

The one policy upon which all elements in the Republican party were agreed was opposition to the further extension of slavery. But within this frame, sentiment careened wildly over how to meet the secession crisis, and the ancient antipathies, both personal and political, of the Whigs, Democrats, Free Soilers, and others further aggravated the situation. "Opinion ranged from the hysterical joy of the abolitionists at the final separation from the slaveholders to the grim determination of a not so vocal minority to crush the movement with military force." [12] Greeley himself probably spoke for widespread Republican sentiment when he said, "If the cotton states shall decide they can do better out of the Union than in it we insist on letting them go in peace." In face of broad public support for this attitude it is easy to understand why Lincoln did not immediately forsake his policy of restricting slavery and present national unity as the fundamental Republican doctrine. Yet the concept of the Union was still firmly, though perhaps subconsciously, held in the public mind. All of the presidential candidates in the recent four-cornered race had spoken of the Union with vibrant emotion, acknowledging its appeal as a propaganda symbol. But not until the South Carolina batteries ringing Charleston Harbor fired a salvo that was directed at this symbol was Northern opinion regrouped into a semblance of agreement.

Aside from policy differences dividing nation and party, Lincoln's immediate problem of selecting a cabinet was intensified by the usual difficulties of a party leader in coping with the jealousies, hopes, and aspirations of ambitious men zealously seeking the summit. Here it was not a matter of dealing with policy antagonisms, but rather the task of working out compromises amidst a climate of congealed hatreds and power struggles of long standing. Since the birth of the modern party system no President-Elect has ever faced a more formidable task of building party leadership than did Mr. Lincoln.

He began by asking Vice-President-Elect Hannibal Hamlin to meet him in Chicago, and here late in November at the home of a friend Lincoln confided his plan for forming a cabinet. What he desired, of course, was a group that would appeal to the followers of Senator William H. Seward of New York, Judge Edward Bates of Missouri, Governor Salmon P. Chase of Ohio, and Senator Simon Cameron of Pennsylvania—all of his principal rivals for the Republican nomination.[13] In December Seward was offered the post of Secretary of State. Seward, apparently pleasantly surprised at Lincoln's magnanimous gesture, wrote Lincoln thanking him and asking for time to think over the offer. Meanwhile Lincoln went on receiving emissaries and letters on behalf of other people desiring cabinet posts, always striving to keep the factional fires within the party under control. Conspicuous among the early visitors at Springfield was Thurlow Weed, who returned from Illinois convinced that it was imperative for Seward to accept the position of Secretary of State. Weed's visit, as it later turned out, had an important bearing upon Seward's acceptance of the post, and this decision in turn was of profound significance for Lincoln in his subsequent trials with his cabinet.

On one appointment Lincoln encountered particular difficulty. Under strong pressure from Pennsylvania, Lincoln notified Cameron in late December that he would at the proper time nominate him as Secretary of the Treasury or Secretary of War, noting that he had not decided definitely which post it was to be. Cameron foolishly showed Lincoln's invitation to a few friends at Harrisburg, and word of the offer soon spread. Irregularities discovered while Cameron served as commissioner to settle the claims of Wisconsin's Winnebago Indians back in 1838 were now quickly exhumed by his opponents, one of whom declared that if Cameron had his just deserts "he would be serving out a sentence in a penitentiary instead of serving in the United States Senate." Allegedly he had given to the Indians depreciated notes on his own bank, and in the publicity that accompanied these charges of corruption he came to be cartooned as "the Great Winnebago Chief."

As these old charges were revived and editors viewed with alarm the appearance of the Winnebago Chief at Springfield, Lincoln found himself in a highly embarrassing position. But he faced up to the occasion without flinching. Writing to Cameron that developments had taken place which now made it impossible to take him into the cabinet, Lincoln suggested that Cameron write to him at once declining the appointment. At the same time he noted that if Cameron did not do so at once "before things change so that you cannot honorably decline," he would be "compelled to openly recall the tender." Even with this warning, however, Cameron had no intention of yielding. And only after two terrible months of pulling and hauling that prompted Lincoln's old law partner William H. Herndon to observe, "Poor Lincoln, God help him," did the President-Elect finally decide on his course: he would take both Cameron and Salmon Chase, whose appointment was being violently opposed by Seward and his friends, into the cabinet.

Lincoln reached Washington on February 23 of 1861 with only two members definitely selected, Seward and Bates. In each of the other cases he was practically certain of the final decision, but the full slate was barely ready before he placed it before the United States Senate on Tuesday morning, March 5. Almost on the eve of the inaugural—March 2—Seward wrote to inform Lincoln that because of changed "circumstances" he was withdrawing his consent to enter the cabinet. This brought a prompt response from the President-Elect, who on March 4 sent off a note asking the New York Senator to reconsider: "The public interest, I think, demands that you should; and my personal feelings are deeply enlisted in the same direction. Please consider and answer by 9 o'clock A.M. tomorrow." He did!

The roster of cabinet nominations which was laid before the Senate on March 5 included the following: William H. Seward of New York for Secretary of State; Salmon P. Chase of Ohio as Secretary of the Treasury; Simon Cameron of Pennsylvania as Secretary of War; Gideon Welles of Connecticut as Secretary of the Navy; Taylor B. Smith of Indiana, Secretary of the Interior; Montgomery Blair for Postmaster General; Edward Bates of Missouri for Attorney General.

An exhausting task was now completed. Undoubtedly the strange conditions of the times demanded that the new President avoid seeking an official family of advisers who seemed likely to pull together in harness, in favor of a decision to represent all segments of the party. It was a cabinet unique in the country's history.

At the subcabinet level Lincoln kept an eye constantly fixed on the need for wisely distributing public positions in order to hold his party together. Soon after he was inaugurated he wrote to Seward defining the hallmark of his policy on patronage: "Justice to all." Brave words, but a goal well-nigh impossible to attain.

Even as Lincoln was completing the formation of his cabinet, Congressmen and Senators were complaining that nothing in their experience approached the clamor of early winter in 1861, as tension mounted over the distribution of the "loaves and fishes." James I. Doolittle, United States Senator from Wisconsin, conveyed the sentiments well with his angry outburst: "I am sick and nauseated with this miserable, selfish clamoring for appointment to office. I sometimes wish I had never recommended a man."

Somehow Lincoln kept a steady head in most matters involving the public pap. In keeping with tradition, he followed the well-trodden path of his predecessors by consulting Senators and Congressmen of his party before making appointments, and on some occasions he even acted against his own judgment in complying with a Congressman's demands for a removal.

Like all party leaders placed in this unenviable position, Lincoln occasionally stubbed his toe. His most disastrous appointment apparently was that of Mark W. Delahay, an old friend from Kansas whom Lincoln nominated for a federal judgeship. This brought a sharp outcry from the bar and the press of the state. "There is not a respectable lawyer in the state that is not absolutely shocked at the appointment," complained one opponent. But after prolonged debate the nomination was finally approved. Yet it had a sad postscript, for so scandalous was Delahay's conduct on the bench that impeachment proceedings were threatened, and to escape disgrace he finally resigned. Despite inevitable slips, however, Lincoln's performance in making appointments was superb—particularly so when we consider that from the time of his election throughout his entire first administration he was treading a narrow catwalk crowded by congressional hostility and jealousy. Essentially conservative in his approach to patronage, as in other matters, Lincoln, once an appointment was made, tried to avoid tampering with the result. "I dislike to make changes in office as long as they can be avoided," he said. "It multiplies my embarrassments." [14]

If—in the manner of many party leaders—he appeared ungrateful to his friends in dispensing patronage, there is a wise explanation in an observation of his close friend, Leonard Swett: It was "because he had nothing to spare, and in the close calculation of attaching factions to him he counted upon the abstract attraction of his friends as an element to be offset against some gift with which he might appease his enemies." [15]

Sizzling away all the while Lincoln grappled with the job hunters, the secession crisis soon started exploding like a string of firecrackers. Three weeks and two days after Lincoln's election, every state of the lower South except Louisiana had instituted a secession movement. And as the last weeks of 1860 passed, the Republican majority in Congress, with few exceptions, could reach no basic agreement either to stiffen federal resistance to the secession movement or to reach a common understanding with the South on any conciliatory measures. Still confident the brush fires would burn out, because they overestimated the strength of Southern Unionism, Republican Congressmen and editors in the North were not disposed to make any concessions.

The Republican party, it must be remembered, was breaking new ground, coming to office for the first time. Like all parties, it was hesitant to assume responsibility for conditions that had drifted to a sad state until it was actually in power. Finally, in assessing the twisting course of events during the first months of 1861, one should not lose sight of the fact that a preponderant element in the public philosophy of Republicanism at this time was "a fixed and indiscriminate hostility to all compromise and all compromisers."

Well into the conflict, both Lincoln and his Secretary of State Seward shared in common a deep faith in the ultimate triumph of Southern Unionism. And as late as July 4, 1861, when Lincoln laid before Congress his request for powers to conduct a war that would reunite the country, he still maintained that within the Confederacy there was much loyalty to the United States. "It may well be questioned," he said, "whether there is today a majority of the legally qualified voters in any state, except perhaps South Carolina, in favor of disunion."

Whatever might or might not have been done to conciliate the South, Republican policy did not temporize in the last hours of sunlight before the war. That the sinews of the secession movement were stoutly bound, however, and that the Confederacy would mount a titanic struggle was never fully perceived.

In the quick swing of military and political crises of 1861, delegates of seven seceding states met at Montgomery, Alabama, on February 4. There they formed a provisional government taking the name Confederate States of America, and on February 8 Jefferson Davis was elected President of the Confederacy. By April events at Charleston reached trigger tension. Federal troops at Fort Sumter refused to surrender to the besieging Confederate forces, and on the morning of April 12 the bombardment of Fort Sumter began. Two days later, as news of the attack reached Washington, Lincoln called a cabinet meeting, following which he issued a proclamation calling for 75,000 volunteers to serve for three months. Simultaneously he called for a special session of Congress to meet on July 4. On May 3 Lincoln called for 42,000 additional men to serve three years or for the duration of the war, again with the expectation of a short-lived conflict.

Meanwhile the critics of Lincoln within his own party found much to criticize. They chafed at his cautious policy toward Fort Sumter, and were impatient that he waited so long before taking aggressive steps to proclaim the authority of the federal government. As the war progressed many Republican members of Congress soon raised another complaint. They resented such unusual acts of the President as the increase of the regular army by proclamation and suspension of the privilege of the writ of habeas corpus. (Lincoln made it clear in his July 4 message to Congress that the constitutional provision respecting the writ of habeas corpus was a provision that "such privilege may be suspended when, in cases of rebellion, or invasion, the public safety *does* require it.") To his critics who insisted that Congress and not the executive is vested with this power, Lincoln countered by noting that the Constitution is itself silent as to who shall exercise the power. Since the provision "was plainly made for a dangerous emergency," he argued, "it cannot be believed the framers of the instrument intended that in every case, the danger should run its course, until Congress could be called together; the very assembling of which might be prevented, as was intended in this case, by the rebellion."

By and large Lincoln's party went along cordially on most issues during the special session of Congress he called in December of 1861. But the organizational mischief which the Radical Republicans were brewing shaped up rapidly. And Lincoln's continued conservative policy toward slavery, coupled with his refusal to take an aggressive position on this issue until his annual message to Congress early in 1862, became a rallying point for criticism of the Commander-in-Chief. Nor was his position as a party leader upgraded by the series of misfortunes which the Union forces encountered on the battlefield.

On July 21, some 30,000 unseasoned troops were routed at the Battle of Bull Run and forced to scamper back to Washington in a highly disorganized condition. That fall only the prudence of Seward and Lincoln avoided war with Great Britain, after the British protested the action of a federal steamer in taking from a British vessel commissioners of the Confederate States to Great Britain.

On the heels of the summer's military disappointment, and in the midst of general restlessness and discontent throughout the North, the 37th Congress assembled on December 6, 1861, for its long session. Its mood was disquieting and filled with distinctly hostile overtones. Now a growing element within the Republican majority was so vigorously opposed to the President's restrained methods of conducting the war that it resolved to force a more aggressive policy upon him. Led by Wade, Chandler, Trumbull, Sumner, and Hale in the Senate, and Stevens, Colfax, Julian, Bingham, and Conkling in the House, they formed the war head of the Radical attack.

The basic assumption of the Radicals was that Congress was ordained by the Constitution as the proper institution to exercise the extraordinary powers essential for the conduct of the war. In furtherance of this objective, therefore, one of their first overt acts to chop down presidential authority was the creation of a Joint Committee on the Conduct of the War. Admittedly this agency was designed to exert heavy pressure upon the President and his subordinates in the domain of military affairs and to destroy Lincoln if possible. Soon the Radicals were beating on the President to adopt a policy that would deal more drastically with traitors, and were equally contentious in pushing demands for a stern confiscation bill. Their over-all policy might be summed up as one aimed at subverting presidential to congressional authority, and at driving Lincoln from the more temperate terrain of the course he had determined to follow in all phases of Union policy.

Spring of 1862 momentarily rekindled some confidence in the Republican administration among people of the North. McClellan's peninsular campaign, which began in April and gradually compelled Confederate forces to fall back, raised hopes that the rebellion might be put to rest within a matter of months. Enthusiasm for the military campaign, moreover, in combination with Lincoln's plan for a compensated emancipation, slowed down the Radical Republican opposition to the President somewhat. But in July the ill-fated peninsular campaign designed to capture Richmond ended in a forced withdrawal because of McClellan's vacillation, and the promise of spring gave way to despair.

This time the President's critics within his party could cry for another scalp, charging mismanagement of the high military command. Why hadn't the President put the gallant Frémont—the noble Pathfinder and Republican nominee of 1856—in full command of the Union forces? And the political predilections of his generals brought even deeper creases to the President's already heavily lined face. From one student of the subject we learn that of the 110 generals in the army of 1861, 80 were Democrats, the most notable being George McClellan—a man with acknowledged pro-slavery sentiments. Here was an issue the Radical Republicans thought they could exploit, and, as the late James G. Randall has observed, the military and professional wisdom of McClellan's selection by Lincoln became lost among charges of treason to the Republican party.[16]

By the fall of 1862, Lincoln's prestige was at an all-time low. Following the second Battle of Bull Run, August 30, Confederate forces had crossed the Potomac and invaded Maryland, and at the Battle of Antietam on September 17 McClellan again was unable to take advantage of his opportunity as Lee began to withdraw back into Virginia. In consequence of mounting criticism against McClellan's direction of the campaign, and the setback in the congressional elections of that fall, Lincoln on November 7 appointed General Ambrose B. Burnside to succeed McClellan. But Burnside, badly walloped by Lee at the battle of Fredericksburg in December, lasted only two months and was succeeded by General Joseph Hooker on January 25, 1863.

Gradually even many of Lincoln's followers reached the conclusion that the President was ineffective in directing his administration. They felt that he was incapable of leadership in both the civil and military branches, and that he was unable to swing his cabinet with him on major policy.

The fire centered on Lincoln's relations with his cabinet compels attention if for no other reason than that it reveals his strength as a leader, rather than weakness. Throughout the war Secretary of State Seward remained a loyal and staunch supporter of Lincoln, and ranking member of the cabinet both in terms of the pre-eminence of his post and his stature with the President. But Seward persisted in thinking of himself as a prime minister—a theory, quite obviously, to which Lincoln never subscribed.[17] Lincoln throughout his entire tour of duty remained an uncompromising champion of presidential government. As one of his successors farther down the road so vigorously phrased it, he declined "to adopt the view that what was imperatively necessary for the nation could not be done by the President unless he could find some specific authorization to do it. . . ."[18]

Initially Lincoln held regular cabinet meetings, but these were soon abandoned after he recognized their futility. No doubt it was one of these early meetings that inspired the story of how he wound up a cabinet discussion, in which he had been opposed solidly by all members, with the remark: "Seven nays, one aye, the ayes have it!"

Early in 1862 Lincoln was forced to take steps to retire Simon Cameron, his Secretary of War, for his shameful mismanagement of the War Department. Most serious of the complaints was Cameron's alleged favoritism in the allocation of war contracts. The Radicals in Congress, of course, had long opposed him, but the cry for his removal came from almost every quarter—from Eastern financial interests as well as from distinguished editors like William Cullen Bryant of the New York *Evening Post,* who wrote, "His presence taints the reputation of the whole cabinet, and I think he should be ousted at once."

Cameron, sensing the tide running heavily against him, attempted to bail himself out by deserting the conservatives to join the Radicals. And in the course of his turnabout he authorized the use of Negro soldiers in the Union forces. But when, without consulting Lincoln, Cameron inserted a recommendation to create an army of freed slaves in his annual report to Congress, the President quickly decided that Cameron had to go. But how to do it? Quickly Lincoln found a ready way at hand:

> As you have, more than once, expressed a desire for a change of position [*he wrote to Cameron*] I can now gratify you, consistently with my view of the public interest. I therefore propose nominating you to the Senate next Monday, as Minister to Russia.

Cameron was subsequently confirmed by the Senate for his new post as minister to Russia, but only after an acrimonious debate. The House of Representatives had no thought of letting Cameron's conduct of the War Department go uncensured, however, and adopted a resolution rebuking him in April of 1862. His conduct in delegating authority to purchase military supplies and to make contracts involving the government, said the resolution, followed a "policy highly injurious to the public service. . . ."

As a concession to the Radicals, Lincoln brought into the cabinet to replace Cameron, Edwin M. Stanton of Steubenville, Ohio—a "war Democrat" who had been Attorney General under Buchanan, and had also served as a legal adviser to Secretary Cameron. Stanton immediately sided with the Radicals in the cabinet, who were hopeful that the new War Secretary "would kick out the West Point trained pro-slavery generals and who, in other respects, would do their bidding." [19] The new War Secretary proved a more efficient administrator than Cameron, and brought far more integrity to the performance of his duties. But his close kinship with the Radicals was distressing to Lincoln. Stanton sided with Chase and the so-called Senate "Jacobins," and undoubtedly took a hand in the plot, after the congressional elections of 1862, to bring about Seward's downfall. But in the case of Stanton, as with others, Lincoln maneuvered adroitly, managing in most instances to keep his enemies at bay.

In all of his actions, the President seemed to pay close heed to the element of timing. It was after the battle of Antietam that he took advantage of the temporary ascendancy of the Union forces by issuing his famed preliminary emancipation proclamation (September 22, 1862). Well aimed and timed, this proclamation blunted some of the more violent anti-slavery opposition to the President. Nowhere is the full measure of the President's own estimate of his leadership more trenchantly stated than in the diaries of his Secretary of the Treasury, Salmon Chase, who recorded Lincoln's observations just before he read his proclamation to the cabinet. Explaining that he had prepared a statement on the subject of emancipation after considering the whole subject in all lights, the President said:

> One other observation I will make. I know very well that many others might, in this matter, as in others, do better than I can; and if I were satisfied that the public confidence was more fully possessed by any one of them than by me, and knew of any constitutional way in which he could be put in my place, he should have it. I would gladly yield it to him. But though I believe that I have not so much of the confidence of the people as I had some time since, I do not know that, all things considered, any other person has more; and, however this may be, there is no way in which I can have any other man put where I am. I am here. I must do the best I can, and bear the responsibility of taking the course which I feel I ought to take.[20]

Here once more we see the consummate politician adroitly managing "his campaigns by ignoring men and by ignoring all small causes but by closely calculating the tendencies of events and the great forces which were producing logical results. . . ." Already he had told his friend Leonard Swett: "I can see emancipation coming; whoever can wait for it will see it; whoever stands in its way will be run over."

While the Emancipation Proclamation broke the force of the anti-slavery opposition, military setbacks soon brought on a new wave of criticism against the administration for its conduct of the war. And now, for the first time since the presidential election two years before, the true test of popular indignation could be measured by the dissent at the polls. Even before the mid-term elections, Lincoln became convinced that he must look for political support from more Democrats and conservative Republicans. He therefore avoided reference to the name Republican in most of his communications. Along with this tendency to soft-pedal the name Republican, the word "Union" began to poke its way into the local level of politics.[21] This development foreshadowed a complete break away from the Republican label in the presidential election of 1864.

That the need for mobilizing public opinion behind the war effort had reached a critical stage became acutely evident as New York, New Jersey, Illinois, Indiana, and even Ohio and Pennsylvania turned in Democratic majorities for their state offices in the fall of 1862. On the congressional side the administration casualties were also heavy in New York, Pennsylvania, Ohio, Indiana, Illinois, and Wisconsin, all of which had cast their electoral votes for Lincoln in 1860. Across the North, the Democratic rebound drove the Republican majority in the House from 35 down to 18.

Once more editors and politicians sharpened their spears and began chanting for radical change in executive policy and urging a drastic head-hunt in personnel. Lincoln's own political supporters in the Senate formally censured his administration when they convened in December of 1862, and now a plan was hatched to blast the President's loyal Seward out of the cabinet. It was hastened and given added impetus by a disastrous defeat of General Burnside in the battle of Fredericksburg on December 13. Three days later, at a secret caucus, nine Republican Senators were chosen to present to the President the case for Seward's removal. The group was known as the Collamer Committee, taking the name of Jacob Collamer, a United States Senator from Vermont. Meeting with Lincoln, the committee instructed him to remove Seward at once, along with all Democratic generals. At the same time it also indicated its intention of challenging the President's exercise of power in the conduct of the war.

Hearing of the scheme to unhorse him, Seward submitted his resignation at once. But Lincoln held on to it and asked the senatorial committee to return the following evening. Then he summoned all members of his cabinet except Seward to meet with the committee. In full command of the situation at this most unusual session, Lincoln skillfully directed the conversation in such a way that he prevented one faction of his party from destroying the other and bringing down his coalition cabinet. In the course of the evening he cornered Chase by forcing him into a situation where he was compelled either to agree with the complaints of the committee or to remain loyal to his chief. Chase managed this skirmish rather badly, and the next day submitted his own resignation. By this act, of course, he enabled Lincoln to play a trump card. With two resignations in hand from the leadership of both factional divisions within the cabinet, Lincoln then asked both Seward and Chase to remain "in the public interest." The plot had failed! More important, Lincoln's stature as a party leader and chief executive had risen, and the intention of driving our presidential system of government into a parliamentary pattern had been checkmated.

By playing off Chase as the leader of the Radical element, against Seward, the foremost of the conservatives, Lincoln used shrewd political strategy to gain the upper hand at the very hour that the disruptive elements of his party were pressing the hardest to bring down his government. In assessing the motives of the Radical Republicans, of course, one is constrained to move with caution. Surely within this group were some figures animated by high ideals and driven by honest conviction. But the group also embraced a motley crew of wreckers. "A more lovely knot of politicians would be hard to find," wrote Professor Randall in his study of Lincoln the President. "Self-important, humorless, itching for power, and scornful of ethical scruple, they sold their wares at their own valuation and paraded behind a front of crusading zeal. Unmerciful in their pressure upon Lincoln, they used the stratagems of patronage, party trickery and propaganda to impose their pattern upon all phases of the war effort."

Against this appraisal are some dissents. Randall's conception of the Republican Radicals is erroneous, says Louis Hacker. "The Radical Republicans had economic and idealistic facets, and they sought a conversion of our economy from a mercantile to an industrial one in a climate of liberty. They of course also wanted to preserve the fruits of their victory. The Radical conception of the war, therefore, was as follows: the South was antagonistic to free institutions and a free way of life. Because the South's politics, ethics, and psychology were dominated by slave owners, this class had to be destroyed." [22]

Even making allowances for the "idealistic facets" of the Radical Republicans, the sum of this argument favors Randall's judgment that the Radical groups were in the main irresponsible in their long-drawn-out vendetta against the chief executive. In their approach to all explosive issues they erroneously insisted on too short a fuse, and dangerously imperiled the war effort of the North by their constant efforts to torpedo Lincoln and the coalition he resolutely held together.

On January 1 of 1863, the formal Emancipation Proclamation was issued by the President. This measure put into effect his preliminary decree of a few months earlier declaring that all slaves in states in rebellion or in states partly in rebellion on January 1,

1863, were to be free from that time thereafter. Now with the more comprehensive anti-slavery policy at last in motion, and the drive of the Radical Senators to force personnel changes in the administration stymied, some of the resistance to the President began to ease off a little in the spring of 1863.

In civil matters, the administration moved ahead with its program for financing the war and strengthening the national economy. The nation already had its first income tax—a measure passed on August 5 of 1861, providing for a tax of three percent on all income in excess of $800. And the first of the legal-tender acts, authorizing the printing of legal-tender notes, had been adopted in February of 1862, followed by similar acts of 1862 and 1863.

In redeeming the pledges of the 1860 platform, the neatest "translation of social pressures into public policies" in all American history, the trump card of Republican Congressmen was the Homestead act, passed in 1862. This measure granted 160-acre tracts of the public domain, free of charge, to all comers who complied with the conditions set down. Ecstatically received by the land-conscious groups, it would prove a great vote-winner for Republican candidates for many years to come.

Lincoln showed no particular enthusiasm for agrarian legislation generally, but he was immensely pleased with the chartering by Congress of the Union and Central Pacific railways under which a huge grant of land was given for building a transcontinental railroad. Railroad promotion had always been a subject close to the President's heart, so much so that he once had hopes of becoming the "Illinois DeWitt Clinton."

Elsewhere, the Republican legislative record included the Morrill Tariff act of March, 1861, marking the beginning of successive tariff increases, which finally reached duties of 47 percent in 1864 under heavy pressure from industrial interests. But this extreme bill left Lincoln with many misgivings and he observed that he signed it only on condition that it be repealed at the end of the war. His wishes for a tariff readjustment were not followed, however, and postwar policies proclaimed themselves vigorously in favor of tariff barriers to check imports.

Late in the spring of 1863 the upward swing in esteem of the administration was suddenly shattered by the bad news of the slaughter at Chancellorsville, followed by another invasion of the North by Lee. But soon the great victory at Gettysburg in July, reinforced by the simultaneous capture of Vicksburg, recharged confidence in the North and refortified belief in the certainty of Union success. From this time on the popular estimate of the President continued to improve, and support for the war was stronger than ever before. The President, though still opposed, must have felt somewhat like Disraeli upon finally becoming prime minister, when he said, "At last I have climbed to the top of the greasy pole." In any case, his ascendancy in his party was fairly well established by March of 1863 when the chairman of the national committee, Edwin Morgan, took the oath of office of the United States Senate.

Soft spots remained here and there; in Missouri, for example, where the Radicals were in open revolt against the administration on the ground that Lincoln was giving far too much deference to the conservative faction of the party. But this year the elections confirmed that he had bounced back from the trough of defeat after the congressional elections in 1862. For in the elections of 1863 substantial majorities were registered for administration tickets in all the loyal states but one.

Whether the successful outcome of these elections had any bearing on his decision or not, the question whether Lincoln would run again was not fully settled in his own mind until just about this time —November, 1863. We know that in the painful days of 1862 he must have doubted his own abilities to lead the nation through the war, because he once suggested to Seward that the secretary run in 1864. Seward, however, having come to admire Lincoln, declined, assuring the President that his re-election was essential to "reaffirm" the indecisive results of the 1860 election.[23]

Lincoln's shaken confidence in his own leadership took a more unconventional turn in 1862, when he offered to give the Union party presidential nomination of 1864 to Governor Horatio Seymour of New York, a Democrat. Unpartisan in the fullest sense, for Seymour was highly critical of the administration, this was a move Lincoln thought might have a moderating influence on the coalition he had been trying to hold together. But Seymour showed no interest when Thurlow Weed arrived at Albany with Lincoln's proposal, and one is left with the impression that all the offer accomplished was to reinforce the conviction of the Radicals that Lincoln was highly erratic and unfit to execute the party program. It is against such a background that the lifting promise of events in late 1863 must be weighed.

Turning into the year of 1864, after running a muddy marathon of well over two years, Lincoln might well have hoped that the force of the opposition to him within his party was spent, and that as it crumbled he could rebuild party unity for the journey ahead. But such was far from the case. The weary years of military defeats, stalemates, and indifferent successes on the battlefields, coupled with disaffection over drafts, higher taxes, patronage conflicts and disputes over the war aims, had left a heritage of badly shaken party morale. So much had these events "shaken the foundation of the Republican party," writes one keen analyst of Lincoln's last campaign, "that the party was in the process of disintegration." [24]

Heterogeneous and ill-compacted when it won its first national victory in 1860, the Republican party had never swung into that harmonious group its well-wishers had hoped for in November of 1860. And now, as 1864 approached, the more fractious elements within the party were actively engaged in dismembering it and building intrigues to discard Lincoln.

Late in 1863 the associates of Secretary Chase started rolling the drums for his presidential nomination, and by February of 1864 this movement developed into a full-blown presidential boom. For obvious reasons Chase was a likely rallying-point for the opponents of Lincoln. To begin with, Chase had an insatiable desire to become President. Lincoln himself always thought Chase "a little insane on the subject of the Presidency." Late in 1864, when he was debating whether or not to nominate Chase to be Chief Justice of the United States Supreme Court, Lincoln said:

> Of Mr. Chase's ability . . . there is of course no question. I have only one doubt about his appointment. He is a man of unbounded ambition, and has been working all his life to become President. That he can never be; and I fear that if I make him Chief Justice he will simply become more restless and uneasy and neglect the place in his strife and intrigue to make himself President. If I were sure that he would go on to the bench and give up his aspirations and do nothing but make himself a great judge, I would not hesitate a moment.[25]

Chase was not without assets as an opponent of Lincoln. As Secretary of the Treasury, he had a patronage of nearly 15,000 places, a resource which James G. Blaine later noted was one from which Chase drew much of his support in opposing Lincoln. The Treasury post also gave him considerable power in financial circles. But the mainstay of Chase's support as a potential rival to Lincoln stemmed from his appeal to the Republican Radicals, or to the Unconditionals, as they were sometimes called. (The Unconditionals opposed making any concessions to the South as a basis for peace, demanding that slavery be abolished, and that the Negro be accorded full political and social rights.)[26] Not exactly harmful to the Chase boom, moreover, was the generous policy of amnesty and reconstruction which was promulgated by Lincoln late in 1863. This plan was jumped upon at once by the Radicals, who complained that free Negroes were given no role to play in the reorganization of the

South, and that the seceding rebels were to be given an opportunity to regain political power.

Chase made extensive campaign treks into Ohio and Indiana to scout support, even suggesting to the governor of Indiana that he would offer him the post of Secretary of State in return for his help. A national Chase Committee was formed, and it came to be known as the Republican National Executive Committee, with Senator Pomeroy of Kansas acting as its chairman.

In the face of the Secretary of the Treasury's obvious bid to overthrow him, Lincoln's reluctance to remove Chase from his cabinet became a subject of intense conjecture at the nation's capital. Even the crafty Thurlow Weed favored the "tipping out" policy. Lincoln knew the dimensions of Chase's effort, and he was certainly concerned about it. Yet he shrugged off every warning: "I determined to shut my eyes, so far as possible, to everything of the sort." Instead of accepting the judgment of those who thought Chase could be stopped if Lincoln would only "kick him out," Lincoln correctly deduced that such a move might drive the Radicals to an open break with his party and destroy all that he had labored to hold together during these painful years. And Weed himself soon saw the wisdom of Lincoln's policy in giving Chase sufficient rope.

Chase was not the only contender for the nomination of the Union party in 1864. Among the radical elements of the party, particularly the Germans, General Frémont had a small but enthusiastic following. Frémont, however, had little support from influential leaders throughout the country, and as his friends despaired of winning the nomination of the Union convention they ultimately launched their candidate under the standard of an independent party.

After February of 1864, the Chase boom was quickly on the wane. One of his persistent problems had been the bickering of various factional elements within the Radical and Unconditional groups. Thad Stevens, for example, had no great love for Chase, nor had Bluff Ben Wade, who was actually hostile to Chase personally. Despite the gloom in the Lincoln camp, where it was believed that Chase was making strong headway, a few discerned the course of events early. One was Joseph Medill, who wrote that he presumed Chase's friends were working for his nomination, but it was "all lost labor. . . . Old Abe has the inside track. So completely that he will be nominated by acclamation when the convention meets." [27] But certainly not all newspapers regarded it with the certainty of Joseph Medill, and in New York City only the *Times* favored Lincoln's renomination early in 1864. This was largely because of Henry J. Raymond's great admiration for Lincoln. Raymond, who would soon become chairman of the Republican national committee, attributed Lincoln's difficulties to the fact that not only were the more violent anti-slavery members of his party dissatisfied, but many distinguished public men resented "his rejection of their advice, and many more have been alienated by his inability to recognize their claims to office." [28]

As the party machinery itself began to creak into action after a long period of disuse, we find chairman Morgan writing to his father at the beginning of 1864: "Mr. L. will be a candidate for re-election. I do not mean to say he will positively be renominated although that is possible." Not long after this the Union Central Committee of New York met, taking the name of Union rather than Republican, and recommended Mr. Lincoln's renomination, word of which was passed along to Morgan. It was then that Morgan wrote to Lincoln, "Dear Mr. President: It is going to be difficult to restrain the Boys, and there is not much use in trying to do so." Both Thurlow Weed, who was using his Albany *Evening Journal* with sharp effect on Lincoln's behalf, and Morgan were reasonably confident at this stage of the pre-convention campaign that, even though Chase's movement was causing quite a stir, Lincoln would be renominated.

On February 20, 1864, perhaps even as the star of Salmon Chase's candidature was beginning its descent, there suddenly appeared in Washington a circular which bore the signature of Senator Pomeroy of Kansas and was labeled "strictly private." Patently a manifesto for Chase, the Pomeroy circular protested that "party machinery and official influence" were being selfishly used to perpetuate the administration. It was essential, therefore, said the circular, that "friends of the Union and of freedom must act." And since Lincoln's re-election was impossible—even undesirable because of his tendency to temporize and compromise—it was quite obvious that the man cut out for the job was Salmon P. Chase. This circular, which was widely quoted in the newspapers, proved highly embarrassing to Chase. Humiliated, Chase insisted to Lincoln that the circular had been issued without his knowledge, and he offered his resignation. Wisely, Lincoln again declined to accept Chase's resignation, for he shrewdly guessed that an acceptance might suggest he feared his talented Treasury Secretary as an opponent, and that he had decided to throw his full weight in with the conservatives of his party.

Appropriately, the machinery for the Republican campaign of 1864 swung into action precisely at noon on Washington's birthday. National committee chairman Morgan prepared a call for a national convention to assemble at Baltimore on June 7. Gideon Welles, representing Connecticut on the national committee, noted that four-fifths of the committeemen favored Lincoln's re-election.[29]

It is interesting to note that a comparison of the 23 names listed on the national committee in 1864 with the 27 members named in 1860 shows only 16 of the original group still on the national committee. Seven were new, and Virginia, Missouri, Texas, and Oregon were now not represented at all. Where unsympathetic state organizations had refused to send representatives, the committee had used its power to fill vacancies. Also of interest is the fact that the New York *Tribune* spoke of the meeting on Washington's birthday as a session of "The National Republican Committee," while the pro-Unionist New York *Times* referred to it as the "National Union Committee," presumably to plug the idea that the call was inclusive enough to appeal to all those wishing to see the rebellion put down.

By the time of the Union national committee's meeting in February, delegates to the national convention had already been selected from New Hampshire, Connecticut, Maryland, and Iowa, and instructed to vote for Lincoln. The President had also received strong assurances of support from legislatures and party organizations in Pennsylvania, California, Colorado, Kansas, Wisconsin, New York, and New Jersey. And on the day following the meeting of the Union national committee, the Lincoln forces struck a hard blow at the Chase candidacy right out in the territory that Chase had counted upon the most. At the Indiana state convention on February 23, Lincoln's lieutenant took Chase supporters off guard by driving through a resolution endorsing the President's re-election.[30]

Sensing the inevitable, Chase wrote to Representative Albert Riddle[31] of Ohio, one of the Republican Radicals, on March 7: "Our Ohio folks don't want me enough, if they want me at all, to make it proper for me to allow my name to be used." But even two days before this date, stunned by his embarrassing lack of support, he wrote to James Hall asking that "no further consideration be given his name." Not all observers were persuaded that Chase really meant to retire from the race, however, and many of his workers continued their activity under cover right down to the time of the Baltimore convention.

Meanwhile, evidence of Lincoln's rising popularity with the people of the North continued to roll into Washington, leaving the Unconditionals and Radicals in a state of bewilderment as they groped for a suitable means of counterattack. But none seemed eminently available at the moment. The friends of General Ben Butler tried to advance him to the front after the eclipse of the Chase candidacy, but this was doomed from the start. Frémont was nominated at Cleveland, May 31, as the candidate of a new party calling itself the "Radical Democracy," but the entire episode roused little enthusiasm among the Unconditionals and Radicals. Its one possible use, said Zachariah Chandler, would be as a rallying candidacy if Lincoln's popularity suddenly took a sharp tumble.

Only one line of strategy remained for the Unconditionals and Radicals as they still hoped to head off Lincoln after failing to build a ground swell for a rival candidate; that was to try delaying the convention. A prime mover in this strategy was editor Horace Greeley, who had been arguing for a September convention date even before the beginning of 1864. Greeley contended that winning the war should take precedence over the presidential election, and his editorials continued to give affectionate pats to Chase, Butler, and Frémont. He also suddenly discovered the one-term principle and indicated his endorsement of the idea. Greeley realized that the effort to sidetrack Lincoln would undoubtedly fail, but he kept trying because he thought he might force the President to move closer to the Radicals. By April Greeley knew the fight to postpone the convention was lost, but it was not until May that others who were agitating for a postponement finally gave up and accepted the inevitable.

If one ray of hope remained for those who sought to retire Lincoln, it could now be summed up in a simple five-letter name: Grant. The North's first great victory in 1862 was led by Grant, who captured Fort Donelson in Tennessee, taking a site of great strategic value to the South, along with 15,000 prisoners.[32]

It was with the great victory at Vicksburg on the nation's birthday, however, and after the defeat of Bragg at Chattanooga in November of 1863, that this hard-hammering general with the unbuttoned tunic and dead cigar began to attract the attention he justly deserved. In March of 1864 Lincoln summoned Grant to Washington "to elevate him to a position that none had held since Washington." Grant was made a lieutenant-general and General-in-Chief of the Union forces. A long search was over. "Grant is the first general I have had," remarked Lincoln to an aide.

Still conducting a last-ditch stand against the President's renomination, the Radicals decided next to bring Grant forward after the collapse of the Chase, Butler, and Frémont movements. With the Union national convention just three days off, a testimonial meeting was scheduled in New York to thank Grant publicly for his magnificent services. But this move was headed off "by the cleverness of Lincoln and by Grant's refusal to have his name brought forward." [33] Invited to attend, Lincoln declined and the meeting was finally controlled by his friends.

In Baltimore on June 7, the delegates to the Union convention were shocked to find no meeting place, apparently because of the connivance of dissident Republicans, who along with Henry Winter Davis were able to rent the hall scheduled for the Baltimore convention. At first it appeared that the convention might move to Philadelphia, but on second thought it was decided to take over Baltimore's Front Street Theatre, where the delegates took their seats without delay. Here the physical arrangements left something to be desired. Warm weather made it necessary to remove the curtains from the windows and the scenery from the stage, and throw the back of the theatre open to the street. Since the theatre was located on one of the noisiest corners in Baltimore, it was very difficult to hear. The speeches, appropriately under these circumstances, were short and to the point. Because the Senate was in session at the time, the chairman of the national committee, Morgan, spent only one day at the Baltimore convention. But his speech calling the meeting to order evoked a tremendous response and underscored the consummate skill of Lincoln as a party leader in setting the stage for a successful campaign.

Before writing his speech, Morgan consulted the President, who suggested an extraordinary idea: the national chairman should use the occasion to propose a constitutional amendment to abolish slavery forever. Here was a concession to the Radicals combined with a strong stride forward in the positions of the President and a very conservative United States Senator. Moreover, in its bold design it reveals in Lincoln a keen perception of the ways of party leadership. Here is a President employing his party chairman in the responsible role in which he ought to be cast—as the President's spokesman on party policy. In sharp contrast to the platitudinous pronouncements so frequently made by party chairmen on such occasions, chairman Morgan said in his brief address:

> It is not my duty nor my purpose to indicate any general course of action for this convention; but I trust I may be permitted to say that, in view of the dread realities of the past and what is passing at this moment, and of the fact that the bones of our soldiers lie bleaching in every state of this Union, and with the knowledge of the further fact that this has all been caused by slavery, the party of which you, gentlemen, are the delegates and honored representatives, will fall far short of accomplishing its great mission, unless among its other resolves it shall declare for such an amendment to the Constitution as will positively prohibit African slavery in the United States.[34]

That evening Governor William Dennison (soon to succeed Montgomery Blair as Postmaster General) of Ohio was selected as permanent chairman, and the convention shifted at once into an executive mood that demanded speed. The tone of the meeting had already been set in the keynote address by Robert J. Breckenridge of Kentucky, who said: "I see before me not only primitive Republicans, primitive Abolitionists, but I also see primitive Democrats, primitive Whigs, and primitive Americans. . . . As a Union party I will follow you to the ends of the earth and into the gates of death; but as an Abolition party, as a Republican party, as a Whig party, as a Democratic party, as an American party, I will not follow you one foot." So the Republican label was dropped from the vocabulary of partisan politics in 1864.

Adopting eleven planks recommended by the resolutions committee, the Republican platform called for a constitutional amendment prohibiting slavery, the fostering of foreign immigration, and speedy construction of a railroad to the Pacific Coast. It also included a plank that was aimed hard at Montgomery Blair, the Postmaster General in Lincoln's cabinet, whose acrimonious attacks upon the Radicals had long ago led to a demand that he be dismissed. The sixth resolution read: ". . . we deem it essential to the general welfare that harmony should prevail in the national councils, and we regard as worthy of public confidence and official trust those only who cordially endorse the principles proclaimed in these resolutions, and which should characterize the administration of the government."

Conspicuous for its absence from the platform was a plank advocating confiscation of rebel property. Happily for harmony, this proposal, which had been energetically argued in the sessions of the resolutions committee, was turned down by the full committee.

On July 8 the convention was ready to select a presidential candidate, and while some Chase literature was still in evidence, Lincoln's nomination was now a certainty. It was prearranged to have Thompson Campbell present Lincoln's name, but Simon Cameron short-circuited this agreement by sending a note to the clerk of the convention with instructions to read it. Cameron's note turned out to be a resolution calling for the nomination of Lincoln and Hamlin. Apparently this was a canny gesture by which Cameron, acting as one of Lincoln's emissaries to make Andrew Johnson the vice-presidential nominee, tried to make it appear that neither he nor Lincoln was opposed to Hamlin. Hence he introduced the resolution knowing full well it would never carry, but hoping it would suggest he favored Hamlin for the Vice-Presidency.

Until Missouri was reached the roll call of the states looked like a unanimous ballot for Lincoln. Then 22 votes were cast for Grant. A Missouri delegate later related that at this announcement he feared the aroused delegates might throw the entire Missouri delegation into the street. But once the roll call was finished, the same delegate who announced the Missouri vote—John Hume—asked for recognition and moved that the nomination be declared unanimous, which was promptly done, Lincoln receiving 506 votes. Not until the din of the brass band playing "Yankee Doodle" was finally brought under control could the delegates turn to the unfinished business at hand, which in this instance turned out to be a historic decision. The hour had arrived to nominate a Vice-President.

In weighing the action that was taken, it is well to remember that American convention practice was still in the process of developing traditions. There was no assumption before the Civil War that a first-term President, much less a Vice-President, could have a renomination for a second term if he wanted it. And the idea that an incumbent first-term President was entitled to a second nomination took a longer time to be accepted by the Republican than the Democratic party. Moreover, today it is now considered a safe proposition that a Vice-President who has succeeded to the Presidency acquires the right to the next nomination of his party. But again this was not at all true before 1900, and probably not recognized as an altogether safe assumption until a stubborn man from Missouri demonstrated it in convincing style in 1948.[35]

The decision to retire Hamlin, therefore, was not so unconventional as one might suppose, though the reasons underlying the move to discard him were highly important.

The leading candidates for the Vice-Presidency were Hannibal Hamlin, Andrew Johnson, Daniel S. Dickinson, and Joseph Holtz. Johnson and Dickinson were both War Democrats. Long before the convention Lincoln had sent Daniel E. Sickles to Nashville, Tennessee, to size up Johnson, the man who had once been a tailor. In the pre-convention period Lincoln also asked Simon Cameron to approach General Benjamin Butler of Massachusetts as a possible running mate. But Butler declined the overture—a decision which he probably regretted.

Some disagreement exists as to how active a hand Lincoln actually took in the selection of his running mate. One writer insists that Lincoln did not engineer the nomination of Johnson.[36] The evidence which suggests that Lincoln did take a hand in the selection of the governor from Tennessee, however, is persuasive, for William Seward, Henry Raymond, and others were all aware of Lincoln's desires. Many factors favored Johnson. He had been a staunch supporter of the Union, and "a recognized friend of labor." [37] He also came from a border state.

As matters turned out, Johnson's nomination still was something of a surprise, even though many delegates knew the President's wishes. On the eve of the convention, Hamlin was thought to be in the lead, and even his manager Senator Morrill did not realize that his candidate would be defeated. But the count on the first ballot, taken June 8, stood Johnson 200, Hamlin 150, and Dickinson 108. In quick succession a rousing speech by a delegate from Tennessee supporting Johnson and a wild maneuver by Governor William Stone of Iowa, who leaped to his feet to cast all sixteen votes of his delegation for Johnson, sewed up the nomination. Governor Stone's action, incidentally, completely ignored "the fact that the majority of the delegates from Iowa opposed Johnson." But it was too late, and the hall was soon spinning with a motion, and seconds, that Johnson's nomination be made unanimous. And this was promptly done.

The Radicals obviously were unhappy. Thad Stevens was infuriated to have a candidate from "a rebel province," while others objected because they thought Seward and Gideon Welles had engineered the nomination—a suspicion not founded in fact, since it is generally acknowledged that Henry Raymond of New York was the facile factotum behind this nomination. Lincoln was pleased, while his secretary Hay wrote in his diary that the convention was one where there had been "little drinking—little quarreling—and earnest intention to simply register the expressed will of the people and go home." [38]

While some of the delegates frolicked in Washington and stopped in to pay their respects to Lincoln on their way home, it was perfectly obvious that despite the convention's work there was an undercurrent of defection sentiment. The Radicals secretly hoped to defeat the ticket. Depressing news again rocked the capital when the heavy casualty lists of Cold Harbor became known, and Lincoln's new general began to be spoken of as "Butcher" Grant. Sherman's advance through Georgia helped dispel some gloom, but during the summer the Radicals mounted another full-scale attack against the President's alleged mismanagement of the war, many of them demanding a new convention and a new candidate.

Late in June Lincoln's brilliant Secretary of the Treasury presented him with another crisis, at a time when the military news was far from pleasant. Following a patronage scuffle over the appointment of personnel in the New York custom house, Chase again offered Lincoln his resignation, feeling that it was clearly a situation where Lincoln must choose between Seward and himself. This time Lincoln surprised Chase with the following reply:

> Your resignation of the office of Secretary of the Treasury sent me yesterday is accepted. Of all I have said in commendation of your ability and fidelity I have nothing to unsay; and yet you and I have reached a point of mutual embarrassment in our official relations, which it seems cannot be overcome or longer sustained consistently with the public service.

Apparently Chase had not intended to resign, but his departure reheated the wrath of the Radicals, who pointed to it as an indication of the President's weakness and his unconscionable willingness to yield to Seward. As Chase's successor, Lincoln appointed Senator William Pitt Fessenden, of Maine. Chase was not the only casualty of the 1864 campaign, for the time was approaching for Lincoln to get rid of his Postmaster General, Montgomery Blair, who was anathema to the Radicals, particularly Thaddeus Stevens. Bad blood also existed between Frémont and Blair. To Blair Lincoln wrote "You have generously said to me more than once, that whenever your resignation could be a relief to me, it was at my disposal. The time has come. . . ."

Lincoln then graciously praised Blair for his services, but the letter breathes firmness in dealing with critical situations in a way befitting a great party leader and chief executive. For a long time it was hypothesized that Lincoln asked for Blair's resignation in order to secure Frémont's withdrawal from the presidential race, but this hardly seems likely, for the President had already promised Ben Wade and Henry Davis that he would remove Blair in return for their support. Today it is more generally accepted that Frémont withdrew because the Democratic party was committed to restoring slavery and possibly also because he came to see his position as hopeless. He insisted that he considered Lincoln's administration "politically, militarily, and financially a failure," and that he was withdrawing out of "consideration for the Republican party."

It was during a downhill trend in popular confidence that the Union party sought to get its campaign off the ground in the summer of 1864. A reaction set in almost as soon as the convention had adjourned. The mighty heave that Grant's army had made in May and June to capture Richmond had become a frightfully costly affair. Moreover, it apparently had failed, and that summer party leaders found it difficult to whip up enthusiasm. For close to a year public sentiment had been building up in favor of the administration, but now the Radicals were beginning to find the going more to their liking, and those who had resolved not to support Lincoln's re-election after his renomination began to speak out. In the President's dismissal of Chase and his pocket veto of the Wade-Davis reconstruction bill they found additional ammunition for the attack by which they hoped to drive Lincoln from the presidential race. Another major weapon was the manifesto prepared by two anti-administration leaders, Senator Wade and Congressman Henry Winter Davis, which was published on August 5. This document, maliciously conceived, was a scathing denunciation of Lincoln's entire policy toward reconstruction. It accused Lincoln of seeking to control the electoral votes of reconstructed states, and it called upon the party to repudiate him. Thereafter Wade and Davis circulated a secret call for a new national convention to select another nominee. But in this instance time was on the side of the President, although a successful canvass that fall looked mighty doubtful. "You think I don't know I am going to be beaten," admitted Lincoln to a friend in August, *"but I do,* and unless some great change takes place *badly* beaten."

The mobilization of the Republican party organizational effort for winning the 1864 campaign was beset by three difficulties. Foremost, perhaps, was that people were pre-eminently preoccupied with the military effort. Detracting also from interest in building a party organization were the distressing military reports throughout the summer, which dampened party spirit. Finally, unlike traditional campaigns, there was really no localized opposition in sight upon which party generals could center their fire. The Democrats had not yet picked a candidate—would not do so in fact until the end of August, almost three months after the Union convention.

Completing their organization two days after the convention adjourned, the Republican national committee selected Henry Raymond of New York as their new chairman, and Edwin Morgan stepped aside after eight years, apparently at his own request. Morgan, however, then became chairman of the Union Executive Committee, a body composed of three members from the Senate and three from the House—an agency, incidentally, that became the center of a factional controversy in 1866. This committee worked closely with the Union national committee, and Morgan himself took a very active part in the campaign, particularly in the matter of raising money. Chairman Raymond was authorized to appoint an additional auxiliary, added for the first time, and known as the Advisory Committee. Located in St. Louis, with a membership of five, this committee functioned as a western arm of the national committee, and as a field office. As the 39 members concluded their organization for the coming canvass, two new men were becoming

known, both of whom would later become national chairmen—
Marcus L. Ward of New Jersey, and William Claflin of Massachusetts.

In August the infectious dejection that sets in on campaigns when
things are going poorly had taken hold of the national committee
and the President himself. After the New York meeting of the Union
national executive committee on August 22, chairman Raymond
dispatched a summation of the discussion to Lincoln, in which he informed the President that Elihu Washburn, Simon Cameron, and
Oliver Morton were all agreed that it was impossible to carry Illinois, Indiana, and Pennsylvania. By his own estimate, Raymond put
down New York as a loss by 50,000 votes. The next day Lincoln,
acting on a premonition that he would be defeated, prepared a
brief note in which he pledged himself to co-operate with his successor between the date of the election and the inauguration in order
to bring the war to a successful close. So concerned was the national
committee that on August 25 the chairman and his executive committee arranged an audience with Lincoln to urge the need for
sending peace feelers to the Confederate States. Calmly Lincoln
went over the ground with the committee, driving home his reasons
why such overtures at this time would be highly inadvisable. How
they reacted is not known, but at least one observer tells us that the
committee "went home encouraged and cheered."

It is difficult to judge at this distance whether the sensory perception of all those concerned with judging public sentiment at the time
was altogether accurate. So low was Lincoln's popularity on September 1, according to one writer, that it appeared the war cry
would be "Oust Lincoln." [39] But another observer, Richard Smith of
the Cincinnati *Gazette,* writing at the time that most observers generally agreed was the period of darkest despair for Lincoln, said: "I
think we shall be able to rally our people around the *cause* and elect
Mr. Lincoln even as it is." [40]

No doubt Lincoln was more popular at the grass-roots level than
politicians were inclined to believe. For politicians—recalling Mr.
Mencken's complaint against editorial writers who write "with their
umbilical cords tied to their desks"—are not always wise in the ways
of popular thought. And in this instance the climate of rumor-infested
Washington very likely tinctured political judgment. But out in the
nation's small communities one index of public sentiment is available that discloses a view of Lincoln's popularity quite different from
the one that writes off his re-election as a lost cause. This index is
the country press. At this level, Carl Sandburg tells us, the small-
town editors who knew the people and their thoughts never wavered

in their support of the Great Emancipator. There is, no doubt, a mite of exaggeration in the notion of Sandburg that these editors always reflected the sentiments of the people whose communities they served. None the less it is true that these small-town editors were speaking with a large measure of authority in reflecting the common will during the dark months of 1864 when most of Washington was convinced of Lincoln's coming defeat.[41]

While Lincoln was not unaffected by the ponderous defeatism that gripped his supporters in the capital, he lost no opportunity to strike a blow for the congressional people who had remained loyal to him. As usual in the exercise of his leadership, in assaying his role in the congressional campaign, he perceived the difference between leading and driving, and showed himself to be a leader who could execute both maneuvers with great skill. There were no overt attempts to purge candidates who had been unfaithful or openly rebellious to his administration. But the long presidential arm shot out swiftly to tap appointees who stepped out of line.

To a Philadelphia friend who complained to Lincoln that the postmaster of the Friendly City was using his influence to defeat the President's friend and supporter, Judge Kelley, who was seeking renomination to Congress, Lincoln wrote snappishly: "Please tell the Postmaster he must find a way to relieve me from the suspicion that he is not keeping his promise to me in good faith." [42] Elsewhere—in Indiana—when Representative George W. Julian complained to the President that his re-election was being jeopardized by the activities of the commissioner of patents, David P. Halloway, also a Hoosier, Lincoln cracked down hard: "Your nomination," he wrote to Congressman Julian, "is as binding on Republicans as mine, and you can rest assured that Mr. Halloway shall support you, openly and unconditionally, or lose his head." That the President prevailed we are assured by Julian in his reminiscences: "It was perfectly evident that the business would now be attended to, and in a few days my name was duly announced, and the work of party insubordination ceased."

In mid-September the heavy overcast that had been darkening party spirits for months lifted abruptly. Behind the change lay several factors. Pre-eminent, probably, were better tidings from the military front. On September 2 the evacuation of Atlanta was begun by the Confederates, and Sherman would soon begin his famous march to the sea. And the national convention called by the conspirators within Lincoln's own party collapsed in failure on September 12. Thereafter, with great reluctance but with noticeable speed, many of the leaders among the disaffected politicians began the political pirouette that brought them into the campaign for Lincoln's re-election.

Meanwhile the third factor in brightening Union party prospects grew out of the action of the Democratic national convention which assembled at Chicago on August 29. Here, amidst rumors that both Chase and Frémont were angling for the Democratic nomination, the Democrats found themselves on the horns of a dilemma. As one observer put it, "they must nominate a Peace Democrat on a war platform, or a War Democrat on a peace platform." It was the latter alternative which the Democrats followed, and as their standard-bearer they turned to "Little Mac"—General McClellan—and the Ohio "Peace Democrat," George H. Pendleton, was selected as his running mate.

The "war failure" plank of the Democratic platform played into Republican hands. It proposed "that immediate efforts be made for a cessation of hostilities, with a view to an ultimate convention of the states." And by failing to spell out whether the South would be called upon to agree that the Union be restored before the armistice, or whether the belligerents would conclude a truce first without laying down any conditions, it struck an ambivalent posture.

Harmful also to the Democratic ticket as the campaign unfolded was the suspicion—widely sown—that the Democratic ranks were haunted by swarms of traitors. This of course was unfounded; but under the circumstances the charge was not easy to shake. In Congress any Democrat who did not support the administration the Radical Republicans promptly bracketed with the Copperheads. What was a Copperhead? A combination of Benedict Arnold and Judas, according to Benjamin Butler, while another figure defined a Copperhead "as a rebel posing as a Democrat." [43] It was a most difficult situation for a party to overcome, and partisans of all faiths can sympathize with Allen Thurman of Ohio, who said at the Democratic state convention:

> Never since God made this world has any party been so infamously treated as has the Democratic party since this war began. Though you give your flesh and blood to put down rebellion, if you do not favor abolition you are denounced as a rebel sympathizer.

The taint, moreover, would outlive more than the war. As Daniel Dickeson discerned, writing of the Democratic party in August, 1864: "Now it has the taint of disloyalty, which whether true or false will cling to it, like the poisoned shirt of Nessus, for a century." [44] It would last twenty years. Nor would this be the end. For Republicans of a nobler mold would be sad to admit that the opprobrium of "twenty years of treason" would be branded indiscriminately on the Democratic party by reckless partisans in the congressional elections of 1954.

True to the traditions of the time, Lincoln did not take the stump during the 1864 canvass. The most active auxiliary of the Republican effort was the Union League of America, which started in Tazewell County, Illinois, in 1862. In combination with subsidiary organizations, the Union League embraced a membership which was estimated at close to a million. Its principal work lay in the distribution of pamphlets and documents.

In the distribution of campaign literature, the Unionists far outdistanced their opponents. The Loyal Publication Society—an organization sponsored by the Unionists to counteract the Democratic organization known as the Society for the Diffusion of Political Knowledge—sent out nearly a million pieces, and the Union executive congressional committee, organized initially in 1864 and placed under the direction of Edwin Morgan and James Holland, sent out approximately six million documents. Certain administration papers, like the Chicago *Tribune,* printed literature and distributed it at their own expense. For sweetening campaign finances, the Union party laid heavy stress upon assessment of office holders. Henry Raymond, chairman of the national committee, also doubled as treasurer. When office holders refused to pay, or were uncooperative in the collection of funds, Raymond "requested and even insisted upon their removal." Late in September, he had a circular sent out from the Union national committee to all employees in the New York customs house, assessing each employee "an average three percent of their yearly pay," for the fall campaign.

Raymond was also careful to cultivate other sources of financial support. To a businessman he wrote: "Your name . . . has been handed to me as having been employed by the Government in furnishing supplies to the Medical Department of the Army during the past year. I take it for granted you appreciate the necessity of sustaining the Government in its contest with the rebellion, and of electing the Union candidates in November. . . .

". . . Please remit whatever you feel inclined to give in a check, payable to my order as treasurer of the National Executive Committee. I respectfully ask your immediate attention to this matter. . . ." Several members of the cabinet contributed $500 apiece, and some contributions were more sizable, such as one from a metals company for $3,000.

Senator James Lane of Kansas was placed in command of the western branch of the Union national executive committee, and he was responsible for collecting funds in the states west of the Mississippi. Both the Union executive committee and the Union executive congressional committee solicited funds, and there is some evidence in a letter of chairman Raymond to Simon Cameron that confusion resulted when different committees attempted to dun the same employees twice.

As the campaign wore on into October, the Democrats decried what they described as violations of civil liberties, which they contended were undermining the Constitution and imperiling the free rights of citizens. They also contended that under Mr. Lincoln's "misrule" clothing had run up to five times its former price, and that everything people "eat, drink, and wear" had risen in similar proportion. In addition they attempted to show that the insistence upon emancipation and a program to free the Negroes was tantamount to sanctioning the equality of Negroes with whites and fostering racial amalgamation.[45]

In vain did the Democrats try to insist upon a recognition of its opponent as the Republican party, and refuse it recognition as the National Union party. As the elections of the "October states" ticked off, a Union victory was foreshadowed. But with the first crucial test in October (Indiana), there was consternation in the Union ranks as the Democrats carried on a heated canvass to drive one of their hated adversaries—Oliver Morton—from the governor's office. So concerned was Morton that he begged Lincoln to send enough troops home to vote in Indiana at election time to assure him a majority. Lincoln himself appealed to Sherman to return some troops to Indiana to vote. But since the general could not spare troops the best that could be done was to send home the sick and wounded soldiers —a tactic which proved unnecessary when Morton won handsomely and his Union party carried eight of the eleven congressional seats. Later the Union party triumphed in Ohio and also in Pennsylvania, though in the Keystone state the vote was somewhat disappointing. While the Democrats were still insisting that McClellan would carry New York, Pennsylvania, New Jersey, California, and many other states that would insure a majority of the electoral vote, the Union party leaders were now exuding optimism. "The elections this year are scarcely worth thinking about," wrote Edwin Morgan on October 13, 1864. Even Chase was writing to Sherman that Mr. Lincoln's victory was now a certainty and the sole remaining question was by what margin.

Late in October, just two weeks before the election, Lincoln advanced a daring plan. Summoning Francis Blair to the White House, he suggested that since McClellan's election now seemed impossible, particularly in view of the October elections which had bolstered Union party confidence and depressed and further divided the Democratic forces, "Why should he not act upon it and help me give peace to this distracted country?" Blair was then commissioned to take Lincoln's proposal to McClellan, inviting him to withdraw in favor of Lincoln's election and bring about a speedy termination of the war. Blair did take to New York the President's offer, under which as an added inducement McClellan was to be made commander of the armies, and his father-in-law would be made a major-general. Not ready to concede by any stretch, however, McClellan refused.

The results on Election Day struck like a thunderclap. Lincoln was re-elected with 212 electoral votes to McClellan's 21. Only three states—Kentucky, New Jersey, and Delaware—landed in the Democratic column. But the electoral count is deceiving, for the Democratic popular vote was 45 percent of the national total. Moreover, the Union majorities in many states were thin as a wafer. In Connecticut the Union majority was 2,388 out of some 86,000 votes, and in New York the majority was 6,749 out of 730,000.

Only in New York and Connecticut did the soldier vote change the result, but even if these states were removed from Lincoln's column he still would have carried the popular and electoral vote of the North. Criticism did follow the liberties taken in removing troops from the front to send them home to vote, however. In Pennsylvania, for example, where party managers were unsteady about their chances, they implored the President to insure results by sending home 30,000 troops from Grant's and Sheridan's armies. Lincoln did not take troops from Grant, but men were eventually brought home from the forces of Meade and Sheridan. Actually, if the soldier vote is not counted, Lincoln carried the state by 5,712 votes. But the additional 14,363 soldier ballots made for a more impressive result.

After the election charges and counter-charges flowed freely for weeks. The Union party was accused of carrying Indiana by a fraud, while elsewhere the Democrats were berated for indulging in the fraudulent practice of substituting McClellan ballots for Lincoln ballots in the original envelopes transmitted to soldiers.

Small wonder that party feelings in many localities developed some touchiness! Said one Hoosier—a Democrat—in commenting on the experience in Indiana: "Indiana soldiers seem to be rather sickly. So one would judge by the number who were at home on sick leave." Quite apart from the soldier vote, however, the results were decisive. Both parties had indulged in slippery practices, including the spreading of crumbs among the foreign-born and newly naturalized persons, and in this instance the Union party undoubtedly had more crumbs to spread. Lincoln's victory would have been clear-cut without the soldier vote, though if we may assume that New York, Maryland, Connecticut, and Indiana would have gone Democratic without the ballots of the boys in blue, the final electoral tally would have been closer—153 to 80 electoral votes.

What may be said of the presidential canvass with respect to the soldier vote also holds for the congressional elections. Here again a good number of Congressmen owed their victories to soldier votes, but even if this group had been defeated the Union party would still have controlled the 39th Congress.

With slightly better than 55 percent of the total vote cast, Lincoln had far outstripped his showing in 1860, when he was a minority President. He also polled 339,308 more votes in 1864 than he had four years earlier, not an unimpressive showing in light of the disintegrative forces within his party and the Union he sought to preserve. Not yet, however, could it be said that the Union party had reached majority status.

In nine states Lincoln's percentage of the total vote cast was lower than it had been in 1860, and a small shift of only a few thousand votes in key states would have given the election to McClellan. Moreover, from the predominantly Democratic areas of the nation —the eleven seceding states of the South—there were no election returns whatsoever, all of which suggests that in popular strength the Democratic party was very likely still the majority choice by a small margin. The one area where Republican growth was spectacular was in the states of the West North Central region, where the vote of 1864 doubled that of 1860 (109,496 in 1860 to 200,776 in 1864). The Republican share of the two-party vote in this region climbed from 33.4 percent in 1860 to 66.5 in 1864. Part of this spectacular increase was undoubtedly due to such benefits as the Homestead act, which encouraged homesteaders to settle here in great droves. Strong anti-slavery sentiment was also an important factor in this area, and surely played an impressive role in the five-to-one victory in Kansas.

A closer look at the composition of voting groups indicates that Lincoln was perhaps somewhat less popular among working-class groups in 1864 than he was in 1860. In fact, if one chooses the seven wards comprising the principal residence of the proletariat in New York City, Lincoln lags far behind McClellan.[46] In New York county the President polled a bare 33.2 percent of the vote, while in the state at large he hit a percentage of 50.4. By and large across the country the Union ticket drew stronger support from the rural areas and the more well-to-do residential metropolitan areas than from the poorer classes and immigrant groups. There were, however, notable exceptions and defections from this pattern in some rural areas. Again as in 1860, a generous measure of Union strength came from the Yankee counties—the counties that were populated by settlers who came from the East or New England. The Irish were predominantly with McClellan in this election, and the Irish Catholics voted heavily for the Democratic ticket, while Protestant denominations, by and large, stood stolidly by the administration.

What did the election finally mean? It indicated, said Lincoln in his annual message to Congress early the next year, "the purpose of the people within the loyal states to maintain the integrity of the Union." It also signified persuasively, as Greeley commented, that slavery was no longer to be tolerated in the United States. In assessing all the causes for the ultimate triumph of the Union party, it is clear that the compacting of multiple mistakes by the Democrats proved costly. "I am here by the blunders of the Democrats," said Lincoln after the campaign, and in this judgment he found many supporters. But, granting that the Democrats stood uneasily on a platform of ambiguities and contradictions, or that they had erroneously called for an immediate peace and had permitted a small minority to dominate major policy at their convention, the leadership of Lincoln in stepping over the tricky ground was still a performance of first magnitude, so much so that by the beginning of 1865 much of the opposition he had encountered within his party was momentarily becalmed, and as the war progressed triumphantly Lincoln's popularity climbed.

Not foreseeable at the moment, of course, was the turn of events after Lincoln's death. For with the death of its President the Union party faded into oblivion and the reborn Republican party was controlled by the Radicals. Never did the Radicals and their sympathizers and supporters in Congress and elsewhere in the North abandon their main purpose of opposing Lincoln to the end, and biding their time to unhinge his policies. Final victory, with Lee's capitulation at Appomattox on April 9, represented for this group a new challenge to impose a program of undiluted vindictiveness on the South.

Between the election and mid-April of 1865, Lincoln moved ahead with a steady stride. In December he was called upon to make a ticklish decision. The death of Chief Justice Taney required the appointment of a successor, and Lincoln was besieged by both the friends and the enemies of his former Secretary of the Treasury, Salmon P. Chase. To those who told Lincoln, "Now is the time to crush him out," the President replied, "Well, I'm not in favor of crushing anybody out! If there is anything that a man can do and do well, I say let him do it. Give him a chance." Mr. Chase was appointed.

In January, 1865, with just three votes to spare, the House, after failure to approve by a two-thirds vote in a previous session, passed the Thirteenth Amendment to the Constitution, forever prohibiting slavery throughout the United States. It was a wild moment as the galleries of the House shook with applause, and outside a battery let go with a hundred-gun salute. It was a proud moment for Lincoln, the day after this action, when a procession marched to his house calling for the President. He was particularly pleased, he said to the crowd, that his own state of Illinois had been the first state to ratify the amendment that very day, and that a former slave state, Maryland, had followed close behind. But for Lincoln, whose leadership had withstood the strains of both his nation and party coming apart, the end was fast approaching. On April 15 a muffled shot in Ford's theatre removed forever the gaunt man in the White House who had taken hold when the tapers of reason were burning low in their sockets.

Ironically he had emerged as a great party leader who found himself without a party to lead—a party divested of its name and a party whose most important congressional leaders loathed his policies and were already plotting to reverse them before his death. Paradoxically (in terms of the future) we find in the first four years of Republican rule the basic contradiction of unresolved party policy —the strong executive vs. congressional supremacy. The day of congressional supremacy was soon at hand, and unhappily for the party a fondness for emasculating the Presidency would cause it to fall upon unhappy times. But that is another story.

Essentially Lincoln was, and remained, a conservative in the sense that he believed the directing of social and economic movement should maintain an orderly pace. But his overriding faith that opportunity in America was limitless a little farther down the road pushed him ahead with the true thrust of a progressive, in thought and action.

What Lincoln breathed into the Republican party was a spirit not soon caught up by his successors. In the abandonment of Lincolnism during the early reconstruction days, so strong was the power of expansion elements that party leaders strayed far from the lessons of Lincoln. Their retreat from Lincolnism led to grave consequences for nation and party. But like flotsam caught up in the central stream of a swollen river, they were driven forward by elements of expansionism the likes of which the nation had never seen. Ahead, opportunity beckoned enticingly; behind, the political footing seemed secure. Had any other party ever taken control of the government, fought a civil war, become hallowed, and distributed homesteads to seal the bargain?

Against such a setting Lincoln would be mightily missed as a national and party leader. On the sad occasion of his assassination even the Baltimore *Sun* had revised its judgment:

> Not alone in the North, but doubtless to a very large extent in the South, had a trust grown up that Abraham Lincoln possessed the qualities of the head and heart that would enable him as readily as any other citizen who could possibly have been chosen, to accomplish successfully the important work of reconciliation, of reconstruction and true national union. . . . This confidence and hope are now rudely dashed down by the diabolical and astounding act of the assassin. . . .

"Power Tends to Corrupt"

Three hours and thirty-eight minutes after the death of Lincoln, Andrew Johnson stood before the Chief Justice of the United States, surrounded by members of the cabinet and Congress. A thickset, dark man who never attended school, he was apprenticed to a tailor at ten, and later taught to write by the schoolmistress he married. Reared in the mountainous regions of eastern Tennessee, Johnson knew poverty from a tender age, and he came to hate the slave-owning aristocracy in the hills where the whites outnumbered the blacks 27 to 1. In his early years he championed the democracy of Jackson and at 21 he organized a workingman's party in Greenville, where he was elected alderman. Soon he was mayor, then off to the lower and the upper houses of the state legislature, and to Congress. Then back home to become governor, and finally off once more to Washington as United States Senator from Tennessee.

With pluck and native ability he fought his way up, wearing off a few of the rough spots as he climbed, but just a few by high Capitol social standards. And now "Andy" Johnson stood before Mr. Justice Chase to take the oath of office and become the seventeenth President of his country. A tailor replaced a rail splitter. A somber man, this Johnson, a man of deep intellectual honesty and moral courage. But he would need more to carry out Lincoln's policies. Even during the lifetime of the Great Emancipator ominous sounds rumbled from Capitol Hill. And even in the heat of a campaign Lincoln's own partisans in the Senate and the House dared challenge their party leader by bringing forth the Wade-Davis manifesto.

The new President brought with him no party, neither North nor South, that would stand behind him. In the eyes of the Radicals, he remained a Southerner elected by the men of the North; a Democrat elected on a Union ticket. Though he possessed none of the personal prestige of the man who saved the Union he must now attempt to carry through his predecessor's magnanimous policy for putting the pieces together again.

Johnson made no cabinet changes. Seward remained as Secretary of State; Stanton stayed on as Secretary of War. Even James Harlan, appointed by Lincoln to the Interior post, but not yet in office, was retained by the new President. Thus the men whom Lincoln had so skillfully chosen as factional representatives rather than personal advisors were kept on. Not until over a year later, July, 1866, did Johnson replace the inherited Radicals, Attorney General Speed and Postmaster General Dennison, with his own men.

Yet from some of this holdover cabinet the new President received devoted service. Seward, critically wounded by the knife thrust of an assassin the day Lincoln was shot—April 14—became his staunchest supporter. But in less than three years the action of one member of the official family might give cause to wonder if this had been the wisest policy.

Lincoln's reconstruction policy that Johnson hoped to carry out was based on the proposition that the Constitution made an indestructible union of states that act neither of government nor of the people could change.[1] Sovereignty of the states resides in its people. The federal government, of course, retained the power to enforce upon the states certain powers delegated to it. But the national government held no authority to enforce those sovereign powers which reside in the states and its people.

Republican leaders in Congress, however, held other ideas on the subject.

In the Senate sat Charles Sumner, the humanitarian whose love of man was wholly intellectual—a man who "loved without passion and hated without warmth." His goal was fixed and no compromise, no deviation was allowed. The war was fought to free the slaves! That was its sole purpose. And reconstruction meant that the freedman must have suffrage. No state government could be republican if the vote was denied, and the Constitution guaranteed to every state a republican form of government. Thus the federal government's course was clear; it must *enforce* equality.

Entrenched on the other side of the Capitol was Thaddeus Stevens, the grim master of the Republican congressional machine from 1861 to 1868. Born during the administration of Washington, he graduated from college during the Presidency of Madison. Now he was in his seventy-fourth year. His flashing eyes still showed with a white-hot intensity under his brown wig. Here was a man who long years since had fought a winning fight in the Pennsylvania legislature for free public schools. Here was a remarkable old man; kindly, yet with the powers of consuming hate. The taunts that his club foot brought from schoolmates had made him combative and harsh-tongued. Thad

Stevens, who once watched terror-stricken slaves slip across his native state of Pennsylvania to freedom, became an abolitionist before there was a party; an emancipator before there was a proclamation. He hated Lincoln for his equivocating, and for him reconstruction was simply the logical outcome of any war between two governments: the conqueror rules, the conquered is ruled. And the road to rule was simple: build a strong Republican party in the South by fortifying the Negro's right to vote.

On this remarkable stage the reconstruction drama began. Three men, the head of the executive and the leaders of the two houses of the legislature, stonily staked the immediate future of the nation on their separate, unwavering philosophical constructs. These were men not given to compromise; it would be winner take all.

Underlying the struggle was a conflict as old as the Union itself —the struggle of the balanced powers between the executive and the legislative: Should the President or Congress reconstruct? It was a struggle whose outcome would shape the whole history of the Republican party. Lincoln, the dominant executive and the party's first President, was dead. The humbling of Johnson, in his footsteps, would deeply involve the next Republican president, Grant, and tag the GOP ideologically as a congressional party.

But to many congressional partisans the battle was not fought on the high intellectual plane of political philosophy and constitutional law. This was a political battle and the only education necessary was a little simple arithmetic. The thirty-ninth Congress, which convened in December, 1865, had 39 Republican senators and 11 Democrats from the Union states. If the 11 reconstructed states were freely admitted they would probably send 22 Democrats to the upper chamber. And this would chop the GOP margin from 28 to 6. Applying the same logic, the House margin would then be 40 instead of 143. Would the reconstruction plan of the man who saved the Union give it back to the foe? Said Thad Stevens, "With the basis unchanged, the eighty-three southern members [of the House], with the Democrats that will in the best times be elected from the North, will always give them a majority in Congress and in the electoral college. They will at the very first election take possession of the White House and the Halls of Congress."

Two weeks after Congress convened on December 4, 1865, for the first time under the new executive the Thirteenth Amendment prohibiting slavery became a part of the Constitution and civil administrations were operating in all former Confederate states except Texas. But though Johnson, like his predecessor Lincoln, would have been happy to have Southern states enfranchise educated Negroes along with those who served in the Union Army, he did not believe that the great majority of Negroes were ready for the vote. And here he ran aground on the key element of the Radical reconstruction blueprint—a plan to build "a solid bloc of voting Negroes in the South." [2] Unable to moderate the combative course of the Radicals by diplomatic concessions to the more conservative and center elements in the Republican party, Johnson soon stood on the bridge almost alone.

Years later, James G. Blaine, recalling his second Congress as legislators scurried to take sides, remembers only five administration Senators in the party's 39-man delegation, and eight pro-Johnson Congressmen out of 141 Republicans.[3] The President's House leader was a distinguished freshman legislator, Henry J. Raymond, author of the first Republican address to the people written at the Pittsburgh convention in 1856, and founder of the New York *Times*. Although an able man, Raymond was hardly a match for the scrappy strategist Stevens. In the Senate Johnson's staunchest support was limited to three men: James R. Doolittle of Wisconsin, James Dixon of Connecticut, and Daniel S. Norton of Minnesota.

The first test of strength came in February, 1866, when Congress extended the life of the Freedmen's Bureau, enlarging its powers and authorizing it to invoke military aid. Johnson wasted no time in vetoing the measure as unconstitutional in peacetime, joining the issue firmly on the same occasion by lumping Sumner and Stevens with Jeff Davis as traitors. On the vote to override the veto, 18 stood with the President against 30 for the bill, thus barely defeating the measure. Johnson had won the first skirmish. Now the "struggle for the two-thirds" was on!

Two courses were available to the Radicals: they could either recruit supporters by admitting new states, or they could try to find a way of removing some of their more conservative colleagues.

Since the former would require enough votes to override the expected veto (which the Radicals obviously didn't have) they chose the second alternative. The target was John P. Stockton of New Jersey, who had been seated over mild protests after a review of his case by the Senate's judiciary committee which gave him a clean bill of health. Now the case was reopened. And the outcome literally rested upon stretcher bearers. For Stockton's colleague, Wright, was ill in Newark at the time, but he was careful to arrange a pair with Maine's Lot Myrick Morrill before he left the Capitol. At the end of the roll-call the vote on the Senator's right to his seat stood 21 yeas, 20 nays. Then the rush for Morrill began as Sumner and the other Radical Senators pressed him to break the pair. "Call my name," said Morrill finally. Morrill voted "nay." But in an instant Stockton was on his feet to protest, for if Morrill could break his pair (with the ailing Wright of New Jersey) then he (Stockton) could vote in his own favor. And so the scheme to declare Stockton's seat vacant again seemed waylaid. Moreover, when the vote was reconsidered the next day a messenger arrived from Newark with word that Wright was to be conveyed to Washington. But the plot was too near accomplishment to run any risk of failure now. The Senate refused any further delay and the vote was again taken. With one defector, who remained in hiding during the roll-call, the conservative Stockton was ejected by a majority of one vote.

In the full flush of victory the Radical congressional leaders then sought new reinforcements through the admission of states. Although the bill to admit Colorado failed, the Radical ranks gained two votes when Nebraska was made a state under the guidance of Ben Wade. Here was mute testimony to the high-handed tactics of the Radical leaders, for Nebraska's vast wilderness held not more than forty thousand persons—less than one-third the number required under existing apportionment for one member of the House of Representatives.[4]

Soon the battle between the President and Congress moved into the "field." First the conservatives cheered on the President at a "National Union" convention held at Philadelphia on August 16 as a lead-off for the midterm congressional elections of 1866. Then the Radicals countered by calling two Philadelphia conventions—one for "Southern Loyalists" and one for "Northern Loyalists," both on September 3. And in the midst of the pre-campaign factional frictions, the pro-Johnson national chairman, Henry Raymond, was ousted at a rump gathering of the national committee. He was replaced by New Jersey's Governor Marcus Ward, hailed as the "Soldier's Friend" because of his wartime Office for Soldier's Business that processed claims for Union troops.

Johnson began his "swing around the circle" accompanied by members of his cabinet, General Grant, and Admiral Farragut. But Andy Johnson was no longer on the stump in East Tennessee and his intemperate words rested as uneasily on his Northern listeners as the expected dignity of the Presidency did on him. From a Cleveland balcony he raged back at a heckler, "I know a man and a gentleman whenever I see him. I have only to look in his face; and if I were to see yours by the light of day I do not doubt that I should see cowardice upon it. Come out here where I can see you. If ever you shoot a man you will do it in the dark, and pull the trigger when no one is by."

Congress's answer was to come out swinging. It appointed a campaign committee composed of one member from each state having a Republican in its delegation.[5] In command of the congressional campaign brigade was Representative Robert C. Schenck of Ohio, a former Union general, actively assisted by Michigan's Zack Chandler and "Black Jack" Logan of Illinois.

Unfortunately, the activities of the congressional campaign committee are obscured by time. But the astute foreign observer Ostrogorski found that it "penetrated more deeply and more continuously into the local political life than could be done by the permanent committee of the national convention." [6] Congress won the day and Republican majorities increased in every Northern state.

Now all that remained was to impeach the President. And the Radicals soon found the excuse. Early in 1867 Congress passed the Tenure of Office bill over Johnson's veto. This law provided that no official whose appointment required senatorial confirmation could be removed without the approval of the upper chamber. It was specifically designed to guard against the removal of Stanton, who was now in league with the Radicals. Johnson challenged the act in February by dismissing Stanton, the Secretary of War he inherited from Lincoln, after becoming convinced that Stanton was a Radical spy and was doing his best to wreck the administration. Under this provocation the House then impeached the President by a vote of 126 to 47 with all "yeas" cast by Republicans, and the opposition party voting solidly against the move. Even the sixteen Republicans not voting were unavoidably absent, with one paired. Eager for the kill, the House then chose seven of the most restive Radicals to present the case for conviction to the Senate: Thad Stevens, Ben Butler, John Logan, John A. Bingham of Ohio, George S. Boutwell of Massachusetts, Thomas Williams of Pennsylvania, and James F. Wilson of Iowa. Since Stevens was in ill health, Butler assumed the actual, though not official, leadership.

Opening with Butler's argument on March 30, 1868, the trial of the President created a new precedent for a judicial proceeding. The cloakroom and hotel deliberations of the Senator-judges, the buttonholing and barroom lobbying, gave it far more the flavor of a national convention. In short, it was, as the always frank Thad Stevens put it, "a purely political proceeding."

Although the Republicans appeared to have the necessary strength for conviction, the outcome was uncertain until the actual vote. Among the handful of wavering Republicans the main focus was on Kansas's young freshman, Edmund Ross, appointed to the upper chamber less than two years before on the unfortunate suicide of

James Lane. Now the Sunflower editor and Union private who was mustered out a major would cast the fateful vote. As he later wrote, "I almost literally looked down into my open grave. Friendships, position, fortune, everything that makes life desirable to an ambitious man were about to be swept away by the breath of my mouth, perhaps forever." [7] "Mr. Senator Ross, how say you?" asked Chief Justice Chase. "Is Andrew Johnson guilty or not guilty of a high misdemeanor as charged in the article?" Ross rose to his feet. The Chief Justice bent forward tensely while the audience listened "for the crack of doom." Then his reply came, "wavering over the air": "Not guilty."

Andrew Johnson, whose "courage passed far beyond the line of obstinacy" (in the opinion of impeachment manager Boutwell),[8] would serve out the few remaining months of Lincoln's term. Bluff Ben Wade, the Senate's president *pro tempore,* would never sleep in the White House. And with Grant already the party's presidential nominee for over a month, a fateful period for the Republican party had passed.

Whether reconstruction and Republicanism would have run a different course had Lincoln lived can never be answered. Possibly Lincoln, the greatest politician the party was ever to know, might have won over those wavering members of Congress who were so quickly driven to the Radicals by the tactless, strongheaded Johnson—Senators like New York's Edwin Morgan and Nevada's William Stewart.

Surely if Lincoln's successor had been able to carry out the milder presidential plan of reconstruction, the sectional solidity of the South would have been considerably modified. Even after the ruinous effects of civil war, some Southerners of stature became moderate Republicans and made sincere efforts to build a two-party system. (Georgia Republicans nominated the distinguished Confederate general James Longstreet for governor in 1884.) But the combined resentment against the Radicals, carpetbaggers, scalawags, and the harshness of early reconstruction policies quickly eclipsed the Republican patches struggling to survive. When most of the Southern states under military reconstruction gave their votes to Grant in 1868 Georgia stayed Democratic (102,822 for Seymour; 57,134 for Grant), and charges "probably true" immediately flew that this was mainly done by intimidation of the Negro Republican vote and other devious devices.[9] The result in any case so disturbed the Radicals in Congress that it became an important reason for Georgia's return to military rule the following year. Never has a Cracker state electoral vote dropped into the Republican column. And never since 1884 has the GOP put up a gubernatorial candidate.

In Georgia as elsewhere in the South, the vituperativeness and vindictiveness of the Radicals as they determined to smite the rebels and confiscate the property of disloyal slave holders not only aroused fierce resentments among a vanquished people: it forestalled indefinitely a solution to growing racial antagonisms. The Radicals well knew that the key weapon with which they hoped to reconstruct the Southern states—Negro suffrage—was meeting heavy headwinds in the North. Section 2 of the proposed Fourteenth Amendment left the matter of suffrage with the states because its framers feared that a direct enactment extending the vote to Negroes would lead to an adverse reaction in the North. And they were right. For Connecticut decided against the Negro by a substantial majority in an election of 1865, and so did Wisconsin and Minnesota. And in New Jersey, Republicans at their state convention decisively defeated a resolution for equal suffrage privileges. (After two defeats Republicans won equal suffrage for Negroes in 1868 but even then they were forced to use deceptive methods on the ballot—concealing the nature of the constitutional amendment with the label "revision of Section 1, Article 7.") In 1868, Iowa granted the ballot to Negroes but Negro Iowans were prevented from running for Congress.[10]

So race bias in the North would take time to conquer. But the Radicals would not permit the problems involved to interfere with their timetable for Southern reconstruction.

During the see-saw struggle of Thaddeus Stevens to exclude the South from the Union until Republican domination was assured by Negro suffrage, Republicans in several of the Northwestern states "differed vigorously from the Eastern leaders of the party on many issues." [11] In Wisconsin, only apathetic support was given the measures to disenfranchise the Southern white man. And to many Badger state politicians, Stevens, Sumner, and other Radical chieftains seemed somewhat fanatic. "Stevens," said the Wisconsin *State Journal,* "was better fitted to lead a minority than to originate measures and to meet the responsibilities that devolve upon a party in power." [12] Elsewhere the same paper said it had more faith in the convictions of the Republican masses in the country than it did in those Republican members of Congress who were "voluble in letting people know how radical they were and how they would punish traitors." [13] And it feared for the establishment of liberty and justice if this group had its way unobstructed.

On another subject, Northwestern Republicans actively opposed the burgeoning plans of Eastern Republican leaders and industrialists to increase the protection of the war tariffs. Like Lincoln before them, Republicans of the Northwest were strongly against higher tariff duties, and Western Congressmen reflected these sentiments between 1865 and 1868.

Yet despite misgivings over Radical leadership, the Northwest remained loyal to the Republican party. In part the continued fidelity was helped by the boom in wheat and lumbering, but another factor no doubt was that the sinews of political organization were being strengthened through the skillful dispensation of patronage. In Wisconsin alone a shrewd state boss, Elisha W. Keyes, held over 950 postmasterships at his disposal. And so the Republican party, though pulling in diverse directions on some issues, held together as it set off on its early postwar course.

And good or bad, a party policy did emerge—one that left a lasting imprint on the Republican party. For the impeachment and trial of the President symbolized the dominance of Republican leadership in Congress.

On another level, it was the first of the perpetual shakeups in party policies and loyalties. The small band of seven Republicans who stood up to be counted with Johnson all left the party, with one exception. Nor were these all men of small stature. In their ranks stood Lincoln's old friend from Illinois, Lyman Trumbull, as well as his Secretary of the Treasury, William Fessenden of Maine. In the second shakedown, the Liberal Republican movement of 1872, Trumbull, Ross, and Joseph Fowler of Tennessee would be actively associated with the Liberals. Later, both Trumbull and Ross would seek office under the Democratic label.

During the impeachment trial all eyes were not turned to Washington. For out in Chicago Republican politicians were getting ready to make a President, and on a bright, clear, invigorating May 20, the fourth Republican national convention opened proceedings. The high spirits of the gathering were understandable. Its clear-cut task was to nominate the "Hero of Appomattox." That Grant voted for a Democrat as late as 1856 made no impression on the assembled delegates or the party rank-and-file. His sympathies were with the Radicals during the impeachment and trial of Johnson and that was faith enough.

For the party that was to make presidential nominees of Union officers as long as they were available, with one exception (and then the vice-presidential nomination was tendered to an ex-general), it was only fitting that its first should be the North's chief of staff. With the formal nomination quickly accomplished, the bunting at the back of the stage was parted, unveiling a huge Thomas Nast drawing of General Grant and a boastful scoff at the Democrats: "Match Him!"

There were few innovations in the platform. The Radical congressional reconstruction policy was endorsed and all forms of debt repudiation denounced, but the fence was straddled on whether the debt should be paid in greenbacks or gold. That the Radicals were disappointed and concerned about the failure of Northern states to enfranchise the Negro is implied by the second plank of the platform. Here the language tiptoes "around the issue of Northern suffrage" [14] by guaranteeing equal suffrage in the South, but leaving it to the "people" in the loyal states. No mention was made of the emerging tariff question, and on another tender subject a compromise was effected by congratulating the 35 senators who voted for impeachment but not following the most radical counsel that recommended denouncing the seven Republicans who supported Johnson.

Without the usual "guidance" from the presidential nominee about a vice-presidential candidate, the convention felt its way through four ballots searching for a balanced ticket. The leading contender was Ben Wade, "robbed" of the Presidency by one Senate vote, with Senators Reuben E. Fenton of New York, Henry Wilson of Massachusetts, and Speaker of the House Schuyler "Smiler" Colfax in hot pursuit. [15]

The break came on the fifth ballot when Pennsylvania threw a sizable block of votes to Indiana's Colfax and other delegations made haste to get on the bandwagon. It would be Grant and Colfax.

Six weeks later when the Democrats met in New York on July 4 at Tammany Hall, they found a new face among their presidential contenders: Chief Justice Salmon P. Chase. But the golden ring was to elude him again. The presidential ambition that Lincoln referred to as "mild insanity" was given short shrift, his highest vote being four! Instead the Democrats turned to Horatio Seymour—a man of considerable intellectual ability, but an unsuitable candidate to oppose Grant. Although the governor of the most populous state, he was little known outside New York, and his "Copperhead" handling of draft riots during the war made him an open target for the Radicals. [16]

"Let us have peace," said Grant, looking to the future in his acceptance speech. But while he enjoyed autumn in Galena, Illinois, those who took to the stump in his behalf held other notions on how to win votes. Orators were quick to remind the North to "vote the way you shot" and to tell Negroes that "the party that saved the nation must rule it." And if more heat was needed there was always New York's Senator Roscoe Conkling to ask, "Are you ready to put your rights, your property and the honor of the nation to be raffled for the murderers of your children and the betrayers of your country?" Although the expression was not coined for another year, some Republicans were already "waving the bloody shirt." [17]

The party left little to chance. Master politician William E. Chandler of New Hampshire, secretary of the national committee, systematically set about raising a substantial war chest from all segments of the business world. Sizable sums tumbled in from Jay Cooke; the Vanderbilts; the Astors; New York's biggest department store magnate, A. T. Stewart; Collis Huntington, whose Central Pacific Railroad was nearing completion; the prominent shipper Moses Grinnel; William E. Dodge of Phelps, Dodge, leaders in the development of Lake Superior copper and Pennsylvania iron; Henry Hilton; and the wealthy lawyer Edwards Pierrepont, remembered for his work in prosecuting John Surratt for complicity in the assassination of Lincoln.[18]

Republican managers worried little in this campaign. In the daily press the ticket enjoyed widespread support and many influential journals, including the *Nation, Harper's Weekly,* the *Independent,* and *Leslie's Weekly,* were all backing Grant.

As results poured in from the September and October state elections, party optimism was confirmed. All went Republican, with the exception of California, where the party polled 49.6 percent of the vote. But the canvass was marked by violence in the South. The "Invisible Empire" of the Ku Klux Klan was founded in 1866, and by presidential election time Alabama alone had ten thousand enrolled Klansmen. Political assassinations designed to keep the Negroes from the polls were reported in South Carolina, Mississippi, and Alabama, while in New Orleans and the outlying parishes gangs of "Seymour Tigers" and "Swamp Fox Rangers" committed wholesale murder.[19]

In the November election, Grant won 214 electoral votes to Seymour's 80. As in 1864, the party carried every New England state and all states in the West North Central region, which now included Nebraska. It was to be the last time they would make a clean sweep in the latter region until 1904.

In Grant's home area, the East North Central states, the party scored an impressive victory, and with Negroes voting for the first time the party was able to carry West Virginia and the Carolinas. But, in Maryland and Delaware—not compelled to enfranchise the ex-slaves before ratification of the 15th amendment—the Negro did not vote and both states went into the Democratic column. An ominous sign for the future unless the party could find a broader appeal for calmer days.

Another sore spot was the loss of New York, home of the Democratic candidate. It was the first time since 1852 that the Empire state yielded a Democratic majority, and the only time except for the weird canvass of 1876 that Republicans would lose New York and win the election. For the moment however, the party could rest easy.

But what could be expected in the later elections from Mississippi, Texas, and Virginia, whose 23 electoral votes were not counted? And some Republicans noted with discomfort that even with an optimum Negro vote many of the states were returning hair-thin majorities. Yet these were problems for another day. For the present it seemed 52.7 percent of the voters agreed with the Kansan who said, "Hell is peopled by two kinds of folks, those who don't read the Bible and those who vote Democratic." [20]

The man who now entered the White House was singularly free from political entanglements. Never had he publicly endorsed the Radical congressional program! And he enjoyed incredibly widespread support, some of it coming from unexpected quarters. Even such violent Southerners as Wade Hampton, late of "Hampton's Legion," and General N. B. Forrest accepted the election of Grant "cordially and heartily." One contemporary expressed the prevailing faith in Grant by saying, "To doubt Grant is to doubt Christ," and long afterward Henry Adams wrote that people tended to feel a parallel between Grant and Washington.

Feeling in no way beholden to the politicians, the President set about picking his cabinet. This selection process was a curious one. Historian John Lothrop Motley was considered for the State department portfolio, but after Grant met him he commented, "He parts his hair in the middle." And that finished Motley. Of the seven department heads, only three were consulted before the inauguration. Grant's choice for Secretary of Navy, Adolph E. Borie, learned of the President's decision from a newspaper. Apparently there was little to commend Borie other than his wealth, accumulated in banking, railroad enterprises, and Civil War contracts, and possibly the fact that "he had contributed heavily toward the purchase of a Philadelphia home for Grant." [21] Neither of the Senators from his state of Pennsylvania had ever heard of him.

The President's selection for Secretary of the Treasury was the merchant prince Alexander T. Stewart, who bothered many Congressmen because they felt he might be dangerous on the tariff question. But in this case the Senate quickly found a statute disqualifying for the office anyone engaged in mercantile trade. A hurt Grant withdrew the appointment.

By the time Grant's cabinet was filled he had violated one of the oldest political tenets: both Boutwell (Treasury) and Hoar (Attorney General) were from the same state, Massachusetts.

As Grant put his faith in men of wealth and business, it seemed to the politicians that his conception of the Presidency was one of "a candy cornucopia from which he is to extract a sugar plum for the good little boys who have given him some of their plum cake." [22] And unquestionably the announcement of his cabinet "broke the spell of Grant's prestige among knowing Americans." But as the skeleton filled out, it became apparent that Grant's cabinet would contain some men of real ability—Secretary of State Hamilton Fish, a former governor of New York who was surprisingly called out of retirement; another former governor, Ohio's Jacob D. Cox, the new Secretary of the Interior; and E. Rockwood Hoar, a member of a political dynasty that included a Congressman father and a brother presently sitting in the House.

For his appointments outside the cabinet the President was also censured. The number of relatives who were finding their way on to the federal payroll prompted one wit to comment, "No President was ever 'got in the family way' so soon after inauguration." A brother-in-law of the President was appointed surveyor of the Port of New York—"Just as if no Civil Service rules had ever been heard of," complained George Julian—and another brother-in-law was reappointed as Collector of the Port of New Orleans. And those who feared a military man in the White House had further cause for alarm when his old staff, Generals Porter, Babcock, and Comstock, joined the executive department.

Yet Grant's initial defeat at the hands of the politicians—the rejection of Stewart's appointment—had a profound effect on him. The soldier President entered the political world at the time that Johnson was being beaten down by Congress. He was convinced that Congress is the policy maker and the President merely the administrator. In his inaugural address he made it clear that he had no policy to "enforce against the will of the people." And Congress would express the people's will. Gradually, in a period that crackled with controversy, a Congressional "Directory" gathered around him, of whom Senators Zack Chandler, Morton, Cameron, Conkling, and Representative Butler were the chief spokesmen. Actually, the "Directory" was composed of eight of the famous Committee of Fifteen— a joint committee of the House and Senate organized by Thad Stevens to examine conditions in the seceded states and with leave to report at any time on whether all or any of these states were entitled to representation.

Among the group, Chandler, the first Republican United States Senator, was the dean. Arriving in Michigan as a young man, he had made his fortune in retail and wholesale dry goods. He became mayor of Detroit when its electorate numbered 3,500, and later signed the call for the Jackson meeting "under the oaks." In the Senate since 1857, the huge man with the imposing fringe of side whiskers was also one of the promoters of the Republican congressional campaign committee.

Probably the most influential member of the Congressional "Directory" was Indiana's Oliver P. Morton. The large, squat Senator was likewise a founder of the party in his state, and later its wartime governor. Now he became the administration's floor leader.

Pennsylvania's Simon Cameron will be remembered as Lincoln's first Secretary of War who was kicked, more sideways than upstairs, to the Russian legation. And Roscoe Conkling, the "Beau Brummel of the Senate," filling a well proportioned frame of six feet three inches, with auburn hair and a golden beard, had broken with his patrons Seward and Weed at the age of thirty. Now, a decade later, he was on the verge of becoming the undisputed political boss of New York.

Grant's House leader, "Stormy Ben" Butler, was a horse of a different color. "Celebrated as the insulter of New Orleans womanhood and a pilferer of silver spoons," the Greenbacker and former Breckinridge Democrat was regarded with suspicion by the Soldier President for his unsound fiscal leanings as well as for his wartime generalship. Butler took great pains to cultivate the President, however, and worked tirelessly to tie himself to the administration.

So two divergent groups, representing economic and political power, converged on the President. Both would wield tremendous influence during his administrations, and their excesses would add the word "Grantism" to the political lexicon.

For Grant, a man who could never make a success in business, those who became so fabulously successful seemed to have almost a fatal fascination. But it was more than merely appointments and special favors that went to business—it was the Republican party. And as the party became the champion of capital it did so with the hearty approval of a great mass of American people. In this fabulous new age of railroads, great industrial expansion, exploitation of a continent gloriously wealthy below the surface, the "little man" too found identification. Even if he would not be "tomorrow's capitalist," today he would share the "American Dream." The Republican party, moreover, far from being a mere front for big business, actually helped to create the conditions that made possible the emergence of modern America. The dominance of industry, while indubitably bringing some evils, resulted in the strengthening of democracy by laying the foundations for a dynamic economic society.

Nor was it an unnatural alliance, this new combine of politician and capitalist. As business looked to Washington for support, aid, and comfort, the businessman looked to the politician as a broker—albeit a broker who sometimes had a little bet on the side.

It was not surprising that some of the nation's vibrant internal expansion should bulge into the field of foreign relations. Under Seward, and with the joyous assent of the radical wing of the party, much thought had been given to the possibility of absorbing Canada. And certainly the plan had been given an added impetus by Great Britain's friendly attitude toward the Confederacy.[23] Now, under Grant, expansionist thoughts turned to sunnier climes. While Grant was unimpressed with some of the more pressing problems of the day, he took to heart the notion of annexing Santo Domingo. Nothing came of the prospect, but it did revive the expansionist dreams of one element in the Republican party, dreams that would recur. It also touched off the administration's break with Sumner. Already miffed by the President's failure to consult him on appointments, he now turned his full vindictiveness on Grant and his advisers. The immediate response was the removal of the Massachusetts Senator as chairman of the foreign relations committee, and his replacement by Cameron. Sumner, once caned into an abolitionist martyr, was now transformed into an anti-Grant martyr.

In time Grant felt compelled to make cabinet changes too, for some appointees of the President's early "independent period" were becoming unacceptable to his close advisers. Resignation was forced upon Cox, who said: "My committal to civil service reform seems to be a load you do not wish to carry, so here's my resignation." The capable Hoar was also disposed of, because Butler regarded him as a threat to his control of Massachusetts and the Southern leaders in Congress demanded cabinet representation in return for support of the President's pet project, the Santo Domingo treaty.

Grant's leadership during his first years gave rise to a growing body of criticism. And his alliance with Congressional favorites provoked counter-movements in the regular party organization. Conkling's inside track on federal patronage alienated Fenton, the New Yorker's colleague in the Senate, and the same situation existed among the anti-Butler men in Massachusetts. In Pennsylvania the machine of ex-governor Curtin, now stranded as minister to Russia, was stalled while the supporters of Senator Cameron reaped the President's blessings. And the Michigan faction, led by war governor Austin Blair, was being systematically replaced by the followers of Zack Chandler.[24]

The reformers were also becoming disenchanted with the President, as soon as it became clear that he favored the radical "get tough" position for Southern reconstruction and sympathized with the protectionist wing of his party. Finally, the dismissal of Hoar and Cox was more than the reformers could bear. In the Senate a revolt was led by Lyman Trumbull of Illinois and Carl Schurz of Missouri. For Schurz it was a familiar trail. A participant in the revolution of 1848 in his native Germany, he was compelled to flee the country, becoming first a newspaperman in Paris and then a teacher in London. Arriving in the United States in 1852, he became a lawyer and during the war served as a general. Again active as a journalist after the war, he was elected to the United States Senate in 1868, sixteen years after coming here.

The first overt sign that the dissidents would take action outside of the party came in 1870. Schurz, in league with ex-Senator B. Gratz Brown, originally a Democrat who served with distinction in the Union ranks, formed a coalition ticket in Missouri. Grant bore down hard on the coalitionists, quickly dispatching the disreputable general, John McDonald, into the state ostensibly as Supervisor of Internal Revenue. But his official trouble shooter couldn't turn the tide and the Liberal ticket was elected by over 40,000 votes, gaining control of the state legislature and the congressional delegation.

As 1872 approached and it became apparent that Grant would again be the Republican standard-bearer, more voices within the party began calling for counter-action. On January 24 the Schurz-Brown group, as the only official Liberal organization, issued a call for a national convention to be held in Cincinnati on May 1.

The new Liberal Republican party attracted the usual disappointed office-seekers and defeated factions. Conspicuous among them were the Tammany Republicans removed from the custom house when Conkling took over the New York state organization, and the predatory crowd of spoilsmen that gathered around Louisiana's Governor Warmoth.

But the movement also boasted more than a fair share of notable figures. The surviving members of Lincoln's cabinet, Welles, Chase, and Blair, joined the ranks, along with the surviving Republicans who voted for Johnson's acquittal, Trumbull, Ross and Fowler. Indiana was represented by George W. Julian, and Ohio by the ousted

reformer Jacob D. Cox. Other notables included Minnesota's Ignatius Donnelly, a former Republican Congressman, who would soon
go on to other movements and other causes; Nebraska's Senator
Thomas Tipton, once admitted to the upper chamber because of his
approved Radicalism during the Johnson crisis; another Senator,
James L. Alcorn of Mississippi, a "scalawag" with aristocratic roots;
Governor Gilbert Walker of Virginia as well as the state's Republican national committeeman, Franklin Stearns; and Maryland's "Union" governor, A. W. Bradford.

Support for the reform movement was also forthcoming from the
nation's independent press—provided that the convention did the
"right" thing. Powerful here were Horace White and the Chicago
Tribune, Samuel Bowles's Springfield *Republican,* E. L. Godkin of
the *Nation,* and William Cullen Bryant and Parke Godwin of the
New York *Evening Post.* Valuable aid seemed likely from the Adams brothers and their contributors on the *North American Review,*
the political columns of the *Atlantic Monthly,* Murat Halstead's Cincinnati *Commercial,* and most of the German press.

When the convention opened it was clear that the independent editors, Bowles, Halstead, White and "Marse Henry" Watterson of the
Louisville *Courier-Journal,* would have nothing to do with the candidacy of David Davis, Lincoln's appointee to the Supreme Court,
who was supported by a shabby troop of Illinois politicians that the
Judge's managers transported to Cincinnati. Far more to their tastes
was Charles Francis Adams, son and grandson of Presidents, as well
as Van Buren's running mate on the Free Soil ticket in 1848 and
wartime minister to England.

On the balloting the early support for Davis turned to Horace
Greeley, candidate of the Tammany Republicans. Greeley was imagined to have strength in the South, particularly because of his
magnanimous gesture in standing bail for Jeff Davis. He was also
presumed to be popular in the West, where he had counselled young
men to go.

But as the lines hardened the reformers upped their confidence
when Adams moved ahead. On the fifth ballot he led Greeley by 51
votes and was within 33 votes of the nomination. Then the drive
snapped. For on the sixth ballot the politicians felt the moment had
arrived to overtake the reformers. And following "one of the
most remarkable stampedes ever seen in a national convention,"
Horace Greeley became the nominee, with B. Gratz Brown as his
running mate.

Despairing of electing their own presidential candidate, the Democrats accepted the Liberal Republicans' ticket and platform. But

accepting the party's most ancient foe to carry its standard was a bitter pill to swallow. Commenting on the general reception given to Greeley's nomination at the Democratic convention in Baltimore, the New York *Times* was charmingly candid: "There was no joy in the fact or if there was it was concealed with most consummate art." [25]

But Greeley's nomination encountered serious opposition from others besides the old-guard Democrats who might be expected to "take a walk." One of the strong factors contributing to the third party movement was the need for tariff reforms. Yet the reform candidate Greeley was an outspoken protectionist! In consequence, under his influence the Liberal Republican platform plumped for a watered-down proposal to refer the tariff question to each congressional district for determination.

To Republicans, the Liberal Republican-Democratic candidate looked like a "soft touch." For years his productive pen had turned out editorials in the *Tribune,* scolding the Democrats for not mending their ways. These could now be turned against him. There were also other targets. His lifelong flirtations with fads, cults, and causes —among them vegetarianism, a crusade against women's corsets, and the new socialism of Fourier and Brook Farm—made him an easy mark for ridicule.[26] Nothing was overlooked.

The tone of the Republican national convention, meeting this time in June at Philadelphia's Academy of Music, was summed up by the remark of one delegate. Told that another delegate was not for Grant, he asked, astonished: "What's he doing here, then?" [27] Well, they knew what they were doing there, and Grant was promptly renominated. The vice-presidential call went to Senator Henry Wilson of Massachusetts—a choice designed to counter Sumner's influence in his home state as well as to exploit Grant's popularity with labor.

To take full advantage of the incongruous slate that had Greeley running as a kind of Republican-Democratic bivalve, the administration set up a "Straight Out" Democratic party as a decoy. Meeting in Louisville, the one-shot party adopted a states' rights platform and nominated Charles O'Conner, a noted New York lawyer, for President and old John Quincy Adams as his running mate. Although both promptly declined, the "party" went ahead with its canvass. Led by the discredited Confederate turncoat, Colonel Blanton Duncan of Kentucky, with the support of "Brick" Pomeroy's copperhead *Democrat* in New York and such extremists in the South as Alexander Stephens, Herschel V. Johnson, and Henry A. Wise, the party feigned an active campaign in a number of states. This "campaign" was played up by the Republican press. (It has even been contended that the "straight out" literature carried Republican congressional franks and was distributed by the party's congressional campaign committee.) In the end, however, the faction's nearly 30,-000 votes proved unnecessary; the GOP might have turned its intrigue to more fruitful schemes.[28]

Once more the party experienced little difficulty filling the campaign coffer. The chief collectors, Bill Chandler and national chairman E. D. Morgan, cousin of J. P. Morgan and prominent financier in his own right, were particularly gratified by the generosity of Jay Cooke. A close friend of the President, Cooke had a more than cordial interest in the success of the administration. Having obtained a government loan the year before, he was now negotiating for another installment. At the same time his Northern Pacific promotion would not be hindered by friendly ears in the White House and Congress. His contributions began with five or ten thousand dollars for the spring election in New Hampshire, although he complained to New Hampshireman Chandler that the state "isn't bigger than one of our wards, and I could carry a ward for $1,000." In New Jersey, Secretary Robeson was allowed $10,000 and Speaker Blaine—"A formidable power for good or evil"—was given a sum for the Maine campaign. Estimates of Cooke's total contributions ran from $40,000 to $50,000 and on up.[29]

The outcome of the ironic contest between one of the founders of the Republican party, running as a Democrat, and the former Democrat, now a Republican President, was an unprecedented victory for the Republicans. The party's proportion of the two-party vote was 55.8 percent. Grant captured all of the Middle Atlantic states, the last time for a Republican until 1896. But the "stay at home" vote zoomed. One estimate has it that "fully one-fourth of the Democrats in these states preferred to go fishing on election day." For the first time New Jersey's vote fell entirely in the Republican column, where it would not land again for a quarter of a century.

Chaos still reigned in parts of the South. And in Louisiana two conflicting sets of "official" returns resulted, prompting the *Tribune Almanac* to comment: "In the counties (parishes) of Assumption, Avoyelles, Lafourche, St. John the Baptist, Terrebonne, and Washington, this pretended vote actually exceeds the number of voters. . . ."[30] Congress finally rejected both sets of returns, while in Arkansas the vote was rejected on the technicality that the returns lacked the State Seal, even though no such seal existed.

The election demonstrated that both the Liberal Republicans and Democrats were placed in an untenable position with Greeley as the nominee. It also showed that they had misjudged the character of the times. Dragging the Democrats along with them, the Liberal Republicans hoped to bury old issues and get on with the "new" tariff, civil service reforms, prevention of further land grants to the railroads, and a return to specie payments.

But out in Ohio, Governor Rutherford B. Hayes was living closer to the people. "The old questions interested me so much that the new ones seem small." Beyond any doubt, said the governor, the number one issue to the American people is the South. And the election proved Hayes and Grant right: the country was still suffering from the "psychoses of the Civil War."

While the formal machinery of the Liberal Republican party lingered on for a spell, its component parts scattered in many directions. In the South, the party served as a "halfway" station, with most boarding trains back to the old homestead in the Democratic party. In the West, the Democrats also gained from the ranks of the Liberal Republicans, but some, like Ignatius Donnelly, joined minor movements and parties springing from agricultural discontent. The Liberal Republicans in the East were a more stubborn lot, striving for a time to be the balance of power between the major parties by going where they could get the best deal. Broadly speaking, "the Liberal movement in all of its diverse manifestations worked decidedly for the interest of the Democrats." [31] Curtin, Julian, Tipton, Senator Benjamin Rice of Arkansas, Walker, Frederick Bromberg of Alabama, and many others were now permanently lost to the Republicans.

The Liberal Republican movement was from the same lineage as the Republican support of Johnson. But where the former left the party by diffusion, the latter departed by overt action. Some of these dissenters were the romantic idealists who had given the Republican party its free soil and abolitionist roots. They were few in number, since the whole free soil vote was hardly more than one-sixth of the Republican vote in 1856. But they were important in shaping the character of the party. Yet now they broke with the Radicals, who were pressing hard for the logical consequences of abolition: Negro equality in the South. Some of the most resolute prewar abolitionists thus turned into postwar "conservatives." The reason perhaps was that the Radicals—men like Wade, Sumner, Butler, and Zack Chandler—had little compassion for their defeated fellows in the South. The Radical line, abolitionist as it was, was one of cold theory, political expediency, or vindictiveness, and one with increasing emphasis on how to get the nation's huge business and industrial potential rolling. And so, having compassion, many of the old Liberty men left their party, which had become foreign to them.

But there have been many attempts to lift the Radicals out of the mean place in history to which they have been so frequently assigned. One of the latest insists that Lincoln would have adopted Stevens's harsh reconstruction policies had he lived to witness the results of Negro rule in the South.[32] The claim is also made that Stevens, far from being the hating, hateful henchman of industry, was the champion of the common man as well as of business, and that his reconstruction policies really brought about substantial benefits to the South. While much is to be said for correcting the notion that the Radicals were in league to crush the South, recasting the role of the Radicals in reconstruction as "fair and statesmanlike" is pushing special pleading too far.

Grant's first administration was remarkably free of scandals, considering the company he kept. Only the unsuccessful attempt of showman-financier Jim Fisk and the shrewd Wall Street operator Jay Gould to corner the gold market tarnished the President—and even then only through the activities of an old scoundrel who was a brother-in-law.[33] The second administration opened happily, but soon ran into trouble.

Extensive congressional bribery was uncovered on the part of the Credit Mobilier, a construction company organized by the large stockholders of the Union Pacific Railroad in a scheme to jack up profits by having the railroad do business with itself. Although the scandalous acts took place before the Grant administration began, and only two of those involved, vice-presidents Colfax and Wilson, were strongly identified with Grant, the "affair" caused distrust of the President's regime. Confidence was also shaken when Sanborn, a Butler henchman, was discovered making sizable profits as an informer on tax dodgers, with the aid of the local internal revenue bureau records.

Later two blockbusting exposures brought the administration into serious trouble. The "Whiskey Rings" were first exposed by a new reformer in Grant's cabinet, able Benjamin H. Bristow, Secretary of the Treasury. The usual methods of the rings were to falsify reports to the government of spirits manufactured and then use forged internal revenue stamps. The whole operation involved collusion with the federal gaugers in the field and with Treasury men in Washington, who gave the tip-off on any adverse moves by high officials. As the illicit picture unraveled the scandal led right up to the White House, to Grant's secretary Babcock, and led in the field to Grant's man McDonald in Missouri, who gathered in more than $2,500,-000 originally devoted to the Republican organization.

The second case of corruption in the official family was brought to light by a congressional investigation of Secretary of War Belknap, who was found receiving bribes from an Indian trader and only saved himself from impeachment by duping the President into accepting his resignation.

Some time after, the administration acquired another stain. Minister to England Robert C. Schenck, a man who won some attention by introducing the game of poker to English society, achieved a certain infamy by unloading an overpriced mining stock on the unsuspecting British public.

In the midst of such disquieting revelations, Congress executed a first-class political boner by granting itself a pay raise. Passed on the day before final adjournment in March, 1873, the appropriations bill rider raised the pay of Senators and Representatives from $5,000 to $7,000 a year. In addition to the raise, the "Salary Grab" act contained a retroactive provision that made the new salary increases apply for the two previous years. The net effect, of course, was that the members of the expiring Congress not only voted themselves a raise, but also a bonus of $4,000 each.

Public reaction was immediate and violent in this instance and many legislators, attempting to undo the political harm, turned their "bonuses" back to the Treasury. So strong was public censure that some 50 out of 252 in the House and 24 out of 74 in the Senate returned the extra money. A few, such as Massachusetts's Representative George F. Hoar, stipulated that their money be expended for education or other specific purposes. No doubt the ill-timed "Salary Grab" was a material factor in the tidal wave that swept the Republicans from power in the midterm congressional elections of 1874. In any case it was forty years before Congress again dared approach the question of raising salaries.

But the early scandals of the Grant administration and the congressional "Salary Grab" were of minor consequence to the fortunes of the party, compared with the Panic of 1873. Business expansion was jolted when a panic swept Vienna in May, spreading rapidly to Berlin and Frankfort, contracting London credit and overthrowing the Paris Thiers in its wake. The already overburdened American banks were unable to carry the load as a full-scale crash hit in September. With the failure of Jay Cooke, too heavily involved in the projected Northern Pacific Railroad, frenzy gripped the business world. Banks and businesses toppled, 89 railroads defaulted on their bonds, over 5,000 concerns went under with an aggregate loss of some $228,500,000, and nearly 3,000,000 wage earners were unemployed. The nation was in the throes of its first industrial depression and the effects would be felt for six dreary years.

During the congressional election campaign of 1874 Thomas Nast, the famous political cartoonist of *Harper's Weekly,* who had done so much to overthrow the Tweed Ring with his jabs at the "Tiger," invented the Republican Elephant. The first appearance of the animal, who was quickly to become the symbol of the party, showed him (labeled "Republican Vote") with a collection of other animals (representing various papers, states, and issues) being frightened by a donkey (the "N. Y. Herald") in a lion's skin ("Caesarism"). The obvious inference, of course, was that the anti-Grant press was scattering the party vote and preparing the way for a Democratic victory. Indeed, a fox resembling Samuel Tilden, the Democrats' candidate for governor of New York, was surveying the chaos from under a bush. But Nast's biting pen could not turn the tide. In the House the Democrats captured 168 seats to the Republicans' 108. Quipped Grant's Postmaster General, "We have met the enemy and we are theirs." And two weeks later, Nast's Elephant was seen plunging head first into a pit.[34] For the first time in sixteen years the Democrats were in control of a branch of Congress. Just ten years after the Civil War, the party associated with the losing side won a national election. While the Republican reconstruction might be considered barbaric by many, the Democratic victory of 1874 seems to give substance to the opinion of Lord Bryce that "there never was a Civil War or a rebellion followed by so few severities."

Another outcome of the off-year election was the appearance of 14 "independents" in the new Congress. These men reflected the agrarian discontent that was directing its fury at the railroads and the manufacturers in the West and Middle West. The Granger movement, starting in 1867, added 9,500 "Granges" during the first half of Grant's second term and now had nearly 1,500,000 members. In Michigan an Independent defeated a Republican; in Wisconsin three reformers went to Congress; and in Illinois the combined assault of the Democrats and Independents reduced the Republican delegation from thirteen to six. "Uncle Joe" Cannon was returned for a second term, but another young man, Adlai E. Stevenson, defeated a Republican to go to Congress for the first time, and Alexander Campbell, later to become "the father of the Greenback party," was elected as an Independent.[35]

For the Republican party—leaders and rank and file alike—this overwhelming defeat showed the desperate need for a party rebirth. Founded upon idealism, the party had grown great in its crusade for ideals. But now its transition to a party of business was bringing difficulties and leading to excesses that might be fatal. And Grant's performance in office had been politically doleful. Now, as nothing else could, defeat at the polls hit home with a wallop to convince the organization that its next presidential nominee must stand for reform.

Whatever thought Grant might have given to another term was now swiftly ended. He announced that he would not be a candidate for re-election, and as if to seal any escape hatch he might have left open Congress passed a resolution declaring a third term unpatriotic, dangerous, and contrary to the American spirit. For the first time in the sixteen years since Lincoln's initial nomination, the party would have an open convention.

The leading contender for the nomination was the Speaker of the House, James G. Blaine of Maine. Through years of party politics he gradually mastered the art of straddling issues—standing now somewhere between the reformers and regulars. As the presidential year approached, however, the main fear of his camp was that he had been prominent too long, and, in the words of Garfield, had been "trying too hard." And shortly before the June convention his candidacy developed more serious drawbacks. Embarrassing questions were asked in Congress. Why had the Union Pacific Railroad, dependent as it was on official favor, paid the Speaker full value for some depreciated securities? And what unsavory part of the deal was in the "Mulligan Letters" that Blaine was trying to suppress? Although he still held widespread support, his nomination, as the New York *Times* soon pointed out, would lead to a "defensive campaign." [36]

A more meteoric possibility was Benjamin Bristow, whose campaign against the "whiskey rings" had endeared him to the reformers, while his management of the Treasury won admiring glances among the financial interests. The secretary was assured the vote of his native Kentucky, through the diligence of John Marshall Harlan, while in major Eastern cities he was heartily endorsed by strong "reform clubs" containing such prominent conservatives as John Jacob Astor, Joseph Choate, Theodore Roosevelt, Sr., William E. Dodge, and John Jay.[37]

Grant's choice for his successor was his Secretary of State, Hamilton Fish, who did not choose to run. His second choice was Roscoe Conkling, commander of the "bread and butter brigade." Since March Senator Conkling had been assured of sixty-nine of New York's seventy votes, the single holdout being George W. Curtis, the editor of *Harper's Weekly,* who had resigned in disgust as Grant's Civil Service Commission chairman.[38]

It was the third week of June when the 756 delegates, their alternates, the press, and thousands of anxious spectators descended on Cincinnati, the "Queen City of the Ohio." The sixth Republican presidential nominating convention, meeting in the centennial year of the birth of the nation, assembled in Exposition Hall, a huge wooden structure resembling "an ambitious and disappointing rail-road depot." Four years earlier it had launched the ill-fated Liberal Republican party. Once more national chairman Edwin Morgan performed the welcoming rites (which he had started in 1856), and as the convention rolled ahead to the nominating speeches fervor and excitement ran high. Pinchback of Louisiana made a bombastic speech for Morton, and Bristow called on the considerable talents of George Curtis and Richard Dana. But by far the most rousing performance was given last by Colonel Robert G. Ingersoll of Illinois, fresh from a successful defense of the Chicago whiskey ring. In his flowing oratory Blaine became a "plumed knight" and his forces expected to put him over on the tide of frenzy that ensued. But the gas lights suddenly failed, nobody ever knowing whether by act of God or a rival candidate's manager, and the balloting was held over until the next day. The delay may well have cost Blaine the nomination.

When the balloting finally began, Blaine led the field with 285 votes, followed by Senator Morton with 125, then Bristow, 113; Conkling, 99; and Hayes, 61. Two "favorite sons," Pennsylvania's Governor John Hartranft, acting as a decoy for Don Cameron, old Simon's son, and Connecticut's Marshall Jewell, the Postmaster General, were holding their delegations in line until the "right" opening appeared.

Blaine's apparent strength, however, was deceptive. All the other candidates were anti-Blaine men, with Conkling and Bristow particularly opposed, and if they could unite on a candidate the "Plumed Knight" would be finished. Blaine's managers were fully aware of this peril for their candidate, which they tried to head off by offering the vice-presidential nomination to Bristow and Hayes. But the anti-Blaine coalition leaders, effective as they were in the early maneuvering, knew they could not hold their delegates in line if the convention became hopelessly deadlocked. Their one hope, therefore, was to find a candidate behind whom they could unite.

The most likely coalition candidate was Rutherford B. Hayes, a former Union general who had served with considerable distinction in the battles of Fishers Hill and Cedar Creek during the West Virginia campaign, and was now governor of Ohio. Adding to his availability were his well known reform sentiments. Here at Cincinnati his cause was ably espoused by a distinguished "Ohio gang" consisting of ex-governor Edward Noyes, Senator John Sherman, and Congressmen Charles Foster, James A. Garfield, and Stanley Matthew.

The strategy, as Garfield wrote Hayes, was to hold the Ohio delegation and "await the break-up which must come when the weaker candidates drop out." The "break-up" came with the fifth ballot!

Connecticut dropped Jewell for Bristow on the second ballot, but there were only minor changes until the fifth. Then Michigan, which had been dividing its vote between Blaine, Bristow and Hayes, threw its entire block to the Ohio governor and the Rubicon was passed. On the next ballot Indiana withdrew Norton in favor of Hayes and Kentucky's twenty-four votes were transferred from Bristow to Hayes by John Marshall Harlan (later to be rewarded for this service by an appointment to the Supreme Court).

By the seventh ballot New York and half of Pennsylvania had come to Hayes and he was over the top. "Thousands of people were on their feet shouting like Comanches." With little opposition the ticket was then completed by the nomination of William A. Wheeler of New York.

A new era was beginning: Hayes's letter of acceptance suggested not only reform, but reconciliation with the South as well. The Democrats, too, promised the nation reform. In their convention the managers of Samuel J. Tilden, with the aid of a private advertising agency, ran roughshod over the Tammany opposition, nominating the New York governor on the second ballot.

From the day of his nomination Hayes ran into trouble with his party. For the Stalwarts (led by Roscoe Conkling and taking this name by way of contrasting their own "stalwart" Republicanism to the reformist sentiments of Hayes, who stood for civil service reform and reconciliation with the South) had no intention of letting the party machinery slip out of their hands. They came to refer to Hayes as a "half-breed Republican," and at the national committee meeting in Philadelphia they overruled Hayes's choice for chairman, his close friend ex-governor Noyes, and elected the supreme spoilsman Zack Chandler. Although the time had not yet arrived when the national chairman was customarily the hand-picked selection of the presidential nominee, the irony of the committee's choice was aptly summed up by the *Nation:* "Just think of a Civil Service Reform party making Zack Chandler chairman of the Executive Committee!"

Once again the campaign, no less than in 1868 and 1872, was based on the bloody shirt. The candidate's instructions to Blaine, embarking on a speaking campaign in Ohio and Indiana, were: "Our strong ground is dread of a solid South, rebel rule. . . . It leads people away from hard times, which is our deadliest foe." [39]

In the East, rain fell on Election Day. And as the first scattered returns trickled in a crowd of 10,000 gathered in front of the New

York *Herald* bulletin board. By midnight it looked like a decisive Tilden victory. For the first time since 1852, Connecticut was tucked safely in the Democratic column. And so was Illinois—for the first time since the founding of the Republican party. Then more depressing news came. It was now certain that the Middle Atlantic region would be Democratic for the first time since 1856 (and the last time until 1912). In the pivotal state of New York the Democratic plurality was over 32,000; in neighboring New Jersey it was 12,-000. Even Ohio—Hayes's native state—gave him an unsteady lead of 50.6 percent of the popular vote.

At the stroke of midnight Tilden seemed assured of 184 electoral votes—just one short of victory, with 166 votes conceded to Hayes. And so, with Tilden leading by more than a quarter of a million votes, Zack Chandler closed up Republican headquarters in New York and went to bed.

Old Zack never revealed his inner thoughts that eventful night. Certainly he would have been an ungrateful man if he harbored any bitter feelings over the defeat of his candidate. For the American electorate had been bountifully good to Zack and his party. They grew up together. In 1857, when Chandler became the first Republican United States Senator, the party was swiftly rebounding from the defeat of its first national campaign. And then the American people gave the Republicans four consecutive terms in the White House while Old Zack stayed in the Senate accumulating seniority.

Now the Washington political landscape would be changing. Come March a Democrat would occupy the White House. The landslide of '74, of course, sounded the warning when the Democrats grabbed control of Congress, and Zack himself went down with the tide. But the party still retained control of the Executive and Zack quickly found himself a cabinet berth as the President's new Secretary of the Interior.

Perhaps a mellow glance over his shoulder at his party's nearly two decades of power comforted Zack Chandler that gloomy night as he climbed into bed. If old Zack was in a philosophical mood, he didn't sleep badly.

6

As New York Goes . . .

In the early hours of the "morning after," 1876, Zack Chandler was abruptly awakened by two men, Bill Chandler and John Reid, managing editor of the Republican New York *Times*. Although Democrat Samuel J. Tilden was now a quarter of a million votes ahead of GOP candidate Hayes and officially only one vote shy of the necessary electoral count, all was not lost. Jubilantly the Republican national chairman's visitors calculated that if Hayes could carry the three remaining carpetbag states, Florida, Louisiana, and South Carolina, he would have exactly the 185 electoral votes needed to elect.

At the moment they proposed to wire Republican officials in the three states to see if they could be held. And their parting instructions to the sleepy chairman were to dispatch competent lawyers into the doubtful territories immediately. At Democratic headquarters the board of strategy quickly followed suit. And to play it safe they threw another counter-punch by contesting a vote in Republican Oregon where an elector was a postmaster and should automatically have been disqualified from serving in the electoral college.[1]

One month later, with the election still hanging fire and tension climbing, Congress convened (December 4). The Democratic House acted swiftly by ordering investigation committees to the contested Southern states, and Republican senatorial investigators were not far behind. But the basic question of how to count the electoral votes when no candidate had a majority remained unanswered.

With no precedents to follow some urged that the Republican president of the Senate, Thomas Ferry, who had succeeded on the death of Vice-President Wilson, should do the counting—thus insuring a Hayes victory. Others contended that the election should be thrown into the House, now controlled by the Democrats—thus sealing a Tilden victory. But what if no President were elected by March 4? Who would succeed to power? And beneath it all was the dank undercurrent of fear that one side might appeal to force, with the Republicans controlling the regular army and the Democrats the National Guards of a minority of the states. What then?

After more than a month an electoral commission was worked out, designed to give neither party any advantage. Carefully blended to accommodate a situation of hardening party lines, the commission was composed of fifteen members—five from each house of Congress and five from the Supreme Court. There were to be three Republican and two Democratic Senators; three Democratic and two Republican Congressmen. And of the four Justices named, two were from each party. The pivotal Justice was to be chosen by the four Justices named to the commission, and it was assumed that the place would go to David Davis, the only Independent on the high bench.

Originally the plan was hailed as a Democratic victory—a judgment borne out by the vote in both houses. For the Republicans felt that with the regular returns from the three Southern states all favoring Hayes the burden of proof for any change was squarely upon the Democrats. But the establishment of a commission now encouraged the Tilden men to believe that this quasi-judicial system, with the support of Davis, would surely be good for at least the necessary one out of the twenty contested votes. (Florida 4; Louisiana 8; South Carolina 7; Oregon 1.)

But on the day the Senate gave its final consent to the proposal, Washington received some startling news from the Mississippi Valley. The Illinois legislature, through a coalition of Democrats and Greenbackers, rather than any Republican collusion, had elected Davis to the United States Senate. The judge thereupon promptly declared himself unavailable to serve on the commission. To fill out the body, Justice Joseph P. Bradley was then chosen, probably because, for the Democrats, Bradley's decision in striking down the Enforcement act made him the most acceptable of the Republican judges. (The Enforcement act of 1870 was aimed at preventing intimidation of Southern Negroes, and prescribed punishment for persons who conspired to "injure, oppress, threaten, or intimidate" any citizen in the enjoyment of rights or privileges secured to him by the Constitution. In a United States Circuit Court case arising out of an attempt to punish persons involved in the massacre of Louisiana Negroes in 1873, Justice Bradley held that the Fourteenth Amendment operated only as a prohibition against state interference with the fundamental rights of United States citizens, and that it did not authorize Congress to legislate generally for the protection of those rights.)

The first decision of the commission came on February 8. Bradley, whose opinion changed "between midnight and sunrise," was true to his party and the Florida case was decided in favor of Hayes. After that all contests would be decided in favor of the Republicans, eight to seven. On February 10, when the Florida findings were officially announced to Congress, the Democrats determined to act. And they succeeded in recessing—a parliamentary maneuver that had the effect of a filibuster. Filibustering was to be the last-ditch Democratic strategy.

But at this point a counter-move was contrived that has been called "the unknown compromise of 1877." Friends of Hayes in that vast news-gathering network known as the Western Associated Press felt the only way to end the filibuster and peacefully inaugurate the Ohioan was to win over enough Southern Congressmen. The WAP, then in the hands of such men as Murat Halstead, publisher of the Cincinnati *Commercial*, William Henry Smith of Chicago, Hayes's closest personal friend, and Joseph Medill of the Chicago *Tribune*, entrusted the negotiations to a former Union general and Confederal colonel, Andrew J. Kellar of Tennessee, and Henry Van Ness Boynton. Kellar, becoming editor of the Memphis *Daily Avalanche* after the war, was aligned in his state with the Whig-industrialist wing of the Democratic party. Boynton, his Northern colleague in this strange negotiation, was a noted military historian and Washington correspondent for the Chicago *Tribune* and other Western Associated Press papers. A bitter critic of General William Tecumseh Sherman, Boynton was feared as a muckraker and gave a powerful assist in exposing the whiskey rings and the Blaine railroad deal. In the last Republican convention he had also been one of the managers of the ill-fated Bristow campaign.

Getting on with their mission, Kellar and Boynton soon found it necessary to form an alliance with the forces of Thomas A. Scott, then at his zenith as a railroad builder. Scott was remembered as Lincoln's youthful "transportation czar" during the Civil War. Now president of the powerful Pennsylvania and ambitious Texas and Pacific, he was anxious to obtain government subsidies, particularly to push the latter line over a southern route to the Pacific. The lead lieutenant in Scott's powerful lobby was General Grenville M. Dodge, famed as the chief engineer of the Union Pacific and now chief engineer of the Texas and Pacific. A steady hand in politics, Dodge served first as a Congressman from Iowa and later as a perennial delegate to Republican national conventions.

The bargain finally struck between the newspapermen, the Scott forces, and the Southern legislators called for an end to the harsh reconstruction policy, a Southern appointment to the Hayes cabinet, and a booster shot for the old Whig doctrine of "internal improvements"—the improvements being aid to the Texas and Pacific Railroad, and presumably other public works assists such as Mississippi levee construction.

The coalition was successful. For on February 20 the filibuster was defeated with the votes of thirty Southern Democrats and Hayes was peacefully inaugurated President of the United States at a secret ceremony in the White House. March 4, 1877, fell on a Sunday, and thus the official swearing-in was to be held the next day. But Grant, fearing that the event might still in some way be challenged, had the President-Elect quietly take the oath in the Red Room on the Sabbath, with the formality repeated publicly on the designated Monday.

Once more a crisis was bypassed—thanks to the American genius for compromise, official and unofficial. Whether Hayes would have been President if a fair count had been possible was another question. The consensus of historical research favors his claims to the electoral votes of South Carolina and Louisiana, but supports the Tilden ticket in Florida, and thus the election of Tilden. But Hayes was now legally President, though the doubts of his electoral paternity would cast a shadow over his four years in the White House. And he entered the Presidency with his party out of control in the House; two years later it would also lose the Senate.

The inauguration of Hayes not only marked an official close to the presidential canvass of 1876, but it brought a virtual end to the "bloody shirt" campaigns. And it also ushered in the first of four consecutive "fifty-fifty" elections, in which neither party would win a clear-cut victory.

In selecting his cabinet, Hayes faithfully redeemed one pledge to the Southerners. For the first time since the war a Confederate was appointed as a department head. David M. Key, retiring Democratic Senator from Tennessee, and the choice of Colonel Kellar, became Postmaster General—a significant gesture for a patronage-laden office usually reserved for the political manager of the administration.

Hayes's cabinet carefully reflected the quality that made him such an acceptable compromise to the Republican convention. In the words of his biographer, "It was a cabinet that was political, but not glaringly so. It was reformist, but not radically so." The able Ohio politician, Senator John Sherman, became Secretary of the Treasury. And Carl Schurz, leader of the Liberal Republican revolt, became Secretary of the Interior. Both would be the President's closest cabinet advisers.

For Secretary of State Hayes selected William M. Evarts—an appointment that was a portent of events ahead. Evarts, who was

Johnson's Attorney General, defended the President in the impeachment trial. And now, somewhat symbolic of the end of Radical reconstruction, he sat in the cabinet of a Republican President. Evarts was a New Yorker, but not a part of the Conkling organization. Conkling was not consulted. Moreover, such older party gladiators as Chandler, Blaine, and Cameron were also boldly excluded from the inner councils of the new administration.

The one member of the old guard who was assiduously courted was Oliver Morton. Benjamin Harrison and John Harlan were kept out of the cabinet at Morton's insistence, and the Senator was permitted to name Richard W. Thompson as Secretary of the Navy, even though the appointee had been an avowed Know-Nothing and had recently published an attack on the Catholic Church. Hayes no doubt was grateful for Morton's support at the convention. And he was also wooing the Hoosier with an eye to the future: he would be a strong match for Conkling or Blaine in a senatorial strategy. But as Eisenhower was to mourn the death of Taft, so Hayes would feel the passing of Morton within six months.[2]

That "this cabinet was the strongest body of men . . . that ever sat around the council table of a President of the United States," [3] as one writer contends, is highly doubtful. But it was a cabinet on which the President could rely for sound advice as the nation entered a painful period of transition.

Initially the "Southern Question" was the most compelling problem and, after some hesitation, Hayes ordered the last federal troops out of the South on April 10. Now with the removal of military support the last carpetbag government fell. The withdrawal, of course, was inevitable. Even Grant, on February 26, admitted that the country was "clearly opposed to the further use of troops in upholding a state government" and promised to recall the troops after the electoral count.

The end of "foreign" rule involved a long uphill struggle for the South. Tennessee cast off its carpetbag yoke in 1869. In 1870 and 1871 the carpetbag régimes toppled in North Carolina, Virginia, and Georgia. Then in 1874 and 1875 Alabama, Arkansas, Texas, and Mississippi returned to "home" rule. And now Florida, South Carolina, and Louisiana, under Radical control long enough to switch the presidential election, were free of the troops and the carpetbaggers.

What could be said of this unnatural alliance of Scalawags, exslaves, and Northern adventurers? Reconstruction, of course, was not all black and white, though novelists might later find it more convenient that way. In the "shocking burlesque upon legislative proceedings," that a Northern journalist, James S. Pike, found in the predominantly Negro South Carolina legislature of 1868, lay "something very real to this uncouth and untutored multitude." Where "seven years ago these men were raising corn and cotton under the whip of the overseer . . . today they are raising points of order and questions of privilege." [4] If in certain quarters the Radicals left behind renewed race hatred, the result of a sudden thrust of power upon a people untutored in its use and uneducated in its purpose, it also left in its wake the foundations of an educational system among other things. For the establishment of Southern school systems generally sprang from the reconstruction period.[5]

When Hayes withdrew the troops, signaling the opening of a "new" South, he also laid plans for a new Republican South. And he aspired to rebuild the Southern wing of the party along economic, rather than racial, lines. As he wrote to John Tyler, Jr., the Republican son of the Whig President, "We cannot hope for permanent success in New Orleans until we can secure conservative support among white men, property holders, who are opposed to repudiation and willing to give to the colored people their constitutional rights." [6] Hayes then set about regenerating Southern Whiggery with the full power of federal patronage to back him up. All through the South he gave jobs to Democrats with Whig tendencies in the vain attempt to pry them loose from their party.

At the same time Hayes attempted to hold the party's Negro support by recognizing their leaders with favors and appointments. Frederick Douglass became Marshal of the District of Columbia although "relieved" of the Marshal's duties as official greeter at formal White House social functions.

But even if the Hayes plan was feasible, the President was not quite politician enough to bring it off. For he not only alienated Republicans in the South, but his designs were frustrated at the polls. In the next congressional elections the party was not even able to fill its slate below the Mason-Dixon line. Six out of eight congressional nominations went begging in Alabama, while in Mississippi four out of six Democrats were unopposed and in Arkansas no Republican ran at all. Just three Republican Congressmen were returned from the South, one each from North Carolina, Tennessee, and Virginia. And in the Senate there were only two Southern Republicans, both holdovers: William Pitt Kellogg of Louisiana, a Southerner since 1865 and on the federal payroll since that date, and Mississippi's Blanche Bruce, an ex-slave who was first tutored by his master's son.

Hayes no doubt felt, as he said in his inaugural address, that he was serving "his party best" by serving "the country best." But few Republicans in Congress believed that his Southern policy was a service to the party. Garfield, the administration leader in the House, could not even risk calling a caucus. Hayes was fast becoming a President without a party.

In consequence he was compelled to meet most of the emerging issues through brisk executive action. He effectively ended Mexican raids into Texas through stern orders to our troops stationed along the border, and he called out the federal troops to protect private property in the railroad strikes of 1877. Standing up to Congress, he also vetoed a bill to exclude the Chinese, which he felt would violate the "most favored nation" clause of our treaty with China. He then called for a new treaty—a pact eventually negotiated by President Angell of the University of Michigan and signed in 1880.

If Hayes intended to live up to his letter of acceptance and his inaugural address, a major "must" was civil service reform. An executive committee, headed by John Jay, grandson of the first Chief Justice, had already reported what everyone knew: In the largest patronage pavilion of the country, the New York customs house, more than one thousand employees had been appointed for political reasons—the reasons being those of Senator Conkling. Hayes reacted with an executive order, in substance an early Hatch act: "No officer should be required, or permitted, to take part in the management of political organizations, caucuses, conventions, or election campaigns." Before the President was finished he dismissed two of Conkling's principal lieutenants, customs house collector Chester A. Arthur and its naval officer Alonzo B. Cornell, son of the famous philanthropist. Moreover, with Democratic aid in the Senate he was eventually able to appoint replacements.

Beyond the halfway mark of Hayes's administration, all eyes as usual began to look to the next presidential election. And although Hayes declared at the outset of his term that he would not be a candidate for re-election, the Democrats, in control of both houses since the midterm elections, felt impelled to manufacture some campaign fodder. The logical issue to reopen, it was decided, was the presidential "steal" of 1876. A committee, headed by Representative Clarkson Potter of New York, went to work with zeal. But what wasn't known to this committee was that a farsighted Senate clerk, a Republican, had failed to return to Western Union some file copies of Democratic telegrams subpoenaed by earlier investigating committees. Bill Chandler, never slow on the uptake, sent several hundred of the most interesting-looking specimens to Whitelaw Reid of the New York *Tribune*. As the Potter committee ground into gear the *Tribune* began publishing a few in the original cipher. The game was for the reader to try his hand at decoding them. Presumably, of course, the *Tribune* didn't know how to read them! But suddenly, at exactly the right moment, the *Tribune* broke the code. One message from Florida to Colonel W. T. Pelton, Tilden's nephew who was living at Tilden's home, read (in translation): "HAVE JUST RECEIVED A PROPOSITION TO HAND OVER AT ANY HOUR REQUIRED TILDEN DECISION OF BOARD AND CERTIFICATE OF GOVERNOR FOR 200,000 [DOLLARS]. MARBLE" To which Pelton replied: "DISPATCH HERE. PROPOSITION TOO HIGH." [7]

Whether or not the various exploits of the nephew were known to Uncle Samuel (Tilden) did not alter the fact that the investigation had blown a gasket. Henceforth the Democrats were declared (though not by the committee) equally culpable for the election irregularities of 1876, and the "martyred" Tilden was removed as an election issue.

The leading administration supporter for the presidential nomination that Hayes would not seek was the Secretary of the Treasury, John Sherman. A seasoned partisan, Sherman was president of the first Republican convention in Ohio in 1855 and went to Congress the same year. After twenty-two years on Capitol Hill, sixteen of them happily spent in the Senate, he entered the President's cabinet. While Hayes might have exerted some influence for his Secretary's candidacy, he was determined to be a bystander in 1880 and would only promise to support Sherman "as far as he could properly, without any unseemly interference." And this, of course, meant virtually no support at all.

Back from abroad—and running hard—was another prominent figure: U. S. Grant, the only Republican ever to serve two full terms in the White House! Shortly after the close of his second term he set sail on a trip around the world. With $25,000 to spend he planned to stay abroad as long as the money held out. Financial reinforcements from fortunate investments, however, extended the tour to nearly two and one-half years. In August Grant wrote to Badeau: "I am not a candidate for any office nor would I hold one if it required any maneuvering or sacrifice to obtain." But in December, 1879, asked in Philadelphia, "Will you not be disappointed after such an ovation from San Francisco to Philadelphia if you are not returned to the presidency?" he replied, "No, not at all, but Mrs. Grant would."

On landing at San Francisco, September 20, 1879, the "Hero of Appomattox" had found that the shortcomings of his presidential years were forgiven or forgotten by a majority of his countrymen and he was once again the most popular man in America. After the lean years of Hayes, Grant's old political cronies were itching for the return of lush days. By early February, Don Cameron was lining up the Pennsylvania delegation for Grant. Later that month Conkling secured the pledge of New York, and in Illinois "Black Jack" Logan won a solid delegation for the ex-President. But Logan's tactics were so high-handed that nine congressional districts immediately entered a protest—one of them being Grant's home district.[8] Grant's preconvention task force promised to be formidable. It would constitute the "triumvirate" of Cameron, Conkling, and Logan—two veterans and a fast-rising protégé.

Don Cameron was a relative newcomer to the national scene, but he had fully learned the rights and obligations of a political boss at his father's knee. Old Simon was elected to the Senate back in 1845, and when he won another term in 1857 his son was now old enough to take over the family banking interests, allowing the Pennsylvania state boss to give his undivided attention to politics. Those who felt that the cold and stiff Don would never have the political acumen of his popular father underestimated the lessons he had learned. Through Simon's influence his son was appointed Secretary of War during the final months of Grant's administration, the same position the father had held, with such disastrous results, under Lincoln. Then in 1877 Simon at the age of seventy-seven decided to retire from the Senate, and Don without incident was elected in his place. Thus power in Pennsylvania was passed on from father to son as the son would later pass it on to Matthew Quay and thence to Boies Penrose—a political dynasty not to be rivaled in the annals of American politics.

The third serious contender for the 1880 presidential nomination was Blaine, who had now moved from his familiar place in the lower house to the Senate. And momentarily at least, after his six years of wielding the powerful Speaker's gavel, Blaine's modest seat in a little supplementary row at the rear of the upper chamber did little to polish his political prestige.

The Southern policy of Hayes made the Republican organizations from that region highly receptive to the overtures of the Grant forces. So hostile were Southern Republicans that any candidate who was felt to have the blessing of Hayes was automatically unacceptable. Of the South's 214 delegates, Sherman was never able to win more than 45. But the Grant years of reconstruction were happy ones for Southern Republicans and now some sixty percent of his support came from below the Mason-Dixon line. And on the final nominating ballot for President at Chicago, 140 of Grant's 306 votes came from the South.

Virtually driven out of the South in 1876, the Southern wing of the Republican party was now just a holdover organization functioning only for the power it could wield in national conventions. It survived on whatever federal patronage was thrown its way, delivering no votes for the national ticket nor any support in the federal legislature. Thus the end of reconstruction brought a new problem for Republican national conventions—the beginning of the "demoralizing influence" that went with the shameful scramble for the votes of the Southern delegates.

Shortly before the convention opened, the Grant strategists, led by Conkling, planned to gain control of the meeting by slipping in their own chairman, who would then enforce the unit rule. The scheme they devised seemed foolproof. Since the chairman of the national committee opens the convention it was decided that Cameron (national chairman and a Grant man) would recognize a motion from the floor to substitute a Grant man for the temporary chairman nominated by the national committee (an anti-Grant man). And on this vote Cameron would apply the unit rule. After this, they reasoned, their temporary chairman would continue the same parliamentary procedure and Grant would be nominated on the first ballot.

Since Grant entered the convention with over 300 votes, an analysis of the delegations suggests that if the unit rule could have been enforced the plan might have been carried out handsomely. But the plan leaked out. The Grant board of directors, moreover, were not reckoning with James A. Garfield. Garfield, recently elected to the Senate for a term to begin the next year, came to Chicago on May 29, five days before the convention opened, as Sherman's campaign manager, and assumed command of the anti-Grant forces at once. And in no time he blocked Conkling's plan and struck a compromise that made Senator George F. Hoar permanent chairman.

When the convention opened Conkling put his principle of solidarity to the test in a new form. Switching signals, he now called for a "loyalty oath" binding every delegate to support the nominee. But again Garfield was ready. Rising slowly, he was promptly recognized by the friendly chairman. In a masterful appeal to the sense of fair play and individualism of his audience, he turned aside Conkling's design while a storm of applause broke over the hall. His fight lost, Conkling wrote across the top of a newspaper, "I congratulate you on being the dark horse," and sent the message over to his opponent, Garfield.

From then on Garfield missed few tricks. When the chairman silenced James Joy, who was nominating Blaine (the New York *Times*, supporting Grant, insisted the galleries were packed with Blaine boosters), Garfield was on his feet pleading for more time for the old gentleman. And when his turn came to nominate Sherman he made no effort to match the flamboyant offerings of the preceding speakers. Instead he won over the gathering with prudence, tact, and a quiet manner.

On the balloting the lines held firm. Grant and Blaine split nearly 600 votes between them, and Sherman's total hovered around 100. Finally, after the thirty-third ballot, Sherman released his votes to Garfield, who had been receiving one or two votes from Pennsylvania. At the close of the thirty-fourth ballot, however, Garfield was on his feet trying to protest the votes he was receiving. But chairman Hoar ruled him out of order, fearing he might say something that would make his nomination impossible, and on the thirty-sixth ballot —an all-time record for Republican conventions—James A. Garfield was nominated for President of the United States.[9]

When the convention reconvened the New York delegation nominated Chester A. Arthur, the ousted collector, for the Vice-Presidency, over the objections of Conkling, who wanted nothing to do with Garfield. As Godkin of the *Nation* wrote, for Conkling to accept Arthur for Vice-President instead of Grant for President was "very like taking a suit of old clothes in lieu of the English mission." [10] But the Stalwarts were to be placated, even over their own objections, and Arthur received the nomination.

Taking a leaf from the Republicans' political guidebook, the Democrats then nominated a former Union general of high caliber, Winfield S. Hancock, and a wealthy Indiana banker, William H. English, who was a strong war Democrat. Even if Republicans wanted to wave the bloody shirt, the records of the opposition candidates gave them no leeway. And when Maine was lost by a combination of Democrats and Greenbackers in September's state and congressional elections, Blaine rushed to New York headquarters to convince the party leaders that the campaign tactics would have to be changed. Blaine's astute judgment was followed, and the Republicans turned their guns on the Democrats' "tariff for revenue only" platform.

In August Grant took the stump and made a few short speeches for Garfield in the East and West. Grant's most conspicuous backer, Roscoe Conkling, also took the field to battle for the ticket. Then just before the election a small daily paper in New York, called *Truth,* published a forged letter, imitating Garfield's handwriting, in which Garfield appeared to be arguing for the importation of cheap Chinese labor. This piece was widely reprinted, and Republican historian Smalley contends that it meant the loss of California and Nevada for the Republicans.[11]

When the popular vote rolled in it was evident that the nation had gone through one of the closest elections in history. The Republican victory over the Democrats was less than 10,000 votes. And since some 300,000 minor party ballots were cast, Garfield became a minority President.

The GOP captured a sizable number of states, though the margins were barely perceptible in some. Party chieftains were up late waiting for Connecticut to return a 2,660 vote majority, Indiana to be carried by 6,625, and New York by 21,033. But at least the three states were back in the GOP column.

The South was now solid—solidly Democratic. And as usual in one-party areas, the vote declined. But in Maine, where the Republicans encountered stiff opposition from the fusion of Greenbackers and Democrats, the vote increased, and Garfield's plurality of 8,868 (53.2 percent of the popular vote) was the closest call any Republican presidential candidate experienced in Maine from 1856 to 1912.

Garfield was well prepared for the task of placating party differences. His political experience "in a State whose people were evenly divided in politics" made him keenly attuned to "the currents of public sentiment." [12] His cabinet could be expected to have a little for everyone. To head the State department went Blaine, receptive to Garfield when his own candidacy became hopeless at the convention, and generous as a campaigner. For Secretary of War Garfield selected Robert T. Lincoln, son of the great President, a Stalwart and one of the "306"—the die-hards who stayed with Grant through the last ballot at Chicago.

Reformers were pleased with the appointments of Wayne McVeagh of Pennsylvania for Attorney General and T. L. James of New York for Postmaster General. And even Southern Republicans could take comfort in one selection. For Secretary of the Navy, Garfield named William Henry Hunt of Louisiana, a native who had aligned himself with the carpetbagger leaders of his state during reconstruction.

The most urgent political problem as Garfield took over the reins was the organization of the Senate, deadlocked with thirty-seven Republicans and thirty-seven Democrats. The balance of power lay in the hands of two Independents, David Davis and William Mahone. And when it became evident that Davis would vote with the Democrats all eyes turned to the Virginian, for if he sided with Republicans the tie-breaking vote of Vice-President Arthur would settle the contest.

Mahone, leader of the Readjusters, had successfully opposed the old "Bourbon" faction of the Democratic party. His rise to power was accomplished with an efficient machine, a large Negro vote, and an economic program of repudiating the state debt (in effect, a demand that one-third of the debt be shifted to West Virginia). When it was learned that Mahone would be with the Republicans, the next question became: What had been his price? It was soon obvious that Mahone received inordinately fine committee assignments for a freshman. But the main agreement was to give two good Senate administrative offices to his friends. And this the Democrats fought with every tactic at their command, the Republicans countering by refusing to go into executive session for six weeks.[13]

When the Republicans broke the deadlock at last on May 4 by their withdrawal of the Mahone supporters, the Senate was confronted with another nomination. And this one gave every promise of decisively influencing the balance of power between Garfield and Congress. It would also shake the factional make-up of the party.

For collector of the port of New York the President sent the name of William H. Robertson to the Senate. Garfield's choice for the powerful post was an old foe of Senator Conkling. Robertson he would remember as one who led a part of the New York delegation against Grant at the 1880 convention. Now the President was openly defying the boss of the Empire state. Moreover, the "half-breeds," Garfield and Blaine, were defying the Stalwarts—shapers of party policy since the Johnsonian era. The Senate was in the embarrassing spot of having either to offend the President at the outset of his administration or to discard the cherished practice of senatorial courtesy. As it laid plans for postponing the day of decision by putting off the Robertson appointment until the December session, the President in a thrillingly bold act withdrew all New York appointments except Robertson's. Conkling's hand was called. It was now impossible to adjourn without sacrificing the state's other lucrative patronage. In a dramatic but silly gesture Conkling resigned from the Senate, dragging along with him New York's junior senator, Tom Platt, who would now spend years living down the derisive nickname, "Me Too." The two Senators appealed to the state legislature for vindication, and with them went Arthur. John Hay wrote in the *Tribune* what many felt: "The Vice-President of the United States still stands at Albany under a sign which reads: 'Political dickering and other dirty work done here!' "[14]

Two days after the resignations, Robertson was confirmed. And in July, as the President lay dying, Conkling and Platt were replaced by two unknowns. For the protagonists of this melodrama, the outcome was decisive in a way few political power struggles are. For Conkling, it was the swift end for one who had labored so long in the service of himself and his party and who represented so much in the history of his time. For Garfield, it meant being the target for a demented killer. For the Republican party, it might have opened a new era under Garfield: under a successor, only time would tell.

Virtually all of the President's first few months was taken up with patronage and appointments. First the selection of the cabinet, then the fight with Conkling, and most of all the hordes of minor office-seekers that burst upon him. For four years under Hayes, patronage channels for regular Republicans were partially blocked by an extended civil service, reformers, and Southern Democrats. Then came the bitter and close presidential campaign. Now it seemed that everyone who even cast a vote expected a suitable reward. Patronage pressure was greater than at any time since the early days when Lincoln was building a new party, and John Hay described the President as "living in a whirlwind, fighting like a baited bull against the mob, hounded down by politicians from morning till midnight."

Amidst the depressing massive jobhunt during Garfield's first months in office, another hard blow threatened to thud home and discredit his administration. From the very outset he was beset by mail frauds on the Star routes in the Far West. Through connivance between contractors hired to carry the mails and officials in the Post Office department at Washington, large sums of money were illegally drawn from the Treasury in payment for services never rendered. The ruse was simple. New contracts were completed for daily carriage of the mail, but in practice the old weekly service was continued on many of these routes while contractors drew pay for a bogus daily service.

Garfield determined to tidy up this mess at once. But his efforts to clean up the scandal brought an outcry from the press. For many of these contractors owned newspapers which they now turned on the President, much to the glee of Conkling, who joyously joined the attack.

All this in the first four months! Then in the tragic course of events from the weird dance of the spoilsmen to the Star route scandals, a small-time politician and half-crazed, disappointed office-seeker bought a pistol. Stalking Garfield for days, he finally stood in wait for him in the railroad station where the President would be passing through to entrain for a class reunion at Williams College. From behind Garfield Charles J. Guiteau fired two shots into the President's arm and spinal column, shouting: "I am a Stalwart and now Arthur is President!"

Through seventy-nine long days the nation waited and prayed. Finally on the evening of September 19 the end came to the twentieth President of the United States, at Elberon where he had been moved in the hope that the sea air might help him. Chester A. Arthur, the New York spoilsman and Vice-President, entered the White House.

The first hint of what influence the Stalwarts would have with the new President came with his appointment of a cabinet. Of the four Easterners and three Westerners he selected, all but one were "Grant men" in 1880. The exception was William E. Chandler, who became Secretary of the Navy. Only one member of the Garfield cabinet was retained—Robert T. Lincoln—a concession to the Stalwarts in the first place. Into the top State department post went Frederick T. Frelinghuysen of New Jersey, a United States Senator off and on since 1866. And into private life went Blaine, to write his *Twenty Years of Congress.* Even the President's fellow New Yorker, Postmaster General James, who was now considered a "traitor" for failing to resign with Conkling and Platt over the Robertson appointment, was retired. Perhaps the most encouraging news was the appointment of Benjamin H. Brewster of Pennsylvania as Attorney General. Brewster was brought into the Garfield administration as special counsel in the Star route frauds and his elevation to the cabinet raised hopes that Arthur would at least attempt to stamp out one area of corruption.[15]

Soon there were other signs that Arthur might try to fill Garfield's shoes. First he refused to remove Collector Robertson. Then during his first Congress he issued a stinging veto of the rivers and harbors bill. For at least a decade this type of pork-barreling was becoming increasingly popular with the legislators. In 1870 it reached $3,-900,000, in 1880 it was $8,900,000, now Congress demanded $18,-700,000. The President returned the appropriation bill to the Hill, stating: "My principal objection to the bill is that it contains appropriations for purposes not for the common defense or general welfare, and which do not promote commerce among the States. These provisions, on the contrary, are entirely for the benefit of the particular localities in which it is proposed to make the improvements. . . ."

Yet, despite several salutary steps ahead by Arthur, as the off-year elections of 1882 approached it was evident that the Stalwarts were still in the saddle. If proof was needed, one might point to Arthur's appointment of Roscoe Conkling to the Supreme Court, an honor the old boss declined.

For Arthur, the congressional elections would test his theory of how to win Southern votes just as the Hayes theory had been put to the test in 1878. The two theories, however, differed considerably. Where Hayes felt that he could win over the Southern conservatives to the party of business, Arthur now distributed his patronage to the "anti-Bourbon" Democrats, those economic radicals who opposed orthodox economic tenets. The policy of the former was to seek an alliance with those who had a natural affinity with the party; the policy of the latter was to ally the Republicans with those who were revolting against the Democrats. Arthur failed, as had Hayes.

Although the Republicans held the Senate, the "landslide" of 1882 saw the enlarged House go to the Democrats 201 to 119, with five Independents and Greenbackers.[16] And in New York, where Arthur forced the selection of a personal friend, Judge Folger, as a gubernatorial candidate, Grover Cleveland won by nearly 200,000 votes. The combined loss of the House and New York was a serious setback to the President's prestige and his chances of gaining the nomination in 1884.

Aware that in three months the Republicans would have to share control with the Democrats, Arthur urged the lame duck Congress to take immediate action on civil service reforms. And despite the long-standing opposition of the Stalwarts to what Conkling called "snivel service reform," the President was still able to get action by both houses, and on January 16, 1883, he signed the Pendleton act into law.

The new law gave the President the power to appoint a three-man bipartisan commission empowered to give competitive examinations, make promotions only from one grade to the next higher, and put appointees on probation for a reasonable time. Arthur's "good faith" was shown by his two Republican appointments, both avowed reformers. One, Dorman B. Eaton, was the author of the reformist *Civil Service in Great Britain.*

Perhaps, as Hayes wrote, Arthur was "driven into reform positions by a public sentiment which he dare not resist," but the fact remains that his administration did much to advance the cause. And the President could take much satisfaction from the salute of the new commission in its *Second Annual Report:* "Our functions cannot be successfully discharged without the constant, firm, and friendly support of the President. That support has never failed."

As a party leader, however, Arthur was not so successful. And as the 1884 convention loomed closer, the field was cluttered with aspirants for his job. One hopeful was John A. Logan, in control of the Illinois delegation and very popular with the rising Grand Army of the Republic. John Sherman was another, not so earnestly in the race this time but still in command of a bloc of Ohio votes. John's brother, General William Tecumseh Sherman, also had a few supporters— soon discouraged by his famous telegram: "I WILL NOT ACCEPT IF

NOMINATED AND WILL NOT SERVE IF ELECTED." It should be noted, however, that what has now become the model declination of a presidential candidate was not sent by a serious contender, but rather by his brother. The reformers, mostly in New England, favored Senator George F. Edmunds of Vermont, a constitutional lawyer with a tireless capacity for picking flaws and raising objections. But above them all stood the ever present, ever willing James G. Blaine.

And Blaine clearly controlled the national committee. When the convention met on June 3, the committee's choice for temporary chairman was already made. He was the notorious Powell Clayton of Arkansas, impeached but not convicted as governor and challenged as Senator on the grounds that his election had been secured by "corrupt bargains," though the charges were found "not proven" by a congressional committee. Powell's selection served notice that the Blaine forces were so powerful that they could ram anything through the convention. But it was also a tactical error that came close to undoing them.

Blaine's campaign at Chicago was in the hands of a group of Southwestern entrepreneurs and politicians, led by Stephen B. Elkins. Having accumulated a fortune in mining and stock raising, Elkins now wintered in New York, where he looked after his land, coal, and railroad interests, and spent the rest of his time in New Mexico, where he was founder and president of the First National Bank of Santa Fe and also kept up a legal practice. His principal pre-convention helpers were Chauncey L. Filley, national committeeman from Missouri, ex-Senator Jerome Chaffee of Colorado, and Tom Donaldson.[17]

The President opened headquarters in the Grand Pacific Hotel, with an organization captained by Frank Hatton of Iowa, First Assistant Postmaster General; George H. Sharpe of New York; Senator Omar D. Conger of Michigan; and Benjamin Butterworth of Ohio, who was appointed by Arthur as a commissioner of the Northern Pacific Railroad after having lost his seat in Congress in the 1882 landslide.[18]

As usual, the delegates reflected all shades of the party spectrum. Political reporters counted eighteen Senators and thirty-five Congressmen in attendance, although only eight Senators and twenty Representatives were actually delegates. There were upwards of one hundred Negro delegates, with ex-Senator Blanch K. Bruce as their recognized leader, and including "Percy Bysshe Shelley" Pinchback of Louisiana, Strobach of Alabama, and John R. Lynch of Mississippi among the ranks. The colorful Mahone ran the Virginia delegation

with almost dictatorial power. Present also were a number of re-
formers and intellectuals, among them George W. Curtis, Theodore
Roosevelt, Henry Cabot Lodge, and Andrew D. White, president of
Cornell University.

A heated contest immediately developed over the selection of the
temporary chairman. Blaine's candidate, Powell Clayton, was offensive to many Republicans, and Lodge challenged the choice from the
floor by nominating John Lynch, the ex-slave and ex-Congressman.
It was a shrewd move, for the forces of Arthur, Edmunds, Logan,
and Sherman quickly rallied to his support and Clayton was defeated, 424 to 384.

Now it was apparent that while Blaine was the leading presidential
contender, he might be turned back by a coalition. Moreover, if factional lines were drawn as in 1880 Blaine's clumsy generalship would
be fatal. But the setting was different after four years. No longer were
the presidential aspirants more interested in stopping Blaine than in
securing their own nominations. The majority of the convention was
not really opposed to the Man from Maine. As Theodore Roosevelt
wrote immediately after the convention, "the second choice of all the
Logan and Sherman and nearly half the Arthur men, was Blaine,
which made it absolutely impossible to form a combination against
him. . . ." [19] For nearly two years rumors had circulated that Logan
and Blaine had reached an agreement by which the weaker would
accept second place, which for Logan would be the Vice-Presidency.
Nearly half of the Edmunds men would "stand by their principles"
and refuse to compromise with any candidate. But Sherman's control
over the Ohio delegation was tenuous. This was immediately apparent from the vote for temporary chairman: Blaine's candidate received twenty-two of the state's forty-six votes. The chairman of the
delegation, Joseph B. Foraker (later governor and Senator), could
be expected to hold them in line for the "favorite son" for a while
(with the aid of a young businessman and newspaper publisher who
was attending his first convention as a delegate—Mark Hanna), but it
was clear that many of the Buckeyes were restive and eager to jump
on the Blaine bandwagon.[20]

Nevertheless, in a convention made jumpy by poor judgment at
the start, it was imperative that the Blaine managers make no more
blunders. They decided on two courses of action: first to beat the
drums loudly enough to convince delegates they were going to win.
Second, once the balloting started, to allow no intermission that
would give the scattered opposition an opportunity to throw in a
neutral candidate. On the first objective, the Baltimore *Sun* tells us,

"Three hundred democratic roughs of Chicago were reported to have been brought into the hall tonight to help in keeping the fire burning, and they were a success." [21] The second objective too was admirably attained.

Nominating speeches ended in the small hours of the fourth day. An adjournment after a single ballot might be disastrous, since opposing commands would have a chance to size up sources of strength as well as spot the weaknesses and act accordingly. So the Blaine managers asked for an adjournment, but their motion was lost. On a second motion, however, the confusion and uproar on the floor was so great that the opposing forces surrendered.

Balloting began the next morning at 11:30. The first ballot showed 334½ for Blaine, 278 for Arthur, 93 for Edmunds, 63½ for Logan, 30 for Sherman, and a few votes for other candidates. [22] Blaine, it was now apparent, was playing the old game of holding back some of his strength. It was also evident that the President had little support outside of the federal jobholders in the Southern delegations. Over half—163—of his votes came from Southern delegates. [23]

On the next ballot Blaine gained 14½ votes, and after the third ballot Sherman triggered the stampede by releasing his delegates. Then on the fourth ballot the Logan men came over to Blaine in a body except for "six delegates from Egypt" (Egypt county, Illinois) who went down shouting "Black Jack forever." Blaine was nominated and Logan received the vice-presidential nomination on a turbulent and disorderly ballot, giving credence to the rumors of a Blaine-Logan deal.

The presidential nominee was obviously the favorite of the men from the states that count. In his column were the total delegations of California, Colorado, Iowa, Maine, Nevada, Oregon, and West Virginia. And he won substantial support from New York, Pennsylvania, Kansas, Michigan, Minnesota, Indiana, Ohio, Wisconsin, Nebraska, and New Jersey. For a more intimate image the letter of a young New York delegate, Theodore Roosevelt, gives the best picture:

> Blaine's adherents included . . . the vast majority of those from the middle and eastern states, and some from New England. These were the men who make up the mass of the party. Their ranks included many scoundrels, adroit and clever, who intend to further their own ends by supporting the popular candidate, or who know Mr. Blaine so well that they expect under him to be able to develop their schemes to the fullest extent; but for the most part these Republicans were good, ordinary men, who do not do very much

thinking, who are pretty honest themselves, but who are callous to any but very flagrant wrongdoing in others, unless it is brought home to them forcibly. . . .[24]

Striking a masterful balance, Republicans were confident of their ticket's cross-country appeal: Blaine the "half-breed," Logan the "Stalwart"; Blaine the "civilian," Logan the former Union general; Blaine the Easterner, Logan from the Middle West.

But this time the Republicans reversed their usual pattern of seeking their vice-presidential nominee in the East and the presidential candidate from the central states. Since Lincoln, the top of the ticket had always gone to the Middle West. Lincoln and Grant were from Illinois, Hayes and Garfield from Ohio. And running mates were taken from the East: Wilson from Massachusetts, Wheeler and Arthur from New York. The logic was simple: the tickets were designed to woo the doubtful areas—the central states and New York. The Democrats liked this strategy too, but reversed the field. Seymour, Greeley, and Tilden were New Yorkers, and Hancock hailed from Pennsylvania. Of the Democratic vice-presidential candidates two were from Missouri and two from Indiana. Now Blaine and Logan would run against governor Grover Cleveland of New York and former governor Thomas Hendricks of Indiana.

The Cleveland-Blaine campaign left a polluted record—one of the worst in American political history. More specific than usual, the Republican platform called for an eight-hour day, an extended civil service, the exclusion of Chinese labor, suppression of polygamy in Utah, regulation of corporations, and reaffirmation of the duty to secure to all citizens all civil and political rights. Actually the party platforms offered no real points of contrast. Even on the tariff question both pledged a revision that would not harm domestic manufacturers. Thus the contest turned upon the personal fitness of the nominees.

In the Democratic camp new "Mulligan Letters" were uncovered, one containing the damaging Blaine marginalia, "Burn this letter." Reopening the controversy of 1876, the Democrats recited, "Blaine, Blaine, the continental liar from the State of Maine," and chanted, "Burn the letter, burn the letter. . . ."

Blaine was also hit from another quarter. A Democratic newspaperman prowling about in a Pennsylvania cemetery found a date on a tombstone showing that a child of Blaine's died just six months after his marriage. But this charge Blaine was able to turn by explaining that originally he was married in Kentucky, but some time later after he settled in Pennsylvania the legality of his marriage was questioned so he remarried.

The Republicans also dug out ample ammunition. On July 21 a Buffalo newspaper broke a damaging story out of the Democratic nominee's past. In banks of headlines it told

A TERRIBLE TALE

A DARK CHAPTER IN PUBLIC MAN'S HISTORY

THE PITIFUL STORY OF MARIA HALPIN

AND GOVERNOR CLEVELAND'S SON

Bachelor candidate Grover Cleveland, it seems, had for many years been supporting the illegitimate son of a widow, one Maria Halpin. Not at all certain that he was the child's father, Cleveland apparently had sufficient doubts to do the "gentlemanly thing." And once the Buffalo paper broke the story, a miserable ditty soon popped into verse: "Ma, Ma, where's my Pa? / Going to the White House! Ha, Ha, Ha!" Cleveland was also accused of mistreating his mother. In the final analysis, however, the outcome of the election suggests that people were more concerned with the public than with the private morals of their next chief executive.

As the campaign wore on, there were several prominent desertions. Many of the Independents, including Schurz and Godkin, could not stomach the old politician who was carrying their party's standard. Soon named the "Mugwumps," they set out to stump the North for Cleveland. And three of the most influential journals in New York city aided the Mugwump movement—the *Times,* the *Evening Post,* and *Harper's Weekly.* Though few in number, the Mugwumps packed a wallop against the Republican ticket in the places it hurt the worst.[25]

Meanwhile, the Republican organization played into the hands of the Democratic opposition. Blaine, the first presidential candidate to tour the country since Greeley, returned to New York for a fundraising dinner on October 29. Held at the fashionable Delmonico's, the affair, which was sponsored by such men as Jay Gould, Cyrus Field, and Russell Sage, would ordinarily have caused little stir. But in the midst of a mild business recession the opposition press quickly made a liability out of this "Mammon's Homage" or "Belshazzar's Feast." And the very same day an even greater albatross was hung around the candidate's neck.

Welcoming Blaine to the city at New York's Fifth Avenue Hotel, the Reverend Samuel D. Burchard turned to the "Plumed Knight" and said: "We are Republicans, and don't propose to leave our party and identify ourselves with the party whose antecedents have been *Rum, Romanism and Rebellion. . . .*"

A fast-thinking reporter on the New York *World* quickly latched on to the remark, and with less than a week until Election Day Democratic headquarters blew it up into a last-minute battle cry. And while Blaine maintained a seventy-two-hour silence before throwing a rejoinder, the opposition hastily scattered handbills at the doors of Catholic churches in New York and other parts of the country.[26]

Again the election was breathtakingly close, and it was three days before the results were made final. Only 23,000 votes separated the two major candidates. Blaine, with 48.3 percent of the popular vote, was barely topped by Cleveland's 48.9 percent. But New York and its thirty-six electoral votes fell to the Democrats' column and that settled it. Cleveland won with an electoral vote of 219 to Blaine's 182. Blaine lost the Empire state by a scant 1,000 votes.

Any number of factors were enough to make the difference: the loss of Irish votes thanks to Burchard's bellicose bellow; the defection of the Mugwumps; the "millionaire's dinner" at Delmonico's; or the votes of the Prohibition party candidate. Since 1872 the anti-barley-corn candidates had made little headway. But this time the Prohibition party nominee, Governor John St. John of Kansas, received over 150,000 votes—25,000 of them in New York—and most of these Prohibitionists were of Republican extraction.

In the election of Cleveland the country might have been following the advice of a Chicago observer: "We are told that Mr. Blaine has been delinquent in office but blameless in private life, while Mr. Cleveland has been a model of official integrity but culpable in his personal relations. We should therefore elect Mr. Cleveland to the public office which he is so well qualified to fill and remand Mr. Blaine to the private station which he is admirably fitted to adorn."

Or the country might have agreed with the New York Democratic chant:

> The *World* says the Independents Did It;
> The *Tribune* says the Stalwarts Did It;
> The *Sun* says Borchard [*sic*] Did It;
> Blaine says St. John Did It;
> Theodore Roosevelt says it was the Soft Soap Dinner;
> We say Blaine's character Did It;
> But We Don't Care What Did It, It's Done.[27]

For Blaine, the defeat was the end of his long, serious quest for the Presidency. His prophecy after the 1876 convention that he was "the Henry Clay of the Republican party" proved true. For the Republican party, it was the first defeat for the Presidency since its initial entry into national politics with Frémont. After twenty-four continuous years in the White House, it would have to learn to be an opposition party.

While President Cleveland struggled to apply "business principles to public affairs," and dueled with a Republican Senate (and often with a Democratic House too), important changes in personnel were taking place in the Republican party. In 1887 Matthew Quay, who at one time held the recordership of Philadelphia—a position reputedly worth $100,000 a year in fees and other emoluments— became junior United States Senator from Pennsylvania, soon to take over the Cameron dynasty. For many years Quay served as trouble-shooter for governor Andrew Curtin, Simon Cameron's old foe. But later he learned to play ball with both Camerons—father and son. Also becoming increasingly active in Republican circles was the department store magnate, John Wanamaker, who for the next thirty-two years would be a power in national party politics. Both men would play prominent roles in the presidential campaign of 1888.

With time on their hands, Republican party leaders now turned to speculating on the next presidential candidate. Blaine, touring Europe in the spring of 1888, was still a mighty popular leader among Republicans. But he wrote in April saying he would not be a candidate, and again on May 17 he wrote from Paris insisting that his earlier letter be considered an unconditional withdrawal of his name. Not until the fourth day of the convention, however, would his friends really give up the idea of bringing about his nomination.

Meanwhile scores of names tumbled into the contention, some serious, others the usual favorite sons. Among them was Benjamin Harrison, a man with illustrious ancestors and a distinguished war record. Harrison had just been defeated for re-election after serving a term in the Senate. Other contenders were Walter Q. Gresham, like Harrison a Hoosier, who served briefly as Secretary of the Treasury under Arthur; Senator William Allison of Iowa; Chauncey Depew, president of the New York Central and Hudson River railways; former governor Russell A. Alger of Michigan; and John Sherman.

Whomever the Republicans nominated would have to face Cleveland in the general election. Breaking the long-standing custom, the Democrats held their convention first, and on June 5 had renominated the President by acclamation—the first such endorsement since Van Buren was renominated in 1840. It was also clear that the campaign would be waged over the tariff, for most of the Democratic platform was devoted to this issue—recommending a "fair and careful revision of the tax laws. . . ."

To this position Republicans were uncompromisingly opposed. At the Chicago convention on June 21 they adopted a plank favoring "the entire repeal of the internal taxes rather than the surrender of any part of our protective system." The platform also favored bimetallism and, with a bow to the growing temperance movement and possibly a thought about the lost Prohibition vote in 1884, declared that it "cordially sympathized with all wise and well directed efforts for the promotion of temperance and morality."

The platform, however, was a mere curtain-raiser to the contest for the nomination. With Blaine seemingly but not really out of the running, touring Scotland at the moment with Andrew Carnegie, the field was wide open. Never before in the history of presidential conventions had so many candidates received votes. Before the decisive eighth ballot nineteen names were entered.

Sherman, the sixth to be placed in nomination, seemed to have a fair chance of winning. He received the strongest demonstration of the day. The seconding speech by Governor Foraker of Ohio amusingly brought an incident that threw the convention into an uproar. Just as Foraker strode to the platform an enormous floral tribute was placed at the speaker's rostrum. Standing several feet high and a foot thick, it was made of red flowers and emblazoned in white with his famous dispatch about Confederate battle flags: "No Rebel flags will be returned while I am Governor." A handsome piece, but embarrassing to Foraker since the flowers were a gift from two inept Chicago women whose brother he had pardoned from the penitentiary the year before, and the crowd knew it.

On the first ballot, with the aid of a memorable nominating speech by Congressman William McKinley, Sherman took the lead. His 229 votes were more than twice the number of his nearest competitor. Next came Gresham with 111; then Depew with 99 (72 in the nature of a complimentary vote from the New York delegation); then Alger with 84; Harrison, 80; Allison, 72; and Blaine, 35.[28]

For the next two ballots there was little change. Then on the fourth ballot Depew dropped out and 58 of New York's votes went to Harrison, who jumped from 94 to 217, just 18 behind Sherman. After the fourth ballot the story that Blaine would be a candidate on the fifth ballot buzzed the convention. A recess was called until 4 P.M., but at this hour the Blaine men got an adjournment until Monday morning. Now the convention became a supermarket for deals, trades, and at least for the leading candidate Sherman what his followers felt to be a "double cross."

Late Saturday afternoon Foraker gave out a statement to the Associated Press saying he had "strained every nerve" in behalf of Sherman, hence he could not be accused of "treachery." Then he said he would henceforth be for Blaine. Cries of treachery greeted the statement at once, and then in the midst of bitter bickering the scene shifted on Sunday.[29] A cable came from Blaine again asking that his Paris letter declining to be a candidate be respected. The "Plumed Knight" was now taken at his word.

Early Monday morning Foraker was awakened by Stephen B. Elkins, who told him the entire Blaine strength including New York would be his if he would accept, but the Ohio governor declined. Nor is it likely that he could have been nominated had he accepted the offer.

There was now little doubt, of course, that Sherman would not be nominated. Although still leading the field, he was five votes below his initial show of strength. Twice before he had been compelled to pen a message of withdrawal. This time he said no. "Let my name stand," he wired Mark Hanna. "I prefer defeat to retreat." When the balloting resumed on Monday, Harrison jumped from 231 on the sixth to 544 on the seventh ballot, and won the nomination on the eighth, when Allison withdrew in his favor and Pennsylvania retired to caucus. On their return, Quay delivered 50 votes to Harrison and the contest was over.

Harrison, the rotund diminutive candidate with the light-gray whiskers, was an eminently available candidate. The name he bore was a vote-catcher. Great-grandfather Benjamin Harrison was a signer of the Declaration of Independence and grandfather William Henry was boosted into the presidency as the Hero of Tippecanoe. Although lacking warmth and charm, he was known for his integrity and independence. Years later, the proprietor of the Washington boarding house where he lived as a Senator reminisced: "At dinner frequently a group of Senators passed Harrison by without speaking as though they didn't care a d——n for him. But what I liked about Harrison was, that he didn't seem to care a G—d d——n for them." [30]

With Quay as national chairman and Wanamaker as chief fundraiser, Republicans set about to put "Uncle Ben right back in his grandfather's place." [31] And they did.

But it was a mighty close squeak. Actually the results were very similar to those of 1884, except that this time the GOP captured all-important New York and Indiana, the former by some 14,000 votes. Ironically, in nationwide totals the Republicans trailed the Democrats by over 90,000 votes, compared with 68,000 in the losing campaign of four years before. While Connecticut went into the Democratic column by 344 votes, the GOP recaptured Indiana by 2,352 votes out of 537,008 cast. And with the struggle raging between the Readjusters and the regulars in Virginia the Republicans came closer to catching the Democrats than at any other time between 1872 and 1928. Cleveland scraped through the Old Dominion by a mere handful—1,605 votes. But across the South the Democratic hold was tightening into a rigid one-party system. Harrison, with 233 electoral votes to 168 for Cleveland, was still the victor in a photo finish. Once again the Republicans lost the popular vote but won the Presidency. While Lincoln in 1860 and Garfield were "plurality" Presidents, Harrison now joined Hayes in winning without a majority of the two-party vote. For the second time the United States had a minority President.

And the Republicans had not only won the Presidency; for the first time since 1875 they would control both the White House and Congress.

On to the First Front Porch

Something troubles the European about the American political system, comments Lord Bryce in his great treatise, *The American Commonwealth:* "He is always asking what the difference between a Republican and a Democrat is because he never gets an answer." Had Lord Bryce's mythical European consulted Senator George F. Hoar of Massachusetts in 1890, he would have received a ready answer:

"The men who do the work of piety and charity in our churches," said Senator Hoar, "the men who administer our school systems, the men who own and till their own farms, the men who perform skilled labor in the shops, the soldiers, the men who went to war and stayed all through, the men who paid the debt and kept the currency sound and saved the nation's honor, the men who saved the country in war and have made it worth living in in peace, commonly and as a rule, by the natural law of their being, find their places in the Republican party; while the old slave owner and slave-driver, the saloon keeper, the ballot box stuffer, the Ku Klux Klan, the criminal class of the great cities, the men who cannot read or write, commonly and as a rule, by the natural law of their being, find their congenial place in the Democratic party." [1]

Brave words, and proud words. But not enough to lead Republican minds away from party difficulties at the moment.

The Republican party was still a sectional party with a fast-fading appeal in the South. Could the party organization here be strengthened? Harrison thought it might. And he elected to follow a Southern policy based upon three main features: a return to reconstruction tactics aimed at protecting Negro voting rights, an effort to attract certain elements of the South by favorable legislation, and an attempt to quell the factional fires between warring Republican leaders of the South.

Unhappily the first of these objectives was forestalled by defeat of the Force bill. Introduced in 1890 by Henry Cabot Lodge (and derisively named by the Democrats) this measure sought to place voting supervisors in each judicial circuit of the country who would watch over registration and report on the reception of voters. Clearly designed to protect Negro voters, this bill passed the House only to run into foul weather in the Senate. Under pressure from Democrats who were filibustering against the Force bill and blocking consideration of the McKinley Tariff bill, Senators Quay and Cameron of Pennsylvania "subordinated the plight of the Negro" to the quick and safe passage of the tariff bill. It was a bitter disappointment to Harrison. And so were his experiences with Southern politicians and Southern legislative measures. But Harrison kept trying to convert the South to Republicanism even as depression pockets in the nation's economy were beginning to deepen.

Harrison, it will be remembered, was a minority President in terms of the popular vote, and though winning in the electoral college had actually lost to Grover Cleveland by a plurality of 98,017 votes. Moreover, though winning control over both houses of Congress, the Republicans ran into strong headwinds in the midterm elections of 1890, largely because of a legislative experiment with the tariff which proved disastrous at the ballot box.

Republican control in the House was a modest one—a working margin, really, of only eight or nine votes, since the division in the Fifty-first Congress stood 173 Republicans, 156 Democrats. On the Senate side the GOP edge was somewhat more comfortable—47 Republicans to 37 Democrats.

From the very outset of this Congress, Republican leaders opposed the demands advanced by the Senators from the West who were making strident calls for a windfall from the federal treasury to help the silver producers. Actually, GOP congressional leaders were opposed to any pressure plays stirred up by the inflation sentiment in the country. And the nation was beset by many inflationary groups because of depressed agricultural prices and the spread of agrarian discontent that was shaping the formation of a new party known as the People's party, or the Populist party. But Republican leaders had other plans than simply holding easy-money advocates at bay.

The primary goal of the party chieftains was tariff revision, and to gain this goal they were forced to strike a bargain with the Congressmen of the West. Not until the administration agreed to the monthly purchase of 4,500,000 ounces of silver did the silver Senators of the West consent to go along with the McKinley bill to lift general tariff levels. For many months the silver bloc held up passage of McKinley's bill until he finally agreed to the terms eventually incorporated into the Sherman Silver Purchase act of 1890.

Under this act the government purchased 4,500,000 ounces of

silver monthly, and thereafter stored either bullion or coin in reserve vaults and issued a special kind of treasury note in payment. The net effect of the Sherman Silver Purchase act was to increase the purchase of silver from thirty million dollars a year—the amount stipulated under the Bland-Allison act of 1878—to fifty million dollars a year. Obviously designed as a windfall to the silver mine owners as well as a sop to those desirous of embarking on an inflationary policy, the Sherman Silver Purchase act rested upon the counterfeit logic that support for the McKinley tariff was worth the price of a small-bore gratuity to special privilege.

The McKinley tariff act, which was the first full-blown Republican experiment with a definite party formula, lifted general tariff levels some 12 percent. Tariff increases on textiles and metal products were particularly drastic, however—so much so that the Treasury department received virtually no revenue whatsoever on imports in this category. During Cleveland's last year in office, it will be recalled, he became worried about a Treasury surplus and decided to send the annual message to Congress urging tariff reduction as a proper remedy for this. And unquestionably the Cleveland proposal for a tariff reduction, to which he devoted an entire message to Congress, was a material factor in bringing about his defeat in 1888. But now under the McKinley Tariff act there was little need to fear for Treasury surpluses. Not only did the steep increase of tariff rates on textile and metal products deprive the Treasury department of revenue, but existing surpluses were eroded away by other provisions of the Tariff act of 1890. Some fifty million dollars of the surplus were raked away by making sugar a duty-free commodity, and an additional ten million dollars was also disposed of by a bounty granted to domestic sugar producers. The Treasury surplus that Cleveland spoke of only a few years back was also siphoned off a bit lower under the Fifty-first Congress by reduction of the internal revenue rates.

Helping likewise to convert a surplus in the Treasury into a deficit was the mounting pressure from army veterans to sweeten pension allowances. By 1890 the Grand Army of the Republic was approaching its zenith in membership. In Ohio alone this year the GAR had enrolled 49,011 members.[2] GAR membership marched steadily with most Republican candidates after the Civil War. But its Republican partiality was particularly evident in the late 1880's when the organization became offended at Grover Cleveland's opposition to the veterans' disability act and his vetoes of hundreds of individual pension bills. In protest, John Raper's Grand Army of the Republic publication portrayed the pension planks of the Democratic party platform of 1888 as a series of ciphers in the shape of an inverted triangle. Mindful of the striking power of this vast veterans' organization, which had now reached the peak of its fighting strength as a pressure group, the Republican Congress generously increased pension legislation from eighty-one million dollars to 139 million during Harrison's four years in office. After constant needling from industry, agriculture, mine owners, veterans, and other groups, the Treasury surplus with which Harrison started quickly receded until it became a sizable deficit at the end of his four-year lease on the White House.

The most notable piece of legislation during Harrison's administration was the Sherman Anti-Trust act, introduced by Senator John Sherman of Ohio on December 4, 1889, and finally approved by the President on July 2, 1890. Designed to outlaw every contract, combination, or conspiracy in restraint of trade or commerce in either the interstate or foreign field, the Sherman Anti-Trust act set up criminal penalties for violations, and provided for the enforcement of the act through federal district attorneys under the direction of the Attorney General. Irritability of the public conscience over monopolistic practices had been growing since the Civil War. In the Panic of '73 the collapse of many jerry-built business enterprises resulted in the absorption, in a great many cases, of the smaller units by the larger interests. Thereafter, as prosperity returned, the larger businesses, now in a strengthened position, continued to plunge ahead and hold their smaller competitors in check. Inevitably, the tendency in many fields of industry and business was toward a form of monopoly control—an outcome bitterly protested by smaller businessmen who insisted that the survival of a competitive order was basic to any free society. And in their attacks upon monopoly these smaller businessmen were joined eagerly by the rank and file of the citizenry who as individual consumers were compelled to pay higher prices because competition was being eliminated.

Monopoly growth, of course, moved ahead not only toward the establishment of huge, carefully organized units that gradually squeezed out small-scale competitors, but it also led to the formation of what we know as "trusts." A trust was simply a combination of several independent firms by means of which they were jointly able to act as a unit through the placement of a majority of the voting stock of each independent firm in the hands of trustees.

Pointing an accusing finger at the trusts, those who looked upon them as repositories of evil generally advanced the following arguments against them: They contended that the over-all effect of building up great monopolies was to destroy competition, that vital ingredient of our economic system which tended to keep prices at a more favorable level for the consumer, and that they tended to drive small enterprises out of business. In addition, trusts were indicted for pyramiding vast fortunes which were not in the transcendent interest of local communities throughout the nation. Finally it was argued that these vast oligarchical combinations which were rapidly building up were becoming so powerful that their domination of legislative policy jeopardized community interests everywhere, and would in the long pull imperil the very existence of free democratic institutions.[3]

Political hucksters never let their audiences forget for a moment that the trusts were responsible for increasing and holding up commodity prices to the consumer. No rally of the day was complete until the audience was duly forewarned that these trusts, perched high on the plateau of special privilege, were becoming more powerful by the hour. So it was that organized combinations such as the Standard Oil trust, the whiskey trust, the sugar trust, and many others, all came to be opposed with great hostility in all parts of the country. Moreover, the same sentiment that crystallized against the trusts also began to shape up into an anti-big business attitude generally.

Not all economists by any means were persuaded that large business organizations were necessarily inimical to the public interest. Moreover in time it would be demonstrated that large-scale organization of business felicitously combined with the skills of technological management, so frequently identified today as "know-how," was a key factor in bracing our high standard of living. But this is another story. In the 1880's and '90's the public conscience cried out against monopoly and trusts, emotionally aroused by the abuses of those Theodore Roosevelt was soon to denounce as "the malefactors of wealth," and stirred up daily by newspaper editors, journalists, and political crusaders. Closely identified with the anti-monopoly sentiment were the demands for control of the railroads and for cheap money, which had long been part and parcel of the agrarian restlessness in the country, and in this period would jell in a movement that was the most important third-party protest since the Civil War.

As we look upon the closing days of the Harrison administration, we need to keep in mind that for a dozen years, from 1880 to 1892, the balance of power between our major parties was extraordinarily close. It was a period that was characterized by an attitude of extreme caution in the platforms of both the Republican and Democratic parties, and in this lull before the storm the issues were stockpiling that would embolden the critics of the major parties to field a challenger in the election of 1892. The close contest between the two parties for control of the Presidency seemed to make the leaders of both major parties hesitant to suggest innovations, and found its counterpart in the political equilibrium which characterized congressional elections of the era. During the same twelve years none of the Presidents could complete his term of office without finding one or both houses of Congress in the hands of the opposition party.

What was happening during these years, of course, was that the nation was winding its way through a kind of economic turnstile—from agrarianism to industrial capitalism. Economically speaking much of the shift toward the new industrial society had already occurred. But as Professor Carleton carefully reminds us, "most people were working out their political and emotional adjustment to it." [4] And in this adjustment, "the Republicans took the lead while the Democrats under Tilden and Cleveland followed a sort of 'me too' policy." These similarities between the parties on policies and attitudes are illustrated in a variety of ways aside from the oft-cited example of hard money.

In the enforcement of the Sherman Anti-Trust law only seven cases had been instituted at the end of the Harrison administration on March 4, 1893, of which only one had been concluded, this being the Tennessee coal case, which ended in victory for the government.

Significantly, we find lack of enthusiasm toward the execution of the Sherman Anti-Trust law in the succeeding Cleveland administration. Moreover, Cleveland's Attorney General Richard Olney, who had appeared against the government in the whiskey trust case, had little sympathy with the Sherman Anti-Trust law. Soon after assuming office he asked for a list of Senators "who might be persuaded to see the thing in the right light," while writing to the Secretary of the Treasury at the same time that the bankers, merchants, and others of Boston were willing and ready to expend some money for repeal of the Sherman law. In his two years as Attorney General Olney took up no new anti-trust cases.

Clearly the prevailing political climate from 1876 to 1894 was one of few clear-cut differences between the major parties. And in some ways it resembled a later period in American politics—the early 1920's—which Sam Blythe once spoke of as an era in which parties were "labels on empty bottles, signs on untenanted houses, cloaks that cover but do not conceal the skeletons beneath them." Into this trough, where clear-cut differences on national policies had been avoided, emptied the discontents of the Greenbackers, Anti-Monopolists, Prohibitionists, and other protest groups, in increasing volume in the late 1880's. And by 1890 the sentiments that would result in a movement known as the People's or Populist party were no longer to be denied.

Essentially, as John Hicks tells us, the Populist philosophy "boiled down finally to two fundamental propositions; one, that the government must restrain the selfish tendencies of those who profited at the expense of the poor and needy; the other, that the people not the plutocrats must control the government." [5] Initially it was the steep decline in agricultural prices that sustained the driving power of this movement. Just as ten-cents-a-bushel flax provoked A. C. Townley to lead farmers on the war path against the railroads, the Minneapolis millers, and the grain exchange in the 1920's, so in the 1880's it was the depressed prices of agricultural products that generated the voltage for the revolt.[6] Following the Civil War, when wheat fell from $1.50 a bushel to 67 cents three years later, the Farmers' Grange was founded. Later, when wheat had climbed above a dollar and then fallen back to 87 cents in 1874, the protest was signified by the organization of the National Greenback party, and the sudden sprouting of anti-monopoly, independent, or reform parties in eleven states. Again, when the price of wheat climbed to $1.05 in 1877 and the Grange movement was on the wane, a drop of 25 cents in the price of wheat within a single year led to the formation of an organization known as the Grand Alliance—the forerunner of the Farmers' Alliance, which in turn formed the organizational skeleton for the People's party. Over three thousand Alliance lodges existed in 1877, when wheat averaged only 68 cents per bushel. Now after wheat had climbed once more to around eight-five cents in 1891, it was on the steep slopes down to forty-nine cents three years later when the National People's party or Populist party was emboldened by the strength of organized discontent to field a presidential candidate who polled more votes than any third party candidate since the Civil War.

Rising swiftly out of the dense thickets of despair in the West and South, the complaints of agrarian groups, inflationists, and mining interests began to jostle confidence in the Harrison administration dangerously in the summer of 1890. The Sherman Silver Purchase act, which went into effect in July of 1890, "failed even momentarily to hush the outcry for free silver." [7] Already the downswing of prices for grain, livestock, and cotton was under way, and in three years the Department of Agriculture would be reporting that the cost of producing wheat and corn exceeded the selling price. In the four years between 1889 and 1893, some 11,000 mortgages were foreclosed in Kansas alone, and over 18,000 covered wagons moved across from the Nebraska to the Iowa side of the Missouri River, in a search for relief from the ruinous conditions prevailing in the Cornhusker state. Notwithstanding the government's policy of buying up silver, the bullion value of the dollar plummeted from 81 cents to 60 cents in 1893. Hamlin Garland, the Iowan, who knew whereof he spoke, summed it up this way: "If ten cent corn and ten percent interest were troubling Kansas, so six cent cotton was inflaming Georgia—and both were frankly sympathetic with Montana and Colorado, whose miners were suffering from a drop in the price of silver."

On the sun-baked prairies of Kansas it was Mary Ellen (Yellen) Lease, "the Kansas pythoness," who personified the spirit in the revolt of the rustics. Irish-born, with a voice that could carry to the next township, "she left a trail of fire through the state." [8] Screaming to huge audiences, and sometimes making use of her skill with polemics, she exhorted the farmers to "raise less corn and more hell," and denounced the East, before whose manufacturers, she said, the West and South were bound and prostrate and little more than slaves. "Our laws are the output of a system which clothes rascals in robes and honesty in rags," she said—a remark which led the New York *Evening Post* to comment: "We don't want any more states until we can civilize Kansas."

Inevitably under these circumstances, demands for a shake-up of the old parties were strong, and the logical beginning for building a new challenger seemed to be the Farmers' Alliance. During the years 1889 and 1890 new members spilled into the order as never before, increasing the plausibility of third party action. By election time in 1890 the drift toward independent political action led to the formation of independent state tickets nominated by Alliance men and their friends everywhere in the Northwest. That fall the Republican incumbent senator from Kansas, John J. Ingalls, widely respected as a cultured and dignified lawyer but tagged by Mary "Yellen" Lease as "a dishonest, soulless, shameless charlatan who suffers from two great robbers, the Sante Fe Railroad and the loan companies," went down to defeat. And in the congressional elections William Peffer, a single-taxer, went to Congress accompanied by "Sockless" Jerry Simpson, the People's party candidate, who had been saying for years of his earlier unsuccessful campaigns: "I haven't a chance to win—but great God, what if I did!" (William Allen White, who was then a young reporter, expanded his title from "Sockless J." to "the Sockless Socrates of the Prairie," a well-merited sobriquet in light of the fact that though uneducated Simpson was a wide reader and intelligent man who was readily familiar with Shelley, Victor Hugo, Robert Burns, Tom Paine, Kent's *Commentaries,* Blackstone, and Henry George.)

What was happening in Kansas, of course, was being repeated

throughout the middle border states. Minnesota had its Ignatius Donnelly—the "Sage of Niniger"—a man of rather remarkable talents whose irregular, reformed Republicanism prompted the correspondent to the New York *Sun* to remark that a reform convention in Minnesota without Donnelly would have been "like catfish without waffles in Philadelphia." Elsewhere Iowa had its James B. Weaver, who cut loose from the Republican party in 1877 to become a Greenbacker and would soon be leading the People's party in a presidential campaign. In the South, perhaps the most spectacular of the young Alliance leaders was thirty-four-year-old Thomas E. Watson. Joining the Alliance, he joyfully made war against the jute trust in 1890, spoke out passionately against the McKinley tariff, and waged a campaign for Congress that has been described as "hot as Nebuchadnezzar's furnace." [9]

All throughout the South the elections ended most gratifyingly for the Alliance. And in the Northwest, operating largely through hastily devised third parties, the Alliance won comparable victories. The Populists picked up some fourteen congressional seats and two Senators, not to mention important successes on many state tickets for legislative and other public offices. Not since the great tidal wave in the elections of 1874 had a Republican majority in the House plummeted so rapidly. From 173 Congressmen in the Fifty-first Congress, Republican strength fell to 88, while the Democratic total lifted from 156 to 231. All over the country Republicans were shaking their heads and wondering what really started the avalanche. Even the architect of the Tariff act of 1890, McKinley, was tipped in his bid for re-election—his first defeat since he went to Congress in 1877. Among the things said to account for his defeat was the device of the Democratic local chieftain who hired an itinerant vender to peddle tin dippers in McKinley's congressional district. His instructions—so it is said—were to greet housewives by asking if they would care to purchase a drinking-water dipper for a dollar. The anticipated reaction to such a statement, of course, was that the housewife would immediately protest such a price as outrageous, with the comment that any fool would know a tin dipper could easily be purchased for ten cents. "I know, madam," was the stock reply of the peddler. "But since the passage of the McKinley Tariff law we are now forced to charge a dollar instead of ten cents."

With the loss of the House, though still in control of the Senate but by a reduced margin, the Harrison administration fell upon hard times, both politically speaking and economically in the country at large. Jubilant with its successes in the November elections of 1890, the Farmers' Alliance was eagerly laying plans in the spring of 1891 to amalgamate the wage earners of the city with the tillers of the soil and reform groups. That May, with some 1,400 representatives of agrarian, labor, and reform groups meeting in Cincinnati, a decision was taken to form a People's party, and in July, 1892, at a second convention in Omaha, preparations were made for launching a presidential campaign. In their platform the People's party promised to restore government to "the plain people," and came out flatly for a graduated income tax, government ownership of the railroads and telegraphs, shorter days for the working man, popular election of United States Senators, and free silver. Then they nominated one of the most insistent inflationists that America has produced, James B. Weaver of Iowa, who led the Greenback ticket for President back in 1880.

Meanwhile President Harrison found himself on the horns of a dilemma. From the outset, perhaps his chief qualification for the honor he had won was his faithful service to the party rather than any distinguished political leadership qualities. A man of somewhat retiring nature, he relied heavily upon the counsel of his Secretary of State, James G. Blaine, to whom he was much beholden for help on his own nomination. At the same time he found himself in a situation where he also was compelled to lean heavily upon others, among whom were Speaker of the House Thomas B. "Czar" Reed of Maine, known for his firm hand in ruling the House, and Senators Tom Platt of New York and Matthew Quay of Pennsylvania. But differences arose between Harrison and Quay almost as soon as the President took office. After his nomination in 1888, Harrison's first choice for chairman of the national committee was James M. Clarkson of Iowa, who was prominently associated with the "Old Blaine Crowd" —the group that really swung the day for Harrison.

Clarkson, however, counseled Harrison not to take him, but to placate the Stalwarts or the "Old Grant Crowd," led by Senator Conkling, by asking Senator Quay to accept the chairmanship of the national committee. Harrison readily fell in line with this suggestion and Quay was named chairman. At the same time, a special office of vice-chairman was created to permit Clarkson to perform the active duties of the office until Quay could take them over in September.[10]

Shortly after Harrison's election, however, the harmony plan hatched by Clarkson went sour. Quay became grumpy over the limp recognition the President accorded him and the antipathy between the two men grew apace. Harrison wanted Quay's retirement, and increasingly so after he very reluctantly made John Wanamaker Postmaster General under the strenuous insistence of his national committee chairman.

Finally in 1891 Harrison decided to lower the boom. Clarkson was commanded to get Quay's resignation and, with Secretary of the Treasury Charles Foster of Ohio acting as Harrison's representative, the President's wishes were fulfilled. Clarkson then ascended to the chairmanship of the national committee.

Many an old-timer in the House who watched the Republican national committee and the new Eisenhower administration deal with patronage in 1953 might well have cast a nostalgic eye upon Harrison's Postmaster General, John Wanamaker, who gave the green light to replacements in the unclassified service. So sweeping was the success of this displacement policy in booming patronage that the Assistant Postmaster General, J. S. Clarkson, was nicknamed the "headsman" for replacing 31,000 fourth-class postmasters within a single year before he himself lost his head in the scuffle. But there is also a shiny side to the story of selecting federal public servants.

Easily forgotten, but long on importance, was Harrison's appointment of a vigorous political mustang to the post of chairman of the civil service commission—Theodore Roosevelt. It was Roosevelt who resolved, if he achieved nothing else, to leave the idea of lofty personnel standards deeply graven on the face of the federal service. Unable to tame him, the political hacks in the Republican as well as the Democratic party became wary of both his bark and his bite during his six years in office.

With the disastrous midterm elections of 1890 behind him, Harrison set out resolutely to mend a badly bruised prestige. But the task proved beyond his reach. Soon after the McKinley Tariff act went into effect his administration began to be troubled by a rise in retail prices. Then, in addition to further difficulties encountered as the Treasury began to experience a mounting deficit, his leadership was threatened from another quarter; intra-family friction within his cabinet and party, or the possibility of it, began to embarrass the administration.

As the shadows convoyed the old year out and a new presidential year—1892—marked another mighty contest for the Presidency, the friends of Secretary of State Blaine began reminiscing about where they had made their mistakes in earlier years and what they could now do about it. Once again they looked fondly upon their hero, the "Plumed Knight," and decided to have another go at the Presidency. The constant conniving of Blaine's friends behind the scenes obviously did little to inspire confidence between the President and his Secretary of State. Nor were their relations improved by Blaine's resignation on June 4, 1892, just three days before the Republican national convention. While Harrison accepted the resignation immediately, both men exchanged notes that were cordial but definitely on the chill side. Privately, to friends, each expressed some of his unhappiness with the other's conduct. Some witnesses, such as Senator Shelby M. Cullom, contend that Blaine did not like Harrison personally, and while he was a member of the cabinet was inclined to do things that would tend to undermine the President. In this view Harrison is said to have felt that he himself had been forced to bear the brunt of the work of the State department for at least a year. Blaine's physical and mental condition also contributed to the strained relations between himself and the President, for he was a sick man during his last year.[11] Presumably the President prepared many official State department documents during this time, and had the originals in his own handwriting to prove it. Allegedly Harrison was also miffed that Blaine took much of the credit for doing this work. Since Blaine died some eight months after the Republican national convention, there is some evidence to support the thesis that Harrison probably had to shoulder a heavy load in the realm of foreign affairs. But in any case, the entire episode was hardly reassuring for the re-election of a Republican President.

Blaine's behavior amidst the maneuvering of his friends to have Harrison discarded marks a curious episode in convention politics. In passing judgment upon his actions, however, two conditions are to be noted—both by way of an apology: first, tradition in leadership succession; second, his health.

For the student of political parties it is easy to overlook the fact that in the lore of nominating conventions the renomination of an incumbent President was by no means the accepted course in an earlier day. Since it was not yet an established precedent in 1892, Blaine and his followers were well within the limits of political propriety in challenging Harrison's bid for renomination. But one may still ask whether Blaine, if he did wish to try for the nomination, was not obligated to pull out of the Harrison cabinet earlier.

The second element to be weighed in assessing Blaine's bizarre behavior, as the convention deadline approached, is his health. Evidently his physical condition left much to be desired, for he was dead within eight months after the nominating convention adjourned. The problem here, of course, still bothers today. "Shouldn't we begin to develop a tradition which might restrain either party from offering a presidential nominee of manifestly doubtful strength?" wrote columnist Roscoe Drummond after the publication of the Yalta papers in the spring of 1955. One may well applaud the sentiment and join the search to find "some acceptable method which would make it less likely to force the American people to vote on a presidential nominee who almost certainly does not have the physical stamina equal to the job?" [12] But how do we find it and to whom do we turn? In the pre-convention warm-up stage of 1948, planted rumors about Michigan's Arthur Vandenberg quickened the velocity of circulation of many newspaper reports that he was a very sick man. Not until an emphatic denial by Vandenberg's physician came from the University of Michigan's hospital at Ann Arbor were these stories finally laid to rest. Improved diagnosis techniques, no doubt, will hasten the day when conjecture about a potential nominee's health can be made with greater assurance, but meanwhile the best we have is an educated guess.

Whatever the state of Blaine's health at convention time in 1892, there was little doubt that he was prayerfully looking for a ground swell. And his friends, many of whom no doubt were sincere, encouraged such hopes when they should have forewarned him. It may well be, as one careful student of the pre-convention campaign period concludes, that Blaine did not "have a genuine desire for the nomination." [13] But the unfortunate timing of his resignation (apparently done in a moment of indignation), the insistence of his friends that they "would rather have *him* dead than anyone else alive . . ." and perhaps Mrs. Blaine's own wish that he be a candidate (allegedly because President Harrison had denied her personal request that he promote her son-in-law over twenty-nine officers who outranked him) all pushed him into the ring.

While the renomination of an incumbent had not yet been elevated to a tradition, the trend of our party system was moving swiftly in that direction. Thus Blaine's friends could only embarrass him by their coltish behavior when they knew full well that the day was at hand when a political party could hardly renounce a President of its own making, however strong the temptation might be. (There were also some bubble-minded agitators who thought that the rejection of Hoover in favor of another candidate would bring a Republican victory in 1932.) What their efforts did succeed in doing, however, was to envelop his candidacy with uncertainty and leave many friends in doubt, and further dismantle Republican national prestige.

Small wonder that the delegates who were threading their way up the Mississippi Valley for the tenth national convention at Minneapolis were not keyed up to the usual carnival mood. The selection of Minneapolis as a convention site was urged on the ground that it would help to offset the growth of the Alliance movement in the Northwest.

Held in the industrial exposition building (later known as the Savage building) on the banks of the Mississippi adjacent to famed

Saint Anthony Falls, the convention was called to order by the temporary chairman, J. Sloat Fassett of New York. Secretary of the Republican national committee for four years, the temporary chairman had served for a brief period as collector of customs for the port of New York, and a dozen years after this convention he was elected to Congress. Even before the chaplain was solemnly intoning the invocation, the effects of the blistering heat (Minneapolis temperatures soared during the three days of the convention) upon a building only recently completed were beginning to tell. From the ceiling resin began to drop from the unseasoned pine onto the sweating delegates below, gumming up their hair, their clothes, and the floor as well as the seats.

On the second day of the convention the committee on permanent organization recommended an obvious choice for permanent chairman—William McKinley, Jr., of Ohio. At the moment, his popularity was probably without peer in the Republican party. Thanking the delegates, among whom were such prominent figures as Platt and Depew from New York, Quay from Pennsylvania, Congressmen Cannon (Uncle Joe), Cullom, and Kohlsaat from Illinois, Spooner from Wisconsin, Teller and Woolcott from Colorado, Brandegee from Connecticut, Ingalls from Kansas, and Crane from Massachusetts, McKinley went quickly to the point of his address in a ringing endorsement of the protective tariff.

"We stand for a protective tariff," he said, "because it represents the American home, the American fireside, the American family, the American girl and the American boy, and the highest possibilities of American citizenship. We propose to raise our money to pay public expenses by taxing the products of other nations, rather than by taxing the products of our own."

Not once during the course of the convention was homage to the protectionist principle laid aside. But a message from the cosmos may have warned of dangers to follow.

On the evening of the third day, just after Chauncey M. Depew asked recognition to present a motion congratulating eighty-three-year-old delegate Colonel Dick Thompson of Indiana on his birthday, the tariff came in for another eulogy. Conducted to the chair for a short speech, Colonel Thompson, who had been a delegate to every national convention of the Republican party since its organization, and who had also served in Congress and in the cabinet, drew the loudest applause of the convention when he stated that the proudest vote he ever cast in his life was for the tariff bill of 1842. But just as he turned to chairman McKinley to tell him he hoped public opinion would vindicate "that great bill which bears your honored name," the feeble filaments in the electric lights of the convention hall began to flicker. Suddenly the entire auditorium was plunged into darkness. No doubt it was an ominous sign that the voting public was still not ready to reverse its judgment on the McKinley Tariff act of 1890, upon which it had spoken so stridently in the congressional elections of that year. In any case, after the lights were restored Colonel Thompson wound up quickly by warning that the Democratic party proposed to destroy the McKinley Tariff act "piecemeal, like rats gnawing at the ropes of a ship and seeking to sink it, while the great craft moves onward and bids defiance to the storm." Bidding farewell on the happy note that he would return four years later at the next Republican national convention—a promise which he faithfully kept—Colonel Thompson bowed off the rostrum to make way for the presentation of the report from the chairman of the committee on resolutions.

Roundly reaffirming the principle of protectionism, the Republican platform drew attention to the growth of tariffs abroad and denounced efforts of the Democratic majority in the House "to destroy our tariff laws. . . ." At the same time the platform paid its respects to the policy of reciprocity adopted by the Republican administration, under which the export trade of the United States "has vastly increased and new and enlarged markets have been opened for the products of our farms and workshops."

The platform urged the "purity of election" in all states for poor or rich, "white or black," and called for an unrestricted ballot in all public elections. On other important questions the platform again pledged Republican opposition to all combinations of capital, organized in trusts or otherwise, "to control arbitrarily the condition of trade among our citizens." It heartily endorsed the Sherman Anti-Trust act, promised a reduction of letter postage to one cent at the earliest possible moment, and commended "the spirit and evidence of reform in Civil Service. . . ."

On the delicate question of currency, the platform drove straight down the middle. Western delegates demanded a declaration for free silver, but the strong opposition of Eastern Republicans forced a compromise which said little other than that the American people by tradition and interest favored "bi-metallism: the Republican party demands the use of both gold and silver as standard money . . ." to the end that "every dollar, paper, or coin, issued by the government shall be as good as any other."

Not unmindful of the growing importance of women in national politics, this convention became the first to declare in favor of using the Women's Republican Association in the presidential campaign, on the motion of Senator Warner Miller of New York. And time was set aside on its fourth day to hear an address by Mrs. J. Ellen Foster, chairman of the Women's Republican Association of the United States. Extolling the services of women in the cause of Republicanism, Mrs. Foster spoke adoringly of "Iowa, my adopted state . . . the beloved daughter of New England's queen . . . thou dost honor thy royalty." Then with a deft dart in the direction of the temperance movement, which was beginning to be felt in American politics, Mrs. Foster commented that "Iowa's corn will feed millions, but by constitutional law [*enforcing local option*] her people have decreed that not one kernel shall be made into poison." So spoke the advance agitators for Prohibition.

On the roll call, there was little doubt by now that the occasion would again be another example of what Mr. Dooley liked to call a "gratification" convention: the renomination of Harrison was virtually certain. But there were more than a few grunts of disaffection, particularly from the followers of the "Plumed Knight." Blaine's son Emmons was much in evidence at the convention, serving as the lead organizer for his father. And he was assisted chiefly by Tom Platt of New York, Mathew Quay of Pennsylvania, J. H. Manley of Maine, and J. S. C. Clarkson of Iowa. No doubt the fact that Harrison was not on the best of terms with Quay, Platt, and Reed put a wrinkle in any plan to ride through a renomination of the President by acclamation.

The real test came on the fourth day of the convention, when the Harrison forces led by Chauncey Depew held a caucus at the market hall. There were 463 delegates present and when exactly 463 votes were cast in support of the report of the Harrison-controlled credentials committee, the outcome was no longer in doubt.

When Colorado was reached on the roll call, Senator E. O. Wolcott rose to nominate Blaine, lauding him for his devotion to the Republican party, and the enrichment and guidance he had given to "two administrations with his sagacity and statesmanship." After a 31-minute demonstration chairman McKinley was finally able to restore order only after warning the delegates that the stamping of feet was imperiling the structure of the building.

Richard W. Thompson of Indiana entered the name of Benjamin Harrison, "the warrior statesman." Thereafter William H. Eustis of Minnesota and W. E. Mollison of Mississippi seconded the nomination of Blaine, while Chauncey Depew did the honors for Harrison, with a salubrious salute to the President's leadership, his "suggestive mind, indomitable courage, intelligent appreciation of situations and grand magnanimity. . . ." Only two nominations were entered.

On the first and only ballot, with 453 necessary for the winner, Benjamin Harrison received 535⅙ votes; James G. Blaine 182⅚; William McKinley, Jr., 182; Thomas B. Reed, 4; and Robert T. Lincoln, the son of the Great Emancipator, 1. During the early stages of the balloting, McKinley, who was fanning himself with a large palm leaf, suddenly became very agitated when a few votes started to be recorded for him. Publisher Kohlsaat, who was sitting with the Illinois delegation, reports that McKinley looked down at him from the rostrum and began to wave the fan at a faster clip. And when Ohio called out its vote as 44 for McKinley and 2 for Harrison, McKinley sprang from his chair to challenge the vote on the ground that his proxy had voted for him. Although the chairman of the Ohio delegation insisted that Mr. McKinley ceased to be a member of the delegation upon his occupancy of the chairmanship of the convention, and that his alternate was therefore legally entitled to vote in his place, McKinley overruled this point of order and instructed his secretary to call the roll of Ohio again. On the second polling of the Ohio delegation, McKinley voted for Harrison, while once again the remaining 45 delegates voted for their governor and favorite son.

With almost 120 votes more than he needed to win, Harrison's nomination was made unanimous by the convention, and he became the tenth presidential nominee of the Republican party. Kohlsaat thought it doubtful that Harrison could have won on a second ballot. Certainly the combined strength of Blaine and McKinley was impressive in light of the fact that this was, after all, a convention wherein there was little recourse other than to renominate the man who had been the steward of the nation's policies the preceding four years. Of the two runners-up McKinley, who actually trailed Blaine by only five-sixths of a vote, was definitely the favorite among the majority of delegates. McKinley votes were scattered among delegates from 25 different states, and on the scratch sheets of those who were thinking four years ahead, he was already ranked for the post position.

Adjourning until eight P.M. of the fourth day, the convention reconvened to take up vice-presidential nominations. Here again the lists were quickly closed. New York presented its distinguished journalist, Whitelaw Reid, who had succeeded Horace Greeley as editor-in-chief of the New York *Tribune* in 1872. Fresh from a tour of duty as our Minister to France (an assignment he had been given by President Harrison in 1889), Reid was eminently available for the post. Not before the convention had been furnished with a hearty laugh, however. While the roll call was proceeding for the vice-presidential nominations, a delegate from Tennessee with a well-lubricated accent rose and said: "I nominate for Vice-President that grand old man from Maine, Thomas B. Reed." "By what right does the delegate from Tennessee propose Mr. Reed?" shouted a Maine delegate, whereupon the Tennessee man tossed back the rejoinder: "By no right, suh. I do not know the gentleman. I wouldn't know him if I met him in the middle of the road, suh, but no man is too big, suh, to be Vice-President of the United States, suh!"

Chauncey Depew wondered whether Reid's fight with the "Big Six" of the typographical union in New York city would have an adverse effect upon his candidacy. Few delegates felt this to be a matter of importance, however, and by this time, as is always the case, most of them were anxious to get on with it and were already itching to break camp and hurry homeward.

Back at the entrance to the baroque red sandstone structure on Hennepin Avenue, known as the West Hotel, a riotous scene followed the adjournment of the convention. As McKinley's carriage approached the hotel, a huge crowd swarmed around it to hoist the Ohio governor on its shoulders and surge triumphantly into the lobby with their airborne hero. Distressed upon discovering that his trousers had been pushed beyond the knee, exposing a broad expanse of skin and garter, McKinley gesticulated helplessly until the crowd finally put him down at the elevator. Up in his room McKinley threw off his clothes and lay exhausted and panting from the insufferable heat while exchanging a few words with his long-time friend Herman Kohlsaat. Just then Mark Hanna entered the room and also began to peel off clothing in the vain hope of getting some relief from the fourth day of excessive temperatures. No one spoke for a while. Then Hanna, after an interval of some fifteen minutes, said: "My God, William, that was a damned close squeak!" What the greatest of all Republican strategists meant, of course, was that McKinley was extremely fortunate in being able to avoid the nomination. Certainly the year 1892 was not a Republican year in Hanna's horoscope, and he had no intention of permitting the candidate he wanted to make President to ruin his chances by running at the wrong moment by history's clock. That very evening the first plans were laid to bring about the nomination of McKinley in 1896.

Meeting two weeks later in Chicago, on June 21, the Democrats took but one day to nominate both their presidential and vice-presidential candidates. For President they again turned to their nominee and winner of 1884, Grover Cleveland of New York, and for Vice-President they selected Adlai E. Stevenson of Illinois, grandfather of the Democratic nominee of 1952. Both were nominated on single ballots. Again the Democrats repeated the pledge in their platform of 1888 calling for reduction of duties that would not imperil domestic industries, and the stage was reset for a campaign that would be fought largely upon this issue.

Both in their platform and in the campaign that followed, Republicans took an unrepentant attitude toward the tariff of 1890, while the Democrats chipped away at the arguments favoring protection on a high-duty basis. Keeping up a running attack throughout the entire campaign, the Democrats exploited the tariff issue by exaggerating what the evil effects of the new tariff rates had been, carrying their arguments on this score to almost absurd lengths. They dragged out the old trick used in the congressional campaign of 1890 with telling effect: sending tin peddlers to country districts with vans loaded with familiar household kitchen utensils whose prices had been marked up to outrageously high levels. At each farm they laid the blame for the sharp increase squarely upon the McKinley Tariff act. For the canning industry, which used enormous amounts of tin, the dire prophecy was made that as a consequence of the higher duty on tin plate there would be a fifteen to twenty percent increase in the price of canned fruits and vegetables. Anticipating the worst, both the manufacturers of tin ware and the canning industry announced immediate advances of from fifteen to twenty percent on their products, and when these prices were further marked up with the idea of magnifying the issue, it is easy to see why the consumer became indignant. Soon the rise in prices on specific articles, which was, of course, a direct consequence of higher duties, was held to be accountable for an extended inflation that covered the entire cost of living.

Unquestionably there had been a rise in the cost of living, but this was described editorially by the New York *Times* as "a moderate" one, which this newspaper estimated for those living in that city for the year of 1891 as a rise of approximately one-fifth. Stated otherwise, said the *Times:* "It will take $1.20 to buy what has been got for $1.00." Since the platform of the Democratic party gave the impression of a sound endorsement of free trade, which was obviously pleasing to the South and the West, there was still some need to avoid alarming Northern and Eastern manufacturers, and accordingly Cleveland's more conservative views on this question were given prominent publicity in the Democratic press of the East and by the Democratic stump speakers working this area. Thus, in his acceptance speech of September 26, Cleveland reaffirmed the policy of moderation he had earlier endorsed in his New York speech of July 20, when he said that the Democratic party was not "recklessly heedless of any American interests," and he now said: "We contemplate a fair and careful distribution of necessary tariff burdens rather than a precipitation of free trade." No matter how he tried, Harrison could not dissociate the economic stresses of the time, which were reflected in the increased cost of living, from the McKinley Tariff act of 1890, and the Democrats gave him no quarter right down to the finish line.

Unhappily for Harrison, his chances for re-election were imperiled at the outset by an incident related to the tariff argument, but very likely producing a greater wallop. It was one of the great misfortunes of his campaign.

Just as the campaign opened it was Harrison's sad lot to be ordering federal troops into action against strikers in the Tennessee and Idaho mine fields, in the railway yards at Buffalo, and in other areas. But it was the Homestead strike, which broke out in the mills of the Carnegie Company on July 6, 1892, that hurt Harrison the most. Following wage reductions in the Carnegie steel works at Homestead, Pennsylvania, striking workers who were trying to prevent a lockout were set upon by a body of Pinkerton detectives that the Carnegie Company had imported to break the strike. Tipped off that the Pinkerton detectives were arriving in two barges on the Ohio River, the striking workers trooped down to the landing barge to greet them. Two days later, after ten of the detectives had been killed and over sixty wounded, the governor of Pennsylvania was called upon to intervene, and he sent in eight thousand National Guardsmen who broke up the strike. With a union's struggle for recognition crushed in this manner, the Homestead affair left a lot of scar tissue. Most of it refused to heal before Election Day, and much of it persisted in the memories of working men who lived through it or heard of it from afar. The effect of the Homestead strike in other areas of the country was that of a delayed-action bomb. Republicans had argued that higher duties were vital for a tariff-protected enterprise like the steel industry, for "the protection of American labor." But the sharp reduction of wages in the Carnegie plant that touched off the Homestead strike hardly lived up to the promise of what the tariff was said to do for the American working man. The entire affair worked to the disadvantage of Harrison and Republicans generally, whether in Pennsylvania or in far-off Idaho. At Coeur d'Alene, where a series of wage cuts provoked miners to start a strike which management failed to end with imported strikebreakers, President Harrison, at the governor's request, also sent in federal troops to crush the uprising. In short, throughout the course of most of the campaign, the Republican chief executive was almost continually in the process of alienating working men.

As Election Day approached that fall it was widely acknowledged by observers that the campaign between the major parties was unenthusiastic. The uniqueness of the contest lay in the fact that for the first time in the history of the country both major party candidates were men who had actually occupied the presidential office. Moreover, it was one of those rare instances when both major party nominees were running against each other in two successive presidential elections.

Except for the tariff, the difference in viewpoint of the two candidates was not deep cut. Both, in fact, were solid conservatives who wished to have no truck with Populism. While a judgment of the two men must necessarily take into account the fact that Harrison was handicapped by his party's performance on the tariff, which the Democrats pointed up as the major cause of the business slump and increased cost of living, Cleveland appeared to proclaim his leadership more vigorously. And the final results showed that Cleveland was far stronger than his party.

The Democrats toppled down in their congressional strength from 231 in the Fifty-second Congress to 220 in the new Congress that went in to office with Cleveland—a highly unusual circumstance for the party winning the Presidency. That the Democratic party was not in high favor with the independent voter at the moment is suggested by the strategy of party leaders in selecting Cleveland's running mate. This time the party turned to Illinois to select for their vice-presidential nominee a former First Assistant Postmaster General, Adlai E. Stevenson, in an obvious effort to shake off criticism that the party had become corroded by the slime of Eastern city machine politics.

Harrison's lack of appeal in many sections stemmed from his strong anti-labor attitude which stretched back to 1877, when as a railroad attorney he prosecuted strikers. He simply was not the kind of a man that people would believe was filled with warm human juices, and that they were glad to follow. The Republican party chieftains intended to rely upon a powerful organization, but Harrison's habit of irritating party workers took the starch out of this plan. Rated according to a theory, advanced by some wag years ago, that the character of each President could be determined by the manner in which he handled his callers and disposed of his visitors, Harrison fell far short of the full mark for a political leader. Thus, reports Indiana's Senator Jim Watson, it was said that Grant, the great soldier, drilled them out; that Hayes, the first of the extreme temperance Presidents, dried them out; that Garfield preached them out; that Arthur smiled and bowed them out; that Cleveland, in his first term, nudged and elbowed them out; that Harrison froze them out.[14]

On Election Day Mark Hanna's judgment that 1892 was not a Republican year was amply confirmed. Harrison, whose popular vote had been topped four years earlier by Cleveland, but who had won the Presidency none the less, lost decisively to Cleveland in the second contest. Polling 46 percent of the popular vote (5,557,000), Cleveland won 277 electoral votes to 145 for Harrison, whose 5,176,000 votes gave him 42 percent of the popular vote. Polling 12 percent of the popular vote, the Populist ticket headed by Weaver showed spectacular strength in the West and South Atlantic regions of the country. Weaver wound up by winning over a million popular votes and 22 electoral votes from Colorado, Kansas, Idaho, Nevada, North Dakota, and Oregon. In addition the Populists sent 10 Congressmen and 5 Senators to Congress. The depth of the Populist protest is also reflected in the fact that their ticket was in either first or second place in 13 of the 44 states, and that they polled votes in every state of the Union.

Both major parties were stunned by the showing of this protest party. But even before the election Democrats in parts of the South saw a fight on their hands and began busying themselves for the struggle ahead. Realizing the danger to their political control as the possibility of a fusion between a Colored Alliance and the Southern Alliance loomed up, many Democratic leaders took no chances in the "black" counties. They persuaded planters to herd their employees to the polls, where they "voted them in droves for the Democratic ticket." [15] One observer reports that in Georgia barrels of whiskey and beer were provided for Negro voters who were "marched to the polls by beat of drums, carefully guarded lest some desert in search of another reward." In Augusta, Georgia, home district of the Populist leader, Tom Watson, the voters turned out to be twice the number of legal voters registered in the community, a condition Watson laid to the wholesale ballot-box stuffing and importation of wagonloads of Negroes from South Carolina to guarantee a Democratic majority.

While Cleveland moved back into the White House with the most powerful victory that the Democrats had won since the election of Pierce in 1852, the Republican forces in the House moved up from the unprecedented low of 88 in the preceding Congress, when they had polled only 27.2 percent of the two-party vote in the congressional elections of 1890. Now they stood at 126 in the Fifty-third Congress, after polling 37 percent of the two-party vote.

Republicans were least affected in New England, where the usual

GOP majority was turned in. There they carried five out of six states. But the loss of Wisconsin, Illinois, Michigan, and Ohio to the Democratic party in the Middle West, in addition to California and New York, was a hard blow to take—particularly since it was the first time since the founding of the Republican party that the Democrats carried the East North Central section and won electoral votes within every state in this region.

Populism won little ground in the East or New England, but across the Missouri the new third party left the major contestants at the post in many areas. In the Rocky Mountain region, nourished by the protests of the small settler, the farmer, and the mining interests, the Populists carried the section and in so doing served notice that a new challenger might be on the way to majority status just as the Republican party began its run back in 1854.

Indubitably, the year 1892 squired out the end of an era for the Republican party. It also marked the close of a twelve-year period that was characterized by the tightest national election contests in the history of the country.

For the Republican party, the ideas and forces making for a liberal capitalism which drew together Democrats like Preston King and William Cullen Bryant, and Whigs like Seward, Weed, Greeley, and Stevens when the new party was born back in 1854, were no longer in the ascendancy. A monopoly capitalism which had learned swiftly the secrets of managing power was rising triumphantly out of the elements that had started so promisingly as the forerunners of liberal capitalism. Inevitably, the bountiful endowments of nature in combination with the lure of limitless opportunities, which encouraged every arrival in America to adopt the mentality of castle owner rather than subject, hastened the development of a monopoly capitalism, frequently short-sighted in the realm of public policy. Astride these unlimited opportunities, what could be more natural than a struggle for leadership succession—to seize a party that had fought a successful war in the name of freedom, become hallowed in consequence of its fight to free the slaves and save the Union, and sealed the bargain by giving the public domain to homesteaders— a struggle by men and interests who saw in this party a popular vehicle for the furtherance and protection of their own enterprises. And as Republican leadership during the post-Civil War period was prevailed upon to strengthen its position by giving away part of the public domain not only to homesteaders but to railroad and mining promoters, sheep herders, cattle men and lumber barons, it attracted supporters who would be temporarily useful in helping to keep the party in power. But at the same time, as the barons of industry and the lumber, railroad, silver, gold, utility, insurance, and other interests moved on toward the acquisition of greater wealth, partly because they had been befriended by Republican policies, they in turn, and often selfishly, sought to twirl the dials of party policy to protect their own interests.

In the endless debate that seeks to know whether the avaricious greed of men and interest groups furthered the interest of the nation in the long pull by speeding the development of its industrial resources and in consequence lifting living standards to levels hitherto unknown or undreamed of, or whether it would have been better to go at a slower pace, keeping the empire builders well leashed, the answer depends upon the lights that one follows. But if there was a fixed figure of political symbolism in the constellation of political ideas in the 1890's, it was that the Republican party was the working ally of monopolistic interests. Surely the Republican party could well be proud of its defense of a free competitive system, for the vibrancy of a free society is furthered by the maintenance of elements of free competition that carry with positions of eminence and distinction certain overt rewards. But the monopolies that sprang up in the last quarter of the nineteenth century were strangling free competition. They were also destroying the confidence that had been so strikingly placed in the Republican stewardship of the nation for so many years.

With the defeat of Harrison in 1892, the coming struggle of insurgency within the party was already dimly outlined. The real flint and steel of the movement was yet to be provided in the way of a national GOP leader. But the prairies were beginning to bristle with challengers anxious to twist the tail of business monopoly and restore the party of Lincoln to an earlier purity. Already young Bob La Follette had served one term in Congress before his defeat in the landslide of 1890, and was readying himself for the coming battle within his party against special privilege. Others from the Middle West would soon be joining him: Dolliver of Iowa, Murdock and Bristow of Kansas, and many others. Soon the power of the pen would also be aiding their cause, with articles like Ida Tarbell's exposé of the Standard Oil Company in *McClure's Magazine,* and Frank Norris's books, *The Octopus* and *The Pit,* attacking railroad abuses and the wheat speculators.

Before 1892, agrarian unrest on the frontier had produced several revolts of consequence and some important political movements. Yet the Populist movement of this year was the most formidable of all. And this revolt is generally acknowledged to be the most significant of all third-party attempts in the history of American politics because of its impact on the major parties. Convincingly, the Populist showing suggested that an act of fission was about to take place which would either split one of the major parties in two or displace one altogether. By and large, however, neither occurred, and the Populist party was swallowed up by the Democratic party. And in the Middle West and in the land of prairie politics generally, the Republicans of an unreconstructed mold still preferred to work for reform within the party of Lincoln rather than to march off under another standard.

Now, very definitely, the agrarian-versus-monopoly-capitalist title bout would begin in earnest and continue for the next twenty-five years. Liberal in its inception, this revolt of the agrarians contained elements within it that would one day tend to be reactionary, just as the liberal capitalism of the 1840's and 1850's held the seeds of monopoly capitalism that rose so swiftly following the Civil War. Somewhere far in the distance, as this struggle was about to begin, would come the voice of Wendell Willkie asking that we re-christen free enterprise as "responsible enterprise." Even then the party was not without its wise men who recognized that some of the excesses of economic exploitation would have to be checked or both the country and party would be ruined. Mark Hanna was one of them. "He was bound," wrote Herbert Croly shortly before he founded the *New Republic,* "by the instinctive consistency of his nature to represent in politics not merely his other dominant interest [*business*] but the essential harmony between the interests of business and those of the whole community." But Hanna found it difficult to persuade many of his business associates to this view.

Thirty-eight years after it was started, with one-third of its first century's existence behind it, the Republican party had foundered in its worst defeat but fortunately was in the position of being able to take on a new pilot who was close at hand. On the record, its ardent champions faced the future not much differently from Senator Hoar, who summed up the blemishes as well as the bright spots of the party with head unbowed. Senator Hoar recited his list of embarrassments for the Republican party as follows: "Five United States judges driven from office by threats of deserved impeachment; four members of the House of Representatives detected making sale of their right of nomination to West Point; the scandals of the Austrian exposition and the Credit Mobilier; four judges of the state foremost in the Union for power and wealth impeached for corruption; Tweed and his accomplices in power in our chief city."

The Massachusetts Senator also noted that he had been humiliated and ashamed every time he thought of other Republican blunders, such as placing civil offices of great states at the disposition of powerful, unscrupulous men, and the issuance of sixty thousand fraudulent naturalization papers in New York for the purpose of carrying an election. Yet with it all, he comments, "I did not think that either the Republic or the Republican party was going to destruction." Among the marvelous achievements of the Republican party, "none is greater than the steady lifting itself and purifying of the public service. . . ." Happy that the addition of new states and new immigration from Europe would reinforce the Republican vote, Senator Hoar closed with a salute to the West and its brave people. "The steadfast, industrious, intelligent Scandinavian, lover of home, lover of country, lover of schools, lover of wife and children," he said, "finds his congenial place in the Republican party."

That he found his home in the Republican party is not to be denied, but that he wanted to rearrange the furniture and make certain restorations that favored earlier party tradition was soon to be demonstrated.

"God's in His Heaven"

"As a rule," exulted national chairman Carter, early in 1894, "the prospects of the party have not been brighter than the prospects of the country. . . . All other considerations aside, should history remain true to itself, the present financial, commercial, and industrial depression precludes the possibility of a Democratic success in 1896, and insures Republican triumph." [1]

Ten years before, the depression of '83 prepared the way for Republican defeat in 1884. And twenty years earlier the financial disturbances of 1873 dipped Republican strength from 55.6 percent in the election of 1872 to 47.9 percent of the popular vote in the contest of 1876.

Now the country was careening into another sidespin of economic panic. Cleveland was hardly in office before the downward descent began. Between April 1 and October 1 of 1893, more than 8,000 commercial firms failed, with liabilities close to $285,000,000. Bank failures were widespread, particularly in the West and South, and 156 railways, among them the Northern Pacific, Union Pacific, and the Erie, went into the hands of receivers. By trade union estimate, unemployment reached four and one-half million in the urban centers, breeding a series of violent outbreaks that left even the calmer elements of the citizenry with uncomfortable feelings in the spinal region.

The worst of the disturbances, of course, was at Chicago. Here the American Railway Union, protesting wage cuts by the Pullman Company, ordered its 150,000 members to stop handling Pullman cars on all railroads. To forestall this action two counter-moves were quickly executed. First a blanket injunction was issued by the federal courts forbidding Eugene V. Debs (organizer of the Railway Union) to interfere with the operation of the railways. Then Cleveland dispatched 2,000 troops to Chicago early in July. Cleveland's justification for the intervention was based on his obligation to protect the mails, safeguard interstate commerce, and uphold the authority of the federal courts. In short order the back of striker resistance was broken and the great labor insurrection was crushed as a direct consequence of federal intervention. But not without leaving an explosive storehouse of ugly feelings in the ranks of American labor. The sweeping character of the injunction and the alliance of government with management burned labor leaders deeply and turned them against Cleveland. Meanwhile Cleveland's difficulties were compounding on another front.

As the gold reserve of the country dwindled down some $30,000,-000 in a six-month period during 1893, Cleveland, a hard-money man, acted to forestall the draining off of our supply of this precious metal. Twice in 1894 he authorized the sale of $50,000,000 in bonds to the public for gold, and the following year he negotiated a loan of some $65,000,000 to the government from J. Pierpont Morgan and a financial syndicate. After these transactions Cleveland not only had the animosity of labor because of his use of troops in the Pullman strike, but he simultaneously alienated the pro-silver wing of his party. Moreover, he also antagonized certain Populist elements who had supported him in 1892. Now they joined in condemning his monetary policy and his negotiations with Wall Street.

By the time the parties squared off for the congressional election contests of 1894, bank failures, unemployment, strikes, railroad receiverships, and Cleveland's championship of the gold standard and deflation were all stirring up discontent throughout the nation. Under these conditions a setback was inevitable. In New England only one of eight Democratic Congressmen survived the elections of 1894. New England's two Democratic governors, elected in 1892, were also retired, and in all states the Democratic slice of the gubernatorial vote dropped sharply from the levels of 1892 and 1890. In the face of these facts and the tendency to misinterpret the presidential election that followed two years later, the comment of V. O. Key is revealing: "The luckless William Jennings Bryan and the Free-Silver heresy perhaps did not contribute as much as is generally supposed to the 1892-1896 decline in New England Democratic strength; New England Democrats moved in large numbers over to the Republican ranks in 1894." [2]

In the Senate Republicans traded positions with the Democrats, gaining control by picking up five seats, leaving a division at the outset of the 54th Congress of 44 Republicans and 38 Democrats. Across the Capitol the overturn in the House was more impressive. Here the Republicans thundered into control by winning 120 additional seats, reversing the Democratic margin of 220 to 104 in the 53rd Congress to 246 Republicans and 126 Democrats in the 54th.

What were the thoughts of these Republicans and their followers? On the tariff issue, long a pillar of Republican doctrine, there were significant defections. In recognition of the low-tariff elements in the Republican party, Grover Cleveland had named Walter Q. Gresham, an Indiana Republican, as his Secretary of State. (Gresham served as Postmaster General under President Arthur.) Already the gathering storm of agrarian dissatisfaction with protectionism was uprooting the high-tariff convictions of many midwestern Republicans, and leading the way for the congressional intra-party revolt of 1910.

Elsewhere the day of the trusts was dawning, and political organizations and machines began to feel, like the slap of a piston stroke, the vibrations of the trust issue. Between 1889 and 1893, sixteen states—ten in the midwest—passed laws regulating industrial combinations. And in 1893, Knute Nelson, a Norwegian immigrant who became a Republican anti-trust governor of Minnesota, issued a call for a convention of midwestern states to convene at Chicago to discuss the regulating of monopoly. No issue cut deeper than the anti-trust feeling, particularly in the Middle West. In 1892 Populist presidential candidate Weaver had claimed there were trusts in everything from oatmeal to watches; now a former Republican Congressman, Ignatius Donnelly, went him one better in purporting to discover an undertakers' trust in the Northwest, adding with a touch of irony that no doubt on resurrection day the dead would awake to find Gabriel controlled by a trumpet trust "with no toots except for spot cash." [3]

Attacks on the trusts not only came from the grass-fed Republican political statesmen of the Middle West, but warnings were also sounded from the bench. "The enterprises of the country," wrote Chief Justice Ryan of Wisconsin, "are aggregating vast political power. For the first time really in our politics money is taking the field as an organized power."

Not all voices, of course, cursed the trusts. There were, it was conceded, "bad trusts." But there were also "good" trusts, as Andrew Carnegie and John D. Rockefeller insisted, whose operation led to lower prices, expanded production, and increased distribution of their products because of their efficient organization. Thus it was folly, so ran the argument, to snaffle the trusts with restrictive legislation.

While everyone talked about the trusts, opinion swayed wildly on what to do about them. Should they simply be regulated when they appeared to be opposed to the public interest? Should they be prohibited altogether, or should they be left entirely free to follow their own unfettered course of economic development? Surely the way to a unified party position among such alternatives was far from simple. Moreover, the significance of the movement toward great industrial combinations was far from being understood by even the more reflective Republicans of the time. Editor William Allen White writes of the trusts:

> Kansas politics was reflecting the iridescent colors of the dawn. I saw the gorgeous picture, I wrote about it but I had no idea of its meaning, of its real significance, and for those who were aware of some vague shadow of the truth, men like Jerry Simpson, Ignatius Donnelly, Thorstein Veblen, and Edward W. Bemus, a Chicago economist—for all those astrologists and seers who were trying to give some account of the forces that were moving the world, I had the deepest scorn. It seemed to me that honesty and good government—that is to say, tax saving, the purification of politics, and personal integrity—were enough to save the world.[4]

So the Republicanism of the middle nineties was a composite of many elements. It represented men like William Allen White and some of his Republican colleagues on the Kansas City *Star* who sought "the purification of politics,"—who "were willing to draw out salaries, hate old Cleveland, regret the frigid ineptitude of Benjamin Harrison, hoot at the Populists, and sputter for the relief of our frustrated spirits." And it included those like Walter Gresham, Colonel William R. Nelson, owner of the Kansas City *Star,* and a steadily growing troop of agrarian dissidents, who damned the protective tariff interests with all the vigor at their command.

At the same time Republicanism embraced a robust free-swinging line of thought that was paving the way for the insurgency of a decade later. So we find Bob La Follette of Wisconsin and Albert B. Cummins of Iowa fighting corruption while admonishing the citizenry to take a more thoughtful look at what was happening to the nation's economy. To the bosses who helped defeat his gubernatorial nomination in 1896 by promising $700 to the Rock County chairman if the seven delegates of this assembly district were delivered to an opponent, La Follette promised a return engagement.[5] And the promise was kept. For in 1898 he became governor of Wisconsin, and in the ensuing years some of his enemies went to the penitentiary.

La Follette also pioneered in the leadership for legislation like workmen's compensation laws, which Wisconsin was the first state to adopt, and through example as a Republican governor set a pace for social reform that was emulated by governors across the nation. Lined up with La Follette, of course, was a fighting array of reform-minded mayors, conservationists, governors, and Congressmen.

It was a hardy lot that led this growing revolt. "There is business in politics," said Detroit's reform mayor, Hazen S. "Potato" Pingree, as he started his first term as governor of Michigan in 1897. "Business in the Republican party forced there by the corporationists. Business in the Republican party in the name of human rights. . . . Unless the Republican party is led back into the spirit of the principles which Mr. Lincoln so clearly stated, it cannot live long as a great party." Like Pingree, one of the first real progressives on the state level, most Republican reformists always stayed Republican, but they expressed their criticism of the GOP with a good deal of heat.

Here, in brief, were the underlying components of Republicanism in the nineties as the nation was about to move into a new era of politics. By this time the old slogan "Vote the way you shot"—representing the heavy favoritism of the GAR for the Republican ticket—was fraying a bit at the edges. But it was still a strong asset at the polls, though from now on its importance to the party would be on the wane.

Related, but quite apart from its own family readjustments, was another series of headliner events that shook the nation as Republicans pointed toward the epochal election of 1896. In May of 1894 General Jacob S. Coxey of Massillon, Ohio, began his march to Washington. Starting from Massillon in an open carriage with Mrs. Coxey and infant son "Legal Tender" Coxey, the general began his march with a hundred men and finally straggled into Washington in July with 1,200. But there they accomplished nothing when they asked for a work relief program that Senators quickly dismissed as "socialism, populism, and paternalism run riot."

On the agrarian front, economic conditions were aggravated by one of the worst droughts in history, which reduced the total crop to one-quarter the yield of the previous year. Meanwhile the Populists continued to agitate, finding ammunition to harass both major parties. Gleefully they caught up an article from *Political Science Quarterly* of December, 1893, showing that nine percent of America's families owned close to 70 percent of the national wealth.

Climaxing the discontent of the middle nineties was the Supreme Court's annulment of the income tax in 1895, which brought about a fresh wave of popular discontent. Though Justice Choate denounced the income tax as "Populistic, socialistic, and communistic," Justice John M. Harlan, a member of the Court at the time, later wrote of the reaction in sobering tones: "There was everywhere . . . a deep feeling of unrest. The nation has been rid of human slavery . . . but the conviction was universal that the country was in real danger from another kind of slavery. . . . Slavery that would result from aggregations of capital in the hands of a few."

Against such social vibrations the greatest master mechanic of Republican politics began to step up the pre-convention campaign of his 1896 presidential candidate. Marcus Alonzo Hanna started his political career as a precinct worker at the bottom rung of the ladder in the early 1870's. As a prosperous Cleveland industrialist, Hanna was far ahead of his time in his views on labor. And curiously the use of strikebreakers in one of his own mines both taught him a bitter lesson about the need for arbitration and brought him into a lifelong friendship with William McKinley. For it was young McKinley who denounced Hanna's own firm of Rhodes and Company when he was defending the strikers who destroyed its property. One might suppose that Hanna would have felt unkindly toward McKinley, who defended the rioting miners notwithstanding bitter community prejudice. But Hanna long afterward relates that he was "strangely attracted to the quiet and methodical" McKinley, who managed his case so well that only one man out of twenty-four was convicted.[6]

Hanna was driven by two burning desires: to refurbish the organization of the Republican party, and to make William McKinley President of the United States. He retired in the 1880's to devote his full energies toward accomplishing both.

Clearly Hanna came closer to being a national Republican boss than any figure in the lore of American politics. "If business is ever to recapture its long-lost leadership in the councils of the nation," wrote Wilfred Binkley in *Fortune* magazine, in the wake of the Dewey 1948 defeat, "it had better study the incomparable party leadership of Marcus A. Hanna, the businessman's finest contribution to the art of politics." [7]

Hanna was a man with a level keel. When his fellow businessmen began to panic over the agrarian unrest of the Populist movement he quieted them. Years later Theodore Roosevelt's Attorney General, Philander C. Knox, recalling an argument between the Bull Moose Roosevelt and Senator Hanna about the Granger movement of the '70's, reports: "Roosevelt thought the grangers were a lot of maniacs." But "Hanna thought they were useful citizens."

Early in his career Hanna recognized the need for bilateral contractual responsibility between management and labor. He "was the first mining operator in the bituminous fields of the United States," testified the secretary of the Miners' Association in 1876, "to recognize the cardinal principle of arbitration in the settlement of wage disputes, and the first to recognize the Miners' National Association." [8] And he became so enraged with George Pullman in 1894 for refusing to arbitrate the great railroad strike, after provoking the strike by a wage cut, that he created a scene in the Cleveland Union Club. "A man who won't meet his men half way is a damned fool," he said. And to someone who protested that at least Pullman deserved credit for his model town, Hanna snorted: "Oh, hell. Model ——! Go and live in Pullman and find out how much Pullman gets selling city water and gas ten percent higher to those poor fools."

Hanna's contributions to the field of industrial arbitration are as significant and durable as those he made to party organization. Commenting on his views of employer-employee relations which led him to take an active interest in the National Civic Federation, Hanna said:

> To have success in conciliation or arbitration, there must be thorough and effective organization on both sides. . . . The employer . . . should go more than half way. . . . I believe in organized labor, and I have for thirty years. . . . Organized labor and organized capital are but forward steps in the great industrial evolution that is taking place.[9]

Very likely Hanna also saw an emerging pattern in America of a classless society of abundance, for to the very end of his life he viewed with contempt those who spoke of classes or castes. When a Philadelphia banker spoke derisively of the "lower classes," Hanna promptly rejoined, "You mean the working man? Or do you mean criminals and that kind of people? Those are the lower classes."

Fortified by these beliefs, Hanna was admirably equipped to bring on his candidate at a critical juncture for our two-party system. Both parties were frightened by the cyclonic yells of the Populists in 1894, and many of the candidates' state platforms of that autumn reflected this unsteadiness. But Hanna seemed to find these conditions to his liking, and once McKinley had the nomination for governor of Ohio safely tucked away in 1893, Hanna began moving him over the rails.

McKinley, of course, had long before impressed audiences across the country, for Bob La Follette speaks of him glowingly at a Chautauqua appearance in 1892, when he visited "Fighting Bob" while on a speaking engagement at Madison. But in 1894 the pre-convention canvass started in earnest, and McKinley began a tour of Republican states on a special train. Foreshadowing modern pre-convention caravans, the McKinley train was equipped with a special baggage car where reporters tapped out their copy as the train pounded across the prairie. After watching McKinley carefully as local politicians boarded the train and were whisked in and out, William Allen White tells us that McKinley carefully avoided talking to any man personally before a crowd, so that no man could say McKinley had made any deal with him, or that any man had his close confidence. "McKinley, the master politician, was given to those hunches which are the result of keen, quick, accurate observation through eye and ear." So steadily did McKinley think in terms of politics that "he lost his private life and private view." One is "compelled to go back almost a century," writes Binkley, "to find the prototype of President McKinley as the gentle but undoubted leader of Congress. . . ." Lincoln, while holding the rank and file, had a wretched time with politicians, and Cleveland lost both these elements in the Democratic party. "It was McKinley's unique achievement to have captivated both." [10]

Unlike Hanna, "a charming and refreshingly realistic man, whose famous corned beef breakfasts (his own recipe from the mining camp) and honest friendliness swung many a doubting delegate or legislator into line," McKinley was more formal. He did not fit as loosely in his harness as his long-time admirer. Careful of stubbing his toe, McKinley had picked his way up the ladder cautiously in Ohio politics, and his knowledge of public opinion and issues was widely admitted. Uncle Joe Cannon, in fact, once remarked that he had his ear so close to the ground that it was full of grasshoppers.

It has been wisely observed that Bryan "faced two opponents in the 1896 campaign"—the Republican nominee and Hanna. And implicit in this statement is the uniqueness of this team that rescued Republican party fortunes in 1896. For "the two men were simply stronger together than apart, and both knew it. McKinley supplied the presence, the speeches, the unifying personality. . . . Hanna supplied the machine." Moving into the campaign for delegates, McKinley and Hanna "were so closely bound together that they merged into a single personality." [11]

Ironically the bilateral contest for the 1896 presidential nomination pitted against each other two men who had fought another close contest some years earlier. In 1889 Thomas Reed defeated McKinley by two votes for the Republican nomination for Speaker, and went on to become Speaker of the House by a narrow margin. A native of Maine, where he engaged in a highly successful career in state politics, Reed went to Congress in 1877 at the age of 37. Here he came to be known for his parliamentary skill, conservatism, dictatorial policies, and "salty speech." Of gargantuan build—six foot three and well over 300 pounds—Reed was nicknamed the "Terrible Turk" during his first session of Congress. A scholar and a man of unbending nature, Reed made his way ahead by his strength. He won the sobriquet "Czar" early in 1890 by his action to forestall dilatory procedures in the House.[12] It was Reed, of course, who successfully pushed through a set of rules giving him more power than any Speaker has ever exercised, including the power to appoint all committees and refer bills to whatever committee he chose. Under his tenure as Speaker, Reed also served as chairman of the powerful Rules Committee. He dominated the House of Representatives in a way that had never happened before.

Long noted for his brilliance, sharp tongue, and wit, Reed's cynicism and biting sarcasm made him far from the ideal presidential candidate. He "is too clever, too strong-willed and too cynical, for a banker's party," wrote Henry Adams in 1896. Moreover, in the course of his congressional service he had alienated many friends. He himself was aware of this, and when his portrait was painted in 1891 by John S. Sargent—not the artist's best by any means—and the painting was hung in the Speaker's lobby adjoining the House chamber, Reed clasped his brow and howled: "My God, now all my enemies are revenged!" But whatever secret thoughts he may have held about his suitability for the presidential nomination, Reed was determined to have a go at it. And he raised his standard early in 1895. To the old political saw, "They might go further and do worse," Reed responded with his own version: "They might do worse, and probably will." And from Reed's standpoint, they probably did.

Actually, by the time Reed entered the race, Mark Hanna—who entered the Republican convention of 1896 with few delegates really knowing him well—had already stolen the march for McKinley. Through his control of Southern delegates and by dint of particularly heavy cultivaiton in the Ohio Valley and Great Lakes regions, Hanna had a majority for McKinley well in hand by late spring of 1896.

The intense feeling that sent to the polls that fall the greatest percentage of eligible voters in presidential election history was reflected in the interest shown in the pre-convention campaign. In Illinois, Hanna selected Charles G. Dawes to organize the McKinley forces. Dawes (a future Vice-President) was a young man said to have had a Napoleonic grasp of the situation. And by January of 1896 the first McKinley club started in the 32nd ward of Chicago enrolled 1,500 enthusiastic men at once. Soon it had a membership of over 4,000, and at the time of the district convention nearly 800 votes were brought out for McKinley in one primary district—a new record for Cook County.[13]

It was to St. Louis that Republicans journeyed this time for their eleventh national convention. And as the clan gathered in a new auditorium some 168 cases of disputed delegate seats had already been settled by the national committee. By now it was apparent that Speaker Reed would make only a limited showing, while McKinley appeared to have the nomination won. But Reed's supporters and friends dominated the platform committee, and this control posed serious difficulties for Hanna.

McKinley's re-election as governor of Ohio by an 80,000 majority under Hanna's tutelage in 1893 made the drive to bag delegates much easier. And Hanna's whirlwind courtship of these delegates put him in a position similar to that of the playful prankster who runs off with the clothes of the boys thrashing around in the old swimming hole. Platt, Quay, and Payne were caught completely off guard. They reacted swiftly—but it was too late. Following the lead of a few who had declared for Speaker Reed in the spring of 1894, Platt and Payne came out for him in June of 1895, and in January of 1896 they conferred with others on a "Stop McKinley" plan. This was to be engineered by having Reed hold New England, Levi Morton taking New York as a favorite son, while others like Harrison and Allison would hold Indiana and Iowa, and Cushman K. Davis would offer himself as Minnesota's favorite son. Not even this combination could upset Hanna's plans, however, and while a spirited struggle for delegates took place in Georgia, Texas, Louisiana, Alabama, Illinois, California, and Nebraska, the fight was gone out of the opposition long before convention time. By mid-April 318 delegates were pledged to McKinley.

In a policy sense, the impending convention represented the first real cleavage in the party since the fissure that developed in 1872 when Horace Greeley, Wendell Phillips, Peter Cooper, and William Lloyd Garrison bolted against Grant and his administration. This time the real dividing issue was the currency plank. The East, or more specifically Eastern financial interests, wanted a simple unequivocal declaration pledging adherence to a single gold standard. Moreover, it was in the East where Speaker Reed drew most of his support and where pockets of resistance to McKinley developed, organized largely by leaders like Platt, Quay, and Lodge.[14]

McKinley himself had been a champion of free silver, but in this convention his party was striped with a tri-color factionalism. Down East the delegates screamed for an all-out declaration for the gold standard, while in the West a noisy minority shrieked for free silver. Lying between the two groups was the temperate zone that embraced those who wished to evade a downright commitment on the monetary issue. It was one of the few times when a major Republican policy difference had not been pretty well watered down by convention time. And the West broke out the storm flags early. At the Colorado state convention in May, 1896, delegates chosen for the national convention were instructed to follow the lead of Senator Teller in demanding a plank favoring unlimited coinage of silver. In effect Teller was given all but explicit power to stage a walkout if his plank was rejected.[15]

Unable to prearrange a compromise between the advocates of bimetallism and a single gold standard, Hanna was driven to drastic action to prevent a factional bolt. Fearing that a platform plank proclaiming gold would "divide the party at the Mississippi River," and well aware that yielding to the free-silver champions might have equally disastrous results, Hanna was forced to abandon his plan for having the convention straddle the issue by highlighting the tariff.

Meeting in Hanna's hotel room the Saturday before the convention, Henry C. Payne, H. H. Kohlsaat of Chicago, W. R. Merriam of Minnesota, and Nicholas Murray Butler wrestled with the money issue for hours. In the end Kohlsaat and Merriam agreed with Payne that a gold plank should go into the platform and Hanna finally yielded. Then he placed his famous call to McKinley, who was staying in Canton. In what may very well be one of the most important long-distance telephone conversations between candidate and manager, he persuaded McKinley to go along with whatever Hanna thought best. In this case it was the gold plank of Wisconsin's Senator Payne—a cleverly contrived measure to appease both those who favored the gold pronouncement and the advocates of bimetallism. The plank read in part: "We are opposed to the free coinage of silver, except by international agreement with the leading commercial nations of the world, which we pledge ourselves to promote, and until such agreement can be obtained the existing gold standard must be preserved." Literally interpreted, this declaration appears to favor free silver. But since a string of international conferences had already shown an unwillingness on the part of European nations to abandon the gold standard, the free silver advocates of the West correctly construed Senator Payne's plank as a defeat for free coinage.

Immediately after the resolutions committee's majority report struck the floor, Henry Moore Teller of Colorado was on his feet to move the adoption of his own substitute for the gold plank, which called for the free and unlimited coinage of silver at the ratio of 16 to 1. Ripping into the majority report of the resolutions committee endorsing the gold standard on the last day of the meeting, Teller set the convention agog. William Allen White watched Mark Hanna:

> The loose muscles about Hanna's mouth twitched irritably as Teller's silver swan song rose and fell . . . his bright brown eyes took the orator's mental and oral measure with merciless precision. But with a rise of passion in the speech his expression changed from a mobile smile to a vicious iron glare.[16]

Finally Teller sat down, weeping, and Hanna grunted in nervous relief. And even before Senator Frank Cannon of Utah denounced the Republican party as the party of oppression, and threatened to bolt, it became evident that a walkout was imminent. Suddenly, while Cannon was still speaking, Hanna's harsh voice cracked above the heads of the delegates: "Go, Go!" Then, as all eyes turned toward the Buckeye ironmaster, Cannon, gesticulating wildly, called for a bolt and spoke of "the parting of the ways," a phrase that was to be taken up many times in the campaign that followed. Instantly Hanna's voice cried out, "Goodbye," and the convention sang out the chant, "Go, go, go," to the speaker on the rostrum.

With Senator Teller at their head, 34 delegates then stormed out in protest, while the convention sustained Senator Foraker's motion that the Teller substitute for the gold plank be tabled. The shooting was over, but not without giving Hanna some anxious moments. For a wider breach within the party had looked perilously close. So tender were the feelings among bimetallism groups that Hanna's decision to accept the gold plank was kept secret for four days. Only one delegate west of the Missouri River favored a gold plank.

In final form the monetary plank was sandwiched in at an inconspicuous spot toward the middle of the party platform, while the first nine paragraphs assailed the Democrats and praised the Republican protective-tariff policy. The last plank called for the admission of women to wider spheres of usefulness and urged their cooperation "in rescuing the country from Democratic and Populist mismanagement and misrule."

For the New York *Times* the bolt marked a new precedent. "It was a disorderly convention," commented the *Times,* "badly officered with perhaps the least efficient Sergeant at Arms, and the most utterly useless corps of assistants ever collected for a similar purpose." [17] The *Times* did, however, pay tribute to the presiding officer of the convention, Senator John M. Thurston, for his composure.

For the first time a platform roused the delegates more than the prospect of a presidential nominating roll call. After Senator Teller left the convention hall (pausing dramatically to shake hands with Senator Washburn of Minnesota at the exit), the business of settling down to the selection of a presidential candidate was anti-climactic. On the first ballot McKinley received 661½ votes out of a total of 930, and was declared the nominee. He was nominated by Senator Foraker of Ohio; the convention minutes record an ovation of twenty-five minutes. Speaker Reed, McKinley's leading contender in the balloting, received 84½ votes, while others winning votes on the first and only ballot were Matthew Quay and governors Morton of New York and Allison of Iowa, in that order.

For McKinley's running mate the convention quickly selected Hanna's choice—Garrat A. Hobart, governor of New Jersey. The ticket therefore "is Hanna's," confirmed the *Times,* while "the platform is the work of the convention." Moreover, it continued: "To the people the ticket is not likely to be as interesting as the platform. If the Republicans shall be successful in November it will be the money plank, not the tariff plank, nor the names of McKinley and Hobart that will win the victory." But there was no doubt that "the wide distribution of the silver bacilli, as suggested by Teller's elaborate farewell, was ominous and threatening."

Hanna, obviously the hero of the hour, was returned to the rostrum after McKinley's nomination for a round of applause and a speech. And instead of waiting the customary two or three weeks to elect its new chairman, the national committee elected Hanna immediately upon adjournment of the convention.[18] For the second time the Republican national committee was to have an "outsider" for its head. Like his predecessor, Thomas H. Carter, whose election smashed a precedent in July of 1892, Mark Hanna was not a member of the national committee.[19]

Three weeks after the Republicans finished their work in St. Louis, the Democrats met at Chicago on July 7. There they became enchanted with Bryan, whose nomination seemed like "the swinging of a firebrand in a powder mill," and the most intense steeplechase that the country was ever likely to see was under way.

Bryan forced the pace by setting out on an 18,000-mile tour in the course of which he spoke without amplifiers to some five million people in 29 states. Meanwhile, Republican bolters, taking the name the National Silver Party, endorsed Bryan and his running mate Sewall. And the Populists also endorsed Bryan instead of naming a candidate of their own, though they did nominate one of their own warriors for Vice-President—Georgia's Tom Watson.

Fretting a bit, Hanna wrote to McKinley from Nantucket, where he was enjoying a little yachting the week following the Democratic convention:

> The Chicago convention has changed everything. It has knocked out my holiday and cruise along the New England coast. The campaign will be work, and hard work. I consider the situation in the West quite alarming as business is all going to pieces and idle men will multiply rapidly. With this communist spirit abroad the cry of "Free Silver" will be catching.

Hanna opened two headquarters, one in Chicago and one in New York. Chicago became the real hub of the campaign, and the management of this office was entrusted to Henry C. Payne of Wisconsin and Charles G. Dawes of Illinois. Hanna was not merely the nominal head of the campaign as chairman of the national committee —he was "the real leader of the committee, the real architect of its plans, the real engineer of its machinery, and to a certain extent the real source of its energy."

One of the first major strategies of the campaign was the decision to keep McKinley in Canton. McKinley himself was the major instrument of this decision. For he considered it somewhat indecent to barnstorm with Bryan, and since he was unwilling to go out and meet the people, a logical counter-move was contrived to bring the people to him. The result, of course, was the first full-blown front-porch campaign, with visiting delegations streaming through Canton in endless procession throughout the late summer and fall.

Almost every detail of these visitations was prearranged with loving care. McKinley was not one to make a Rum, Romanism, and Rebellion slip. Or, as Herbert Croly has it, "the candidate was not taking any chance of a reference by some alliterative chairman to the party of Silver, Sacerdotalism, and Sedition." So, when delegations of editors, ministers, farmers, railroad workers, Negroes, Catholics, Germans, and others indicated their desire to migrate to Canton, an advance understanding was reached on the words to be exchanged between delegation chairmen and the presidential candidate.

Ten to twenty times a day McKinley stepped on to his front porch in stately stride, outfitted in a white vest and cutaway, and occasionally wearing a black hat. Often he spoke of the perils of the cheap dollar for the working man, and customarily he fired a parting shot at the silver Democrats for churning up class antagonism. "In America," he said, "we spurn all class distinction. We are all equal citizens and equal in privilege and opportunity."

A unique feature of Hanna's campaign direction was the degree of integration he achieved among party organizations at the national level. At the outset he decided to absorb the staff of the National Republican League, and early in the campaign he reached an agreement with chairman Babcock of the Republican congressional campaign committee that the work of this agency was to be enlarged and made subject to the direction of the national chairman. Another major innovation was Hanna's installation of a full-blown commercial bookkeeping and auditing system. By this device the chairman could for the first time in party history account for and control the flow of national committee funds.

Hanna's unshakable calm and fine sense of balance appear all the more remarkable as we reflect on the tornado tempo of the times. Hanna "had no sympathy for his frightened friends who chattered of 'revolution.' 'You're just a lot of damned fools,' he told frightened members of the Cleveland Union Club."

Hanna's low moments came between mid-August and early September when the advance "sixty-day" polls were taken. He believed that if the election had been held in August or September Bryan would have won. And he was also convinced that if his "damn fool" friends had prevailed and made the campaign an "orgy of class hatred," the Democrats would have won. Instead both Hanna and McKinley insisted upon composure. They argued "as if the people had brains, and by insisting that the Republican party stood for no class or region, but for America."

The organizational engine that Hanna built left the politicos panting. At the end of the campaign he had 8,000 Republican speakers in the field. Over 120 million copies of 275 different pamphlets in English, German, Italian, Polish, Yiddish, Greek, Swedish, and other languages were distributed across the nation. Both in numbers and in the quality of speakers of ability the Republicans outdistanced the Democrats in this campaign. The national committee took full measure of their resources. It organized a body of 1,400 campaigners whose expenses were paid, and dispatched them into every hamlet and country schoolhouse where there seemed to be a need.

Part of Hanna's strategy was saturation bombing with campaign literature. Over a hundred million campaign leaflets were sent out from the Chicago office; twenty million left the New York office. In this massive distribution scheme, the country weeklies with a combined circulation of about a million and a half received three and a half columns of pre-digested campaign matter every week, while other country weeklies with a circulation of a million were given plates and mats, with appropriate cartoons, on a weekly basis.

Much of the material in these campaign leaflets was drawn from McKinley's speeches and the pronouncements of leading Republicans on sound money. The most effective one, apparently, was a lengthy conversational tract of some forty pages dealing with the subject of silver. Protectionism, however, as Hanna always wanted, did gain more attention toward the close of the canvass.

Just as many businessmen were beginning to panic when Bryan took the stump, his massive body swinging one way and then the other like a mighty gun turret on a swivel before crowds the likes of which had never been seen in American campaigns, Hanna found a new ally who joined him from the West at a critical moment. On August 15, James J. Hill met Hanna (by accident, reports Hill) in New York city, at a moment when the national chairman was deeply discouraged. While the press was gossiping that the national chairman had gone east for the sole purpose of raising funds, Hanna told Hill that he was so disheartened he was thinking of quitting. But the Empire Builder had another thought in mind. He took Hanna on a series of "mad cab rides" up and down Manhattan that undoubtedly set a new mark in the annals of party finance.

Jim Hill, who once bought huge quantities of coal from Hanna's mines, was able to vouch for the national chairman's integrity, and he convinced the industrial and financial giants of the East that Hanna, unlike most professional political hacks, who reputedly wasted at least half the money given to them and pocketed the other half, would get every last cent of mileage out of the dollar. Hill took Hanna to the House of Morgan, to the Pennsylvania Railroad offices and those of the New York Central, and convinced the leadership of these far-flung enterprises that the shadow of Populism and Bryanism was falling upon this happy land, and that only a miracle could save McKinley.

How much money was raised in this campaign will be debated until the end of history's clock. The national committee reports raising about $3,500,000—$3,000,000 from New York, and the rest from Chicago. This figure is commonly doubled, and some students like Matthew Josephson place the estimates at from ten to sixteen and a half million dollars—the latter no doubt far ahead of the mark. In any case the $3,500,000 set forth in the audited account of the national committee tells us a good deal about this campaign as we compare it with the 1892 campaign. Four years earlier, the committee reported a total expenditure of a million and a half dollars, though it is true that in 1892 the committee finished the campaign $200,000 in debt.

How was the money spent in 1896? Some $13,000 went into the general office for staff salaries, while the bureau of printed matter spent approximately $452,000 in printing and $32,000 in salaries. To the speakers' bureau went $140,000; for the assistance of local and special organizations, $276,000; and somewhat over $903,000 to state committees.

Contributions spilled in so generously in the closing days of the canvass that the national committee wound up its affairs with a handsome surplus. The largest campaign contribution, incidentally, came from the Standard Oil Company, which contributed $250,000, and years later—1908—Charles Evans Hughes's sensational investigation of life insurance companies revealed that the New York Life, Mutual, Equitable, and Prudential companies made contributions to the Republican national committee for the 1896 presidential campaign totaling $21,000; in 1900, $80,000; in 1904, $148,-702.50.[20]

On into October, Hanna's confidence climbed, and there was much sense in his comment about Bryan's missteps: "He's talking silver all the time, and that's where we've got him," said Hanna. For by now the grudges against the privileged—this attitude "garnished with poverty, drought, grasshoppers, high freight charges and other miseries and impositions" which had lined up a great following behind the Great Commoner in midsummer—"could not be held together on the single question of the standard of value." [21]

Hanna was far in advance of his time in employing the tools for measuring public opinion.[22] Alarmed in September at the results of a careful private poll indicating that the sure Republican state of Iowa had some 30,000 voters who with Populist support might drive the state into the Bryan column, he ordered several elaborate surveys to be taken in the corn belt and other doubtful states. Then he hustled speakers into Iowa and the states which had been Granger strongholds, armed with materials to sell McKinley, gold, and protection, and to stop Bryan. When a second private poll in mid-October indicated Iowa was safe, he quickly shifted his energies toward Michigan, Ohio, and Illinois.

By the third week in October the turbulence of the campaign was shaking the paving blocks in every city in America. Little boys were running through the streets yelling

McKinley drinks soda water.
Bryan drinks rum;
McKinley is a gentleman,
Bryan is a bum!

Charges and counter-chargers crackled in the crisp autumn air, and an intense excitement gripped the nation. On October 19 chairman Jones of the Democratic national committee alleged that "The great corporations, with scarcely an exception, and many of the large employers of labor are engaged in a concerted effort to coerce their employees to vote against their conviction. . . . The working man is being robbed of his *rights* as an American citizen by an appeal to force and fraud." To this Hanna promptly countered on October 20 that the accusation was absurd, adding that Republicans would not possibly resort to such "un-American" measures. Actually, however, evidence that some manufacturers made contracts contingent upon McKinley's election is incontrovertible. And the example of the head of the Steinway piano works, who was reported as saying, "Men, vote as you please, but if Bryan is elected tomorrow the whistle will not blow Wednesday morning," was probably not unique.

How effective some of these threats were we have no way of accurately determining. Certain it is that they aroused bitter enmity. One man, in any case, was pretty sure about what this type of persuasion would accomplish. Told that such threats would boomerang against the Republicans because of resentment at such an un-American practice, Senator Teller, the Colorado Republican who had bolted to support Bryan, shook his head in disagreement: "Boys, I'm afraid it beats us. If I were a working man and had nothing but my job, I am afraid when I came to vote I would think of Molly and the babies."

On October 31, the Saturday before election, Hanna brought his campaign to full throttle. In New York a Sound-Money parade included some 150,000 people, and was estimated to have been witnessed by over a million. During the entire day and evening the city was regaled with marchers blowing tin horns, waving flags, and driving floats.

Election Day brought an astonishingly high number of voters. In this greatest outpouring in our history in terms of proportional turnout, McKinley received 7,112,000 ballots—51% of the popular vote—to 6,733,000, a shade less than 47%, for Bryan. It was the first time a Republican candidate had won a majority of the popular vote in a presidential election for a quarter of a century. In the electoral college, of course, McKinley's margin looked far more impressive: 271 to 176.

The total vote represented an increase of two million over the 1892 election, and the significance of the Democratic vote is better understood if we remember that Bryan's total was larger than that polled for the Democratic candidate in 1900 or 1904, and even larger than Woodrow Wilson's vote when he was elected in 1912. Over half of McKinley's total vote came from eight states: New York, New Jersey, Pennsylvania, Ohio, Indiana, Illinois, Michigan, and Wisconsin. In these states Bryan ran far behind McKinley. McKinley carried 23 states, Bryan carried 22.

How close the election was is indicated by the fact that a shift of less than 50,000 votes in close states that Bryan lost, such as Indiana and Oregon and others, would have meant his election. The Democrats actually won more counties than did the Republicans—1,551 for the Democrats to 1,163 for the Republicans.

No election in American history is more heavily embroidered with theories purporting to show what really happened. "The usual interpretation of the outcome," says V. O. Key:

> . . . is that the manufacturers and financiers of the East succeeded in persuading the workers to help them beat off the threat of the embattled debtors of the West. Superficially this is what happened, but the struggle was not purely sectional. The issue of men against property was fought in every section, and McKinley, the "advance agent of prosperity," annexed nearly everywhere a greater proportion of the increased outpouring of electors than did Bryan.[23]

The primary difficulty of most interpretations—or perhaps one should say misinterpretations—of the election of 1896 comes from a concentration on that single election rather than on a comparison with the election of four years earlier. Even in 1896 the Democrats were strongest in the poor, working-class immigrant sections of New England cities. But, as has been demonstrated in a recent study of critical elections, "the same relation had existed in sharper form in 1892. In 1896 the Republicans gained in the working class wards, just as they did in the silk stocking wards over their 1892 vote."[24] The Republicans successfully placed the blame for unemployment upon the Democrats, while simultaneously promoting the doctrine that the Grand Old Party was the party of prosperity and the "full dinner pail."[25] What we really had then, at least in New England and most likely elsewhere in the East, was not a sharpening of class cleavages, but a situation where the voting reflected "more a sectional antagonism and anxiety, shared by all classes, expressed in opposition to the dangers supposed to be threatening from the West."[26]

It was a supreme triumph for Hanna as he cabled to his friend McKinley on election night, "God's in His Heaven, all's right with the world." In Canton the President-Elect went to his bedroom to pray. How Hanna must have smiled as he thought of the jitters and shivers of the gold bugs that Bryan had scared so stiff that he couldn't get any campaign contributions out of them, and of others whose spite led them to take another course. "Many of my friends," wrote John Hay during the campaign, "are saving money for the purchase of suitable residences in Paris."

McKinley, "wise with the ancient lore of politics, crafty with the ways that win men and hold them," had turned back the Great Commoner. Of Bryan, some have declared like Richard Hofstadter that he "could no more analyze the issues of his day than the Confederates could realize the obsolescence of slavery"; others agree with Henry L. Mencken, who said that he would be remembered as democracy's "supreme impostor." But "what his enemies could not understand," wrote Charles E. Merriam, "was that people are as much interested in knowing about their leader's heart as in knowing about his head, and that sympathy no less than intelligence plays its part in the great process of popular control." In this judgment is the clue to some of the change in Republican party fortunes that came in the years ahead.

The very success of industry made the campaign of 1896 a notable one. The railroad system was near completion, and the intensive industrialization of the country was proceeding at a breakneck clip. In this setting Hanna's scheme was "simplicity incarnate." He believed high tariffs kept foreign goods made with cheap labor out of American markets. Since politics controlled Congress, and it was Congress that made high tariffs, it followed that those who benefited from the high tariffs should contribute the money that influences elections and controls politics. So Hanna's idea was not particularly utopian. "He was not tinkering at the abolition of poverty, for instance. His was simply a device to provide for more work, more sweat, more business, more dividends." [27]

Thus Hanna was not "just another rich man buying his way to power," as Herbert Agar reminds us, but he was a pioneer in the economic tradition of America.[28] For the present, at least, a majority had declared in favor of a capitalistic system, and labor seems to have distrusted the agrarians of the West whose chance against the money power failed to bring into clear focus a reassuring alternative." "All one's friends," wrote Henry Adams, "all one's best citizens, reformers, churches, colleges, educated classes, had joined the banks to force submission to capitalism; a submission long foreseen by the mere law of man."

The contest had been conducted at a time when some questions of social reform, issues of conservation and the need for broadening the base of economic democracy had barely surfaced. Winding out of the campaign, however, was a rising consciousness of the social responsibilities of government. Almost at hand was the day when the desires—now subconsciously held—for a positive philosophy of government action as well as one of a government of restraint would emerge. City worker and agrarian were both becoming familiar with the uncertainties flowing from an advancing industrial urbanism and rapidly rising and falling markets often aggravated by adverse weather conditions. Thus McKinley came to the Presidency not only at the end of a century, but also toward the end of an era, in which the policies that streamed from great industrial and financial concentrations had largely followed their own course of natural development. The transition might have been far more difficult had not Hanna and McKinley lifted politics to a high "level of competence."

Both Hanna and McKinley were unshaken in their faith that an advancing industrialism, aided by protection, was the essential road to happiness. But both were aware that the success of the Republican ticket in 1896 was largely due to the recapture of industrial workers in the East lost in the 1892 election. McKinley agreed with Hanna that labor should have the right to organize and demand a fair share of the profits. As to the certainty of these profits he was completely confident, for he believed high tariffs added to the wealth of the nation by stimulating production that led in turn to more profit which finally shook down into more full dinner pails.

On their return from the inauguration exercises on March 4, 1897, retiring President Cleveland turned to McKinley and said gravely: "I am deeply sorry, Mr. President, to pass on to you a war with Spain. It will come within two years. Nothing can stop it." At the moment McKinley was extremely happy, and felt that war could be avoided. But thirteen months later, April 21, 1898, Cleveland's prophecy was fulfilled.

McKinley's first cabinet largely gave way to another team during his first term, and for the most part the replacements were abler men. Initially the Postmaster General's post was offered to Hanna, who declined because he wanted to be a United States Senator. To negotiate this, McKinley appointed ailing John Sherman Secretary of State. This move, of course, left the Ohio Senator's seat vacant, and Hanna was appointed to the Senate, taking office on March 5, 1897. The selection of Sherman, however, was much criticized, for as Henry Adams acidly remarked, "John Sherman, otherwise admirably fitted for the place, was notoriously feeble and quite senile," and his appointment constituted "a betrayal of an old friend, as well as of the State Department." Sherman's enfeebled condition did worsen as events drifted toward war, and a year after his appointment he resigned. His replacement by John Hay, another Ohioan, brought a distinguished figure to the post, and when further replacements brought in Elihu Root as Secretary of War and Philander Knox as Attorney General, the new administration could quite properly jubilate over the distinction of its cabinet.[29]

On the legislative side one of the first concerns of the new administration was with tariff rates, and in 1897 the Dingley tariff act was passed, putting the Republican party on record again for high protection. On money, Republicans were still far from united, but in an effort to redeem a platform pledge McKinley did appoint an official commission to confer with representatives of France and Great Britain in 1897 on the possibility of establishing free silver as a currency medium under international agreement. Because of his intuitive political sense that it might be well to leave the gold issue alone for a time, McKinley avoided pushing this issue—a strategy well founded. For in the months following his assumption of office, a wave of prosperity billowed across the nation, accompanied by a startling increase in the nation's gold supply (due in part to improved methods for extracting the precious metal, and also to new discoveries in Alaska, Australia, and South Africa). In the same period, moreover, the condition of agriculture improved, and a foreign crop-failure in 1897 shoved up wheat prices to a new high on the American market.

Not until March of 1900 did Congress finally act on the gold standard pledge in the Republican platform of 1896. Now, with substantial gold reserves, and fears over the scarcity of currency largely removed, the case for silver inflation lost its momentum. And so in March of 1900 Congress passed the Gold Standard act, which declared other forms of money redeemable in gold on demand, and enlarged the supporting reserve fund to $150,000,000. Moreover, to avoid the difficulties of the Cleveland administration, the Gold Standard act set up the gold reserve as a separate and distinct account which was not to be drawn upon for current revenue deficits.

On February 15, 1898, the first dramatic incident in the chain of events that would confirm Cleveland's inaugural prediction jammed the nation's wire services. The U.S.S. *Maine* was mysteriously blown up in Havana harbor. Two hundred and sixty lives were lost, and this blow, combined with American sympathies for Cubans after the alleged atrocities committed by the Spanish as a result of the Cuban insurrection of 1895, whipped up an intense war fever. The story, of course, of the part played by the American press in winding up American public opinion to the breaking point is well known. "The old, the young, the weak, the crippled—all are butchered without mercy," cried Joseph Pulitzer's New York *World,* while William

Randolph Hearst's *Journal* shrilled away about Spanish atrocities, and even financed an expedition to rescue a young Cuban girl who had been sent to prison for treason. Only two weeks after the sinking of the *Maine* the Chicago *Tribune* was beating the drums for war, saying in part: "Will one delay follow another until the patriotic ardor of Americans has cooled down? . . ." [30]

Despite the appalling clamor for war, McKinley genuinely wanted peace with Spain, and so did Mark Hanna along with a great many other responsible Republican leaders throughout the country. But the noisy elements were too powerful to allow the difficulties between the Spanish and United States governments to be peaceably composed. And the tone of many Republicans made it difficult for McKinley to remain calm. "It is time someone woke up and realized the necessity of annexing some property," cried Senator Shelby Cullom of Illinois: "We want all this Northern Hemisphere." At the same time Henry Cabot Lodge was saying, "From the Rio Grande to the Arctic Ocean there should be but one flag and one country." And Theodore Roosevelt, who had written to Lodge in 1895, during the Venezuelan crisis, that the "clamor of the peace faction has convinced me that this country needs a war," was even more belligerent when he became Assistant Secretary of the Navy in McKinley's cabinet. The President was a "white livered cur," he said, for even thinking twice before attacking the Spaniards.

Under such conditions it was extremely difficult for a man of McKinley's political sensitivity to put on the brakes. Whatever his inner thoughts, McKinley decided to leave the decision to Congress, and on April 20 Congress chose war.

In the exchanges between this government and Spain before the war broke out, the demands which the President made upon the Spanish government were reasonable. Moreover, there is good reason to believe that if McKinley's steady and dignified pressure had continued the President could probably have obtained Cuban autonomy or independence, or possibly even annexation to the United States, without war. Under heavy pressure at home, however, the President sent a message to Congress, not advocating war but indicating his displeasure with Spain's behavior and referring to "the intolerable condition of affairs which is at our doors."

McKinley has been criticized for not taking the responsibility of a war declaration upon himself. Had he done so, his position in this crisis might well have been stronger in history's judgment. Yet not only was he under tremendous pressure, but Congress would probably have declared war even if he had come out against it.

Happily the war was a short one, for Spain proved to be weak and inefficient. From the standpoint of military preparedness, our own nation was woefully weak. But fortunately the Navy was in good shape, thanks in good measure to the foresight and energy of the able young Assistant Secretary of the Navy, Theodore Roosevelt. Yet it was Roosevelt who by laying plans to attack Spain in the Far East as well as in the Caribbean soon had McKinley on the horns of another dilemma. Should the United States now annex the Philippines, with its eight million inhabitants? Late one night, following a tour of the Middle West, with both ears carefully cocked to catch public opinion, and after struggling with the Philippine question in prayer, the President found the answer: "One night late it came to me this way—I don't know what it was but it came! (1) That we could not give them back to Spain—that would be cowardly and dishonorable; (2) That we could not turn them over to France or Germany—our commercial rivals in the Orient—that would be bad business and discreditable; (3) That we could not leave them to themselves—they were unfit for self-government—and they would have anarchy and misrule worse than Spain's war; (4) That there was nothing left for us to do but to take them all, and to educate the Philippinos, and uplift and civilize and Christianize them as our fellow men for whom Christ also died." The communion with his conscience thus established, McKinley cabled to his commissioners in Paris, then negotiating a peace with Spain, to hold the islands, and as compensation Spain was given $20,000,000.

A ten-weeks war drastically altered the position of the United States in the community of nations. If the war with Spain was Roosevelt's "finest hour," for all its exciting drama, including the charge up San Juan Hill at the head of his Rough Riders, it was also something else—something far more. It was an event in which others like him perceived a new greatness in the nation's destiny. "It was for him a device by which the United States assumed, at last, its proper place as a responsible world power."

Within the compass of a single administration the nation had waged war on Spain, made Cuba a protectorate, and added Puerto Rico, Guam, and the Philippine Islands to the American empire as unincorporated territories. In the same period the Hawaiian Islands had also been annexed. Soon the United States was taking the lead in another step of far-reaching significance directed toward maintaining international stability and promoting international justice. This it did in September, 1899, when Secretary of State John Hay addressed a note to the major powers urging an " 'open door' policy for all nations in China—to declare themselves for equality of trade, identical tariffs, harbor duties and railroad charges in all of the areas that they controlled." Within a year the United States was sending 2,500 American soldiers to join an international relief expedition to subdue the Boxer uprising in China. Thus in swift successive strokes the United States found itself far from its continental borders, pawing daringly in the world of international diplomacy.

Many Republicans looked upon the results with high satisfaction, viewing them as perfectly consistent with the development of a trading empire which the National Republican Daniel Webster had promoted and Lincoln's Secretary of State Seward had advanced. And to men like Jim Hill, the powerful railroad magnate, the linkage of the Orient to the golden grain fields of the Middle West, serviced by his Great Northern Railway, was a dream come true. Not without significance is the fact that the black and red emblem that Minnesota and Dakota farm boys saw stenciled on the sides of Northern Pacific cars as they rushed across the prairies to Seattle was the Yin and Yang symbol of ancient China.

John Hay wrote to Roosevelt, "It has been a splendid little war." But many discerning Republicans were apprehensive over this new imperialism. The Republicans who now joined the anti-imperialist movement "were almost without exception Republicans of the older generation, former supporters of Frémont and Lincoln who believed they were carrying on the tradition of the party's anti-slavery days in opposing colonial expansionism." [31] Though the Philippines were annexed, years of guerilla warfare followed. Some Republican Senators, like Hoar, Justin Morrill, and former Senator George Franklin Edmunds of Vermont, protested the annexation of these distant territories on constitutional as well as moral and strategic grounds. They felt these acquisitions would prove to be a mistake in the long run. But a majority of the citizenry—at least at that time—was not overly concerned. And a new nationalistic fervor induced by the war, in combination with a bristling prosperity, brought the McKinley administration up to presidential convention time in 1900 primed for the contest to decide whether it was to be recommissioned for the next quadrennium.

Quite apart from the prosperous economic condition of the country, however, and the popularity acquired through success in the domain of foreign relations, another portent pointed to the success of the Republican party in 1900—the midterm elections of 1898. "The precedents of the past half century delineate an important law of American politics," writes Cortez Ewing in his study of congressional elections from 1896 to 1944: "Success in a presidential election will go to that party which already has majority control of the

House of Representatives." [32] There were exceptions to this rule—Garfield's election in 1880 and Harrison's in 1888, and a long time later Truman's surprising upset of 1948. But far from losing support at the midterm elections, the Republicans upped their margin by 7 seats in the Senate, winning a total of 56 seats in 1898, while in the House they lost 19 seats, still keeping control by a safe margin of 185 to 163.

Long before convention time in 1900, it was apparent that both parties would nominate the same candidates they did in 1896. Bryan still held an enormous following, and McKinley's popularity made him certain of a renomination. So when the Republican clan gathered at Philadelphia's exposition auditorium on June 19, 1900, outside of the platform and the usual round of morale-building war whoops for the Grand Old Party, only one real issue faced the convention—the Vice-Presidency. Vice-President Hobart had died on November 21, 1899, and another running mate had to be found for McKinley.

As national chairman Hanna opened the convention a touch of nostalgia gripped the hall. Many of the old faces and tested troopers of previous conventions were gone. And new ones were showing that would be occupying pre-eminent positions in national party councils for many years to come—some for the next quarter of a century. So we find names like Cushman K. Davis and Knute Nelson of Minnesota, Phillip Goldsborough of Maryland, Boies Penrose of Pennsylvania, Albert J. Beveridge of Indiana, Frank Lowden of Illinois, and Frank B. Brandegee of Connecticut. The temporary chairman was Senator E. O. Wolcott of Colorado, and the permanent chairman was also a man who was going to be heard from increasingly during the next twenty years, Henry Cabot Lodge of Massachusetts.

In a touching ceremony, the 13 survivors of the first Republican convention at Philadelphia in 1856 were introduced one by one.[33] Then, after a routine try at reducing Southern representation, led by Senator Quay of Pennsylvania, the convention settled down to scold Democrats.[34]

The platform was adopted by unanimous vote, but it is hardly of interest here, nor was it really of interest in the campaign that fall. McKinley's popularity was enormous, and the only real problem facing the convention was finding a Vice-President.

High on many lists was the young Colonel Roosevelt who had been elected governor of New York in 1898. Thomas Platt, "the easy boss" of New York Republicanism, had been "a mite apprehensive" about taking Roosevelt as a gubernatorial candidate, but he gave in because he realized he needed a romantic figure to keep the Democrats out of Albany. But, as John Blum tells us, "virtue alone would not have convinced Platt, had not the Colonel guaranteed to meet him half way."

Roosevelt promised to "treat with and work with the organization," "see and consult the leaders—not once but continuously—and earnestly try to come to an agreement on all important questions with them. . . ." But, he solemnly warned, "When we come to . . . anything touching the eighth commandment and general decency, I could not allow any consideration of party to come in." Apparently "this was good enough for Platt, who also professed to believe in the Decalogue. It provided, he reckoned, the matter and cadence for first-rate campaign orations." [35]

After his election Roosevelt did keep his pledge to Platt to consult and to reward, by giving Platt a generous crop of appointed plums. But he also graded the yield scrupulously. And there were times when he refused to go along on appointments, as he did in refusing to reappoint Platt's incumbent Superintendent of Insurance. The man was "a stench in the nostrils of the people" of New York, said Roosevelt.

Roosevelt's first-term success as governor of New York, together with his colorful, violent speeches, made him a natural candidate for the Vice-Presidency.

At first Roosevelt vigorously refused, insisting he wanted nothing more at the moment than a second term as governor of New York. But his skirmishes with Platt gave the New York boss the idea that he ought to be unloaded from the Empire state and cast into that cavernous bin of anonymity known as the Vice-Presidency. He was, of course, "wrecking the Platt machine quietly, almost stealthily—but certainly." So Platt determined that Roosevelt must go. But it was not so simple as it seemed. For Mark Hanna not only had a low opinion of Roosevelt, but he was still smoldering over Platt's sponsorship of Reed in the 1896 convention, and he resented the fact that Platt had forced the gold standard into the Republican platform that year. But Hanna either misjudged the ability of Platt to put Roosevelt's nomination over, or he thought that Roosevelt was only a noisy sophomore who would probably not accomplish much in the Vice-Presidency anyway.

It was Senator Foraker who nominated McKinley for his second term in a convention hall built to accommodate 16,000, but acknowledged now to hold at least 20,000. For nearly two days beforehand, Hanna had sat on the platform, usually concealed from the convention audience by a group of his fellow national committeemen.

When McKinley was nominated, he jumped up on a table, "grabbed a pampas plume and began to yell like an Apache for five minutes."

For the Vice-Presidency Hanna preferred Cornelius Bliss, his strategy being a business ticket. But Platt by this time had formed an alliance with his fellow boss, Matthew Quay of Pennsylvania, who had long nursed a grudge against Hanna for voting against his admission to the Senate in 1899, and in light of Roosevelt's enormous popularity it was not a difficult matter to bring about the New York governor's nomination. Even at the last hour, however, Roosevelt was insisting he would not accept the nomination. Then, while he was waiting for an elevator in the Walton Hotel, Platt's brother approached him and asked him to come up for a talk with Senator Thomas Platt. "An hour later," reports Nicholas Murray Butler, "T.R. rejoined us in our headquarters; his tail feathers were all down. The fight had gone out of him, and he changed his former tune to that of 'I cannot disappoint my Western friends if they insist. I cannot seem to be bigger than the party.'" Roosevelt became the vice-presidential nominee by 929 out of 930 votes, for to the end he withheld his own vote.

Now, the deed done, Hanna moaned to Roosevelt's sponsors: "Don't you realize that there is only one life between this madman and the White House?" But here Hanna erred, for Roosevelt understood his calling with a coolness that Hanna greatly misjudged. And so did Hanna misjudge Roosevelt if by madman he meant radical. For, once he was in power, his bite was never so formidable as his bark.

Roosevelt was a master of group diplomacy, with a remarkably coherent and consistent philosophy throughout the years he exercised executive power as governor of New York and as President of the United States. "His profession molded him," writes John Blum, and as a "conscionable professional, Roosevelt was not a mere opportunist. He did not, like many of his liberal contemporaries, expect new laws and theories in themselves to provide good government." And in administering laws or policies as they had to be applied to specific situations he became a master adjuster. Thus he concerned himself primarily "with processes and instruments" rather than with "finalities." In this sense he was basically conservative, but it was a conservatism tempered by a sincere belief in causes and deep understanding and sympathy.

His appeal to followers is legendary; so is his ability to lead and organize. "He sounded in my heart the first trumpet call of the time that was to be," said Will White, rushing home after his first casual meeting with Roosevelt to tell his wife. Roosevelt, said John Hay, "could organize the unorganizable by sheer personality."

That his nomination struck an immediate responsive chord is given a well-documented touch by *Harper's Weekly,* a journal that opposed Roosevelt's nomination (because it preferred his re-election as governor of New York). "It is probably true that the nomination of Governor Roosevelt is the most popular move the convention could have made. And that it will serve to strengthen the ticket in certain sections of the country is an undoubted fact." But looking ahead, the same publication thought it saw a new institutional change in prospect for American government.

> We cannot escape the conviction that the old order of things is about to change, and that the vice presidency, instead of being a graveyard of political ambition, will turn out to be something radically different—*something like a dynamo, for instance, with a large number of live wires attached to it.*[36]

Leaving the convention behind, Hanna, who had resisted Roosevelt's nomination to the end, told McKinley, "We have done the best we could. Now it is up to you to live."

With Bryan renominated unanimously and running this time with Adlai E. Stevenson of Illinois, Cleveland's Vice-President, the return match of the principals who had tilted against each other in 1896 got under way. Bryan was again endorsed by the Populists and the Silver Republicans, but silver by this time was a limp issue. The Great Commoner's assault weapon in this campaign was Republican imperialism. But a majority of the nation was in no mood to listen. The hero of San Juan Hill, often delivering thirteen talks in a day, took over the brunt of the speech-making, rousing "the traditionally expansionist West to such a frenzy of enthusiasm that Bryan was repudiated in the very cradle of Populism." For better or worse, Americans wanted some part on the stage of world politics, and this proved helpful to the Republican cause. One could rail against the consequences of economic expansionism, economic exploitation of territories, or of economic imperialism. But the fact was that there was something more involved in this heady enthusiasm of the American people for their entry into world diplomacy.

On the domestic side, the prosperous times spoke for themselves. Mark Hanna, again McKinley's campaign manager, emphasized everywhere that the return of good times had been brought about by the Republican party. Hanna, who had been elected himself in 1898 for his first full term in the Senate, had coined the term "stand-patter" during this campaign, and it was now his intention to demonstrate that the prosperous conditions of the times simply flowed from this stand-pat conservatism. "Full dinner pail" posters were plastered on every possible wall, and this emblem served to symbolize the redemption of the Republican party pledge to the American people for a healthy economy.

That fall, while the vice-presidential candidate roamed the countryside, a new gun opened up. Mark Hanna, the national chairman, took the stump. And he did so in face of an adverse warning from the President, who feared he would be assassinated as a wicked old capitalist. "Return to Washington and tell the President that God hates a coward," barked Hanna to an emissary from the White House.

Speaking to crowds that were frequently larger than those turning out for Roosevelt, Hanna waded into the heart of the Populist strongholds. "What about the trusts?" quacked a farmer boy, well aware that this was the day's touchiest issue. "Well what about 'em?" snorted the national chairman. "All you boys have got foolish reading the papers. You'll see that big combinations of capital end up by forcing down prices. Why's one wagon company sell your dad his wagon ten dollars cheaper than the next one? That's what comes of these big combinations in the long run. . . . Any old Grangers in the crowd here? . . . Good morning. . . . I ask you this. Didn't the Grangers combine to run up prices so's your families could live comfortably, and didn't you fight the railroads like Sam Hill, to get rates regulated? Of course you did! It was sound business and good practice. Anybody abusin' you people now? All right, combine and smash 'em." [37]

Everywhere Hanna drew attentive crowds as he defended the integrity of an economic system under which he had seen the United States prosper so mightily. And even those who remained unconvinced or failed to fall under his spell had a word of praise. "By heaven, he has sand," exclaimed his old anti-monopolist opponent Tom Johnson—the reform mayor of Cleveland who had fought Hanna to a draw.

The calmness of the political summer in 1900 belied the intensity of preparations under way. Hanna was busy pulling the inharmonious elements of the party together for a second heat with the challenger from Nebraska. Only after a long talk with Roosevelt did he appoint an executive committee which the *Review of Reviews* pronounced "as strong a fighting body as the party ever had to wage its battles." Cornelius Bliss again served as treasurer, and Perry S.

Heath of Indiana resigned as First Assistant Postmaster General to take up his old place as secretary of the national committee.

Until 1896, the national headquarters had always been in an old brownstone private house on Fifth Avenue. Now the New York national headquarters occupied space in the Metropolitan Life Building at Number One Madison Avenue, while once again the Western headquarters in Chicago came to be regarded as the real operational base. Hanna made it perfectly clear that he was in the business of merchandising doubt to the voters about Bryan, and selling McKinley on prosperity. He considered it quite proper to pay a farmer or laborer for getting to the polls. But he considered it entirely improper for a firm to demand a definite service for a contribution, even by implication, and he may have set a precedent by returning a $10,000 check to some Wall Street bankers who suggested such an arrangement.

Betting again on the Middle West as the critical battleground, the Republicans sent out three-fifths of their campaign material from Chicago. At the peak of the campaign in October an estimated 7,000 speeches were being made every night—with 600 orators being managed from the headquarters of the Chicago office alone.

Seventy different documents—80,000,000 pieces—were employed at a cost of about one million dollars, and once again a tremendous effort was mobilized in appeals to minority groups.

The verdict that fall gave McKinley 7,218,491 votes to Bryan's 6,360,000. With the total vote somewhat smaller than in 1896, McKinley received a larger proportion—51.6%—to Bryan's 45.5%. McKinley carried a total of 28 states this time, with 292 electoral votes to Bryan's 155. A remarkable comeback had been staged by the Republican party in the West, which in part may have been due to the energetic campaign of the vice-presidential nominee. For this time McKinley carried Nebraska, South Dakota, Kansas, Utah, Washington, and Wyoming, all of which went to Bryan in 1896. Bryan's most notable gains were in New England, where McKinley had carried every single county in 1896, and also in the Middle Atlantic region.

Jubilant over the results, McKinley, who now became the first President since Andrew Jackson to be re-elected by a majority of free votes in face of a strong opposition party, said: "I can no longer be called the President of a party. I am President of the whole people."

Riding along with this presidential sweep was an increased majority for the Republicans in both houses of Congress. In the Senate the Republicans picked up an additional three seats; in the House they added thirteen.

After the election, while Platt and Quay prematurely enjoyed a few quiet chuckles on how they had outmaneuvered Hanna by exiling Theodore Roosevelt to the Vice-Presidency, someone asked Senator Platt if he were going to attend the inaugural exercises. "Yes, I am going to Washington to see Theodore Roosevelt take the veil!" he said. He spoke too hastily. For Roosevelt intended from the outset to make the Vice-Presidency a stepping stone. But not quite so soon.

Meanwhile McKinley, enjoying his triumph to the hilt, embarked on his self-styled role as "President of the whole people." That spring —1901—he made a tour of the West Coast by train on a trip that was supposed to bring him back to Buffalo, New York, on June 13. For this was to be President's Day at the Pan-American exposition which had opened on May 1. But Mrs. McKinley's illness (she was a chronic invalid) in El Paso, Texas, on the return from the West, forced the cancellation of the President's appearance on June 13—a day that would have found Leon F. Czolgocz (pronounced Cholgosh) back on a farm in Ohio instead of at the Temple of Music in Buffalo with a revolver in his hand wrapped in a handkerchief. But a foretaste of trouble was not to come for three more months.

"Now That Damned Cowboy Is President!"

🐘

The first sign of it came at 6:30 on the evening of September 4, as the McKinleys arrived from their Canton, Ohio, home aboard a special train on the Lakeshore and Michigan Southern Railway. As they pulled into Buffalo an inexperienced young artillery officer, in charge of the battery for the presidential salute, had placed the guns too close to the tracks and the concussion from the blast blew out a few windows in the train, "causing Mrs. McKinley to faint."

But the exposition was a gala event, and amidst festive floral tributes and the inventive wonders of the world that was to be, the incident accompanying McKinley's arrival was quickly forgotten. Next day, 100,000 people crowded into the fair grounds, and at least 50,000 of them heard McKinley deliver his President's Day address. It was his valedictory—very likely the most notable speech of his career.

A high-tariff man from infancy—a symbol of protectionism—he informed his audience that economic changes had led him to modify his own belief in the direction of reciprocal trade and the freer flow of commodities between nations. "Isolationism," he said, "is no longer possible or desirable. . . . The period of exclusiveness is past." It was a startling admission, coming as it did from a man who passionately believed that the full dinner pail could only adequately be stocked when the nation hiked up its tariff rate.

Next morning McKinley visited Niagara Falls. When he returned that afternoon for a reception to be given in his honor at the Temple of Music, one of the exposition hosts greeted him with: "I am glad to see you back in Buffalo, Mr. President." "Yes," the President answered, "and I don't know whether I'll ever be able to get away."

At the moment the nation was free from the sectional bitterness that preceded Lincoln's assassination, and the intense factional strife that had embittered partisan tempers twenty years earlier at the time of Garfield's assassination. But McKinley's associates were not at all happy about his contemplated public appearance at the Pan-American exposition, and his secretary, George B. Cortelyou, anxious because of rumors after the shooting of King Humbert that there were anarchist plots to kill the President, urged McKinley several times to cancel the reception. But the President always replied, "Why should I? No one would wish to hurt me."

Shaking hands with hundreds as they filed past him in the Temple of Music that afternoon, McKinley was well flanked by Secret Service men, and perhaps 50 guards of one sort or another who were stationed near or in the Temple. But as the President reached out to clasp the hand of a slender young man of slight build with a dull moody expression, Leon F. Czolgosz—an anarchist—pushed the President's hand aside and lunged forward, firing two shots through his handkerchief, one shell striking McKinley in the breastbone, the other ripping into the left side of his abdomen. Shivering, the President straightened up to his full height, looked at Czolgosz in astonishment, then slumped into the arms of the men around him. He did not lose consciousness. As he lay on the floor while soldiers rushed forward, beating Czolgosz with rifles and fists, the President called out: "Be easy with him, boys."

How it might have been prevented or how a President who insists upon such appearances can ever be adequately safeguarded is still an unsolved problem. "We never thought for a moment he had a revolver with him," remarked Secret Service agent Samuel R. Ireland sadly. "He was the last man in the world we would pick out of a crowd as dangerous."

From Czolgosz came the statement, "I thought it would be a good thing for the country to kill the President." Czolgosz said further that he thought the President was "an enemy of the good working people," and that "McKinley was going around the country shouting prosperity when there was no prosperity for the poor man." [1]

For several days the President's condition improved, so much so that on September 10 Vice-President Roosevelt, who had hurried to Buffalo after the shooting, left again to go mountain climbing because of the optimism of McKinley's physicians. But in the afternoon of September 12, following the best hours the President had had since the shooting, his pulse suddenly weakened. And on the evening of September 13 he said farewell to his wife, his last words being, as the physician jotted them down: "Good-bye, all, good-bye. It is God's way, His will will be done." He died the morning of September 14. At 3:35 that afternoon Roosevelt, who had been summoned back to Buffalo, was sworn in as President in the home of Ansley Wilcox some eight blocks from where his predecessor lay in state. [2]

With Roosevelt at the time he was sworn in were six of the eight members of McKinley's cabinet. Interestingly, the two not present, John Hay, Secretary of State, and Lyman J. Gage, Secretary of the Treasury, who were both in Washington, were the very two that Roosevelt had in mind to replace at once. Summoning his old friend, Herman Kohlsaat, Roosevelt said that he was going to ask both Hay and Gage for their resignations and was about to make Elihu Root Secretary of State. But this move was discouraged by Kohlsaat, who pointed out that the stock exchange had closed on McKinley's death, and that the press was filled with rumors about uneasiness in the market over what might happen when it opened tomorrow. The reason for this uncertainty, argued Kohlsaat, was that Roosevelt was considered a "bucking bronco" in finance, and any announcement from him that he was going to fire his Secretary of the Treasury might start a panic. It was persuasive advice which Roosevelt took at once; he dashed immediately into the adjoining room, where six of McKinley's cabinet members were waiting, to say: "I have changed my mind. I am going to keep all of you!"

Next day the funeral train left for Canton with one intensely bitter and melancholy man aboard it. It was Mark Hanna. Damning Roosevelt up and down, Hanna said to Kohlsaat: "I told William McKinley it was a mistake to nominate that wild man at Philadelphia. I asked him if he realized what would happen if he should die. Now look, that damned cowboy is President of the United States!" [3]

Few men ever entered the Presidency with the assets of Theodore Roosevelt. A man of considerable intellectual stature, a brilliant conversationalist and widely read, he was easily the most versatile man in politics since Jefferson. Yet he never remained aloof in the rarefied seclusion of intellectuals, nor did he flinch from working with the political bosses. It was characteristic of him from childhood to be deeply interested in the elemental mechanics of political power. Warned by his friends, who felt it odd he should want to enter the legislature in the 1880's, that his associates in politics would be liquor dealers, grooms and low politicians who inhabited livery stables, he answered: "In that case they belong to the governing class, and you do not. I mean, if I can, to be one of the governing class."

His success in the legislature was immediate, and from there he went on to distinguish himself with a long list of public honors. When Benjamin Harrison made him a civil service commissioner—a post that amounted to little for the first six years of its existence—Roosevelt lifted the assignment to national prominence by bringing 20,-000 federal employees into the merit system and out from under the old spoils arrangement. Whatever he did, attending a national con-

vention as a delegate, running for mayor of New York against the
single-tax advocate, Henry George (he lost, although not to
George), serving as Assistant Secretary of the Navy, travelling extensively in the West, administering law enforcement as president of
the New York city board of police commissioners, or running the
state of New York as governor, he fell to the task with the enthusiasm
of a Sousa march and the perceptive insights that bred success. "The
thing which the Gods gave Roosevelt in excess was energy," observed his old friend William Allen White.

> He was gargantuan in his capacity for work. It was one of those
> utterly unthinkable coincidences . . . that a man of Roosevelt's
> enormous energy should come to the presidency of exactly that
> country which at exactly that time was going through a transitional
> period—critical, dangerous, and but for him terrible—between an
> old, rural, individual order and a new highly socialized order.

A man of impetuous nature, Roosevelt suited the times admirably,
and when he took office on September 14 his mastery of the techniques of politics and government had become accomplished fact.

For the duration of McKinley's unexpired term, Roosevelt did not
press Congress for a spate of reform legislation. Instead, he directed
his energies wisely toward gaining control of the tap-roots of his
party. If he appeared to do this, as some of his critics have said,
with seemingly "indecent haste," it was partly because he fully
sensed the growing responsibilities of executive leadership in a changing world, and the imperative need for developing commensurate
authority within the presidential office to discharge these growing
obligations. One way toward this goal, obviously, lay in becoming
the number one signal-caller of the party. Moreover, the need for
getting into the quarterback position as quickly as possible was accentuated by the fact that the party was being ruled as never before
by its first national boss, Mark Hanna. And Hanna's dislike of Roosevelt was almost but not quite so intense as that of Speaker Reed
for McKinley. On the day of McKinley's funeral Reed let out a blast
of bitterness against the late President to Will White that White
described as "a torrent of wrath, a cold, repressed New England
cascade of icicles."

After Roosevelt took over, Hanna's old time adversary, Senator
Matthew Quay, with a seasoned look at the impending party struggle, sized up the situation accurately. Trouble was in the offing, he
predicted, because "we have two executive mansions"—the White
House and Hanna's suite at the Arlington Hotel.

In so many ways the two men were strikingly different. Yet they held much in common and were of similar mind on the relations of capital and labor. In policy matters Hanna, on his own motion, supported Roosevelt in the liquidation of the Northern Securities Company, the first trust-busting move of the President, and he was an active supporter of the President's stand on conservation policies and in eliminating tariff duties on Cuban imports. Roosevelt himself spoke generously of Hanna:

> No man had larger traits than Hanna. He was a big man in every way and as forceful a personality as we have seen in public life in our generation. I think that not merely I myself, but the whole party and the whole country have reason to be very grateful to him for the way in which, after I came into office, under circumstances which were very hard for him, he resolutely declined to be drawn into the position which a smaller man of meaner cast would inevitably have taken; that is, the position of antagonizing public policies if I was identified with them.

Whatever respect Roosevelt had for the "master mechanic," however, he showed no sentimentality about his demolition of Hanna's organizational control. Striking out boldly in the Middle West, the heartland of Hanna's political province, Roosevelt went against the counsel of his devoted friend, William Allen White, in Kansas, where he chopped off "Uncle Mark's" control by replacing a Hanna stalwart in the post of Commissioner of Pensions. Not only did Roosevelt demobilize Hanna's forces in the Middle West in short order, but he also set about destroying Uncle Mark's suzerainty in the South. He did this in a way that shocked many of his admirers.

Rescuing from exile James S. Clarkson—the man known as the "headsman" in the Harrison administration for his flagrant violation of civil service regulations—Roosevelt appointed him collector of the port of New York. Since Hanna himself kept Clarkson up in the bleachers during the McKinley administration and the spoilsman expert had come under such bitter attack from reform organizations, his new appointment was immediately jumped upon by many critics, particularly those who were ardent supporters of civil service. To these critics Roosevelt gave short shrift and had a ready answer. Mr. Clarkson, he said, had announced an intention to adhere to Civil Service, showing, he added, "a rather good spirit."

Behind the appointment, of course, was a simple strategy. Not only was Clarkson an influence in his native Iowa and throughout the Middle West because of his influence on the National Republican League, which in some places actually supplanted the Republican organizations, but he had a deep familiarity with the patchwork Republicanism of the South. Long a friend of the Southern Negro politicians, "Clarkson took particular pleasure in converting organizations which Hanna had made 'lily white' to the 'black and tan' of the carpetbag tradition." In this circumstance, of course, Roosevelt could well take both a moral and a political satisfaction. Occasionally Roosevelt permitted one of Hanna's agents to hold power, but his intention was clear from the outset, and that was to construct a personal organization of his own within the Republican party. This he did without apology. To the end he followed the policy of consulting established organizations, but even here he offers an interesting postscript on his own practice: "It is one thing to say that I shall consult the organization in making appointments; it is an entirely different thing to say that I shall consult no one but the organization. . . ." Thus Roosevelt consulted Senators and Congressmen, including Hanna, but how often did they have the last word?

In the exchange of power between Roosevelt and Hanna over the Republican organization, it is doing no disservice to Hanna to say that Roosevelt did raise the level of competency in the federal service. This he did not only on the bench, where his appointments were distinguished, but also in many subordinate appointments involving the simplest sinecures. He was well convinced that character and capacity could coincide with a fervently proclaimed partisanship.

Recognizing the inevitable, Hanna did not fight back. He supported Roosevelt's policies and, except on rare occasions, backed his appointments. Hanna was wise enough to see that the resources of the Presidency were in the hands of a man who was without peer in knowing how to use them.

Systematically dismembering Hanna's personal political control with one hand, Roosevelt began simultaneously to gesticulate to the galleries with the other, speaking with a voice that betokened a new era of governmental action. The flight of the years had convinced Roosevelt that the day was at hand for a new relationship between business and politics. Not yet ready for it in McKinley's tour of duty in the White House, the country was fortunate that in the transition to a new readjustment in this relationship it was in the hands of men who believed earnestly in a system of state-aided business, and who served this system faithfully. Hanna and McKinley, as Agar writes, may have been looked upon as old-fashioned, "but they were the right men to preside over the transition. Without them the 'progressive era' might have been strangled in its cradle, to the pleasure of the socialists and of the belated pioneers, the Left and the extreme Right." [4]

Roosevelt started off his early career in a far more conservative frame of mind than McKinley. But through successive stages he experienced a "personal conversion" in his social outlook that gradually led him to advocate a high degree of paternalism in government. He was quick to sense that certain transformations in the relationship between government policy and the national economy were inevitable. Roosevelt had long believed that to raise the standard of living for the mass of people did not necessarily require a reduction in the standard of "the fortunate few." And in reflecting upon the future course of society, he saw an emerging way of life without extremes of poverty and wealth. In the drive for such a goal, he confided, "the sphere of the state's action may be vastly increased without in any way diminishing the happiness of either the many or the few." Socialism he dismissed as neither necessary nor probable, but he did insist that a completely laissez-faire hands-off policy was unthinkable for the road ahead where the "greatest victories" were "yet to be won."

With his first message to Congress, in December of 1901, Roosevelt began laying the groundwork for the propagation of his view. He acclaimed business concentration as a natural and desirable development, and said he was opposed to legislation prohibiting large-scale combinations. What he desired was not to abolish competition but to make the chances of competition more even. Thus he demanded legislation to eliminate the abuses of huge business combinations, while at the same time retaining their advantages. In the same address he asked for broader regulatory controls over railways, and protective legislation for women and children in all industries directly or indirectly working for the United States government. One other subject he touched upon was to become a favorite theme: conservation.

From his earliest boyhood nature had been an all-consuming interest for Roosevelt. Not only was he interested in such subjects as biology, but he also found in the great expanse of nature a kind of spiritual solace that served him well in times of crisis. When his first wife died two weeks after the birth of his first child, Alice, and his mother died suddenly the following day, he fled to the Dakotas, where he remained on the prairies for almost two years. All his life his enchantment with the great outdoors led him to take a devoted interest in conservation policy. In this area, moreover, he achieved conspicuous successes. While his predecessors had set aside some 40,000,000 acres of woodland, Roosevelt added 148,000,000 more, notwithstanding the protests of the grazing interests, cattle men and lumber men of the West. The year after he left office in 1909 it was reported that through his reclamation projects, irrigation programs, and dam construction, more than 3,000,000 acres of farmland had been so improved that results were an increased annual profit of $75,000,000. Notable advances were made in all phases of conservation. Names like that of Gifford Pinchot, whom Roosevelt appointed to head the division of forestry in a systematic effort to retimber denuded forest lands, have become landmarks in the history of conservation.

Again toward the close of his second term Roosevelt scored another long advance in the field of conservation, setting a precedent by summoning state governors for a conference on the subject in 1908 to set the stage for federal-state co-operation. Eighteen months later, forty-one state conservation commissions were already in existence, and Roosevelt had finally succeeded in making the nation conservation conscious.

Roosevelt's first message to Congress failed to bring forth an accolade from that body, but it struck a widespread responsive chord across the nation. And thereafter he met with continued success, bringing into his speeches railroad and trust regulations, labor problems, and other social questions that were bedeviling the nation.

In the summer and autumn of 1902 he took his appeals directly to the people, stumping New England and the Middle West. Everywhere his theme was the same: greater federal regulation and the pursuit of a program he abstracted into two words—the Square Deal—which, broadly stated, called for greater fairness for labor, capital, and the public as well. Soon the Progressive revolt, a long time in the making, burgeoned into a full-blown crusade as a new factional element of Republicanism in the Roosevelt era.

The Progressive movement essentially was a mixture of economic discontent and of middle-class protest against the plutocratic influences that were in danger of gaining ascendancy in our society. It also embraced certain moral and religious overtones that gave it a power which speeded its political acceptance. Fanned by famous exposés of the time, such as Ida M. Tarbell's "History of the Standard Oil Company," running in *McClure's Magazine* in 1902 and 1903, and such works as Thomas Lawson's *Frenzied Finance,* a stark account of the Amalgamated Copper Company, Lincoln Steffens's *The Shame of the Cities,* and Upton Sinclair's *The Jungle,* giving a sordid account of the Chicago stockyards, the Progressive spirit kindled a lusty drive for reform. In each person was the latent desire to be the dragon slayer in moving toward a better society. And no man knew better than Roosevelt how to raise those dragon-slaying instincts to the surface. His shrill denunciations, the piercing quality of his epithets ("malefactors of wealth"), and what a New York police captain called, after Roosevelt's death, "the fun of him," all combined to dazzle the country and confirm the fact that he was "the most tremendous thing that could have happened to American progressivism." [5] "The battles Roosevelt fought," said Mark Sullivan, "had they been waged by a La Follette or a Bryan, or even a Grover Cleveland, might have had the somber sourness of a puritanical crusade." But Roosevelt emitted vibrations "like a master tuning fork," setting the "whole atmosphere of the country atingle." [6]

Early in 1902 Roosevelt started to move against the trusts. On February 18, his Attorney General, Philander Knox, began proceedings to bring about the dissolution of the Northern Securities Company for violation of the Sherman Anti-Trust act. The Northern Securities Company, which emerged from a battle for control of the Great Northern Railroad between the rail titan Edward H. Harriman of the Union Pacific and the Hill-Morgan interests, was a merger of the holdings of this triumvirate in the Great Northern, Northern Pacific, and Burlington railways. Its effect, of course, was to establish a railroad monopoly in the Northwest. Morgan was amazed when he heard the government was going to prosecute his company, and he hurried off to Washington to tell Roosevelt: "If we have done anything wrong, send your man [*in this case Attorney General Knox*] to my man [*presumably one of Morgan's lawyers*] and they can fix it up." But to this Philander Knox replied: "We don't want to fix it up; we want to stop it."

The year 1902 also brought the great anthracite coal strike in Pennsylvania, which Hanna had tried to forestall but failed because George F. Baer, president of the Philadelphia-Reading Railway and spokesman for the mine operators, persuaded Morgan, whose railroads controlled the coal fields, that Hanna was wrong and that the miners had no real grievances. But on May 12, 1902, 147,000 workers left the mines, and the strike persisted until late fall. Eventually schools in many parts of New York were closed to save fuel and the East as well as the Middle West became critically concerned over coal stocks, which were at famine level. For months the mine operators steadfastly refused all requests of the United Mine Workers to meet with the anthracite workers for the purpose of discussing grievances.

With winter coming on and matters still at an impasse, the President, angry with the arrogance of the operators after months of patient effort to compromise the dispute, decided to intervene in the transcendent public interest. While the employers persisted in denying his right to interfere he made known his intention of seizing the mines and operating them as receiver while he appointed an arbitration board to settle the controversy. By this gesture he drove the owners to accept arbitration by a commission which he promptly appointed. Again he emerged as a master of the political arts in an approach to an explosive problem. The anthracite strike involved nearly 150,000 men and ultimately meant a loss to the miners and owners of close to a hundred million dollars. Once the strike was settled, incidentally, with the granting of a ten percent wage rise and a shorter work day, the anthracite industry was without serious trouble until after World War I.

On the legislative front Roosevelt managed one significant regulatory measure in 1903 with the passage of the Elkins act, a measure designed to end the rebate abuse by prohibiting railways from making variations in the published rates and inflicting fines for violations not only on the railways but on shippers as well. In 1903 Congress also created a Department of Commerce and Labor, acknowledging the coming of age of the labor movement and the need for stimulating trade and business as well as restraining it.

By now Roosevelt's public stature was forcing a more attentive attitude from Congress. In office less than two years, this young Republican President—the youngest man ever to assume the Presidency—was reaching dizzy heights of popularity. Roosevelt was able to garnish his serious achievements by living riotously with his romping children, much to the joy of the nation. Life at home, reports his dear friend Hermann Hagedorn, was pretty much of a "strenuous bedlam," with politicians, writers, editors, naturalists, and "celebrities of all kinds in constant attendance." And life elsewhere was pretty much the same in tempo, whether he was seeing more people in the first few months of his office than his predecessors had in a term, or drawing a bead on a grizzly.

On October 23 in 1902, 150,000 miners had gone back to work, and on November 10 Roosevelt went bear hunting in Mississippi. No President has ever enjoyed such a press as the Republican Roosevelt. When cartoonist Berryman's imaginative pen included a Teddy Bear in a caricature of Roosevelt on the bear hunting expedition, the Teddy Bear became a national vogue in American life. It was not only repeated millions of times, but was worked into dialogues on the stage, in small talk, and in jokes everywhere, while toymakers took such advantage of it that it became more common as a child's plaything than the traditional woolly lamb. Thereafter even at presidential conventions a sure way of bringing down the roof was to hoist a giant Teddy Bear up from the rostrum and suspend it in midair over the howling delegates.

Wherever he turned up some incident occurred that made his

audiences giddy with excitement. Speaking from the capital steps in Minnesota during the 1904 campaign, he was flanked by Governor Van Sant, a man filled with warm human juices who abhorred violence, despite gallant service as a Captain in the Civil War. His peaceful nature was legendary. As a young aide hurriedly slipped Prince Albert coats onto Roosevelt and Van Sant after the festivities, a mix-up occurred. Van Sant reached into his pocket, presumably for a scarf, and out came a Colt revolver with a six-inch barrel which he dangled limply while the crowd howled and Roosevelt roared. T.R. was taking no chances with his Secret Service.[7]

In some quarters, however, Roosevelt's forceful intervention in the coal strike, his proposals to Congress for stricter regulation of the trusts, his initiation of the suit to dissolve the Northern Securities Company, and his round-house swings at plutocracy as he raced about the country, were breeding anxiety. Some of his critics, in fact, were spreading the word that his mannerisms denoted a tendency toward the abnormal and that he was dangerous.[8] Certain elements in big business were therefore eager to bring about his retirement. To do so, they turned to Mark Hanna, whom many had been urging to seek the nomination against Roosevelt ever since 1901. But Hanna, "knowing politics better than Wall Street did," knew there was not even a remote possibility of bringing about his own nomination. He listened patiently, but he knew that Roosevelt's popularity was such that he could never wrest the nomination away from him. It is not definitely known that Hanna wanted to be President, though the evidence suggests that he might have. In any case he would have preferred to replace Roosevelt in 1904 with a candidate more in the mold of William McKinley. But if Hanna could not have the nomination himself, he did feel that as national chairman, and with some control still in his hands, he might manage the pre-convention strategy in such a way as to make it appear that he was responsible for Roosevelt's nomination in 1904. In this way he hoped to place Roosevelt under some obligation. At the same time, of course, Hanna was pleased with the way the conservative press was splashing him with editorials and with the attention he was receiving because of a fund raised "to put him over."

Unfortunately for Hanna, the plan was stopped cold, catching him in an embarrassing bind. Lying in wait for a chance to nip his prestige was his long-time local rival, Joseph Benson Foraker, senior Senator from Ohio. And in the spring—May, 1903—Foraker saw just the opportunity to bring Hanna into a head-on collision with Roosevelt under circumstances in which Hanna could only come off as the loser. At the Ohio Republican state convention, scheduled for June,

Foraker proposed that a resolution be introduced declaring the intention of the delegates to support Roosevelt next year. "As our candidate for the Presidency." Immediately Hanna was placed in the position of having to declare his own candidacy or support the resolution. Obviously, he knew he could not become a candidate then and win, and yet to oppose the resolution would not only antagonize Roosevelt but might well cost Hanna his Senate seat when he came up for re-election in 1904. "All the cards were in Foraker's hands," as Mark Sullivan writes, and he played them superbly.

Deeply shaken by the position into which he had been driven, and fearing that to let the resolution pass would strengthen Foraker's grip on Ohio at his expense, Hanna reacted recklessly in a moment of rage. Wiring the President, he said: "THE ISSUE WHICH HAS BEEN FORCED ON ME IN THE MATTER OF OUR STATE CONVENTION THIS YEAR ENDORSING YOU FOR THE REPUBLICAN NOMINATION NEXT YEAR, HAS COME IN A WAY WHICH MAKES IT NECESSARY FOR ME TO OPPOSE SUCH A RESOLUTION. WHEN YOU KNOW ALL THE FACTS I AM SURE YOU WILL APPROVE MY COURSE." Then Hanna suggested to the press in a public interview that Foraker's maneuvering had forced him to take this stand as a matter of principle. His reasoning seemed a mite fuzzy, and so it struck Roosevelt. Already some twenty states had endorsed Roosevelt, and he had no intention of permitting Hanna to find a way out of the trap that Foraker had set. "The time had come to stop shilly-shallying," he decided, "and let Hanna know definitely that I did not intend to assume the position, at least passively, of a suppliant to whom he might give the nomination as a boon." Quickly Roosevelt dispatched a telegram to Hanna forcing the issue: "I HAVE NOT ASKED ANY MAN FOR HIS SUPPORT. I HAVE HAD NOTHING WHATEVER TO DO WITH RAISING THIS ISSUE. INASMUCH AS IT HAS BEEN RAISED, OF COURSE, THOSE WHO FAVOR MY ADMINISTRATION AND MY NOMINATION WILL FAVOR ENDORSING BOTH, AND THOSE WHO DO NOT WILL OPPOSE." With further indecision untenable, Hanna capitulated in the only decent way now open to him, with a wire to the President: "I SHALL NOT OPPOSE THE ENDORSEMENT OF YOUR ADMINISTRATION AND CANDIDACY BY OUR STATE CONVENTION." With this exchange there was no longer any doubt that a shift in power had taken place within the Republican party, leading to complete control by Roosevelt. Increasingly thereafter Roosevelt referred to Hanna in his public pronouncements with "the whole Wall Street crowd." Not quite certain that Hanna, or perhaps his Wall Street allies, had given up all hope of a fight, Roosevelt wrote confidently to a friend in January of 1904 that he was certain he could beat Hanna even if all the Wall Street money was behind him, and that Hanna "would get the majority of

the delegations from no state excepting Ohio. . . ." But this prophecy was never tested, since Hanna died on February 15, 1904, four
months before the convention. Roosevelt's nomination was now a
certainty, and for the first time that a Vice-President had succeeded
to the Presidency in the Republican party he was assured a nomination if he wanted it.

Writing to William Allen White about ways to win over the leaders
of the party for the nomination in 1904, Roosevelt said: "If my
nomination is to come at all, it has to come at the initiative of the
people. I know that this has a rather demagogic sound, but I do not
mean it in a demagogic way. What I mean is that I want it understood that the prime movers in forcing my nomination are men like
you . . . like the farmers, small businessmen and upper class mechanics who are my natural allies—I mean who are naturally against
populism and who sympathize with my appeal for common sense,
courage, and honesty. . . . I want to make it evident that I am
pushed by the professional politicians in response to the pressure
from these kinds of men and not merely on their own initiative."

For the first time in three campaigns there was really no single
pre-convention manager. But Roosevelt characteristically arranged
that the two men now selected to run the actual convention
were men of towering strength, each in his own right. For temporary
chairman he selected Elihu Root, now his Secretary of War, who
would be remembered as the man who introduced the chief-of-staff
structure, giving the United States a new military establishment—
a reform long overdue. And for the permanent chairman, Roosevelt's choice was Joseph G. Cannon—"Uncle Joe," Speaker of the
House—a political powerhouse whose prestige in Congress made him
a mighty important ally.

Meeting in Chicago on June 26, the convention was probably not
nearly so exciting as any of its predecessors for a half-century, so
completely certain was the nomination of Roosevelt. From the outset
the convention was smoothly controlled by leading Senators of the
party, including Lodge, Depew, Gallinger, Fairbanks, Beveridge,
Foraker, Spooner, Dolliver, Platt, Collom, Hopkins, and McComas.
In his keynote address, Elihu Root reviewed the adoption of the
gold standard and dealt at some length with the efforts of the United
States to establish a republic in the Philippines and to salvage the
Monroe Doctrine. If the keynote had a theme which was really the
theme of the whole convention, it might be expressed in one phrase,
wrote Francis E. Luepp in *The Outlook,* and that was "America at
last a citizen of the world." For the most part domestic concerns were
played down in this convention in sharp contrast to the reminders

that the United States had come of age and was taking its rightful part in the community of nations and would henceforth be a power to be reckoned with. Only one scuffle of any consequence developed, and this was over which Republican faction of Wisconsin was to enjoy regular standing in the Republican party—raising a question, incidentally, not settled by the convention but ultimately by the courts.

Moving the nomination of Roosevelt, Frank S. Black of New York pumped up to the summit of his speech for the final peroration —a classic in convention auctioneering:

> He is not conservative if conservative means waiting until it is too late. He is not wise if wisdom is to count a thing a hundred times when once will do. . . . He is no slender flower swaying in the winds, but that heroic fibre which is best nurtured by the mountains and the snow.

What were the thoughts of the delegates as the President was nominated by acclamation? Many—perhaps a great many—would have preferred another candidate. "The bulk of delegates who came to this convention at Chicago came to vote for Roosevelt not because they wished to but because they had to," wrote one commentator. "They would gladly have voted for Hanna had he been living and willing, or for Cannon had he been eligible. After three years of Roosevelt—well, that was almost enough for their taste. They sat in silence when Mr. Knight of California said to the delegates: 'The party needs him more than he needs the party,' and when Mr. Cotton of Minnesota told them: 'The people sent you here and you are to do their bidding.' " [9] Clearly, in an era before Gallup polls, there was no way of telling what the inner convictions of the convention body really were. But there was a gap between the thinking of the delegate leadership and the rank and file of the party, who wildly acclaimed Roosevelt.

For the Vice-Presidency, the convention quickly endorsed Senator Charles W. Fairbanks, the senior Senator from Indiana, by unanimous vote. Conservative, Fairbanks generally followed the urge to "stand pat."

In the platform imperialism was not a factor this time, and the chief points of interest were the planks on the regulation of corporations and trusts. Speaking of combinations of capital and of labor, the platform declared: "Such combinations, when lawfully formed for lawful purposes are alike entitled to the protection of the laws, but both are subject to the laws and neither can be permitted to break them." Some observers declared this plank to be out of harmony with the delegates, the presumption being that the more stand-pat element would have preferred no mention of trust regulations.[10] Actually, of course, the plank did not commit the party to any action. But Roosevelt, animated by the spirit of the party's rank and file, was determined to move ahead.

The platform again upheld the principle of protective tariff, but in a gesture of compromise after the protest of Albert Cummins a year before, the platform eased somewhat its intractable high tariff position of earlier years. On this matter it provided that "rates of duty should be readjusted only when conditions had so changed that the public interest demanded their alteration"—small comfort, perhaps, to the would-be tariff reformers of the Middle West, yet indicative of doubts that would not be silent. At the time, however, even this admission was regarded as something, and to some Western Congressmen it represented a concession.

Not without its humor, the convention enjoyed its chief laughs from its permanent chairman, Uncle Joe. Wielding a gavel "as large as a butcher's mallet with a fair-sized broomstick for a handle," he waved it aloft "like a music master's baton." And, like Hanna, he had some earthy advice upon which delegates could reflect as they scampered home from Chicago. "There is not one of you that raises chickens, as I do," said Uncle Joe, "but what understands that when an old hen comes off the nest with one chicken she does more scratching and makes more noise than the motherly hen that is more fortunate with twenty-three. Our friends the enemy will have the enthusiasm; we will take the votes in November."

Two weeks later, against Bryan's wishes, the Democratic convention nominated the conservative Alton B. Parker, a New York judge, relatively unknown, and as his running mate ex-Senator Henry G. Davis of West Virginia. The Democratic platform blasted Roosevelt for "executive usurpation of legislative and judicial functions," and charged him with conduct in office which was "erratic, sensational, spectacular, and arbitrary."

While Judge Parker unquestionably represented a more conservative approach to economic and social questions than did Roosevelt, the New York *Sun* put it well in speaking for many a business-motivated person when it said: "We prefer the impulsive candidate of the party of conservatives to the conservative candidate of the party which the business interests regard as permanently and dangerously impulsive." Thus the businessmen, large and small, the Morgans, the Harrimans, and the upper-class mechanics and small businessmen that Roosevelt so earnestly desired as followers, fell into line behind the President. Elihu Root himself had made a special trip to New

York before the convention to address the Union League Club, where he told this group in no uncertain terms to stop this nonsensical talk that Roosevelt was not "for" the right people. And he took the hide off some Wall Streeters in pointedly discussing for what sort of people Mr. Roosevelt was "unsafe."

In the 1904 campaign Roosevelt therefore not only had the support of big and little business, but he also stole some of the Democratic thunder and broke up the Democratic monopoly of championship of the underdog. Bryan himself complained that Roosevelt had stolen the lance used by the Great Commoner in the two previous campaigns.

Pridefully Roosevelt pointed to his role in lengthening the arm of the federal government to conserve the nation's resources and to curb monopoly abuse. In foreign affairs Roosevelt could likewise point to large achievements. By offering his "good offices," he successfully intervened to terminate the war between Russia and Japan, and vigorously reminded the Kaiser of the Monroe Doctrine in warning him to steer clear of Venezuela, and he won signal successes in many other areas. In one administration, as John Blum sums it up, "Roosevelt had struck for peace, magnanimously assisted the victims of centuries of Spanish oppression in both hemispheres, twisted the lion's tail, planted Old Glory in two outposts, nourished it elsewhere, and presumably defied the strutting Prince of Wilhelmstrasse, whose fleet so recently had dared to embarrass Dewey's at Manila." [11] Small wonder that the Democrats made little of foreign policy in the campaign of 1904.

Yet Roosevelt, far from taking any chances, not only fretted about what the Democrats might do, but decided to armor-plate his own position a little more securely as he stepped off into the campaign, to discourage any small incipient revolt by the right wing of his own party. To do this he wisely selected George Bruce Cortelyou for chairman of the national committee. It was a shrewd decision, for Cortelyou, formerly McKinley's personal secretary, had stayed in this post under Roosevelt until the Department of Commerce and Labor was created in 1903, when Roosevelt made him Secretary. Wealthy, with unlimited contacts in the business world, Cortelyou had access to the giants who had helped finance the McKinley campaigns of 1896 and 1900, and was an admirable choice in every way. Well familiar with the party organization, Cortelyou operated perhaps too smoothly for some of the party professionals. Yet he was not "a namby-pamby," and while he was not chosen as "an unswerving devotee" there was little danger of his doing what his chief could not approve. Cortelyou not only doubled up in positions but actually functioned as a kind of triple-threat quarterback in this campaign by serving simultaneously as chairman and secretary of the national committee as well as financial manager of the campaign.

Behaving like an expectant father during the campaign, Roosevelt left nothing to chance. "I have been told that there is a little lukewarmness among the Methodists . . ." he wrote to the chairman of the national committee. "Cannot they be got at?" Then he suggested that his old friend the Reverend Ezra Tipple, general secretary of the Methodist Conference, be sent for.

And to an influential Catholic in New York he wrote expressing his own conviction that some day there would be a Catholic President of the United States, recalling in the same letter that he himself had tried to bring this about in 1884. In his appointments, of course, Roosevelt had already put in office Catholics, Methodists, Jews, Negroes, and labor leaders, all of which was repeatedly emphasized with great force during the campaign. So was Pension Order 78, which Roosevelt approved in March, providing lower ages for eligibility for veterans' pensions.

As the canvass progressed, Roosevelt thoroughly enjoyed the organizational side of it, as well as his own participation, and he took a hand in this work with the seriousness of a field marshal plotting the movements of his troops. "I want you particularly to see Dr. Formaneseck," he wrote again to the office of the national committee, "because I feel he could be of immense assistance among the Bohemians, perhaps especially in Illinois." To the national committeeman of Indiana, he wrote: "Colonel Edward G. Hall has been one of our most vigorous and successful workers. He knows the voter of German birth or antecedents as few other men know him. . . . I do not think we can afford to take any chances in Indiana. . . ."

Avoiding factional identification where he could not compromise differences between the warring elements, he stayed clear of Wisconsin until the State Supreme Court decided in October that the La Follette ticket was the legal Republican ticket. Then he jumped in at once, demanding that the conservative elements fall in line, and while this result was never accomplished, the decision leaving the congressional campaign largely in the hands of the Stalwarts and the state-wide contest under the direction of La Follette helped to make the state safe for Roosevelt.

The election returns in, Roosevelt was elated. In an overwhelming tribute, the voters gave the President 7,628,461 votes—a two-and-a-half-million lead over Parker (5,084,000). Roosevelt's slice of the two-party vote was 56.4 percent, Parker's 37.6 percent, with

336 electoral votes going to the President, compared with 140 for Parker. Parker's showing was very poor, for he polled a million fewer votes than Bryan had received in 1896 and 1900, and this time there was an increase of over 400,000 in the Republican vote. Notified of his triumph on election night, Roosevelt said, "I had no idea that there would be such a sweep." To his son Kermit he confided, "I am stunned by the overwhelming victory we have won. . . . This was the day of greatest triumph I have ever had or ever could have, and I was very proud and happy." On election night, however, he also made a pledge which he would later regret. "The wise custom which limits the President to two terms regards the substance and not the form, and under no circumstances will I be a candidate for or accept another nomination."

Telling Mrs. Roosevelt, "I am no longer a political accident," Roosevelt turned at once to the design of a program for Congress. For the moment some of the inharmonious elements within his party seemed within his mastery, a circumstance that gave him much pleasure. Yet after 1904 the rifts within the party would become wider. Just as 1904 rolled to an end, his commissioner of corporations, James R. Garfield, issued a report urging congressional legislation to bring all corporations engaged in interstate transactions under federal regulation. The report, writes George Mowry, sent a shiver "through the nation's business circles." It was "the shower before the storm." And only a month later Roosevelt threw the follow-up punch before Pennsylvania's portals of financial and industrial leadership—the Union League Club of Philadelphia. Speaking before men who had heretofore regarded his messages to Congress as moderate and who had just contributed generously to his campaign, Roosevelt said that business had become so powerful that a broad increase in governmental supervision was imperative. Business, he went on, was now interstate in scope, and no free people could tolerate the private use of "power conferred by vast wealth," without granting to government "the still higher power" of guiding its employment in the national public interest.

The gauntlet down, he busied himself at once with the legislative struggle about to commence.

In watching Roosevelt spar with Congress for advantage, one is reminded of the statement once made by Disraeli in the great nineteenth-century struggle over free trade in England. "Free trade," remarked Disraeli, "is not a principle. It is an expedient." Sensing that there was a goodly number of Republicans, along with independent Democrats, who had "a very strong feeling in favor of what I prefer to call an amendment rather than a revision of the tariff law," Roosevelt said that he felt it "is dangerous to undertake to do anything, but that it is fatal not to undertake it. . . ."

Obviously family differences within the Republican party over the tariff were of real and not imagined significance. In the West the agrarians clamored for a reduction of rates, and elsewhere, such as in Minnesota and Massachusetts, among flour, shoe, and woolen manufacturers, there was sentiment for reciprocity agreements with Canada, which presumably would bring cheaper raw materials and enlarge the export market. With beautiful timing Roosevelt sent a message to Speaker Cannon on November 30, 1904, suggesting that while it was desirable to keep the present tariff law, above all things, there might well be some points that ought to be amended and certain schedules changed. Cannon, the arch-priest of protectionism, was startled by this message, and while he may have pondered about its consequences, Roosevelt had no notion of permitting a collision to develop. "His problem," writes Blum, "was to talk of tariff revision firmly enough to frighten the old guard but gently enough not to alienate them." If, of course, he was able to gain certain modifications, all well and good. But his driving strategy was railroad regulation, and in January, 1905, clarifying his position to a friend, he wrote: "I am having anything but a harmonious time about the tariff and about the interstate commerce. . . . On the interstate commerce business, which I regard as a matter of principle, I shall fight. On the tariff, which I regard as a matter of expediency, I shall endeavor to get the best results I can, but I shall not break with my party." Then with characteristic skill he dropped a note to Cannon two days later: "Stop in here as soon as you can. I care very little for what the newspapers get in the way of passing sensationalism; but I do not want the people of the country to get the idea that there will be any split or clash between you and me on the tariff or anything else."

No clash ever did develop between Roosevelt and his party on the tariff, though there were considerable disappointments in the West. But he did succeed, by adroit maneuvers, in persuading the House to take action on railway regulation. Then he turned to the equally or perhaps more difficult task of getting the Senate to follow a similar course. To describe the infighting that Roosevelt undertook for the bill giving the federal government the power to make railroad rates would, as Mark Sullivan observed, "achieve dramatic unity," for it was one of Roosevelt's greatest legislative struggles. His chief antagonist in this scrap was Senator Foraker of Ohio. Now the man who had aided him in cutting down Hanna delivered 86 speeches against the Hepburn railroad rate bill, calling it revolutionary, contrary to the spirit of our institutions, and finally "a cheat, a humbug, and a fraud." Yet in the end Foraker was the only Republican, and one of just three Senators, who voted against the bill.

Again Roosevelt had triumphed through his impressive ability to lead Congress. And in this success as in others behind and before him, as Blum reminds us, his striking "ability to work within the structure of government, like his facility in managing the party, depended less on his arresting manner than on his appreciation of the institutions that shaped American political life." Like Edmund Burke, who was fond of saying that public life "is a situation of power and energy," Roosevelt delighted in operating within a concourse molded by institutional development. He followed the ground rules, though the measures by which he sometimes managed to steal a base have often come in for criticism. And like Burke, Roosevelt was a firm believer in time—"that great respecter of all change"—as the formidable ally for the battles ahead. Time was not only a respecter of change, but in the political process it meant for Roosevelt the opportunity to recharge the batteries while he scanned the field ahead for the next leadership battle of principle. It was for this reason that he paid such great heed to keeping a factional truce within his party, contriving constantly to reconcile in equilibrium opposing elements in order to gain time for the next assault.

Speeding along the legislative program, Roosevelt's second term produced in 1906 not only the Hepburn act, which incidentally also finally eliminated free railroad passes—a practice long abused as a source of political influence—but also the adoption of the Meat Inspection and Pure Food acts. This law brought all meat sold in interstate commerce under federal supervision and forbade under penalty the sale of "deleterious drugs and patent medicines."

Next year corporations received the additional curb of being forbidden to make campaign contributions in federal elections. In the same year Roosevelt appointed an inland waterways commission to investigate the possibility of relieving some of the freight congestion on the railroads and to study measures for preventing the destructive floods on rivers, particularly the Mississippi. Soon, on the basis of reports from this commission, appropriations began to flow from Congress for the planned development of the nation's rivers and canals and lakes. So energetically did Roosevelt throw himself behind the fight for conservation that Robert La Follette, who mistrusted Roosevelt on so many occasions, paid him the highest tribute for his work in this area when Roosevelt left the presidency in 1909.

Two of the more notable anti-trust prosecutions instituted under Roosevelt were the actions against the sugar trusts and the Standard

Oil Company of Indiana. In 1907 conviction of several officers was obtained in the sugar trust case, and over four million dollars was recovered for fraudulently withheld import duties. The same year the Standard Oil Company of Indiana, a subsidiary of Standard Oil of New Jersey, was prosecuted for making secret rebates on its freight shipments over the Chicago and Alton Railroad. In charge of the prosecution was Frank B. Kellogg of Minnesota, later United States Senator and Secretary of State under Calvin Coolidge. It was a clear indication of the drift of the times that Judge K. M. Landis of the federal district court imposed a fine of $29,240,000 for a total of 1,462 separate offenses. Though this decision was ultimately reversed by the circuit court of appeals, the dramatic character of the criminal prosecution left the great bulk of the nation's citizenry with an unchanged feeling about the defendants' guilt. "Trust-busting" came to be synonymous with the Roosevelt administration. Quite a contrast to the day when the laws to restrain railways and trusts were flagrantly violated, and when Roosevelt could report the rail tycoon Edward H. Harriman as saying "that he could buy a sufficient number of senators and congressmen and state legislators to protect his interests and when necessary he could buy the judiciary."

It was the day of the Square Deal. It was also the day when a growing band of Republicans who were in Congress or holding down state governorships and other public offices were growing restive by the hour, and were hoping to proclaim the Square Deal even more vigorously as the policy of the Republican party. The Liberal Republicans and the Mugwump factions had been largely composed of people who were splitting away from the leadership of Grant and Blaine. Now the term Insurgent was about to join the vocabulary of Republican politics and would be employed with increasing frequency in the immediate years ahead. The "hotbed of Insurgency" was in the agrarian states of Kansas, Nebraska, Minnesota, Wisconsin, and Iowa, and the movement also spilled over into the Dakotas and into Indiana. Distrustful of urbanism, the Insurgents were strongly motivated toward social reform, and in earlier stages Insurgency was vitally connected with railway abuses. By the turn of the century names already beginning to have a familiar ring in this movement were Dolliver of Iowa, Murdock of Kansas, and La Follette of Wisconsin. La Follette, one of the first Insurgent leaders to arrive in the Senate, found himself somewhat alone when he first came to Washington in 1906.

"The money that was expended to defeat La Follette and his wing would, his admirers claim, construct a railroad from California to

Maine," wrote one commentator in 1906. Under La Follette as governor the Wisconsin legislature passed a constitutional amendment providing for an income tax in 1905. Governor Albert Cummins in his campaign for renomination in Iowa also declared in favor of an income tax, while other midwestern figures rapidly surfacing to contest for Republican leadership were calling for similar action. The *North American Review* declared: "The breakup of the Republican party in the middlewest is no mere figure of speech. Actually the Progressives and Conservatives are too far apart, not alone on personalities, but on the vital questions of the hour." [12]

1906 not only brought La Follette to the United States Senate, it also saw the re-election of John A. Johnson as governor of Minnesota, a Democrat in a Republican stronghold who had been elected governor for the first time in the very year that Theodore Roosevelt carried the state by a 161,000 plurality. In North Dakota the revolt against corporations, particularly railroads, was also fully under way, and here the Republican radicals defeated the machine controlled by Senator Kittridge.

What was the tinder for the revolt in the first instance? Where did the responsibility lie? By and large with the railroads and corporations. "Who shall be the master?" asked Cummins, declaring himself for the Republican nomination for governor for the third time in Iowa. "The corporations that are to be regulated, or the people in whose name the regulation is imposed?" In Iowa, a generous share of the Insurgents' revolt could be laid to the efforts of the Chicago, Burlington and Quincy Railroad to control the organization, while in Minnesota similar resentment grew out of the attempts of the Great Northern Railroad to influence Republican party policy.

Insurgency also looked favorably toward tariff reform and the freer flow of trade. So it was, as one writer put it, that the principles of the Insurgents revolved initially around the three R's—reasonable freight regulations, reciprocity, and revision. The movement also took in other matters, like the demand for direct primary elections, which the state of Wisconsin was the first to adopt in 1905.

Gradually the band of Insurgents enlarged. It came to include men like Bristow, Bourne, Dixon, Dolliver, Beveridge, and Cummins of Iowa, who reached the Senate in 1909, after popularizing "The Iowa Idea"—a program calling for regulation of corporations and tariff reduction. For speaking ability perhaps La Follette and Beveridge had few superiors. La Follette was noted for his consummate skill in driving home hard-headed facts in a flamboyant style, and Beveridge for his sheer brilliance of oratory. Slashing out against the abuses of the railroads in a two-and-a-half-hour speech at St. Peter,

Minnesota, La Follette was thrown to the floor by a bolt of lightning striking a tree outside of the auditorium just as he reached the climax of his speech. Stunned and a bit dazed for the moment, he rose to his feet, shaking his fist at the sky, saying, "Even the Gods agree." Self-reliant and courageous, La Follette was intolerant of compromise, and this intolerance often drove him too far in opposing constructive compromise—a characteristic which may well have prevented La Follette from ever becoming a presidential nominee of his party.

It was a distinguished group that came to be identified with the Insurgency, including men of many different temperaments and abilities. Moses E. Clapp—the Black Eagle—of Minnesota personified the more easy-going Insurgent who often straightened out matters when the Insurgents fell to quarreling amongst themselves. Most of these men had distinguished themselves in significant ways before they came to the Senate. Clapp was an eminent Attorney General of Minnesota, while Bristow of Kansas had done a stem-winding job of cleaning out Post Office department fraud as Fourth Assistant Postmaster General under McKinley, and later served Roosevelt admirably as commissioner of the Panama Railroad.

Critical though some of them occasionally were of Theodore Roosevelt, most of them never went so far as La Follette, who said in his autobiography:

> Roosevelt's most savage assault on special interests was invariably offset with an equally drastic attack upon those who were seeking to reform abuses . . . demagogues and dangerous persons. In this way he sought to win approval both from the Radicals and Conservatives. This cannonading first in one direction, then in another, filled the air with noise and smoke which confused and obscured the line of action, but when the battle cloud drifted by and quiet was restored, it was always a matter of surprise that so little had been accomplished.

Because this description is exact, writes Herbert Agar, this is how "Roosevelt held together his extraordinary personal following and gave his country rest from too-great anxiety during a time of transition. 'When the battle cloud drifted by,' one thing at least had been 'accomplished': the nation was not divided into irreconcilable classes or regions." [13]

It was Roosevelt who provided the real flint and steel for the Insurgent movement, "combining in equal proportions the attributes of St. Paul and St. Vitus," as Lord Morely states it. He dramatized the issues of railroad regulation, trust-busting and conservation, all of which were later swept up as a part of the Insurgent program. But

Roosevelt was also much more than the flint and steel of the Insurgent movement. For while the din of industrial strife was growing
louder, it was the great genius of this man to make the moderate
reforms of the Square Deal "acceptable to a solid majority." No
President has done it better. In the midst of the reform movement
in the nation's economic and political machine, Roosevelt did not get
carried away to seek revolutionary change, but rather by adjustments and improvements he sought "to make it run better without
skipping a beat." Roosevelt labored hopefully in the tradition of what
Frederick Lewis Allen describes as our "basic principle of unrevolu-
tionary and unsystematic and experimental change. . . ." [14] Years
later—1919—while planning for his nomination in 1920, Roosevelt
re-sounded his political creed in his noblest conception: "I wish to do
everything in my power," he said, "to make the Republican party the
party of sane, conceptive radicalism. . . ." He wished further, he
added, to avoid "merely . . . criticism, delay in reaction . . ." and
to prepare a liberal platform "satisfactory to conscientious, practical
and courageous men. . . ."

Roosevelt saw clearly, as he stated with ringing emphasis time
and again, that "the corporation has come to stay, just as the trade
union has come to stay," to which he always added, "and both must
bow to the popular will." It was his belief that in our own unsystematic way of patchwork revisions of our political and economic system
we evolve our way not toward socialism but past socialism—a destiny well within our grasp.

Roosevelt "deprecates any suggestion that he had genius" writes
Hagedorn, attempting to convey something of the personal magnetism
of T.R.

> But his ardor was beyond the ardor of other men; the intensity, the
> glow, of his living, the fervor of his caring, were, indeed, a form of
> genius, and one that was rare in his country's history. Men felt it in
> him as they felt first love, or the birth of a first child or the first
> challenge of death, and went from his presence with a sense that
> their lips had been touched with the burning coal and they had be-
> come capable of doing what they had not dreamed they could do.[15]

That Roosevelt left a splendid record as President, both in
achievement and in inspired leadership for a changing order, is there
for all men to see despite his shortcomings and his failings. That he
would run amok and wreck the party he loved so dearly, because of
an uncontrollable desire to rule, is another story.

The Lost Moose

It has been quite a spell—almost a half-century—since the Chicago convention of 1912, which, as Mr. Dooley confidently predicted, turned out to be "a combination iv th' Chicago fire, St. Bartholomew's massacre, the battle iv th' Boyne, the life iv Jesse James, and th' night iv th' big wind."

No convention was ever quite like it. "The stormiest in our history," declared Senator Lodge in a eulogy of his lifelong friend, Colonel Roosevelt.

How this collision of two huge monolithic factions shaped up is one of the great dramas of Republican party history—a drama filled with passions and principle, crumbled friendships, tragedy and triumph. It is a salty story, one that still stirs the memories of those who participated and either stayed with Taft—the amiable island—or marched out to the tune of "Onward, Christian Soldiers" to stand with Roosevelt a mile away at Armageddon.

"Of course I would have liked to have stayed on as President—any strong man would," wrote Theodore Roosevelt six days after he had seen William Howard Taft inaugurated as his successor. "But I am more than contented to be back in Sagamore Hill." Within two months Roosevelt was hunting in East Africa, in the territory we now know as the Mau-Mau country, flashing back the word: "I am absolutely contented. I haven't thought of politics since I left New York."

The statement of course was absurd. For a man with the cut of Roosevelt's jib had obviously been thinking of politics every time he drew a bead on a hippo. His passion for politics was matched by few, and his great love of the craft made him excel in it.

Theodore Roosevelt and William Howard Taft began their friendship back in 1890 when they both occupied subordinate government posts in Washington. Roosevelt at the time was a civil service commissioner, and Taft Solicitor General of the United States. As the years passed this friendship ripened, and after Roosevelt became

President he offered Taft an appointment on the Supreme Court while the latter was Governor General of the Philippines (an appointment he had accepted from President McKinley). Even after Taft declined Roosevelt persisted, writing: "Dear Will: I am sorry, old man, but . . . I shall have to put you on the Supreme Court. I am very sorry. But, after all, old fellow, if you will permit me to say so, I am President and see the whole field. . . ." Again Taft refused, though he found it difficult to turn the President down. But in 1904 he did accept appointment from Roosevelt as Secretary of War, and back in Washington the two men caught up their friendship with great gusto, after a separation of many years.

"Roosevelt," remarked Mark Sullivan, "loved Taft and admired him extravagantly—admired him to a degree that almost reached a kind of generous envy." Though Roosevelt always felt Taft should go on the Supreme Court and again urged him to accept an appointment in 1906, he also thought of Taft for the Presidency. And Taft, turning down his second chance to go on the Court because he felt his appointment to the Philippines "imposed something in the nature of a trust to me personally," always made it clear to his friends that he preferred the Court to the Presidency. "Never," wrote Mrs. Taft, "did he cease to regard a Supreme Court appointment as vastly more desirable than the presidency."

Why did Taft not accept an appointment to the Court instead of permitting himself to be drawn into the presidential race? Here the answer seems to lie with Taft's family, and certain intimate friends who thought him highly capable of fulfilling the Presidency. So "out of the conflict between his heart's desire and the worthy ambition of those close and dear to him," Taft made a formal statement in the fall of 1906 that brought him into the presidential race. Though there was some chance that the popularity of New York's governor, Hughes, might bring him to the front as convention time drew near, it was quite obvious that Taft would be nominated with the enthusiastic blessings of Theodore Roosevelt, who was determined to install him as his successor.

Meeting in Chicago on June 16, 1908, the fourteenth Republican national convention was called together by Harry S. New of Indiana, chairman of the national committee, successor to George B. Cortelyou when the latter resigned to become Roosevelt's Postmaster General. (Cortelyou became Secretary of the Treasury in 1907 with the retirement of Leslie M. Shaw of Iowa.) But it was Henry Cabot Lodge, the permanent chairman, who turned the hall into a tornado just as he began to speak. Touched off by Lodge's reference to Roosevelt: "He is the most abused and most popular man in the United States today," the hall exploded with a roar and for forty-seven minutes the convention cheered, clapped, stamped, whistled, and howled, while delegates beat umbrellas and canes against the floor, chairs, and gallery rails. Thirty minutes after the demonstration began a giant Teddy Bear was hoisted to the platform, surrounded by chats of "Four, Four, Four Years More," and when the tumult finally died down the demonstration had surpassed the record set after Bryan's cross-of-gold speech of 1896.

Whether Lodge actually held a letter from Roosevelt in his pocket at the time he spoke that would have put a stop to any move for a third-term nomination is uncertain. But he did say, after the delegates permitted him to continue, that the President was determined to retire on "the fourth of March next. His refusal of a renomination, dictated by the loftiest motives and by a noble loyalty to American tradition, is final and irrecoverable. Anyone who attempts to use his name as a candidate for the presidency impugns both his sincerity and his good faith, two of the President's greatest and most conspicuous qualities, upon which no shadow has ever been cast."

On the third day of the convention, an oppressive heat wave with a rising humidity accompanied by "disgusting coal smoke and cinders," heated up tempers as the resolutions committee got ready to submit its report. Again the issue was the submission of a minority report from Wisconsin embodying several proposals of the La Follette Republican faction, calling for the direct election of Senators, physical valuation of railroads, and publicity for campaign expenditures. That the chairman of the resolutions committee was pretty exercised over the minority report is shown by his question to the convention: "Will you stand by the report of the majority, or will you take the socialist democratic utterances of Wisconsin?" None of the minority proposals was adopted, but the one calling for direct election of Senators did receive 113 votes.

Several favorite sons were placed before the convention—Speaker Cannon, Robert La Follette, Charles W. Fairbanks of Indiana, and Charles Evans Hughes of New York. But as anticipated, Taft went over the top with a bang on the first ballot, rolling in 702 votes (necessary to nominate, 490), and his nomination was immediately made unanimous. By a curious coincidence it was just as the clerk called for the vote of the Ohio delegation that Taft passed the number of votes necessary to nominate, so his native state actually had the honor of nominating its own candidate. Taft's manager, Frank Hitchcock, also made something of a mark for convention prophecy when Taft received only one less vote than Hitchcock, a week before, had predicted he would receive, and the loss of that vote could be accounted for by an absent delegate.

Several names were mentioned for the Vice-Presidency—including Dolliver and Cummins of Iowa and Kellogg of Minnesota. But James S. Sherman of New York, a representative of the stand-pat wing, quickly became the favorite and was nominated on the first ballot. Sherman, from upstate New York, had represented the Utica district in Congress for twenty years.

Out in Denver two weeks later at the Democratic national convention, Bryan, the "peerless leader," climbed to the rostrum after two nights without sleep, just as dawn was breaking. His purpose was to second the nomination of Senator Cockrell of Missouri. But when he declared he was returning the commission that the party had twice bestowed upon him, the party responded in a frenzy by recommissioning him for a third try at the Presidency.

As Republican field marshal for the 1908 campaign, Frank H. Hitchcock, the new national chairman, was eminently well equipped. A native of Ohio and a graduate of Harvard, Hitchcock was Cortelyou's assistant when the latter headed the Republican national committee. Moreover, he had also soaked up a few tricks about politics as First Assistant Postmaster General. The kind of man who does things well with both hands, Hitchcock at one time was an assistant biologist in the Department of Agriculture, where he formulated what are known as the Hitchcock regulations for the protection of the seal herds off Alaska.

Silent and secretive,[1] Hitchcock rarely forgot a face, seldom spoke on the record, and developed his own filing-card system for every person who called on him. A great believer in the Hanna strategy of winding up a campaign with a whirlwind finish in September and October, Hitchcock was criticized for letting Bryan get too much of a head start in the summer months. But Hitchcock kept his own counsel despite a batch of critical letters berating his strategy. Looking over the field, he decided that Indiana had the best precinct organization, and selected the precinct polls taken by Hoosier party workers sixty days before elections, then thirty days, and finally a week before, as a model for twenty Western states. Then he mobilized fifty thousand poll takers to canvass five million voters. Moreover, all poll takers were paid, because of Hitchcock's desire to reduce the number of professional salaried orators that were put in the field in previous campaigns. The new national chairman had far greater faith in salaried canvassers than in professional orators, and he preferred to confine speaking to the big batteries.

Both presidential nominees made extended speaking tours. Taft, admonished by Roosevelt, "Hit them hard, old man!" soon caught the fancy of his audiences as he swung his 354-pound frame around the country. Praising the Republican platform that eulogized Roosevelt for combating "the abuse of wealth and the tyranny of power," Taft called for further regulation of trusts and tariff revision. Revision he interpreted as a promise to scale tariff schedules downward. Roosevelt, meanwhile, heaped lavish praise on Taft all during the campaign, and to an English friend he wrote: "Always excepting Washington and Lincoln, I believe that Taft will rank with any other man who has ever been in the White House. He and I view questions exactly alike."

Toward the end of September Wall Street became alarmed that stocks were breaking because of the report that Bryan was roaring across the countryside, carrying everything before him. And now a second flurry of letters reached Taft and Roosevelt urging that Hitchcock be jettisoned. But the fears from the financial centers proved groundless, for on Election Day Taft won handily, though not so impressively as Roosevelt. He carried 321 electoral votes to 162 for Bryan. In popular figures, the distribution was 7,679,000, or 51.6 percent, for Taft, and 6,409,000, or 43.0 percent, for Bryan. Taft was weaker than Roosevelt had been in the Middle Atlantic and North Central regions, though stronger in the South and far West. Interestingly, he was much weaker in his own native state of Ohio and in Pennsylvania than Roosevelt had been four years earlier.

Outside of the South Taft lost to Bryan in only four states: Oklahoma, Nebraska, Colorado, and Nevada, and even here Bryan's margin of victory was only 19,000. Three-fifths of the Taft electoral vote actually came from states west of the Alleghenies. "Yet within a year, no statement was more generally accepted than that the 'West' was the enemy's country. In that it was opposed to the leadership of the dominant faction of the Republican organization and dissatisfied with the Taft administration." [2]

Trouble-time for Taft arrived with the opening of the Sixty-first Congress on March 15, 1909. Roosevelt, it will be remembered, in the interest of winning other legislative battles, allowed tariff revision to sideslip, thus reviving the criticism that, while he had proclaimed himself as a convinced free-trader in his biography of Thomas Hart Benton, he had not lived up to it. And now the new Congress, summoned to consider tariff revision, was under heavy pressure from the Middle West to pare down the tariff rates of the Dingley act of 1897, long believed to be an important factor in the rising cost of living. Complicating the bitter intra-party struggle about to begin over this issue was the equally explosive subject of Speaker Cannon's re-election. Insurgent opposition to Cannon had been a major cause of Republican patches of discontent in the West, a fact Taft himself recognized in a letter he wrote to William Allen White. "Very early in the campaign," said Taft, "I thought of encouraging a movement to beat Cannon, but I found that he was so strongly entrenched . . . that it was impossible."

Unhappily for Taft, he became involved in the struggle to dethrone the Speaker in a way that incensed the growing band of Insurgents now in open revolt against Cannonism. Actually Taft could ill afford a knock-down drag-out fight with the "Dry Smoking" Speaker, who chewed cigars into tobacco strips and was equally at home on the stump or behind the Speaker's rostrum, where he ruled the House with an iron fist. But it was Taft's unfortunate lot to say a kind word about the Speaker just at a time when prudence should have suggested either silence on his part or a more adroit comment. Taken up by the newspapers, Taft's statement that the Speaker had promised to assist him loyally in carrying out the pledges of the Chicago platform soured relations between the President and the Insurgents at once. Believing almost to the end that Taft was their ally and would ultimately throw his prestige of office and patronage powers behind them, the Insurgents became embittered over what they felt was the President's desertion—a blow from which Taft never recovered.[3]

That Taft never really changed his mind about Cannon, however, is apparent from a letter he wrote to Philander Knox late in 1909. Here he reaffirmed his belief that Cannon ought to announce his retirement in advance of the next general election. "The American people are decent, clean, pure minded people as a whole, and they do not approve of vulgarity and blackguardism in daily conversation for publication of their public men; and Cannon has driven from him by this characteristic, many who would support his general policies, and has made many doubt his sincerity of purpose and his patriotic devotion to duty. . . ." Obviously the Speaker's way with stories conveying "an outhouse odor" displeased William Howard Taft. Nor did Taft's sense of equity and fair play permit him to accept the concentration of autocratic powers which the Speaker had drawn to himself through control of the House rules.

In the end twelve Republicans from the Middle West and one from the West voted against Cannon—not enough to defeat him, yet sufficient to record a warning. But thirty-one Republicans from the Middle West and West were able to defeat a motion to adopt the former rules of the House, which, of course, Cannon passionately desired. The day for the complete overthrow of the Speaker was not yet at hand, but a beachhead had been established by defeat of the motion to readopt the former rules. When the re-elected Speaker announced the appointment of new committees, the tempers of Insurgents shot up again. Of the 61 House committees, chairmanships for 44 of the most important committees had been given to the Representatives from eight states. Pennsylvania had ten and Illinois (Cannon's home state) seven, followed by New York and Massachusetts with six each. Representatives from twenty-five states were given no chairmanships, and of this group sixteen were thoroughly Republican states with a total of 52 Representatives, 30 of whom were men with more than one term's experience. In the face of this treatment, the Insurgents kept their disgust fresh.

Meanwhile, as Congress pushed on with legislative business, Taft was able to swing certain revisions for lower tariff rates through passage of the Payne bill in the House. But in the Senate the high-tariff advocates, led by Nelson Aldrich, chopped the Payne bill to pieces by adding 847 amendments, undoing most of the reductions proposed by the lower house. And when the bill finally emerged as the Payne-Aldrich bill, and was signed by Taft on August 5, 1909, it left the nation with "a tariff wall . . . a very little higher rather than a very little lower."

To critics who denounced this deviation from the platform, Senator Aldrich rejoined that the platform pledge for "revision" did not necessarily mean downward—an argument promptly scalded by Republican Insurgents. Now for the first time the Insurgents in the Senate were able to mount an attack of sharp striking power. Led by La Follette, and joined by Dolliver, Beveridge, Cummins, Bristow, Knute Nelson of Minnesota, Crawford of South Dakota, and Brown of Nebraska, the Insurgents embarked on one of the hardest-fought legislative struggles in the annals of the Senate.

And then Taft stirred up the Insurgents even more by flipping out a word of praise for the hated Aldrich. He praised the Rhode Islander as an able statesman and the "real leader of the Senate," and then went on to pay tribute to the Aldrich plan for the establishment of a central bank—a proposal which already had the Middle West seething against its author. " 'Leader of the Senate'—we will jar that myth in the next few years," wrote the ailing Dolliver to his friend and Senate colleague Beveridge. "Wait for the results my boy. . . . With Pinchot knocked out and Aldrich put in command I think you can hear a lion roar in East Africa." And if you couldn't it wouldn't take long.

For, three days later, on September 17, 1909, at Winona, Minnesota, beside Lake Pepin, Taft squeezed the trigger against the Progressives by describing the new law as the "best tariff bill that the Republican party has ever passed and therefore the best tariff bill that has ever passed at all." That did it! From that moment on Taft was thought of as irrevocably aligned with the forces of reaction. The Winona speech also had one other important result: "It started the 'back from Elba' movement for the reelection of Roosevelt in 1912." More than one prominent Republican Progressive announced he would look to Africa for the next GOP nominee.[4]

And Taft was soon seared with another hot iron. In the summer of 1909 Gifford Pinchot, head of the Division of Forestry, had denounced his superior, Secretary of Interior Ballinger, for failure to put more zeal into the federal protection of water-power sites and coal lands. At the same time Pinchot accused his chief of secretly conniving with special-interest groups bent on plundering the public domain. Taft, convinced that the Pinchot charges were both unfounded and unfair, fired him for insubordination in January of 1910. Everyone agreed that under the circumstances he had no choice except to dismiss Pinchot, but the incident brought a head-on crash between the conservative and Roosevelt wings of the party.

Pinchot was a Roosevelt intimate, and no subject touched the lips of the Progressives more frequently than the conservation of natural resources. To spare the President further embarrassment, Ballinger resigned as Secretary of the Interior, but the damage was already done, and there was no way of relieving the situation. Pinchot raced off to Italy to join Roosevelt upon his return from the African safari and gave him a first-hand report on what the Progressives now believed was a turnabout on the home front. Meanwhile, as the Insurgents were beginning to rally around Roosevelt and longed for his return, the Republican regulars were moving in closer to Taft.

Soon after the Ballinger-Pinchot controversy, the word spread— untrue, of course—that the President was not only "unconcerned" about upholding the conservation policies started by Roosevelt, "but that he was willing that the natural resources of the nation should fall again into the hands of greedy private corporations." [5] Such an assumption was obviously false, and Ballinger was later exonerated by public investigation. But during the interim a cloud hung over Taft's reputation for at least two years.

By March of 1910 the Insurgents were ready to turn out in full fighting force to finish the job they had set out to do a year earlier. On March 19, the Insurgents rallied 42 Republicans to join with the Democrats in passing a resolution stripping the Speaker of the House of most of his personal power.

Not only had the Speaker come to appoint all committees through the course of the years, but by his domination of the rules committee he was also able to restrict debate and call the signals for the entire legislative process. Aroused at the stand-pattism of Cannon in blocking progressive legislation, and upset at the exercise of his unusually broad prerogatives, the Insurgents with George W. Norris at their head now sounded the tocsin of revolt that would shake Republican voting habits drastically that fall. Along with fellow Insurgents Victor Murdock, John M. Nelson, Miles Poindexter, and Charles A. Lindbergh, Sr., Norris managed to trim the Speaker's powers so that while Cannon was not removed from office he no longer could appoint the rules committee or be one of its members. And the Democrats carried the change a step further the following year, when they won control of the House, by making all committees elective.

Cannonism was a subject that bordered on incitement to riot as the Republican party began to pull apart. How deeply some Insurgents were upset by it is well expressed by the fact that Senator Norris's brief autobiography in *Who's Who in America* included the line: "Led fight in Ho. of Rep. which overthrew 'Cannonism.'"

By June 18, 1910, the day Roosevelt returned to New York from the jungles of Africa and the capitals of Europe, he was well acquainted with the factional fires now raging within the Republican party. But he soon discovered that he stood in a changed relationship to the party leaders. In New York, where the governor, Charles Evans Hughes, struggled against elements of a Republican machine that were conducting a fierce fight against his bill for primary elections, Hughes begged Roosevelt as a patriotic "boss-hating" citizen to help him. Roosevelt at once dispatched a telegram to Albany urging Republicans to back Hughes. But Roosevelt's influence with this group was no longer formidable, for now that he was out of office they no longer feared him.

Aware that the political football, like the gridiron pigskin, sometimes takes some queer bounces, even the old-time Republican professionals were not quite prepared for the complete deterioration of the friendship between Roosevelt and Taft during the summer of 1910. Some of Roosevelt's friends tried to prick him with exaggerated tales to serve their own ends; they complained to him on his return that both his friends and family had been treated cavalierly by the White House, and they soon had him believing it. Even more easily exploited was the story that Taft's half-brother Charles was openly attacking Roosevelt in the Cincinnati *Times Star*. But what incensed the Colonel above all was the incontrovertible fact that Taft was breaking his pre-election promises by working in harness with Aldrich and Cannon rather than with Beveridge and Dolliver.[6]

Taft, watching developments and posted by his own lookouts, did not take kindly to the Colonel's behavior either. Getting madder by the hour, he sent an "ultimatum" to Roosevelt in July through Lloyd Griscom. What Taft proposed was that in return for Roosevelt's unequivocal endorsement the President agreed to dump Cannon and Aldrich as advisers and to give Roosevelt a counselor's voice in the administration. This tender, of course, was immediately rejected by Roosevelt, and the relations of these two men as well as the fortunes of the party hastened toward ruin.

The elections that fall ended the complete control of the national government which the Republican party had held for fourteen years. Gradually during this period, as enormous aggregations of capital assumed greater control over natural resources and the means of transportation, the Republican party, following popular demand, embarked on a policy of stricter control of industrial development. And it was from the Western political leaders that the greatest pressure came for more adequate control over corporate power. Moreover, the new alignments within the Republican party first appeared in the states of the Mississippi Valley.

For almost a decade of this fourteen-year power span, the Insurgency that had been needling the stand-pat element of the Republican party did not acquire sufficient strength to assume dominant control of the Republican national organization. And Roosevelt's leadership, perhaps because he sensed the urgency of Western protests and was able to secure some of their demands, may have postponed an earlier serious clash between the Insurgents and the more stand-pat elements of Eastern Republicanism. But the 1906 election demonstrated that Insurgency was climbing, and by the fall of 1910 the high tide was reached. Thereafter the act of fission which finally took place in 1912 looked ominously near.

Even in Vermont, where the off-year Republican plurality rarely fell below 20,000, pluralities in elections for governor, legislature, and two Republican Congressmen were reduced to around 17,000 in the mid-September elections of 1910. The decline was attributed to the high cost of living, part of which was blamed upon the tariff.

Close by in the neighboring state of New Hampshire, the regular Republican machine met with disaster. There Colonel Bertram Ellis, Republican candidate for governor, backed by the powerful railway organization, long a dominant force in New Hampshire politics, was defeated by state senator Robert Perkins Bass, an energetic Republican Progressive who campaigned for more equitable taxation. In California, where the first Republican convention was held under the new primary law, the meeting was overwhelmingly dominated by Progressive Republicans; while in Michigan Senator Burroughs, long noted for his bony stand-pattism among Republican regulars, was defeated by Congressman Townsend, another Progressive.

The ascendancy of the Progressive tide in 1910 also brought a heady victory in Wisconsin. La Follette, up for re-election, encountered the concentrated opposition of the national Republican organization. But his Progressive allies accepted the challenge by entering the Wisconsin campaign and turning the state into a battlefield upon which the eyes of the nation were focused. Here also the result was an overwhelming victory for La Follette, coming at a time when it could only be interpreted as something of a broad sectional endorsement of this pioneer of Insurgency.

The shooting over, the Republican party wound up in the Senate with 10 fewer seats in the Sixty-second Congress than it had in the Sixty-first, and it lost control of the House by dropping 57 seats, a tidy gain for the Democrats. For progressive Republicanism won an all but complete shutout over the President. By the end of September, 41 incumbent GOP Congressmen had been defeated, and of this group only one, Charles N. Fowler of New Jersey, could be called an Insurgent. But the great bulk of the remaining 40 defeated incumbents were upset by acknowledged progressives.

And in the Senate the progressive parade grew apace. All Republican Insurgents were returned, and new reinforcements were added with the arrival of Miles Poindexter of Washington, John D. Works of California, and Asle J. Gronna of North Dakota.

Stepping aside in 1911 as the Insurgents arrived to replace them, many Republican lame duck Congressmen wore thin smiles and wondered about the next round. At least one man felt certain of the outcome. The party was so badly split, said Roosevelt, that it would go down to defeat in 1912.

In the state elections, the party also hit serious trouble. Republican rule was abruptly broken in New Jersey when Woodrow Wilson moved from the presidency of Princeton University to the governor's chair at Trenton. And in other parts of the nation state after state elected progressive governors committed to driving through their legislatures tax and regulatory measures controlling corporations.

Moving quickly to quell some of the revolt within his party in the winter of 1911, Taft asked Congress for a reciprocity agreement with Canada, calling for a reduction or an abolition of duties on many Canadian foodstuffs and raw materials, in return for similar concessions on American farm machinery and other commodities. Since this measure did not affect Eastern manufacturers, Republicans from the Atlantic Seaboard were willing to go along with Taft. But in the Midwest and Far West, the farming and lumbering interests looked askance at the possibility of Canadian competition. And the Democrats exploited this Republican breach by helping the President carry through the tariff revision toward the close of the special session which Taft had called for this specific purpose. In consequence Taft won little favor for his efforts with the Canadian reciprocity bill. The real clamor for revision had been general in nature, and by failure to redeem the party pledge of 1908 with the Payne-Aldrich bill, Republican congressional leadership paved the way for the debacle of the 1910 midterm elections. A genuine revision of the tariff in any case might have lifted the tariff question out of politics and spared the Republicans their crushing defeat of 1910. Moreover, had Taft "tried one-tenth as hard to secure real tariff revision in the special session of 1909 as he tried to force his Canadian tariff bill through the special session of 1911," he probably would have succeeded. But even his failure to bring about a downward revision of the tariff, while damaging to Taft, might not have cost him so dearly in party prestige if it were not for a fatal miscalculation on his role in the midterm elections of 1910.

Proclaiming the Payne-Aldrich tariff act to the voters as most satisfactory, Taft used the power of the presidential office to punish the Republican Senators and Congressmen who had worked for tariff revision. Even Senator Dolliver, who had been stumping for the Republican party since he was 21 years old, and at Taft's own request was one of two men who bore the heaviest brunt of the speaking engagements in Taft's 1908 campaign, was singled out in the Taft purge of 1910. Neither Dolliver nor other Insurgent Senators had opposed the President on other matters. Nor had they criticized him for signing the measure. But for voting against the Payne-Aldrich bill on final passage, the President together with members of his cabinet decided to try and read them out of the party and secure their defeat. Like Franklin D. Roosevelt's attempted purge much later in American political history, the Taft try in 1910 was unsuccessful. For Taft, it meant one more demerit stripe on the record of his presidential leadership.

Notwithstanding his misguided leadership and the throbbing revolt that mounted against his administration, Taft actually accomplished several constructive reform measures in a "quiet untheatrical way." "A conservative by temperament, he found it impossible to resist the liberal spirit of his day, and the statute book of his administration actually recorded greater victories for progressivism than had

been won in the seven years of his predecessor, the first Roosevelt." [7]
In 1910 Congress passed the Mann-Elkins act, putting sharper teeth
into the Interstate Commerce law by extending the commission's
authority to cable, telegraph, and telephone companies. During 1909,
in response to a recommendation from Taft, Congress also tackled the
problem of campaign expenditures. The result was a law enacted in
1910 requiring political committees and candidates for Congress to
file their campaign receipts and expenditures with a public officer. This
measure, subsequently amended and extended, still stands as a basis
of Federal corrupt-practices legislation. (In 1911 an amendment extended the law to cover primary expenditures and to limit the amount
of expenditures.) Under Taft's leadership Congress also enlarged the
scope of federal activity in conservation by providing for the purchase
of forest lands surrounding the headwaters of navigable streams in
certain eastern areas of the United States.

During the last year of the Taft administration a Children's Bureau and a new Department of Labor were created, and before he
left office two important constitutional amendments were launched.
The first—the Sixteenth Amendment—submitted to the states at
Taft's suggestion in 1909, was a proposal to empower Congress to
levy an income tax without the requirement of apportionment among
the several states according to population. Settling controversy that
had existed since the Supreme Court decision of 1895 denying the
constitutionality of a statutory income tax, the Sixteenth Amendment
finally established the authority of the federal government to levy an
income tax. It was ratified shortly before Taft left office in 1913.
The second important amendment initiated under Taft was the seventeenth Amendment, proposed by Congress in 1912. This called for
the direct election of Senators by popular vote instead of leaving the
choice to state legislatures, and was ratified just three months after
Taft left office.

Because he lacked Roosevelt's dramatic qualities, many of Taft's
solidly constructive contributions were obscured from the popular
view. Easily forgotten is the trust-busting work of the Taft administration. Under the leadership of the able Attorney General George W.
Wickenham, almost twice as many prosecutions were conducted
against business consolidations as had been instituted during the
Roosevelt regime. But, as one commentator put it, "the great prestige
of Roosevelt, which he gained by being the first to grapple with the
great monopolies, could not be shared by any successor of his who
simply carried on the work of trust-busting." And by midterm, no
doubt, Taft must have looked back sadly upon some of those joyously

engaging evenings he had spent with his predecessor, and remembered the night when Roosevelt sank back into an easy chair after a White House dinner with the Tafts, closed his eyes, and said:

> "I am the seventh son of a seventh daughter and I have clairvoyant powers. I see a man weighing 350 pounds. There is something hanging over his head but I cannot make out what it is. . . . At one time it looks like the presidency, then again it looks like the Chief Justiceship."
> "Make it the presidency," said Mrs. Taft.
> "Make it the Chief Justiceship," said Mr. Taft.[8]

Bucking biting headwinds, Taft had little if any peace after 1910. On January 21, 1911, the National Progressive Republican League was organized in Washington, D.C.[9] Bypassing economics, the Progressive League's statement of principles started off by declaring its intention of restoring the Republican party to the people, then advocated the direct election of United States Senators, direct primaries for all elective offices, direct election of delegates to national conventions, and the submission of a constitutional amendment for the initiative, referendum, and recall. Obviously a political casing was beginning to form that would lift the factional differences in the Republican party from a sectional to a national level.

Beginning in July of 1911, several Insurgents who had been urging La Follette to become a candidate for President started an active campaign on his behalf, and on October 16 300 delegates organized a Progressive Republican convention in Chicago to endorse La Follette's candidacy. No published list of delegates is available, but it was generally acknowledged that, of the two committees set up by this convention, three-fourths of the membership came from the West.

While La Follette held a strong appeal for many Insurgents of the West, the Roosevelt charism was still casting its spell. And now he was entreated by hundreds of old friends to snap back into the fight. "I am not and shall not be a candidate for President," he was saying in the summer of 1910. But by the time the Republican national convention of 1912 was ready to meet, he was saying Taft was "useless to the people." [10]

La Follette, on the other hand, carried on an aggressive campaign. But he gradually became discouraged because he felt Roosevelt was using him as a stalking-horse, and in a sense La Follette was correct. For as he worked over the trans-Mississippi country and elsewhere, winning converts to the Progressive Republican cause and helping build an organization, there were more than a few hints from Oyster

Bay that Roosevelt might later come along to reap the benefits of this important preliminary skirmishing and wrest the nomination from La Follette by popular demand.

Tired and distraught over the illness of his daughter, and discouraged by the duplicity he sensed in Roosevelt's conduct, La Follette suddenly terminated his candidacy on February 2 because of what the press reported as a physical and nervous breakdown. Speaking at Philadelphia before an audience of several hundred leading magazine publishers, writers, and newspaper correspondents, La Follette created a bad impression by re-reading and stumbling over parts of his speech. His wife and daughter have called reports of his collapse exaggerated, but in any case newspapers captioned their headlines to suggest that La Follette had collapsed and that his presidential campaign was through.[11]

However embroidered newspaper reports of La Follette's collapse may have been, his candidacy was not taken seriously after this event. But La Follette did not withdraw in favor of Roosevelt, as alleged in some quarters; on the contrary, he felt that he had been given a fast shuffle in the preliminary presidential sweepstakes.

That very month Roosevelt's candidacy began to soar. Even before the La Follette speech of February 2, a Roosevelt Republican national committee had been set up in Chicago (January 31), and the president of this organization, Alexander H. Revell, hastily fired the next cartridge. He called a meeting for February 10 at Oyster Bay, predicting that Roosevelt "will respond to a sense of duty." Attended by governors from eight states,[12] this meeting adopted a resolution calling upon Roosevelt to run and T.R. himself, off to Columbus, Ohio, for an address before the constitutional convention of Ohio on the 21st of February, let the cat out of the bag. In a carefully contrived slip he told a reporter, "My hat is in the ring."

Squaring away for battle, the Roosevelt forces immediately organized to enter their candidate in the presidential primaries, which Roosevelt soon carried in a sweep all the way from New England to the Pacific coast. In the thirteen preferential primary states Roosevelt won 270 delegates to 68 for Taft. In three, Pennsylvania, Illinois, and California, representing the East, Middle West, and Far West, Roosevelt carried the primaries overwhelmingly. And in Minnesota, where the Taft people claimed victory to the very end, the Roosevelt sweep was equally decisive. Even in Massachusetts and Maryland, regarded as invincible Taft strongholds, the Taft forces were put to rout. Taft himself thought he might salvage the situation in his native state of Ohio, but here again his case was hopeless when the Ohio primary delivered 34 delegates to Roosevelt, fourteen to Taft.

Initially Taft's pre-convention campaign management was in the hands of his secretary, Charles D. Hilles of New York. But early in February it seemed wise to open campaign headquarters outside of the White House, and Congressman William B. McKinley of Illinois was put in command. This appointment represented a sharp break in tradition, for McKinley was already the chairman of the Republican congressional campaign committee, a post which he continued to retain after he became director of the Taft pre-convention campaign. Obviously it was a highly unusual arrangement to take the head of a general committee, which presumably spoke for the entire party, and simultaneously use him to direct the private campaign of one candidate for the presidential nomination. But these were abnormal political conditions, and they led to an abnormal political convention. In fact, two conventions.

The first—the fifteenth Republican national convention—met at Chicago on June 18. Here in an atmosphere as tense as that of a powder mill, the delegates watched Victor Rosewater of Nebraska, chairman of the national committee and publisher of the Omaha *Bee,* call the meeting to order, and wondered whose prayers would be answered as the chaplain invoked a blessing that "every prayer and every work of ours" be happily ended.

Almost at once, as the duel began between Taft's floor leader Jim Watson of Indiana (also chairman of the credentials committee), and Herbert S. Hadley, governor of Missouri and a Roosevelt supporter, everyone sensed that prickly feeling that history was in the making. The overriding issue, of course, was the seating of the temporary roll, and here the national committee dominated by Taft gave the President an initial edge which Roosevelt could never overcome.

Acting as the first court on the contested delegation cases, the national committee denied Roosevelt at least fifty votes to which he appeared clearly entitled (Governor Hadley claimed 72).[13] What this did to Roosevelt's chances for the nomination can be shown by counting noses on the first convention vote. By a shade more than a bare majority, 558 to 501, the Taft forces succeeded in electing their candidate for temporary chairman, Elihu Root, over the Roosevelt candidate Francis E. McGovern of Wisconsin. Clearly if the national committee had seated the 50-odd delegates to which Roosevelt was entitled, the Colonel could have won the first trial heat and held control of the convention on through adjournment. But the followers of the Rough Rider lost the battle right in the opening hours when Hadley's motion to seat 72 Roosevelt delegates in place of the Taft delegates on the temporary roll submitted by the national committee was defeated on the floor of the convention.

After this setback the outcome was never in doubt. In vain did Hadley cite the precedent of 1864 when Thaddeus Stevens's motion was adopted providing "that all contested cases be laid over and that the delegates from such states shall not be entered on the roll until the credentials shall have been sent to a committee on credentials and reported back." (Missouri sent two delegations in 1864.) And when Jim Watson tried to shake off this precedent by saying that there had been no national committee in 1864, Hadley had him there. For the committee was very much in existence, under the leadership of Edwin Morgan. But it made little difference what was said where the power lines were as tightly drawn as in the 1912 convention.

What happened, of course, was that soon the credentials committee, acting as the second court on seating contests, followed most of the decisions of the national committee, and then reported to the convention separately on each contest. Now as the convention voted to sustain the credentials committee in one case after the other, most involving Southern delegations (283 of Taft's delegates came from 23 hopelessly Democratic states, while 350 Roosevelt delegates came from 25 states normally Republican), "the turbulence and disorder . . . bordered on riot."

The gross malapportionment of convention seats at the 1912 convention, of course, was a direct result of the steady decline of the Republican party in the South during the preceding three decades. This malapportionment alone distorted the representative character of the convention, but it should also be remarked that several presidential primaries in that year confounded the misrepresentation even more.

Soon Roosevelt, long aware that he had been stopped, sent word to the convention from his Congress Hotel headquarters, through Henry J. Allen, that his delegates would not vote on any proposition. And the reasons for his action, he said in a message read by Allen from the rostrum, were that "robbery and fraud" controlled the convention and that it was no longer a Republican convention but an illegal and unofficial body.

Taunted by the word "steal," the Taft supporters kept a stony silence during some of these assaults, barking back sullenly at the worst of them. In the end, as the convention proceeded to the nominating roll call for the Presidency, Roosevelt supporters sat mute while Warren G. Harding placed Taft in nomination. Finally, at 9:28 P.M. five days after the convention first met, William Howard Taft was renominated, with 349 Roosevelt delegates refusing to vote.

Two men, reported on-the-scenes observer Henry L. Stoddard, were responsible for the plan that held a majority of delegates for Taft— William Barnes, national committeeman from New York, and Elihu Root, then a Senator from the Empire state. Barnes—"the acknowl- edged master of thirty out of forty-eight national committeemen"— originated and "piloted in committee the work of unseating enough delegates" to control the convention. And Root, who Roosevelt re- marked always did his best for his clients, "certainly did in that con- vention." In fairness to Root, however, his ruling that delegates whose seats were contested could vote in every case but their own was not without an inherent logic. For to rule otherwise could lay the precedent for disqualifying hundreds of delegates from voting simply because formal contests were instituted against them which were essentially phony proceedings and without basis in fact.

Tactically, the Roosevelt camp committed some minor errors in their floor generalship. "The Roosevelt managers were almost con- stantly in disagreement as to what should be done," observed Hadley. And one of the chief embarrassments was that "our most skillful lead- ers and ablest advisers were not in the convention as delegates." In consequence, "whenever we agreed on a proposition someone would say, 'Borah you take care of that.' But he would reply 'I am not a delegate.' 'Well then let Kellogg handle it.' " [14] But Kellogg was not a delegate either and so the ball rolled from one to the other—to Garfield, Pinchot, and the rest—as each was compelled to sidestep, leaving few available who were familiar with convention procedure. Whether these difficulties made the difference between victory and defeat, however, no one can say.

Losing no momentum after the President's renomination, the Taft forces then renominated James Schoolcraft Sherman for Vice-Presi- dent, with Sherman receiving 595 votes and 352 delegates abstain- ing this time.[15] Now the convention folded into a quick adjournment. It was 10:29, an hour and one minute since Mr. Taft's renomina- tion. But events were already ticking off like a time-bomb at Or- chestra Hall less than a mile away.

While the fifteenth Republican national convention was nominat- ing Taft, Theodore Roosevelt—twenty-sixth President of the United States—declared himself a presidential candidate and announced the formation of a third party. He would, Roosevelt made clear, step aside if this third party genuinely decided upon another candidate, but he left no doubt that he was bristling for the fight. And he was ready with a new war cry. The cardinal principle of the new party, he cried to the faithful gathered at Orchestra Hall, must be: "Thou shalt not steal."

There in the dying hours of the Republican convention, Roosevelt was nominated for President on an independent ticket. No public announcement of the decision to form a third party was made until late in the day (Saturday, June 22), and when the word was finally sent out about the plan to meet at Orchestra Hall police reserves were hastily summoned to handle the huge crowds that gathered at the site on Michigan Boulevard. William Prendergast, Controller of New York, who was to have presented Roosevelt's name at the regular GOP convention, now nominated him as the new party's standard-bearer. Then as telegraph and telephone linesmen rushed frantically about the hall stringing cables and installing wires to flash the word of Roosevelt's nomination across the nation, Governor Johnson of California swung into a two-fisted attack against the leadership of the Republican convention: "A national committee has endeavored to assassinate the Republican party." And that, he maintained, was the principal reason for this meeting—"to erect upon the ruins another party that represents progress."

One reason for the informal nomination of Roosevelt, besides the psychological advantage of playing up the size of the bolt, was to effect a temporary organization. In a sense the representatives of twenty-two states who composed the notification committee to tell Roosevelt of his nomination stood as the sponsors of the new party. And they laid their plans swiftly, for the very next day after Roosevelt was nominated at Orchestra Hall a call went out for a state convention in Illinois and schedules were being drafted to organize the Progressive party state by state for a new national convention.

Six weeks later most of the Roosevelt diehards were back in Chicago once more for a convention described by the New York *Times* as "a Methodist camp meeting done over in political terms."

With the rampant Bull Moose on their victory banners, the delegates gave attention to Senator Beveridge's keynote speech as he reached for a high one: "Knowing the price we must pay, the sacrifices we must make . . . the assaults we must endure . . . we enlist for the war." That started it, but to sharpen the effect, the dignified Beveridge added a little fun of his own by ripping off his collar as a howl went up from the delegates.

The rest was routine. William A. Prendergast again nominated Roosevelt, and the "cross country ticket" was completed with the addition of California's Hiram Johnson as running mate. Then a platform of Progressive principles was drawn up, and the delegates sped away with the charge of the indomitable Roosevelt still ringing in their ears: "To you men and women, who have come together here to spend and be spent in the endless crusade against wrong, I say now . . . We stand at Armageddon and we battle for the Lord."

But to battle for the Lord often takes time, particularly in politics. And only ten weeks remained to organize a national party.

Looking at the platforms of the Republican and Progressive parties, the voter could find a few similarities. Both favored limitation of campaign funds, improvement of inland waterways, establishment of agricultural credit, and conservation of natural resources. Both platforms also paid respect to the principle of protectionism, though the Progressive plank denounced the Payne-Aldrich bill for going beyond what was necessary in protecting industries so that they could pay liberal wages and still compete on equal terms with foreign competitors. But in other areas there were important differences.

The Progressive platform called for a federal commission to regulate trusts and business consolidations, an easier method of amending the federal constitution, a popular referendum for court decisions that invalidated state laws, and woman suffrage. And in a plank called "social and industrial justice," much highlighted during the campaign, the party asked for both national and state laws to promote the health and improve the condition of laborers, to prohibit child labor, and to regulate wages and hours. Another conspicuous plank in the Progressive platform favored the initiative, referendum, and recall, although all three were limited to state action.

Waiting for Roosevelt to scamper out and smite the wicked and for Taft to defend the record, voters anticipated quite a political fare in the summer of 1912—a triple fare, in fact. For at Baltimore on June 25 the Democrats named Woodrow Wilson on the forty-sixth ballot, with Thomas R. Marshall, governor of Indiana, as his running mate. Now for the first time since 1860 a three-cornered presidential race was promised in which all three candidates would receive substantial support.

In the reasonably boisterous campaign that followed, Roosevelt, stouter and slower than in 1900, rarely mentioned Taft, centering most of his attacks on Wilson. Everywhere people thronged to see him, on many occasions to be turned away because of overflowing auditoriums. And never did his unerring instinct for drama fail him. "Stand back! Don't hurt the man!" he shouted after being wounded by a bullet during a speech in Milwaukee, seeing the crowd surge toward the would-be assassin. With the bullet in his chest, he still continued to speak, waving aloft a bloody handkerchief.

Stumping for his "new nationalism," Roosevelt called for a strong government, as strong as it needed to be for promoting the liberties of the downtrodden against the greed and oppression of those in higher stations of life. Clearly Roosevelt and Wilson were the two most talked-of men in the campaign. For Taft by temperament was out of place in this battle. On Election Day he was a poor third in the running, polling 3,486,000 votes against 4,118,000 for Roosevelt. With Wilson garnering 6,296,000 popular ballots, the Republican split gave victory to the Democratic candidate, though interestingly the Democratic proportion of the popular vote fell from 43.1 percent in 1908 to 41.9 in 1912. In the electoral college the final count stood Wilson 435, Roosevelt 88, Taft 8. Taft carried only two states—Vermont and Utah, while Roosevelt won in Minnesota, Michigan, Pennsylvania, South Dakota, and Washington, and carried 11 of 13 electoral votes in California. Interestingly, the split within the Republican party did not reflect a sectional clique despite the fact that Roosevelt's popular vote was generally highest in the Middle West and the Far West.

After four years streaked with bitterness, the parting of the ways would be long remembered. Taft, in a moment of overstatement as he opened fire against his Progressive opponents on Lincoln's birthday in 1912, said he could find no parallel except in the French Revolution: "These extremists are not progressives," he said. "They are political emotionalists or neurotics." Nor was uncourtly conduct held back in the Roosevelt encampment. Roosevelt not only taunted Taft with betraying Republican principles, but he also pointedly referred to the past relations of these two close friends: "It is a bad trait to bite the hand that feeds you."

What did it all amount to? The real distinction in the GOP, felt the *Review of Reviews,* "is not so much between Progressives and Conservatives as between the coalition of selfish interests on the one hand. The machinery of the party has come to a great extent under the control of self-seekers and special interests." This is by way of suggesting a pat oversimplification, of course, for the "self-seekers and special interests" were scrambling to reach the choirmaster's loft in the Progressive party just as they seek control in any party. And within the Progressive movement there was "abundant evidence of the coexistence of illiberalism and reform." Some of the militant Progressive Republicans who saw so clearly the need for social and industrial reform failed completely to see the growing tendency for nations, both old and new, to co-operate and even federate in international organizations. Others fled to the extremist fringe of politics.

But however the detractors chip away, there developed in the heart of Republican Insurgency and Republican Progressivism a new faith that regenerated the roots of popular confidence in government itself. And in the continuity of party life it was the contribution of the Bull Moose party to elevate and preserve this faith.

Roosevelt genuinely resented Taft's trucking with the most conservative leaders in his party and, though a conservative, Roosevelt developed a basic distrust "for representatives of predatory wealth . . . accumulated on a giant scale by iniquity . . . by oppressing wage workers, by manipulating securities, by unfair and unwholesome competition, and by stock jobbing. . . ." So clearly in fact did he develop this theme in his annual message to Congress in 1908 that he alienated such supporters as Nicholas Murray Butler, Root, and Lodge. Yet in the same years he was also sorely trying many Progressives.

La Follette, publishing his *Autobiography* in 1913, complained that the Progressive movement in the Republican party made greater headway in Taft's first two years than in Roosevelt's two terms. And this, he concluded, "was largely due to the fact that Taft's course was more direct, Roosevelt's devious." Such other Progressives as Bristow, who served as Fourth Assistant Postmaster General under Roosevelt, were similarly disturbed. Bristow found him a much less satisfactory superior than McKinley had been because he was temperamental and impulsive, "and given to jumping to conclusions without hearing both sides of an issue. . . ." [16]

If all of these judgments tend to focus on Roosevelt's ambivalence, they also bring out the illogicality and unprogrammatic nature of our party system as it works its way ahead, blurring and compromising conflicts before they become irreconcilable. And Roosevelt was so unerringly a spokesman for this system of politics. One can be amused or even sneer at publisher and large United States Steel stockholder Frank A. Munsey's remark about Roosevelt's charge to the 1912 Progressive convention: "While splendidly progressive, it is at the same time, amply conservative and sound." But this was simply another way of saying what inner conscience tells so many voters, and Roosevelt sensed it, knew it.

In the aftermath of 1912 it would have been expecting too much for Roosevelt to fade gracefully from the scene, even if he had so desired. For he was too committed to his many admirers, and they knew that he alone was peculiarly suited to lead the way for a Republican comeback. Roosevelt, moreover, still thought Wilson was too much oriented toward states' rights and that his program lacked a "Hamiltonian centralization," in which Roosevelt had such faith.

Remarkably clear-headed in some political judgments—if a bit zany in others, such as his anti-German hysteria when World War I broke out—Roosevelt saw earlier than others the wisdom of junking the Progressive party after the elections of 1914. He quickly saw what Beveridge and others wished to ignore: that while the Progressive party pulled a remarkable presidential vote in 1912, it made little headway in the congressional and local elections. And he was certain that the climate was not favorable for the Bull Moose to organize enough precincts to become a major party. It would be quite impossible, he insisted, to hold the party together; there were no "loaves and fishes."

The midterm elections in 1914 confirmed his judgment. The Republicans lost five seats in the Senate that year, leaving them with 39 to the Democrats' 56, and in the House gained some sixty seats, giving them 193 to 231. But running on the Progressive party ticket was hard. Barely a dozen Progressives were elected to Congress.

No one was quite prepared yet to write an epitaph for the Progressive party, however. Nor was anyone quite certain how the Bull Moose and Elephant could get together in the same lodge again, particularly with Roosevelt around. What everyone did know was that after 1910 Roosevelt was a frustrated man. But what few suspected was that after 1910 he was a tired and in many ways a prematurely old man and that after 1914 he was a sick man.

Now would come a strange interlude for Republicans of all hues in the party prism, and an inevitable adjustment. In 1912, sixty-two Negroes were delegates. By 1924 there were only thirty-two, a drop brought about primarily because of reduced Southern representation—another outgrowth of the collision in 1912. Negroes were also without membership on the national committee between 1912 and 1920.

Unable to moderate the differences that exploded at Chicago, the Republicans and Progressives were still at loggerheads as 1916 approached. Roosevelt Major, as Mr. Mencken would later identify him, still believed he had the answer: "What I have advocated . . . is not wild radicalism. It is the highest and wisest kind of conservatism." But the days of the Bull Moose were numbered and his prospects for taking control of the Republican party were slipping. Soon there would be quite a few lost moose looking for a party.

Defeat by the Shade of a Shadow

For quite a spell as the presidential quadrennium rolled around again, 1916 looked like another double-entry engagement for the Republicans. And another tri-cornered contest, with Wilson romping over the finish line gaily ahead, was the one thing Republicans feared most. But how to avoid it? Particularly with the partisans of both the Republican and Progressive camps still licking their wounds over the split of 1912. Hopefully men of good faith in both factions induced their national committees, which met in January of 1916, to set the dates for their two presidential conventions for the same week and in the same city (Chicago). But it was a hope bedeviled from the outset by many factors that militated against a happy reunion.

For the Progressives, defections back to the Republican party had been serious. In the 1914 elections, gubernatorial candidates Gifford Pinchot and Raymond Robbins had lost in Pennsylvania and Illinois. And in the House of Representatives the Progressive Republicans wound up with two less seats than they had after the 1912 election. Sizing it up in December of 1914, Theodore Roosevelt remarked to William Allen White that the campaign seemed to him like "whipping a dead horse." But the horse was not quite dead, though his knees had buckled dangerously.

Roosevelt was still the idol of the Progressives, and with such a standard-bearer in view the pulse beat of the "Bull Moosers" began to quicken early in 1915. Once again the Colonel's friends besought him to make the run and declared their intention of nominating him, needling him with the argument that he owed it to the Progressive Republicans to make the fight—win, lose, or draw. But the old Rough Rider had no desire to have a repeat billing of the 1912 encounter and go down to defeat. He wanted none of the heroics of martyrdom this time. He had carried the lamp against plutocracy in 1912, he reminded his advisers. This time he did not want to be in the position of the batter who made a sacrifice hit. Nor did he wish to become the pathetic spectacle of a perennial third-party candidate, for the experience of General Weaver with the Greenbackers and Populists always disturbed him.

As always, however, the old warrior found it difficult to close the door completely, and this kept alive the hopes of the left wing in the Progressive movement which was determined to have him as its candidate. But if the left wing of the Progressives was dead set upon having Roosevelt as its nominee, the right wing of the Republican party was equally dedicated to keeping him up in the bleachers. Not only did the latter group want no part of him as a candidate or as a counsel in party affairs, but it earnestly desired, if at all possible, to keep him from throwing pop bottles at the contestants for the GOP nomination. In firm control of the national committee, but chastened by the experience of 1912, the conservative Republicans hoped to freeze out Roosevelt. At the same time they knew that some conciliatory gesture was needed to woo back the disgruntled Progressives. Yet their obsessive hatred of Roosevelt prevented them from hatching any plan that could reunite the team behind him.

Communication between the Republicans and Progressives was maintained in these days by two groups that had been working intensively, beginning in 1915, to put the party out on the road again in one piece. In the Progressive party it was the more conservative-minded wing, led by George Perkins, political representative of the House of Morgan, that took the lead in trying to bring the two parties together. At the January, 1916, meeting of the Progressive party national committee in Chicago, the harmonizing or compromising wing of the party won some ground in a resolution that was adopted, stating: "Our people are seeking leadership—leadership of the highest order and most courageous character; leadership that will draw to itself for the country's benefit the unselfish and patriotic services of its ablest citizens. The surest way to secure for our country the required leadership will be by having if possible, both the Progressive and Republican parties choose the same standard-bearer and the same principles."

In the realm of tactics, the harmony element in the Progressive camp was quite willing to take the nomination of Theodore Roosevelt by the Republican party. Likewise it was amenable to accepting the Republican vice-presidential nominee, notwithstanding the fact that a ticket headed by Roosevelt was unthinkable to the GOP directorate in the saddle at the moment. Simultaneously, however, this suggestion was also unacceptable, if not downright offensive, to left-wing Progressives.

What a majority of the Progressives, or the real Bull-Moosers, wanted was a blitzkrieg convention that would nominate Roosevelt quickly and then adjourn. The strategy here was to force the Republican party to take Roosevelt as its nominee or face the dreary consequences of certain defeat with three parties in the field. As the plan shaped up at a conference the Progressives held before their convention, the Bull Moose wing decided to nominate Roosevelt and then to follow one of two alternatives: either (1) to entrust their central committee with authority to accept the Republican vice-presidential nominee; or (2) to nominate a Vice-President of their own and empower their central committee to scratch their candidate later and accept the Republican vice-presidential nominee.

Of some comfort to the Bull Moose Progressives as they laid their strategy was the fact that the Republicans seemed unable to call up a strong candidate. Elihu Root was mentioned, but the distinguished former Secretary of War was already fourteen years older than Roosevelt. Even if nominated and elected President he would be inaugurated at the age of seventy-two. Root's stature and acclaim among some groups were running high at the moment, for his work as chairman of the New York state constitutional convention in 1915 had shown him once again as a man of uncommon ability and insight in the realm of public affairs. But the rejection of proposed amendments by the people on a referendum vote damaged his prestige and undoubtedly hurt his presidential chances.

Among other presidential hopefuls, most were favorite sons. Three prominently mentioned were Senator Cummins of Iowa, Senator Sherman of Illinois, and former Senator Theodore E. Burton of Ohio, who was pledged the unanimous support of the Ohio delegation. Another person—a newcomer—who decided to have a fling at politics was the Michigan industrialist from Dearborn, Henry Ford. Surprisingly, Ford came out ahead of Michigan's United States Senator, William Alden Smith, in the Michigan presidential primary, and he also nosed out Senator Cummins in the Nebraska primary.

Actually, the pre-convention campaign of 1916 was of a very different stripe from that of 1912. Four years before there had been a series of mighty contests in the presidential primaries in such states as Ohio, Pennsylvania, Massachusetts, Illinois, California, New Jersey, and Maryland, in which two principals collided with one another in direct contest. But in 1916 not one of the men who were most talked about from Maine to California was entered in a primary.

The names most noisily debated were Root, Roosevelt, and Charles Evans Hughes, of whom the first was disqualified by age, the intentions of the second were wrapped in uncertainty, and the third kept insisting he could not be a candidate. Despite Hughes's disclaimers, however, his star was rising steadily in the spring of 1916.

In October of 1910 Charles Evans Hughes, after a brilliant tour of duty as New York's chief executive, resigned the governorship to take his seat as an Associate Justice on the Supreme Court of the United States, where he was still serving in 1916. As the pre-convention campaign of 1916 warmed up, Hughes was mentioned by both the Progressive and Republican parties as a possible Presidential nominee, though there was little doubt that the Republicans were the ones taking him most seriously as a candidate. Three denials were issued by Hughes protesting the use of his name, one to Bascom Slemp, who later became Calvin Coolidge's secretary, another to Henry A. Wise Wood of New York City, and a third to state senator Charles H. Brown of Massachusetts. To the latter Hughes apparently tried to ring down the curtain on talk of his candidacy by simply saying: "I cannot permit the use of my name." But the friends of Justice Hughes thought otherwise, and acted so. Undoubtedly Hughes had a sincere desire to remain on the bench, but he could not bring himself to say "no" in the General Sherman formula.

Renowned for his work in the Armstrong investigation of life insurance in New York, and for his progressive record as governor of the Empire state, Hughes appealed to Republicans as the kind of candidate who might persuade a majority of the Progressives to crawl back under the tent-flap of the GOP. He had been described by Roosevelt in 1915 as "safe, sane, and progressive." The thought was that Hughes could be presented as a mild-mannered dragon-slayer who fought corruption with both hands, and whose heart was slightly left of center—where all healthy hearts are normally located, as Geoffrey Crowther of the London *Economist* is fond of saying. George Perkins quietly began to work for nomination of Hughes in the Republican party, with the ultimate hope that he would then be accepted by the Progressive party and the long-sought fusion would come to pass. Perkins, who in effect appointed himself "receiver of the Progressive party after 1912," Harold Ickes tells us, was willing to have Roosevelt as the nominee of both the Republicans and Progressives if the matter could be arranged without too much effort. But he was also perfectly willing to settle on another candidate, provided he could have a hand in his selection. This he made clear in discussing the Progressive party's "declaration of principles" with newsmen early in 1916 when he said: "We are all hoping that both the Progressive and Republican parties will agree on a candidate, *and it will not necessarily have to be Colonel Roosevelt.*" [1] Thereafter it became increasingly clear that the Republican and Progressive parties could never unite on Roosevelt. From this moment Perkins began to reveal his hand.

Throughout most of the pre-convention capers, Hughes kept insisting that he could not run, while Roosevelt, taking counsel with himself and a few close friends, concealed his own plans. But during the entire interim both parties—the Progressives and Republicans—moved merrily ahead, gradually pushing both Roosevelt and Hughes to the point where their nominations were virtually assured by convention time. In order for Perkins's strategy to work, there were two political musts: first he had to see to it that Hughes would not reject the nomination if tendered by the Republican party: thereafter, he had to persuade Roosevelt that as the Progressive party nominee he would be unable to win the Presidency in a three-party tussle, and the sensible thing would be to withdraw. The Perkins plan carried.

During the spring Hughes talked with William Howard Taft, then a professor of constitutional law at Yale, presumably about the possibility of Hughes's being nominated and under what, if any, conditions he could accept the nomination. And on April 11, Taft wrote a long letter to Hughes in which he communicated his opinions that Hughes was going to be nominated, that he was the only one who could reunite the Republican party, and that he would be elected. Taft also urged Hughes not to decide whether to accept or reject the nomination until the convention acted.[2]

In the absence of other front-running candidates, and supported by the presumption that rejection of a presidential nomination actually tendered is highly unlikely, there was little difficulty in keeping the Hughes candidacy airborne. Unlike 1952, when two candidates—Taft and Ike—were both within a whisker of enough votes to secure the nomination, no one except Hughes was within a mile of the nomination in 1916, and the risk involved in staying with Hughes until the situation jelled a little more was not too great. After all, only one major party candidate—the Democrats' Horatio Seymour in 1868—had tried to refuse the nomination after it had been tendered him, and he had not been allowed to decline.

That Hughes would accept the nomination if offered apparently became known to George Perkins some time in the spring, for Perkins's behavior seemed to be based on this premise. Throughout the campaign, Perkins sought to promote a fusion of Progressive and Republican forces behind the candidacy of Hughes.[3] Certain it is in any case that Perkins and some of his Republican friends were more than reasonably confident Hughes would accept.

The possibility that Roosevelt might win the Republican nomination in addition to that of the Progressives was extremely remote. But the strategists in both parties for fusion behind Hughes could never be completely sure that Roosevelt would dismount after the Progressives had nominated him. Perhaps he might ride off into battle again as he did in 1912, when he said, "We stand at Armageddon." Against a lone-wolf candidacy, however, was one element that constantly disconcerted Roosevelt about the Progressive party. Several friends had complained to him from time to time that some strange species had washed up into the ranks of the Progressives. Mindful that Roosevelt abhorred the thought of being used by a lunatic fringe, Perkins and his friends lost no opportunity to exploit this point. Actually, the Progressive party, including its Bull Moose left wing, was composed of followers with a moderately progressive political outlook and was in no sense a body of irresponsibles. Like all parties born under similar circumstances, of course, the Progressives had a few among their ranks who proclaimed themselves in a way that suggested wild economic beliefs and political heresies. But these were definitely in the minority and in no way reflected the character of the great majority of those who had left the Republican reservation in 1912 and still maintained a kind of roving Insurgency.

With both parties readying their plans for the formal organizational machinery of their respective conventions, the likelihood that they could reunite behind a common standard-bearer steadily diminished. On the Republican side a senatorial "soviet" gave an effective demonstration of power in the organization of the convention, just as it did four years later, when a dark horse from Ohio jumped the leading contenders on the tenth ballot to win the nomination. Harry Daugherty, national committeeman from Ohio, was already planning to move his future dark-horse candidate up to the front, but not too fast. Accordingly, when the national committee was wrestling with the delicate problem of how to mollify the Progressives and still assure the old-guard control of the convention, Daugherty quietly asked: "Why not Warren G. Harding for temporary chairman?" Clearly Harding was no Roosevelt-worshipper. He had demonstrated that in 1912 when he himself nominated William Howard Taft for a second term at the Republican convention. At the same time the Progressives held no congealed hatred for Harding. With this for a recommendation, the national committee quickly selected Harding as temporary chairman. And so the man who went to his first convention as an alternate with Harry Daugherty in 1904, his second as a delegate in 1908, and nominated President Taft for a second term in 1912, became the temporary chairman of the convention in 1916. It would take another jump: "Gee, but he'd make a great-looking President," Daugherty had told his faithful friend Jesse Smith, walking along a stream during an early summer morning; "we'll put it over sometime, Jesse!" [4]

For the keynote assignment Harding was eminently available. He had as yet made no enemies, and his immediate task was to make friends. Harding plunged into the preparation of his keynote address with a stout heart, determined to make it his greatest effort. But the senatorial cabal that was determined not to let the convention get out of hand, and which included such men as Reed Smoot of Utah, W. Murray Crane and Henry Cabot Lodge of Massachusetts, Jim Watson of Indiana, and Boies Penrose of Pennsylvania, demanded to have a look-see at his labors and then have a go at it themselves. What they turned up with was not a retread, but practically a new talk from start to finish.

"It's rotten. I wrote a good one," said Harding to Finley Peter Dunne, "but my friends in the Senate made me put things in—the tariff, reciprocity, public lands, pensions, and God knows what, and now it's a rag carpet." [5]

Called to order at the Chicago Coliseum on June 7, 1916, by Charles D. Hilles, chairman of the national committee, the sixteenth Republican national convention began without lusty enthusiasm. The convention hall was not overcrowded, never a happy sign, and the overtones of apathy among both delegates and visitors were quickly picked up by the press correspondents assigned to the Coliseum. They called it the mausoleum. Handicapped by a dispirited audience, Harding hammered down his charge to the Progressives right at the outset. Reaffirming that a party is a volunteer organization and must find "strength in the enlistment of volunteers who find the nearest or best expression of their individual convictions in our party declarations," he conceded that "there can be no treason in withdrawal if our declarations fall short in their appeal. But I am old fashioned enough to believe," he went on, "that in popular government party success and party capacity for service to the nation must lie in making the will of the righteous majority the willing pledge of all." Digging his cleats into Progressive backs a little more, he called upon the Progressives to return—that "the banners of harmony" might be unfurled. "No apology has been asked," he said, "no forswearing is required. This is not the time for recriminations, it is the day of reconsecration." Taking one well-aimed passing shot at the popular idol of the Progressives, he noted first that he did not believe "there is really a reactionary Republican bearing credentials to this convention." Then, welcoming delegates present who wished to emphasize their progressivism, he solemnly admonished that such a person "is expected to do his part in making our party a reflex of the best thought and the best intent of sincere committal to the uplift and progress of the American people, thereby strengthening party purpose instead of magnifying individual belief. . . ." Thereafter Harding turned to the political and economic topics of the day, deploring our unpreparedness, flogging the curse of militarism. Turning for home, he touched upon a theme of which Republicans can well be proud to this day.

Noticing the ever widening demands of new relations in the community of nations, and the development of corporate diplomacy, Harding's words seemed to anticipate Wendell Willkie's *One World:*

> One century of marvelous development has led us into another century of international sponsorship. This mighty people, idealizing popular government and committed to human progress, can no longer live within and for ourselves alone. Obliterated distance makes it impossible to stand aloof from mankind and escape widened responsibility. If we are to become the agency of a progressive civilization and God's great intent, and to believe otherwise is to deny the proofs of American development, we must assume the responsibilities of influence and example, and accept the burden of enlarged participation. The cloistered life is not possible to the potential man or the potential nation.

Mr. Dooley (Finley Peter Dunne) thought the keynote "dismally unsuccessful," and noted that the orator had suffered the additional indignity "of having his audience walk out on him." The New York *Times,* however, thought the speech deserved a better reception than it had received. Certainly it made quite an impression on some of those in attendance. Mark Sullivan, for example, quotes Will Hays as saying that he thought that it was very important in developing Harding's acquaintance among the men who go to conventions.

But the speech cut the Bull Moose Progressives to the quick. Treating the Progressives somewhat as if they had been a band of misguided truants who had been led into their folly by a bumptious, irresponsible leader, Harding's speech sought to dispel the notion that the Republicans were in collision in 1912. "We did not divide over fundamental principles, we did not disagree over a national policy. We split over methods of party procedure and preferred personalities."

Still refusing to recognize the nature of the issues that had sprung Republicans apart in 1912, the right-wing Senate coterie that guided the Republican convention of 1916 was making it inordinately difficult for those who walked out four years before to return to the party fold. Many never would.

Paralleling the regular Republican convention in time and place, the Progressive party convention met on the same day—June 7—under the able leadership of Raymond Robins, who was the presiding chairman. Robins was acceptable to both factions of the Progressive party and made a masterful statement of the Progressive battle cries upon taking the chair.

As the two conventions paced each other, with the Bull Moose Progressives ever hoping to force the hand of the Republicans by nominating Roosevelt quickly and then disbanding, the situation was not without its comic touch. One can almost see William Allen White glued to a telegraph ticker backstage in the Progressive auditorium. A Bull Moose Progressive, White had the duty of monitoring the proceedings of the Republican convention, and if the nomination of Hughes proceeded with too great speed, of slipping the news to the little group of Progressives who had determined to nominate Roosevelt first. Over at the Coliseum Donald Richberg (later director of the National Recovery Administration under Franklin Roosevelt) was performing similar signal duty at the Republican convention. "Old Curmudgeon," Harold Ickes, was also in on the plan, along with Gifford Pinchot of Pennsylvania. Through this signal corps work the Progressives hoped to get the jump on the Republicans.

But while the Bull Moosers were perfecting their own intelligence system and arranging the battle posts for their floor leaders, a master plan for interlocking the participants of the right-wing Progressive salient with the Republican convention was also being eased into execution. For months George Perkins and Frank Hitchcock, national committeeman from New Mexico and former Postmaster General under Theodore Roosevelt, had been quietly doing some spadework to bring about the nomination of Hughes. Both Perkins and Hitchcock were in the Progressive party, but more than anything else they wanted the two parties brought together, and thought that Hughes was the man to do it. Their strategy was intent on keeping the Progressives from nominating Roosevelt and adjourning. It was also based on the assumption that the Republicans would nominate Hughes. Once Hughes was nominated, they felt that they could induce a majority of the Progressives to endorse his nomination and that the disheartened remnants who would be dissatisfied with Hughes would no longer have anything to gain by nominating Roosevelt. Not only would they have nothing to gain, but in such a situation they would almost certainly have no candidate, for Perkins had already been building the necessary doubts to make Roosevelt gun-shy of the Progressive convention.

At the same time Perkins was maneuvering to line up the Progressives behind Hughes as a fusion nominee, he was also counseling Roosevelt. During the convention week he had a direct telephone line from his own hotel room at the Blackstone in Chicago to the Colonel's library in Oyster Bay, New York. Presumably this telephone wire was to be open only to James R. Garfield, the floor leader at the Progressive convention, Hiram Johnson, Raymond Robins, Gifford Pinchot, and William Allen White.[6] As matters turned out, however, few among this group knew of the existence of the wire except Perkins, and instead of really being concerned with Roosevelt, as the former President thought he was, Perkins was working to nail down the nomination of Charles Evans Hughes.

In the early preliminaries while the Progressive convention was more or less marking time, a conference committee was appointed from the membership of both conventions to try and secure a conciliation between the Republicans and Progressives. This committee, requested by the Progressives and known as the "Peace Committee," was composed of Reed Smoot, W. Murray Crane, A. R. Johnson, William E. Borah, and Nicholas Murray Butler on the Republican side; among the Progressives were George W. Perkins, Charles J. Bonaparte, Horace Wilkinson, Hiram Johnson, and John M. Parker. The committee not only failed to produce a compromise, which probably few expected it to do anyway, but had little effect one way or the other on the well-laid plans of Perkins. In the course of the week Harold Ickes and George Perkins finally had it out as the game of each became apparent to the other. Perkins knew that Ickes and the Bull Moosers were determined to nominate Roosevelt before Hughes was nominated by the Republicans, and Perkins was equally determined to block this move. At the same time Ickes was completely aware of Perkins's strategy and the interests Perkins was serving. Considering the proficiency of each with invective, the scene that followed must have been a good one. Only a few hours before the Progressives nominated Roosevelt, Perkins insisted to Ickes that it was unkind to think he was trying to bring about the nomination of Hughes. "Why should I wish that?" he asked piously: "Hughes is the man who besmirched my name." [7] (As a result of Hughes's investigation of insurance companies, Perkins had been arrested on a warrant charging grand larceny of close to $49,000 from the New York Life Insurance Company, and though later released he received some unfavorable publicity.) But whatever his resentment over the past, June, 1916, found Perkins plugging backstage for Hughes.

Late in the week—Friday—word finally came to the Progressive convention that the nominating speeches were beginning in the Coliseum. On this cue the left-wing Bull Moosers attempted a premature nomination of Roosevelt which failed. While chairman Robins was about to recognize the person selected to place the nomination, another delegate moved the convention adjourned, doing so apparently, if William Allen White's account is accurate, on a signal from George Perkins.

That afternoon White himself received a message that Colonel Roosevelt wished to speak with him at once on the direct wire in Perkins's room at the Blackstone Hotel. Exasperated because he had heard from none of the five with whom he was expecting to be in constant communication throughout the week, Roosevelt demanded to know the score from White. White, not having known of the wire's existence, explained to the Colonel that he felt certain none of the others knew about it. Roosevelt then said it would be a great mistake to nominate him, no matter what happened at the Republican convention, and began rattling off names he felt the Progressive convention should consider. White attempted once more to emphasize the respectability of the Progressive delegates. The tip-off on Perkins's hand probably came in the surprised reaction of Roosevelt, who immediately responded by saying that this was the first statement of confidence in the responsible character of the convention he had heard from anyone. Apparently on the basis of reports flowing from Perkins's room at the Blackstone, from a few bankers, industrialists, and newspaper proprietors such as Frank Munsey and Henry L. Stoddard, the Colonel a few days before the convention had made up his mind irrevocably against accepting the Progressive party nomination. Two days before the nomination of Hughes a letter from Roosevelt was in Perkins's hands. Though White, Pinchot, Garfield, and perhaps a few others may have known of the existence of the Colonel's letter and his determination not to accept the nomination of the Progressives a couple of days before the nomination of Hughes by the Republicans, it was confidential and not for distribution.

However they may have despaired at the Colonel's decision, the Bull Moosers determined to go ahead and nominate Roosevelt in any case. Their plans called for Bainbridge Colby to nominate Roosevelt Saturday morning. The platform of the Progressive party had been adopted by the resolutions committee and logically its acceptance by the convention should have been the next order of business. Colby, though out of order, asked for recognition and obtained it. But when chairman Robins recognized Colby, Perkins, who was seated on the platform behind the chair, sprang to his feet and rushed to the speaker's rostrum, speaking in a distracted voice. Reconstructing the scene years later, Harold Ickes reports that no one knew exactly what Perkins was trying to say. While Robins, the chairman, shoved Perkins away from the rostrum and back into his chair, Colby nominated Roosevelt in a few words. Compacted in the ten-minute demonstration that followed was an emotional outburst and a deafening tribute that impressed the crustiest of the seasoned newspaper correspondents. Thereafter Hiram Johnson seconded the Colby resolution and the nomination was made. John M. Parker, former governor of Louisiana, was then nominated for Vice-President. The hour was high noon. No word had yet been communicated to the convention from the man of the hour at Oyster Bay.

Meanwhile, moving beyond the tedious strain of all conventions— the nominating speeches—the gathering at the Coliseum was now at the balloting stage. The day before—the third day of the convention, June 9—the results of the first ballot gave: Hughes, 253; Weeks of Massachusetts, 105; Root of New York, 103; Cummins of Iowa, 87; Theodore Burton of Ohio, 82; Charles W. Fairbanks of Indiana, 72; Theodore Roosevelt, 67; Lawrence Y. Sherman of Illinois, 63. On the second ballot Hughes climbed to 328½—170 short of the nomination. At this time, as the convention adjourned for the night, there was still no complete assurance that Hughes would be nominated, but almost everyone assumed that he would. Perkins, however, could not take Hughes's nomination for granted, and just what was going on in his mind as he tried to reach the rostrum at the Progressive convention Saturday forenoon no one knows.[8] The likely explanation is that he wanted to read the Colonel's letter.

That afternoon—following the adjournment of the Progressive party after the nomination of Roosevelt, Hughes surged ahead on the third roll call at the Republican convention to win the nomination with 949½ votes, and it was immediately made unanimous. For the first time a major party had drafted its presidential candidate from the Supreme bench. Charles W. Fairbanks, Vice-President under Theodore Roosevelt from 1905 to 1909, was nominated as Hughes's running mate. The sixteenth Republican convention was now history. But a final postscript that turned out to be significant in the campaign was yet to be written.

Reconvening later in the afternoon for a session devoted to raising money, laying plans for the coming campaign, and some contented clucking at having nominated Roosevelt, the Progressives stayed in session late. Over a hundred thousand dollars had been raised for Roosevelt, and the pledges were still forthcoming. Watching the scene from a press box with Ida Tarbell, William Allen White felt "a kind of terror such as a train dispatcher might feel who had two engines approaching on the same track." Where was the letter? Hughes was nominated, and the Republicans were busily packing their soiled linen to return home. Had the letter from Roosevelt to Perkins been withdrawn? Had the unpredictable Colonel changed his mind, or was Perkins simply withholding it?

Late in the day a blockbuster dropped on the convention. In stunned silence the throng heard the last words as the letter was read: "But your candidate I cannot be." Arising in indignation the delegates tore up photographs of the Rough Rider, threw Roosevelt badges on the floor and stamped on them, and drifted out of the convention hall in angry disorder. More than a few would leave the Republican party for good, and more importantly they would carry thousands away with them. Perhaps most significant of all to the fighting faith of a political party was that the disillusionment of even those who remained would be reflected in the families they were raising at the time. Many of their sons, as we shall see, were active leaders in the Democratic party only a generation distant. Many Progressives, including Harold Ickes, supported Hughes that fall, but did so with the feeling that this might be the last trip.

June 10, 1916, marked more than a simple parting of the ways of two factions within the Republican party. It was definite confirmation that the Republican leadership, which had failed to heed the voices of Insurgency in 1910 and 1912, had by 1916 become deaf to Progressive Republican sentiments. "My despair came," said William Allen White, reflecting on the day's events, "because I did not realize what had happened. It was merely ebb tide. Since the Civil War destroyed slavery in this country and the tide went out with Reconstruction and the corruption of Grant's day, a new tide had been flowing in, and for fifteen years since the century's turn had been pounding upon the rocks of privilege, and of social and economic injustice, crumbling them here and there, and making inroads upon bastions and ramparts. This Progressive movement was a part of a revolution and as I stood there heartbroken upon the shore at ebb tide, I did not realize how soon and how strong the tide would come flowing in, and what rocks, and docks, and earthworks would melt in that flowing current."

Late in the evening of Election Day, November 7, 1916, Chester Congdon, one of the wealthiest copper and steel industrialists in America, phoned from his home in Duluth, Minnesota, to an old political crony in St. Paul. He asked him to arrange a small breakfast at the St. Francis Hotel the next morning on a matter of great urgency. Leaving at once, Congdon drove to the capital city of Minnesota, arriving in time for the scheduled breakfast meeting with four men prominent in Republican circles. As the little group began their meal, barely 300 votes out of 387,397 told the story of the slim lead that Hughes held over Woodrow Wilson in Minnesota. Over and over the copper magnate kept imploring the group to find him an attorney who could immediately arrange for the impounding of the ballot boxes of Minnesota's three-thousand-odd election districts. Rejecting one nominee after another as not tough enough for the job that lay ahead, and reminding his friends of the prize at stake, Congdon brought his clenched fist down on the table with a powerful stroke and said, "Damn it, gentlemen, what I want for this job is a man the dogs won't urinate on." [9]

At this moment Woodrow Wilson himself believed he had been defeated, and had already devised an ingenious plan, suggested to him by Colonel House, to bring about the immediate induction of the President-Elect into the chief executive's office. This was to be accomplished by having Vice-President Marshall resign and then having Secretary of State Lansing resign, whereupon he would appoint the President-Elect, Charles Evans Hughes, to be Secretary of State. This accomplished, Wilson would then resign and Hughes, as next in line under the statutory succession law at that time, would ascend into the Presidency. But whatever Wilson thought about his possible defeat, and however confident of victory Republicans may have been in the immediate post-election hours, the result was still anybody's guess for three days to come. If Hughes led Wilson by the slim margin of 359 votes in Minnesota, elsewhere the presidential contest was equally close, if not closer. It was the tightest presidential battle since the Cleveland-Harrison tilt of 1888.

In New Hampshire, Wilson led by 76 votes out of a total of 87,-000. In New Mexico he won by 30 votes out of 65,000, and in North Dakota he was ahead by 1,725 votes out of 108,000. Not until the final California returns came in three days later were Wilson's doubts finally dispelled. For Republicans, defeat came hard.

By commonly accepted standards, Hughes was an ideal candidate, and he fought gamely within the conduct code to which he rigorously conformed. But his inexpert feel for politics, combined with incredibly bad handling by his advisers, very likely cost him the election. Aside from the broad appeal of Wilson's New Freedom, however, perhaps the most compelling circumstance of Hughes's defeat was the widespread conviction that Woodrow Wilson would keep the country out of war. Shrewdly assaying this point, Wilson turned it to his advantage on every possible occasion. Late in the campaign he spoke of it tellingly to the disadvantage of the Republican candidate by saying: "There is only one choice as against peace and that is war. A very great body of the supporters of that party outspokenly declare they want war, so that the certain prospect of the success of the Republican party is that we shall be drawn, in one form or another, into the embroilments of the European war." Adding credence to the Wilson statement, of course, were the intemperate broadsides of Theodore Roosevelt, who believed that Wilson had been cowardly and who desperately wanted the United States to get into the scrap. Though he did not speak for the Republican party, Roosevelt none the less symbolized the hopes and aspirations of millions of Republicans, and his identification with interventionism was harmful to Hughes. It was particularly harmful because of the German vote, which favored American neutrality in the European conflict.

Yet quite apart from the effectiveness of the Democratic slogan, "He kept us out of war," any number of other factors might be cited that were equally responsible for the defeat of Hughes. Chief among them was the failure of Hughes to comprehend the domestic issues of the day. After six cloistered years on the Supreme Court, he was pathetically unaware that the joists which once held the Republican party together had been badly weakened by the split of 1912 and the failure of the right-wing salient to make concessions in 1916 at convention time. Visiting with William Allen White in Estes Park, Colorado, late in August, Hughes asked: "What are the Progressive issues? I have been out of politics now so long that I am not familiar with it. Just how should I express my sympathy with the Progressive movement?"

By impulse, Hughes was moderately progressive. He had been one of the leading champions of the direct primary at a time, interestingly enough, when Theodore Roosevelt had not only opposed it but had even used Hughes's endorsement of the primary as a reason for opposing Hughes for the Republican presidential nomination in 1908. But as Hughes squared away to meet the 1916 campaign requirements, he seemed far out of touch with the demands for social and industrial justice that had impelled so many voters to follow Woodrow Wilson's New Freedom, or at least give it another four-year lease, or make common cause with the Progressives. Laws establishing minimum wages, the eight-hour day, old-age pensions, workmen's compensation, and the prohibition of child labor were the natural campaign grist that year. Yet Hughes never seemed to realize that the electorate wanted some forthright words on these matters.

Hughes was also quite unpopular with labor, at a time when mass industrialism was bringing up the labor vote to a point where it could be of decisive significance in American politics. And during his campaign Hughes assailed the basic eight-hour-day clause of the Adamson act—a social objective that even the labor antagonist, Uncle Joe Cannon, supported before he became Speaker of the House. Interpreting Hughes's opposition to the eight-hour day to mean that he favored the repeal of the Adamson act, the Railway Brotherhoods

supported Wilson almost to a man. "Hughes," writes Professor Binkley, "by unnecessarily appearing to threaten the repeal of the Adamson Act, apparently threw to Wilson the electoral vote of Ohio and
California, and thereby lost the election." [10] Hughes lost the highly
industrialized state of Ohio by some 80,000 votes out of over a million cast. In California he lost by slightly under 4,000 votes. Actually
a shift of 1,904 votes would have swung this state to Hughes, and it
seems likely that his inept handling of the labor issues was particularly fatal here. Not only did workers experience misgivings over the
attack on the eight-hour day, but encouraged by Democratic speakers
they recalled the fact that Associate Justice Hughes had voted to impose a treble-damage penalty on the Danbury Hatters for a boy-
cott they had maintained a dozen years before when the case was
reheard in the Supreme Court in 1914. Workers involved in this case
had their homes sold over their protests, to pay $240,000 damages,
which was added in 1914 to the $60,000 they had already paid. Not
exactly a happy backlog for a presidential candidate.

From the very inception of his campaign Hughes also labored under another formidable handicap—the shadow of Theodore Roosevelt. Roosevelt was angry with Hughes for not taking a more decisive stand in urging that the United States be brought into the war.
Moreover, he was particularly incensed when the German-American
Alliance endorsed Hughes, and he didn't hesitate to say so to his
friends. And here is an interesting aside (for which we are indebted
to Hermann Hagedorn):

At a small luncheon shortly after Hughes was nominated in 1916,
Roosevelt told a group of young writers, including Hagedorn, what
he really thought about "Charles the Baptist," as he was fond of
calling him. Fully conscious of Hughes's integrity and great ability,
he pulled no punches in explaining exactly why he did not like him.
Then just as the party broke up the Colonel said: "Of course, you
understand that what I have said is not for publication. If you quote
me I shall repudiate you, and be right in doing so. Saying these
things to you is one thing. Saying them to the public is quite another.
You men understand that I want to see Mr. Hughes elected and
want to do everything in my power to help him win. You know that
my personal feelings about Mr. Hughes will in no wise effect the
vigor of my support. But the public does not know that. If the
public hears that I don't personally like Mr. Hughes, it will jump to
the conclusion that I am half-hearted in my support. That will be
untrue. So, in repudiating you, I shall be the one who is telling the
truth." [11]

"I have always wondered," Hagedorn tells us, "whether the great

Colonel wasn't trying to eat his pie and have it too—to enjoy, that is, both the luxury of untrammelled utterance and the security of reticence." But it did not help presidential nominee Hughes.

Publicly Roosevelt was loyal to the core and unstinting in his efforts to campaign with all his old-time vigor for Hughes. But privately he continued to call Hughes a "bearded iceberg," and "only a pink-whiskered Wilson." Some confidences were bound to be betrayed, and these comments, spread among party organization men, surely diluted their enthusiasm.

In another respect, the ebullient Colonel was still more damaging to the Hughes candidacy. Roosevelt had been heating up the branding irons to apply some of the choicest derisive adjectives at his command to Woodrow Wilson. Going after his old enemy with unconcealed delight, he accused him of cowardice, of using weasel words, and of bearing the responsibility for the deaths of the screaming women and children who had sunk forever beneath the frigid waters of the Atlantic following the sinking of the *Lusitania*. And while Roosevelt talked about Wilson, and Wilson referred to Roosevelt, nobody spoke about Hughes. In consequence, the contest at many points seemed to settle down to a duel between Wilson and Roosevelt, with Hughes benched on the sidelines. Actually, some of Hughes's friends felt he should be kept off the stump because they thought him ineffective as a speaker. But there can be little doubt that the shadow of Roosevelt spreading over him kept him from being out in front where presidential candidates belong.

With war closing in and becoming more and more the center of attention, the campaign found Hughes still nimbly evading the issues. In his acceptance speech at Carnegie Hall on July 31 his mood seemed unchanged: conciliatory and slightly confused. Whisked about by Republican stand-patters who seemed mainly concerned with fencing off the Progressives and preventing them from getting near Hughes, the Republican nominee experienced a trying campaign. Not quite matching Wendell Willkie's 1940 campaign record of being domiciled six weeks in a Pullman train, Hughes none the less carried on the fight with a will in keeping with presidential campaign tradition. He traveled extensively in a railroad car appropriately named the Constitution, and surprised many a doubting Thomas by his amiable manner on the hustings. In Colorado he even descended into the bowels of the earth where, with the aid of a miner's cap, he crawled into a coal shaft, finally emerging with well-sooted whiskers in proof of his descent. But in all his travels his gravest campaign experience befell him in California. Since stories of the Hughes snub of Hiram Johnson in 1916 are legion, the circumstances surrounding the event call for a word of introduction. Several accounts, fortunately—in particular the recollections of Frederick M. Davenport, and the studies of George E. Mowry and Merlo Pusey—have provided us with a reasonably clear picture of what happened upon that fateful occasion.[12]

Accompanying Hughes on a campaign trek across the continent, Davenport was asked by Hughes to handle a sheaf of telegrams which for some reason had been neglected. Almost immediately Davenport, who started to work on this batch of telegrams at St. Paul, Minnesota, discovered the first overt signal of what Hughes was going to meet in California: "The vast and bitter controversy between the Hiram Johnson Progressives and the Crocker-Keesling Republican machine in the state, in a life and death struggle for control." [13] The conflict, as painfully evident from the telegrams, was simple. Hiram Johnson's manager for his senatorial campaign wanted Johnson to preside at the Hughes speech in San Francisco. William H. Crocker of the Southern Pacific Railway, and the ruling party leaders who belonged to his organization, had another nominee in mind. As governor of the state, Johnson was obviously the logical man to introduce Hughes, but his opponents contended that since Johnson was running for a new office—for the United States Senate—and the primaries were only two weeks away, it would be unfair to give Johnson such a pre-eminent position at the expense of the Republican candidate running against him, who happened to be a candidate put forward by the Crocker machine. While selection of a presiding officer for the Hughes meeting was simply a detail of the developing controversy, the real issue at stake ran far deeper. It was part and parcel of a very deep division along economic and political lines involving a fight to the end between Progressive policies and standpattism in the California commonwealth. Not only did it involve the rapidly expanding state of California, but symptomatically it represented a struggle that was being fought nationally.

Seeking advice as to what should be done, Hughes, at the suggestion of Davenport, wired national committee chairman William R. Willcox to bring together Chester Rowell, Johnson's campaign manager, and William Crocker for the groups opposing Johnson, at Portland, Oregon, where Hughes would speak before going on to San Francisco. Behind this move was the hope that some agreement could be reached in Portland before Hughes entered California. Receiving the request to act as intermediary, William Willcox wired Crocker from New York City on August 11:

HAVE TELEGRAM FROM MANAGER OF THE HUGHES TRAIN WHICH SUG-
GESTS BOTH YOU AND ROWELL MEET THE TRAIN IN PORTLAND ON
WEDNESDAY, AUGUST SIXTEENTH, AND TRAVEL WITH GOVERNOR HUGHES
TO SAN FRANCISCO AND TO WITHHOLD FINAL ARRANGEMENTS ABOUT
CHAIRMAN UNTIL THEN, UNLESS YOU HAVE COME TO AN AGREEMENT.

Rowell replied immediately that he would be there, but on the same
day Crocker wired as follows: "REPLYING TO YOUR TELEGRAM TODAY,
ALL ARRANGEMENTS FOR CALIFORNIA HAVE BEEN COMPLETED."

Republican national chairman Willcox even earlier in the game
had indicated to California's national committeeman Crocker how he
felt about the controversy that was developing in California. As
early as July 13 he had wired to Crocker that he did not feel the
national committee or the presidential candidate should have to intervene in a local matter of this nature, and then added: "I might
personally say, but not officially, that I think there is some force in
the governor of the state, supporting the presidential candidate, having the privilege of presiding at one of the meetings." This telegram
was actually sent at the instance of Hughes.

At Portland, Johnson's manager Rowell appeared and went over
the whole issue with Hughes, but Crocker failed to show up, reiterating by wire instead the arrogant message that all arrangements
had been completed. Speeding from Portland to the California border, the Hughes train was greeted at the California line by Crocker
with a group of tame Progressives in tow. Since Hughes was not up
yet, Crocker talked with Davenport, insisting from the outset that
Hughes be kept away from Johnson at all costs. Not once during
the entire journey to the Golden Gate did Crocker let up on this
argument, and thereafter he continuously harped on it throughout
the state. "Crocker, the Southern Pacific aristocrat," remarks Davenport, "seemed to me then and seems to me now, as I look back upon
it, to have been the archetype of the *laissez-faire* Bourbon of the
period, without an iota of political or national sense."

That night, before a jammed civic auditorium in San Francisco, it
was Crocker who rose to introduce Hughes. Just as he was about to
speak someone, possibly a plant in the gallery, rose and yelled,
"Three cheers for San Francisco's favorite son." Whatever the impetus behind this remark, it caught Hughes off base. Admittedly
Crocker was a philanthropist of high personal prestige—even the
Johnson representatives stressed this point. Not unmindful of
Crocker's reputation in the latter regard, Hughes teed off in response
to the Crocker eulogy with the politically highly unfortunate remark: "I salute with you San Francisco's favorite son."

In the throes of violent industrial growing pains at the moment, the state of California was very likely the most progressively Republican state in the Union. With three eminently successful gubernatorial campaigns under his belt, and having become the first California governor to win both nominations under the cross-filing system, Johnson enjoyed a following that outnumbered the old-time Republican machine by a preponderant majority. Johnson was the personification of the noble crusader fighting privileged plutocracy; Crocker, the symbol of Southern Pacific machine rule, with its record of corruption and contempt for policy in the public interest.

Unknowingly, says Davenport, but "with innocently unhuman relations to his surroundings," Hughes then proceeded to stub his toe even more seriously: "I come," he said, "as the spokesman of a reunited Republican party, to talk to you of national issues—*with local conditions I have no concern.*" This was more than the Progressives could take. For many years the followers of Johnson had looked upon their uplifting struggle as one of national import, and momentarily they took this rebuke personally, forgetting, of course, that as governor of New York Hughes himself had carried the lance against the very kind of corruption and machine rule they were fighting.

If the misstep at the San Francisco evening speech was not enough to jar California out of the Hughes column, an incident that occurred the following day certainly was, and more demonstrably so. Scheduled to deliver a speech at noon before the Commercial Club in San Francisco, Hughes was urged by his advisers to cancel the talk because of a strike of the waiters' union around the Bay of Oakland. Since the Commercial Club was directly in the center of these labor difficulties, it was hoped that Hughes would abandon the talk. Always the perfectionist on his commitments, however, Hughes insisted that he get on with the speech as scheduled. Meantime, Hughes's personal manager, Charles W. Farnham, went to see the head of the waiters' union to ask him if he could hold up a walkout on the part of the waiters at the Commercial Club until Hughes had given his talk. To this request the head of the waiters' union was perfectly reasonable, but laid down one condition: "The men will stay on their jobs during the luncheon," but "there is to us a very offensive placard hanging in the window of the Commercial Club, declaring against our hopes and purposes. All that we ask is that the placard be taken down from the window of the club while our men are serving the luncheon." Hughes's manager then hurried to see Crocker, who was an influential member of the club, and asked Crocker to see what he could do to have the placard taken down. Nothing was done, however, and Hughes's manager next went to see another party sachem on the local committee arranging the luncheon, to see if he could get the placard taken down. "Take down those placards?" the politician said. "Not on your life. We have got these labor bastards in this town where we want them at last, and we are not going to let up on them at all." [14]

Nothing was done. Hughes spoke and recruits to serve the luncheon were gathered from outlying scab restaurants. But the waiters' union wrote its own postscript to the incident on Election Day. As Davenport reminds us, "the labor bastards" had their own inning in November. Looking at the election statistics for the area, and the heavy Wilson majorities, one might easily conclude that Hughes lost the election in the Oakland Bay region.

Of all the Hughes mistakes, the most publicized was his subsequent failure to meet with Hiram Johnson in Long Beach, California. From the time he first crossed the California line Hughes had been surrounded by a cordon, directed by national committeeman William Crocker and state central chairman Keesling, that never relaxed its guard lest he rub shoulders with the Progressives. Literally, Hughes was unable to ride in an automobile without Keesling or Crocker or both. If he was to be photographed, he had to be surrounded by the most notorious practitioners of stand-pattism that could be produced.

At Long Beach, California, Sunday afternoon, Johnson and Hughes were within four floors of each other in the Hotel Virginia. A large reception for Hughes was arranged at the hotel by the manager, who happened to be a strong supporter of the Crocker faction. Meanwhile Johnson, who had just returned from an exhausting week on the stump shortly before the reception, learned at the reservation desk that Hughes was expected soon. Thus the manager knew that Johnson was there and that Hughes was on his way. But Hughes was never informed of Johnson's presence in the hotel. Later that evening when Hughes returned to Los Angeles and the newspapermen who had discovered that Johnson had been in the Long Beach hotel all the time told Hughes about it, Hughes said to Davenport: "If I had known that Johnson was in that hotel, I would have seen him if I had been obliged to kick the door down."

After Hughes's defeat both California factions sought to explain to Eastern Republicans that they were blameless for what happened. Carrying a letter East dated November 28, 1916, Johnson's campaign manager Rowell, now the new state central committee chairman, brought Johnson's own account of what happened in Long Beach. Johnson confirmed that the manager of the Hotel Virginia knew that he was upstairs during Hughes's visit, and noted that the manager was with Hughes during every minute of the reception. Johnson also noted that the men surrounding Hughes knew of his presence. He also related that later in the evening he had granted an interview to Hughes's personal manager, Farnham, who had gone to Los Angeles accompanied by Francis V. Keesling in the hope that something might be done to undo the damage that had been wrought Hughes by the failure of the two to meet that afternoon. Referring to Keesling's presence, Johnson's letter comments: "In as forceful language as I could command I explained the activities of Crocker and Keesling; that these activities were dictated solely by a desire to use our presidential candidate, and that they preferred my defeat rather than Hughes' success.

". . . I told Farnham that, from the instant Hughes' coming to California was announced, the trip had been used by Crocker and Keesling and those acting with them, not for the benefit of Hughes, but for their petty ambitions, and that they might again control California's government. . . .

". . . I made the statement directly to Keesling and to Farnham that Crocker and Keesling had publicly said they would be for Wilson if the commonest courtesy were shown to Progressives." This, incidentally, Keesling denied, claiming that he had merely stated that Republicans would revolt if Hughes had anything to do with Progressives. Johnson's letter ends on the note that, in response to Farnham's plea that he go to Sacramento and there preside over a later meeting where Hughes was to make an address, he sent a reply to Farnham the next morning stating ". . . for me, even at your suggestion, to wire Mr. Hughes and for him to reply, or for me to preside at his Sacramento meeting, would be misunderstood and misinterpreted and maliciously distorted," and closed by wishing Hughes the best for his success.

In a letter dated November 24, four days before the date of the Johnson letter, William Crocker made public his own explanation of the California disaster. Once more he offered the lame excuse that the "exclusion" policy which sought to keep Johnson away from Hughes was simply enforced on the ground that "all candidates for election in the primaries should be excluded from the Governor Hughes meetings." He then went on to say that there was no thought of excluding the Progressives generally from Hughes meetings—which was, of course, absurd and everyone knew it.

Irascible and inclined to be crotchety, Hiram Johnson himself is not without a generous share of the blame for what happened in California on Election Day of 1916. He, after all, knew that Hughes was present and might have, in common courtesy, closed in the gap of four floors to shake hands with the presidential candidate and exchange a few pleasantries with him. Here was a time when he mistakenly nursed his hates and must share in the blame for what eventually happened. Yet, given the vapors of discontent that were rising out of the dissatisfaction with the Crocker-Keesling misrule, perhaps it may have been asking too much for Johnson to exercise more dispassionate control. Looking back, it seems all the more unfortunate that this incident which played such a momentous part in Republican party history was brought about largely by the bubble-headed childishness of two men already condemned to fade into the wings of party history—William Crocker and Francis Keesling. The simple but sad truth of the matter, as Merlo Pusey reminds us, was that through most of California Hughes was squired about and "presented to the people by political leaders who were about to lose their shirts."

Unknown, of course, until the judgment scrolls are some day unrolled, is what might have been our course if Hughes had been elected. One school leans to the theory that Germany, though badly misjudging Wilson and the United States, had certain grounds for believing that Wilson would not fight if he were re-elected. That Hughes would fight was an eventuality German intelligence agents never doubted. Had Hughes been elected—so the argument runs—Germany would never have unleashed her submarine attack upon American merchant shipping because of the fear that it would bring immediate war, and in consequence World War I would have been a much more limited military conflict. In this case Germany might not have been plunged into the economic ruin that followed, which provided the seed-bed for the Nazis, who led the world into a second world war. Carried one more turn, the argument holds that if only things had been otherwise in 1916 even the prospect of a third world war might have been avoided. But all this is wishful thinking.

Statistics finally claimed a victory for Wilson on the third day following the election. Surprising as it may have been to Hughes, Wilson, and many observers who had noted the Republican gains in elections of September and October with the thought that they carried promise of a Hughes victory, the Democratic presidential candidate carried 30 states, Hughes 18. Wilson's 49.2 percent of the national vote was the smallest slice of the total popular vote (except for his own 41.8 percent vote in 1912) that any victorious presidential candidate had received since the election of 1888. Hughes's 46 percent of the popular vote was also greater than any losing candidate had received in the same period—a circumstance brought about by the fact that the minor and third-party vote was a negligible factor in the 1916 campaign.

The vote in 1916 reflected intense voter interest, in that the total ballots exceeded those of 1912 by 3½ million. Some of this, no doubt, was brought about by the extension of suffrage to women. In Illinois, for example, the total vote increased by a million over that of 1912. Hughes polled nearly a million more votes than had ever been cast for a Republican candidate. Moreover, in computing the percentage score of Hughes as a presidential candidate in relation to his party's congressional ticket, his mark of 114.9 percent equaled that set by Theodore Roosevelt in 1904, which was the best showing of either party's candidate in relation to the vote of his congressional ticket from 1896 to 1952 (Eisenhower's mark of 119 percent in 1952 was the highest). But Wilson's great increase of nearly three million votes over his 1912 mark enabled him to carry three states, Ohio, New Hampshire, and California, none of which had been Democratic in a two-party contest in any election up to this time. Wilson ran behind Hughes in New England, the Middle Atlantic states, and in the East North Central section, but his lead was very large in the West South Central and the Rocky Mountain region, as well as in the East South Central and South Atlantic sections. In county totals Wilson led in 2,039, approximately two-thirds of the nation's counties, while Hughes carried 976, the smallest number in the Republican column in a two-party contest until the Republicans were defeated in 1932. Unmistakably, the German vote went to Hughes, though it is interesting to note that the Democratic national committee issued a sensational and ridiculous statement on October 22 that Hughes had met with German-American groups and made a deal with them. In particular, Roosevelt's bellicose speeches threw thousands of German votes to Wilson.[15] At the final count the popular vote stood: Wilson, 9,129,606; Hughes, 8,538,221. By electoral count the score was Wilson, 277; Hughes, 254.

In the congressional elections the Republicans gained some ground. Two years earlier the Democrats had won two additional senators, bringing their total after the 1914 midterm elections to 64, a majority of 16. But in the House their majority was reduced in the same year from 47 to 29. Some comfort to Republicans, therefore, lay in the fact that the Democratic majority in the Senate fell from 16 to 10 in the 1916 elections, leaving the Senate divided as follows: Democrats 53; Republicans 42; Independent 1. In the House the Republicans won 216 seats, against 210 for the Democrats. But 9 independents were elected, and enough independents joined forces with the Democrats to organize the House.

Contrary to the embroidered accounts of motion pictures and reckless raconteurs, Hughes was not unprepared for defeat. The story that he retired on election night thinking he was the next President does not square with the facts. Nor is there any truth in the tale that a newsman, told imperiously by Hughes's son, "The President cannot be disturbed," replied: "O.K., when he wakes up just tell him he's no longer President." When the New York *World* and other papers conceded Hughes's election, and begged for a statement, Hughes said, "Wait until the Democrats concede my election." To a crowd gathered outside the Hotel Astor where he was staying, he showed additional caution: "If I have been elected President, it is because the people of this country think that I'll keep my shirt on in an emergency. I'll start right now by not yielding to this demand when I'm not positive that I have been elected."

One by one the causes for Hughes's defeat were pieced together by the morning-after quarterbacks. In the Kansas City *Star* Henry J. Haskell had written of Hughes's appearance in Kansas City: "His speech here gives me the impression of being perfunctory and of indicating no comprehensive grasp. . . . If the independent voters of the Western counties are to be persuaded to replace President Wilson by Mr. Hughes, they will have to be convinced that he is more than a critic, that he has a great program." Hughes was uniformly criticized for pussyfooting. John Palmer Gavit, a former Hughes supporter from his governorship days, wrote a piece for the New York *Evening Post* magazine, November 18, entitled "What Hughes Was This?" It was a sharp attack on Hughes, flogging him unsparingly for standing cowed before the dissension in his party's ranks.

"Longing for one swish of the club of Theodore Roosevelt," or "just one blast from the old Hughes trumpet of the New York days," Davenport wistfully suggests that "one sharp uppercut delivered by Hughes would have forced an outworn party philosophy and the personal pique of 1916 Republicanism to bow before him." Uncomfortable at family quarreling in public, Hughes went about the campaign slightly mystified, never daring, never knowing quite how to throw the kind of body punch he had dealt so fearlessly in his attacks on corruption in New York. In the choice of William R. Willcox as his national chairman, Hughes had also made a serious mistake. Though an able public servant, as he demonstrated when Hughes first appointed him to the public service commission of New York City in 1907, Willcox did not know the terrain of practical politics, and was regarded as a "blunderhead" by President Taft.

With the 1916 canvass complete, the Bull Moose party that had started out so jubilantly in 1912 was now laid finally to rest, though officially its demise did not take place until February, 1918, in St.

Louis. With only a vice-presidential candidate (Parker) in the field on the national ticket, the Progressives won a mere 42,856 votes—carrying just 5 counties. But the spirit that had been kindled in the years leading up to 1912 was far from dormant, though no one any longer seemed capable of organizing it in a way that could again challenge the leadership of the Republican party in a national election.

Theodore Roosevelt was tired and, the election over, he turned his energies again to needling Wilson. This time, once America had been drawn into the war in the spring of 1917, Roosevelt used every lane of approach he could think of to persuade the President to raise a division of troops under his command to be sent immediately to the western front of Europe. But in all such requests to raise a division of "mounted" infantrymen, Roosevelt was icily repulsed. Secretary of War Baker would reply: "Your letter will be filed for consideration should the occasion arise." Finally, Roosevelt even went to call on Wilson at the White House to make the request in person, but the man whom Roosevelt had called a "sophist," a "pacifist," a "logothete," a "trained elocutionist," and "neither a gentleman nor a real man," was not disposed to honor his request. How strongly Roosevelt felt about the chance to go to Europe at the head of a division is suggested by the quip he made just before the Wilson visit, when he told a friend: "I will promise Wilson that if he will send me to France, I will not come home alive." Clearly there were perfectly sound military considerations for not acceding to Roosevelt's request. None the less there were also psychological factors, which apparently Wilson failed to see but the French did, in favor of playing along with Roosevelt. As Clemenceau wrote to Wilson: "At the present moment there is in France one name which sums up the beauty of American intervention—Roosevelt. You are too much of a philosopher to ignore that the influence on the people of great leaders of men often exceeds their personal merit. The name Roosevelt has legendary force in this country at this time. Our poilus ask 'where is Roosevelt?' Send them Roosevelt—it will gladden their hearts." Wilson remained unmoved.

Soon thereafter a misfortune befell Roosevelt. A form letter from the War department informed him of son Quentin's death—shot down over enemy lines. That fall his vigor began to leave him, and though he went on making speeches on preparedness, as he had done the evening he had been informed of his son's death, he was noticeably failing. He still toyed occasionally with thoughts of once again leading the Republican party to victory. But he was indifferent about the subject and to one friend who asked him about the possibility of his nomination in 1920 he replied: "Since Quentin's death the world seems to have shut down upon me. If my other boys do not come back, what would the presidency mean to me? . . . But if I do consent it will be because as President I could accomplish some things that I should like to see accomplished before I die, and by George if they take me they will take me without a single modification of the things I have always stood for!" The chance never came.

For over a year after the 1916 election, Woodrow Wilson enjoyed a unity hitherto unknown to an American President. During 1917 party opposition was practically unknown, so much so in fact that in speaking of the deference to the President one writer noted that "Senators of sovereign states, and leaders of parties, grovelled in their marble corridors, so terrified were they of public opinion." But in 1918 the partisan honeymooning was abruptly challenged, and party warfare was revived when Wilson called for the election of a Democratic Congress in the midterm elections of 1918, on the grounds that the Republican Congressmen had been anti-administration. This charge appears to be cut out of whole cloth when one examines the roll-call statistics for the period. On 51 roll calls dealing with war measures between April, 1917, and May, 1918, the average Republican support had been 72 percent, against 67 percent for the average support from Democratic members of the House. Since Wilson himself had declared that "politics is adjourned," a year before he demanded the election of a Democratic Congress, his reversal in 1918 in light of Republican support during the period left both him and his party in a vulnerable position.

On Election Day the voters gave Republican congressional candidates 1,200,000 more votes than they gave Democratic candidates, and partisan strife took up where it had left off a year and a half before. Almost from the day that Wilson requested the election of a partisan Congress, the Democratic party leadership began wobbling. Weary with the strains and anxieties that batter a wartime President, Wilson was beginning to lose the physical vigor and certainly the patience and tact to reassert his leadership over his own party. Thus, after six disastrous years, here was a rift in the clouds through which the sun was beginning to shine for the GOP. But, looking up at the sunlight, who could tell what was ahead? True, the Progressive party as an organization had expired. But by no means all of those who had mourned the party's passing when Roosevelt had refused to become its candidate at the 1916 convention were ready to slip back into the Republican ranks as second-class members. Yet the Republican stewardship, which had really misunderstood the Insurgent revolt of 1910 that cut the Speaker's powers, misread the true nature of the bolt in 1912, and misled the campaign of 1916, was once again inclined to view the Progressive element as a fractious minority. Even now it was laying plans that imperiled the future of the party.

"Say Boys, Let's Nominate Harding"

It was 102 degrees Fahrenheit that day early in June of 1920. And up to this time the first national party convention to meet since adoption of the 18th amendment had failed to respond—perhaps, as Mr. Mencken suggests, because "it was quite impossible to wring anything properly describable as enthusiasm out of a crowd with lakewater in its carbureters." Pausing in the midst of his address to the seventeenth Republican national convention at Chicago, Frank Willis, governor of Ohio, started to say, "Say boys, let's nominate Harding": and then as an afterthought began over: "Say boys and girls . . ."

For the first time the convention broke loose. It was on its feet, in its first spontaneous burst of enthusiasm, in a demonstration that surpassed the showing of Lowden and Wood, who were the leading contenders for the Presidential nomination. Shrewdly, assaying the fact that women would vote in the 1920 election for the first time, Willis, who later became Harding's successor in the Senate, brought down the house. In no time at all the phrase, "Say boys and girls . . ." was taken up by various delegates and heard almost like a password at the delegation caucuses.

Obviously it was not the speech of Frank Willis alone that turned the trick and changed Harding from simply a favorite son to a front-running candidate. But in the setting of the 1920 convention it gave Harding a timely assist. It was not a great speech—quite the contrary: a combination of "oratory, grand opera, and hog-calling," to quote Mark Sullivan's pithy description. Yet it was effective, and not only because it lasted just eight minutes.

For one thing, the speech of Willis stood out in sharp contrast to the dull, pedestrian effort of Henry Allen, governor of Kansas, who placed the name of General Leonard Wood in nomination. Edited and watered down by Wood's board of strategists, it had emerged almost as spineless as Disraeli once described a revised speech—"so altered, remoulded, remodelled, patched, cobbled, painted, veneered,

and varnished, that at last no trace is left of the original. . . ." Allen
knew the speech would be a dud, and his delivery revealed his own
lack of faith in it. Though a few critics have contended that Allen
deliberately delivered an uninspired speech to ruin Wood's chances,
such a theory is so unfounded that it hardly deserves comment. Allen's
case was in no way like that of Garfield, whose brilliant nominating
speech for Sherman was a factor in bringing about his own nomination for the Presidency. Any crude betrayal could only injure Allen,
which he certainly knew. He also knew that he would be suspected
of a double cross even before he made the speech, but he none the
less felt constrained to carry out his commitment as a conscientious
soldier in the ranks.

Not since James Polk became the first "dark horse" candidate to
win a presidential nomination had this term been applied with the
frequency that it came to be associated with Warren Harding. Little
mention was made of Harding as presidential timber early in 1920.
Actually several observers supposed that Harding entered the Ohio
presidential primary not for the purpose of winning the presidential
nomination, but rather to uplift his prestige for what he expected
to be his campaign for re-election to the United States Senate. Even
in his own state, Harding had a hard time of it. A bitter fight for
delegates in the Ohio presidential primary finally resulted in 39 delegates for Harding and 9 for General Wood. Beyond Ohio's borders,
Harding had not more than a few handfuls of delegates. Of just
65½ votes that he received on the first roll call at the national convention, over half were from his native state. But while the handsome Ohio Senator appeared to be limping along all during the
pre-convention campaign, certainly he was not without formidable
political allies. Moreover, at least some of Harding's supporters were
confident Harding was not a riderless horse who suddenly lunged
forth from the shadows of political oblivion at the last moment to
steal the presidential nomination.

At least five months before the convention, Harry Daugherty, then
an Ohio lobbyist, had boasted that Harding would be nominated in a
"smoke-filled room," some time "after the delegates had been allowed to play for a while with their own candidates." [1] And on
February 21 he was quoted in the New York *Times* as saying:

> I don't expect Senator Harding to be nominated on the first, second
> or third ballots, but I think we can afford to take chances that, about
> eleven minutes after two, Friday morning of the convention, when
> ten or twenty weary men are sitting around a table, someone will
> say, "Who will we nominate?" At that decisive time the friends of
> Harding will suggest him and can well afford to abide by the result.

While this was undoubtedly a piece of exaggerated embroidery, later events proved there was more behind the remark than the folly of a braggart.

Harding owed much to Daugherty, not simply because the former doggedly kept him in the race when it seemed hopeless, but for a helping hand up the successive rungs of the political ladder. In the 1908 national convention, Harding made his first appearance as an alternate-at-large, accompanied by Daugherty, then a delegate from Ohio's seventh congressional district. Four years later, during the bitter 1912 Ohio primary fight when Roosevelt took 34 delegates, leaving Taft with 14, Harding and Daugherty were again allied. The Taft forces won the four delegates-at-large, two of whom were Harry Daugherty and Warren Harding. Thus the association between Harding and his strategist was one that stretched through many political battles.

As the time neared for Will Hays, chairman of the Republican national committee, to gavel the 1920 convention to order, the pre-convention campaign was still in a highly fluid state. To begin with, had the "damn cowboy," as Hanna had called him, lived, it is generally agreed that Theodore Roosevelt would have been the Republican nominee in 1920. Not without a scrap, of course, for the right wing of the party had been flaying Roosevelt and his supporters upon every possible occasion since the debacle of 1912. None the less, as the situation unfolded in the years following Hughes's defeat, Roosevelt seemed to take the center of the stage once more as the most likely nominee. But death stilled this possibility early in January of 1919 and with it the hopes of millions who were awaiting the word from their idol.

Death came to Roosevelt while his thoughts still turned lovingly on the future of his party. Found at his bedside the morning after he died in his sleep was a scribbled note that became Will Hays's most prized possession: "Hays—see him; he must go to Washington for 10 days; see Senate and House; prevent split on domestic policies."

The leading triumvirate at convention time were Leonard Wood, Frank Lowden, and Hiram Johnson. A long-time advocate of preparedness, and originator of the Plattsburg officers' training program, General Wood had wide popular support. In the course of a distinguished career he had been Theodore Roosevelt's commanding officer during the Spanish-American War, chief of staff of the Army, and governor general of Cuba, where he continued the splendid work of ridding Havana of yellow fever.

Wood showed the greatest strength among the three leading contenders in the initial presidential balloting. He also had the support of many former friends of Roosevelt. His political manager, John T. King, was to have managed TR's 1920 campaign had he lived.

Lowden, governor of Illinois, was an able administrator whose leadership in pushing across a comprehensive state reorganization plan in 1917 began a nationwide series of adminstrative overhaulings by various state governments. He was also a person highly esteemed by farmers and won most of his support from the farm bloc states. Johnson, one of the most contentious opponents of the League of Nations in the Senate, enjoyed the reputation of a militant Progressive, and found most of his support among groups attracted by Republican Insurgency. Trailing the top three contenders were Governor Sproul and Senator Knox of Pennsylvania, Harding, Governor Coolidge of Massachusetts, and Herbert Hoover of California. Also mentioned, and having some support in the New York delegation, was Nicholas Murray Butler, president of Columbia University.

Midway in the pre-convention campaign a damaging bomb was dropped that had a crippling effect on both the Wood and Lowden campaigns and very likely cost one or the other the presidential nomination. Campaigning in North Dakota three or four months before the convention, Hiram Johnson struck out boldly with a savage attack on the money that was pouring into the headquarters of General Wood. Sensing a lively piece in this speech, which received very little national recognition, Louis Seibold, a political reporter for the old New York *World,* persuaded his managing editor to let him work up a story. First a call was placed to Senator Borah suggesting that a congressional investigation might be useful, and when Borah demanded facts Seibold set out to get them. He left at once for Bridgeport, where he saw John T. King, who had recently been removed as one of the factotums in the Wood campaign. Thoroughly discontented with his treatment, King turned over a list of Wood contributors to Seibold and the latter promptly published the list of "fat cats" on the front page of the New York *World.* With E. L. Doheny, a millionaire oil man, heading the list, each of the men was to raise a million dollars.

Once in possession of this information, Senator Borah cut loose with a Senate speech demanding an immediate inquiry, and a committee headed by Senator Kenyon of Iowa was appointed. The committee was composed of four Republicans and two Democrats.

Subsequent disclosures of the Kenyon committee brought embarrassment to both Wood and Lowden. On May 21, 1920, the committee published figures that had been obtained from duly sworn witnesses which showed Wood contributions of close to a million and three-quarters dollars. Reported contributions for Lowden were only $414,000, but the discovery of a questionable use of funds in Missouri (of which Lowden had no knowledge whatsoever) also brought unsavory publicity to the camp of the Illinois governor.

Undoubtedly the revelation of Wood's campaign expenditures was a serious jolt to his chances for the nomination. Samuel Hopkins Adams called it a "catastrophe," and writes: "Without the Kenyon Committee exposures, it is almost certain that the ex-army man, with his unimpeachable record of public service, the personal respect and liking which he commanded, and the efficient organization behind him would have swept the convention." [2] In Lowden's case the Missouri incident was probably less damaging, though one writer at least seems to have felt otherwise.[3] It is interesting to note that, in writing his book years later, Harry Daugherty claims to have started a counterattack against Wood by sending an emissary to stir up Borah. To most careful students of the period, however, this seems an exaggeration.

Quite apart from the effect of revelations that Wood had many "fat cat" contributors, and the disclosure of misuse of funds for Lowden in Missouri, the real reason that both their presidential bids stalled was fairly simple: neither candidate, nor his manager, could manage the necessary group diplomacy to come even close to the 493 votes needed to nominate. Wood, who started by leading with 287½ votes, touched his peak on the fourth ballot with 314½. Lowden, teeing off with 211½ on the first ballot, climbed gradually until he and Wood reached almost a stand-off. Johnson struck his maximum strength of 148 on the third ballot, while Harding plugged along with his 60-odd votes slightly behind Sproul throughout the early balloting.

For two days 984 heat-baked delegates and their alternates agonized while the deadlock between Wood and Lowden grew tighter. By the eighth ballot, with the general and the governor still running nip and tuck, the Harding strategists knew the time was close at hand to exploit the convention's hunger for a compromise. They were not unprepared.

It was now late afternoon Friday, the 11th of June. Saturday, presumably, was the day most delegates expected to be homeward bound. By this time chairman Henry Cabot Lodge, who served as both temporary and permanent chairman of the convention, was convinced that a compromise had to be worked out.

Actually, Lodge's dual-duty tour in itself gives some insight into the hardening lines of power that gradually crimped the decisions of the 1920 convention. Early in the spring, Beveridge had been proposed as temporary chairman for the convention. So nearly settled was this decision that Beveridge had even written a keynote speech. But though Beveridge was opposed to the League, the conservative senatorial group designated Lodge for the temporary chairmanship, and it was commonly asserted after this that the permanent chairmanship would go to Beveridge. Yet once again the senatorial cabal that seemed to stay quietly in the wings until it was time to take a direct hand in the 1920 nomination took over. Instead of becoming permanent chairman, Beveridge was shunted into the background. Will Hays of Indiana, it will be recalled, was chairman of the national committee. Jim Watson, also of Indiana, was the name the senatorial cabal used to head off Beveridge as permanent chairman. Long before the convention met they agreed to support Watson for chairman of the platform committee. Just an hour before the time a permanent chairman was to be selected at the national convention in Chicago, the resolutions committee met, and named Watson chairman without a hitch in the plan. Thereafter word of Watson's selection was hurriedly conveyed to the committee on permanent organization, with the pious thought that since it would be presumptuous to honor another Hoosier with the permanent chairmanship Lodge should be continued in the post. And so Lodge doubled in brass, while Beveridge filed away his undelivered speech.

Following the eighth ballot Lodge used his power to force an adjournment. After a hurried conference with Senator Smoot of Utah, a motion of adjournment was entertained. Since the ayes were quite inarticulate, Lodge asked for the vote again. This time an overwhelming chorus of noes thundered from the Lowden and Wood camps, but they went unheeded by chairman Lodge. Down came the gavel and with it the simultaneous announcement that the motion had carried and that the convention would reassemble Saturday.

It had been a hectic week. To his wife Senator Beveridge had written: "The Presidential muddle grows worse and worse. The delegates are desperate—literally so. No candidate will do, and they don't know where to turn." And to Albert Shaw, the noted editor of *Review of Reviews,* he later wrote: "The things that went on on the inside were perfectly amazing." [4]

What was demanded, in the way of a candidate who could meet the qualifications of those in a position to throw the nomination, narrowed down to a few specific things. The nominee, as one writer noted, should be a man who had opposed the League of Nations, and yet one who would champion a League with American reservations, so as not to give offense to that large body of Republicans who favored some form of league. He also had to have a perfect attendance record within the party and was not eligible if he had played truant in 1912. In addition, "he must be democratic and genial, not aristocratic; he must be of that persuasion that the Senate would be able to assert its constitutional position; and he must be safe in that the Senators could trust him to listen to the reasonings of its leaders." [5]

Who could fill the shoes of such a candidacy? Not Wood, for he struck the senatorial cabal as a man who would not go along easily. Nor would Lowden do, with his reputation for firmness of decision. Hiram Johnson was obviously out because of his bolt with Roosevelt in 1912 as well as his uncompromising opposition to the League. When Johnson began to fade, Borah tried to coax sentiment for a Knox-Johnson ticket which would balance an Eastern conservative with a Western Insurgent, but he found no support. Even Johnson was opposed to it. Colonel George Harvey thought of Will Hays as the man of the hour who could fill the slot, but while Hays was well liked within the party he had little general appeal. Herbert Hoover was aso a name that crept into conversations wherever candidates were mentioned, but it was quickly dismissed for want of better party credentials. Wasn't he really a Democrat? Certainly he had not kept his name out of some Democratic primaries, where incidentally he ran quite well. And so the names filed by, with the finger of fortune pointing closer to Harding all the time.

Throughout the week Harding had despaired of his chances. To Nicholas Murray Butler he said, "This convention will never nominate me," then added wistfully, "I am going to quit politics." And for his friend George B. Harris he left standing instructions that if he didn't get the nomination Harris was to return to Columbus immediately and file his name for re-election to the Senate.[6] Dejected and disheartened, he neglected even his personal grooming. William Allen White saw him with a two days' beard, looking little like the "fine statuesque figure, all tailored, and pressed" that he usually presented. Many others also noticed Harding's disheveled appearance and commented on his apparent defeatism. Even Mrs. Harding, who had stoutly maintained that Warren was in the battle "until hell freezes over," was shaken in her confidence and held an uneasy eye on the mounting bill for their suite at the Congress Hotel. The high rental for their rooms worried her, though her fears were groundless since Jake Hamon's check for $25,000 would take care of this.

No thought of dropping out appears to have crossed the mind of Harry Daugherty. Carefully collaring good will where he could, he instructed his workers not to argue but to talk up Harding as a second choice when they struck delegates favoring Wood or Lowden. While others fretted that Harding was falling out of the race when he slipped from 65½ on the first ballot to 61 on the fourth, Daugherty knew better. He had "loaned a few votes," well aware of the fact that while any slippage is usually fatal to a front runner, a low man in the race can afford it.[7] How correct he was!

Meanwhile the nocturnal drama that would always be known as the "smoke-filled room" was beginning to jell. The exact chronology of what happened that Friday evening and early Saturday morning has never been set down. Nor has there ever been full agreement by the principals of the cast. But one incontrovertible fact is clear: the conservative Republican senatorial leadership called the play.

Stepping into an elevator in the lobby of Chicago's Blackstone Hotel around 8:30 P.M., Friday evening, ex-Senator Murray Crane of Massachusetts, a delegate-at-large to each Republican convention since 1888, greeted Senator Frank Kellogg (later Secretary of State under Coolidge) of Minnesota: "Frank, you better come up tonight. We're getting this thing up for the finale." [8] Always a punctual retirer at 9:30, Kellogg could not be induced to break with habit, not even by the enchanting prospect of engineering a presidential nomination—of "sittin' in where there's somethin' doin'," as Harding's crony Jesse Smith might have put it.

Beginning with a dinner in Colonel Harvey's suite at the Blackstone, attended by Harvey, Senator Curtis of Kansas, who became Vice-President under Hoover, Senator Brandegee of Connecticut, and Senator Lodge of Massachusetts, the wheels started turning to break the stalemate. Sensing that Lowden and Wood were hopelessly deadlocked and that the delegates, many of whose financial resources were running low, would be in no mood to sanction an adjournment until Monday, this group began winnowing the field as a kind of unofficial steering committee. Calling the session a conference would be a misnomer, for throughout the evening between twelve and fifteen of the same participants were running in and out of the room. "Once when I looked in," commented Senator Wadsworth, "they were acting like a bunch of chickens with their heads cut off." As the evening wore on different emissaries and party leaders arrived, most of them presumably with deliverable votes at their disposal. Among the callers were New and Watson of Indiana, McCormick of Illinois, Murray Crane of Massachusetts, Calder and Wadsworth of New York, Joe Grundy of Pennsylvania, and Nicholas Murray Butler. Not present, but heard, was a man far to the east who had that very night rallied from a coma that his physicians thought was the end—Boies Penrose. Early in the game, Penrose had given some thought to Harding as a presidential possibility. But after hearing a speech of Harding's before the Pennsylvania Manufacturers' Association, he complained that Harding wasn't the man of parts he thought he was. "He should have talked more about the tariff and not so much about playing the cymbals in the Marion brass band." Now at the zero hour, having just regained consciousness and hearing of the deadlock at Chicago, he turned to his secretary, Leighton C. Taylor, and said: "Call up King, and tell him to throw it to Harding." [9]

Two conspicuous absentees from the political soiree at the Blackstone were Will Hays and Harry Daugherty. Nor did any supporters of the two leading contenders come before the senatorial patriarchs who were serving as unofficial pallbearers for Lowden and Wood.

Sometime before midnight tentative agreement was reached and an emissary left the room, presumably to seek out Harding. But the decision of the conference was still conditional. There appears to be little doubt, however, that the matter was pretty well settled. At 11 P.M., reports Samuel Hopkins Adams, Jacob Meckstroth of the Ohio *State Journal* saw Harding coming out of the *Journal* headquarters with Myron T. Herrick. The change that had come over Harding in a few short hours seemed unbelievable to Meckstroth. In a jaunty mood, Harding beamed as Herrick said to reporters: "You can say that Senator Harding will be nominated on the first ballot tomorrow."

Two hours later (1 A.M.) and just a few blocks away, Harding appeared at the suite of Colonel Harvey in the Blackstone. One detail remained: a leading question must be put to the Ohio Senator before the offer could become final. With only Harvey and Senator Brandegee in the room, Harvey, by self-appointment, shot the question in the kind of Olympian style for which he was noted. Several versions of this question have been reported. The one which seemed to find most credence immediately after the event was the following:

> "Senator, we want to put a question to you. Is there in your life or background any element which might embarrass the Republican Party if we nominate you for President?"

For the record, the recitation of the question to Mark Sullivan a day and a half later, after Harvey had time to embellish it a little, also bears mention:

> "We think you may be nominated tomorrow; before acting finally we think you should tell us, on your conscience and before God, whether there is anything that might be brought against you that would embarrass the party, any impediment that might disqualify you or make you inexpedient either as a candidate or as President."

Harding, taken aback, asked leave to mull it over. Harvey left him alone in a room and rejoined Brandegee while the man who would become the twenty-ninth President of the United States communed with his conscience.

What thoughts coursed through his mind as he weighed the question that had been put to him remain a matter of conjecture, though it is fairly certain that two matters troubled him. Since his political past was untouched by scandal, it is reasonable to assume that what his questioners were seeking to find out was whether there was any truth to the stories about Harding's involvement with a woman and that he was part Negro.[10]

At the very time Harding was brooding over Harvey's question, there were in Chicago both Nan Britton, allegedly the unwed mother of his child, and William Estabrook Chancellor, a professor at Wooster College in Ohio who had written several pamphlets which were then being circulated among rival headquarters, stating that Harding had Negro blood.

For several minutes Harding hung on the horns of a dilemma. Publicity about Nan would be dangerous. Several people knew about them. Yet he must have felt that he could trust Nan as well as the people who knew. In the case of the Negro story the difficulty was that newspapers had already published testimony from people who contended that there was Negro blood in the Harding family. For Harding to mention either the affair with Nan or the Negro story, if only to call them closed incidents, or to say that they were without substantiation, very likely would have spelled the end of his candidacy. He decided against saying anything about them and after ten minutes walked in and told Harvey and Brandegee that there was nothing embarrassing in his background.

This done, his nomination was practically assured. Daugherty's wild prediction had come true.

Messengers carrying the news of the decision of the "fifteen men" were dispatched at once to other headquarters, where they reported that Harding was a shoo-in for the nomination and that everybody had better board the bandwagon. The Wood camp let it be known that they would stick it out to the finish, and Lowden also said he would not withdraw while there was a fighting chance.

Meanwhile confidence radiated. So certain of the outcome was the little group that had selected Harding that Senator Smoot made a public statement detailing how the cat was to be skinned. Next morning Wood and Lowden would be given another chance on the first roll call. Wood's total, he said—and here he was wrong—would fatten a little, but not threateningly. That afternoon, after all the competitors had been afforded the chance to show their strength, Harding would get the nod.

Saturday morning Charley Curtis visited the Kansas delegation to say that it had been decided to "give Harding a play" after one or two more ballots. That afternoon he returned to tell his fellow Kansans that now was the time to break for the Ohio Senator. Similar promptings were going on in every cranny of the convention hall and delegation headquarters.

On the fifth roll call—the first to be taken Saturday forenoon, Lowden passed Wood, contrary to Smoot's prophecy. He led by four votes, 303 to 299. Then Wood made it an even draw on the sixth ballot when the vote stood 311½ to 311½, and on the seventh drew ahead of Lowden by 312-311½. The eighth ballot brought the curtain down on the hopes of Lowden and Wood. Wood fell to 299, and Lowden to 307.

Meanwhile the star for the man from Marion, Ohio, was beginning to rise. From 78 on the fifth ballot he rose to 89 on the sixth, 105 on the seventh when he passed Johnson, and 133½ on the eighth. "Watch Harding," was the word that swept the hall.

At this critical juncture, the Harding forces requested a recess; just why, no one seems to know, for with everything going their way it seemed a poor time to give the opposition a chance to recharge the batteries. Which is precisely what Wood and Lowden tried to do. Communicating by telephone they agreed to combine forces and attempt to force an adjournment until Monday. Will Hays, chairman of the national committee, was receptive to this idea and said he would use his influence to lengthen the recess until Wood and Lowden could regroup their battle lines to carry a motion for adjournment. The actual motion to adjourn was to be made by a man named Alvin T. Hert, national committeeman from Kentucky. But here the plan miscarried. A frailty in human judgment led to the selection of the wrong man for so responsible a task. Hert was on the verge of breaking for Harding and taking Kentucky with him, though he was supposed to be a representative of Lowden.

With the recess time long since elapsed, Lodge grew irritable, and after informing the stop-Harding forces that he could not hold off much longer he grudgingly allowed another ten minutes. Still Hert did not return to the hall, and when the ten minutes were up down came the gavel as chairman Lodge barked at the clerk to call the roll of the states: the ninth ballot.

While the states were voting, Hert returned. To the frantic inquiries of the Lowden-Wood floor leaders about where he had been and what about the adjournment motion, he countered with a lethal punch. He voted the Kentucky delegation for Harding. Later Hert defended his position with the lame excuse that if Lowden stayed in the race, Wood was certain to win, hence he preferred to defeat Wood rather than stay loyal to the man he was pledged to support.

Kentucky's bolt early in the parade of the states increased the din in the hall, and at the end of the roll call, Harding had 374½ votes, followed by Wood 249, Lowden 121½, and Johnson 82. The end followed swiftly.

On the tenth and final ballot—more than any in Republican convention history save the 36 in 1880, Harding won the presidential nomination with 692½ votes. Amidst screechings to make it unanimous, chairman Lodge declared that Warren G. Harding of Ohio had been unanimously nominated for President. Though the official proceedings of the convention for 1920 so record Harding's nomination, the fact is that it was not unanimous. La Follette's Wisconsin delegation, 24 strong, grimly voted "no."

And so Warren Gamaliel Harding was given the highest honor that his party had to bestow. "I feel," he said, "like a man who goes in with a pair of eights and comes out with aces full."

And so Ohio, like Virginia a "mother of presidents," added another son to the lists. This had been the seventeenth Republican national convention. In ten of these seventeen, sons of Ohio emerged as Republican nominees for President. Hayes, Garfield, McKinley (twice), Taft and Harding were actual residents of Ohio when nominated, while Ulysses S. Grant and Benjamin Harrison, who were each nominated twice, lived elsewhere at the time of nomination. Four conventions yielded Ohio vice-presidential nominees. Reid in 1892, Fairbanks in 1904 and 1916, and Dawes in 1924 were Ohio's vice-presidential sons, though none of them lived in Ohio at the time of nomination. How striking the record of Ohio has been in Republican politics is forcefully called to mind by a speech of Senator C. C. Dill at a memorial service for Senator Frank Willis eight years after the unique 1920 convention. Said Dill: "Every Republican president who has entered the White House by the votes of the people since the Civil War has come directly from Ohio or been born in Ohio." The other two Republican Presidents who entered the White House stepped in via the Vice-Presidency. Herbert Hoover in 1928 was the first one to break the Ohio spell.

Born in Blooming Grove, Ohio, November 2, 1865, the eldest of eight children, Harding was raised in Marion, where his father practiced medicine. Because his mother wanted him to be a preacher he went to Iberia College (no longer extant); he studied law for a short time, taught school, and by a fortuitous combination of circumstances became the editor and publisher of a small paper, the Marion *Star,* in 1884 at the relatively young age of nineteen. Newspaper work and printing continued to fascinate him throughout his life, and few things gave him more genuine delight than the chance to discuss composing problems or newsprint in the sad days he had in the White House. He also liked music and, equipped with a fair musical ear, he became a first-rate performer on the alto horn in the Citizen's Cornet Band of Marion.

In politics, Harding got around the bases modestly well. Starting out in the state senate in 1899, he became lieutenant-governor in 1904, was defeated for the governorship in 1910 and was elected to the United States Senate in 1914. Not an architect of ideas nor a person with resolute leadership qualities, he was disposed to follow the political maxim that the way to get along is to go along. He had no illusions about himself and throughout the full distance of his political ascent he approached each new assignment with a deep-felt humility. Driven onward and upward by his ambitious wife, there were many times that Harding wanted out. But, like Gladstone, he discovered that "it's easier to get into politics than to get out." Now he was the Republican presidential nominee at a promising time. With Woodrow Wilson stricken by a fatal illness and the reaction against the "ins" beginning to bruise the Democratic party, 1920 looked like a good year for the GOP.

Not often does the pulse beat of a national convention quicken over the nomination of a Vice-President. But it did in 1920, in this charged atmosphere of power plays. After Harding was nominated word quickly slipped around that it was to be Lenroot. Senator Medill McCormick told the Kansas delegation "that on the slate it was written that Irvine Lenroot should be nominated for Vice-President," but on this one the delegates rebelled. A United States Senator from Wisconsin, Lenroot had been speaker of the Wisconsin House under La Follette's administration as governor, but by this time his earlier Insurgency had cooled considerably. What really mattered in his rejection for the Vice-Presidency, however, was the old breaking-point rule of group politics that the party members will follow leaders so far and no farther. When the leaders tried to place a second Senator on the ticket something snapped. The delegates revolted.

Lenroot was nominated by Senator McCormick, whose speech was seconded by Governor Herrick of Ohio and that same Hert of Kentucky who had swung from Lowden to Harding. Then a loud voice began baying for recognition far over on the north side of the convention floor. It was Wallace McCamant—*not even a member of the convention,* but the chairman didn't seem to mind. By this time delegates were drifting out of the hall and observers were spilling from the galleries, and what McCamant said few were able to hear. But what he did amidst the clatter of crashing seats and shuffl-ing feet was to nominate Calvin Coolidge. The nomination—so the official proceedings tell us—was then followed by "an outburst of applause of short duration, but of great power." Michigan seconded the Coolidge nomination and in rapid order Maryland, Arkansas, Connecticut, and North Dakota lined up behind the Bay state can-didate. When these states were joined by Illinois, Nebraska, Nevada, and Vermont, Coolidge could no longer be stopped. On the first and only ballot, Coolidge received 674½ votes to 146 for Lenroot. Even Wisconsin joined in to make the final vote unanimous this time.

Far off in Boston Coolidge was listening quietly to the proceedings with his wife. He suddenly perked up as the news of the warm re-sponse to McCamant's speech reached him. After several long dis-tance calls he finally cradled the telephone and quacked to his wife crisply: "Nominated." "You're not going to take it, are you?" she inquired. "I suppose I'll have to," he answered.

In the fading sunset of the 1920 convention what the party directorate failed to recognize was that by selecting the type of leader they did they were "emasculating the great office of the Presi-dency, and were seriously damaging if not dooming their party." It would lead to association with a policy which Sam Lubell accurately characterizes as "one of the most basic of all Republican contradic-tions," a "fondness for a weak President." [11] Amidst the compelling urgency for the exercise of leadership and legislative guidance at home as well as abroad, the attraction for Presidents who abstained from vigorous leadership would speed the decline of the party.

Romanticized accounts of the "smoke-filled room" have over-drawn the role of George Harvey. Harvey wanted Will Hays, and even as late as Saturday afternoon he was trying to promote Hays rather than Harding. And Lodge, also immortalized as a smoke-filled-room kingmaker, did not want Harding. More important, how-ever, was the fact that the stalemate of leading contenders Lowden and Wood made Harding a logical person to call up. A handsome showpiece, he was a popular figure with the delegates. Moreover, he was a "regular"—something not true of Lowden and Wood. And so with "the majority of delegates hostile to Wood, utterly out of sym-pathy with Johnson, and the fund scandal compromising Lowden," [12] Harding appealed to organizational men. No doubt he would have picked up many delegates even without the smoke-filled room.

Weighing the 1920 nomination story in the balance, probably no other convention had been so completely dominated by a Republican contingent from the national legislature. Whether by accident, con-spicuous desire for change, or both, the influence of the congressional

wing of the party in more recent times has been lessening. Not only
have fewer Congressmen been serving as actual delegates, but their
influence has also declined as that of governors has ascended in the
matter of leading state delegations. In part this change may stem
from the long lockout on federal patronage that kept GOP Congressmen and Senators from building strength by dispensing jobs.
Their influence henceforth may also be checked somewhat by the
Hatch act, which restricts the political activity of most federal employees. But in all likelihood an element of sociological change that
runs deeper has also had a restraining influence on Republican
legislators in national convention affairs. The political pigmentation
of the country varies so widely that there are still many tight islands
of thought among Republican congressional districts, just as in the
Senate some members speak for tight islands. In the House, these
areas—often known as "safe districts"—are likely to be represented
by persons whose views lag behind the central stream of thought of
the party. Yet seniority advances these men to committee chairmanships, where they are thrust into positions of great power in steering
the course of party policy. But a growing urbanization in the past
generation has forced Republican candidates who run for a statewide office to attend to "the movement of urban thought," which, as
one writer capably puts it, "in our day is restless." This has meant,
of course, that many Republican governors have managed to get
their candidacies airborne by making an appeal that shows some
awareness of urban interests. In consequence, as such men as Dewey,
Herter, Warren, Lodge, McKeldin, and others have been elected, the
influence of the Republican congressional wing at national conventions has received a formidable challenge. Certainly the curbing influence of gubernatorial strength has been a significant factor in the
outcome of every convention from the nomination of Alfred Landon
in 1936.

Initially no accolade greeted the Harding nomination. To begin
with, men like Will Hays were not sold on Harding. The nation's
number one Republican paper, the New York *Herald Tribune,*
thought it a victory for the stand-patters, while the *Evening Post*
and the Cleveland *Plain Dealer* felt the nomination signified domination by the Senate ring. The New York *Times* did not hesitate to use
the brass knuckles, and labeled the nomination "the fine and perfect
flower of the cowardice and imbecility of the senatorial cabal." [13]

That the campaign would not be a free-fisted match was sug-
gested at the very outset. Meeting at San Francisco the last week in
June the Democrats nominated the publisher, James M. Cox, for
President and a former assistant Secretary of the Navy, Franklin D.

Roosevelt, as his running mate. Now the strange campaign was on.

Seriously weakened by illness, Boies Penrose, ringmaster of Pennsylvania Republican politics for a quarter of a century, issued a statement that the issue of the campaign would be "Americanism." Asked by Talcott Williams what the word "Americanism" meant, he replied: "Damned if I know, but you will find it a damned good issue to get votes in an election." On the type of campaign that was to be waged, Penrose counseled wisely: "Keep Warren at home. Don't let him make any speeches. If he goes out on a tour, somebody's sure to ask him questions, and Warren's just the sort of damn fool that'll try and answer them."

The advice of Penrose was not carried out to the last dotting of the "i" and crossing of the "t." Harding made a few speeches. But the campaign was designed to keep his utterances on public questions to a minimum and to pick his audiences carefully. For such strategy, the Front Porch campaign was a natural.

Emerging on the curved side porch of his modest home, set off with dignity by a fine stand of stately elms and maples, Harding could lean over the white balustrade, shake hands with the leaders of visiting delegations, and then make a speech no longer than today's "whistle stop." It proved highly effective, partly because Harding really loved people and threw himself into the handshaking ordeal effortlessly and vigorously; once he told a friend, "This is the most pleasant thing I do."

All summer long special trains, bands, glee clubs, and caravans of people representing different organizations and groups arrived at Marion while Harding used his home as a nerve center.

The "Hays harmony platform," as the 1920 convention platform was often called, finally emerged with the usual spongy spots of party platforms—"fusions of ambiguities," as Wendell Willkie liked to call them. It contained pledges for economy, tax reduction, rapped Wilson briskly and, thanks to the efforts of Senator Borah, Senator McCormick, and delegate William Allen White, included a plank granting to labor the right of "collective bargaining" in labor disputes, with "representatives of their own choosing." The latter phrase, incidentally, was Samuel Gompers's own and had been presented to Senator Borah personally by the long-time head of the American Federation of Labor. Curiously, the 1920 platform also contained a pledge to work for the diplomatic recognition of Russia —an item that most Republican orators conveniently overlook in laying all foreign-affairs troubles at the doorstep of Franklin Roosevelt's recognition of the Soviet Union in 1933.

One of the friction points that needed immediate greasing was the party policy on the League of Nations issue. The resolutions committee agreed to a statement giving a gentle endorsement to the World Court, but no one sewed together a statement that was acceptable to both the isolationists and internationalists. In desperation, the internationalist group appealed to Elihu Root, who was about to sail for Europe. An internationalist, Root recognized the realities of the situation, and determined to get something in the platform that would not slam the door against negotiations to join the League. What he finally came up with resembled an oil slick. "It was fearfully and wonderfully made," writes William Allen White. "It meant nothing except that it frankly did mean nothing, and we accepted it. It was that or defeat on the floor."

With this background on the platform fight over the League issue, it was natural that insuring harmony for campaign purposes was a matter of high priority in getting the party into working harness. As the campaign wore on into autumn, a group of thirty-one distinguished Republicans announced that they favored a League of Nations, but that they also preferred Harding for President. The Committee of Thirty-one, as it was called, included A. Lawrence Lowell, president of Harvard University, and Messrs. William Howard Taft, Herbert Hoover, Charles Evans Hughes, Nicholas Murray Butler, Roger Straus, George Wickersham, Ray Lyman Wilbur, Jacob Gould Schurmann and William Allen White. Its chairman was the former Senator and Secretary of War, Elihu Root. Speaking forthrightly, Taft said, "Even if the risk of war to the United States would be greater by entering a league to enforce peace . . . does not the United States have a duty . . . to join a league?" Clearly it would not do to ignore such a formidable group as the Committee of Thirty-one. The way out of the dilemma was not easy. Nor has the issue of isolationism vs. internationalism been one that the Republican party has been able to resolve ever since.

During most of the campaign Harding walked a tight wire on the League issue. Toward the end of August he gave two speeches that had some friendly gestures for an association of nations not unlike a proposal advocated by Elihu Root. Pro-League supporters took some measure of comfort in this stand. Instantly, however, the League's enemies swung into action. Beveridge wrote to Harding: "Might it not be well for you to cut the Gordian knot—to cut loose from the whole miserable business, and say, simply, plainly and positively, that we will have nothing to do with the League in any shape or form." Senators Borah and Johnson then had a go at Harding, with the result that the candidate sidestepped the issue for quite a time. In late September, however, he indicated that he favored a "rejection" of the League.

Meanwhile two advisers the national committee had assigned to Harding to help him in the tight places devised a scheme to take some of the crackle out of the issue. Richard Washburn Child, a fiction writer, and editor George Harvey proposed a world court, and a reconstructed league which would rest upon the court, and a loose association of nations functioning through what was to be known as a Conference.

The articulation of the scheme drawn up by Child and Harvey, of course, was consciously kept misty, the real purpose being to make it easier for proponents of the League to stay with Harding and yet not give offense to the isolationists. For the most part the dodge worked, though the leaders of both groups had many misgivings.

On other matters Harding took his cues largely from the party platform. He asked for tax reduction, but said that he was for continuance of the excess-profits tax and high levies on large incomes. As for the touchy subject of Prohibition, he simply acknowledged that it was "impossible to ignore the Constitution . . . and unthinkable to evade the law."

Few campaigns have generated less bitterness. The candidates had a cordial regard for one another, and neither threw any low punches. Only one serious blemish marred the conduct of the campaign against Harding, and this in no way was inspired by the Democratic opponent, James M. Cox.

Once again the old rumor that Harding had Negro blood was dusted off for use against him. This time it was dressed up in a genealogical diagram by Professor William Estabrook Chancellor of Wooster College, who described himself as an "anthropologist, ethnologist, and genealogist." Carrying his investigation back to the seventeenth century, Chancellor purported to show by a diagrammatic sketch that Harding had mixed blood. Not only did he conduct such investigations but actually printed them in leaflet form. One such leaflet was addressed "To the Men and Women of America," then added: "Warren Gamaliel Harding is not a white man. May God save America from international shame and domestic ruin."

How many such leaflets were actually distributed and who paid for them is not known. Strangely, the professor himself held no grudge against Harding, but simply had an obsession against Negroes. Democrats disclaimed any connection with distribution of the leaflets, and Joe Tumulty, Woodrow Wilson's secretary, reports that when approached by a person who thought they might be used for campaign material, Tumulty turned him away, saying, "I'll have nothing to do with it."

At Wooster, Ohio, the president of Wooster College summoned a meeting of his trustees, and after Chancellor was given a hearing his resignation was requested by unanimous vote. Chancellor complied, though some of his students protested. At his hearing he stated that Harding's nomination was a plot to bring about Negro domination in this country, and that while he had been superintendent of schools in Washington, D.C., he had himself been the victim of Negro persecution.

Late in the campaign the firecracker that Professor Chancellor had lit seemed to call for some kind of counter-offensive. Special correspondents were sending out long stories to their papers each day from Marion, and accompanying them with private messages for their editors. At this juncture Harding, who had then left the Front Porch for a whirlwind short tour, called a press conference, presumably for the purpose of issuing a denial of the Negro charge. Exactly what happened cannot be documented, but one person who preferred to remain anonymous reported that just as the candidate was about to issue a statement Mrs. Harding came in unexpectedly and insisted the matter be dropped. No formal denial ever followed.

The campaign, as it ground to a close, seemed to be going moderately well. It had been well financed under the capable direction of the party treasurer, Fred Upham of Chicago, and it had been skillfully organized by one of the best chairmen the national committee ever had—Will Hays of Indiana. A man who really understood the chemistry of politics, Hays hugged close to the rule that politics is an art of the possible. And you don't overreach yourself. Hays knew the limitations of his candidate. He knew it would be a mistake to permit his candidate to rush around the country and "bloviate"—a word used by Harding himself to describe how he liked to pontificate generalities in a florid oratorical style. Harding's kind of oratory was already beginning to be outmoded, and his English, when he was left to his own resources, "was the worst I have ever encountered," said H. L. Mencken. "It reminded me of a string of wet sponges." Hays was aware of it.

Hays also knew the mood of the country. Waste motion and undistributed campaign literature did not fit his idea of conducting winning campaigns. Moreover, he believed in party workers who held grass-roots credentials, and not interlopers who bounded into campaigns with periodic regularity. Sending sometimes as many as three telegrams a day to local workers out in the field, he managed to give them the heady feeling that they were looking right over his shoulder and planning major moves in the campaign. Again and again he admonished his workers: "Things don't just happen. They're brought about." Seldom has the Republican party had so effective a field general.

Election Day brought the word "landslide" back into the Republican vocabulary. Polling 60.3 percent of the popular vote, Harding captured a larger share of the total vote than Franklin Roosevelt would command in retiring Herbert Hoover twelve years later. He carried 37 states and nearly two-thirds of the counties. The 26,748,-224 million votes cast in 1920 represented an increase of eight million over 1916. While the Democratic vote remained almost exactly the same as it had been in 1916, the Republican total practically doubled. "Not a single county was carried in the Pacific section by the Democrats, and only thirteen in the Mountain section, where in 1916 there had been 223." [14] Compared with 1916, the Democratic vote proportionately (there were 8,000,000 new voters this year) suffered a loss in every state in the Union except South Carolina and Mississippi.

On the congressional side, the Republican score was also not unimpressive. The Congress that took office with Harding on March 4, 1921, was composed of 59 Republicans and 37 Democrats in the Senate, and 300 Republicans and 132 Democrats in the House (there were two vacancies and one independent).

In the aftermath, opinion tended to agree that the major factors in the victory were the attacks on Wilson and his foreign policies, and the secret weapon of American politics known as the "desire for a change." It would be ten years before the Republicans lost control of Congress, twelve before they lost the Presidency.

In the flush of victory, an earlier outburst of Mrs. Harding was momentarily forgotten: "I can see but one word written over his head if they make him President, and that word is Tragedy." Although his wife's premonition was quickly put out of mind, Harding was not unmindful of the fearsome responsibilities ahead. His old friends at Marion, and the Elks, the Loyal Order of Moose, and other organizations that gave him farewell testimonials noted a brooding composure in him and remarked about it.

Hoping to be the best-loved if not the best President, Harding placed his trust in the Deity. Not all of his friends did.

"How do I Get Out of the Senate?"

Hurrying to answer a roll call a few days after his defeat for renomination to the United States Senate in 1922, Harry S. New encountered a frantic woman who apparently was completely confused by the many complicated passageways that so often confound visitors to the Capitol building. "Won't you please tell me how to get out of the Senate?" she begged. "I've been running around in circles for at least half an hour, and I simply must get out." "Madam," said New, bowing graciously, "I suggest you try an Indiana primary."

Except for the election of 1820, when Monroe was elected without opposition, no party had ever experienced such a triumph as that which befell the Republicans in 1920. Yet in the face of this extraordinary record, and despite the fact that whispers of a tumultuous scandal were hardly yet heard, the Republican party suffered defeats in many parts of the country. The only notable Republican victories in 1922 were won by Progressive stalwarts who had left the reservation in 1912 to follow Theodore Roosevelt. Gifford Pinchot, repudiated by the regular Republican organization of his own state, was elected governor of Pennsylvania by a margin of 250,000 votes; Robert Howell was sent to the Senate from Nebraska with a handsome majority; and the embattled warrior Hiram Johnson returned to the Senate from California by 340,000 votes.

Elsewhere the fortunes of the Republican regulars were quite different. In the seven states of Wisconsin, Idaho, Iowa, Minnesota, North Dakota, South Dakota, and Nebraska, voters took a perverse posture toward the national leadership of the Republican party in the elections of 1922 (and the 1923 special elections). Disapproval of control by the Republican national organization was expressed either by direct affiliation with the Non-Partisan League or the Farmer-Labor party or by the character of Republicans elected. In North Dakota, where A. C. Townley had been accepting postdated checks to help finance his Non-Partisan League, Lynn Frazier was elected to the United States Senate as the League's candidate by over

100,000 votes. Moreover, though the League began to lose ground after 1922, it was still strong enough to menace the regular Republican organizations in many states. It had already added a formidable beachhead in Minnesota, and was making efforts to homestead a place in South Dakota, Montana, Kansas, Oklahoma, Nebraska, Iowa, and Wisconsin.

Up in the central Northwest, the newly foaled Farmer-Labor party gave further evidence of growing discontent with national GOP leadership by scoring its first impressive victory in Minnesota. After one term in the Senate, Frank Kellogg was dethroned in 1922 by the Farmer-Labor nominee, Henrik Shipstead, a handsome candidate who had trained for a political career by filling molars and fitting dentures. While the Republican gubernatorial candidate, Jacob Preus, was successful in the same election, Magnus Johnson, his Farmer-Labor opponent, defeated him the following year in a special election to fill the Senate vacancy caused by the death of the venerable Viking, Knute Nelson.

In Wisconsin the return of Robert Marion La Follette to the Senate for a third term by a 300,000 vote margin also conformed nicely with the protest pattern of 1922. But it was in Iowa that the direction of party affairs within the Republican fold itself was most effectively unhinged. In a special election to fill the Senate seat vacated by the resignation of William S. Kenyon, Smith Wildman Brookhart, a lusty Bedouin, took the Republican nomination in easy stride and went on to win the general election by 167,000 votes.

That fall the Republican seats in the House fell from 300 in 1920 to 221; in the Senate from 59 to 52. It was in the primaries, however, that the strongest hints emerged of what was about to happen.

What was prompting these ripples of revolt that led voters to page Beveridge from political retirement to contest the organization-backed candidacy of Harry New in Indiana? What explained results like Frazier's election in North Dakota, Shipstead's and Magnus Johnson's in Minnesota, and "Wildman" Brookhart in Iowa (newspapermen were fond of setting off his middle name in quotes)?

Many news editors professed to see in the election results of 1922 a return to what they characterized as that "instability in the public mind" and "the idiosyncrasies of public opinion" that were ravaging the land in the days when the direct primary, initiative, referendum, and recall were demanded by "Sockless" Jerry Simpson and "People's Party Peffer." Surely much of the impetus for these upheavals came from discontent over the agricultural depression of 1921-22, low prices for farm commodities, and the inability of Republican na-

tional leadership to get an effective agricultural relief program off
the ground. The country was, after all, in its first agricultural depression of the century.[1] In 1922 the protest followed the rims of the
hardest-hit congressional districts and states. In Brookhardt's campaigns in Iowa, for example, he ran the strongest wherever the livestock or cash grain prices were the lowest or where drought conditions
were the worst.[2]

No doubt the turbulent tones of the 1922 Middle Western protest had an intimate kinship with those of an earlier era when the
battle cries of reform were first sounded by La Follette, Bristow, Norris, Beveridge, Clapp, and others. But the "alliance of left wing economics and isolationism," as Sam Lubell reminds us, was another
important ingredient in the Republican reverses of 1922 as well as
of other setbacks during the twenties.[3] Many Progressives of the
Northwest felt that their crusade for reform had been betrayed by
the war, and were now openly hostile to any participation in foreign
affairs. Charles Lindbergh's father, a former Minnesota Congressman who had bitterly opposed our entrance into the war, encountered
a few people who protested his stand by getting off streetcars when
he boarded them in 1918. But, by the early twenties, he found far
more who thought he had been right. Behind this resentment an ancient distrust was reviving—a feeling that the East regarded the
states of the Northwest as merely distant provinces whose inhabitants
were to be regarded as colonials. Thus the preoccupation of the East
with foreign affairs meant to the farmer and small businessman of
the Middle West the neglect of unsolved problems at home. This
they deeply opposed, and not unnaturally turned to the leadership of
such rebels of reform within the GOP as Norris, Norbeck, Borah,
Johnson, La Follette, and others who fought Old Guard leadership.

More subtle changes in town-farm relationships were also beginning in the twenties which would soon affect the traditional dominance the Republican party enjoyed among the rural voters. The
farmer was insisting that the town not be simply an outpost for business interests, but identify its own interest increasingly with the
farmer. And to encourage such a change in attitude they happily
hooked their political fortunes onto the coattails of the Progressive
GOP Senators—the "sons of the wild jackass." But the depth of discontent among farmers of the area and what the gradual stockpiling
of political grievances was doing to the traditional ties of party loyalty were seen only by a few.

How deep a change was being wrought in party loyalties was not
to be fully apparent for another decade, when the Republican party
was tumbled from power after a twelve-year lease on the Presidency,

and thereafter went down to five successive defeats before regaining office. But even the subsequent results of the ballot box, which after all proclaim themselves more effectively than any other measurement device in politics, did not reveal the full story of the break in Republican loyalties that was beginning in the early twenties.

Since the inception of the GOP the Middle West had been one of the principal supports of the Republican party. For the first thirty years after the 1854 Republican meeting under the oaks at the grove in Jackson, no Democrat could snare Michigan's electoral vote until Grover Cleveland broke the spell in 1884, and what was true of Michigan was by and large true of all the West North Central states. Moreover, what happens in Michigan is worth watching, for if the Republican party loses Michigan for good, "it has lost the nation for good." For very likely just as Michigan, Ohio, and Illinois go, with their mass industrialism in combination with broad agricultural interests, so goes the nation.

Had the shift in farm-belt voting sentiment been solely one of gradual defection from the once preponderant Republicanism of this region, in favor of the rise in Democratic registration that has been on the increase for the past twenty years, this alone would be a matter of compelling seriousness. But looking behind the ballot box, the element of grave concern for the Republican party lies in the young men who were born in the immediate post-World War I period and in the early twenties, who today are the leading officers in the Democratic party in this region.

Today most of the Democratic state chairmen and leaders in the farm belt states, of whom Carl Thompson of Wisconsin, Orville Freeman of Minnesota, Joseph Robbie of South Dakota, J. A. Loveland of Iowa, Clayton Strout of Nebraska, Marvin Harder, Paul Aiken, and D. C. (Buzz) Hill of Kansas are typical, are in their thirties.[4] And a majority of them come from Republican families and Republican backgrounds. It is in this circumstance that the Republican party faces its greatest problem of manning the dikes: how to attract and hold a vigorous following among the youth of America.

After the Civil War, when the Republican party took on a conservative coloration, it could not draw upon an educated aristocratic leadership as conservative parties have sometimes been able to do elsewhere. In consequence the GOP found itself at various times taking orders from first-generation masters of industry, commerce, and finance, many of them geniuses to be sure, but none of them entirely dedicated to policies of statecraft that served the transcendent public good. By 1922—almost three generations from the party's birth, and after it had ruled the Republic for 50 of its first 68 years—

staunch Republicans were siring sons who would be the potentates of the Democratic party by 1950. Many of the sons and daughters who during this period grew up surrounded by Republican families and environments have, of course, remained faithful to the party of the Great Emancipator. And several have labored diligently to re-tread Republican platforms and programs with more progressive principles. But, beginning in 1913, the removal of such a large group of earnest young men from Republican backgrounds to the Democratic party, where they quickly ascended to positions of lead-ership, was a significant loss to Republicanism.

It may well be that, like many political movements, to a genera-tion growing up through a decade of riotous living followed by one of depression the Republican party and many Republicans themselves appeared to have outdistanced their major fighting faiths and their fighting formulae. The single issue that had united the splinter par-ties and political remnants of 1854 had long since fallen into disuse. Nor did there appear to be any sizable group within the ranks of the GOP which was seriously interested in reactivating the work that began with Lincoln's Emancipation Proclamation. When the sixteenth Republican national convention convened in 1916, there were only twenty-five Negro delegates in the convention, the smallest number ever present since Negroes were accorded full recognition. And in 1919 a Tennessee Republican, John W. Farley, published a small monograph in which he argued that the Republican Radical leader of the Civil War period, Thaddeus Stevens, was wrong in wanting to enfranchise the Negro. Taking nine counties, where over fifty per-cent of the Negroes in Tennessee lived, to validate his argument, Farley attempted to show that wherever Republicans made an appeal for the Negro vote their activity caused more Democrats and inde-pendents to turn out at elections and vote against Republican nom-inees.[5] Concluding also that Southern whites were more migratory than Negroes, he contended that the million or more Southerners who had moved to the North by 1910 found Negro literature put out by the Republicans highly offensive. Obviously Farley was not expressing the majority sentiments of his party, yet his arguments appeared to spark few vigorous rejoinders. Far from the fighting faith that once stirred them to action, the Republicans in 1920, as the brilliant but bitter Negro sociologist William E. B. Dubois com-mented in the *Nation,* were "not losing much sleep over the Negro." Not without validity also were the complaints of Dubois that many Republicans joined hands with the South in disfranchising the Negro, and that they fostered a system which encouraged the practice of buying up certain Southern delegates to the party's conventions.

Not only had the fighting faiths of Republicans in the twenties seemed to recede distantly into the mists of the past, but the GOP partisans were also without a national leader who could conceptualize these faiths dramatically and simultaneously devise new fighting formulae. It had been quite a spell since that searing hot August day in 1910 when Teddy Roosevelt tipped his toes into the dust of Osawatomie's Main Street (John Brown's middle name was Osawatomie) and roused the Kansas townfolk with the ringing battle cry: "I stand for the square deal." Roosevelt had passed away at his Oyster Bay home on Long Island, January 6, 1919. That he had many faults, that he was inconsistent, that his progressivism was too much a matter of expediency to suit the La Follette wing of the Republican party, and too unpredictable and heretical for the stand-pat wing, was freely admitted. Yet beyond all his shortcomings, and the blemishes he left on the record of the American political scene, he had one overriding quality—he was "incorrigibly human." "Which is one of the reasons, I suppose," wrote his close friend Hermann Hagedorn thirty years after his death, "why thousands who knew him at close range or only from afar still feel his spell, and wish, on dark nights, that he were somewhere around." [6]

But Roosevelt was not around as the Republican leadership groped uncertainly and fitfully to meet the challenge of events in the early 1920's. And many of those who had marched behind his banner were now weak of heart or were toying with the idea of riding off under a different party standard. Certainly their sons would be reared in a climate where defection from the GOP might readily be anticipated. So it was that the drive of the little group of progressives who started to change the dominant character of the Republican party from the once "almost solid phalanx of stand-patters" at the turn of the century now was without a national leader.

Early in the summer of 1923, Warren Harding left the oppressive heat of Washington on the first leg of his long trip to Alaska. He did not, however, leave behind the heavy anxieties that had been bedeviling him for many months. By this time the internal pressures bearing upon the President's mind were indescribably awesome. For some months rumors had circulated about a marauding gang of small-bore politicos who were organizing commercialized political vice on a shameful scale. Harding himself had long been aware of the problem, for it began to descend upon him the moment he was elected. He had, in fact, complained of it distressingly to a number of persons, including William Allen White, whom he sent for after he had been in office about a year. On White's first visit to the White

House the President spoke of a "bunch" who were going to call on him that very afternoon, "good friends of mine from Ohio, decent fellows that I have worked with for thirty years." The "good friends" that the President referred to were, of course, under indictment for violating an anti-trust law and what they intended to ask him, said Harding, was to dismiss the indictment. Agonized by the situation about to confront him, the President cried to White: "I can take care of my enemies all right. But damn my friends—God damn my friends, White, they're the ones that keep me walking the floor nights!"

A year after this, the cabal of influence hucksters and his own inability to say no had placed Harding on the steep slopes of a volcano. What was about to happen might perhaps be best described by a term Paul Elmer More once used: "an explosion in a cesspool." Now it was no longer only a matter of the noxious group of characters, headed by Jesse Smith, who sold federal favors from that much publicized little green house on K Street. Beyond the unbelievably corrupt transactions of a semi-public character, and the sale of governmental favors for whatever the traffic would bear by the little gang operating from K Street, the word had passed around that these scandals had touched the cabinet itself.

On March 4, 1923, just two years after he was sworn in, Albert Bacon Fall resigned as Secretary of the Interior. A former United States Senator from New Mexico and an associate justice on the supreme court of that state, Fall had been an incongruity from the start in the important post of Secretary of the Interior. It was surely unwise to elevate an anti-conservationist to such a post when the Republican party could lay legitimate claim to conservation leadership under men like Theodore Roosevelt and Gifford Pinchot. But Fall turned out to be more than an anti-conservationist. Unhappily he also turned out to be a corruptionist.

Though he had been out of the cabinet for several months when Harding started his trip to the north from which he would not return alive, the full measure of Albert Fall's trespasses against the public domain were not yet known. Even the extent to which a case against him would be pushed was not entirely clear. But the night Harding talked briefly with William Allen White in a Kansas City hotel suite on his way west, and suddenly asked to be excused when Mrs. Fall came to the door, the President probably knew that a real blockbuster could no longer be kept from dropping on his administration. What was said remains unknown, though Senator Capper later reported that the President stayed with Mrs. Fall until the very moment he was scheduled to make a speech that night, and that he returned excited and obviously worried.

Fall's transgressions against the Republic not only forced his resignation from the cabinet—ultimately they led to prosecution and imprisonment. What he had done was to persuade President Harding to sign an executive order (which the Supreme Court later declared illegal), transferring the management of huge oil reserves belonging to the public domain from the jurisdiction of the Secretary of the Navy to Fall's own Department of the Interior. Thereafter, for handsome considerations, Fall leased these government properties to various oil owners. While complicity was not proved against Secretary of the Navy Denby in this transfer of oil reserves from one executive department to the other, complacency was, and Denby himself resigned from the cabinet under pressure from Harding's successor Calvin Coolidge on March 18, 1924.

The great oil scandals, of course, marked but one of the effronteries of the Harding administration. Elsewhere there were many others. Another cabinet member who turned out to be a storm center of contention was Attorney General Harry Daugherty. Against the better judgments and express protests of several of the party's most powerful and respectable luminaries, Harding had appointed Daugherty, who had been an attorney for several large corporations. After the 1920 convention, of course, the President had reason to feel under heavy obligation to Daugherty. But as those who counseled against the appointment anticipated, soon after Daugherty moved into the Attorney General's office the milking began. His little coterie of friends who moved in with him started using his name and the office for corrupt purposes in total disregard of the public interest. Protection against prosecution, for which large sums were exacted, was one facet of this abuse of the public trust. There was also set up a system of toll transactions, involving the horde of people seeking soft sinecures somewhere in the ark of the federal service. Moreover, to screen these activities and hold possible detractors at bay, selected agents in the Department of Justice were used to spy upon those who protested or threatened disclosure of any irregular practice.

Nor was the sordid side of these years confined solely to abuses within the preserves of the Interior, Navy, and Attorney General's offices. The Veterans' Bureau too became seriously involved in graft. Will Irwin, who did a series for the North American news syndicate on the malpractices of Colonel Charles R. Forbes, who headed this agency, estimated the total cost to the taxpayers at $200,000,000. Director Forbes, like the Secretary of the Interior, was convicted and sent to jail. Elsewhere several millions in worthless foreign bonds were permitted to be sold to the public. Actually the full measure of cases involving bartering for privileges will probably never be known. Not since the days of the Grant administration had predatory desires run so rampant among men holding positions of public trust. How Secretaries Hoover and Hughes, with their impeccable reputations for honesty and integrity, must have felt as their cabinet teammates became steadily more tarnished, pales the imagination.

The Attorney General was indicted and put on trial for faithlessness to duty for his alleged part in causing the American Metals Company to be released from the Alien Property Custodian's office. Set forth briefly, the facts leading to the Daugherty indictment were as follows: The American Metals Company, said to have been owned by a German concern, was taken over and sold during the war, and the proceeds from the sale were sequestered by the Treasury Department. Following the war, the owners of the American Metals Company set about to get the property back, contending that the concern had not been German-owned, but was actually a Swiss property. Richard Merton, representing the owners, came over from Germany and arranged with John T. King, a New York financier and active Republican who left Wood in the middle of the 1920 preconvention campaign to support Harding, to have the American Metals Company removed from the Alien Property Custodian's office —a move which would have been altogether proper if consummated through the available legal channels for such action. This was to be done by first getting the consent of the Alien Property Custodian's office to release the property and then acquiring the approval of the Attorney General's office. For this service King was paid $441,000.

Subsequently, however, it was discovered that of the $441,000 King had been paid ($391,000 of this sum was in Liberty bonds), $50,-000 in bonds passed to Alien Property Custodian John W. Miller. Moreover, an additional $50,000 in bonds was shown to have reached Jess Smith, Daugherty's close crony and the man who shared an apartment with him at Washington's Wardman Park Hotel. Alien Property Custodian Miller was convicted and sent to jail. Jess Smith, however, who had deposited bonds totaling at least $50,000 from the lot which had been paid to King in the bank of Daugherty's brother at Washington Court House, Ohio, had long since committed suicide when this fact became known.[7] Smith deposited the bonds in an account marked "Jess Smith Extra No. 3," a political account which was directed by Daugherty and had been opened by Daugherty when he first started his pre-convention campaign for Harding's nomination.

Under this circumstantial evidence Daugherty was indicted for conspiring to "defraud the United States of its governmental functions and rights and of the honest, impartial, and unprejudiced services" of its Attorney General. At the trial in October of 1926, Daugherty marshaled strong evidence to show that he had nothing to do with the release of the American Metals Company except to affix his signature to decisions made by other officials. On this matter Daugherty was backed up by both Alien Property Custodian Miller, who took full responsibility for the decision that the metals company be released, and by the Assistant Attorney General, who assumed full responsibility for the approval given to the release by the Attorney General's office. Daugherty's refusal to take the stand in his own defense and submit to cross-examination, however, shocked the public. At the time Daugherty's assigned reason for not taking the stand emphasized his close confidential relations with President Harding and seemed to suggest, or at least was interpreted to mean, that he was seeking to protect Harding from scandal. In his book, published subsequently, Daugherty maintained that he refused to take the stand and submit to cross-examination because "it would have amounted to a breach of the public trust on my part." [8] Whatever the reasons behind Daugherty's refusal to testify, the effect of his action was to direct new suspicion on the entire Harding administration —a suspicion that was heightened when the jury deliberated for sixty-six hours before failing to convict.

While public indignation rose as the misconduct of several high public officials was brought to light, the antipathy for what had happened did not lead to punitive action against the Republican party at the ensuing national election. This time the party won a reprieve, with death itself acting as the intercessor, that kept the ill-fated Harding administration from running ahead to more ruinous depths. And thereafter the party passed into the hands of a better element.

En route to San Francisco on his return from Alaska, Harding became ill at Seattle, where he appeared to be suffering from what was diagnosed as acute indigestion. On re-examination, however, his seizure was found to have been caused by a cardiac condition and his doctors advised immediate cancelation of his scheduled appearance in San Francisco. This Harding refused to do, insisting that a night's rest would restore his vitality. But on his arrival at San Francisco, though he rejected a wheel chair, his gait was unmistakably unsteady as he walked into the Palace Hotel, where he promptly went to bed under his doctor's orders. Within a few hours he was struck by pneumonia, from which he rallied, so much so, in fact, that on August 1 his attending physician announced that he had passed the crisis. Yet two days later—August 3—he was dead. He died instantly from a blood clot in his brain. Listening to Mrs. Harding read Sam Blythe's warm profile of the President in the *Saturday Evening Post,* "A Calm View of a Calm Man," Harding smiled and said, "That's good." Then, as he asked, "Go on. Read some more," a sudden change came over his face, and without warning he slumped back dead. For the first time in many months his face looked unharried.

Not even his passing escaped conjecture—leading in this case to the widespread circulation of a yarn that he had been poisoned. Though Surgeon General Dr. Charles E. Sawyer, Dr. Ray Lyman Wilbur (then president of Stanford University and later Hoover's Secretary of the Interior), and others who signed Harding's death certificate urged Mrs. Harding to have an autopsy, she refused. While her action was completely understandable it was cited by many to support the theory that she had resorted to a mercy killing to spare her husband the disgrace that would follow the exposure of scandals in his administration. Another rumor had it that her jealousy over the alleged affair between Nan Britton and the President led her to dispose of her husband by poison. Moreover, the fact that she was present a little over a year later when Surgeon General Sawyer died under circumstances which were reported in the New York *Times* as "almost identical with the manner of the death of the late Warren G. Harding . . ." churned up the rumor traffic anew. Even today some doubts—however hesitant—still persist over the causes of Harding's death. The late Frederick Lewis Allen in his *Only Yesterday* suggests that both the possibility of suicide and that of poisoning were "very plausible," while Oswald Garrison Villard, speaking more unequivocally in his *Fighting Years,* states: "I am one of those who lean to the belief that there was foul play in his [*Harding's*] death."

But the view that there was absolutely no mystery involved in Harding's death is borne up by the strongest of evidence. Writing in the *Saturday Evening Post* shortly after Harding's death, Dr. Ray Lyman Wilbur, who had been president of the American Academy of Medicine, catalogued the causes of the President's death in precise terms.[9] At stake was his professional reputation, which had never been impugned in any way—and the same, of course, may also be said for the eminent physicians who were in attendance at the time of Harding's death and jointly signed the death certificate. For the many vague rumors about Harding's death Mark Sullivan finds "there is no faintest justification," and in this judgment he is supported by the searching inquiry of Samuel Hopkins Adams, who concludes that all indications seem hardly controvertible "that there was nothing abnormal about Harding's death." Perhaps the final post-script is yet to be written that will remove all suspicion from a death which was befogged by so many rumors and such bizarre conditions. And when it is, present data indicate it will confirm without a shadow of a doubt that Harding died of natural causes.

Unexpected as it was at the moment, Harding's death was hardly a surprise to those who knew of the mounting mental torments he had undergone during the brief period he occupied the White House. It had been a "Tragic Era," to be sure, yet not altogether bereft of sunlight, as a few historians have led us to suppose.

Not all of Harding's cabinet appointments were men of midget morality or mediocre ability. "Back to normalcy" gave us several shining examples to the contrary.[10] The three H's—Hughes, Hoover, and Hays—were all signally able men. Hughes made several vigor-ous efforts in the direction of greater American participation in for-eign affairs. A supporter of the League of Nations at the time our entrance was blocked by the Senate in 1919, Hughes labored dili-gently to rebuild the prestige loss the United States suffered after its rejection of the Covenant. The Washington Arms Conference, of which Senator Borah and Secretary Hughes were the principal archi-tects, marked a new milestone for American leadership in interna-tional co-operation. Suggested by the Republican Progressive from Idaho, William E. Borah, this conference was called in 1922 to dis-cuss naval armaments. For Hughes the Disarmament Conference was one of his greatest hours. His speech proposing actual disarmament by the great powers won accolades from every quarter.

With the advantage of hindsight available to us, the Disarmament Conference strikes us today as little more than a prayerful gesture toward the impossible. Yet it is equally clear that in taming power for the maintenance of a peaceful community of nations there must be many false starts. And not the least of Secretary Hughes's contri-butions was that, in an era when diplomatists despaired of America's insular attitude, he demonstrated that this nation could work in har-ness with other nations in striving to build collective security.

Against hostile opposition, Hughes plugged steadily for the ad-herence of the United States to the World Court. He also set about determinedly to repair the relations between the executive and Con-gress in the conduct of foreign affairs which were so badly ruptured in the twilight of the Wilson administration. Hughes advised Har-ding not to make the mistake of Wilson in ignoring minority-party representation when congressional representatives were appointed on delegations to international conferences, and the President took his advice. Harding himself, incidentally, indicated an awareness of the fact that while constitutionally the executive and legislature held a partnership in some aspects of foreign relations, by and large the President must be the voice of America in the field of foreign affairs and negotiations.[11] Unhappily the limitations of Harding's resources, combined with the prevailing winds of isolationism, prevented him from more forceful exercise of this principle. But experience in both the Senate and Presidency taught him that the President should be in the driver's seat in foreign affairs, and that in juggling the domestic political strategy for necessary support, representatives of the minority party must be officially called into the play.

In Herbert Hoover, Harding had a Secretary of Commerce of uncommon ability. Hoover engineered the kind of reform within the Department of Commerce that all careful students of public administration recognize as the most effective in the long pull. Not the sweeping reshuffling, consolidating, and renaming administrative reorganizations which are proclaimed by noisy trumpets and so often fail to be effective, but the patient, piecemeal, and continuous day-to-day changes in administrative practice which bring lasting results. Hoover's policies for the encouragement of business enterprise, criticized by many, will be commented upon later here.

Outside of Hughes, Hoover, and Hays, the Harding cabinet appointments were of mediocre caliber with one exception, and that was Andrew Mellon. Unquestionably an able financier, Mellon was one of the wealthiest men in America. But he was the head of the Aluminum Corporation, and he seemed to keynote the tie between the administration and special interests. Like other highly successful business magnates, Mellon never gave evidence that he was sensitive to the peculiar demands of public life, or aware of the signally different problems between managing a vast private enterprise and one of the great executive public offices.

The most far-reaching constructive imprint that the brief Harding incumbency made on the face of the federal government was the creation of the Bureau of the Budget. It has sometimes been said that it took the assassination of a President (Garfield) to give us a merit system, and a world war to bring about a budget system. Both, it should be remarked, were undertaken by Republican administrations. Incredible as it seems today, no provision was made for an executive budget system until the passage of the Budget act of 1921. This law created a Bureau of the Budget, which not only prepares the annual budget for the President but today is the principal government agency aiding the President in overseeing the management of the sixty-odd bureaus, commissions, and departments with their two million employees that make up the federal government.

During Harding's incumbency the ascendancy of vested interests without a sense of responsibility, and without vigorous monitoring restraints by the administration, eventually cost the Republican party and the country a dear price. "The national income was fabulously high, unemployment was relatively low," as Eric Goldman notes, but the chief difficulty, as economists have long pointed out, was that "the control of the country's industries was steadily concentrating and the returns from the increased national wealth were not proportionately distributed." [12]

With official encouragement from the administration, great mergers began taking place in the fields of utilities, finance, industry, trade, and transportation. Inevitably these mergers led to the domination of American industry, transportation, and finance by gigantic corporations, so that by 1933 no more than 594 corporations, capitalized at 50 million or more dollars each, owned 53 percent of all the corporate wealth in the country, while the remaining 387,970 owned 47 percent.[13]

To many, the Republican policies of the twenties that encouraged the development of giant corporations appeared to be a negation of the "trust-busting" commitments of the party in the McKinley and Theodore Roosevelt administrations. Certainly the combinations and consolidations that were promoted in the twenties by the paternal policies of the government were designed to decrease competition. Herbert Hoover, a man who deplored the waste that stemmed from competition, actively promoted the preparation of codes for cooperative activities among trade associations and corporations. Summing up the fruits of these policies years later, Hoover proudly proclaimed, "We are passing from a period of extreme individualistic action into a period of associational activities." [14]

Many of the mergers in the twenties, of course, could be defended on the ground that they eliminated some of the waste that stems from competition. Included in this category were certain mergers and recommended combinations of railroad transportation systems, submitted to and endorsed by the Interstate Commerce Commission. But the same could not be said for other combinations. With the growth of interlocking directorates and the additional device known as the holding company, the outcome inevitably was the concentration of power in fewer hands.

Essentially the problem to be feared in permitting and encouraging the growth of huge structures of corporate power was not bigness itself. On this score alone, the Republican party need make no apology, for bigness despite its curses also meant astounding developments in new technology and brought cheap consumer goods within reach of millions. Interestingly enough, some thirty years after the fabulous period of the twenties we have one of the most vigorous defenses of "bigness" in our industrial society coming from one of the leading luminaries of the New Deal era, David Lilienthal, formerly chairman of the Tennessee Valley Authority.[15] But the "bigness" of the twenties represented a form of unbridled economic activity. It resulted from a drawing together of the forces that Theodore Roosevelt had once denounced as "predatory wealth." And as corporate power passed to fewer hands during a period of tremendous postwar expansion, the responsible exercise of this power in the public interest did not grow apace.

Too preoccupied with other matters to function as "responsible enterprise," as the late Wendell Willkie hoped to recharacterize "free enterprise," many business and industrial empires of the twenties embarked on policies with the cozy confidence that whatever was good for business was good for the country. The patent truth of the matter, of course, was that it wasn't, as the crash of 1929 showed.

But while the business world was more united and more articulate in promoting its public relations in the twenties than in the McKinley period, some of its component parts held together within the fold of the Republican party in uneasy amalgam. Enshrined in the political traditions of the businessmen of the West was a deep distrust of Eastern capital and big aggregations of corporate wealth. Out in the "rhubarbs" one sure-fire method on the hustings of getting blood to pound in the veins of many small businessmen was to mention the wickedness of Wall Street. In this attitude Harding was typical. He possessed the Middle Westerner's "indifference to, if not contempt for, New York finance, distrusting any business that was bigger than Ohio business."

Still the small businessman, with minor defections, remained loyal to the Republican party. Whatever misgivings the small businessman of the Middle West had about corporate size, the architects who engineered these huge structures of corporate power held a certain fascination for him. In their domestic outlook these small businessmen probably inclined toward a more progressive posture during the twenties than did the business leaders of whom they were critical in the East. At the same time they were part of the spine of isolationism that found such broad endorsement throughout the Middle West for so many years. A generation later, the small businessman of the Middle West would probably be looked upon as more conservative than many of his fellow Republicans among the financial and industrial leaders of the East. In the 1948 Republican pre-convention campaign he would be supporting Taft more probably than Dewey; in 1952, Taft rather than Eisenhower.

Laid to rest after two years and four months as President and head of the Republican party, Warren Harding had suffered from a basic difficulty that could be summed up in a brief profile once given him by his father and related by the President in an off-the-record speech. "Warren, it's a good thing you wasn't born a gal," said his father. "You'd be in the family way all the time. You can't say no." [16]

That Harding was personally innocent of any participation in the corrupt practices of his administration and that he in no way profited from them seems to be the considered judgment of careful scholars of the period. That he must bear responsibility for not taking firm, resolute steps to check these abuses is equally clear, since he appointed the men who committed them, and could hardly have been unmindful of some of the things that were happening. Moreover, he and his party share responsibility not only for the moral missteps of his administration but for the general orientation of governmental policy.

Although he had real affection for the common people, and tried to understand them, Harding was ill suited for his post. In searching for the truth after listening to the arguments of first one group and then another, Harding literally had to "paw" for it, as Jud Welliver of the White House staff related. And altogether too frequently he had "to take the luck of the road to get it." Lacking the resources of a vigorous leader, Harding hastened Republican acceptance of a doctrine that seemed to favor emasculation of the presidential office. By weakening the presidential office Republican leaders inadvertently were endangering the future success of the GOP, for the Presidency had become a rallying point of decisive importance.

Summoned to duty by the Senate cabal that sought to devitalize the chief executive's office, Harding went along with this concept, thus repudiating the views of his Republican predecessors Lincoln and Roosevelt that the presidential powers should be exercised to the utmost. But even though he was disposed to accept a caretaker view of the Presidency, there were times when his own conscience, along with the factors that have promoted the ascendancy of this office in our political system, urged him forward. Most conspicuous of such examples was his initiative in bringing about the abolition of the twelve-hour day in the steel industry. When Elbert H. Gary, head of the United States Steel Corporation, said on May 25, 1923, that it was "not feasible" to abolish the twelve-hour day, Harding wrote him of his disappointment at the continuance of this practice "that should be obsolete in American industry." In the same letter he also suggested that on his Alaskan trip he would have occasion to say a word about the twelve-hour day—a hint which apparently influenced Mr. Gary to change his mind, lest the President drop a public remark that might well become a campaign issue. In any case what one writer calls the "most salient advance of Harding's presidency, the most positive achievement wrought by his own effort," [17] was announced in a news story which by a twist of fate coincided with the day of Harding's death. On August 3, 1923, the Iron and Steel Institute rescinded its resolution supporting the twelve-hour day—a decision casting off an archaic relic long opposed by labor in the steel industry. For this advance Harding merits a generous word of thanks.

Sullied by the scandals that overtook his friends, the dark side of the ledger has all but crowded into obscurity the more noble impulses which Harding showed. At times he could comport himself with a show of strength passing the highest test of statesmanship. Typical was the time he was petitioned to pardon the socialist leader, Eugene Debs, by Oswald Garrison Villard, Monseigneur Ryan, William Allen White, and a few others. After Ryan had spoken for the group, Harding thanked those present for the manner in which they had presented the case and said it would get his immediate attention. Then a woman suddenly shocked the entire assemblage by blurting out: "Mr. President, that's no way to answer us. We demand a yes or no answer." Whereupon Harding drew himself erect, and as "a certain gentle dignity enveloped him," then said:

> My dear woman: You may demand anything you please out of Warren Harding. He will not resent it. But the President of the United States has a right to keep his own counsel, and the office forbids me to reply to you as I should like to if I were elsewhere.

"A flutter of applause" followed as the full measure of Harding's eloquent command of the situation quietly sank into the group.[18] Debs, by the way, was subsequently pardoned.

Surely the Harding heart was larger than that of many who have held the Presidency. But a fatal streak of softness divested his generous impulses of their authority and caused them to be misread as weaknesses. Belatedly, Harding came upon the hard realities of what Samuel Hopkins Adams later wrote in the concluding line of his novel on the Harding administration: "Friendship in politics undermines more principles than fraud, and gratitude is a worse poison than graft."

The hallmark of the Harding requiem as written by the unworthy acts of his friends who violated the United States penal code was to become scandal. Yet the scandalous behavior of his convicted appointees, along with the trespasses of those who escaped conviction, played a lesser role than is commonly surmised in the requiem that was written for the Republican party by American voters a few years hence. "Historians may yet conclude," Wilfred Binkley reminds us, "that the Republican party suffered immeasurably more from the social lag of the party ideology in the heyday of the adulation of Calvin Coolidge than from the maladministration of the Harding years in the White House." [19] On the congressional front, the American voter—often a perverse character who likes to split his ticket—tipped his hand on what he thought of this lag by sending one wave of Republican stand-patters into retirement in the primaries of 1922. Not a personal rebuke of Harding at this early date, it was simply one more example in which our electoral history abounds, wherein the sovereign voter tends to look upon presidential and congressional elections as two unconnected events.[20] On this occasion it was the most conservative cabal of the Republican party that took the pasting, and it was at this group the protest was aimed, not Harding.

Once the disenchantment process set in against Harding personally as the misdeeds of certain appointees were disclosed, the "austere disinfectant" applied by Coolidge did much to cushion the immediate shock. But simultaneously the Coolidge decision to allow the general economic policies of the Harding period to drift by default to more conservative extremes set the fuse on a delayed-action time bomb that exploded with the depression. When this happened the allegiance of millions of Republican voters was permanently severed.

Coolidge, much more than Harding, disliked urging views upon Congress. "I have never felt that it was my duty to attempt to coerce Senators or Representatives, or to make reprisals," he said. "The people sent them to Washington. I felt I had discharged my duty when I had done the best I could with them. In this way I avoided personal opposition, which I think was of more value to the country than to attempt to prevail through arousing personal fear." Reluctant to consolidate his position with Congress as the party policy leader, Coolidge would not busy himself with the task of persuading Congressmen to get legislation passed. Even when he performed his constitutional duty to inform Congress on the state of the Union it was done in such a *pro forma* fashion that Congress often found it impossible to discover what he really thought. Nor did Harding's successor believe that he bore any responsibility for directing public opinion, as did both Theodore Roosevelt and McKinley. Coolidge even more than Harding was unwilling to articulate what he wanted and leaned more heavily on the theory that the Presidency should not be active and reformist but should simply protect the established order of things. Under Harding the dynamic character of the Presidency as envisaged and practiced by Lincoln, McKinley, and Theodore Roosevelt was deactivated; under Coolidge, except for functions of a strictly administrative nature, the office became inert. Coming when the complexities of vast technological change pointed to the need for more concentrated legislative leadership through the ascendancy of the Presidency in our political system, the choice to mothball a theory of presidential leadership under which the Republican party had managed its most notable achievements was ill-fated. What was needed and what people were increasingly seeking was guidance from a leader who could manage the slippery imponderables of public opinion; a leader who could unite opinions and fuse them into a common meaning. More than ever before, the times called for a President who—within limits—believed his office should be autonomous and self-directing, not servilely subordinate to the supreme legislative power of Congress. Now this idea was quarantined. Today the party is still divided over lifting the ban.

"Iowa Started Out to Smash the Windows a Little"

🐘

It was after midnight when the messenger who had whisked over from Bridgewater, the nearest Western Union night station, drew up alongside the white New England cottage. Racing across the headlights while the heated engine of his motorcar was still ticking in the cool summer morning, he began pounding at the door. "What's wanted?" barked Colonel John Coolidge, as he lit a coal-oil lamp and thrust his head through a window. "President Harding is dead," shouted the excited messenger, "and I have a telegram for the Vice-President."

Two hours later—at 2:47 A.M., August 3, to be exact—Calvin Coolidge took the oath as thirtieth President of the United States from his father by the light of a kerosene lamp.[1] Thereafter—even as motorcades began descending upon the little cottage from all sections of New England and from as far away as New York city, the new President blew out the lamps and went back to bed. His first thought about the job had been: "I believe I can swing it." Appropriately, the place was Vermont.

Taking over the reins in the Green Mountain state seemed an auspicious start for the taciturn Coolidge. Not exactly the shrine of Republicanism, little Vermont had risen steadily in the hearts and minds of Republican men. Opposed to the Democratic party since the time of Jackson, it was the only state in the Union that gave its electoral vote to William Wirt, the anti-Masonic candidate when Jackson was re-elected in 1832. Endeared to Republicans more recently for her vote in the presidential election of 1936, when Maine and Vermont were a minority of two, this was not the only time when Vermont was one of a Republican total of two. In 1912, Vermont and Utah were the only two states that supported William Howard Taft.

That Coolidge might need the kind of loyalty of which Vermont had given so generously to the Republican party could be readily conceded. For it could hardly be called a happy time at which he became the sixth person to ascend to the presidential office upon the death of a chief executive.

In taking command, the new President avoided anything suggestive of a defensive posture, and wisely decided to roll with the punches. Restoration of public confidence in the stewardship of the national government was uppermost in importance and he knew it. Moreover, with a general election just a mite over a year away, he also knew that the time was short.

Coolidge began his major task of finding replacements for those who had abused the public trust in his predecessor's administration with a quiet earnestness that was to serve him in good stead throughout the five years, seven months, and a day that he was to remain in office. In the choice of a new Attorney General he was most fortunate in bringing Harlan Fiske Stone into his cabinet. Dean of the law school at Columbia University, Stone was a noted craftsman of the law, and a person of unimpeachable character. By coincidence he had been a classmate of Coolidge's at Amherst College, though apparently Coolidge could not remember him despite the relatively small size of the class. Starting off with a vigorous housecleaning in the Department of Justice, Stone took over his duties early in April of 1924 and continued in his post until he received an appointment to the United States Supreme Court the following spring.

In overcoming a situation of demoralized leadership in the government as well as within the Republican party, Coolidge profited by two fortuitous circumstances. First and foremost was his own popularity and the extraordinary way he fitted the times.

He was known as a dour, reticent, and humorless figure, and few imagined that he would become one of the most popular American Presidents. Yet he did.

Effortlessly symbolizing the steady middle-class virtues of thrift, industry, frugality, and honesty, Coolidge caught the popular fancy like a home run with the bases loaded. To a generation toying dangerously with installment buying, speculation, and personal extravagance, the parsimonious Yankee seemed the ideal housekeeper for a White House tenant.

The facts that Coolidge had disdained use of an official car to which he was entitled as Vice-President, preferring instead to drive his own Model T Ford, and that he occupied half of a two-family house in the small city of Northampton, Massachusetts, were regarded as reassuring by his fellow citizens. Among other qualities that struck a responsive chord, Coolidge gave the appearance of being a good sport. Though painfully shy, he did his level best to put up with the buffoonery to which Presidents are often subjected, whether it involved wearing the plumed war bonnet of a Sioux chieftain or the monstrous ten-gallon headgear of the range. Everywhere people hooted, as the piscatorial enthusiasts did when they heard he used worms instead of flies for trout fishing. But they liked him!

The second element that helped Coolidge jack up the badly mauled reputation of his party after Harding's demise was the method he finally chose to deal with the oil scandals. Dredged to light by congressional investigations, these scandals had already resulted in the resignation of Secretary of the Interior Albert Fall, and by mid-March, 1924, Secretary of the Navy Denby was also forced to resign. With a Democrat from Montana, Senator Thomas J. Walsh, as the principal spear-carrier, the congressional investigations into the oil conspiracy were causing some shocking disclosures, and not unnaturally the Democrats were anxious to continue them.

Impatient with Coolidge for not swinging the axe at once, several members of his party were calling for Denby's scalp early in 1924, and were urging action. Senator Borah demanded Denby's impeachment as the only constitutional method of removing him, while from Indiana, Beveridge, who could no longer restrain his long-suffering conscience at the outrages of his party, wrote to Gifford Pinchot: "The nasty mess in Washington must be cleaned up, and the whole place fumigated and sterilized. These investigations must not be allowed to peter out. . . . They must go on until every last person— and I don't care who he is—who has been faithless to the public interest is at last exposed, and if possible punished." [2]

Elsewhere other prominent Republicans joined the chant in demanding immediate action from the President to remove certain officials, fearing that every day's delay was seriously imperiling the party's future. But Coolidge was not a man to be hurried. As he once complained to Judson Welliver, "Theodore Roosevelt was always getting himself in hot water before he had to commit himself upon issues not well defined." It seemed to him, added Coolidge, "that public administrators would get along better if they would restrain the impulse to butt in or be dragged into trouble. They should remain silent until an issue is reduced to its lowest moral terms, until it boils down to something like a moral issue."

Convinced that the situation had reduced to a moral issue by April of 1924, Coolidge got ready to cock the hammer. He began by arranging for a thoroughly dispassionate legal inquiry into the questions raised by the congressional investigations. For bolstering public confidence, his choice of strategy could hardly have been improved. What he did, in fact, worked so well that many objective observers wondered why Harry Truman didn't take a cue from the

Coolidge experience at the time the irregularities among certain tax collectors were bubbling to the surface in 1951.

Though Coolidge cracked out, "Let the guilty be punished," at a press conference, his inner emotional distress at the oil deals was laid bare just once. And this was to Herbert Hoover.

"Some people think they can escape purgatory," he said. "There are three purgatories to which people can be assigned: to be damned by one's fellows; to be damned by the courts; to be damned in the next world. I want these men to get all three without probation." [3]

He appointed two special prosecutors, one a prominent Democrat noted for his integrity, Senator Atlee Pomerene of Ohio, and the other a Republican, Owen J. Roberts, who later went to the United States Supreme Court. Their duties were to take appropriate legal proceedings on all questions about the leasing of the public domain which had been raised in the course of the congressional investigations. In making the appointments, moreover, the President stipulated that the special prosecutors should report to him instead of to the Attorney General. The result, of course, was that Fall, who had received a $100,000 bribe in a satchel from Doheny, and $300,000 from Sinclair, was packed off to jail where several others who had held high positions in the Harding administration later joined him.

Indubitably, by taking a strictly unpartisan approach to the prosecution of persons suspected of misconduct in office, Coolidge effected an important morale-builder for regaining the public confidence. In embarking on this course of action, Coolidge also received several assists, none perhaps as important or more articulate than that given by the 1916 Republican standard-bearer, Charles Evans Hughes. Keynoting the Republican state convention in New York on April 15, 1924, after the Teapot Dome disclosures had rocked the country and dimmed the Republican outlook, Hughes said: [4]

> Let it be understood that we do not condone wrong; we extenuate no crime. . . . We would bring to the bar of justice every dishonest official and every perverter of administration in or out of office. . . .
>
> Neither political party has a monopoly of virtue or rascality. There are crooks in every community and in every party. Now and then, one gets into office. Let wrongs be exposed and punished, but let not partisan Pecksniffs affect a "holier than thou" attitude. The corrupting currency may be found in Democratic satchels. One who is corrupt is as faithless to his party as to his government. Guilt is personal and corruption knows no party.
>
> Today, counsel of eminent ability and unimpeachable integrity, selected from both the great parties by a Republican President, are taking appropriate legal proceedings by which all the questions which

have been raised as to the leasing of the public domain will be threshed out, every public interest will be safeguarded and every guilty person punished. These cases are in the courts where they belong and the courts will decide. It would be foolish, false, and unpatriotic to breed distrust either of the integrity of the government or of the soundness of American life. That would be to assail the honor of the hosts of officials devoting their lives with unselfish fidelity to the country's interests.

The true measure of the impact that Hughes's speech had in divesting the idea of Republican corruption from the popular mind is difficult to assess. But no doubt Pusey is close to the truth in his brilliant biography of Hughes when he states that the candor and sense of proportion of Hughes in that speech "had much to do with turning the public mind away from oil toward the rising tide of national prosperity."

By the time of the Republican national convention at Cleveland in June, 1924, Coolidge had purged the entourage known as the "Ohio gang," which he had inherited as a liability. And Coolidge by now had worked himself firmly into the driver's seat as titular leader of the Republican party. But this had taken some skillful broken-field running, for at the time he succeeded to the Presidency there were a number of leaders being boomed as "sure bets" to block Coolidge's nomination in 1924. But by the early fall of 1923, only Hiram Johnson and governors Lowden and Pinchot were ranked as serious rivals.

The story of how Coolidge cleared the field begins with the appointment of his personal secretary. In August of 1923, the President appointed C. Bascom Slemp to the post instead of Edward T. Clark, his secretary as Vice-President and the man who it was assumed would receive the appointment.

C. Bascom Slemp of Big Stone Gap, Virginia, from 1907 until 1932 was very likely the Republican party's most influential Southerner. A man who made a fortune in the coal and timber business in southwestern Virginia, Slemp was first elected to Congress to succeed his father in 1902, and he represented the ninth district (Virginia's only Republican congressional district) for fifteen years until his appointment as Coolidge's secretary.

As Congressman and Republican national committeeman, Slemp became a power station in all phases of party affairs. The Democrats sent big names into the "fighting ninth"—Senators Martin and Swanson, and Congressmen Glass and Flood, but they could not defeat Slemp, who showed great skill in turning back the entire weight of the state organization. Using the same tireless energy and shrewdness he applied to his local fiefdom in southwestern Virginia, Slemp also became a man to reckon with at national conventions because of his control of Virginia delegations. Even in 1912 when "a stampede to Theodore was narrowly averted," Slemp's dominant control of Virginia party affairs as state chairman gave Taft 20 of 24 delegates to the national convention.

But in the course of becoming such a powerful leader in the land of "Caretaker Republicanism," Slemp acquired a slippery reputation for his methods that brought on a wave of criticism when Coolidge named him as his personal secretary. The elevation of a party "tax-collector" to a post involving such an intimate relationship with the President brought an immediate outcry. "An endorsement of jobbery in politics" came one protest, while the National Association for the Advancement of Colored People charged that "every association of the race, political, social, or otherwise," opposed the choice.

Yet Coolidge apparently knew what he was doing. Slemp proved a real ally in helping Coolidge slip into undisputed control of his party before convention time. Slemp, however, was unable to work with Coolidge's national chairman, William M. Butler. They quarreled bitterly because Slemp opposed Butler's decision to humiliate Henry Cabot Lodge by not giving him a convention assignment for the first time in a quarter of a century. Perhaps Coolidge had not forgotten Lodge's estimate of him when he was nominated for Vice-President in 1920. Slemp offered his resignation to Coolidge three days after the convention. But a grateful President did not accept it, and Slemp remained with Coolidge a few more months—until January, 1925. Just why they parted has not been revealed. Certainly the faith in Slemp's ability to help Coolidge win the nomination was not misplaced. But the fires built under Slemp by the press very likely persuaded Coolidge that it was time for Mr. Slemp to move on.

While Coolidge's nomination was no longer doubted quite some time before the convention, the vice-presidential nomination was another matter. Three times in forty-two years a Republican Vice-President had succeeded to the Presidency. The odds on ascendancy, therefore, were not something to be casually dismissed despite acceptance of Daniel Webster's sentiments by many men in declining vice-presidential nominations: "No thank you, I do not propose to be buried until I am really dead and securely nailed in my coffin."

This time Calvin Coolidge sought his running mate in one of the Middle West universities. His choice was Marion L. Burton. Once president of the University of Minnesota, Burton was continuing a distinguished career as president of the University of Michigan at the time he was considered for the vice-presidential spot on the Republican ticket. But Burton won little widespread support among professionals and his candidacy burned out quietly.

Among the real possibilities, the name of William E. Borah became one of those most frequently heard. Great pressure was brought to bear on this leonine-featured man from the West whom "Idaho was proud to accept on his own terms." Then serving his third term in the United States Senate, Borah had refused to have any truck with a few members of his party who tried to blunt the investigations.

There was another compelling reason for wanting Borah on the ticket. While Coolidge had purged the government of dishonest officials, he very definitely followed the strongly conservative economic policies of the Harding regime. If anything, he was disposed to be more friendly than Harding to big business, and in office he proved more acceptable than Harding to Eastern capital. Not unmindful of growing unrest within the progressive flank of the party, the right wing, which was firmly in the saddle, thought the presence of Borah on the ticket would greatly strengthen Republican prospects. It was also thought that a progressive to balance the ticket would help override the opposition to Coolidge from particular pressure groups. Even before the 1924 campaign proper got under way there were portents that suggested Coolidge might be in trouble. In the Northwest his party was threatened with a secession in the Bad Lands, and farmers everywhere were complaining against the President, who they felt had been unsympathetic to their plight. (He was already known to be against the McNary-Haugen bill for the relief of agricultural distress, a measure he later vetoed.)

Elsewhere Coolidge had other problems. Postal employees were hostile toward him because he vetoed their salary increase. The veterans, vigorously organizing, were unhappy with Coolidge because he killed their bonus. And finally, out in Indiana where the President's party was mixed up sordidly with the activities of the Ku Klux Klan, there were evidences that the Negro vote of the Hoosier state was hostile to the GOP.

Altogether the election prospects were not encouraging, and the draft of Borah as a running mate for Coolidge appealed to the conservatives as a step that would lengthen the odds against a Democratic comeback. But the fancy footwork to maneuver Borah into the rumble seat of the ticket failed. Borah would have none of it.

So after bobbling the names of Kenyon (formerly a Senator from Iowa and then a judge of the federal circuit court of appeals), whom they rejected, and Frank Lowden, Governor of Illinois, who refused, the delegates turned to Charles G. Dawes.

Another Ohioan by birth in the long list from the Buckeye state who won distinguished honors from the Republican party, Dawes was a banker who had served as Comptroller of the Currency in the first McKinley administration. During the war he rose from a major to the rank of brigadier general and eventually became chief of supply procurement of the American Expeditionary Forces. In 1921, following establishment of the Bureau of the Budget, he was appointed its first director, and in 1923 he became chairman of the reparations committee that brought forth the well-known "Dawes Plan" for German reparations payments. A resident of Chicago, Dawes had participated in Republican national conventions as a delegate, but had heretofore held no elective public office. With Dawes nominated, everybody sat back to see what the Democrats were going to do. They had not long to wait.

Two weeks later the Democrats convened at Madison Square Garden to enact a scene of political carnage that proved to be one of the most formidable weapons of the 1924 Republican campaign chest. In a pitched battle, of which a blow-by-blow account was broadcast for the first time in the nation's history, the Democrats took 103 ballots before they emerged with their nominee, John W. Davis. The prolonged deadlock between the forces of Alfred E. Smith, governor of New York, and William Gibbs McAdoo of California all but decimated the ranks of the Democratic party. Some notion of the heat which this internecine family quarrel generated is indicated by the vote on a resolution to denounce the Ku Klux Klan which finally lost by 542 3/20 to 541 3/20. Whatever the merits of their candidate, who was concededly an able man—"one of the fastest candidates ever nominated to receive the poorest ride," said Frank Kent—the Democrats came up to the starting post ill prepared.

Not only were the Democrats hard beset with their own internal problems of reuniting behind their standard-bearer, but they were also threatened from another quarter. Since December, 1923, the drums of discontent had been rolling among several political groups for either an independent presidential candidate or the formation of a third party. Meeting at Cleveland in July, delegates coming principally from four groups—the followers of La Follette in Wisconsin, Non-Partisan Leaguers, railroad brotherhoods, and the Socialist party —ratified a nomination that had really been agreed upon in advance.[5] Before balloting began, the national committee of the Progressive party convention asked La Follette to run and he accepted. Senator Burton K. Wheeler of Montana became his running mate.

Though the Progressive ticket wound up winning only the 13 electoral votes of Wisconsin, and while La Follette proportionately did not do as well as Roosevelt had in the three-cornered fight in 1912, his close to five million popular votes were more than any third-party candidate ever received. Thus, added to the discomforts they had already suffered as a result of their historic Madison Square Garden hassle, the Democrats now had a third party to contend with. Actually the absence of the Progressive party from the field would not have meant a Democratic victory in any case. But the third party was one more trying factor for the already demoralized Democrats.

Squaring off for the campaign, Coolidge made it clear that he would base his appeal for re-election on a straight program of honesty, efficiency, and economy, in the domestic realm, and for affiliation with the World Court in foreign relations.

While Davis campaigned vigorously, and tangled with the Progressives over their platform proposal to trim the power of the Supreme Court, Coolidge stayed on the sidelines, content to leave to General Dawes most of the oratorical jousting. Dawes took over in a style which the party professionals unexpectedly found quite pleasing. His mannerisms, underslung pipe, and cracker-barrel profanity went over well on the stump. And when the occasion demanded he could also trade blows with his opponents in a roughhouse style.

Standing above the triangular contest by his own choice, Coolidge stepped down only to reaffirm the record. "It is well for the country to have liberality in thought and progress in action," he said, "but its greatest asset is common sense. . . . The people want a government of common sense." Sloganizing this theme into campaign battle-cries, Republican strategists urged voters to "Keep Cool with Coolidge." Elsewhere the theme was embroidered into such hopeful persuaders as "Coolidge and Common Sense," and "Silence and Success." Finally, voters were told that it was "Coolidge or Chaos."

On one occasion Coolidge threw a body blow aimed hard at La Follette. In the midst of several press attacks against La Follette as a "Bolshevik," Coolidge dropped the comment in a prepared speech that the issue of 1924 was "whether America will allow itself to be degraded into a communistic or socialistic state or whether it will remain American." Unhappily for La Follette the usual handful of bubbleheads that often embarrass third-party movements did the honors for his 1924 candidacy. In his camp, reports Russel Nye, were the vegetarians, theosophists, goo-goos, moonbeamers, uplifters, and single-taxers. As Allen McCurdy remarked, in noting that the Liberty Bell was the emblem of the La Follette party: "The crack is getting bigger every day."

The real thing that carried Coolidge to easy victory, of course, was the fact that the nation was riding high on the crest of a business boom. Even in the farm belt, where there was every reason to believe the Republican ticket might encounter a stern rebuke, a threat never materialized. After three years of hard times, agricultural prices blossomed in the summer of 1924 to the point where in August they reached their highest point in forty-seven months.

Coolidge, with over fifteen and a half million votes, received 54.1 percent of the popular vote, while Davis, with some eight million ballots, garnered only 28.8 percent. La Follette, with 17 percent of the popular vote, cut deeply into the strength that Davis might otherwise have had, and the Wisconsin Senator actually ran second in California, Idaho, Minnesota, Montana, Nebraska, North Dakota, South Dakota, Washington, and Wyoming.

With Coolidge elected, conservative continuity of the Harding economic policies was assured. Discussing the "Old Guard at Bay" in the June *Outlook* of 1924, Stanley Frost had seemed certain that the Old Guard would be weaker at the Cleveland convention than it had been since Roosevelt's days. This was not wholly because of the deaths of Senators Murray Crane and Boies Penrose, he suggested, but rather for lack of replacements. When Mark Hanna and Nelson Aldrich passed from the scene, he recalled, other men stepped into their places. But since 1920 the gaps simply had not been filled.

If the Old Guard was without the services of men who could hold the fort in legislative battles with the skill and bruising vigor of those who led it in an earlier era, few people noticed it. Certainly the steady maintenance of the Coolidge policies did not suggest that the Old Guard had stopped calling the signals. Throughout the full time of Coolidge's incumbency, the pressure from the farm bloc continued to harass administration leadership, but this revolt of Republican dissenters did not seriously impair administrational control, as it did during the succeeding Hoover administration.

Coolidge, though no strings were attached to him, was, in the well-chosen words of William Allen White, "the natural ally of organized capital, those vast amalgamations of wealth which controlled the banks and so had suzerainty over major commodities of the land." The comment of a financial expert, heralding his election, is typical of the affection and confidence with which he was regarded at the time: "Not in memory of this generation has a president sat in the White House in whom the financial interests have more confidence."

Without even some of the mild misgivings of Hanna about certain abuses of the free enterprise system, Coolidge gave business a free hand in the full expectation that the words of the Cincinnati *Enquirer* the day after his election would come to pass: "The United States faces the greatest period of prosperity it has ever known."

But while the sunny summits of prosperity were being reached, some of the mistakes were also accumulating for a sinister recoil.

To Coolidge's mind, untutored in the ways of the new mass industrialism which was swiftly transforming the American economy, the thought of social protections seemed unthinkable. Thus he opposed unemployment insurance for the reason that laborers would receive payments they did not "earn." In tax policies, Coolidge went along in complete accord with Andrew Mellon, upon whom he bestowed the title, "the greatest Secretary of the Treasury since Alexander Hamilton." And with them both went Congress.

With an unprecedented debt of twenty-four billion dollars facing the country at the end of World War I, the Republicans had repealed the wartime excess-profits tax with the Revenue act of 1921, and brought about successive income tax reductions in 1924 and 1926 under the leadership of Andrew Mellon. Though the debt of the Civil War had been liquidated in a generation, and there was some reason to believe that prosperous conditions of the twenties might make it possible to discharge the debt of the first World War with similar dispatch, Mellon counseled against such a policy. In his *Taxation, the People's Business,* put out in 1924, he contended that if income and inheritance taxes were cut radically, money earmarked for the Treasury would be diverted into productive enterprises and stimulate employment.

Under ordinary conditions his policy for encouragement of investment was desirable. And even today it is impossible to say whether a stricter tax policy might have brought about substantially different results. But it seems likely that heavier taxes would have slowed down the speculative spree the nation indulged in between 1924 and 1929. Moreover, it should also be noted that even with three successive tax reductions the war debt, which stood at twenty-four billions in 1920, had been filed down to sixteen billions in 1930.

In another area of economic policy, the likely consequence of misguided action could be assessed with greater certainty. Under the Fordney-McCumber tariff of September 19, 1922, Congress established the highest rates in the history of the Republic. Duties on such items as pig iron and textiles were restored to the old level of the Payne-Aldrich tariff law of the Taft administration, while increases imposed on commodities such as chemicals, toys, dyes, and hardware ranged from 60 to 400 percent. To provide some elasticity, the law empowered the tariff commission to recommend to the President lowering or raising duties by as much as 50 percent, but this proviso had little effect. Harding and Coolidge used their discretionary authority thirty-seven times, thirty-two times revising rates upward. And the five articles on which duties were reduced were bobwhite quail, paint-brush handles, mill feed, cresylic acid, and phenol.

The immediate result of this high-protection policy was a series of retaliatory measures enacted by various foreign countries, including some of our best customers, like Great Britain and France. Imposition of these high duties, of course, also struck a body blow at the ability of European nations to pay off their war debts to the United States in the form of goods. All in all, the resumption of high protectionism by Republican administrations in the twenties set in motion a policy incredibly short-sighted in its conception. By exhuming a page from the past and reaffirming a high-tariff policy Republican leadership ignored the rapidly changing world conditions that had prompted even such an ardent advocate of protectionism as McKinley to change his mind a generation earlier.

The expedient of protectionism, useful for the encouragement and promotion of infant industry, as Hamilton had wisely argued, could now only do disservice to the general economic health of the nation in the long run. But there were few reminders of McKinley's own reversal on the tariff question to keep Republican leaders from hiking up tariff duties disastrously in the twenties. The decision to elevate a rusty policy into something of a hallowed principle was made without regard to either the warning of McKinley or the unmistakable changes in the tempo of the times. It would prove to be a costly error for our trade relations with other nations. Moreover, it would turn out to be a serious political error at home, for the promises they made in the name of high tariffs and what they would do to maintain employment and a high standard of living were to haunt the Republican leaders later, in the dark days of the early thirties.

Midway in the Coolidge incumbency, with the conservative leadership appearing firmly entrenched, the administration met an abrupt challenge. Just as had happened in the midterm elections of the Harding administration, a family protest was raised within the Republican party itself. But this time the neighbors could hear the argument better. By June 5, 1926, the Baltimore *Sun* could report: "In every Republican senatorial primary so far this year, the candidate who has based his campaign on support of the national Administration has been beaten. This circumstance," added the *Sun,* "is coming to have great significance with those whose eyes are glued to the weathervane to note the direction of public opinion." In Oregon, Senator Stanfield, a staunch supporter of the Coolidge administration, was defeated by Frederick Steiwer, while elsewhere perhaps

the two most important administration stalwarts to be defeated for renomination were Senator George Wharton Pepper of Pennsylvania
and Senator William B. McKinley of Illinois.

Down in the tall corn state of Iowa, however, the biggest Republican primary debacle took place. Reaching for his fifth term in the
United States Senate, in a tour of service that began in 1908, Albert
Baird Cummins was defeated in the GOP primary by Smith "Wildman" Brookhart. If Iowa "had tumbled a ton of dynamite down on
the dome of the national Capitol," commented one correspondent,
"it could not have produced a greater explosion in Washington."

Sizing up the voter verdict from the home base, the Des Moines
Register teed off its analysis with a bit of sound prophecy: "Iowa
started out to smash the windows a little, and nobody knows where
this smashing will end." Little did the Republican leadership know
how violent the "window smashing" would soon become and to what
depths it would carry the Grand Old Party.

But who could tell in 1926 that a bare half-dozen years later the
Republican party would be routed from office, not to regain the
Presidency again for the next two decades; that the combined electoral vote of its presidential nominees in the four succeeding elections
after 1928 would be insufficient to capture the White House?

More ominous still for the party future, who could foresee that a
generation distant—in midpassage of the twentieth century—the
Gallup Poll (January, 1950) would show that only 32 percent of
the voters considered themselves Republicans, while 48 percent professed allegiance to the Democratic party and 20 percent preferred
to call themselves independents? Who could possibly know that after
1932 the Republican party would be directing all manner of frantic
appeals to the voters? It would solicit but not win back labor, talk
"blood, sweat, and tears" to the farmer while the Democrats simply
mailed him a check, and go right on losing national elections.

No, despite the primary upsets, 1926 for most Republicans
hardly seemed a year to festoon the party with crepe. Yet it should
have been. Once again the party leaders were warned, but paid no
attention to the storm signals because only the farmers were turning
against the GOP as yet. But in their uncritical reliance upon an economic system to make all necessary self-adjustments, Republicans
failed to see that certain repairs and refinements were needed if
prosperity was to be stabilized. And so they could not see the long
decline that lay ahead for the party. Of the lights that now guided the
Republican party only a few faint rays filtered through from the
beacon that beckoned to the little group of disgruntled Free Soilers,
Whigs, anti-slavery Democrats, and others who attended the party

birthsites at Ripon, Wisconsin, and at Jackson, Michigan, back in 1854. Teddy Roosevelt's Rough Riders were now only ghost riders in the sky. From the compelling issue upon which Republicans had united to drive to power under the leadership of Lincoln, the party sideslipped. In the 1920's its leadership seemed content to ride to power double-harness, bestride the twin mounts of the grain pit and Dun and Bradstreet, complacently indifferent to the areas of disaffection that were beginning to tire of the Republican voting habit.

Already noticeable, yet missed by most, was the uniformly sharp decline of GOP voting strength in our twelve largest cities.[6] Between 1920 and 1924 the metropolitan pluralities for the Republican presidential ticket fell from 441,000 to 137,000 in New York City, from 32,000 to 18,000 in Boston, from 63,000 to 5,000 in San Francisco, and from 51,000 to the point where the Republicans lost Cleveland by 7,000. Carrying all twelve major cities in 1920, which, of course, was not a normal election year, the Republicans won ten in 1924, six in 1928, and only one by 1932.

If urban discontent with Republican policies did not proclaim itself noisily in the twenties, the protest from the farm belt did. Here one of the clearest indications of the division within the party showed up in the vote on the McNary-Haugen bill for farm price supports in the spring of 1924.[7] With the exception of the Congressmen from the industrial districts of California, Denver, Kansas City, St. Louis, and Minneapolis, every Republican delegation west of the Mississippi River voted for passage of this controversial bill. Together they constituted one-half of the Republican caucus in the House. That Western voters mightily favored this action is also suggested by the fact that in the fall general election 129 out of 161 representatives who voted for the McNary-Haugen bill were returned to Congress. Moreover, at least half of the rest were superseded by men running on the same platform. Among the farm bloc west of the Mississippi there were just six changes in the House, two in the Senate. In the Senate the farm bloc could also muster about half the Republican vote, and this meant that there were two Republican blocs of approximately equal strength in collision: the farm bloc of the West and the business bloc of the East.

As always the play of special interest was doubtless a potent factor in explaining the lineup of Western Republicans on the McNary-Haugen bill. Some supporters no doubt were prompted by much the same crass sentiments that the Farmer-Labor Senator Henrik Shipstead identified himself with when the Baltimore *Evening Sun* in 1923 quoted him as saying that he was "sent down here primarily to lead the farmers up to the treasury trough for a hearty feed of public funds." Yet a more subtle division, though imperfectly identified at the time, was also widening the discord within party ranks. A brief and unimportant exchange between Mr. Mills of New York and Mr. Green of Iowa during a debate concerning a gift tax in the House of Representatives serves to illustrate this point. Mr. Green wanted to enact the gift tax on the ground that it would increase revenues from the surtaxes and estate taxes by serving as a barrier to evasion. Mills, on the other hand, opposed high surtaxes and increased estate taxes, and argued that to relieve the wealthier groups from such taxation would be best for the country. Coming from Iowa, Green, not unnaturally, lined up with the Western view of the times, which favored taxing the rich to relieve the poor. The interesting contrast between these two Republicans, however, lay not in economic disagreement, but rather in their difference in social attitude. Heating up his attack, Mr. Mills asked Mr. Green if the Iowa Congressman would tax the gift of a $10,000 necklace given by a man to his wife at Christmas. Almost jubilantly Mr. Green came back with the rejoinder "that it would be most desirable so to tax ostentation." Congressman Green was not a follower of La Follette or his group, and had always been counted as a regular Republican until the fight on the Mellon tax plan opened. Yet here was an attitude that spoke for countless thousands of Republicans who seemed to find it increasingly difficult to make themselves articulate to the leadership of the Grand Old Party. Out in the Middle West and West a mild semi-radical social theory was developing along with mildly radical economic tendencies directed more immediately toward the relief of agricultural distress. For the most part the Republicans of this stripe in the Middle West and West might best be described as progressive-conservatives or Tory-radicals whose party allegiance was a matter not to be taken lightly. But they looked uneasily at the urban management of the Republican party from the industrial and financial East.

Though kicking up the traces occasionally, Western Republicans had—with exceptions like 1912—managed to hold together for many years in a political alliance with the Republicanism dominated by the business world of the East, however uneasy the alliance proved to be at times. But by the middle 1920's this alliance was about ready to snap, and while the fracture never did come all at once, one Republican salient gradually pulled away to cast its political allegiance elsewhere. Once in motion, this parting of the ways led to a remarkable change in the political complexion of Middle-Western Republicanism. Equally drastic changes were to influence the political tincture of New England Republicanism. In both instances the changes would not be fully apparent for at least another decade.

One of the favorite Grundy grumbles (Grundy was a leading Pennsylvania industrialist and former president of the Pennsylvania Association of Manufacturers, long a power in Republican politics) during the 1920's was that the Middle-Western rustics in the Republican party who came from "the backward states" were continually upsetting his plans. Looking at the roster of names of men who served as the Middle-Western representatives in the United States Senate, it is not difficult to see what Joe Grundy meant. In this period we find such names as Norris and Howell of Nebraska; Norbeck, the prairie radical from South Dakota; Bristow and Capper of Kansas; Brookhardt and Dolliver of Iowa; La Follette and Blaine of Wisconsin; Ladd and Frazier of North Dakota; and Couzens of Michigan. Here was the band of veterans that gradually began replacing in the corn and wheat states the type of stand-patter that had been personified by the Ingalls, Thurston, Allison, and Spooner kind of Republican in the early 1900's. From 1910 until the middle twenties the progressive type of Republican was on the increase, while the stand-patter was declining in so far as Middle-Western representation was concerned. And the progressive type, of course, had been roving the land pouring out ideas and programs unacceptable to conservative Republican leadership.

If we look at New England in the middle 1920's, the type of Republican in the senatorial contingent stands out in marked contrast to what we find in the Middle West. From Connecticut we have Bingham and Brandegee; from New Hampshire Moses and Keyes; from Rhode Island LeBaron Colt and Metcalf; and in Maine, Frederick Hale. Only a couple of years earlier—in the early 1920's—Massachusetts had been represented by W. Murray Crane and Henry Cabot Lodge. That the foregoing represented the hard-shell conservative wing of the Republican party hardly requires explaining. A generation hence, in the early 1950's, the configuration of sentiment among the Senators of New England and the Middle West would be just reversed. The leap of twenty-five years would bring us to such names from New England as Margaret Chase Smith of Maine, Flanders and Aiken of Vermont, Tobey of New Hampshire, and Lodge and Saltonstall of Massachusetts—all obviously representing the progressive wing of the party. But out in the Middle West the roll call would include Dirksen of Illinois, Jenner and Capehart of Indiana, Ferguson of Michigan, McCarthy of Wisconsin, Butler of Nebraska, Bricker and Robert A. Taft of Ohio—all very definitely in the conservative camp.

Once the dust settled and the Midwest rejoined the Republican party, the new GOP spokesmen stood in sharp contrast to their predecessors of the twenties. It was Clyde Reed, a middle-of-the-road Republican, who spoke for "John Brown's Kansas," and the very conservative Kenneth Wherry who spoke for George W. Norris's Nebraska.[8] Clearly the primacy of liberal leadership for the Republican party had passed from the Middle West to New England. What were the reasons behind this shift? Certainly they are complex and no single explanation will suffice.

One reason why progressive Republican leadership slipped away from the Middle West and sent the frontier regions back to the Northeast is very likely to be found in New England's economic geography. A leader for many years in the nation's economic growth, New England has lost ground over the last generation.

From 8.2 percent of the nation's flow of income to individuals in 1929, New England's share was reduced to 6.7 percent during the ensuing twenty years. Again, while the national average increase of income in the United States was 139 percent for the period 1929 to 1949, New England's income was up 95 percent. And taking per capita income, the growth for the region was 67 percent, compared with 96 percent for the entire nation during the same twenty-year period. The per capita income of New England residents, it should be noted, was still above the national average in 1929. But while it was 124 percent of the national average in 1949, the per capita income for New England in 1949 was down to 105 percent. Finally, among other factors it should be noted that employment in New England's factories in 1949 was below the peak reached in 1919.

Beset by a slower rate of growth than the national average, and exposed to the familiar hardships that the entire country experienced during the depression and recession era, New England might be expected to reflect some of the uneasiness of her economy in her political behavior. Forty-three percent of her population was in the labor force in 1940, compared with 40 percent for the nation as a whole. And some New England residents—notably in a few areas of the region where factories were moved to other sections of the country—were living within at least the marginal shadows of a depression in the early 1920's.

New England, a highly industrialized area with a large labor force dependent upon employment, has (with the exception of Massachusetts) demonstrated a certain willingness to hold to its traditional Republican loyalties. But simultaneously this region has registered a dissent against traditional GOP policy by reflecting more progressive sentiments in the party primaries. And so the primary candidates who have been trying to retread the party with progressive ideas have been winning out in the New England primaries. One might ask, of course, why the same disposition to send progressive men to Congress has not been reflected in as broad a way in the House elections. Here the answer in large part would seem to turn on the fact that to win on a statewide basis a candidate has to compromise with forces that have altered the entire economic structure of the state, such as those we have just discussed, while in the House elections he has only to satisfy the peculiar interests of a single district—the interests of the "tight little islands." In the House, moreover, the urban districts are decidedly underrepresented, and this aggravates the condition in the Republican party where the "safe districts" have tended to be rural and conservative.

In the pulling and hauling that went on as the Republican party appeared to adapt itself to the changing needs and conditions of a rising urbanism in New England, while the progressivism of the Midwest in the middle twenties rapidly declined, certain differences are to be noted. Initially, it should be recalled that many of the farm bloc groups of the Midwest during the middle twenties were basically quite conservative. The radical cast given to the farm bloc by what was sometimes held to be the "collectivist" attitude of such groups as the Non-Partisan League, the Farmer-Labor party, or the Progressive party was by no means characteristic of all the members whose voting habits placed them in this interest-group configuration. Some collectivist and radical inflections that developed within such groups as the Non-Partisan League and Farmer-Labor party were inspired by leaders of the urban wings of these groups, a few of whom were socialists. These latter, however, were often in disagreement with the viewpoint of the agricultural sector of this alliance, and when they dared to expose themselves they opposed the McNary-Haugen bill. None the less, by means of certain disingenuous appeals at times, and aided by the widespread distress in agricultural economic conditions, the urban-directed wings of these third-party movements kept up the working alliance with the farm bloc throughout most of the twenties.

At bottom, what was really rankling farm bloc members was their distress over the turbulent conditions of the agricultural market and their unhappiness at the urban management of the Republican party. In combination these two factors led to interesting results in the dissolution and resurgence of Republican party strength. The farm belt states were the first to revolt in the rapid defection from the Republican party in the late twenties and early thirties. But the farm belt states were also the first to return to the Republican fold after the successive debacles of 1930-32-34 and '36.

When these farm belt states returned, however, where were the old agrarian liberals of the Republican party? Beginning with the comeback in 1938, the Republican Senators and House members from the Middle West who started slipping back into the United States Congress were by and large in a very different band of the political spectrum from those who had occupied these seats in the twenties. Now the men who came from "the backward states," as Grundy used to call them, were more likely to agree with the Pennsylvania political tycoon than with their fellow legislators from New England. Gone now was the agrarian liberal group that Senator George H. Moses of New Hampshire had in mind when he rose before the New England Manufacturers' Association on November 7, 1929, and said, "Mournfully I prophesy that the program of these *sons of the wild jackass* who now control the Senate will probably go forward to complete consummation." Increasingly the old agrarian liberalism of the 1920's had a hard time of it in trying to adjust to the new industrial liberalism, despite huge farm programs with their subsidies and price supports. Another factor accounting for the absence of the old liberal agrarianism in the Republican party is that the small businessman feels more aggrieved at government regulation than at big business. Also complicating the position of the liberal Republican agrarian is the matter of isolationism, which has proved as divisive an issue to the Republican party as the question of race relations has to the Democrats.

Against the more conservative leadership that has characterized the Middle West since the GOP comeback in the late thirties, many protests from within the party are being heard. But the processes of adjustment grind slowly in an area once pre-eminently agrarian and now beset by the problems of integrating huge industry. (In the Chicago area alone some ten thousand new industries have sprung up since the end of World War II.) Meantime, the configuration of power within the largest Republican region of the nation retains a definitely conservative orientation.

Where matters would finally lead as Republicans began to pull apart in the middle 1920's, and how the forces operating within our society would come to shape the party future, were not easily discernible at the time. That even some kind of reshuffling would take place was seen only by a few. From the general election results of 1926 the unsteady conditions of Republicanism could not be foretold, though they were surely indicated by the primaries of that year. In the Senate the GOP clung to the same balance of 1924—52 Republicans and 42 Democrats (and two Farmer-Laborites)— while in the House they actually picked up 25 seats, which gave them 247 to 182 for the Democrats. With such results the Republican leadership failed to experience that chill that more thoughtful party members could feel. Four years later it was too late.

The Hinge of Defeat

Calvin Coolidge was tidying up his office that day of March 3, 1929, methodically cataloguing his correspondence in anticipation of his departure for New England. Had he looked at the financial page of any newspaper that morning, which he undoubtedly did, inveterate news reader that he was, the headline would have read: "FEDERAL RESERVE BOARD WARNING DISREGARDED WITH ORGY OF SPECULATION AGAIN IN FULL SWING."

Perhaps the outgoing President had misgivings about the speculative spree which the Federal Reserve Board was already trying to ease off. But few could foresee the ruinous ravine into which the market would dive only seven months hence.

Under this mild and pleasant sky of March 3, Mr. Coolidge was continuing a policy strictly followed from the day his successor was elected. "The best thing I can do for the Hoover administration is to keep my mouth shut," he confided to friends in the early winter of 1929. And if he was concerned as he looked forward to the incoming Hoover administration, he kept his own counsel in his own amusing way as he turned aside efforts to smoke him out. Asked by the wife of a publishing representative what had worried him most of all, he reflected a moment, then replied: "The White House hams; they would always bring a big one to the table. Mrs. Coolidge would always have a slice and I would have one. The butler would take it away and what happened to it afterward I could never find out." Then somewhat wistfully he added, "I like ham that comes from near the bone."

Had Coolidge wished a second nomination he could have had it. Nor can we doubt that his election would have followed.

Coolidge, concluded William Allen White, was a perfect democratic expression of the dominant voices of the day. He had "pitchforked the muck of oil and petty graft from the Augean stables of the White House," but thereafter "he let in, all smartly frock-coated, plug-hatted, high-collared, bespatted and smugly proud, an-

other crew which was to devastate his country more terribly than
Harding's greasy playfellows." [1] All of which is to say, again, that
Coolidge more than Harding persisted to the end in a boundless faith
in the indestructibility of unbridled free enterprise—a conviction as
solid in his mind as the granite of his native Vermont.

Whether he sensed what was coming has often been a subject of
intense conjecture, leading some observers to conclude that a foretaste of what the future might bring led him to decline to run in
1928. But whatever he saw ahead, he moved with and not against
the ascendant forces of the day—the forces that were driving the
nation toward an overexpansion of credit facilities and dangerous
excesses in installment buying. (Conservative estimates placed the
amount of automobiles sold on installment plans in 1927 at around
60 percent, and approximately 15 percent of all goods sold were
sold on the installment plan.[2])

While the feverish pace of business activity inspired confidence in
the idea of "Keeping Cool with Coolidge," it also overinflated this
confidence by speeding up the velocity of the riotous living in the
roaring twenties. How much so is well conveyed by Arthur Mize-
ner's biography of Scott Fitzgerald—*The Far Side of Paradise*
—when he explains how Scott and his wife Zelda expected only joy
out of life and quarreled bitterly when disappointed. "We grew up
founding our dreams on the infinite promises of American advertising," Zelda once said. "I still believe that one can learn to play the
piano by mail, and that mud will give you a perfect complexion." Across the half-dozen busy years Coolidge was in the
White House, the nation's morals, business, and politics bounced as
crazily as a runaway automobile.

Calvin Coolidge was a pallid performer on the hustings, and not
a man who believed in leading Congress. His legislative record after
1924, in keeping with his strategy of riding the tide, is not a conspicuous one. Twice Coolidge vetoed McNary-Haugen bills for farm
relief—in 1927 and in 1928—and among the last-minute bills
which reached his desk on March 3, 1929, the most important that
he signed was the measure known as the Jones act, providing for
increased penalties for violation of the Volstead prohibition act. Yet
if the domestic legislative achievements of the Coolidge program
were not of striking dimension, the President, about to embark on
retirement, could look back with satisfaction on a signal achievement
in foreign affairs. For on August 27, 1928, the diplomatic notables
of 63 nations had assembled in Paris to sign the first pact ever to renounce war as an instrument of national policy.

History knows few treaties as brief as the Kellogg Pact. Sixty-three nations agreed in Article I "That they condemn recourse to war for the solution of international controversies, and renounce it as an instrument of national policy in their relations with one another." Under Article II they agreed "That settlement or solution of all disputes or conflicts of whatever nature or whatever origin they may be, which may arise among them, shall never be sought except by pacific means."

The paternity of the Kellogg Pact takes us back to 1918 when the Chicago lawyer, Salmon O. Levinson, urged a pact for the outlawry of war. Pre-eminent also in the take-off of this idea was Professor James T. Shotwell of Columbia University, who persuaded Aristide Briand to submit a proposal while the latter was Premier of France. But Briand's proposal called for "a pact of perpetual friendship," to be concluded solely between France and the United States, on April 6, 1927, the tenth anniversary of America's entry into the first World War. Happily, however, Coolidge's Secretary of State Kellogg struck out for a pact of more corporate dimensions. And after receiving Briand's proposal for a bilateral pact, he replaced the suggestion with his own plan for a multilateral treaty.

Ready at last with his reply to the French government, after painstaking preparation, he went to see Coolidge on December 28, 1927. Reading the proposal with great care, the President with customary brevity asked his Secretary of State: "We can do that, can we not?" After receiving Kellogg's assurances, Coolidge nodded: "All right. Go ahead."

Thereafter Kellogg faced formidable obstacles both at home and abroad. But in both operating theaters he met with success, managing with considerable skill to line up bipartisan support in the United States Senate. Obviously the Kellogg-Briand Pact had its frailties. Some critics have even termed it an absurdity because it lacked the necessary means of implementation for enforcement. Yet despite its limitations, the Kellogg Pact remains a milestone in the continuity of international law. Moreover, in light of the experiences of the last quarter of a century that have given us new insights into the ways of aggression, it will undoubtedly have an important bearing on the future course of confederative action for the maintenance of peace.

A generous word is due Mr. Coolidge and his Secretary of State Kellogg for the effort behind the negotiations of this historic multilateral pact. And its mention at this point brings to mind that the loose generalization depicting the Republican party of the period as predominantly isolationist has long been distorted. "The widely accepted assumption that the United States was isolationist from 1920 through 1932 is no more than a legend," writes Professor William A.

Williams. Nor was there "an intense isolationism on the part of [its] legislators with regard to membership in a world organization." [3] George Grassmuck has also demonstrated that from 1921 to 1933 the Republicans in both houses of Congress were more favorable to both army and navy measures than were the Democrats, and that eighty-five percent of these same Republicans in that period supported international economic measures and international agreements.

That there were figures in the Republican party who could appropriately be described by what we term today "isolationist," there can be no doubt. But too often references to the isolationist posture of many prominent statesmen of the period are misleading. After World War I some of the early Progressives of the Republican party who never were enthusiastic expansionists like Theodore Roosevelt, became firmly anti-expansionist. These men, concludes Williams, in no way wished to deny the power of the United States in world affairs, nor did they think "that the nation could become self-sufficient and impregnable in its strength." What they did maintain "was that any effort to run the world by establishing an American system comparable to the British Empire was both futile and un-American."

Far from championing a virulent isolationism in the 1920's, the leadership, particularly of Secretary of Commerce Hoover and Secretaries of State Hughes and, later, Stimson, was consistently directed toward support of the idea of a community of interests among the industrialized powers of the world. The "community of interests" would be led by an American-British alliance, the avowed goals being "order, stability, and social peace." This postwar concept of the community of interests was the intellectual offspring of Herbert Croly's *The Promise of American Life,* and Herbert Hoover's *American Individualism.* And it enjoyed the support of labor leaders Samuel Gompers and Matthew Wohl as well as the blessings of Owen Young of management and Bernard Baruch of the financial world. Eventually these ideas aspired to use American economic power for building and maintaining the co-operation they sought in other parts of the world. "Internationalization through the avoidance of conflict" was to be a key objective. Toward this end Hoover himself transformed the Department of Commerce from an agency whose concern was primarily with interstate commerce to one that concentrated increasingly on foreign markets and loans and the control of import sources.

The goal of these men was not imperialism in the traditional sense of that abused term, and by no sense of the imagination could the program be called a negative foreign policy. Essentially the long-range objective was the building through American leadership of a world community regulated by agreement among the industrialized nations. Applying the same idea to Latin America, Secretary of State Hughes stated succinctly: "We are seeking to establish a pax Americana, maintained not by arms but by mutual respect and good will, and the tranquilizing processes of reason."

Thus the far side of Republican belief as interpreted by Republican leaders Hughes, Hoover, and Stimson was that through example the genius of American technological advance in industry might speed up the elevation of living standards in different parts of the world, while simultaneously strengthening the American economy.

It is to the above tradition that President Coolidge belonged, though he was perhaps not so vigorously dedicated as were his fellow Republicans Hoover and Hughes. And as he pulled out of the Union Station in Washington while a large crowd waved a thunderous farewell on March 4, 1929, his five and one-half years deserved to be judged in this perspective.

Whether Mr. Coolidge would really be entraining for Northampton on March 4, 1929, was a well-guarded secret until August 2, 1927, when he first issued the laconic statement from his summer headquarters at Rapid City, South Dakota: "I do not choose to run for President in 1928." Given out on the exact anniversary of that early morning in August of 1923 when he had taken the oath of office from his father at Plymouth Notch, Vermont, his statement at once set politicians panting. What did it mean? Was he susceptible to a draft? Was he deliberately injecting confusion into his intentions to strengthen his own position for the remaining days he had in the White House? Or was it an irrevocable decision to retire? No one could say for sure.

Meantime, the name of Herbert Hoover, frequently mentioned but muted for reasons of propriety until the President had made some kind of announcement, now leaped into discussion throughout the land. In the South, Colonel Horace Mann began a drive for Hoover delegates at once, aided by such old-time professionals as Bascom Slemp of Virginia (formerly Coolidge's secretary), Colonel R. B. Creager of Texas, Perry Howard, the Negro boss of Mississippi, and Ben J. Davis, national committeeman from Georgia.

As the Hoover campaign warmed up, Coolidge admirers who wanted him for another term kept up their hopes. But to the national committee, on December 6, 1927, he said crisply, "My decision will be respected."

On another front, a movement was hastily organized to help Coolidge respect this decision. Prepared and introduced into the Senate by Robert M. La Follette, Jr., of Wisconsin, was a slickly slanted anti-third-term resolution which said that failure to observe the third-term tradition would constitute a precedent "unwise, unpatriotic, and fraught with peril to our free institutions." On February 10 this resolution passed the Senate by a vote of 56 to 26. Some of those supporting it, incidentally, among them George W. Norris of Nebraska, later contended that it ought not to be applied to Franklin D. Roosevelt in 1940. Once passed, this cleared the air a little more on the Republican pre-convention race, and more names began to crop up as possible candidates. Topping the list were Charles Evans Hughes, Senator Willis of Ohio, James Watson of Indiana, General Pershing, and former governor Frank Lowden of Illinois.

In the presidential-primary states, Hoover had setbacks, particularly in Nebraska, Illinois, and Indiana, where he was defeated by favorite sons. But the real battle was fought elsewhere, and despite a whispering campaign attacking Hoover's Republican orthodoxy, and reminders that he had been in the Michigan presidential primary of 1920 as a Democrat, his campaign headquarters were able to report honestly on the eve of the convention that with 545 votes necessary to nominate, Hoover was assured of 673.[4]

In Kansas City, where Mr. Mencken reported "the booze sufficient for all demands," it was just 10:03 A.M. on June 12 when chairman of the national committee W. M. Butler banged down the gavel and called the convention to order. From the standpoint of technological progress, new advances were much in evidence. The nine microphones on the speakers' rostrum could now blare a speaker's voice to all corners of the auditorium. Pictures taken at the convention were hastily developed in airplanes speeding to distant parts of the land, where they appeared in local newspapers the next morning.

Keynoting the meeting was Senator Simeon D. Fess of Ohio, an ex-college-president whose tendency to pontificate inspired editor Mencken to snort about "such preposterous bladders" that now ran the Republican party. Noting the absence of long-time leaders as he moved about the convention hall, Mr. Mencken found himself "gushing tears every time I think of old Boies Penrose, that hearty Buck, and Henry Cabot Lodge. Even Uncle Joe Cannon in this gang would look like Socrates." [5] Speaking from memory Senator Fess said: "Today we are in the longest period of sustained business prosperity in our history. To continue it free from the cycle of business depression is the prime concern. . . ." But for the delegates more important things were going on than the speechmaking of Senator Fess, whose performance the *Times* summed up by saying: "The speech as a whole may have been learned and able, but it was certainly dull." [6] More important to the delegates than the keynote speech on this day was the news that Andrew W. Mellon, Secretary of the Treasury, "recommended" to the 79 members of the Pennsylvania delegation that they give their vote to Herbert Hoover. Almost at once Idaho and New Jersey fell into step behind Pennsylvania, and on the first day of the convention everyone knew that the nomination of Hoover was sewed up. But first there was work to do.

Only one fiery flurry picked up the tempo of what otherwise goes down as a tame convention, and one conspicuous for its lack of sensational deviltries. And this was over the fight for repeal. But despite Senator Wadsworth's eloquent appeal to the committeemen to vote as they drank, the proposal was turned down.

Except for the prohibition plank, where the aim was to say nothing and "yet satisfy both ends," the platform of some 30 planks and 7,000 words caused little excitement. Though conceding the "serious condition of agriculture, chiefly due to surplus crops," the platform repudiated the McNary-Haugen plan for the regulation and disposal of surplus crops, in favor of voluntary co-operation between farmer and government. On hard drink, of course, the plank recommending continuance and vigorous enforcement of the Eighteenth Amendment pleased no one. The one stirring round of applause came when Senator Robert M. La Follette, Jr., of Wisconsin, read a section of the resolutions committee's minority report after reminding the delegates that of the 35 planks which the progressive Wisconsin delegation had offered Republican conventions since 1908, 32 had been enacted into law. But the youthful La Follette pleased the galleries more than the delegates, and his report was voted down.

Placed in nomination by his old friend John L. McNabb, after Alabama yielded to California, Hoover shook loose a demonstration of twenty-four minutes.[7] Then Jim Watson of Indiana, Curtis of Kansas, George Norris of Nebraska, and Senator Guy D. Goff of West Virginia were placed in nomination, and one die-hard delegate from Ohio (ex-Congressman Ralph D. Cole) also managed to nominate Coolidge. But the nomination of Hoover was executed quickly, with the Californian winning 837 votes on the first roll call.

Turning to a man who had been against Hoover's nomination, the convention nominated Charles Curtis for Vice-President on the first ballot, completing a team that set a precedent in American political history. For the first time in either party both candidates hailed from states west of the Mississippi. At one time Hoover desired the nomination of George Norris, believing that the Nebraska Insurgent Norris would add to the strength of the ticket, but Norris had no interest in the Vice-Presidency.

The ticket was a strong one. By nominating Hoover the Republican party professionals made some concession to independents, because he was not thought of as a party regular. Curtis, on the other hand, was a party conformist, highly popular in the Middle West and a man with warm friends in both houses of Congress.

In Herbert Hoover the Republicans called up a nominee of stainless character and striking record. Born at West Branch, Iowa, in 1874, he had a career divided into three periods, the first ending with his graduation from Stanford University at the age of 21. The second—1895 to 1914—led to success as a mining engineer and in the management of various industries both here and abroad. It was during these years that he won a world-wide reputation for international installation of American methods and materials, and for his knowledge of international economic affairs. After 1914, Hoover devoted himself exclusively to public service, winning his next accolade as director of Belgian relief—an engagement he himself modestly described as "the biggest wholesale grocery job in history." Serving as United States Food Administrator under Woodrow Wilson, he entered President Harding's cabinet in 1921, where he continued to serve throughout the administrations of both Harding and Coolidge until his nomination for President.

Looking at the nomination neutrally, V. O. Key evaluates Mr. Hoover as follows: "Herbert Hoover came to the presidency with greater ability and greater promise than his immediate predecessors. A man of humanitarian impulses, great knowledge, demonstrated administrative capacity . . . fate dealt with him worse than he deserved. Crisis after crisis was his lot, and he met them as they came, sometimes skillfully, but sometimes ineptly. A recalcitrant Congress did not ease his task. During his entire administration a Democratic-Progressive Republican coalition controlled the Senate at critical moments." And to this appraisal, of course, should be added the fact that during the last two years of his administration the Democrats held complete control over the House of Representatives.

Within a week after his nomination, Hoover's personal choice, Dr. Hubert Work of Colorado (Secretary of the Interior), was elected chairman of the Republican national committee. The promptness of this selection led the New York *Times* to comment on the speed with which Mr. Hoover had reached for the throttle as the new head of the party. Senator George Moses of New Hampshire became chairman of the national committee's eastern division with headquarters in New York, while Congressman James Good of Iowa headed the western division. Some grimaces greeted this selection because the international wing of the Republican party disliked Moses's isolationism, and Charles Burrill of Boston joined with the

Scripps-Howard newspapers in asking for his removal. But Hoover kept the quarrel under control throughout the campaign, and no serious rift developed. Hoover delivered his acceptance speech at Stanford University on August 11, 1928, and made just six major addresses during the campaign. Rejecting ghost writers, he insisted upon an interval of two to three weeks for preparing each address.

On many of the subjects touched in this campaign Hoover, who held a great admiration for his opponent Alfred E. Smith, reports that there was no great difference between Smith and himself.[8] But the issues that really mattered were prosperity, prohibition, agricultural relief, water power, religion, and to a lesser extent governmental economy and reorganization, and foreign affairs. And the one that cut deepest was prosperity, and by long odds. The good times of the country were emphasized by the Republican national committee on every occasion, and eventually symbolized in the campaign slogans —"A Chicken in Every Pot," and "Two Cars in Every Garage."

Against the advice of his managers, Mr. Hoover insisted upon an address late in the campaign lining up the issue of the American system squarely for the Republican party "as opposed to all forms of collectivism." Here Mr. Hoover laced into his campaign an ideological tone that was to be characteristic of his long trek across the stage of American politics. "Every expansion of government and business," he said, "means that government in order to protect itself from the political consequences of its errors and wrongs is driven irresistibly and without peace to greater and greater control of the nation's press and platforms. Free speech does not live many hours after free industry and free commerce die. . . ."

Again in his inaugural address Mr. Hoover interpreted his election as confirmation of "the determination of the American people that regulation of private enterprise and not governmental ownership or operation is the course rightly to be pursued in our relation to business." Obviously there was wide concurrence with these beliefs within the Republican party. But for Hoover reliance on private initiative was a principle which he believed should be proclaimed time and again and it became the theme song of practically all of his speeches. So, apparently agreeing with André Gide's epigram that everything there is to say has been said before, but since no one listens we must say it again, Mr. Hoover believed this a far too important message to neglect. "Socialism," he warned, "does not contain the divine spark, but implies the crowd mind." And after a quarter of a century his speeches still ring with the same sentiments.

The religious issue in the 1928 campaign was a form of bigotry pounding far beneath the operational plane of the candidates. Governor Smith, a Roman Catholic, was attacked for his religion even before the campaign got under way, and Hoover hoped to remove the issue from politics in his August acceptance speech at Palo Alto. "I come of Quaker stock," he said. "My ancestors were persecuted for their belief. . . . By blood and conviction I stand for religious tolerance, both in act and in spirit. The glory of our American ideals is the right of every man to worship God according to the dictates of his own conscience."

Obviously no statement by either one of the candidates could deflect the winds of intolerance over this issue. And surely Smith's religion led many a Democratic voter to defect. But Hoover felt that Smith might have aggravated the situation by his Oklahoma speech insisting that his religion did not disqualify any man from public office. While Smith was completely right, said Hoover later, this gave bigoted Protestants a chance to come out in the open, particularly in the South, where Smith was hurt the most.

Austere, as he read speeches that stretched at least an hour in length, Mr. Hoover conducted a dignified campaign that failed to arouse any great upsurges of emotional warmth. But the reputation of both candidates as men of outstanding ability evoked a tremendous interest, and on Election Day this interest was expressed vigorously in the fact that nearly eight million more people voted than in 1924. It was nearly twice the vote cast in 1916. The Hoover vote was the highest for any presidential candidate up to that time, and the first to pass twenty million. Moreover, Hoover's 21,391,993 ballots represented an increase of more than five and a half million over the Coolidge total four years earlier. Hoover carried 40 states, while Smith carried 8 with a total popular vote of 15,016,000. In popular percentages it was Hoover 58.1 percent, Smith 40.8 percent, while the electoral count stood Hoover 444, Smith 87. By far the most unique feature of the canvass was the Democratic defection of five Southern states into the Republican column for the first time since Reconstruction days—Virginia, Florida, North Carolina, Tennessee, and Texas. Despite the spectacular Republican victory, however, the vote of Al Smith was not unimpressive. For he won nearly as many votes as Coolidge polled in 1924, and his total exceeded that of the previous Democratic candidate, John W. Davis, by more than six and a half million.

Actually, the Democratic presidential candidate made galloping gains in all the New England states, particularly in Massachusetts and Rhode Island. And digging below the surface of gross election figures "it becomes apparent," observes Key, "that a sharp and durable realignment also occurred within the electorate, a fact reflective of the activation by the Democratic candidate of low income Catholic urban voters of recent immigrant stock. In New England, at least, the Roosevelt revolution of 1932 was in large measure an Al Smith revolution of 1928, a characterization less applicable to the remainder of the country." [9] Under the cover of another Republican triumph, the GOP plurality of 163,000 in the nation's twelve largest cities in 1920 fell away entirely in 1928 before a Democratic plurality of 38,000. Smith broke the Republican hold on our great cities.

Something of the new pattern of American politics that would throw the weight of a rising urbanism more behind Democratic candidates of the future was beginning to show. The rural Main Street, mainstay of the Republicans, would hold insufficient recruits in the next five successive tries at the Presidency.

Now, with the campaign won, Herbert Hoover could enjoy a telegram from his chief, far up in the wilds of northern Wisconsin. Not one word had been uttered by Coolidge throughout the entire campaign, though he did consent to be photographed with Hoover. Said Coolidge: "MAY GOD CONTINUE TO BESTOW UPON YOU THE POWER TO DO YOUR DUTY."

In the congressional races, the new Seventy-first Congress would have eight additional Republican Senators for a total of 56, while in the House the Republicans picked up 30 seats to lift their total to 267. Momentarily, at least, the President-Elect appeared to have a handy working majority, but as we have already seen these numbers were deceptive, for from the very outset Hoover encountered difficulties with his Congress. In the Senate a so-called "coalition" consisting of a dozen Republican Senators combined with the Democrats to harass the new President almost as soon as he took office.

With the election over in November of 1928, the country at large was in a prosperous and expansive mood. But in seven short months from the time of Hoover's inauguration the tornado that had been coiling for months struck with tremendous force. It was obvious beforehand that business was receding, but so frantic was the speculation that contrary to previous cycles the market price of stocks continued to climb, notwithstanding business reverses. The end which had to come is grimly portrayed in Frederick Lewis Allen's *Only Yesterday:*

> The big gong had hardly sounded in the great hall of the Exchange at 10:00 o'clock Tuesday morning before the storm broke in full force. Huge blocks of stock were thrown upon the market for what they would bring. . . . Not only were innumerable small traders being sold out, but big ones too. . . . Again and again a specialist in a stock would find himself surrounded by brokers fighting to sell

—and nobody at all even thinking of buying. . . . The scene on
the floor was chaotic. . . . Within a half hour of the opening the
volume of trading passed three million shares, by 12 o'clock it
passed eight million, by half past 1:00 it had passed twelve million,
and when the closing gong brought the day's madness to an end, the
gigantic record of 16,410,030 shares had been set . . . the average
prices of fifty leading stocks, as compiled by the New York *Times,*
had fallen nearly 40 points.

Then came three and one-half years—September, 1929, to Jan-
urary, 1933—when thirty industrial stocks fell from an average of
364.9 to 62.7 dollars per share (based on Dow-Jones Index). A
group of twenty public utilities dropped from 141.9 to 28 dollars
per share, while twenty railroad stocks sank from an average of
180 to 28.1 dollars per share. Meanwhile estimates of the American Federation of Labor, probably somewhat high but a reasonable
guide none the less to what was happening, placed the number of
unemployed in October of 1930 at 4,639,000, a figure which rose to
7,778,000 in October, 1931; 11,586,000 in 1932; and 13,000,000
in the spring of 1933. Instead of easing off after the first few
months, the depression deepened, and with the failure of the Credit
Anstalt Bank in Austria during the summer of 1931, and England's
abandonment of the gold standard in September of that year, there
were repercussions which further aggravated conditions at home. In
1931 American business failures rose to almost 29,000, with liabilities of $736,000,00, while the same year saw nearly 2,300
bank suspensions, entailing a loss of $1,690,000,000.

Faced with such calamitous collapse on the domestic front, along
with a striking decline in America's foreign trade, Hoover mobilized
a series of constructive efforts to stave off further reverses. And
though Hoover remained the stolid defender of private initiative and
a laissez-faire attitude toward government, his actions none the less
brought government directly into economic rescue operations with
several projects and ideas later taken over by the New Deal.

Immediately after the stock market crash, Hoover called a series
of conferences that resulted in the expenditure of several hundreds
of millions of dollars by the federal and state governments and private corporations. To alleviate agricultural distress, the administration had already passed the Agricultural Marketing act some four
months before the stock market crash. This law authorized the Federal Farm Board to create a grain stabilization corporation and a cotton stabilization corporation, whose major purpose was to raise the
prices of both commodities. Both corporations did enter the market
in 1930, and by purchasing cotton and grain and "futures," kept the

price levels of these commodities somewhat higher than world market averages for a time.

Meanwhile, as crisis after crisis mounted, Republicans lost their footing in the midterm elections of November, 1930. When the returns were in they appeared to hold a slim majority with 220 seats to the Democrats' 214, but fate played an unsuspected role in the drama that followed. Between the November election and the convening of the Seventy-second Congress in March, 1931, so many Republican Congressmen died that the Republicans lost control of the House, and the Democrats organized the committees and elected their own speaker. A more serious blow could hardly have befallen the harassed chief executive. In the Senate as the Seventy-second Congress opened the Republicans held eight fewer seats, dropping their total to 48 against 47 for the Democrats, with the balance of power resting with Henrik Shipstead, the Farmer-Laborite from Minnesota. Hardly an encouraging position for a chief executive while the nation was floundering in its gravest economic crisis.

Adding also to the President's discomfort were bonus marches and the encampment of several thousand men in the nation's capital; they were eventually driven out of Washington without loss of life by the Army chief of staff, General Douglas MacArthur. Nor did it add to Mr. Hoover's popularity to veto a bonus bill which Congress promptly passed over the President's veto. Releasing almost a billion dollars, the net effect of this bill was to give some temporary relief to needy veterans, while simultaneously making Mr. Hoover still more unpopular with the distressed farmers and unemployed who clamored for more direct relief.

In January of 1932 the Hoover administration succeeded in persuading Congress to create the Reconstruction Finance Corporation, with a capital of five hundred million dollars, and with power to incur debts up to three times that amount. Initially designed to aid the financing of agriculture, commerce, and industry, the authority of the RFC was enlarged by a new act passed in July authorizing it to lend $1,800,000,000 to states, cities, and other governmental agencies for self-liquidating public projects and for direct public relief. Additionally the federal government was authorized to spend $322,000,000 on public works. To relieve foreclosure victims, Hoover also obtained the Home Loan Banks from Congress, under a special act authorizing the creation of from eight to twelve banks, each with a capital of five million dollars and with a share in a government subsidy of $125,000,000. The Home Loan Banks, of course, were also designed to aid in the building of new homes.

By October 1, 1932, the RFC had advanced funds to almost

6,000 financial institutions and railroads, and had granted loans to 37 states for public works and relief of the unemployed. Criticism was made of the RFC on two grounds: (1) that it involved the distribution of public credit to some of the incapable business leaders who had helped bring about the depression, and (2) that this type of trickle-down operation was too slow in taking effect. Yet there is no disputing that the RFC helped in a formidable way during one of the most acute periods of the depression. This agency, moreover, was one that the Roosevelt administration gratefully inherited and relied on heavily for many years.

Despite progress along several fronts, distressed conditions yielded slowly. Wheat, after dropping to 40 cents, finally fell to 25 cents a bushel. Considering that even under ideal conditions the farmer needed 80 cents a bushel just to break even, it is not difficult to see that someone was getting hurt. And as embattled farmers commenced banding together to prevent foreclosures, the sullen mood of the unemployed lines of the cities spread to the rural sections.

In his own estimate of these years, Mr. Hoover sets forth three major themes: (1) That from October 29, 1929 to April, 1931, the depression was "a normal recession due to domestic causes, beginning with the stock market slump"; (2) that it did not become "the *great depression* [*italics are Mr. Hoover's*] until the European economic and financial crisis of 1931"; (3) and finally that this country was well on its way out of the depression by 1932, but suffered a relapse because of public apprehension over President-Elect Roosevelt's policies. (Mr. Hoover also holds that the depression continued through the successive Roosevelt administrations until World War II brought an end to various economic problems including unemployment.)[10]

In the 1920's Hoover issued warnings against speculation, and in the year 1925, in his annual report as Secretary of Commerce, he strongly condemned the Federal Reserve Board credit inflation policy, which was stimulating stock market speculation. Whether economists would accept Mr. Hoover's description of the crash in October of 1929 as a "slump" is highly questionable, but the fact remains, as Mr. Hoover contends, that the depression was aggravated by the European financial crisis of 1931. The real issue arising out of the leadership in these years, of course, was whether the obligation for direct relief rested with local communities, as Mr. Hoover insisted, with federal aid coming only as a last resort, or whether the federal government should have stepped in sooner. Today, obviously, with carefully built-in plans for economic emergencies, the question of federal government action would not be "should it step in," but rather "when" to set the machinery in motion. But Hoover fought doggedly for individual initiative and for local governmental responsibility, though he did initiate several of the measures that the New Deal was later to expand hugely.

Much political capital has been made of Mr. Hoover's pronouncements during these days of depression that only a slump had overtaken the country and that the business downturn would be quickly reversed. "On this subject," remarked the Baltimore *Evening Sun* many years later, "he is, to put it as kindly as possible, a sitting duck." Two days after the stock market crash of October 29, 1929, the President did issue a statement that echoed around the globe that "the fundamental business of the country, that is production and distribution of commodities, is on a sound and prosperous basis." And he was also quoted as saying in March, 1931, "Prosperity is just around the corner" (which Mr. Hoover emphatically denies). But while the statements are even today found serviceable for Democratic minstrel shows, it is only fair to recall that Hoover was not the only one who erred on the side of optimism in the years 1929, 1930, and 1931. A famous economist said he was "certainly optimistic," while the motor mogul Henry Ford proclaimed, "These are really good times but only a few know it." Meanwhile a mail order executive reported: "Comparatively few people are reached by this crash." Alfred P. Sloan, President of General Motors, commented: "Now everybody will get to work," and a Chicago banker said it "would surprise many to know how good business is." Either through misjudging the signs or fearful of dehydrating optimism, men like Secretary of the Treasury Mellon found "nothing in the present situation that is either menacing or warrants pessimism," while his cabinet colleague Commerce Secretary Lamont noted that "as weather conditions moderate we are likely to find the country as a whole enjoying its wonted state of prosperity," and columnist Arthur Brisbane observed that "all the important millionaires are planning to continue prosperity."

The three and one-half years of Hoover's steady struggle against the harrowing economic trend of the nation reveal a man reacting quite differently under the strains of the Presidency than an earlier career might indicate. As the Great Humanitarian of the twenties, Hoover was regarded as the very "incarnation of American liberalism." His denouncement of Attorney General Daugherty's injunction against striking railroad employees at a cabinet meeting persuaded Harding to have it withdrawn. And Hoover himself was denounced by the steel barons, Schwab and Gary, for his attack against the twelve-hour day as "unsocial and uneconomic," and for his speech defending collective bargaining before the Boston Chamber of Commerce in 1920 drew applause "that would not have waked a nervous baby." Others looked askance at his advocacy of free noonday meals for schoolchildren in some areas, proposals to curtail "inherited control of tools of production by increased inheritance taxes," and to "tax earned incomes much lower than interest, dividends and rent."

What transformed the Herbert Hoover, the ardent conservationist and champion of the League of Nations, who wore the liberal livery of the early twenties so proudly, into the symbol of ultraconservatism? What led him to insist upon a balanced budget as the depression deepened instead of wheeling up in a hurry his own earlier proposal to boom government public-works construction in times of unemployment? The shock of the initial impact, no doubt, to a man who had sincerely proclaimed the approaching end of poverty, had a profound effect upon him. And as this wore off somewhat, only to be replaced by an orgy of outcries berating him for the depression, it further hampered his adhering to the more boldly imaginative course that Herbert Hoover, the Secretary of Commerce, might have elected to follow. Against the ultraconservatives of his party and to his credit he stood his ground. He was completely out of sorts with Andrew Mellon's depression formula, which he says was: "Liquidate labor, liquidate stocks, liquidate farmers." But thrown on the defensive the "Great Engineer" became increasingly convinced that a large part of the nation's grief under the onslaught of the depression could be traced to our infection by a socialistic virus imported from Europe. And in exhorting his countrymen to hasten the development of a vaccine born of the free will to combat the spread of socialism he made large assumptions: Al Smith's defeat was partly caused by "snuggling up of socialists," and George Norris was a "devoted socialist." Both Mr. Hoover and his fellow Americans were looking for scapegoats on which to hang the depression, but while the nation was not held accountable, Mr. Hoover was. And all the while he was rethinking his own ideas on the alternatives to combat the depression he gradually found himself more isolated from his party leaders in Congress. For a period of almost two weeks while the Democrats tore into him in the Senate with the wildest attacks, not one Republican rose in his defense.

Working through the crises of the spring of 1932, Hoover found an increasingly quarrelsome Congress, as more of the progressives of his own party moved to fight side by side with the Democrats. And the division in Congress made it all the more important that the President hold his forces together. So it was that majority leader

Jim Watson begged him not to assail the Senate's relief program as "playing politics at the expense of human misery," and sought to dissuade him from further outbursts, not always successfully.

Someone once said that the President of the United States to be successful must be 90 percent politician and 10 percent executive. And here is where Mr. Hoover fell down. While the legislative record laid out end to end is more impressive than one would expect in light of the obstacles, the unanswered question remains how much more might Hoover have accomplished or how much was his administration handicapped by his lack of political touch. Hoover had little patience "with the politicians' willingness to accommodate." For Hoover the true test was that a matter must be administratively sound rather than politically possible. Thus while compromise was the lodestar of Theodore Roosevelt's politics it came hard for Hoover. And unlike Roosevelt, Hoover was incapable of sensing the need for dramatic appeals. For today's "space merchants" who specialize in the techniques of communication, Mr. Hoover would not ring the bell. That he himself sensed this is confirmed in his *Memoirs*, where he states wistfully that he discovered that dramatics had greater appeal than honest administration.

With party affairs and matters of party leadership, Mr. Hoover had an inexpert hand. He had little use for the rough and tumble of politics. Roosevelt, on the other hand, found "much the same pleasure" in hunting moose or bagging elephants. Hoover accepted the custom of party patronage as inevitable, and to his credit modified the ground rules. But he found the operations in this realm distasteful. While Coolidge had entrusted Southern patronage to the shrewd and calculating C. Bascom Slemp, Hoover set up independent committees within most states to recommend appointments. He also slid in a notion of his own that altered the custom of senatorial recommendations on judicial nominations by submitting lists of men "whom we could approve" to the appropriate Senator.

Whatever Hoover's difficulties in manipulating the political wand, it was his misfortune, of course, to enter the White House at a time when the heirs of Insurgency within his party were cutting adrift. And many of these heirs—the sons of the wild jackass—were not cut from the same cloth as the Insurgent group that formed between 1900 and 1910. Borah was not Bristow, but more often "the leading liberal [who] votes with the other side when the pinch comes." And like others he often emitted contradictory noises. Some of the "sons of the wild jackass" had real starch in their spines and fought on principle in the image of their Insurgent forebears. But this was perhaps the most critical of all periods of readjustment for the Republican party, and it brought to the front all variety of muckers who based their politics on the divine right of farmers. This was hardly surprising. For the nation has long lionized the farmer and it was considered one of the greatest assets of a burgeoning political career to have been born on a farm. Bernard Baruch has said: "Agriculture is the greatest and fundamentally the most important of our American industries. The cities are but branches of the tree of national life, the roots of which go deeply into the land. We all flourish or decline with the farmer." So with the farmer declining amidst depressed agricultural prices of the twenties, embryo political careers built on the farmer continued to prosper.

"Oddly enough," writes Richard Hofstadter, "the agrarian myth came to be believed more widely and tenaciously as it became more fictional." [11]

A good deal of the strain on the Republican party for many years to come emerged from the ambiguous character of the so-called agrarian Republican radicals, many of whom hitched their star to the corn-crib and their minds to the past. For they failed to recognize that "the United States was born in the country and has moved to the city." And while the farmers once were quite ineffective as a pressure group "when they were numerous, competing, and unorganized," they now "grew stronger as they grew relatively fewer" and became more "tenaciously organized." Frequently pro-isolationist, many of the self-styled agrarian radicals were basically unsympathetic with the mass industrialism that was rolling across the corn belt. Unlike the gallant troop of Progressives who led what was primarily an urban movement and who saw more clearly that bigness was here to stay and the best approach to reform was to control, not destroy it, too many of the sons of the wild jackass underestimated the nature of the industrialism that was overtaking the midlands of the United States. And so they went about spouting syllogisms on the virtues of the small farmer or small businessman. And their impatience with the need to adjust to the newer techniques of mass industrialism and the mass politics it produced retarded Republican adjustment to the newer responsibilties of government.

With the nation always in a state of "becoming," the nature and tempo of the party's adjustment to new social and economic conditions presented critical problems for Republicans as the time came to defend the record in another campaign. Standing on the sidelines in the spring of 1932 as Republicans prepared for their defense of the title, columnist Walter Lippmann tried a little summing up of his own in a look at the last twelve years of Republican rule. Recalling Republican promises of 1928 and what he termed the "hard actualities of unemployment, deficits, and bankruptcies of 1932," Lippmann wrote: "The Republican regime of the last twelve years is not necessarily responsible for the present calamity merely because it claimed the credit for the preceding prosperity. . . . If the Republican policies brought disaster in the last twelve years it is useful to know that the Democrats might have done no better." [12] The two main errors of Republican policy, continued Lippmann, were the withdrawal from European affairs in 1921, and the decision to erect tariffs which would effectively close the American market to the importation of European manufactured goods, and in particular the policy of the Hawley-Smoot act of 1930. This bill, of course, which only the diligence of Pennsylvania's Joseph Grundy brought through the Senate, was finally passed by a vote of 44 to 42 in March of 1930, and set up the highest tariff schedules in American history. Among some 20,000 separate listings there were almost no decreases. And far from having the effect of helping farmers and manufacturers, it was generally agreed that the Hawley-Smoot tariff rates aggravated the slackening of commerce and industry, because one nation after another abroad responded to this act by raising its duties on our products, causing overseas markets to dwindle.

The Republican delegates who convened at Chicago on June 14, 1932, were determined to put up the best battle they could to fight the pessimism of the times. But their task was overlaid with difficulties. "The Republicans," as Arthur Krock said, "must renominate a hardtime President, whose administration has accordingly been unpopular, and they must find words to uphold the acts of his administration. . . . Without admitting failure in anything, they must swallow many things said in 1928 and imply promise of later achievement. They must find a goat on which to lay the burden of the depression, and he cannot be an American or a Democratic goat. He must be part Democratic and part cosmic." [13]

Prior to the convention, mutterings were to be heard that another candidate should be found. Even the Chicago *Tribune* urged that the party look "elsewhere" for a leader. Some Republicans secretly hoped that Calvin Coolidge could be induced out of his retirement to run for another term. But few of these suggestions could be taken seriously. For the Republicans knew they had to run on their own record, and in Herbert Hoover those who had come to know him and work with him recognized a leader of uncommon integrity and ability, whatever his other shortcomings.

Opening the convention in an auditorium one-third unfilled, national chairman Everett Sanders presented handsome Lester J. Dickinson of Iowa for the keynote address.[14] Reminding delegates that

Republican candidates had been occupants of the White House "for all but sixteen out of nearly seventy-two years," Senator Dickinson called for the renomination of Herbert Hoover. This the convention promptly did, only minor catcalls ruffling the proceedings.

That stubborn agitator "repeal" crashed convention lines once again, to the embarrassment of the convention management, this time blowing up into a floor fight for acceptance of the minority report of the resolutions committee. Led by Nicholas Murray Butler and Senator Bingham of Connecticut, and urged on by the lusty cheers of a pro-wet Chicago gallery, this contest carried over into the early morning hours. But even Bingham's stark statistics about the 16,000 youths who were arrested for intoxication in Cleveland, and his account of the 7,000,000 tons of coal still unmined because of no market for it in breweries where it was formerly used, failed to sway enough delegates. By a vote of 681 to 472, the minority plank was turned down. Not, however, without leaving behind a trail of frustration. Party unity may have been achieved, as the New York *Herald Tribune* put it, "but at a ruinous cost in disappointed hopes and outraged convictions." Elsewhere the Chicago *Tribune* concurred by denouncing the majority plank (calling for a new amendment to permit each state to determine whether liquor could be manufactured and sold within its borders) as a "flagrant fraud."

The only really riotous behavior of the convention came on the nominating roll call for the Presidency. When Oregon was reached, a delegate appropriately named Sandblast gave a rousing stump speech to nominate former Senator Joseph Irwin France of Maryland. Just as he was placed in nomination, France made a dash for the rostrum, where he was halted by the permanent chairman, Bertrand Snell, and later removed from the convention hall by the police. (France, not a member of the convention, held only a proxy for an Oregon delegate.) The scheme here, of course, was to have France withdraw in favor of Coolidge and stampede the convention for the man from Plymouth Notch. But the Hoover managers were not caught unawares, and it was hardly a coincidence that as soon as Sandblast started speaking something went wrong with the amplifying system. Their fears were groundless, however, for by this time the convention never dreamed of recommissioning Mr. Coolidge. Hoover received 1,126½ votes, Coolidge 4½, and France 4.

Six men were entered in the vice-presidential nominations, largely because of the general feeling that advancing years and his reputation as a "dry" did not make Curtis an ideal candidate. Charles Dawes very likely would have been nominated except for his withdrawal, and after that neither Hanford MacNider nor General John

G. Harbord, the next leading contenders, could overtake Curtis.[15]

Two weeks later, in the same hall, the Democrats chose Franklin Roosevelt and John Garner for their ticket, and in September both candidates took to the stump, Roosevelt on an aggressive campaign that carried him into 37 states. In the months that followed Mr. Roosevelt made general charges that the Republicans had catered to big business at the expense of the "forgotten man," and criticized the handling of the depression. But except for the issue of prohibition, he did not enunciate a clear-cut party line that presented discernible alternatives of policy between the parties. Roosevelt, moreover, promised faithfully to balance the budget, and criticized Hoover severely for what he termed reckless financial policies. "The nationalistic, collectivist note" in some of Roosevelt's appeals, writes historian Arthur Ekirch, "was accompanied by incongruous avowals of faith in the traditional, limited-government ideal of the Democratic party of Jefferson and his successors. But in 1932 a linkage of essentially contradictory ideas did not bother either Roosevelt or the electorate. Rendered desperate by the Depression . . . the American public was not inclined to inquire extensively into the logic of the Democrats' case." [16]

Handicapped by the defection of several Progressives, Hiram Johnson of California, Bob La Follette, Jr., and George Norris, all of whom declared for Roosevelt, the Republicans were on the defensive. And though Hoover spelled out the many expedients he had undertaken to ease the strains of the depression, the desires of people from all walks of life—rich, poor, middle-class, farmers, workers—were for a change. In consequence Roosevelt won the Presidency with a vote of 22,809,638, or 57.4 percent of the popular vote, while Hoover in defeat had 15,758,901 votes—39.6 percent of the two-party vote. Carrying 40 states in 1928, Hoover carried only 6 in 1932, with a total of 59 electoral votes. The full dimension of this shift perhaps can be even better appreciated by noting that Roosevelt carried 2,721 of the nation's 3,050 counties—the greatest number ever carried by a candidate for the Presidency. It was nothing short of an earthquake. In the same sweep the Democrats picked up 12 Senate seats to give them 59, and 99 additional seats in the House for a total of 313.

Amidst the clamorous life of the big cities, only in Philadelphia were the Republicans able to hold on. And here the Republican city machine that held a lease on power for 67 years still managed to control an incredible vote right into the early thirties under the leadership of William S. Vare. But part of the story of how it was done shines through the municipal jobholders' register. Of 119 inspectors in the Philadelphia bureau of weights and measures in 1933, 98 were Republican city committeemen; of 32 mercantile appraisers, 23 were members of ward committees; of 92 real estate assessors, 55 were precinct committeemen.[17] Not until 1949 did the demise of the Philadelphia machine finally take place, but elsewhere GOP urban citadels fell long before. In 1932, of the cities with 100,000 inhabitants or more, the Democrats carried 91, the Republicans 15; in 1936 the Democrats upped this to 104 against two for the GOP.

Meeting with the President-Elect and his adviser Raymond Moley on November 22, Hoover began at once to outline the case for some kind of strong joint declaration of public policy between himself and Roosevelt. The alternatives as Hoover depicted them were clear. Either a plan with the joint backing of the two leaders could be put forward as an earnest of our interest in international economic stability or the war debts would drift to default on December 15. In the latter case urgent issues of monetary stabilization and tariff revision scheduled for consideration at the forthcoming World Economic Conference would drift aimlessly until spring.

Out of this conference, however, characterized as one of "bristling formality," nothing emerged but disappointment. "Roosevelt," reports Raymond Moley, "felt Hoover capable of acting without his concurrence, and that until noon on March 4th it was Hoover's baby." But the notion that it was "Hoover's baby"—a phrase which Roosevelt used in a jocular aside to the press on war debt exchanges —was not an idea to which some critics took kindly. "In rejecting this method [*Hoover's suggestion*] Governor Roosevelt obviously displayed more tact than courage. . . ." said the New York *Times*.[18]

Early in 1933, the depression moved into its most acute stage. By now business had shrunk to less than 60 percent of normal, and in January, 1933, commodity prices dropped to the lowest point since the beginning of the depression. In February more trouble followed when leading banks in Detroit closed on Valentine's Day, and the state of Michigan declared an eight-day banking moratorium. Thereafter, other states followed until, by March 2, 21 states in addition to the District of Columbia either had established moratoria or their banks were operating under special regulations.

For forty days, spreading in its acute stage from the last week of January to March 5, the nation drifted toward disaster while Hoover vainly appealed to President-Elect Franklin Roosevelt for a reassuring statement on gold, money, and budget policies. The problem after the Detroit banks had closed was to resume payment and turn back an incipient nationwide panic. But between February 14 and 25, no less than eight specific Hoover proposals for remedial action were defeated or obstructed.[19] Meanwhile Hoover appealed to Roosevelt on February 17 for a statement of policy to help check gold withdrawals and currency hoarding and to spare the nation from a complete banking paralysis. But by February 27 he still had no reply from the President-Elect, on which day he addressed a second appeal to Roosevelt urging him to announce his intention of assembling Congress in extraordinary session on Monday, March 6. But once again Roosevelt laid the delay on the lame excuse that his secretary failed to send his reply "through an assumption . . . that it was only a draft letter." And on the very day that Roosevelt finally did answer, Arthur Krock's column in the *Times* carried a report that Roosevelt preferred not to call Congress until some time in April.

That history records the nation as making progress toward recovery in the latter half of 1932 is now beyond dispute. "There is very good statistical evidence which goes to prove . . . the world depression reached its low point in mid-summer of 1932," wrote Walter Lippmann in November of 1933, while three years later— June 18, 1936, the same writer added: "The historians will . . . see that President Hoover, Secretary Mills, Governor Meyer [chairman of the Federal Reserve Board] had hold of the essence of the matter in the spring of 1932 when . . . they arrested the depression."

It was a sad but proud group that gathered to bid farewell to President and Mrs. Hoover as they left Washington on March 4, 1933. Yet few Presidents could leave office enjoying more affectionate devotion than Mr. Hoover held from those who had served him during the previous four years. It was, by common agreement, one of the fiercest devotions that any man has ever enjoyed who has held high public office. And it was a devotion that would persist to the end of his life. Twenty-two years later, in writing of the staggering contributions of the Hoover commission (officially known as the Commission on Organization of the Executive Branch of the Government), Arthur Krock said: "No one has a wider acquaintance with Americans of great capacity in all the Commission's appointed fields of inquiry." And "no leader in this country has been served with more devotion by persons of that caliber." Noting that the first Hoover commission made 275 recommendations of which 72 had been enacted into law, Krock guessed that many of the 350 recommendations of the second commission's labors would not "withstand the fires of political controversy." Yet by common consent "they are the capstone of an enduring tower of public service that is unique in American history." [20] For this, Herbert Hoover is not to be denied even by the atrocity-story agents who blamed him for the depression.

Bewildered at the spectacle that unfolded, the likes of which Washington had never seen, in the first months after the New Deal came to power in 1933, the Republicans went along in granting Mr. Roosevelt the emergency powers asked for to combat the depression. Not yet ready for the period of readjustment which necessarily had to precede a comeback, Republicans came gradually if somewhat dazedly to accept the grim reality that the hinge of defeat involved a new realignment in the two-party system in America, in which the Republican party had been transformed from a majority to a minority party. And if confirmation was needed, this fact was reconfirmed in the midterm elections of 1934 when the Democrats became the first party in history holding power to increase its majority in both the Senate and the House. In the Seventy-fourth Congress the Democrats began with an additional 10 seats in the Senate, bringing their total to 69, along with an increase of 9 seats in the House, lifting their forces to 322. In the same year more Republican governorships toppled across the land, and the Democratic whirlwind began churning down to sweep up other elective offices long held without breach by the Republicans. In Iowa, all three supreme court posts up for election in 1934 were filled by Democrats. The election of 1932 was no ordinary election. This canvass and those succeeding it "substituted a national realignment for an extreme sectional alignment everywhere in the country except in the South. And thereafter the monopoly of one-party states which the Republican party enjoyed in the North since . . . 1896 was permanently destroyed."

A lesson not readily realized is that the politician is a most important figure in stabilizing the power relationships of the community. And in the protracted period of business ascendancy, the Republican party had produced few, if any, politicians with Mark Hanna's grasp of the ingredients of successful political organizational leadership. What had been happening perhaps is well summed up by the elder Senator Henry Cabot Lodge's remark in 1910: "The businessman dealing with a large political question is really a painful sight." Implicit in the statement of Lodge is not only the inability of some businessmen to comprehend fully the pros and cons of major questions of public policy. Equally important is their failure to understand the elements of politics, which is essentially the profession of compromise. By training as well as approach the politician and the business executive are two different animals. Actually it was Coolidge who pushed hardest for the concept of the party as the political fiefdom of business. In ten short months Coolidge remade the party by taking it away from national committee control.

Coolidge gave his leadership frankly, openly, proudly, to American business by direct rather than by indirect control. Heretofore for fifty years his party had served business through the leadership of politicians. They assumed to arbitrate between capital and government, between the people and organized plutocracy—government invisible and never quite brazen. Coolidge in a few months had wrecked that political liaison. He destroyed the arbitration myth by putting much of the control of the Republican party directly into business without moderation of the political machine.[21]

The decline of the politician as a middleman became a serious matter. As the unrest of the middle '30's settled upon us, with sit-down strikes and riots, and such third parties advancing to power as the Farmer-Labor party in Minnesota under Floyd B. Olson upon a platform calling for state ownership of certain heavy industries, some business leaders panicked. Still refusing to believe that a new day was at hand which could only be moderated and modified by a restitution of confidence in the Republican party, these leaders fell back upon practices as unlikely to succeed as trying to plug up holes in a sieve. And in some cases the desperation of this type of leadership to stay the progress of the Democratic onslaught and the advance of the more radical parties of the left could only worsen the prestige and integrity of the party of Lincoln. Summoning a long-time political leader in one three-party state of the Middle West, where a Republican gubernatorial candidate looked like a sure loser, one of the nation's largest milling magnates suggested he would like to have the Democratic candidate withdraw. Then he proposed that the sum of $10,000 would be paid to the candidate if he withdrew from the race and threw his full support to the Republican candidate. "What I want," he said, "is an honest schwindler. There are only two conditions. Be certain that he is a schwindler, but equally certain that he is an honest one!" How Mark Hanna would have cringed had he lived to see the revival of the same pattern of panic and political ineptness that he had so deplored forty years earlier!

Plumbing the Depths

Hardy old Maine and Vermont, quipped those who had recovered their senses of humor as they crawled out of their storm cellars the first Tuesday after the first Monday in November of 1936: at least they stayed in line during the holocaust. Surveying the carnage in the wake of Roosevelt's remarkable sweep, Republicans were compelled to reflect upon some disenchanting facts.

In 1920 Warren Harding pulled down an aggregate vote of 16,-141,536. When the final tally was marked up in 1936, the Landon vote was 16,679,583. Harding's percentage of the two-party total in 1920 was 60.2 percent; Landon's in 1936, 36.5. In 1920 the Democratic presidential candidate polled 9,147,353; in 1936 the Democratic candidate had trebled this figure, winning 27,904,949 votes, while the Republican vote more or less stood still. Biting into realities, Republicans were forced to concede that in sixteen years their total vote in national elections had remained practically stationary, while that of Democratic presidential standard-bearers had multiplied three times. Adding to the unpleasantness of the election postmortem was the further statistic that if the Bull Moose campaign of 1912 be disregarded, only one Republican presidential candidate since 1856 had polled less than 40 percent of the total vote.[1]

Hard on the heels of the discouragement from the presidential election was an equally distressing result—the slippage in the congressional contests. In 1934 the Democratic party had completely upset tradition by having the first administration since the Civil War actually to gain congressional strength in the midterm elections. Leading Republicans in the congressional balloting by 4,000,000 votes, the Democrats wound up with more than 70 percent of the total membership in Congress. After this bitter setback of the Republicans there was more to come. Following the general elections of 1936, Republican voices in the Congress were reduced to 17 in the Senate and 89 in the House, the lowest in the party's history.

Standing by, the Republican congressional contingent watched the

Democrats redeem some of the campaign promises of the Bull Moose Progressive platform in 1912, and in several instances continue measures inaugurated by Herbert Hoover, pushing some only a step and others a long stride forward. The Agricultural Adjustment act, embodying means to control production, was a measure which Hoover's Federal Farm Board had long since concluded would be necessary. The Grazing act, setting up machinery for the regulation of the use of public ranges, made concrete many of the recommendations of a commission that had been appointed by Hoover to bring about ways and means of preventing overgrazing. Elsewhere a securities regulatory act became law that called forth a reminder from the Bull Moose Progressive platform of 1912. Twenty years back it was a Bull Moose plank that had bemoaned the fact that citizens were "swindled" out of millions every year by investing their savings in stocks baited by "highly colored prospectuses" and urged that it was the duty of government "to protect its people from this kind of piracy." In other instances the Democrats retained measures inaugurated by Hoover that seemed to be functioning successfully in easing some of the economic strains of the depression and in rebuilding confidence.[2] Most conspicuous of these was the Reconstruction Finance Corporation, the agency for priming business activity by means of loans and government refinancing.

The Democratic administration, of course, also redeemed several former pledges of their own, even some from the platform of 1908. It also launched new agencies like the National Recovery act, the Tennessee Valley Authority act, and the Home Owner's Loan Corporation agency, which was created and given an appropriation of three billion dollars to stave off foreclosures on home owners. In addition the Democratic administration sped through measures creating such controversial agencies as the Civil Works Authority, the Works Progress Administration directed by Harry Hopkins, and many others.

Slightly bewildered by the breathtaking speed with which some of the New Deal program was driven through Congress, and held at bay by the crushing superiority of the Democratic majority during Roosevelt's first term, Republican Congressmen rocked uncertainly as they groped for a defensive strategy. Only a few members of the House and a very few members of the Senate, from the safe Republican districts, such as those of Dan Reed in upstate New York or Harold Knutson in Minnesota, could say what they thought without fear of swift reprisals at the polls. It was a belittling experience for those used to governing as the majority party.

In the face of the Republican congressional losses in 1934 and further reverses in 1936, the Republican legislative leadership had something in common with a football coach whose squad is up against a far more powerful team midway in the season, but still has several important engagements remaining on the schedule. Should he throw caution to the winds in the hope of at least keeping the score down, thereby incurring heavy personal casualties? Or should he have his boys simply play heads-up defensive ball and wait for the breaks—the old Michigan strategy of "Hurry-up" Yost, a "pass, punt, and a prayer"? Wisely after the disastrous election of 1936, the Republican minority of 17 in the Senate found the answer in the man they elected minority leader, Charles L. McNary of Oregon. "Let the boys across the aisle do the talking," said "Charlie Mac" at a party caucus early in 1937. It worked.

But it was frightfully difficult not to move in on the attack, even though it caused further legislative casualties and did little to restructure a positive creed for the Republican party consistent both with the principles upon which it was founded and with the age in which it lived. One of the great difficulties of the period was that so many of the Republicans in Congress hailed from the safe districts, the tight little islands of thought. Many of these legislators were simply out of step with the thinking of the rank and file American voter. As one writer put it crisply in an election post-mortem appearing in the *Atlantic Monthly* early in 1937: "We Republicans, if we are to devise a brand of conservatism with a chance of winning the nation back to the Republican party, must recognize that it will require elements beyond wealth in the present and fear of the future." [3]

Struggling to reset its course and regroup its forces to speed the day when it could travel on the open road again with a faith based on something deeper than a hopeful promise to do something better, Republican party leadership struggled with several misconceptions. Most serious was the erroneous conception that the methods of consumer manipulation, which have long been applied successfully in various advertising departments, can be carried over into politics to rebuild good will for a political party. These techniques may be successfully applied to particular candidacies in American politics, for the Senate, House of Representatives, and even the Presidency in a given situation. But they do not restore faith in the political party, nor will they be successful except under certain specific conditions. This was a basic factor in the misdirection of the campaign of 1936.

"Where is the Republican grand and gaudy enough to polish off Dr. Roosevelt on election day?" challenged Mr. Mencken as 1935 folded into history on December 31. What the times called for was a "true spine rattler," someone like "Roosevelt Major" (Mr. Mencken's sobriquet for Theodore Roosevelt). But where was he?

In 1934 and '35 former President Herbert Hoover, not permitting himself to rust in inactivity, took to the radio to direct a few well-placed shots at the New Deal administration. With a new-found sense of humor, he noted sadly that the proliferation of New Deal agencies such as the WPA, NRA, AAA, and others, would shortly use up the entire alphabet, with nothing left after XYZ had been reached. But, he added sardonically, after all, "the Russian alphabet has 36 letters instead of the English 26." On the serious side, Mr. Hoover did attempt to point out that the New Deal administration could not legitimately homestead every reform it now laid claim to, and that many of these measures had their genesis in Republican administrations. Because the popular mind associated him with the depression, and many Republicans simply thought he lacked glamour, an anti-Hoover sentiment developed in one segment of the Republican party leadership that determined to devise a kind of Hoover-containment policy. Curiously, the temperament of many of these anti-Hoover leaders was not out of line with the ex-President's own conservative position. John D. M. Hamilton, for example, who became a leader of Alfred Landon's pre-convention campaign for the presidential nomination, and later the chairman of the Republican national committee, was the eastern director of the national Taft-for-President organization in 1952. In following their impulses to keep Hoover under blankets and seek a presidential candidate who could not easily be denounced as a lackey of Wall Street or the errand boy of vested interests, the group of businessmen who were working to take over the direction of the Republican party in 1936 thought they had found their dream candidate far out in America's heartland on the sunbaked prairies of Kansas: Alfred Mossman Landon.

Landon stood out peculiarly amidst the Republican ruins of the times. One of seven Republican governors in the entire United States, he was the only state chief executive who had survived two Democratic landslides. Actually he had been elected governor in 1932 in the Democratic sweep and re-elected in 1934 when Republican governors, Congressmen, and Senators were toppling throughout the nation. On the face of it, his vote-getting record seemed impressive, but one needs to read behind the circumstances of both these elections for part of the explanation. In each contest an independent candidate was in the gubernatorial race for the Kansas governorship. John R. Brinkley, the notorious goat-gland doctor, who was barred by the state medical board from practicing in Kansas and for many years an object of pursuit by the Federal Trade Commission for making pretentious radio claims for his patent nostrums, ran as an independent in each election, drawing thousands of votes that would have otherwise gone to the Democratic nominee. Though Landon was an industrious, earnest candidate, there seemed little doubt that Brinkley's candidacy was a major factor in his two elections.

In 1935, however, the reasons for choosing Landon as the 1936 standard-bearer continued to advance. Landon's father had been a Bull Mooser in 1912, and with this thought in mind there was additional hope that he could be put forward as a true liberal.

In December of 1935 William Randolph Hearst, accompanied by Arthur Brisbane and Paul Block, journeyed to Emporia to offer Landon the support of his newspaper empire. Much was made of this visit, and the presence of Hearst's private railroad car on an Emporia sidetrack, by Harold Ickes and others. But Landon dodged Hearst's request that he become an avowed candidate immediately and he never committed himself on accepting Hearst's support. For a time it looked as though the matter might come to a head in California when Hearst entered and supported a Landon slate in the presidential primary. Happily for the Kansan, the Hearst slate was defeated by Hoover delegates.[4]

Early in 1936 as important personages drifted to the Kansas capital at Topeka to see Landon, editor William Allen White, still cordial in his support of Landon, noted that "political geography does not make a President" and that he still has to measure up to certain requirements. By the spring of 1936, it was fairly evident that Landon would be the front-running candidate all the way and was apparently a shoo-in for the nomination. Only one challenger appeared anxious to have an active go at it himself, and that was Colonel Frank Knox, publisher of the Chicago *Daily News,* whose friends advised him early in the game that he really had no chance. None the less Knox did enter the Illinois primary without opposition, and at convention time he had most of the Illinois delegation. In another state where he made an effort—Minnesota—he actually had a majority (13 out of 22) of the state delegates at convention time, and he also had some support from New Hampshire, where he owned a paper at Manchester.

Discussed but never taken too seriously was the prospect that Herbert Hoover—The Chief, to many devoted followers—might still sweep the convention and be drafted at the last minute. Hoover carefully kept a discreet silence on this subject, maintaining always that he was not a candidate but never denying that he would accept the nomination in the remote and outside chance that it would be offered to him. Always a bridesmaid but never the bride, the hardy veteran from Idaho, William E. Borah, was another man prominently mentioned during the pre-convention campaign. But Borah gave little encouragement to such talk.

Curious—but difficult to take seriously—was the possible candidacy of another figure that has been divulged to us recently. Complaining in his *Diary* that he was sorry he had not resigned a year earlier from the Roosevelt administration, former Secretary of the Interior Harold Ickes has this to say:

> When I was approached with the proposition that if I should resign there was a good chance that I might be nominated for President on the Republican ticket, I did not take it seriously. At that time Landon had barely been mentioned. The build-up for him had not started. In the end he was built up because those opposed to this Administration had no one outstanding with any real standing and reputation in the nation. I do not say that the thing would have come my way, but I think the probabilities are that Landon would not have been thought of as a candidate. At any rate I would have had as good a chance as anyone for the nomination.[5]

Who the Republicans were that approached Ickes he does not say, which is all the more reason, we may suppose, for believing that "Old Curmudgeon" himself was playfully pulling his own leg.

From the very outset of serious presidential candidate speculation the build-up of Landon proceeded with great speed. Late in 1935 he was hardly known outside of Kansas, and prior to his nomination he had made just two political speeches and appeared on one radio interview. The one thing that seemed to be known about him was that he was an economy man in favor of balancing budgets, and had balanced the budget of Kansas. During the pre-convention period he was completely noncommittal on the issues of the day.

By the time temporary chairman Senator Frederick Steiwer of Oregon delivered his keynote address at the national convention in Cleveland on June 9, Landon's nomination was conceded. For the most part the convention was not one charged with exciting overtones. Even during the keynote speech the only warm response from the audience came from chairman Steiwer's continuous reference to New Deal effronteries with the phrase "for four long years! . . ."

The one dramatic moment of the convention was the demonstration that followed Herbert Clark Hoover's speech, as he closed with: "thank Almighty God for the Constitution and the Supreme Court." For a few moments after Hoover's address pulses quickened among his old loyal supporters who thought that by some miracle the con-

vention would rise upon its feet and demand his nomination by acclamation. At best these were only prayerful hopes, however, and
the political amateurs directing Landon's campaign who dominated
at this convention were quite prepared to take over, as Hoover smil-
ingly backed away from the rostrum into the wings. Described as "a
strange convocation of the quick and the dead" (referring to the
young Western liberals and the Old Guard Senators), the 1936
convention never again hit an intensive pitch of enthusiasm, once
the echoes died away from the accolade following Hoover's speech.

Arizona yielded to Kansas to permit presentation of Governor
Landon's name first and, once it was discharged into the ether, thousands of sunflowers, the official flower of Kansas, began waving wildly to the tune of "Oh! Susannah." All stop-Landon opposition collapsed and he went over on the first ballot by acclamation.
Meanwhile Colonel Knox, whose advisers had counseled him that his
own candidacy was hopeless, had left Cleveland and was journeying
east by motorcar. At noon the next day while stopping in a filling
station he heard over the radio that the Republican ticket would be
"Off the rocks with Landon and Knox." Several other vice-presidential nominee possibilities had been mentioned, including the president pro tempore of the United States Senate today, H. Styles
Bridges, who was then governor of New Hampshire. Someone was
said to have raised the objection to Bridges that it would give the
Democrats an opening for the slogan: "Landon Bridges falling down."
Colonel Knox had been a Bull Mooser in 1912, and had actually
been a Rough Rider under Teddy Roosevelt in the Spanish-American
campaign. So with two Middle-Westerners for candidates—both of
them ex-Bull Moosers—the Republicans started out bravely, though
definitely without a battle plan, to take on "the Champ," as Wendell
Willkie said four years later he hoped to do.

In their 1936 platform the Republicans invited all men and all
parties to join with them in defense of American institutions, to
pledge themselves to the maintenance of the Constitution and the
preservation of free enterprise. They condemned as "unworkable"
unemployment insurance and old age annuities which had been provided for by the Social Security Act. In the field of labor relations
they proposed that labor have the right to bargain through representatives "of its own choosing without interference from any source."
This construction would seem to require some modification of the
Wagner act—the National Labor Relations act. Finally they pledged
themselves to "balance the budget" and to maintain a "sound currency."

It was in a little grove of oaks on the Tam O'Shanter golf course, a mile or two from West Middlesex, Pennsylvania, his birthplace, that Landon opened his campaign on August 22, 1936. Unhappily for his listeners, as Mr. Mencken's ringside account tells us, "the difference between his loudest shout and faintest whisper was probably no more than two decibels." And before long, even the professionals, "who believed that his colorless voice might be teased and tortured into something resembling a Kiwanis baritone, with maybe even some of the dulcet overtones of tenor," gave up in despair. Traveling through little towns in Pennsylvania where he had spent his boyhood, he talked to the townsmen of different regions, recalling incidents of his great-grandfather's life and sharing with them some of his own remembered experiences. Friendly in an engaging way, with an approach reminiscent of the cracker barrel, he was not the kind of candidate who alienated people by his appearance. Yet at the same time he did not make converts to the Republican standard, nor did he manage to change the belief that the Republicans caused the depression.

Though by coincidence he happened to have the initials of Abraham Lincoln, the moment he ceased to be the legendary figure which he had been built up to be before the convention and stepped off into his own person for the campaign, Landon revealed some of his shortcomings. As Churchill, asked to comment upon his rival Attlee, once observed: "He is a nice, modest man, with a good deal to be modest about." His thin voice, with a Midwestern twang that sounded like a cross-cut saw slicing through a knot, was a poor match for the resonant tones of candidate Roosevelt. But quite apart from these personal matters, Landon also found himself in the uneasy position of advancing many contradictions in his campaign.

Ostensibly he symbolized economy. Yet he favored government programs of such dimensions that they would have been as unattainable within a balanced budget if he were President as they were under Roosevelt. The Kansas governor flogged Roosevelt's relief policy, but he also took considerable pains to offer his assurances that he would continue relief. Denouncing the Democratic reciprocal trade program, he none the less asserted that he was not against the trade pact program. The latter ambiguity, or contradiction, incidentally cost Landon the support of the Baltimore *Sun*. Throughout much of the campaign the *Sun* had hopefully looked for a forthright declaration from the Republican presidential candidate on the reciprocal trade treaties which would enable the *Sun* to give him their unqualified endorsement. Though he was strongly anti-New Deal, Landon's failure to be really clear as to what he meant on this issue brought forth an editorial from the *Sun* that while they could not support Roosevelt in the forthcoming election, they decided to sit this one out.[6]

Elsewhere, Landon decried government interference with agriculture in his farm speeches, but at the same time submitted a program for crop insurance which would have planted the government firmly in the business of controlling free markets. Actually, where the focal points of the Republican campaign should have been drawn, Landon never defined the indictment against Roosevelt with convincing clarity. One of these issues was suggested by Roosevelt himself at a press conference a few days after his re-election, when he commented that he felt his opponent had failed to exploit the most vulnerable spot on his first-term record—his weakness as an administrator. Landon spoke of confusion, but he failed to join the issue in such a way as to call attention to the most compelling of all contemporary problems of government, that of getting the multifarious agencies of government working in harmony and not at cross-purposes, and organized in such relationship to each other that a conscientious chief executive can confidently oversee their management.

But the prime issue which the Republican nominee left untouched, and the one which should have been brought into sharp focus, was the issue between statism and freedom as a future economic pattern, and the right to develop a classless society where everyone shall have an equal opportunity to get ahead and where no doors are closed to ability and zeal. At times Landon squared off to strike an incisive blow and was applauded for it. This happened when he lashed out at the act requiring a teacher's oath (to support the Constitution) in the state of New York. But for the most part he simply could not stir the popular imagination.

Yet admittedly Landon was up against overwhelming odds. With 12,500,000 workers unemployed and 20,000,000 on public relief, the power of New Deal spending counted heavily. Amidst many discouraging signs against the outcome, two events held out hope, both misleadingly. Late in September, in what was heralded as a bold campaign stroke, Landon made a hurried trip to Maine, just before the state general elections. The idea behind the move was to give Landon a chance to demonstrate his coattail power. As usual, the Republican ticket won in Maine, and the Republican presidential nominee carried the state in November. But as Maine goes so goes the election meant no more that year than what the Democrats said it did: as Maine goes, so goes Vermont. Even more misguiding was the ill-fated *Literary Digest* poll, which on the eve of the general election in November showed Landon winning with more than 300 electoral votes. Using telephone directories and automobile registration lists for the ten million sample ballots they sent out, what the directors of the poll failed to realize was that in this period millions who had never voted before were people without telephones. Disastrous for the poll also was the fact that it failed to make allowances for the circumstance that people who drive Cadillacs or Buicks are several times more likely to answer such a mail poll than those who drive second-hand Fords, Chevrolets, and Plymouths.

On the managerial side, the 1936 campaign bumped along in somewhat the amateurish fashion of the one to follow in 1940. John D. M. Hamilton started with some real handicaps, to be sure. Upon taking over the post of national committeeman he found that the office of the national committee did not even have a list of the county chairmen. Moreover, he found that in many counties there were no chairmen and that in several areas heretofore considered Republican there was no organization whatsoever. On the financial side it could not be said that the chairman faced an unstocked treasury, for the nine million dollars that the Republican national committee spent that year was an unprecedented amount. Admittedly, of course, the Republicans were up against the spending policies of the New Deal, with its largess for the employed, for those on relief, and for the more unfortunate segment of the population generally.

In actual campaign arrangements the amateur touch was easy to discern, and the absence of the steady hand of a Will Hays easy to detect. A humorous but unhappy incident in Evanston, Illinois, is typical. Invited to board the Landon campaign train at Evanston, a former Republican governor of Illinois, then in his eighties, was carefully kept in the cool confines of a basement during a scorching summer day lest the excitement prove too much for him and injure his health. After he had been brought down to the station several times on false alarms through misinformation from the dispatcher, the train finally appeared while the old gentleman waved a sunflower, with photographers present waiting to snap his picture with candidate Landon. But instead of stopping the train roared on through, leaving the ex-governor a pathetic spectacle, waving a drooping sunflower. And again, at Fort Wayne, Indiana, when the Landon train came to a stop it was blanketed from the crowd by a train standing on the next track.

As an auxiliary arm of the Republican effort, the Liberty League, founded in 1935 to save the country from what it termed the perils of the New Deal, also joined the assault. Herbert Hoover's characterization of the group, however, as "one of the humors of the times" is particularly apt. Composed of several wealthy Democrats including Jouett Shouse, Irénée Du Pont, and John J. Raskob, formerly chairman of the Democratic national committee, this organization, as Mr. Hoover waspishly commented in refusing to join it, "had supported the election of the New Deal."

During the 1936 campaign the League set up quite a clatter and carried on a campaign reminiscent of the "only eighteen more shopping days till Christmas" idea. But the Liberty Leaguers hardly made a dent with their "Ten more weeks to save the American way." In Hoover's judgment the "personalities" that ran it were so out of favor in the country that it "boomeranged" to aid Roosevelt.

Meanwhile the wiseacres close to the betting odds saw clear indications that both Maine and the *Literary Digest* poll were wrong, and badly so. On Election Day the earlier prediction of Jim Farley, which he himself had no faith in, made him the clairvoyant overnight. With only Maine and Vermont loyally planted in the Republican column, many wondered if the Republican party was going the way of the Whig and Federalist parties and if this was the beginning of the end. Carrying only 459 of the nation's 3,000-odd counties (Hoover carried 372), Landon's popular vote—36.5 percent—was just a whisker better than that of Democratic candidate Cox when he was inundated by the Harding landslide in 1920. In an increased total vote of about 6,000,000 ballots over the combined totals for 1932, the gain for the Democratic ticket was 4,500,000, approximately one-third of which, interestingly, came from three states—New York, Pennsylvania, and New Jersey. The Republican increase was slightly under 1,000,000 votes.

Almost everywhere Republicans might search the election map they could find little comfort. Earl Brown, writing for the Negro Journal, *Opportunity,* in December, 1936, estimated that over 2,000,000 Negroes voted in the election that year. This was the first time since Reconstruction, he said, "that a majority of Negroes voted for a Democratic President." The change of political allegiance for the Negro was also felt in other areas besides the presidential contest. Republican Negro Congressman Oscar De Priest was defeated by a Democratic Negro, Arthur Mitchell, who had lived in De Priest's district only six years. Of the sixteen Negroes who were elected to state legislatures that year, eleven were Democrats.[7]

In one area, however, the showing of Alfred Landon is not to be denied. Unfortunately even here his performance escaped notice in the tide of post-campaign comment. Throughout New England generally Landon actually fared better than Willkie in 1940 and Dewey in 1944. Particularly is this phenomenon noticeable in Maine, where the Republicans almost lost in 1940; New Hampshire, where the 1940 GOP nominee lost by a larger margin than in 1936; and Vermont, where the Republican ticket was weaker than in 1936.

Perhaps the reason for Landon's better showing than either Willkie or Dewey in New England lies partly in the growing internationalist tendencies of the region and partly in the class composition of the parties. Traditionally GOP territory, New England as an area is relatively speaking internationalist, strongly industrialized, and Catholic. Since 1928, the Democratic party has become more and more identified with internationalism, pro-labor policies, and pro-Catholic sentiments. Thus the lengthy Republican tradition has been affected by new forces, particularly in southern New England.

Looking back on a campaign that many observers found reminiscent of the class divisions of an earlier alignment in the presidential campaign of 1896, Republicans grew restive over the clobbering they had received in 1936, fell out amongst themselves again on how to hit the comeback trail. Dipping back into party experience, more than a few Republicans recalled the happy experience of the Advisory Committee on Policies and Platform which functioned as a research unit before the 1920 campaign. Set up by the national committee in 1919 as an important element in the strategy laid to recapture political power, the Advisory Committee on Policies and Platform was "to investigate the existing needs and conditions affecting specific problems that would have to be considered by the national convention; to gather facts and data; to invite a full expression of leading Republicans; and to submit its recommendations and the material it collected, in convenient form, to the Resolutions Committee of the National convention for the consideration of that Committee and also of the Convention."

In view of the difficult problem of postwar adjustment, the number of compelling social and economic problems was staggering, and happily the Advisory Committee was able to recruit a distinguished staff. Albert J. Beveridge headed the subcommittee on Law, Order, and the Administration of Justice, one of 18 subcommittees that were organized, and over 100,000 questionnaires were sent out to elicit information on subjects including regulation of high cost of living, conservation, problems of capital and labor, postal service, war risk insurance, and many others. This research experiment, notwithstanding judgments to the contrary by some Republicans, was effective in shaping the form and substance of its decisions, taken later by the resolutions committee.[8]

The Advisory Committee that started off so promisingly, however, gradually shook down into simply a one-man agency collecting data on persons and events, most of which could be extracted from a newspaper morgue. In 1936, some time before the death of the man who handled this work (J. Bennett Gordon), it became obvious that the Research Division would have to be reinvigorated if it was to be an effective auxiliary to national campaigns. In February, Dr. O. Glenn Saxon, professor of Economics at Yale, was appointed director of the Research and Editorial division of the national committee, and during the campaign of 1936, a decision was made to operate the Research Division on a permanent basis. Thereafter a library of some 6,000 volumes was built up, a staff recruited, and in 1938 research services were provided by the staff for the congressional campaign committee of both the House and Senate. Down to substandard size, the tiny group of Republican legislators in the 75th Congress found the week-end briefing of the research staff—a plan recommended by chairman John Hamilton—particularly useful for speeches, public statements, and minority committee reports. From time to time the Research Division also issued a number of memoranda: "The Tyranny of New Deal Taxation," "The Labor Record of the Republican Party," and "Social Security." By far the most spoken of was "Promise and Performance," a pamphlet issued during the 1936 campaign that contrasted Roosevelt's utterances and Democratic party planks of 1932 with the New Deal actions of the ensuing four years.

Prompted again by the desire to stir up party spirit when morale was at a low ebb was a somewhat different approach to policy research, suggested in 1937 by former President Hoover.[9] Early in the latter year, Hoover published his proposal for a midterm party convention, a meeting patterned after the regular national convention each quadrennium, but devoted exclusively to the delicate business "of working out afresh the party position." Republican Congressmen mustered little or no enthusiasm for the proposal, but the GOP rank and file did, and by November 5 when the national committee met, the popular demand for action was so strong that opponents of the idea sought a compromise. The result was the creation of a program committee of 100 whose duty would be to report its findings to the national committee. Selection of the program committee was entrusted to the executive body of the national committee, and after some delay Dr. Glenn Frank, former president of the University of Wisconsin, accepted the post of chairman. One of his first duties was to enlarge the membership of the program committee, for it had already become apparent that more than 100 would have to serve if the committee was to represent adequately a cross-section of the party. Eventually close to 200 were selected, including lawyers, manufacturers (6), labor leaders (2), clergymen, and various other representatives of the professions and business. The average age of the committee members was under 50, and ten were under 35.

Outlining the task of the committee in broad strokes, chairman Frank said at the first meeting at Chicago in March, 1938:

> This Commission must make an utterly honest and objective audit of the New Deal . . . must rethink, restate, and reinterpret to the nation the political and economic circumstances of this new age— must, as its contribution to the counsel of Republicanism, create a comprehensive report of policy respecting the long array of stubborn problems confronting us as a people. . . .

Designating two vice-chairmen—one a woman, Frances Bolton (who later succeeded her husband as the Representative of Ohio's 22nd Congressional district)—the program committee divided the country into nine regions and began its efforts to get subcommittees working on policy throughout the nation. What inspired one member at the meeting to call it "the most remarkable political meeting since the Constitutional Convention of 1787," however, began to look less promising a few months later. By the time of the committee's second meeting, in August, the slippery imponderables of its task were beginning to blunt earlier enthusiasms. The key subcommittee on fundamentals got all snarled up over the nature of the fundamentals and fretted constantly lest what it was writing down as fundamentals could not be "distinguished from platitudes." Even more discouraging were the skirmishes between committee members and Congressmen over party strategy, and tiffs about what was right or wrong for the country as a whole.

Just before the second meeting of the committee Dr. Thomas H. Reed was made director of studies for the program committee and he did manage to arrange a number of round tables for the August meeting that revived some of the lost spirit. But some of the members chafed at jocular catcalls from the press that the GOP was going back to school again, and the idea that the committee could ever aspire to become a vigorous national molder of party policy began to die on the vine. GOP Congressmen of course were not pleased at the prospect of being committed or embarrassed in any way by a national program, particularly one that they had no hand in devising. Moreover, it was becoming increasingly evident to the program committee that the scope of the plan it had once envisaged was beyond reach. This decided, the idea of a national policy body was abandoned in favor of a revised plan whose purpose was to produce an exhaustive report on the needs and desires of the American people—

a report that was to be submitted to the national committee before the end of 1939, presumably for use in drafting the 1940 platform.

Useful though it had been in bringing Republicans together from the far-flung environs of Maine to California, the program committee experiment burned out quietly, but not without leaving its mark. As a practicable measure for restoring the party to power it mustered little confidence. As an idea worthy of revival, however, it has continued to have force. A similar proposal was warmly endorsed by the Political Parties Committee of the American Political Science Association in its report of 1950 and was urged as a strategy measure by several prominent Democrats in 1954.[10] To date the Republican program committee of 280 laymen and women that gathered in 1938 still represents the only time a major political party has held a national midterm convention that aimed to structure party policy.

If Republicans were distressed at the accuracy of Farley's farsighted prediction on the 1936 outcome, there was also some comfort, though they did not know it, in one of his post-election asides. While Democrats were cackling jubilantly that the Republican party was now a "corpse," Farley said he was much distressed at the magnitude of the Democratic sweep and that in it he saw disintegrating factors that would serve the Republican cause. They soon did.

Within two months after the new Congress took office in 1937, the antithetic elements that comprised the Democratic party and had thus far been held together so skillfully under the leadership of Franklin Roosevelt started dismembering. Almost imperceptibly at first, the growing antagonisms within the Democratic party that began in February continued to harass the administration to the steady advantage of the Republicans. Perhaps Mr. Mencken's conjecture was right when he reported the day after election that Roosevelt "must be entertaining certain stealthy qualms today. He now carries all the burdens of omnipotence." [11]

Initially it was the introduction of the President's proposal to "rejuvenate" the Supreme Court. This measure, if adopted, would have permitted the President to increase the size of the Court up to a maximum of fifteen by giving him authority to appoint one justice for each member of the Court who was beyond the age of seventy. Caught without advance warning, many staunch supporters of the administration were shocked by what they considered the President's audacity in calling for the introduction of such legislation, and in a very few weeks the tinder had been set for a serious revolt within the Democratic senatorial contingent. It was at this point that the very capable leadership of minority leader Charles McNary came into play. His "Let the boys across the aisle do the talking" became the byword of Republican strategy. Incredible as it seems, all 17 members held their fire, resisting temptation and bombardment from indignant constituents to get on the firing line and save the Republic from this diabolical plan. Actually, of course, the proposal had a certain antecedent in the Progressive party platform of 1912, which had demanded the restriction of the Supreme Court's power in order that the people might have "the ultimate authority to determine fundamental questions of social welfare and public policy." But Franklin Roosevelt's design to "pack" the Court was calculated to bypass change by constitutional amendment, and it touched off one of the most acrimonious debates in the nation's history.

Under the leadership of two Democrats, Senators Wheeler of Montana and Burke of Nebraska, the Democrats laid their strategy to bury the President's proposal.[12] From the outset they were in constant touch with minority leader Charles McNary, who was quietly marshaling his small task force of 17 Republicans into an "operation silence" maneuver. Most formidable of his immediate problems was that of dealing with former President Hoover. Learning that the ex-President was about to make a nationwide broadcast calling upon the nation to rise up in arms against the Supreme Court bill, McNary found an intercessor to try and head Hoover off. "Who's trying to muzzle me?" queried Hoover angrily to the friend who relayed the suggestion that he not make the talk. None the less the speech was canceled, for a time at least, and the Republicans preserved their silence. And so McNary, the man who went to the United States Senate in 1917 and at his first Washington press conference parried a question on what his favorite legislative interest was with the reply: "Nuts" (he raised filberts in Oregon), piloted his dozen and a half Republicans through the darkest days of '37, when their strength was at its lowest ebb in Republican history. With the death of majority leader Senator Joseph Robinson of Arkansas in the summer of 1937, the demise of the President's Supreme Court packing proposal was a certainty and a wide-open rift had developed in the Democratic party. It was at this time that John Garner, the Vice-President, acting as the official pallbearer for the Democratic opponents of the bill, went to the President and asked him how he wanted the story: "With the bark on it or off it?"

Shortly after, another legislative measure took the front center stage position in a controversy that also derived to the advantage of the Republicans—the Administrative Reorganization bill. This proposal embodied many desirable features, including several formerly advocated by President Hoover. But its introduction, coming on the heels of the ill-fated Supreme Court bill, led to popular charges of dictatorship and allegations that the President secretly desired to set himself up as a supreme omniarch in defiance of our sober system of checks and balances. In any case this legislation stirred such a furor that it worked to the advantage of the Republicans.

Combined with these two proposals a third and more all-pervasive factor soon served Republican political interests: the recession that set in early in 1937. In face of certain economic reverses, murmurs of discontent began to be heard, and with them the cause of Republicanism experienced a gradual uplift.

Early in 1938 still another impetus was given to the Republican comeback. Franklin Roosevelt decided to make several candidates for re-election walk the plank. He failed. Moreover, by trying to purge such Democratic Senators as Millard Tydings of Maryland, Guy Gillette of Iowa, Walter George of Georgia, and others in the Senate as well as the House, he injected further elements of dissension within his party. By now things were looking up for the Republicans and they were on the trail of a comeback. In the fall elections not only did they gain sharply in the House and Senate, but for the first time in six years new GOP governors were elected. Some of them would be heard from, and mighty soon. Out in Minnesota, 31-year-old Harold Stassen became the first Republican governor in eight years by defeating the regime of the Farmer-Labor party. In New York Thomas E. Dewey, then only 38, lost out in the gubernatorial race to the veteran and very popular Herbert Lehman by only 58,000 votes. And out in Ohio a man who had served his apprenticeship ringing doorbells, and gradually worked himself up to be speaker of the Ohio Assembly and would one day become "Mr. Republican" of the United States Senate, won his first term in what Gladstone called "the world's greatest deliberative body." Taking seats in the 76th Congress in January, 1939, were 164 Republicans in the House, compared with 89 two years earlier; 23 Republicans in the Senate, against 17 earlier. With 1940 just around the corner, the presidential batons began twirling early.

"We Want Willkie"

🐘

First in the field this time, but not in his later two tries, was Thomas E. Dewey, fresh from his triumphs in the prosecution of racketeers in New York city as special prosecutor for Mayor Fiorello La Guardia. Aided by skillful managers and strong financial support from the purse of Ruth Hanna McCormick Simms, the Dewey pre-convention campaign as early as December, 1939, was making remarkable headway, particularly in light of the fact that the young prosecutor had never yet held public elective office. Also in the field and making solid strides with committed delegates early in the pre-convention foray was Robert A. Taft, who at convention time had lined up approximately 200 delegates, chiefly from the South and Ohio. By December of 1939, with Roosevelt still not saying whether he would or not, but acting very much like a candidate who would accept a draft for a third term, Dewey and Taft were the most discussed Republican candidates.

Then, early in 1940, a man tired of the carping about the state of domestic affairs from many of his business associates, and with some ideas of his own on what was the matter, decided to shake the dust off his feet and get into politics. Listed in the 1940 edition of *Who's Who in America* as a Democrat (he had, however, voted for Alf Landon in 1936, according to a story published in the New York *Sun* in mid-January), and almost unknown to Republican party leaders as late as January, 1940, he began a campaign that rolled along with the speed of a prairie fire. And while many professionals were still shaking their heads that it couldn't happen, he stalked off with the presidential nomination on the sixth ballot. In all the sprints for the presidential nomination, nothing touches that of Wendell Willkie.

Willkie publicly referred to his candidacy for the first time in an address at Wooster College in Ohio on January 29, 1940. In response to a question he said: "I am running for President. Of course, it is not going to happen, but if the nomination were given to me without strings, I would have to accept it. But I couldn't go out and

seek delegates and make two-sided statements. I value my independence." [1]

Beginning to catch the public eye with a fortuitous appearance on
the popular quiz program, "Information, Please," April 9, he moved
ahead by leaps in the public opinion polls if not in actual delegate
strength. Even as late as April the Willkie campaign for the presidential nomination seemed little more than a buzz and was not taken
seriously by party professionals. But from then on, masterminded by
Russell Davenport, who had resigned as editor of *Fortune,* and aided
by Oren Root, Jr., and the Midwestern publishers, the Cowles
brothers, the Willkie campaign gained momentum rapidly. His popularity rose steadily in the public opinion polls until, by convention
week, for the first time in the entire pre-convention period he ranked
first among the popular choices.

Discouraged by the grievous defeat of Landon, businessmen did
not find it difficult to believe that in Willkie they might have a
marketable commodity at the ballot box. Here was a man, they reasoned, who embodied a fierce faith in American private enterprise.
Said Willkie in 1935, "I want to say to you that no duty has ever
come to me in my life, even that in the service of my country, which
has so appealed to my sense of social obligation, patriotism and love
of mankind as this, my obligation to say and do what I can for the
preservation of public utilities privately owned." But while Willkie
could proclaim his faith in private enterprise militantly, there were
also other facets to his thinking that gave him broad group appeal.
An internationalist who believed in the extension of aid to England
and France in their all-out struggle against Hitler, his views were
well received by Republicans of New England and the Atlantic seaboard. At the same time his Hoosier background was not exactly
a handicap. "It pays off to look like an Indiana farmer on Wall
Street," he once remarked.

To the casual observer, the spectacular advance of the Willkie
candidacy had the general appearance of being inspired by a spontaneous demand of the rank and file of the party that he be the nominee. It is doubtful, however, if a short pre-convention campaign has
ever been planned with more political acumen than that of Willkie
in 1940. Once the organization began to take shape money flowed
into the Root headquarters at an incredibly swift pace, making possible some elaborate plans to be unleashed at convention time. One
of these called for a deluge of telegrams from the grass roots to delegates at the Philadelphia convention. Eventually these telegrams
were delivered by the bushel basket, all urging the nomination of the
former president of the Commonwealth and Southern Company.

Meeting in Philadelphia June 25, 1940—the day the French Armistice went into effect—with Harold Stassen, governor of Minnesota, as temporary chairman delivering the keynote address, and Joseph Martin, minority leader in the House, as permanent chairman, the convention seemed likely to be a riotous affair almost from its inception. Filled with many earnest-looking bespectacled young men, the galleries had the look of a sophomore class in political economy and its partisanship was evident from the outset. The galleries, concededly two-thirds pro-Willkie, kept chanting throughout the entire proceedings "We want Willkie."

Among the candidates some tenderness had also developed. Initially Harold Stassen had indicated his willingness to support Dewey and had invited Dewey to Minnesota to speak at a major rally in Minneapolis in December of 1939. But as the Willkie star began its ascent, Stassen late in the pre-convention campaign accepted the post of convention floor-manager for the Willkie forces. The recruitment of the energetic Minnesota governor was an important element of strategy for Willkie, who needed some Middle-Western outposts.

During the convention Willkie, wearing a straw hat tilted at a rakish angle, violated modern convention tradition by ambling around hotel lobbies buttonholing delegates and asking them to vote for him. At convention time his strength appeared to be about a hundred votes, and Willkie himself predicted that he would be nominated on the fifth or sixth ballot.

Willkie's first big break came the day before the convention opened—July 23—when Governor Baldwin of Connecticut stepped out of the race, with an announcement that he would second the Hoosier's nomination. This gave Willkie 16 delegates from the Nutmeg state. A second important reinforcement arrived when Stassen "without any prior hint and five minutes before a scheduled meeting of his state delegation told Roy Dunn, National Committeeman from Minnesota, that he would support Willkie." [2]

Leading on the first three ballots with something over 300 votes, followed by Taft with around 200, Dewey was unable to increase his strength and gradually began to lose his footing. On the first ballot the vote stood: Dewey 360, Taft 189, Vandenberg 76, and Willkie 105—the latter scattered among 25 of 53 states and territories. Not even a favorite son, Willkie got only nine of Indiana's 28 votes on the first ballot, and eight of the 92 from New York. Thereafter, however, the shift to the fast-rising Hoosier took place swiftly, amidst tumultuous cheering. On the second ballot he rose to 171, moved ahead of Taft with 259 on the third, and overtook Dewey on the fourth with 306. On the fifth roll call, Willkie had climbed to the point where he began to look unbeatable—429—and on the sixth he went over the top, after which a motion was quickly adopted to make his nomination unanimous.

In a convention of this type—a kind of supermarket for deals and trades of all sorts—the possibility of some kind of coalition to stop Willkie remained open in the early balloting. Pennsylvania, for example, with a favorite son in its governor, Arthur James, and a huge bloc of 70 votes, was holding out against Willkie and in the proverbial nomenclature of conventions was said to be "for James until hell freezes over." But agreement upon a candidate to head the coalition, and the insurmountable problems of delivering to the coalition choice votes pledged to other candidates, forestalled all such attempts. Hoping perhaps to play the decisive role, Pennsylvania waited too long and Wendell Willkie became the twenty-first Republican nominee.

It was now 1:57 A.M., Friday morning, and as Willkie listened elatedly to a message from Herbert Hoover being read to the convention—"My congratulations. The result of a free convention of a free people will carry you to victory"—he faced a distasteful decision. Traditionally the presidential nominee has a strong voice in the selection of his running mate, and in this case it was well known that Willkie was committed to support Raymond Baldwin, governor of Connecticut, for the Vice-Presidency. But his advisers now argued that Willkie was too much identified with New York, not Indiana, and that the Republican ticket must not have another Easterner. Charles L. McNary of Oregon was suggested as the ideal candidate, and Willkie himself summoned Baldwin to explain the pressure that was now being put on him. The Connecticut governor took this major disappointment graciously, and then Willkie got off another hurried call to Joe Martin, who was already asleep, to see if he would ask McNary to accept. This McNary did at once, bringing to the completed ticket (he was nominated Friday afternoon with 896 votes, Dewey Short receiving 108, H. Styles Bridges 2) a legislator of a rich and varied background who enjoyed the reputation of being one of the most loved characters in the Senate.

McNary was a true Westerner. His ancestors had followed the overland route of the Oregon trail, and he had been born in Salem, Oregon. A graduate of Leland Stanford University, he became successively a lawyer, district attorney, dean of Willamette Law School, state supreme court justice, and finally a United States Senator in 1917. While some argued that it was incongruous to place a champion of public power on the same ticket with a known opponent of public power development, it is extremely doubtful that this alone lost Willkie any votes.

Of all the candidates who seemed to have what it takes to get around the bases, Wendell Willkie looked the most likely to make the grade in the early summer days of 1940. His bison build and handsome appearance made him a striking figure on the stump. His energy seemed boundless, and in the public eye he had the advantage of not seeming to be a presidential nominee hand-picked by the party professionals. Though there were grumbles, the party regulars who thought him an interloper put on their working gloves and resumed their local stations throughout the country ready to do battle for him. And Willkie himself in the initial stages gave evidence of a certain humility and showed a degree of willingness to defer to the judgment of the regular party leaders.

That he stood an excellent chance of winning is attested by a Gallup poll immediately after the Republican convention (July 11), which gave Willkie 47 percent of the popular vote to 53 percent for Roosevelt if FDR became a third-term candidate. Almost immediately, however, Willkie was given to brash utterances that disturbed many GOP leaders and to them seemed unnecessary.

By this time it was almost self-evident that Franklin Roosevelt would be renominated. Though Garner had given his consent to have his name presented at the Democratic convention, and there was some talk of a coalition to stop Roosevelt, being a realist Garner was prompted to make the brittle remark privately that without the President's support no candidacy was better than "a can of stale beer." Commenting on this situation, Willkie told newsmen he wanted to take on "The Champ" and would be satisfied with nothing less. Brave, bold talk, but the party professionals shook their heads and looked at one another silently. What they wanted was to elect a Republican President, and having gone against the Champ in two bruising battles before, they would not be unhappy if he decided to step aside.

It has been alleged many times by different writers that the course of the European war, particularly the fall of France and her surrender in June of 1940, had a swift impact upon the American presidential campaign and steadily diminished the chance of Willkie's election. In part there is a real case for this argument. But often the argument has been pushed too far, to the neglect of the mistakes and shortcomings of the Willkie campaign. By the time Willkie was nominated, Germany had already overrun France and the surrender had taken place. Unquestionably the commencement of heavy bombardment of England in September of 1940 and the ensuing Battle of Britain reawakened the American conscience to the grim realities of the war and our proximity to it. But it should be recalled that the

Republican nominee was in substantial agreement with Roosevelt on pronouncements in foreign affairs, and that in this area Willkie took his stand unequivocally. Always well-informed on American affairs, the London *Economist* gave a lusty cheer for this concurrence at the time Willkie was nominated.[3] And Roosevelt himself thought of Willkie's choice as a "godsend" for the country, "because it eliminated the isolationist issue from the campaign and reassured the world of the continuity of American foreign policy." [4]

On the party platform, Republicans had tiptoed tenderly in the matter of extending aid to nations "disturbed by invasion." "We favor the extension to all peoples fighting for liberty, or whose liberty is threatened, of such aid as shall not be in violation of international law or inconsistent with the requirement of our national defense." The restriction of aid to the confines of international law, of course, was inspired by isolationist sympathizers who were really for declaring an unqualified neutrality. But, quaint people that we are in our political customs, it is the campaign pronouncements of the candidate rather than the platform planks, as every schoolboy knows, that strike home with the voters. And here the earnest Hoosier spoke out unequivocally for aid to overrun nations.

Some Republican speakers did call the Democratic party the "war party," while the Democrats answered such talk by calling attention to several outstanding isolationists in the Republican ranks.

Whatever the dimensions of the impact of foreign affairs on the course of the campaign, the crest of Willkie's popularity, reached immediately after his nomination, slackened off as the campaign wore on. His much-heralded acceptance speech at Elmwood, Indiana, in late July, was a lusterless performance. Thousands came from adjoining areas, but despite the valiant efforts of Homer Capehart, who was in charge of arrangements, the heat and the inadequacy of roads and parking facilities took the edge off his audience's receptive mood even before he began his speech. And the speech itself did little to fire the imagination. Willkie not only forgot the manuscript of his speech, which had to be rushed to him at the last minute, but, inexperienced as he was, he had failed to have it triple-spaced, as all speakers do for easy reading and to make eye contact possible with the audience and newsreel cameramen. Worst of all, he had not gone over the talk alone or in consultation with party advisers.

Highly effective before a small group, Willkie never quite carried off a speech before a huge gathering. Also most unfortunate for his health and for his campaign was his complete failure to learn how to husband his physical resources. In consequence, by mid-September his voice was giving him trouble and from then on he was under the constant treatment of a laryngologist. Toward the close of the campaign his voice was gravel-edged and there were times when his words came over the microphone almost in a stage whisper.

Willkie's campaign train, reminiscent of a group of Boy Scouts off to a jamboree, was roundly cursed by one local delegation of Republican party officials after another as it made its way about the country. With many amateur strategists roaming about the train, "chain smoking like their chief and planning new devices such as pretty girls handing out windshield stickers," tried and true party workers often found it difficult to get aboard and their ideas usually had no hearing. "Will you tell me what goes on here?" asked J. Wells Farley, a Boston attorney and member of the board of overseers of Harvard University, furious after he boarded the train because he could find no one to brief on arrangements for a Boston speech. "I will tell you," answered Pierce Butler, Jr., a Willkie aide and son of the late Supreme Court Justice: "This place is like a whorehouse on a Saturday night when the madam is out, and all the girls are running around dropping nickels in juke boxes." [5] In consequence it was Willkie's running mate, Charles McNary, who had to do most of the hand-pumping among local party leaders.

Try as he might, Willkie never quite succeeded in shaking off the Wall Street association with which the Democrats were constantly brushing him. "Just a simple, barefoot Wall Street lawyer," Harold Ickes labeled him. (But Willkie had him there. "My office is on Pine Street, a block away," he said.) All through the campaign Willkie labored doggedly to throw off this stigma. Having started his politics arguing at the breakfast table with his father, he had finished law school at Indiana University, then gone to Akron where he became an important corporation lawyer. From Akron he had finally been summoned to the citadel of corporate finance in New York, as his opponents liked to remind voters, there to become chief counsel and later president of Commonwealth and Southern. In vain did Willkie plead that at heart he was really a small-town boy, and that he would rather be associating with his hogs and chickens than his most important clients on Wall Street.

The Wall Street association damaged him with Democrats as well as with many Republicans outside of the East. The inbred distrust of the West for Eastern capital still carried over to bother Republicans in the area, and this, combined with his party unorthodoxy, they found hardly reassuring. Hadn't he said, "Party lines are down!" at his Elmwood acceptance speech? And hadn't he gone on to underscore the remark by saying: "Nothing could make that clearer than the nomination by the Republicans of a liberal Democrat who changed his party affiliation because he found democracy in the Republican party and not in the New Deal"?

The isolationists who hated Roosevelt grew steadily cooler toward Willkie as the campaign wore on. "When he swallowed the Roosevelt foreign policy," grumbled Henry L. Mencken in the Baltimore *Sun* on September 15, "all the rest of the New Deal rumble-bumble went down with it, and he has since presented the spectacle of a man choking on his own false teeth."

Late in the campaign—October 25—the United Mine Workers' leader, John L. Lewis, growled an endorsement of Willkie over the air that may well have done more harm than good. Lewis, embittered by this time from a personal feud with Roosevelt, insisted that he be given an opportunity to make an hour's speech over a national hook-up that would cost $45,000. He also declared he would not speak under the auspices of the Republican national committee. Though reluctant to assume such a burden, the Democrats-for-Willkie finally agreed to pay for the radio time, induced by the dubious prospect that Lewis might spin 4,000,000 votes into the Republican column. Threatening to resign as president of the CIO if Roosevelt were re-elected, Lewis made a speech that newsmen thought of poor caliber and very likely injurious to Willkie's campaign. Certainly chairman Hamilton thought so as he read a telegram after the speech sent to him by a prominent labor leader: "AFTER TONIGHT I CANNOT DO ANYTHING TO HELP YOUR BOY." [6] Noticeable also following the speech was John Bricker's slackened enthusiasm for the campaign. And Arthur James, Pennsylvania's governor, never made another speech for Willkie.

Like Landon, Willkie found it difficult to state a program. In his acceptance speech he had told his Hoosier friends, "The New Deal does not distribute wealth, it distributes poverty!" But his plea for unlimited production, with no mention of a plan that held out promise for keeping up purchasing power, was not effective in wooing back the body of voters who had been persuaded, by Roosevelt's reduction of complicated Keynesian economics to the simple logic of "pump priming," that their needs and interests were interlocked with New Deal policies.

Toward the end of the campaign Willkie's nerves, frayed by something like 28,000 miles of travel (18,500 by train, 8,800 by plane, and several hundred by motorcar), chain-smoking, endless conferences, and three or four speeches a day, led him into some slips of brash behavior.[7] On one occasion, when he was quickly challenged by the Democrats for his statement that Roosevelt had been instrumental in the partition of Czechoslovakia under the Munich pact,

Willkie could only come back lamely that he had been "misquoted." Obviously there were many factors that caused Willkie to overreach himself in moving into the attack. Exploiting their incumbency, the Democrats took advantage of the fact that Roosevelt was staying at the helm during a momentous crisis in the history of American foreign relations, and implied that he simply could not be bothered by a young upstart like Willkie snapping at his heels. In consequence, billboards advocating Roosevelt's election spoke of him as the commander-in-chief, and on all possible occasions an attempt was made to clothe Roosevelt with gold braid, suggesting powerfully his constitutional position as commander-in-chief of the armed forces. And his frequent photographs on cruisers or battleships, with the long cape he liked to wear flapping in the breeze, again served as a reminder that he was still guarding the ramparts in the nation's hour of peril. Turning the tables effectively, the Democrats also dredged up the slogan that had been used by Republicans in the Hoover campaign of 1932, "Don't change horses in the middle of the stream." Also injurious to Willkie in certain areas were the underhanded stories about his German ancestry, implying pro-German sympathies.

A scurrilous screed was issued in October by the Negro division of the Democratic national committee which attempted to link Willkie's parents and his wife's parents with a statement by Hitler that "Negroes are lower than apes." The same document also identified him with neo-Nazi fanatics, while other unsigned leaflets were sprinkled around the country attacking Willkie's sister for marrying a German naval officer (she was actually married to Commander Paul E. Pihl, United States naval attaché in Berlin).

Willkie was also given a thoroughgoing tarring by the liberal press. He had, of course, the bulk of the nation's press behind him, including the New York *Times* (the third time in 56 years for a Republican presidential candidate—McKinley in 1900 and Taft in 1908). But the liberal press struck out at Willkie savagely, calling him a "fixer" for Wall Street and private utilities, a "condottiere," and a man who would hire out to the highest bidder.

All these factors, of course, tended to throw Willkie off balance at times, often with costly results. Yet if one looks at his inexperience, and judges him in the light of the bitterness that was injected into the campaign, his performance in many ways was truly remarkable. On one occasion he even had to suffer the indignity and personal hurt of seeing splatter on Mrs. Willkie a rotten egg that had been intended for him.

Long before the autumn leaves began drifting down from the beeches and lindens, there were signs that Willkie just could not mount the speed to close the gap. On October 6 the Gallup poll showed Roosevelt leading with 56 percent of the popular vote, Willkie trailing with 44 percent. Asked, regardless of whom they were for, which candidate they expected to win, 60 percent of the respondents in a poll picked Roosevelt, 23 percent named Willkie.

By any standards, Willkie's final vote can only be regarded as an extraordinarily handsome performance. Polling 22,230,018 popular votes, against 26,890,401 for Roosevelt, the Republican nominee won the largest vote in the history of the party up to 1952, and topped the best effort of a Republican candidate heretofore by close to six million votes. Percentagewise Willkie won 44.7 percent to Roosevelt's 53.9. While FDR led again in the great cities, he lost ten states, giving Willkie 82 electoral votes to 449 for Roosevelt. Willkie's greatest strength was in the West North Central region, which he carried, but perhaps more significant was the fact that the margin of victory for Roosevelt in the Middle Atlantic and East North Central sections was slight. Landon had carried only 459 counties throughout the nation in 1936; Willkie pulled 1,147 counties into the Republican column in 1940. County by county there was an unmistakable drift away from previously high Democratic pluralities, and the Republicans seemed well out of their disastrous 1932 and 1936 slumps. In the Senate, Republicans could also take new heart, for they captured five additional seats. They fared less well in the House, where they dropped from 169 to 162 seats.

"How could we lose?" cried Mrs. Willkie. "We tried so hard!" By 11:00 P.M. on Election Day the stern truths of the outcome were already evident. But Willkie would not concede. Not until the following morning—Armistice Day, November 11—looking much shaken, did he finally appear and announce that he had dispatched a telegram to Franklin Roosevelt extending congratulations.

For one explanation nothing more illuminating can be cited than an interview of Samuel Lubell with William J. Galvin, Democratic leader in a Charlestown ward of metropolitan Boston. This particular ward—populated by longshoremen, packers, waitresses, and minor city employees—gave Roosevelt a four-to-one margin. "Probably no section in the country gained more under the New Deal," said Galvin, then proceeding to list specific benefits which the people living in this community had derived: "Hundreds got pay raises under the wage-hour law; more hundreds of seasonal workers are having slack months cushioned by unemployment insurance benefits. The NYA [National Youth Administration] is helping from 300 to 500 youths; at the worst of the depression thousands held WPA jobs; of 1,500 persons past 65 in the ward, more than 600 receive old-age assistance; another 600 cases are on direct relief and get aid for dependent children. Charlestown is a food stamp area; the WPA improved its bathing beach; a new low-cost housing project will relieve some of the ward's congestion." [8]

In the same post-election survey Lubell, sent by the *Saturday Evening Post* to sift down the election returns in particular precinct areas of great cities to see what he could discover, suggested some interesting correlations between presidential voting and prevailing rents. In seven Minneapolis wards where rents were less than thirty dollars, Roosevelt ran ahead by a margin of better than two and a half to one. In four wards where rentals ranged between thirty and forty dollars, Roosevelt ran just slightly ahead, while in three wards where the average rents exceeded forty dollars, residents voted for Willkie five to three. The breaking point between Roosevelt and Willkie in Minneapolis seemed to be in the wards with rents around forty-four dollars, while in Pittsburgh the dividing point between Willkie and Roosevelt appeared to be between wards where rents averaged somewhere between forty-five and sixty dollars.

Dr. Gallup's analysis of the presidential vote of 1940 showed that in addition to capturing, by two-to-one margins, income groups receiving below twenty dollars a week, Roosevelt also won a majority of the groups receiving from twenty to fifty dollars weekly.

Most cheering to Republicans was their comeback among the farmers, suggested by Willkie's capture of 57 percent of the Midwestern farm vote, against only 44 percent who had supported Landon. Part of this defection away from Roosevelt stemmed from discontent with Democratic agrarian policies, but another factor was the defection from Roosevelt among farmers of German extraction. Thus Lubell notes that in 1940 Roosevelt's proportion of the major party vote dropped off roughly one percent throughout the country. But of the twenty counties in the United States where his loss was in excess of 35 percent—"five times the national average"—19 "are predominantly German speaking and background." [9]

Willkie lost the election primarily in our twelve great cities, carrying only one city—Cincinnati—with a population above 400,000. But hopeful for future Republican campaigns was the fact that the Republican vote was starting to climb in many cities—a circumstance of desperate importance if the Republicans were to find the winning combination. What Willkie might have done had he been able to build depth in party loyalty and had he not been viewed coolly by the Republican machines as too much the amateur and a renegade Democrat, is worth no more than passing comment. It is interesting to recall, however, that as the 1952 pre-convention campaign got under way the strategists guiding both the Eisenhower and Taft efforts took great pains to remind all of their lieutenants that there are 170,000 precincts in the United States and that it was one of the misfortunes of Wendell Willkie that Republican precinct leaders in many of these districts lost heart by early forenoon on Election Day, simply because they had not been made part of the show during the long campaign. During the critical opening period of the campaign "he was dragging his heels on seeing important Republican leaders." [10]

With the United States moving closer toward involvement in World War II, a majority of the Republicans in Congress began supporting a doctrine which the Republican party, departing from its tradition before 1919, had embraced on an increasing scale: isolationism. A majority of Republicans voted against the Burke-Wadsworth bill in September of 1939—the first peace-time conscription measure in United States history, providing for the registration of all men between the ages of 21 and 35 and the induction into the armed services of 800,000 draftees. Most embarrassing to Republicans, however, was the House vote for extension of the conscription act for the duration of the emergency, which passed by a single vote —203 to 202—just before the Pearl Harbor attack in 1941. Throughout the tortuous prewar period, many Republicans in the House and Senate went along with President Roosevelt in support of policies dedicated to all-out aid to Great Britain and other countries resisting Hitler's aggression. But a majority of Republicans during this period voted otherwise and spoke otherwise. Relations between the titular head of the Republican party, Wendell Willkie, and the dominant Republican faction in the Senate and House were not pleasantly amicable. Thus Willkie's post-election statement that he intended to lead a "loyal opposition," carried little weight with the majority of GOP Congressmen, many of whom felt that he had thrown away his chance for election by not taking Roosevelt savagely to task for his interventionist policies.

Meanwhile, undeterred by the coolness of GOP Congressmen, Willkie visited England, where he conferred with Winston Churchill and other British leaders, then returned to this country to speak eloquently in support of far greater effort for the aid of gallant Britain. And in the congressional elections of 1942 the Republicans all but captured the lower house of Congress. Winning 208 seats, against 218 for the Democrats, and nailing down nine additional seats in the Senate to bring their total to 37, the Republicans were in the strongest position they had been in in Congress for a dozen years. That the vote was a portent for better things to come in 1944 for the GOP was not to be inferred from a careful look behind the statistics, however. It was an extremely light vote, brought about by a combination of factors. One element that held the vote down, of course, was the usual apathy that characterizes our midterm elections in contrast with congressional elections in a presidential year. But the enormous internal migration of working men to different war industries scattered all over the country left large numbers disfranchised because of residence requirements. Inductions into the armed services also drew upon an age group in which studies on voting preferences showed that a majority were inclined to support the Democratic party. Another factor involved the exactions of war, which are never taken without some grumbling, and not uncommonly find expression in voting against the "ins."

At the state level two enormously gratifying victories lifted GOP hearts everywhere. In New York the feat of Tom Dewey in becoming the first Republican governor in the Empire state in a quarter of a century served notice that here was a man soon to be heard from. At the other end of the line Earl Warren's election as governor of California was equally welcome and encouraged Republicans to believe they were at last ready for a contest on the Presidency.

The following year a non-isolationist salient began taking a firmer mold within the Republican congressional forces and also among Republican governors. With postwar problems in view, the efforts of Secretary of State Cordell Hull to introduce a bipartisan element into American planning efforts were welcomed from the Republican side of the aisle in the House as well as in the Senate. And at the governors' Mackinac conference during the summer of 1943 Dewey and others in the Republican fold took the lead in the issuance of a declaration that called upon the United States to take its rightful place in the community of nations in a collective peace effort.

During 1943 Wendell Willkie brought out his book *One World,* a swift-moving tract embodying impressions he had gleaned the year before on a 31,000-mile trip to Africa, the Middle East, China, and the Soviet Union. Tellingly the hard-hitting Hoosier pointed out that the war was not "a simple technical problem for task forces. It is also war for men's minds." Everywhere, and particularly in Asia, he noted that the common people had misgivings about Allied war aims, and he deplored the attitude of those who opposed social change, urging delay simply because of the present crisis. "After the war, the changes may be too little and too late." Willkie's publishers, Simon and Schuster, estimated they might sell 250,000 copies of *One World.* Barely two months after its publication, sales climbed over the million mark, and within two years to two million.

Turning from 1943 into 1944, Willkie held a curious position within his party. Like Gladstone, of whom it was once said, "He is liked better out of doors than in the house," Willkie had a following among rank-and-file Republicans that was far greater than he enjoyed in the Congress. In the popular mind he was a figure standing above the party battle who called the shots as he saw them. He had fought valiantly for the passage of the lend-lease bill in 1941, and when it finally made the grade he was accorded a generous share of the credit for its passage. On occasion he could be flippant, as he appeared to be before a congressional committee when he brushed aside a remark that he had made in the course of the 1940 presidential contest as merely a bit of "campaign oratory." The fact was, of course, that in making this statement Willkie was simply unmasking a truth concerning many campaign statements which most candidates are reluctant to disclose. "I think [it] one of the most courageous things any man ever said in public life," remarked William Allen White soon afterward. "It was not discreet, but it was deeply honest. Only three times in public life have I seen such honesty. The pretension that a candidate's utterances are omniscient when everyone knows he is talking damned nonsense is one of the large reasons why the American people lose faith in democracy." [11]

On every side the big question looming before the followers of both political parties was: Will Willkie retake the Republican presidential nomination in 1944? Against him the odds were formidable. By many Republicans Willkie was regarded as a huckster of the "me-too" variety. Some, in fact, alleged that his "me-tooism" was merely the opportunist politicking of a corporation executive to defeat Franklin Roosevelt. The same group of critics also held an uneasy view of what they conceived to be Willkie's erratic tendencies, and they bracketed him with the "tame millionaires" like Ed Stettinius, Averell Harriman of the Union Pacific, and William L. Batt, president of SKF, that Harry Hopkins was maneuvering into high posts of government during the war.

The nomination had come easily for Willkie in 1940. He had won it without ever really getting to know the substructure of Republican party organization, and he had not taken the time to learn it since. With this in mind he started out determinedly and boldly to make up for lost time late in 1943 and early in 1944. By and large, however, his personal strategy was unchanged from the unorthodox methods he used in his pre-convention build-up of 1940. It was still based upon broadsides issued to the people by which he hoped to bring about his nomination through a popular upsurge rather than through patient preconvention politicking for individual delegates.

Early in 1944, with Dewey again keeping his own counsel as to whether he intended to run, Willkie gave out a statement that he intended to meet the challenge of isolation head-on in his campaign for the Republican nomination. Moreover, he said, he had decided to file in the April Wisconsin presidential primary.

Advised against this move by his own counselors, Willkie went ahead none the less. But the real reason for Willkie's running, writes his close friend and biographer, Joe Barnes, "was that he could do nothing else." With the California primary closed to him because of Governor Warren's candidacy, Willkie felt he had to run in what he admitted was the worst state for him in the country, with the possible exception of Illinois. That the Republican party should abandon the false doctrine of isolationism and return to its pre-1919 tradition was for him a matter of deep faith. Journeying to Wisconsin, where he knew he was staking his political future, Willkie began speaking in scattered Wisconsin communities, including the shrine of Republicanism at Ripon. There he said the founding of the Republican party "represented an honest effort on the part of men to extend the areas of freedom," that it came to power in 1860 because it "dared to take a stand" on the issues of the day, and that it had maintained its vitality because "it was a flexible vehicle capable of generating within itself new ideas and principles."

Punching hard at both the reactionaries in his own party and at the Democrats, who he said had "deadened incentives," Willkie thrust all of his energies into a ten-day whirlwind tour. And as he did so the contrast between himself and his rivals became sharper each day. "He seems to have about the same talent for suppression of his personal opinions that Theodore Roosevelt possessed," commented the Baltimore *Sun*'s distinguished editor, John W. Owens, "and he lives in a day which presents vastly more and bigger subjects to awaken ideas. Perhaps people think he 'talks too much,' but he continues to be out with his thoughts. Probably he thinks he can lose the presidency and live, but has doubt that he could survive as a sphinx."

For ten days Willkie slogged through late spring snowfalls—to Sheboygan, Green Bay, Oshkosh, Appleton, Milwaukee, Manitowoc, and many other Wisconsin communities. Everywhere his theme was much the same. "A political party can never stand still," he said, ". . . those leaders of a party who insist upon applying old formulas to present problems merely because those formulas worked in the past are damaging the party and will eventually destroy it. For they are standing still, whereas the world around them moves." On the subject of foreign relations, he was equally outspoken in his criticism of one wing of the Republican party. "Help me save the party from those forces that back away from the sacred obligation of putting the full strength of this nation behind the war," he pleaded at Green Bay. "No nation can live alone and to itself in this modern world." [12]

Warming to the task he had assigned himself, Willkie was immensely pleased with the large, responsible throngs that greeted him at every stop. But as the campaign progressed Willkie encountered much to discourage him. He expected large support for General Douglas MacArthur, whose campaign was being headed by former governor Philip La Follette, though MacArthur himself was publicly contending that he was not a candidate. But Willkie did not expect the name of Commander Harold Stassen to be entered in the Wisconsin primary, and though Stassen did not indicate publicly that he was a candidate he apparently did nothing to have his friends withdraw his name from the Wisconsin primary. His failure to do so distressed Willkie very much, for he felt that Stassen's name on the ballot would tend to split internationalist sentiment in Wisconsin— which, of course, it did.

Stunned by the results of the Wisconsin vote on April 4, in which Willkie won not one delegate out of 24, the crestfallen crusader announced that he was quitting the race. Dewey had won seventeen delegates while Stassen, as Willkie feared, had won four, and MacArthur three. The fact that he had received a complete rebuke made up Willkie's mind to abandon the race irrevocably. Had he been able to establish even a small beachhead in this region, Willkie would have kept in the race. But his complete shutout made it "perfectly obvious," he said, that it would be futile for him to continue.

Actually, had Willkie not been so headstrong and had he not been determined to collide head-on with the prong of isolationism in terms of political geography, the ensuing pre-convention campaign for the Republican nomination might have been quite different. What lasting imprint Willkie's brief but gallant leadership might have made on the party no one can yet tell, least of all Willkie, for in five months he was dead. But more than a few Republicans were aware at the time that he had served the party well, and that in pleading for the renunciation of isolationism he had rendered a signally lasting service. Others would have to discover it later, if not by 1944, 1948, or 1952, surely at some time not too distant, if the party was to survive. What Willkie really did was to try to redirect Republican energies to a realization of what McKinley had told his fellow partisans long ago: "The period of exclusiveness is past. . . ."

Willkie died depressed that his ideas appeared to have made such a little dent on the Republican party. But the big, frolicsome, earnest, and hard-driving Hoosier had opened the way unknowingly for some important conversions to follow. Less than a year away the long-time isolationist Arthur H. Vandenberg would be stepping out to pick up the standard where Willkie fell. And with Vandenberg's passing (1951), which was deeply despaired by Republicans who approved of his bipartisan efforts for a constructive foreign policy, another convert was emerging from the wings to take his place—Alexander Wiley of Wisconsin.

"Death cannot quench a dream," commented the Indianapolis *News* on October 10, 1946, two years after Wendell Willkie came home to Indiana "to return to the rich earth from which he sprang." Looking at the words graven on the book at his grave in Rushville, the *News* invited living men everywhere to reflect upon Willkie's creed, among the lines of which we find:

> Whenever we take away the liberties of those whom we hate we are opening the way to loss of liberty for those we love.
> The moral losses of expediency always far outweigh temporary gains.

Six years later, in an editorial, "Wendell Willkie, 60," on what would have been the Hoosier's sixtieth birthday (February 18, 1952), the New York *Times* put it this way:

> Wendell Willkie has been deeply missed during these past seven years, and there is every reason to believe that he will continue to be missed for a long time to come. . . .
> He was a man of courage and of honesty—two virtues of which there is never a sufficient supply in public life. He was a visionary and a realist, a conservative and a liberal, an independent thinker never afraid of the unorthodox or the unconventional. "I won't be dropped into a mold. I want to be a free spirit," he said. He was as American as the countryside of his native Indiana, and America could do with more men like Wendell Willkie.

Now and again a man appears in American politics who has the qualities which make him a center of political thought—a man unlike so many leaders who are forever catching up in their positions. Willkie was such a man—a natural, for want of a better name, who stood firmly in the storm center while the tides of party thought and feeling swirled around him and his ideas.

Following Willkie's dramatic withdrawal from the presidential race after his disastrous defeat in Wisconsin on April 4, the Republican pre-convention fight looked mighty like Dewey all the way.

Keeping up a discreet no-comment attitude publicly, Dewey and his boy-wonder team, headed by Herbert Brownell, kept busy in the field, sewing up delegations and carrying on a successful harvest of delegates. Actually Dewey's nomination was threatened only by the remote possibility of an emotional crusade to draft MacArthur or some grievous mistake on the part of Dewey or his managers that might give John W. Bricker, governor of Ohio, some chance for the top prize. Bricker had the Ohio delegation under an informal agreement that, in return for Bricker's support in 1940, Robert Taft would step aside to open the way for Bricker's candidacy in 1944.

By convention time at Chicago on June 26, 1944, Dewey's managers had already been able to negotiate a majority before the balloting began. So certain was the outcome that Dewey's name was the only one to be placed in nomination (by Dwight Griswold, governor of Nebraska). Immediately thereafter, Bricker of Ohio bowed out of the race in a gesture of unity. Then Senator Joseph Ball of Minnesota withdrew Minnesota's favorite son, Harold Stassen, and the first and only ballot was taken. Dewey received all the ballots on the roll call except one lone vote for MacArthur.

Off to its fourth start against perennial candidate Roosevelt, the Republican party found itself held together in uneasy amalgam. By no means dispelled were the lingering doubts of the party professionals who had been unhappy with Willkie in 1940 and felt not much more kindly disposed toward the efficiency crew from Albany whose smooth drive for a successful nomination left them gaping at the post. Willkie, they grumbled, was at least a friendly man with warm human juices in him—a man of parts—if you did manage to get to see him. But greeting the new presidential nominee was like shaking hands with a frozen chocolate éclair. Disturbing the serenity of party loyalty still more was the fact that quite apart from those Republicans who knew they didn't like Willkie and were pretty certain they disliked Dewey, there were numbers who had pinned their hopes on Wendell Willkie. "Surely," wrote William Allen White in a tribute to Willkie in the Emporia *Gazette*, "the Republican party, which came to power more than eighty years ago under Abraham Lincoln by saving the country from disunion and by freeing four million slaves, the Republican party which guided the country while the continent was settled . . . cannot be so craven that it would conspire to steal into victory with no issue but Bricker and a bellyache." Willkie himself had declared that without a firm forward-looking world and domestic policy the GOP would fail in the 1944 election. And when the Willkie pre-convention campaign collapsed, the faith of many Republicans in a victory for 1944 collapsed with it. Thus Dewey began his first bid for the Presidency beset by handicaps within his own party that were hardly conducive to success.

Troublesome from the start were circumstances that permitted Dewey's opponent to take a more Olympian attitude toward campaigning than he had against Willkie in 1940. In Western Europe the American offensive was well advanced, while in the Pacific Theater, after the slow but steady build-up of amphibious assaults in 1943, matters were beginning to look up. Roosevelt said he expected to be too busy to engage in political debate, and besides he had no personal taste for campaigning. Therefore, he announced, he expected to devote little if any time to either. He did say, however, that he expected to speak out from time to time and report to the nation the facts as he saw them. Which meant, of course, that his formal addresses on reports of the war's progress, as President and commander-in-chief of the United States armed forces, did double duty as campaign talks.

As in 1940, the avowed differences between the Democratic and Republican presidential nominees on foreign policy were slight. Dewey announced at the outset that in the interest of national security he would refrain from any criticism relating to the war effort. Moreover, the nature of the campaign and the national emergency led to the highly unusual arrangement under which Dewey's adviser on foreign affairs, John Foster Dulles, met with Secretary of State Cordell Hull during the campaign for the purpose of keeping in focus, on a bipartisan basis, the major lines of our foreign policy.

Dewey campaigned industriously, reiterating his theme that the administration was composed of a group of tired old men who were no longer capable of meeting the challenge, and that the times called for a new team. He also argued that "it took a war to make jobs under the New Deal," and that the misguided efforts of the Democratic administration to bring about economic recovery had failed to lift the United States out of its depression. Not until September, after his return from a 21-day tour to Hawaii and Alaska, did the President make his first 1944 campaign speech, delivered from the deck of a destroyer in the Puget Sound Naval Yard. Roosevelt emphasized conduct of the war and foreign relations throughout the campaign and on the domestic side refused to debate home-front issues.

In a sense the fourth-term campaign of Roosevelt came as an anticlimax. After he had defied the third-term tradition successfully in 1940, the argument against another term appeared to be less persuasive in 1944. No doubt the Republican nominee was hurt somewhat in this election by Roosevelt's mild swing to the right. This slight swerve attracted the support of some business and professional groups, notably in New England and the Atlantic seaboard areas, who disliked Roosevelt's domestic policies but felt there should be no breach in his handling of foreign affairs.

Dewey was also hurt by the silence of the 1940 GOP standard-bearer. As late as October 8, no word on how he would vote had been spoken by the ailing Hoosier who was fighting for his life in a New York hospital. That day, just before dawn, he died from an acute cardiac condition that followed the toxic effects of a strepto-coccic throat infection. No one knew how he would have voted.

The most notable defection in the Republican ranks was that of Senator Joseph Hurst Ball of Minnesota, who suddenly announced in September that he had decided to support Roosevelt because can-didate Dewey was equivocating on the issue of foreign policy. Ball himself had been a member of the resolutions committee at the Re-publican convention that drafted the plank on foreign affairs, and his bolt angered Republicans everywhere, but particularly in his na-tive heath of Minnesota.[13] Many of them predicted at the time that it would be his first and last elective term in the Senate—a prediction which Hubert Humphrey helped along by defeating Ball in 1948 by a quarter of a million majority.

On Election Day—the first while the nation was at war since 1864—a huge vote was cast. Though two million below the re-cord-breaking total of 1940, it was still ten million beyond pre-election estimates. This time Roosevelt's percentage of the total vote dropped below his mark of 1940. Nominee Dewey received 22,-017,592 votes; Roosevelt 25,602,646. Percentagewise it was Dewey 45.8; Roosevelt 53.8. Dewey carried twelve states and could take some comfort in the fact that his vote in the Middle Atlantic and West North Central regions of the country was greater than that of the Democratic presidential ticket. Continuing their move-ment toward the Republican party which started under Willkie, the farmers helped Dewey pick up close to 200 new counties. Dewey won 1,344 in 1944, compared with Willkie's 1,147 in 1940.

In the House elections the Republicans lost some ground, dropping to 190 seats as against 208 in the previous biennium, but in the Senate they pulled one more seat away from the Democrats to give them 38.

On the Trail to a Comeback

It began suddenly on January 10, 1945. Arthur H. Vandenberg had the floor and was firing a shot that made editors perk up at their copy desks throughout America and brought an accolade the likes of which few Senate speeches of modern times are apt to get:

> There are critical moments in the life of every nation which call for the straightest, the plainest, and the most courageous thinking of which we are capable. We confront such a moment now. It is not only desperately important to America, it is important to the world. . . .
> The thing . . . we need to do, Mr. President . . . is to frankly face the postwar alternatives which are available. . . .
> There are two ways to do it. One way is by exclusive individual action in which each of us tries to look out for himself, the other is by joint action in which we undertake to look out for each other.
> The first is the old way which has twice taken us to Europe's interminable battlefields within a quarter of a century. The second way is the new way in which our present fraternity of war becomes a new fraternity of peace. I do not believe that either we or our allies can have it both ways. They serve to cancel out each other. We cannot tolerate unilateral privilege in a multilateral peace. . . .

Here was an elder statesman of the Republican party, a man who had gone to the Senate in 1928 and had been re-elected in the Democratic landslide of 1934, striking a new note of counsel for his party on the eve of the President's departure for the Yalta Conference. Moreover, he was asking from the administration a straightforward guileless trust in the legislative phase of diplomacy—for a genuinely unpartisan approach to the critical demands of the hour in foreign affairs. Heretofore Vandenberg had moved forward and away from his former isolationist thinking with a certain bounce, but as one man expressed it, he still liked to pause now and then "to assure stragglers that he understands their feelings." From this moment onward, however, the name Vandenberg became the hallmark of legislative leadership in foreign relations.

Less spectacular in his ascent to leadership, Robert A. Taft had already inherited the mantle of leadership in domestic affairs by dint of an incisive mind and an expenditure of energy dedicated to the legislative process that has seldom been equaled. By common consent, Taft was felt to have one of the best minds in the United States Senate—a judgment sometimes qualified by his opponents to the effect that he had the best mind in the Senate "until he made it up."

Serving an apprenticeship in precinct politics, Taft had gone to the Ohio legislature at an early age and had been speaker of the House in that body before being elected to the United States Senate in 1938. Clearly dedicated to the proposition that the function of the minority party is to oppose, Taft mounted an attack against New Deal-Fair Deal policies that he never permitted to relax.

In his fifteen years in the Senate Taft came to have a unique position in the annals of Republican leadership, and there was something very special about him that made him quite unlike any of his contemporaries. "The nation came to rely upon his character," said Walter Lippmann, "as something apart from his politics, and upon the quality of his mind rather than upon his political opinions.

"He was the very opposite of the hollow men with their fabricated personalities. The inner man was the solidest part of Taft, and at the core he was so genuine and so just, so rational and so compassionate that he commanded the confidence of men when he could never convince them."

Where Taft would land with both feet upon the more striking issues of the day was something no one could ever quite predict. On such matters as public housing and federal aid to education, Taft took a stand which many of his party thought too advanced, and he was criticized for it. Several of Taft's more conservative colleagues made some carping criticisms of him back in 1947. "We actually have a hard time keeping him out of the lap of guys like Claude Pepper," said John Bricker. "Actually," continued Bricker, "I hear the Socialists have gotten to Taft."

Years later Taft also was to shock members of his own party as well as those of the opposition with a comment he made in a speech to the National Canners' Association early in 1953, on the subject of Communists in universities. It depends upon the subject taught, observed Taft, noting that he thought there were instances where the presence of a member of the Communist party on the faculty of a university would not be objectionable.

Selecting for himself an assignment to the Senate committee on

Labor and Education when Republicans organized the 80th Congress in 1947, Taft plunged directly into the explosive area of labor-management relations. And while Taft engrossed himself in this subject as well as others in the fields of welfare, education, and taxation, his Republican colleagues in the Senate and House prepared themselves for other assignments in this brief but controversial interlude known as the 80th Congress—"the worst Congress in history," according to President Truman.

The possibility of a dispassionate review of any congressional session is a dim one in any case. Moreover, in the case of the 80th —or "Eighty-worst" Congress, as the Democrats jeeringly spoke of it—a balanced judgment becomes all the more difficult because the attack mounted against this Congress was most successful in burying the constructive side of the record by concentrating its fire on a few issues. This is particularly true of the Taft-Hartley act, where the law was denounced as a "slave-labor act," and its supporters portrayed as selfish ogres bent on restoring labor to chatteldom.

Forgotten, but not the least in importance among the legislative enactments of the Eightieth Congress, was the Hope-Aiken bill for farm price supports—a measure generally acknowledged as one of the best agricultural bills to be drafted in many years. And in the realm of foreign affairs the voting record was far from the isolationist wall that has been so often alleged. On the European Recovery act—the Marshall Plan, which was a far-reaching program for aid to foreign nations—thirty-one of the Senate's forty-nine Republicans voted for the bill to carry it, 69 to 17. In the House, where the measure won, 329 to 74, 171 Republicans out of 245 voted for it. On the Greek-Turkish aid appropriation of four hundred million dollars which swept the House early in 1947, 287 to 108, the margin of Republicans in favor of the bill was smaller than on the Marshall Plan. None the less, 127 Republicans voted for this appropriation leading to the adoption of the so-called Truman Doctrine, while 94 voted against it.

Any comparison of Democratic and Republican voting records on foreign-aid measures will, of course, reveal far greater opposition from Republicans. It should also be noted that quantifying the voting record is sometimes deceiving. Thus, while the roll-call results may show that a majority of Republicans supported particular foreign-aid measures on final passage of a bill, this does not always tell the full story of crippling amendments submitted by Republicans to induce changes. Yet the fact remains that a majority of Republicans did support our far-reaching foreign aid program.

Another shiny postscript to the record of the Eightieth Congress was the Taft-Wagner-Ellender bill on public housing. Admittedly a very modest postwar beginning in a field of compelling urgency, the measure offered some testimony at least that not all Republicans were stone-age gorillas oblivious to the need for redressing social blights. But all such constructive measures were quickly drowned by the noisy tempest that arose over the prime target of those seeking to discredit the Eightieth Congress: the Taft-Hartley act.

The Taft-Hartley act, which sought to balance the bargaining rights of management and labor, restricted some labor prerogatives and abolished others. Under the law, enacted in 1947, the union shop was circumscribed closely by regulated elections conducted by the National Labor Relations Board, deduction of union dues from an employee's envelope was to be permitted only upon written author-ization by the employee, unions were made subject to suit in federal courts for damages incurred through violation of collective-bargain-ing agreements or union participation in jurisdictional strikes or secondary boycotts, unions were chargeable with unfair labor prac-tices such as coercion of employees in the choice of a bargaining agent, and employers gained the right to petition the National Labor Relations Board for elections whenever they believed a union no longer represented a majority. In addition the Taft-Hartley act out-lawed the "closed shop," stipulated a cooling-off period of sixty days following labor's notice of a termination or change of contract be-fore striking, and employers were permitted to make anti-union statements so long as they were free from threat of economic reprisal or offer of reward.

Taking no hand in the preparation of the Taft-Hartley bill as it moved along to final passage (becoming law only after Congress overrode a presidential veto), organized labor leaders immediately denounced the measure as hostile to labor rights. Admittedly there were sections of this act which labor groups found particularly ob-noxious that required redress, and Senator Taft himself was one of the first to urge that the law be modified by several amendments. But labor would have none of it, and as an issue with which to flay the Republicans in the 1948 presidential and congressional campaigns the Democrats found the law heaven-sent. In 1949 labor again spurned Taft's proposals to amend the law and consistently thereafter the position of labor and many Democratic leaders was that nothing would satisfy on this issue other than outright repeal. Actually the law was not the bogey that labor and Democratic party orators berated it as, and privately many prominent Democrats admitted that it could be changed satisfactorily through amendment. But in 1948, as in later years, the temptation to use it as a whipping post and exploit it politically as the "slave-labor act" was something the Democrats could not resist, and they made the most of it. In 1948, while attacks against the act hurt Dewey, they were probably much more serious for Republican congressional candidates, who suffered heavy casualties in the nation's urban and mixed districts. The Democrats held many urban voters in the congressional elections of 1948 whom they lost in the presidential election of the same year.[1]

Less prominent in the attack against the Eightieth Congress, but a significant issue none the less among the bruising blows struck by the Democrats in the fall of '48, was the Knutson bill for an income-tax reduction. Vetoed twice by President Truman in 1947 and passed in 1948 over the President's veto, the probable effect an income-tax reduction had upon many voters at this particular postwar juncture is most convincingly demonstrated by Congressman Knutson's own fate. Going to Congress in 1917, Knutson cast his first House vote on April 6, 1917, and on this occasion he was one of fifty members who voted against our declaration of war on Germany. Thirty years later he was still in Congress, having survived the Democratic landslides of the thirties and risen through seniority to the chairmanship of the House Ways and Means Committee in 1947. But in 1948 Knutson, whose hold over the Minnesota Sixth District had been regarded as unassailable, went down to defeat. Why? The late Congressman's own valedictory is perhaps the most effective testimony.

"The Democrats said my bill was a 50-50 bill—gave a horse to the rich man and a rabbit to the poor man."

"It helped lick me all right," said Knutson wistfully, "but it was the best tax reduction bill ever passed by a United States Congress, and in the long run will confer greater benefits on the country than any other legislation I have had anything to do with." [2]

One further matter involving the Eightieth Congress which eventually worked against Republican success in the 1948 general election was primarily an error of omission rather than commission: the failure of the Congress to authorize the Commodity Credit Corporation to support declining grain prices. In this case the likely consequences did not become painfully evident until the close of the presidential campaign. How these factors spelled out the GOP defeat is a story embracing one of the greatest upsets in the annals of the American ballot box, and one that commands a closer look.

Moving into the pre-convention period of 1948, ever confident that victory lay just ahead, several Republican presidential aspirants began their limbering-up exercises early. First to declare himself was Harold E. Stassen, who defied orthodoxy by making a public announcement a full year and six months before the 1948 presidential convention that he was a candidate for the nomination.

While Harold Stassen was setting something of a record by traveling over 30,000 miles in his pre-convention efforts to corral delegates, Dewey, after his fashion of 1944, carefully avoided any sharp commitments either on his intentions or on major political and economic issues until the last stages of the pre-convention campaign. Still the titular leader of the party, and recovering some lost prestige by his re-election in the New York gubernatorial election of 1946, Dewey was very definitely a factor to be reckoned with.

Returning to the national competition after his unsuccessful bid for the nomination in 1940, Senator Taft planted himself in the pre-convention campaign with both feet. Soon he joined with Stassen and most of the nation's press in challenging Dewey for his failure to square off and meet the issues as well as to make a forthright statement on his availability.

Other names in the 1948 convention were Vandenberg of Michigan, Earl Warren, governor of California, and General Douglas MacArthur. In a sense the Vandenberg candidacy was never full-blown. Like Borah, Vandenberg was regularly discussed every four years but he never made the grade. This time, while there were indications that fortune might smile upon him differently, there again were factors that caused the party to bypass him. One difficulty was the failure of Michigan's senior Senator to give his friends the green light and permit them to organize a drive for delegates. To the public generally he let it be understood that he was not an active candidate. At the same time he took some pains to underline the fact that he would not be against accepting a draft. That there be no misunderstanding, Vandenberg suggested to the press that any man who said he was not interested in becoming President of the United States would simply be telling an untruth.

Harmful also to the growth of a real Vandenberg boom was the oft-repeated whisper that his health was in serious jeopardy and that he had but a short time to live. These stories were denied by Vandenberg's own personal physician, but the rumor persisted and was undoubtedly a factor in discouraging supporters from rallying under his banner. One further element that kept the presidential nomination from going to this very able Republican also bears remark. Vandenberg at this particular juncture was in a weakened position simply because he was such a recent and strong convert to internationalism. Known for many years as an isolationist—and a vigorous one—Vandenberg had a career that could enable one columnist who admired him to speak of him none the less as the outstanding example of a presidential possibility who had stood squarely on both sides of every important political question in American politics during the past fifteen years. Clearly Vandenberg's orientation on foreign policy after 1945 was coming to be greatly admired, but in 1948 it savored too much of New Dealism for a great many Republicans who would actually be called upon to make the choice.

Unhappily, the combination of these several factors conspired against Vandenberg's nomination. That he rather than Dewey might have defeated Harry Truman in 1948 seems at least a reasonable possibility, since there are ample grounds for believing that Vandenberg at the head of the ticket might have inspired greater loyalty throughout the Republican ranks than Dewey and his team subsequently did. Additionally, there is certainly every reason to believe that his forthright pronouncements for vigorous American co-operation in the field of foreign affairs might have attracted greater numbers of independent and Democratic votes than did the campaign speeches of Dewey on this issue. Be that as it may, in March, 1951, Arthur Vandenberg died of a lung cancer, his place assured in the annals of history, though he was denied the opportunity to lead his party along the course he had courageously chosen.

Earl Warren of California still appeared as "the best-known unknown in American politics." And he had added mightily to his reputation as a vote-getter when he became the first Republican governor to win both the Republican and Democratic nominations in the 1946 California primary as he made his bid for a second term. Not since Hiram Johnson won both party nominations for the United States Senate had such a spectacular victory been recorded in California. Known for his integrity, honesty, and record of progressive achievements, Warren as in 1944 was still having a difficult time in raising his candidacy to major-league status. No serious attempt was made at national organization, and by and large his candidacy was that of a lustily cheered favorite son, backed, to be sure, by the delegation that happened to be the third largest in the convention, with 53 votes.

MacArthur, though disclaiming ambitions to be the presidential nominee, did permit the use of his name in a few places, but his command with the occupational forces in Japan kept him far from the scene of political activity. Moreover, his refusal to return to the United States in 1946, and indeed his refusal to return at any time until his dismissal in April of 1951 by President Truman, was a definite handicap to his followers.

On his own motion the most sought-after candidate removed himself from the list irrevocably, early in 1948. To those who hoped to draft him as the Republican presidential nominee, General Dwight Eisenhower stilled all such thought with a letter addressed to a New England publisher who had requested permission to file Ike's name in the New Hampshire primary. Said Ike in a telegram on January 23, 1948: "I AM NOT AVAILABLE FOR AND COULD NOT ACCEPT NOMINATION TO HIGH POLITICAL OFFICE. . . . IT IS MY CONVICTION THAT THE NECESSARY AND WISE SUBORDINATION OF THE MILITARY TO CIVIL POWER WILL BEST BE SUSTAINED AND OUR PEOPLE WILL HAVE GREATER CONFIDENCE THAT IT IS SO SUSTAINED, WHEN LIFE-LONG PROFESSIONAL SOLDIERS, IN THE ABSENCE OF SOME OBVIOUS AND OVERRIDING REASONS, ABSTAIN FROM SEEKING HIGH POLITICAL OFFICE. THIS TRUTH HAS A POSSIBLE INVERSE APPLICATION. I WOULD REGARD IT AS UNALLOYED TRAGEDY FOR OUR COUNTRY IF EVER SHOULD COME THE DAY WHEN MILITARY COMMANDERS MIGHT BE SELECTED WITH AN EYE TO THEIR FUTURE POTENTIALITIES IN THE POLITICAL FIELD RATHER THAN EXCLUSIVELY UPON JUDGMENT AS TO THEIR MILITARY ABILITIES." Noting also that "POLITICS IS A PROFESSION, A SERIOUS, COMPLICATED, AND IN ITS TRUE SENSE, A NOBLE ONE . . ." Ike also said, as he looked upon the American political scene, "I SEE NO DEARTH OF MEN FITTED BY TRAINING, TALENT, AND INTEGRITY FOR NATIONAL LEADERSHIP."

Not even this powerful statement managed to abate the talk that Ike might still be drafted. But gradually the fact that he was unavailable came to be accepted, and the pre-convention campaign settled down to a race that began to look increasingly like Dewey versus the field.

Withholding formal declaration once again, Dewey was pushed ahead by his team of assistants headed by Herbert Brownell, who roamed about the country in a quiet but earnest way, sewing up delegates. The New York governor was off to a fast start. The full weight of his organization was thrown into New Hampshire, where he won the nation's first primary, and it was not until the Wisconsin primary in the first weeks of April that Dewey met his first reverse. Belatedly Dewey made a last-minute dash out to the Badger state, where he finally took off his gloves in a vain attempt to rescue a situation which his advisers had suddenly discovered might have a critical impact on his candidacy for the presidential nomination. He arrived too late, however, with the result that Harold Stassen carried off a majority of the Wisconsin delegates. From here on in, in response to his advisers' admonitions that if he really wanted the nomination he would have to go after it, Dewey took on the stance of a fighter who knows he is in danger of being outpointed and that his only chance of insuring a victory is by a decisive knock-down.

The opportunity to redeem a sagging candidacy presented itself in the Oregon primary in May; there followed one of the most celebrated presidential primary contests on record.

Losing on the same day in both the Wisconsin and Nebraska primaries, Dewey had not suffered a serious loss in delegate strength, thanks to his efficient organization, but his prestige had been winged, and talk of his being stopped grew steadily after these two losses. Confident of his momentary advantage, Harold Stassen issued Dewey a challenge that he hoped would be his undoing. For Stassen it was a grievous mistake.

Anxious to speak out in favor of a bill to outlaw the Communist party, introduced by Senator Karl Mundt of South Dakota, Stassen challenged Dewey to debate him on the merits of this proposal. And so midway in the Oregon campaign New York's gang-busting governor met Minnesota's roving ex-governor and settled down to an old-fashioned debate that was broadcast on a nationwide hook-up. In the duel between two former district attorneys, Stassen soon found the scrimmage against a man whose business was prosecution a mighty rough hassle. In his crisp, systematic style, Dewey took after his opponent and soon held him in a hammerlock. Mr. Stassen, he said, had erred when he argued that Russia's failure to outlaw the Communist party had been an important factor in bringing the Bolsheviks and the Communist party to power. Citing chapter and verse, Mr. Dewey proceeded to show that the Czarist government had on several occasions issued decrees and passed legislation designed to outlaw the Communist party, and that these measures were in no way helpful in manning the dikes against the onslaught of Communism.

No designated referees, of course, issued a decision on the Stassen-Dewey debate. The jury in this case was the American press and public. On the proposal to suppress the Communist party, commented Joseph Alsop, "Stassen was defeated," and the fact that "this proposal was thus rejected does credit to the political decency and above all the common sense of the voters." [3] But quite apart from personal conviction on the merits of the issue at stake, the weight of the judgments from the press and public opinion gave Dewey this inning. And the event also showed the New York governor's resources in the give and take of a debate.

How much the debate had to do with the eventual outcome in the Oregon primary is purely conjectural. Certainly Dewey had no intention of permitting the outcome to rest on the debate.[4] For days Dewey stumped the state by bus, making six or eight speeches daily, on some days as many as ten. How much money was expended in this brief but all-out campaign is anyone's guess. One advertising concern estimated that the amount of money expended for radio time and other expenses was approximately $100,000 for each of the two candidates, and at least one estimate has it that the Dewey forces spent close to a quarter of a million dollars. Summing up the results the Portland *Oregonian* wondered if perhaps the intensity with which the Oregon primary had been waged had not been carried a notch too far in terms of its importance in the national picture. Elsewhere other editors were inclined to agree. But of one thing that emerged from this race we can be relatively sure: thereafter Dewey's campaign stature was on the upswing, while Stassen's steadily declined. Commenting on the situation, columnist Alsop reported that for Stassen, "the question has now become whether the Republican nomination can be secured not for himself but for Arthur H. Vandenberg or some other Republican who is not a bitter Stassen enemy." [5]

When the chairman of the committee on arrangements, Walter S. Hallanan of West Virginia, called the twenty-fourth Republican convention to order in Philadelphia on June 21, 1948, a Dewey deadlock appeared out of the question. Taft, busy with his heavy burdens in the United States Senate, had carried on neither a fully active nor a carefully directed pre-convention campaign, as he did four years later. Vandenberg, the most eminently available candidate of the dark-horse stripe, was most anxious that he not exploit his leadership position in the Senate. For this reason he waited perhaps until it was too late to let the Michigan delegation push him seriously.

Unmindful of his critics, who were inclined to agree that he had pursued the Presidency in a manner that suggested the "humorless calculation of a Certified Public Accountant in pursuit of the Holy Grail," Dewey and his managers had everything swimmingly their way by convention time. To those who said he was ruthless, his managers retorted that what America needed was a hard-hitting, wiry contender who stalked his political enemies relentlessly and gave them no quarter. Mindful of the unkind quips about his size and personality, allegedly inspired by Alice Roosevelt Longworth's "He looks like the bridegroom on a wedding cake," and her subsequent remark in commenting upon his chances for election following his second nomination—"How can you expect a soufflé to rise twice?" —Dewey's managers no longer attempted to conceal his size or certain aspects of his personality. Instead it was emphasized that he had taken his small stature in stride, and that in matters of personality, while he publicly behaved with a certain amount of reserve, he liked to romp around at home with his two sons. He was also portrayed as a person who could talk to people of any station in life.

Working through the usual preliminaries of reports on contested delegations and other matters that precede the nominating roll calls, the convention paused on Tuesday evening—June 22—to hear from the then only living ex-President of the United States, Herbert Hoover. It was his fourth address to a Republican national convention since his defeat in 1932. Almost prophetically, as he turned to the final paragraph of his speech, Mr. Hoover said: "If you produce nothing but improvised platitudes, you will give no hope." Looking back later many wondered, as they listened to the theme song of the subsequent campaign, the plea for unity, whether the result on the first Tuesday after the first Monday in November of 1948 might have been different if a different course had been followed. But in this ecstatic emporium few thoughts were defeatist.

Leading off on the nomination speeches, Senator Edward Martin of Pennsylvania placed Thomas E. Dewey in nomination. Next to be presented was Taft, who was placed in nomination by Senator John Bricker of Ohio, and third was Earl Warren, presented by Dr. Robert Gordon Sproul, president of the University of California. The fourth was Harold E. Stassen, placed in nomination by Congressman Walter Judd of Minnesota. Then the name of Raymond E. Baldwin, governor of Connecticut, was followed by that of Arthur H. Vandenberg, who was nominated by Kim Siegler, Michigan's governor. The final candidate to be presented was General Douglas MacArthur, just as he was at the 1952 convention.

Late Thursday afternoon (June 24), amid stifling heat and humidity accentuated for the first time by powerful lights for television cameras, which may have raised the temperature to the highest point ever recorded in a national political convention, the secretary began calling the roll of states for the first ballot. Not unexpectedly, Dewey wound up with 434 votes, followed by Taft with 224, Stassen third with 157, then Vandenberg with 62, who was trailed by Warren with 59 and Green, governor and favorite son of Illinois, with 56. Moving to the second ballot the Dewey forces signaled for some of the votes they had loaned on the first roll call, and this time the New York governor gained 81 votes for a total of 515, followed by Taft with 274 (a jump of 50 votes), and then Stassen, who slipped 8 votes to wind up with a total of 149. Among the other candidates, Michigan stood fast for Vandenberg with 62, Warren dropped 2 down to 57, and the favorite sons all but disappeared. Taft's big increase had come from the 56 votes of Green of Illinois, while Dewey's total was sweetened by the addition of almost all of New Jersey's 35 votes, which had been cast as a token vote for its governor and favorite son Driscoll on the first ballot. With some still hoping for a stop-Dewey miracle, an adjournment was called after the second ballot.

As usual under such conditions, the adjournment was to no avail. And the frantic conferences between Senator Taft and Harold Stassen in a freight elevator to escape the prying eyes of reporters could not at this late hour give birth to a working coalition. The brief recess of three hours between 5:00 and 8:10 P.M. simply sealed the result that everyone already knew was a foregone conclusion. During this interim the leading candidates prepared their release statements, and when the convention convened that evening chairman Martin recognized Senator Bricker of Ohio, to read a statement on behalf of Robert A. Taft. Since an analysis of the situation showed that a majority of the delegates would support Thomas E. Dewey on the third ballot, said Taft, he was releasing his delegates and asking them to vote for Dewey "with all their force and enthusiasm, and I hope the selection will be unanimous." Thereafter similar statements were read for Warren, Vandenberg, and MacArthur, and Stassen himself appeared on the rostrum to release his own delegates. This done, the convention cast a unanimous ballot for Dewey.

And so the 1944 presidential nominee became the first defeated Republican candidate in the party's history who had returned to receive a second nomination. Looking skyward, one or two news writers thought they saw the outline of a rainbow stretched in a noble arc over the Philadelphia auditorium just as candidate Dewey and his wife entered the hall before his acceptance speech that evening. But had they looked closer they would have perceived not a rainbow but an angry yellow sky that hung menacingly over the auditorium as Dewey began his remarks.

Laying down the trademark of his campaign, Dewey delivered a brief speech of some twelve hundred words in which he used the word "unite" or "unity" a dozen times, mentioning it in almost all of the paragraphs, and assured the convention that the next government of the United States would rest on teamwork. Next day the delegates met for the windup, which in this case was to select Earl Warren as the vice-presidential nominee.

If there were any doubts over the certainty of victory at the time of the Republican convention, the succession of events in the month that followed served to dispel them. The attempt of James Roosevelt and others to boom a draft-Eisenhower movement for the Democratic convention underlined the fact that morale was wobbly in the Democratic camp and that there was little confidence in the ability of Harry Truman to win the Presidency under his own steam. Also encouraging to Republican prospects was the bolt of several Southern states following the successful attempt of Senator Hubert Humphrey of Minnesota to have the minority report on civil rights of the resolutions committee adopted in the Democratic platform after a hard convention floor fight. The walkout of these delegations, of course, ultimately led to the formation of a States' Rights ticket, more popularly known as the Dixiecrat party. And if the foregoing was insufficient to encourage a jaunty optimism among Republicans, there was still another divisive element that threatened the Democratic party and presumably would work to the advantage of the Republicans: the launching of a third party and a third-party ticket headed by Henry Wallace—the Progressive party of 1948.

Yet in the midst of these many discouragements and defections, Harry Truman demonstrated that he was not without resources. Calling a special session of Congress—known as "the turnip Congress"—late in the summer, Truman charged that this had been made necessary by the failure of the Eightieth Congress to discharge its responsibilities, notably in the field of housing. Judgments of course may differ as to either the justification for the calling of this special session or its strategic effect on the subsequent course of the election. But one thing is certain, and that is that by summoning Congress Truman acquired a certain initiative in laying at the doorstep of this Republican-controlled body certain consequences which he quickly and effectively exploited in the ensuing months.

For a crackling example, we need only look at how this was accomplished in an attack against Republican farm policy in five Midwestern states, under circumstances of agricultural discontent which Louis Bean has aptly described as the "green uprising." Farm income among the Middle-Western states had been extraordinarily high in the postwar years. None the less, by the summer of 1948 farmers were worried because of a decline that had set in on most prices. As the campaigns of both parties began in earnest, following traditional opening-day guns on Labor Day, Republican farm leaders became increasingly puzzled by the statements of top party figures on GOP agricultural policy.

On September 2 Harold Stassen emerged from a conference with Dewey in Albany and told reporters that the government purchase of fifty million pounds of lard caused "lard and all prices to skyrocket," and that Truman had deliberately attempted to sustain high food prices in face of bumper crops. Later, in response to Mr. Truman's Labor Day speech in Detroit, Stassen dropped the remark that farm prices were too high and by implication suggested that Republican policy could not sustain such high price supports for farm commodities. Reaction to this statement was swift. One Middle-Western editor of a large agricultural journal wired Dewey that in his judgment such a statement had overnight cost at least 25,000 votes in both Wisconsin and Minnesota.

Meanwhile, President Truman began to step up his attack. In September both party nominees had been invited to address the National Plowing Contest at Dexter, Iowa. Governor Dewey, however, declined, largely on the advice of his managers, who pointed out that Iowa had gone Democratic only three times since 1872: in 1912 when Teddy Roosevelt and Taft had split the GOP vote; in 1932 when corn was selling at ten cents a bushel; and again in 1936. Moreover, it was argued, the polls showed Dewey leading with 55 percent in Iowa against 39 percent for Truman. But Truman went to Dexter, and in a speech which became famous among the cornbelt states he told a crowd of 80,000 farmers that on the grain storage issue the Republicans had "stuck a pitchfork in their backs." Speaking of prices he said: "We are planning to aid the farmers of America to meet their pressing problems and avoid catastrophe . . . The reactionary Republican answer is to let prices crash to the bottom." What Truman was referring to was the action of the Republican Congress in slipping a clause into a bill renewing the charter of the Commodity Credit Corporation, which forbade the government to store grain.

By now there had been a bumper corn crop, too great by far for commercial storage companies to handle. Unless the farmers could get storage for their corn, they could not get loans from the Commodity Credit Corporation under the price support program. With such loans, farmers could hang on to their grain, wait for prices to rise, sell their grain and repay their loans. If prices did not rise, the government kept the grain and the farmers kept their loans, though without such loans the farmers would have to dump immediately on a falling market. Obviously this was a vulnerability that the farmers felt keenly as they kept an uneasy eye on falling prices, and Mr. Truman was beginning to make some of them gunshy of Republicans.

Again farm leaders urged Mr. Dewey to come out with a ringing speech on farm policy when he later came to Des Moines. But, whatever the reason, Mr. Dewey responded with a speech on his general philosophy of government, stating that his national goal was the unity of all interests. Unfortunately for the Republican party, the farmers of the Middle West seemed more concerned at the moment with market conditions than they were with political abstractions. Between September 1 and October 1 corn had dropped from $1.78 a bushel to $1.38, and by November 1, the week before elections, corn prices had fallen to $1.21 a bushel. Pacing this decline was a drop in hog prices, which fell from $27.40 per cwt. on September 1 to $24.70 on October 1 and $21.80 on November 1. What the farmers thought about this was most convincingly demonstrated among these agricultural states on Election Day.

Iowa, pre-eminently the land of the corn-fed hog—with 54 of the leading hog-producing counties and 42 of her counties among the 200 wealthiest agricultural counties of the nation—gave Dewey a victory of 47,000 votes over Franklin Roosevelt in 1944. Yet it went for Truman by 28,000 votes in 1948—a Democratic net shift of 75,000 votes. Looking at the results, particularly in the corn-hog states, in a post-mortem after the election, H. L. Mencken, the sage of Hollins Street in Baltimore, gave full marks to Mr. Truman: "The Missouri Wonder was roving and ravaging the land, pouring out hope and promise in a wholesale manner, promising the farmers a continuance of the outrageous prices that are reducing the rest of us to eating only once a day."

Almost four years after Dewey's defeat in 1948, one of the foremost Republican authorities on agriculture, Senator Aiken of Vermont, brought a serious charge against the Truman administration. He claimed before the Senate Agricultural Committee that the Democratic administration had deliberately allowed farm prices to drop, and thereafter successfully blamed the Republicans for this decline. Senator Aiken contended that the Democrats had maneuvered the situation as follows: In the spring of 1948 Congress had amended the farm price support law to restrain the Department of Agriculture from building, buying, or leasing its own storage space for farm crops. The purpose of this measure, of course, was to enjoin the government from competing with privately operated storage elevators and warehouses. That fall, as Senator Aiken pointed out, agricultural prices began to drop, and when farmers applied for government loans to store their crops and support prices, Department of Agriculture officials refused to make loans unless farmers could show that their crops were properly stored. The joker here, as we have seen, was that the farmers were unable to find storage space because the Department of Agriculture was prevented from providing space under the amended farm price support law. Actually, however, the commercial space then available was only 60 percent filled. These manipulations, which Senator Aiken maintained lost the farmers at least one billion dollars because they had to sell their crops at prices below the official support level, embittered farmers throughout the Middle West, and prompted them to turn against the Republicans.

By way of reinforcing his charge that the Democratic administration rigged the situation to bring about a drop in farm prices, Senator Aiken told the Senate Agricultural Committee that in 1949, almost immediately after the election, the policies of the administration were suddenly switched. Acknowledging that the new Democratic Congress changed the price support law to permit the government to build or lease storage space, Mr. Aiken reminds us that precious little government building or leasing of storage space was actually done. Using quite different tactics, government officials made loans on grain which farmers were forced to leave on the ground. They also loaned money to farmers to build their own storage bins. They further offered guarantees to use commercial storage space, and in addition government officials found airplane hangars, oil storage tanks, and even idle ships, along with other usable storage bins, to store 1949 harvests and support prices. Almost all the expedients adopted under this program, insisted Senator Aiken, might well have been followed in 1948. Had this been done, he said, farmers could have obtained loans for grain on the ground in 1948 just as they did in 1949. Moreover, government officials could have made a survey in 1948 to see if commercial storage space was available, and had this been done government officials could have arranged for the use of such space just as easily in 1948 as in 1949.

Prompt rejoinders were issued to Senator Aiken's charge by Democrats, the gist of their argument being that because of the bumper crop, the huge harvests of 1948, and a slight recession in business conditions, prices would have declined anyway. This Republicans conceded, but they also made the telling point that there was no need for prices to have fallen so far and that there had been a deliberate effort to panic the farmers and blame the Republicans.

That the Republicans received a lethal punch from the farmers at the ballot box in 1948 there can be no doubt. Looking at the election totals in five Middle-Western states, all leaders in corn-hog production, it is apparent that Dewey lost four narrowly:

Ohio	7,107	out of 2,898,475
Illinois	33,612	out of 3,955,818
Iowa	28,362	out of 1,016,398
Wisconsin	56,351	out of 1,238,269
Minnesota	209,349	out of 1,176,583

Dewey lost these states by a total of 334,781 out of 10,285,543 votes. Had he carried all five Dewey would have had 275 electoral votes, nine more than needed, while Truman had 217.

Glancing at the tally sheet, Dewey won 21,991,290 votes in 1948 against Truman's 24,179,623. Actually Dewey's vote was slightly less than his popular vote of 1944 (22,017,592), although it should be remembered that 1948 marked a low turnout for both parties. In percentages, Dewey received 45.3 percent (four years earlier he won 45.8) of the major two-party vote, while Truman garnered 49.9 percent. Wallace, the Progressive party candidate, received 2.4 percent of the total vote cast, and Thurmond, the States' Rights candidate, also received 2.4 percent. Dewey carried sixteen states, which gave him 189 electoral votes; Truman carried 28 to wind up with 303 electoral votes, and 38 votes went to Thurmond. In county-wide totals, Dewey slipped from the 1,338 which he carried in 1944 to 1,186 in 1948. Geographically, "the agrarian wing of the GOP, particularly in the North Central section, was relatively weaker in 1948 than four years earlier," Professor Holcombe reminds us, while "the industrial wing, particularly in the Northeast, was relatively stronger." [6]

Unusual in more ways than one, this was the first presidential election since 1916 in which the winning candidate actually won with less than a majority of the total vote cast, and very likely it was also the first time that a presidential candidate won an election while actually running behind his congressional ticket. Among other political curiosa of the 1948 election was the fact that while 49,362,798 ballots were cast on November 2 only 48,680,416 were marked for President. What this meant, of course, was that 682,382 voters balloted for state, county, and local candidates, but failed to make a choice for the highest office in the land. There were 16 states that showed a greater aggregate vote than the total vote for President. Although the entire vote was 1,400,000 above that of 1944, the number of potentially eligible voters had increased during the four-year period by more than ten million. Hence the turnout was shockingly low, and probably less than 51 percent of the eligible vote.

If we look at the voting pattern in the cities, the showing of Dewey in 1948 is distinctly more favorable. While the Republican ticket carried only 39 percent of the two-party vote in San Francisco in 1940 and 1944, Dewey netted 48.8 percent in 1948. In Philadelphia, where the Republican national ticket won 40 percent of the major party vote in 1940, and 41 percent in 1944, Dewey made it 49.0 per cent in 1948. In all but two of the 12 major metropolitan areas—St. Louis and Pittsburgh—Dewey's slice of the two-party vote on a percentage basis was an improvement over the GOP metropolitan record of 1944.

As in 1940, the clue to party voting habits in the cities seemed to be related to rentals. For quite some time it was observable that the districts which ran more consistently Republican were those with the highest rentals, most of them suburban. By 1948, however, the steady population drift to the suburbs was really beginning to make an imprint on metropolitan voting profiles, and undoubtedly this trend redounded to Dewey's benefit. But in the districts of intermediate rents which have been the most doubtful for both major parties, the situation was quite different. "These are the districts," writes Professor Holcombe, "in which the Republicans made the greatest gains from the Democrats at the election of 1946, and in which the Democrats in turn made the greatest gains from the Republicans in 1948." Driving it home vividly with an example in Cleveland, Sam Lubell puts it this way:

> Outwardly at least there seemed nothing unusual about this . . . street. Each two story frame dwelling had its lawn in the front and garage in the rear. If stained-glass windows and scrolled, oaken doors in some houses hinted at a lost elegance, the lady cigar trees shading the sidewalks and the "no through trucks" sign at the corner stamped the street as still fair-to-do, middle class. Driving by one would hardly give those houses a second glance. Yet it was here that Thomas E. Dewey lost his chance at the presidency.
>
> To have beaten Truman, Dewey should have swept streets like this one, with homes ranging in value between $15,000 and $20,000. Actually he managed only to break even.[7]

Overwhelmingly Republican in the twenties, these intermediate rental districts have become "break-even zones," says Lubell, by a factor of "timing" which lifted many newer middle-class residents who had a rough time in the depression to a more prosperous status. And to many such persons, he adds, "Truman rather than Dewey seemed the conservative candidate." Thus the "1948 voting was done in the shadow of threatened depression and Dewey's vague campaign talks left deep fears about what he might do in case of economic collapse. The harshest fact about the 1948 voting from the Republican viewpoint was how many ordinary conservative persons feared a Republican victory."

So it was that "to an appreciable part of the electorate," the Democrats appeared to have "replaced the Republicans as the party of prosperity."

"How could so many wizards be so thumpingly wrong?" wondered H. L. Mencken as he rolled out a column like a merry mortician the morning after the election. "And how could enlightenment play so scurvy a trick upon its agents?"

> What had Dewey to offer against all this pie in the sky? Virtually nothing. His plan in the campaign as that in 1944, was to chase what appeared to be the other fellow's ambulance. He seemed eager to

convince everyone that he was for everything that Truman was in favor of, but with much less heat. Never once in his canvass, so far as I can recall, did he tackle Truman's buncombe and blather in a frank and forthright manner.

His literati have been blamed for this tender gurgling, but it seems to me the fault was his own. The late Al Smith in the campaign of 1928 was afflicted by literati even more literary, but he got rid of them by tearing up their speeches and striking out on his own. To be sure, he didn't win, but that was surely not because he did not make a good fight, it was simply because the Bible-searchers everywhere had become convinced that if he got to the White House the Pope would move into the cellar.

Dewey had no such handicap and yet he came to grief in the grand manner. His defeat ran against all probalilities and was complete, colossal, and ignominious. Its springs, I believe, are to be sought in the defects of his own personality. He is by nature cute but cautious. . . . He addresses great multitudes as if they were gangs of drowsing judges, all of them austere in their hangmen's gowns, but consumed inwardly by an expectant thirst.

Truman made no such mistake. He assumed as a matter of course that the American people were just folks like himself. He thus wasted no high-falutin rhetoric upon them, but appealed directly to their self-interest. Everyone of them, he figured, was itching for something, and he made his campaign by the sempiternal device of engaging to give it to them. A politico trained in a harsh but realistic school, he naturally directed his most gaudy promises to the groups that seemed to be the most numerous, and the event proved he was a smart mathematician.

Neither candidate made a speech on the stump that will survive in the schoolbooks, but those of Truman at least had some human warmth in them. . . . While Dewey was intoning essays sounding like the worst bombast of university professors, Truman was down on the ground. . . . He made votes every time he gave a show, but Dewey lost them.[8]

Harsh words these were, albeit impishly spoken—words the bulk of which were grimly applauded by many Republicans. Smarting under defeat, Dewey offered no excuses, publicly acknowledged no basic misdirection of his campaign. That the directional lights of the party should not signal a turn to the right, however, was a belief he clung to courageously.

Two years later, in a brace of lectures delivered at Princeton University, he would argue his case more persuasively. Stabbing at reactionary as well as radical groups who demand "that our parties be sharply divided, one against the other in interest, membership, and doctrine," he hit hard:

"These impractical theorists . . . want to drive all moderates and liberals out of the Republican party and have the remainder join forces with the conservative groups of the South. Then they would have everything neatly arranged indeed. The Democratic party would be the liberal-to-radical party. The Republican party would be the conservative-to-reactionary party.

"The results would be neatly arranged, too. The Republicans would lose every election and the Democrats would win every election. . . ." [9]

Here was an argument that no member of the Taft wing of the party was willing to let pass unchallenged. Next time—as matters began to take shape—it looked like a knock-down fight for control against the Dewey forces right down to the last gavel rap.

Does No Mean Maybe?

Among the old saws about birthplaces of American Presidents, few are more commonplace than the remark that Ohio is the "Mother of Presidents." Seven sons of the Buckeye state have occupied the White House—a record equaled only by the Old Dominion. This record, along with the achievements of the Senate majority leader, "Mr. Republican," in the early 1950's quickly suggests why, after a long unproductive spell, it was beginning to look as if Mother was pregnant again. At least this was the view of a powerful number of Republicans as they laid aside their frustration after Dewey's defeat and thought about a new standard-bearer for 1952.

For seventeen hours and seventeen minutes after the closing of the polls, the presidential vote of the 1948 general election hung in the balance. Not a long period by most standards, but long enough for Thomas E. Dewey and the faithful supporters who watched the scene of political carnage caused by a stubborn man from Missouri. So close was the contest that it seemed entirely possible that the election of the President might be thrown into the House of Representatives. But behind the final outcome—in which the Republicans were successful, as one comment put it, "in snatching defeat from the jaws of victory"—lay a shattered ten-year dream.

True to American traditions, one of the first questions at Dewey's press conference on Wednesday, November 3, 1948, was an inquiry about his intentions: Would he seek the presidential nomination once more? "Never again," said Dewey. Shelved by many authoritative voices in his party as an elder statesman—at the comparatively ripe age of 46, as he sardonically put it—Dewey returned to Albany, acting for a time like a man who was done with national politics, but not actually saying so. Dewey in the popular as well as the party professional mind had become a boy wonder emeritus. As early as December, 1948, Hugh Scott, chairman of the Republican national committee, boldly predicted that the choice of their 1952 national convention would be either Senator Robert A. Taft or General

Dwight D. Eisenhower, and that in his opinion Dewey did not and should not aspire to the nomination again. Simultaneously other Republicans took note of the fact that Dewey had twice led his party to defeat and began to look elsewhere. At the same time, Taft became increasingly prominent as "Mr. Republican."

As the 1950 midterm congressional elections approached, several things pointed toward a titanic struggle for party control and for the 1952 presidential nomination. Meeting at Omaha early in 1949, the national committee immediately became embroiled in a hard-fought duel to remove Dewey and his followers from party control. By the uneasy margin of four votes (54 to 50), chairman Hugh Scott, a Dewey man, clung to his post after three days of recrimination and name-calling, leaving the Taft-Stassen coalition against Dewey momentarily stopped. But the respite was short-lived, since the Taft-Stassen forces won an important major concession under which Scott agreed to appoint a new executive committee giving representation to all groups to replace the one he had just appointed dominated by Dewey supporters. Unable to direct affairs effectively under these conditions of crumpled confidence, Hugh Scott soon resigned in the interest of party harmony, and was succeeded by Guy Gabrielson of New Jersey, a spokesman for the Taft wing, following an election of the national committee on August 4, 1949. From this time forward through the 1952 national convention the followers of Senator Taft were in firm control of the national committee.

Midway in 1950, and timed to have an impact on the fall general elections, a public challenge to the conservative-led forces in the party came forth from two sources—the first by way of a "Declaration of Conscience" issued by seven GOP Senators, the second from a group calling itself "The Republican Advance."

The background for the first challenge—the "Declaration of Conscience"—goes back to August 13, 1946, a day that many Republicans would like to drape with crepe. On this day a decision was made at the polls that brought to an end the long lease of the La Follettes on Wisconsin public offices, a period that stretched almost a half-century—46 years, to be exact. During all these years, the La Follettes—father and sons—held either the governorship or a seat in the United States Senate. For six years son Philip was governor while his brother Bob held down a seat in the Senate. But in 1946 the brilliant tour of family service came to an abrupt conclusion in the August Republican primary. Robert La Follette, Jr., was nosed out in his bid for renomination to the Senate by a bare 5,000 votes. For his followers defeat came hard. It was at the hands of a political unknown—Joseph R. McCarthy.

Limited to eight days of personal campaigning because he felt it his duty to press for passage of the La Follette-Monroney Congressional Reorganization bill of 1946, La Follette was beset by several formidable handicaps as he set sail for re-election that year. Prominent among those obstacles was the presence of a well-tuned organization aiming at unseating him. Tom Coleman, Republican state central chairman, had been so impressed by the work of Victor Johnston for Harold Stassen in the 1944 Wisconsin presidential primary that he persuaded Johnston, a former Minnesota newspaper man who had done public-relations work for Stassen, to stay on and accept the post of executive secretary to the state committee. This Johnston did, and during the next two years worked hand in glove with Coleman as they readied their plans to unhorse La Follette. Moving into 1946, the man who had fought unsuccessfully to twist the Republican nomination away from Senator Alexander Wiley in 1944—Joseph R. McCarthy—was again a contender and this time he was the candidate of Coleman and Johnston.

Complicating La Follette's position still further as the primary date loomed closer in the summer of 1946 was the fact that only that spring he had called upon his Progressive followers to forswear their allegiance to the Progressive party which had been started in 1934. Speaking to the Progressives at their Portage conference on March 17, 1946, he urged their return to the Republican party. Arguing against alignment with the Democratic party, La Follette noted that the Democratic party "is now stalled on dead center. Although it is the party in power with a clear majority," he added, "it has been unable to act with sufficient unity of purpose to meet the urgent problems of today."

Winding up a 45-minute extemporaneous speech, La Follette then said: "I am convinced that the Republican Party of Wisconsin offers us the best opportunity for the advancement of progressive principles. Wisconsin has always been a Republican State—and by this I don't mean a reactionary state. Some of the most far-reaching legislation ever enacted anywhere in America was enacted in our State when Progressives were in the Republican Party. . . ." [1]

Two months later—May 19—La Follette shook off the tattered Progressive party label in a simple statement: "I am running for re-election to the United States Senate under the same banner that I first ran under in 1925 and again in 1928—as a Progressive Republican." But safe return to the family fold was not in the cards for Bob Jr. on this trip.

To worsen the odds at the last moment, the unopposed Democratic candidate McMurray, who thought McCarthy would be easier to defeat in the general election, astonished everyone by buying full-page advertisements in several daily newspapers the day before election attacking La Follette's isolationist tendencies. In a final blow —very likely the critical one—La Follette was smitten from another quarter. His political discomfiture in the latter instance was brought about by the Communist-dominated Milwaukee CIO Council. Angered by La Follette's rejection of the uncritical Soviet Union eulogy line, the County CIO Council in Milwaukee (Wisconsin has an open primary) openly solicited votes for McCarthy in labor circles—this notwithstanding the record La Follette had marked up as one of the staunchest supporters of organized labor as well as of civil rights.

The results probably should have been foretold. Yet the retirement of La Follette in a turnout that barely embraced 30 percent of the registered voters still came as something of a shock. Wisconsin, under the elder La Follette, had become something of a political laboratory for the rest of the nation. The Badger state had the first direct primary law for statewide office, the first effective state regulatory agency for controlling railroad rates, and the first comprehensive plan of workmen's compensation laws. The defeat in 1946 of Bob La Follette, Jr., a man who had been at the storm center of Progressive Republicanism for half a century, seemed to signal a change.

Unlike the elder La Follette, who struck Washington with the impact of a powerful Middle-Western meteor, McCarthy gave no spectacular indications when he took his Senate seat early in 1947. He took Victor Johnston to Washington with him as his administrative assistant and demonstrated an active interest in national politics by agreeing to take the title of Stassen's campaign manager in Wisconsin in 1948 and to run as one of Stassen's delegates in the presidential primary.[2] Yet not until February 11, 1950, did the name McCarthy receive more than a dutiful nod in the nationwide press. For the next four years at least, rarely did it recede from prominence.

At Wheeling, West Virginia, McCarthy made a radio speech on February 9 in which he charged that he had the names of 57 persons who were either members of or loyal to the Communist party. In the same speech he also made reference to 205 persons who he said were still on the State department's payroll despite the fact that they had already been declared unfit for government service by President Truman's security officers. Not only did this dramatic charge hit the nation like a thunderclap, coming as it did in the wake of the conviction of Alger Hiss for perjury following the revelation of the famous "pumpkin papers" by Whittaker Chambers. It also touched off an acrimonious debate over just what figures McCarthy actually used in his speech. In a subsequent investigation by a subcommittee of the Senate judiciary committee, headed by Senator Millard Tydings of Maryland, the contention was made that McCarthy said at first in the Wheeling speech that he had the names of 205 Communists working in the State Department, and later—February 11—reduced the figure to 57 when challenged. This McCarthy denies in his book *McCarthyism: the Fight for America,*[3] but in a six-hour speech to the Senate on February 20, he reduced his number of names to 81. Whatever facts could be validated in the numbers game that followed about the precise figures used, however, were soon overshadowed by the drama that began to unfold on the larger loom of national political life. Without waiting for his critics to reload, and amidst demands that he produce the list of 57 names and step aside from his congressional immunity, McCarthy rocked the headlines even more dramatically a few weeks later.

On Sunday evening, March 26, Drew Pearson declared he would reveal the name of the man McCarthy had designated before a closed Senate committee hearing as "the top Soviet espionage agent of the United States." The man, said Pearson, was Owen Lattimore, author of numerous works on the Far East, director of the Far Eastern division of OWI during World War II, and at the time a lecturer on the staff of the Johns Hopkins University. Again McCarthy later maintained that he had not called Lattimore "the top Soviet espionage agent in the United States," but three days later he did name Lattimore as the person against whom he had laid charges before the Tydings committee—evidence, he said, upon which he was "willing to stand or fall."

Thereafter it was only a matter of a few more weeks before the term "McCarthyism" was a part of our working political vocabulary. In a matter of three years it was going into dictionaries.

During the sulfurous scuffles that followed McCarthy's charges against various people, his methods of attack brought a chorus of denunciations. For three months almost all such protests came from members of the opposition party or editors, journalists, and columnists. But on June 1, 1950, the McCarthy methods of accusation without representation and the sticky methods of some of his agents in searching for evidence brought a round rejoinder from the floor of the Senate, sponsored by seven Republicans. Entitled a "Declaration of Conscience," the statement began: "We are Republicans. But we are Americans first."

It is as Americans that we express our concern with the growing confusion that threatens the security and stability of our country. Democrats and Republicans alike have contributed to that confusion. . . .

Taking aim at the Wisconsin Senator, the Declaration went on:

> Certain elements of the Republican party have materially added to this confusion in the hopes of riding the Republican party to victory through the selfish expectations of fear, bigotry, ignorance, and intolerance. There are enough mistakes of the Democrats for Republicans to criticize constructively without resorting to political smears. To this extent, Democrats and Republicans alike have unwittingly, but undeniably played directly into the Communist design of "confuse, divide, and conquer."
>
> It is high time that we stopped thinking politically as Republicans and Democrats about elections, and started thinking patriotically as Americans about national security based upon individual freedom. It is high time that we all stopped being tools and victims of totalitarian techniques—techniques that, if continued here unchecked, will surely end what we have come to cherish as the American way of life.[4]

Signed by Senators Irving M. Ives of New York, Charles W. Tobey of New Hampshire, George D. Aiken of Vermont, Robert C. Hendrickson of New Jersey, Edward J. Thye of Minnesota, Wayne L. Morse of Oregon, and Margaret Chase Smith of Maine, the "Declaration of Conscience" blew hope like a fresh gust of clean wind into the ranks of Republicans who had despaired of reckless attacks on character and of the wanton disregard of civil rights by men who piously proclaimed their acts as the rightful concomitants of congressional inquiry. Accompanying this declaration, Margaret Chase Smith added a postscript by way of a public statement, one which very probably had something to do with Senator McCarthy's later move to have her "bumped" from the Senate rules committee. Said Senator Smith: "It is high time we remember that the Constitution speaks of trial by jury instead of trial by accusation."

As if in anticipation of the "Declaration of Conscience," another GOP group, also concerned lest the Republican party be only "against" instead of "for" positive goals, spoke forth from the citadel of American freedom—Philadelphia. Assembling in the Friendly City on June 30, 1950, under the temporary chairmanship of Henry V. Poore, a New York attorney and former president of the New York Young Republican Club, 50 GOP partisans from ten states,[5] calling themselves "The Republican Advance," drafted a statement of progressive principles "to found a new political era." Governor

James Duff of Pennsylvania, fresh from his triumph over the Grundy organization in a heated contest for the United States senatorial nomination, addressed the conference, the membership of which also included the editor and writer, Russell Davenport, who was the principal adviser of Wendell Willkie in the 1940 campaign. One unidentified spokesman for the group, disclaiming any idea of bolting from the party, explained the purpose behind the meeting to rally liberal-thinking Republican members of Congress, state party leaders, and rank-and-file workers for the coming elections:

> . . . We want to give the party some new helpful ideas. We think we can show the leaders how the Republican party can be sold to the voters.
>
> The Republicans have failed to sell themselves by attacking the product of the Democrats. They have not presented satisfactory alternatives to the Democratic projects they have attacked. The way we look at it Ford couldn't sell his motor cars if all he had to tell his customers was what was wrong with the Chevrolet.[6]

Twenty-one Republican members of the House of Representatives endorsed the declaration issued by the Republican Advance, which was a rather remarkable document in that it dealt with specific proposals for social welfare (such as the Ives-Javits health bill), and discussed in detail economic, agricultural, and international-affairs recommendations. The statement was also noteworthy because of the shiny send-off it received from a large part of the metropolitan press. Listing the early achievements of the Republican party, the Republican Advance statement of principles then addressed itself to the ideas that it considered requisite for keeping the Republican party lustily alive:

> The new challenges of our time are dominantly social in nature. They have given rise to certain goals that are deeply desired by the people and that are in fact essential to the preservation of freedom in an industrial society. Such goals include a reasonable security for old age, adequate medical care available for all, insurance against unemployment, year-round work, better education, better housing, protection of the rights of labor, aid to agriculture—to mention only the most conspicuous. The implementation of such goals has become necessary to that basic security without which a free society cannot long endure.
>
> For seventeen years the Democratic party has been faced with these challenges: yet it has proposed only one solution to them, namely, the unlimited extension of governmental control of the people. The Republican party, on its side, has always stood for a strong Federal government, and many of its leaders will agree that the appli-

cation of this principle during the past two decades has brought about necessary reforms. Yet to try to solve all issues by one single remedy is a form of political bankruptcy. The inevitable end of that road is a new form of slavery—slavery to the state.

The rank and file of the Republican party has opposed this bankrupt kind of thinking. And they will continue to do so. Nevertheless, alternative solutions have been too slowly evolved. Too often the party has been permitted to be maneuvered into a position of purely negative opposition; too often the appearance has been created that the party is not merely anti-Socialist but antisocial.

The situation is made worse by the fact that many Republicans who have frankly espoused some of the important social goals have been accused by members of their own party of being "me too." This accusation displays a lack of clear thinking that seems almost fantastic. In the first place, if the goals are right and just, then, as a responsible political party, we must accept them; we are not against the concept of private property just because the Democrats purport to be for it. But secondly, the accusation of "me too" completely misses the real issue.

The real issue against the Democrats does not lie with the goals. The truth is that many of these goals are wholly consonant with traditional Republican aims; they typify the kind of goals that the party has always worked to establish in its long battle to free the common man. They are of the essence of true Republicanism. And they are wholly achievable under our free economic system. The real issue with the Democrats lies with the means of achieving these goals.

Thus the Republican task today is twofold. First, the party should not merely accept, it should provide enthusiastic leadership for the social goals that have become so necessary to the health of our society. But secondly, it should develop new means of achieving these goals without enslaving the people. In the case of the medical goal, a group of Republicans have already made a proposal that demonstrates how this can be done. Instead of vesting total responsibility in government, this proposal gives strong government encouragement to mutual efforts on the part of the people themselves toward the goal of adequate medical care. The party must now set to work to frame legislation of this kind in other fields, placing the prime, though not the sole, burden of social advance upon the people rather than upon the government.

. . . The right to life is as fundamental to freedom as the right to liberty; and in an industrial society, in which men and women are dependent for their livelihood upon economic factors wholly beyond their control, the implementation of the right to life becomes largely an economic matter. It gives rise to certain rights, here called social rights, which can be implemented only by providing protection from economic hazards for such individuals as cannot hope adequately to insure themselves. These hazards include unemployment, old age, accident, ill health, disabilities, etc.

Most modern societies recognize these social rights. But they can find no way to implement them except by giving the government monopolistic powers over the people's lives. It is the pressing task of the Republican party to develop means by which the primary responsibility for the implementing of these rights can be carried by the citizens themselves: for by no other means can the free economic way of life be maintained.

This does not mean that the government should play no part in making these social rights real. On the contrary, it is government's role to provide substantial assistance. Such assistance may take the form of direct grants. More importantly, however, legislation should be devised defining the responsibilities of private parties and at the same time providing incentives for their fulfillment.[7]

Hailing the political prescription of the Republican Advance as "Republican Yeast," the New York *Times* welcomed the statement because: "it seems to us that the thinking of the Republican party has become a little musty." Particularly gratifying, said the *Times,* was the following statement of the Republican Advance, which came close to explaining Republican adversities in recent years: "Too often the appearance has been created that the party is not merely anti-socialist but antisocial." Continuing, the *Times* editorial noted that the United States "needs two strong political parties. It runs the risk of having only one strong political party if the Republicans lag too far behind the times. That is why we agree with the authors of this statement that many of the social objectives on which Democrats now seem to have a monopoly are 'wholly consonant with traditional Republican aims,' and that the party's real issue with the Democrats 'lies with the means of achieving these goals.' "[8]

The nation's number-one Republican metropolitan daily, the New York *Herald Tribune,* flushed with pride on the statement of the Republican Advance. "It is characteristic of the document's approach," said the *Tribune,* that it should place civil rights at the center of its analysis (as it has always been at the center of orthodox Republicanism), advancing from here to a definition of freedom which includes the satisfaction of men's social needs."[9]

Far from joining the accolade of the New York *Times* and New York *Herald Tribune,* the Republican national committee made it clear through a spokesman that it would ignore the document of the Republican Advance and continue its work of compiling a list of what it construed to be the mistakes of the Truman foreign policy.

These mistakes were held to be particularly the misdirection of policies in the Far East. From Senate minority leader Kenneth Wherry of Nebraska the Republican Advance got another cold stare. After reading the Philadelphia statement of the group, he said he stood foursquare on the February, 1950, statement of the Republican national committee. Then, taking careful aim at the liberal band who drafted the statement, he added: "If any group of Republicans wants to back a man for the presidential nomination they ought to get on that platform and get to work."

From Colonel McCormick's Chicago *Tribune,* the response was not unexpected. "This document," said its lead editorial, "appears to have been drafted by Russell Davenport, one of Henry Luce's former editors of the *Time-Life-Fortune* axis, who in 1940 was a leading drum beater for Wendell Willkie when that retreaded New Dealer hijacked the Republican presidential nomination." Willkie "was a sucker" on such matters, said the self-styled World's Greatest Newspaper. "This is the old 'One World' stuff in a new package," sniffed the editorial, concluding: "They can call themselves 'the Republican Advance,' but what they are is the New Deal rear guard." [10]

Drawn in this fashion, the issues that divided Republicans became more evident as two monolithic factions of great striking power got ready to collide with one another in a knock-down battle for the presidential nomination. Over a year before the Republican Advance statement, the friends of Robert A. Taft, with an eye on his all-important bid for re-election to the Senate in 1950, succeeded in pushing through a referendum measure in Ohio that provided for a switch to the Massachusetts-type ballot. Adopted by the voters of Ohio in November, 1949, the new ballot made it no longer possible to vote a straight party ticket by marking a single X at the top of the ballot: thereafter the voter was required to mark his choice for each office on the ballot. Commenting on the shift to this type of ballot, which facilitated ticket-splitting, Congressman George Bender of Cleveland, a Taft supporter, stated that the change would mean an additional 100,000 votes for Taft in the 1950 senatorial contest. Before 1950 it had also been agreed by a group of Taft supporters, including David Ingalls, later Taft's campaign manager, that if Taft won re-election in his senatorial contest by a margin greater than 250,000 votes, he should definitely try again for the presidential nomination. Thus the preliminary moves of one of the most prominently discussed presidential candidates were being carefully charted well over two years in advance of the 1952 convention.

The midterm elections produced several important upsets on the senatorial side, though the successes of the Republicans in the House of Representatives were hardly more than those normally anticipated for the party out of power. Certainly they were far less than those the Republicans enjoyed in 1946, when they gained 55 House seats and 12 Senators. Actually the Republican gains in the 1950 contest were the smallest of any non-presidential election since 1934. Republicans picked up five Senate seats in 1950, the most notable upsets being the defeat of Democratic majority leader Scott Lucas of Illinois and Millard Tydings of Maryland (a veteran of four terms). In the House the Republicans won an additional 28 seats, but were still far short of control.

On the gubernatorial front, the GOP had a much faster track performance in 1950. For the first time since 1930, a majority of the state governorships were in the hands of Republicans after the 1950 general election. In the Rocky Mountain region the inroads were particularly gratifying. Here Republicans won governorships for the first time since 1928 in Arizona and New Mexico, and carried off the chief-executive station in Nevada for the first time since 1930. Utah elected a Republican governor, her first in ten years, Wyoming installed her first Republican chief executive since 1938, and Colorado her first since 1944. While four years earlier there were but two GOP governors in the entire Rocky Mountain region, 1950 saw the election of seven out of eight. Far to the east one other state in the habit of electing Democratic governors also helped to swell the grand total. Maryland, by the largest majority ever given to a gubernatorial candidate, elected Theodore Roosevelt McKeldin, sending up the score for GOP chief executives to 28. Hardly an unimpressive showing under circumstances which also saw the re-election of Dewey in New York and Earl Warren in California—each for third terms. Warren won his unprecedented third term, incidentally, with the greatest plurality ever given any California candidate. At least with such a large number of state governorships in Republican hands, the way was now clear for a greater organizational effort behind a presidential drive even if the congressional results of 1950 suggested some voter uncertainty with Republican performance.

The return of Taft to the Senate by a thumping margin of 437,000 votes—the greatest plurality ever given an Ohio Senator—was a much heralded event.[11] Admittedly he was running against a weak challenger; he also received a friendly nod from Ohio's greatest vote-getter, Democratic governor Frank Lausche ("I admire Robert Taft"). During the 1950 senatorial campaign Lausche actually dropped the remark that he "might" vote for the Republican candidate. Taft's win in 1950 after his wafer-thin margin of 17,000 in 1944 lifted his 1952 presidential prospects enormously, and from this moment on Ohio thought she might have another President.

While observers may differ, the first serious salvo of the 1952 Republican pre-convention campaign seems to have been a declaration by Thomas E. Dewey in the autumn of 1950. During a TV appearance on "Meet the Press" he set at rest two years of speculation about the possibility of his taking another crack at the Presidency. Said Dewey: "I'm definitely and finally removed. I removed myself by letter eighteen months ago, and that is beyond consideration." At the same time he responded to further prodding about whether he had a candidate in mind by saying:

> Well it's a little early, but we have in New York a very great world figure, the president of Columbia University, one of the greatest soldiers of history, a fine educator, a man who really understands the problems of the world and if I should be reelected governor and have influence with the New York delegation, I would recommend to them that they support General Eisenhower for President if he would accept the draft.

The following day, October 16, 1950, Dewey's suggestion for the Republican nomination drew a prompt disclaimer from General Eisenhower, who said he had "had no change in sentiment about the presidency."

It was a year later to a day before the first formal announcement was made by an actual candidate. But the interim bristled with activity. Various scouting expeditions were dispatched to sound out sentiment among state party chairmen and the county and precinct leaders in the nation's 3,000-odd counties and 170,000 precincts.

An added touch of personal drama excited the Republican pre-convention campaign in the spring of 1951. President Truman dismissed General Douglas MacArthur from his United Nations, Allied, and United States commands in the Far East on April 11. With newspapers noting that only Lincoln's dismissal of General George McClellan on November 5, 1862, had been more sensational, MacArthur returned from Japan to address a joint session of Congress on April 19, 1951. From this speech to the climactic moment when the shift of the Minnesota delegation to Eisenhower clinched the latter's nomination on July 11, 1952, the name of MacArthur was never wholly out of the running as a possible dark-horse Republican nominee. No national organization on his behalf was ever fully realized, but MacArthur ran second in an October 14, 1951, poll of the delegates to the Republican national convention of 1948

(Taft led). In a Gallup poll released November 6, 1951, based on a cross-section of all voters, Eisenhower led the field of candidates in both parties with 28 percent of the total vote, but MacArthur and Truman were tied for second place, each with 13 percent.

The most intensive early activity of the pre-convention period was probably the survey organized on behalf of Senator Taft. Shortly after the midterm elections, David Ingalls and Ben E. Tate took off for all sections of the country to determine if there was a ground swell for Taft, and if so to lay the foundation for a later effort to win convention delegates over to the Ohio Senator.

During this period General Eisenhower was recalled to active duty as Commanding General, Supreme Headquarters, Allied Powers in Europe. Eisenhower's designation as Supreme Allied Commander in Europe was ordered December 19, 1950, by the Atlantic Council in Brussels and by President Truman. To the dismay of many of his supporters, he left his post at Columbia and was bade good-bye at the Washington airport by the President on January 6, 1951, without having made any public statement as to his political party affiliation.

Several months later (September 9, 1951) Eisenhower's old friend, Roy Roberts, president of the Kansas City *Star,* said Ike had confided to him that he was "a good Kansas Republican." Meanwhile, during the summer of 1951, many Republican Congressmen, governors, and party leaders visited Eisenhower at his Paris headquarters. These conferences led to many rumors but no firm information. At the end of the summer the one significant statement regarding the Eisenhower candidacy came from Sherman Adams, governor of New Hampshire, at the governors' conference in Gatlinburg, Tennessee. On September 30, 1951, Adams stated that General Eisenhower's name would be entered the following March in the New Hampshire presidential primary, and that this time, in his opinion, it would be allowed to stand. Another item of interest from the same meeting was the endorsement of Eisenhower by several Republican governors. These included Peterson of Nebraska, Adams of New Hampshire, Arn of Kansas, Dewey of New York, Kohler of Wisconsin, Thornton of Colorado, and Langley of Washington. The list of state chief executives who appeared to be in Ike's corner at this time began to suggest an impressive beachhead of organizational support.

Senator Robert A. Taft was the first to throw his hat into the ring as an avowed candidate for the presidential nomination. On October 16, 1951, Taft announced his candidacy, set forth the reasons for his decision to run, and outlined his plan of campaign.

Within a month—November 14, 1951—the second formal candidacy for the Republican presidential nomination was announced from Sacramento, California. Contrasting with Taft's statement of 1,200 words, Earl Warren declared himself with a very brief announcement: "With all humility, I have concluded to become a candidate." He said that he would enter the California primary, but that he was undecided on out-of-state campaigning. In addition he called attention to the fact that he felt the Republicans must present a "definite, constructive, and workable program for the nation," and that they could not hope to win "solely on the mistakes of the present twenty-year administration."

The most elaborate formal entry into the race was that of Harold E. Stassen. On leave from his post as president of the University of Pennsylvania, the former governor of Minnesota announced his candidacy in a 3,000-word address sponsored by the Friends-of-Stassen Committee on December 27, 1951. Among proposals offered in support of his candidacy, Stassen called for "old fashioned honesty" and a "solid dollar anchored to a modern gold standard."

Not until January of 1952 did the Eisenhower candidacy, befogged with doubts for so many months, begin to clarify. Late in December of 1951, Senator Henry Cabot Lodge flew to Paris, conferred with Ike, and returned to Washington. Walking into a packed press conference at Washington's Shoreham Hotel promptly at noon on Sunday, January 6, 1952, Lodge began:

> I have been asked by Governor Sherman Adams of New Hampshire to enter General Eisenhower as a candidate for the presidency on the Republican ticket in the New Hampshire primary. I have assured Governor Adams that General Eisenhower is in to the finish. General Eisenhower has personally assured me that he is a Republican. . . . I invite you to check this in Paris. . . . I am speaking for the General and I will not be repudiated.

Next day, January 7—one year to the day since Eisenhower had taken up his SHAPE command—the following message came from Supreme Headquarters, Allied Powers in Europe:

> Senator Lodge's announcement of yesterday as reported in the press gives an accurate account of the general tenor of my political convictions and of my Republican voting record. He was correct also in stating that I would not seek nomination to political office.
> . . . Under no circumstances will I ask for relief from this assignment in order to seek nomination to political office and I shall not participate in the pre-convention activities of others who may have such intention with respect to me.
> Of course there is no question of the right of American citizens to organize in pursuit of their common convictions. I realize that Sena-

tor Lodge and his associates are exercising this right in an attempt to place before me next July a duty that would transcend my present responsibility. In the absence, however, of a clear-cut call to political duty, I shall continue to devote my full attention . . . to the task to which I am assigned.

With the Lodge announcement, several prominent newspapers endorsed Ike's candidacy at once. Most notable was the New York *Times.*

January, 1952, closed with a promise of the first test of strength for three of the Republican presidential candidates. On January 17 Ike's name was filed in the New Hampshire preference poll, and on January 27 his failure to withdraw it—the tenth day after it had been filed—gave tacit consent to the filing. January 29, one day before the last day for filing, the names of Taft and Stassen were entered in New Hampshire, thus assuring a three-cornered contest.

Late in February the eyes of the nation drifted to the snowbound regions of New Hampshire where one presidential candidate was making his bid *in absentia,* while the other two were conducting vigorous campaigns. Eisenhower, with Lodge as his campaign manager and seven former New Hampshire governors in his camp, was not without important support despite his absence; Taft and Stassen concededly had an uphill fight. Thus on March 1, after the first returns trickled in from Waterville Valley, a community of seven that had wrested the crown from two other villages for being the first to vote in the nation's 1952 presidential primaries, the trend for an Eisenhower victory was soon established. Final result: Eisenhower 46,661, Taft 35,838, Stassen 6,574, with scattered write-in votes for others. Said Ike from Paris the next day: "Any American who would have that many other Americans pay him that compliment would be proud or he would not be an American."

The second major popular test followed quickly in Minnesota on March 18, where a new presidential primary law was being inaugurated. Taft had refrained from entering the Minnesota primary in deference to Stassen as a favorite son, although Stassen was challenging Taft in Ohio. An attempt to put Eisenhower on the ballot had been thrown out because of defective petitions, and the only presidential candidate on the ballot other than Stassen was a relatively unknown person who said he was pledged to MacArthur. Here the results could hardly be described as anything but a Minnesota thunderclap. Stassen was a plurality victor with 44 percent of the vote, but over 100,000 write-in votes were cast for Ike. With the ballots finally tallied, Stassen led Eisenhower by only 20,000 votes. From Rocquencourt, France, Ike on March 20 said he was "astonished" at the results and indicated that he might soon return to take an active hand in the campaign.

Not every round was won by Ike in March, however, despite his win in New Hampshire and his remarkable write-in vote in Minnesota. On the same day as the Minnesota primary—March 18—the state convention in North Carolina completed the election of a delegation that eventually gave Taft 14 votes, Ike 12.

In the March polls based upon a cross-section of all voters, Ike led the field among possible candidates for both parties, but in polls of Republicans the race between Taft and Ike was very close. On March 2, before any primaries were held, Taft led Ike 34 to 33 percent in a Gallup poll of Republicans. MacArthur was given 14 percent, while Warren and Stassen trailed, each with 6 percent. Rival supporters of Taft and Ike reported their estimates of first-ballot strength to the New York *Times* on March 2 as 579 for Taft, 549 for Ike (needed to nominate: 604).

The two primaries in March gave Ike a sturdy boost, but the Taft organization appeared to be working well. Thus by the end of March no one could be reasonably certain of the Republican convention outcome—no one, that is, except the Navajo *natahni* (medicine man) who conferred an Indian blessing upon Taft at a ceremony at Albuquerque on March 17. Forced to use a hastily concocted substitute because he had left his own feathered wand at home, the *natahni,* when asked by reporters what he thought of the Ohio Senator's chances, said: "Maybe fine before ceremony. But the wand had chicken feathers instead of turkey feathers. So now Taft is finished."

Laboring hard in late March, the Taft organization stepped up its efforts in Wisconsin and Nebraska to recover from the New Hampshire defeat. Taft won his first primary victories in Wisconsin and Nebraska on April 1. In Wisconsin, he won 24 delegates, with a substantial lead over Earl Warren and Harold Stassen.

With Taft scoring two important primary victories in Wisconsin and Nebraska, the question of Ike's seriousness as a candidate again surged to the front. Party professionals again shook their heads, discounting the possibility of a nomination for a candidate who seemed so reluctant to get into the lineup and actively bid for delegates. Senator Lodge, national chairman of the Eisenhower-for-President committee, once more took off for Paris, arriving on April 3. The day before, Ike had sent off a letter to Defense Secretary Robert A. Lovett asking to be relieved of his duties: "As of now, I consider that the specific purposes for which I was recalled to duty have been largely accomplished," he wrote. A little over a week later—April 11—the White House announced that Eisenhower would be relieved of his duties as NATO Commander on June 1. For the first time it was clear that Ike would return before the national convention.

By mid-April Taft, unchanged in the posture he had assumed from the outset, was stressing four main points: (1) The New Deal-Fair Deal philosophy, he alleged, had brought about ruinous conditions from which the country was hoping to find some way out. (2) A Republican national standard-bearer had never squared off against this philosophy; that is to say, the party's presidential candidates had always compromised and temporized instead of moving in to attack. (3) Only he, Robert A. Taft, could conduct the campaign that could present the alternatives to the country, and this in turn was the only way that the Republicans could win. By implication, Taft and his supporters also suggested (4) that generals were admirably suited to wage war, but inept at the game of statecraft and civil affairs.

The helmsmen directing the Taft organization appeared also to follow four general policies: (1) In their appeal for support they underscored the fact that Taft fully understood the value of overt rewards for the party faithful—that he was an organization man and a purist in the belief that regular party leaders should be recognized. (2) It was further stressed that Taft was not an interloper; that deservedly he had become the leading spokesman of the opposition to the New Deal-Fair Deal; he was "Mr. Republican." (3) In substantiation of the second point, much was made of the fact that among Republican Congressmen Taft was the favorite. (In a poll of the 201 House Republican Congressmen taken by Representative Walter Norblad of Oregon in February, 81 of 144 responding were for Taft while 37 supported Eisenhower.) (4) Particular attention was paid to the South, where Taft had received strong delegate support in his nomination bids of 1940 and 1948, and to the Middle West.

In so far as attitudes toward other candidates were concerned, another policy of Taft's deserves remark. Throughout the entire preconvention campaign, he took particular pains not to attack Earl Warren. And on one occasion when Warren was bitterly assailed by a group within his own state, Taft said persons calling themselves Republicans who employed such "smear" tactics were undermining the party and that their attacks on Warren were malicious.

Eisenhower's managers hammered away with three central themes: (1) The party needed a winner, and the general's popularity was indisputable. Heavy efforts were made to drive across the results of the polls showing Ike to be the strongest Republican candidate. (2) Ike, it was argued, not only could win the Presidency, but was the only man who could pull a Republican House and Senate safely into port. Writing in *Business Week,* March 29, 1952, editor Gabriel Hauge (director of research of the Citizens for Eisenhower and later administrative assistant to the President on economic affairs), stressed the importance of Eisenhower's ability to help the ticket: Arthur Krock and other writers took note of the fact that this would be a persuasive argument when the infighting got really close among the professionals. (3) Ike understood military and foreign-affairs problems, the most compelling issues of the day.

In addition to plugging all three arguments, the Eisenhower strategy sought to enlist the support of a majority of the Republican governors—an extremely important group since governors more often than Senators or Congressmen control their state party organization.

Coming into the home stretch of the pre-convention campaign it still looked like a photo finish. May brought the Ohio primary which, as expected, delivered 56 firmly pledged votes into the Taft column. Then late in May came the Texas affair. What was thought to be another routine exercise by party professionals was challenged by an uprising that had the force of a Texas twister. Outnumbered and outvoted at the county conventions in the larger Texas counties, the Taft forces were still able to control the Texas Republican state convention on May 27 at Mineral Wells—a development that led to a rump convention the same day by Eisenhower supporters who had been denied seats at the regular convention. Each convention then proceeded to name separate slates of delegates to the national convention, thus continuing a contest over Texas's 38 votes that was not finally resolved until the third day of the national convention in July. Probably no single factor in the entire pre-convention struggle had a greater bearing on the nomination than did the Texas controversy.

California loomed as a significant test in 1952, not because anyone seriously supposed that Earl Warren would be defeated in the presidential primary, but for another reason. Throughout the pre-convention campaign Warren appeared on the scratch sheets of most political observers as a likely dark horse or compromise candidate. Many professionals predicted a close race in which a deadlock between Taft and Ike might be possible. The real hope of the Warren supporters was that if the two leading contenders became hopelessly stalemated, the convention would then turn to California's first three-term governor. Despite the diatribes of the anti-Warren faction, the California governor won the June 3 primary by a two-to-one vote.

Held the same day, the South Dakota primary brought Eisenhower and Taft before the voters for the last popular test before the national convention. By the thinnest of margins, Taft won a slate of pledged delegates by 64,695 to 63,879 after an intensive campaign in which the Ohio Senator appeared in the state himself for five days. In the course of the South Dakota campaign, Taft was the recipient of a favorable telegram from General MacArthur. Eisenhower, making no personal appearances in the state, declined to call his close runner-up vote a moral victory. Said Ike: "When you go to war, it's win or lose."

Throughout the entire pre-convention campaign, no other Republican presidential candidate was able to offer a serious challenge to front-runners Eisenhower and Taft. Actually there were just two others who had declared themselves in the race: Stassen and Warren. Warren made only one foray for delegates outside of his own state and the neighboring state of Oregon, where he was defeated, and his venture in Wisconsin netted him just six delegates.

Stassen's campaign limped badly in 1952, compared with his showing in 1948, when he was able to muster 150 delegates on the first ballot. Not so well financed as previously, Stassen did not travel in a chartered plane from state to state as he did in 1948, but rode in a regular commercial airliner. He inaugurated a series of television broadcasts in February, but here again his appearances were made at 11:15 P.M., an hour when the time is approximately half the cost of a choicer time between 6 and 11 P.M. Except for Minnesota, where he won 24 of 28 delegates, Stassen won only a single delegate in 1952.

Eisenhower's return from Paris to take charge of his own campaign was a vital matter in raising his candidacy off the ground during the final month before the national convention. Arriving in Washington on June 1, he retired from the Army on June 2. At the same time, in a letter to Secretary of Defense Robert Lovett, he waived the $19,541.80-a-year retirement allowance to which he was entitled, because he wished to "feel free to deal with Republican national convention delegates" without anybody accusing him of violating regulations or "embarrassing the government or the Army." This announcement by Eisenhower measured the distance from his statement of January, 1948, which removed him from the New Hampshire primary: "I am not available for and could not accept nomination to high political office."

When Eisenhower made his first political speech of his campaign at Abilene, Kansas, on June 4, it prompted a sharp philippic from a Taft supporter, Congressman Carroll Reece: "It looks like he's pretty much for mother, home, and heaven." After a period in Colorado, Ike then returned to the Morningside Heights residence that he had occupied as president of Columbia University. Here, after the fashion of the old-fashioned front-porch campaigns, Eisenhower proceeded to receive delegations from different states.

Both the Eisenhower and Taft organizations exuded optimism throughout June, with the Taft supporters taking a somewhat more confident posture. Claiming 588 delegates on June 23, the Taft strategists consistently advanced the theme that Taft was going over on the first ballot, that the delegates committed to him were rock-ribbed in their loyalty, and that anyone who had doubts about the outcome had better climb aboard the bandwagon. Moreover, the confidence that prevailed in the Taft camp was not unwarranted. With a firm majority in the national committee, Taft supporters named General MacArthur as convention keynoter on June 10, and selected a Taft man, Walter Hallanan, as temporary chairman.

Throughout the pre-convention period and up until the end of June, the Taft managers seemed more sure-footed about the nature of the nominating process and the deadly necessity for nailing down delegates; during the same period, and particularly during the earlier months, Ike's managers seemed to be thinking more in terms of an election than a national convention nomination. From April onward, however (a time that coincided with more active participation by Herbert Brownell), the direction of Eisenhower's campaign seemed more perceptibly oriented to the strategy of acquiring delegates rather than winning over the one out of every five persons that some analysts call the independent voter. Ike himself began declaring publicly that he believed in recognizing the regular party workers. In his Abilene speech, moreover, he tried to puncture complaints about his alleged recent conversion to Republicanism, stating that he would support Taft or any other Republican presidential nominee if the platform followed the Republican declaration of principles of 1950.

The big surprise of the pre-convention period, little realized at the time, was the tremendous impact those precinct, county, and finally state convention meetings had in Texas on May 3, 6, and 27. With Taft supporters firmly in control of the Republican national committee, the final disposition of the dispute over the seating of the contesting Texas delegations seemed likely to favor the Ohio Senator. But what appeared at the time as merely a Southern family quarrel gradually became the factor that unhinged the Taft drive for victory. The Texas "steal," as press, radio, and television took up the chant, was a story that spread throughout the nation.

Eager for an issue that would halt or at least slow down the momentum of the Taft campaign, Eisenhower strategists prepared to make the most out of the promised conflict over the seating of Texas delegates. Backers of Robert Taft in Texas, said Ike on June 21 at

Dallas, were guilty of "a betrayal of the whole Republican party and its principles" when they "deliberately and ruthlessly disenfranchised" the majorities that voted for another candidate at the precinct and county conventions. "In this case" he added, "the rustlers stole the Texas birthright instead of the steers." To this charge Taft backers issued a rejoinder perhaps best represented by the nationwide newspaper advertisements run on June 23, which stated that the Texas dispute was a case of Democrats trying to "nominate the strongest candidate for themselves" and "the weakest candidate for the Republicans." Eisenhower leaders were also accused of urging Democrats to sign a pledge that they were Republicans in order to participate in Republican nominating activities, on the assurance that this would not prevent them from voting in the Democratic primary.

On this note of charges and counter-charges, the Republican preconvention campaigns steamed to a close on July 6. As delegates and alternates converged on Chicago the Saturday and Sunday before the convention opened, the box score of the candidates, as revealed by the final tabulation of the Associated Press, was:

	Uncontested	Contested but temporarily seated	Total
Taft	458	72	530
Eisenhower	406	21	427
Warren	76	0	76
Stassen	25	0	25
McKeldin	24	0	24
MacArthur	5	0	5
Wedemeyer	1	0	1
Uncommitted	115	3	118
	1,110	96	1,206

In the Gallup Poll that had been released on June 19 Eisenhower was favored over Stevenson in a trial heat by 59 to 31 percent, and over Kefauver by 55 to 35 percent. Both Democrats led Taft, Kefauver by 50 to 41 percent, Stevenson by 45 to 44 percent. The inference was clear, that Ike could lick either of the two Democrats but that either of them could defeat Taft.

Nominations, however, are decided by delegates and not by public-opinion polls. On the eve of the convention the Taft forces appeared clearly to hold the upper hand. Many of Ike's backers were privately admitting that they didn't quite see how Taft could be stopped. They found out how on the opening day of the convention.

20

The Big Draft

Ninety-six years after nominating John C. Frémont at their first national convention in Philadelphia in 1856, the Republicans convened at the International Amphitheatre in Chicago, July 7, 1952, to select their twenty-fifth candidate for the Presidency of the United States. Of the twenty-four previous candidates, only ten had been defeated; fourteen were elected, three of them for a second time. But after twenty years out of executive power, the Republican party was hardly in a position to take anything for granted.

The fact that Republicans had somehow been unable to bring about any combination or coalition of forces to insure at least one victory in the last five starts underlined the bitterness behind the struggle for the nomination in 1952. Both factions were in fundamental disagreement on the causes for previous defeats. Taft supporters insisted that the "me-tooism" of Republican presidential nominees in the 1940, 1944, and 1948 campaigns had failed to present an alternative to the voters. The only way to win, they argued, was to mount an aggressive attack against the New Deal-Fair Deal. Thus Senator Taft urged an all-out offensive against the "complete failure of the Truman, Acheson, and Marshall" foreign policy, and the "socialism" of the administration's domestic program.

The Eisenhower forces counseled a different course of action. They contended that the Republican party should not assume a posture of negativism, but adopt in its stead a policy that would keep social and economic reforms intact. Essentially the Eisenhower supporters argued that the Republican party was a conservative party whose true calling was the pursuit of a mildly progressive program that would strive to refine and improve the social reforms of the previous twenty years.

Throughout the entire pre-convention campaign and during the week of the convention itself, Taft and Eisenhower leaders endeavored to identify their candidates with these two different approaches to Republican strategy and to keep them from becoming blurred. It was this basic rift over what the campaign battle cries should be that prompted some of the die-hard Taft delegates to declare on the day Ike was nominated that they would sooner vote for Truman.

Once again, as in 1912 when the Bull Moosers stormed out of the Taft-dominated convention hall at Chicago to stand with Theodore Roosevelt at Armageddon, the critical fight in the 1952 nominating contest centered on who would control the contested Southern delegations. In 1912, the outcome had been the domination of the regular Republican convention by William Howard Taft, a disastrous split in the party, and defeat in November. In 1952, the results were strikingly different.

Amidst tense conditions, the national committee began its crucial hearings on the delegate contests on Tuesday, July 1. From their inception, these hearings were punctuated by sharp clashes—a prelude to even more bitter wrangling that followed later. Touched off by argument over whether the proceedings should be broadcast and televised, the hearings went on for four days. Supporters of General Eisenhower argued that the nation was entitled to sit in on the hearings. Senator Taft said he was agreeable to live broadcasts, but his followers took a different view. They argued that broadcasts were not conducive to a judicial atmosphere; their view prevailed by a vote of 60 to 40.

Ninety-six delegate seats were in dispute when the national committee began its hearings. Of these, twenty-eight involved local factional or frivolous contests that had little special interest for either Taft or Eisenhower supporters. The legal and procedural merits in most of these cases were reasonably clear. The committee dealt with them rapidly—some, such as the Mississippi contest between the Black and Tans and the Lily Whites, were a regular quadrennial event—and the committee's decisions in these cases were final for all practical purposes. But the real struggle to see who would carry the mail developed over 68 seats in three southern delegations: Georgia, 17; Louisiana, 13; and Texas, 38. Georgia, with the entire state delegation at stake, was the first of the three to be heard.

For twenty years there had been two Republican parties in Georgia. Each maintained the official apparatus of a party hierarchy, one known as the Tucker faction, the other as the Foster. In 1944 and 1948, the national committee and the convention had seated the Tucker faction delegation, and it was the Tucker faction that retained membership on the national committee and official recognition from national headquarters up to the eve of the 1952 convention. In 1952, however, the committee voted to seat the Foster faction delegation, a decision that would have given Taft all 17 delegates if upheld by the convention.

The Louisiana contest involved 13 of the state's 15 seats; two Taft delegates were not in contest. Here the "regulars" were led by the national committeeman, John E. Jackson, a strong Taft supporter, while the pro-Eisenhower insurgents, who were driving to take over state leadership, were led by John Minor Wisdom. The proceedings in Louisiana had been much like the more-publicized events in Texas, but had taken place within a registered party membership, unlike the confused legal situation in Texas. Nevertheless, the national committee proposed to settle the Louisiana contest by giving Eisenhower two delegates and allowing Taft to retain eleven.

For Texas, where 38 seats were at stake, the issue presented to the national committee was whether to seat the slate led by the Taft leader, national committeeman Henry Zweifel, or the delegation headed by H. J. Porter, an Eisenhower backer. The Zweifel slate was 34 for Taft, 4 for Eisenhower, while the Porter slate divided 33 for Eisenhower and 5 for Taft.

Opening the national committee hearings on the delegate contests with two unanticipated proposals, chairman Guy Gabrielson began by reading a telegram from former President Herbert Hoover. Hoover suggested that each side select "an eminent citizen, not one of their own managers, to sit with me and see if we could find a basis of agreement." Next Gabrielson read a letter from Senator Taft that contained a detailed analysis of the Texas situation on a district-by-district basis. The letter concluded with an offer to compromise the contest by splitting the delegates 22 for Taft, 16 for Eisenhower. This proposal, in the words of Senator Taft, was "so generous that its equity cannot be questioned." Adjourning the meeting at this point to await a reply from Eisenhower leaders, chairman Gabrielson soon had a tart rejoinder to both offers. To the Hoover proposal, Senator Lodge, speaking as Eisenhower's manager, said: "I cannot imagine anything more undemocratic than for three men in a private meeting to arrogate unto themselves the power to disenfranchise many thousands of Americans." His reply to Taft's offer was equally blunt: "General Eisenhower is a no-deal man."

The national committee voted through the Taft proposal, giving Taft 22 and Ike 16 delegates, by a 60 to 41 vote, following which the Eisenhower leaders reiterated their pledge to carry the fight to the convention floor. They also sought to exploit the issue not only in Chicago but in every hamlet and crossroads in the nation. Meanwhile General Eisenhower himself, en route from Denver to Chicago by special train, took up the theme at every whistle stop with references to "chicanery," "star-chamber methods," and "smoke-filled rooms."

Elsewhere several offstage events, probably not all of them planned by the official Eisenhower managers, were moving merrily along in Houston, Texas. There the governors of the 48 states were holding their annual conference. Officially, the business of the conference was well publicized and had little to do with national politics. But most of the 25 Republican governors were present, and their private conversations doubtless turned in the direction of Chicago. On July 1, just as he was leaving the conference, Thomas E. Dewey of New York sent a telegram to the national committee urging that the credentials hearings be opened to television: "LET THE PEOPLE SEE AND HEAR THE EVIDENCE." With governors Adams (New Hampshire) and McKay (Oregon), he sent a strongly worded message on the same day urging that the Porter delegation from Texas be seated.

The most important of the Houston actions, however, took the form of a delayed-action time bomb. This was the manifesto signed by 23 of the 25 Republican governors, prepared privately under leadership never identified, and released in a press conference at Houston held jointly by governors Dan Thornton of Colorado and J. Bracken Lee of Utah on July 2.[1] The manifesto urged that contested delegates not be allowed to vote in the national convention until after the contests had been settled. It was a simple proposal with obvious public appeal, and subsequently in amended form, of course, became the basis of the Langlie Fair Play amendment to the national rules. As eventually became clear, it was this Fair Play amendment that torpedoed Taft's chance for the nomination.

The governors' manifesto came as an obvious shock to the Taft leaders and to the officers of the national committee. Heretofore under the long-standing rules and practice of both major parties, the temporary roll of delegates as made up by the national committee was always the basis for opening the convention. Delegates on the temporary roll, contested or uncontested, could vote on any question, with one exception, and that in the Republican party only: when the credentials committee report on permanent seating was received, contested delegates on the temporary roll could not vote on their own contest. But they could still vote on other contests, as well as on any question that might come before the convention before contests were permanently settled.

Quite obviously the strategists in far-off Houston foresaw that the contested Taft delegates from Louisiana and Texas would vote to seat the Taft delegates from Georgia, and that they might swing the decision.

Replying to the governors' manifesto with a long statement of carefully reasoned argument citing historical precedents, chairman Gabrielson also slipped in a few stout political blows of his own. After admitting that the convention had the power to adopt the proposed new rule if it so desired, he suggested that in consequence:

> We would make it possible for ruthless, selfish men to prevent any delegate from voting in the next Republican convention—merely by filing contests in every state and territory. And we would be taking this step, not in justice, equity or fair play, but for temporary political expediency.
>
> It is difficult for me to understand why some of those who controlled the Republican National Conventions of 1944 and 1948 did not seek such a rule then, but demand it now.[2]

On this note the issue was clearly drawn, and gave promise of rocking the convention right from the outset.

The assembly convened in the air-conditioned emporium at the Chicago stockyards shortly before noon on Monday, July 7, to hear the first of the 150,000 words that would be hurled at them in the course of five days of oratorical outpourings. There were 1,206 delegates, with 604 needed to win the nomination. This time there were more women delegates and alternates than ever before—128 delegates and 252 alternates.

Soon after chairman Guy G. Gabrielson had gaveled the convention to order on Monday, the promised fireworks began to explode. Immediately after Senator Bricker offered the usually routine motion to adopt the previous rules, Governor Langlie was on his feet with a substitute resolution which provided in substance that no delegate whose seat was in contest could vote in the convention or committee until the contest was finally resolved.[3] (The number of such delegates involved in the Langlie substitute resolution was 68.) In some amplifying remarks, Langlie sought to make it clear that those who supported the proposal were insisting that the delegations of Georgia, Texas, and 13 of 15 delegates from Louisiana should not be seated nor participate in committees until their qualifications had been approved by a majority of the convention.

Langlie's proposal quickly sparked an acrimonious debate. The Taft forces opposed the move, insisting that it was a sorry business to be changing the rules once a contest was under way, while Eisenhower supporter Dan Thornton, governor of Colorado, cried: "Lincoln believed in change, and I believe in change."

Adding to the confusion that churned the course of the debate was an amendment offered by Congressman Clarence J. Brown, a delegate from Ohio. Mr. Brown argued that seven of the Louisiana delegates who were included as "in contest" in the Langlie resolution had been declared the legal delegates by the Republican state committee of Louisiana. This action, he stated, was in complete conformity with Rule 4, Section (b) of the Republican national convention as adopted in 1948, which read:

> All contests arising in any State electing District Delegates by District Conventions, shall be decided by its State Convention, or if the State Convention shall not meet prior to the National Convention, then by its State Committee; and only contests affecting delegates at large shall be presented to the National Convention.

The contest on seven delegates, therefore, contended Brown, was decided by the state committee of Louisiana. Then he offered a motion to amend the Langlie resolution by deleting seven district delegates from Louisiana because these delegates were not, in his judgment, under contest before the national committee and therefore should not be under contest before the convention. Thus it was the Brown amendment to the Langlie substitute resolution that the delegates were actually voting on when the first test of the convention came.

Debate will long continue as to the merits of the political and parliamentary strategy embodied in the Brown amendment. Possibly it represented a desperate attempt to retrieve a situation already almost lost. It presented a narrowly legalistic issue in which the technical merits were somewhat on the Taft side of the case. But the basic provision in the existing national rules to which Brown appealed was one that many delegates were no longer prepared to tolerate. In any event, the main debate in the convention was over the merits of the Langlie proposal as a whole. And in the confusion of the convention hall, with neither proposal available to many delegates in written form, fine distinctions were impossible. For all practical purposes, the vote on the Brown amendment was to be the vote on the Langlie proposal.

When the vote came, after two hours of debate, the Brown amendment was defeated 658 to 548. On motion by a Taft delegate, the Langlie proposal was then approved unanimously without a roll call. And on this note the curtain rang down on the first crucial test of convention strength. Taft, said the wiseacres, had been stopped.

Not all of the delegates who voted against the Brown amendment had made up their minds to vote for Eisenhower. But the 548 who voted for the amendment were the rock-ribbed portion of the Taft support. And 548 was short of the 604 votes necessary to win the nomination. (On Sunday Taft had announced that he had 537 telegraphed pledges to vote for him.) Taft had almost certainly lost his chance to win on the first ballot. The situation of the Taft forces was rather accurately diagnosed by a man with some skill in such matters: "I am afraid," said Harry S. Truman with a broad smile when informed of the convention vote, "that my favorite candidate is going to be beaten."

Tuesday and Wednesday it was the credentials committee that occupied the front center stage position. In a sense the credentials committee was the second court to sit in judgment on the delegate contests, the first having been the national committee. The court of last resort would be the convention itself if the losers were to appeal the decision of the credentials committee.

This time the contest disputes were televised and motion-picture cameramen were permitted to film the proceedings. When a vote was finally put to the committee on the Georgia contest, it sustained the national committee action by 30 to 21, voting to seat the pro-Taft delegation of 17 from Georgia.

Wednesday, in an unexpected move before the credentials committee, the Taft forces proposed to give the entire 13 Louisiana delegates in contest to Eisenhower, instead of splitting them 11 for Taft and 2 for Eisenhower. Apparently intended by the Taft leaders as a peace overture and as a measure to remove the stigma of the Texas "steal" talk that had attached itself to Taft's candidacy, the Louisiana proposal met quick rebuff from the Eisenhower managers. Both contests—Georgia and Texas—said Senator Lodge, would still be brought to the floor, since they "are stains on the integrity of our party that we must erase if we are to go to the people with clean hands and ask them to have faith in our party to lead the nation in the years that lie ahead."

After the unanimous vote to seat the 13 pro-Eisenhower Louisiana delegates, Taft supporters on the credentials committee quickly fell in line for the final contest hearing on Texas. This contest drew the closest vote of the credentials committee hearings. By a margin of 27 to 24, the committee voted to seat the "compromise" delegation originally proposed by Taft himself, which gave Taft 22 and Eisenhower 16 of the Texas delegates.

Finally delegate Ross Rizley of Oklahoma, chairman of the credentials committee, climbed to the platform to deliver his report on contested delegations. Knowing a decisive test was at hand that would probably decide the presidential nomination, delegates impatiently fingered programs and campaign buttons, hoping to get on with it. They had not long to wait. Immediately following chairman Rizley's motion recommending that the Georgia delegates on the temporary roll be seated, state senator Donald W. Eastvold of Washington presented the minority report of the credentials committee.

Young (32) and earnest, Eastvold presented a case structured strictly along factual lines, sounding quite academic at times as he interpolated court citations into his prepared text. In contrast, Senator Dirksen of Illinois, with his eloquent ecclesiastical style, blossomed out with a skilled blend of Biblical and Fourth of July oratory. Though many disagreed violently with his position and what he said, by common consent Senator Dirksen's speech was recognized as the dramatic highlight of the 1952 Republican convention. One speaker for the minority report had likened their cause to that of Diogenes treading the streets in broad daylight holding a lantern aloft in search of "an honest man." Dirksen, however, tuned his voice to the mellifluous pitch of a French horn and sought counsel in what Paul said upon sacred parchments: "Come let us reason together." He expressed doubt as to whether in an emotionally charged concourse like the convention hall his words could have any effect. None the less he felt compelled to try. And try he did.

Shaking a finger at the New York delegation to the left of the speaker's rostrum, where Dewey, the delegation chairman, was seated, he noted that the Republican party "had a habit of winning conventions and losing elections." Later when he mentioned Dewey by name, and reminded him of the support he had given him in 1944 and 1948, the New York governor was loudly booed. "We followed you before," thundered Dirksen, "and you took us down the path to defeat." At this point booing became general and the convention was in an uproar. Some delegates, moved by the Dirksen oratory and his direct attack upon the party's titular leader, were booing Dewey. Others, including most of the New York delegation and other Eisenhower supporters, were booing Dirksen.

Whether the Dirksen oratory helped or harmed Taft or actually altered one vote is surely a matter of conjecture. No doubt a large number enjoyed his effort to spank Tom Dewey in public, but they also were simultaneously filled with doubts as to whether this public reproach, before a nationwide television audience, was in the best interests of the party.

Again, it was the vote that counted. For the second time the Eisenhower drive for the presidential nomination scored an impressive convention victory. On the roll call vote for acceptance or rejection of the substitute minority report on Georgia, the convention divided 607 yes, 531 no. The pro-Eisenhower, Tucker delegation was seated.

Unlike the Georgia contest, the Texas delegate dispute never reached an actual vote by the convention. A surprise motion by a

Taft delegate that the convention "unanimously support the substitute motion to adopt the minority report" put a quick end to the long controversy that started deep in the heart of Texas early in May. Thirty-eight happy Texas delegates belonging to the Porter faction trooped in to take their seats, the permanent roll of the convention delegates was immediately adopted, and at 1:45 A.M. on July 10 the convention recessed.

Why had the Taft forces yielded the Texas fight before a vote was taken? To most observers the answer seemed obvious: anticipating an adverse vote as in the case of the Georgia contest, the Taft strategists sought to avoid another roll-call defeat. Was the presidential nomination now beyond Taft's grasp? It began to look so.

Readying themselves on Thursday for the supreme moment—the nominating roll call—the delegates to the 1952 convention first were called upon to consider several far-reaching changes in the national rules. In 1952 revisions were unusually extensive. The first nailed down the temporary rule of the Langlie "Fair Play" amendment—that no delegate on the temporary roll whose right to be seated was being contested could vote in the convention or in any committee until the contest was finally decided. Another change was directed at the problems bubbling out of the Texas controversy —the determination of who is legally entitled to participate in Republican precinct, parish, and county caucuses, conventions, and mass meetings. Heretofore the national rules merely specified that participants be "legal and qualified voters." As revised the rule now permits the "governing Republican committee of each state or territory to prescribe additional qualifications not inconsistent with law."

Striking at another goblin, the 1952 convention also revised its apportionment formula. Since 1916, in consequence of reforms following the convention of 1912, party rules had required at least 1,000 Republican votes within a congressional district to qualify for a single congressional district delegate, and at least 10,000 for two congressional district delegates. The 1952 amendment raised to 2,000 votes the figure necessary to qualify for a single district delegate.

Among other changes, the most important was the enlargement of the national committee. Here state party chairmen were added to the national committee as third members for every state that currently received passing marks as a Republican stronghold. A state can now make the grade on any one of the following tests: (1) a Republican majority in the last presidential election, (2) a Republican majority among the whole number of the state's representatives in both houses of Congress, (3) a Republican governor. This would have added about 20 members to the national committee on the basis of the situation as it prevailed in July 1952; after the Eisenhower sweep in November, another dozen state chairmen, more or less, were added.

The idea for adding state central chairmen to the national committee originated in the Middle West and was spearheaded by a member of the Taft delegation from Wisconsin. Ostensibly the motivation arose from a combination of two desires: first, to squeeze down the influence of the Southern states by giving increased representation to areas more likely to produce Republican majorities and, second, to increase the influence of state party officials.

Most Northern states could expect to qualify for the third membership much of the time. But like many such proposals, the new rule takes no account of state size, increasing the representation of Vermont as much as New York. Moreover, the new rule is potentially dangerous to the large states where Republican victories cannot always be taken for granted. Large states could lose a part of their representation on the national committee, under such a rule, at a time when they were most likely to need it. Yet in 1952, with the scent of victory in the air, this fear seemed remote; and for the most part the large state delegations that were for Eisenhower supported the change. Clearly the new rule will have the effect of stepping up the influence of the Republican governors in the national committee, since a sitting governor usually controls his state party chairman. Some of the Taft followers were inclined to view the change askance, although Senator Taft himself outlined a similar proposal in 1950. But the real furor stemmed from a source that had been disregarded by the sponsors of the proposal—from the female representation on the national committee. Heretofore each state had been represented on the national committee by one man and one woman. The implied assumption of the new rule, however, was that the state chairmen who were to be added would inevitably be men. What followed was a pitched battle in the perennial warfare of the sexes, in which women delegates at Chicago found themselves making common cause with most of the Southern delegations in a losing battle. (The rule was adopted by a vote of 683 to 513.)

Few major rifts were encountered over the GOP platform in 1952. As the plank on foreign policy finally emerged it met the demands of the Taft forces for a sharp attack on the alleged failures of the Truman administration, but it also met the demands of the Eisenhower supporters for endorsement of continued European aid.

The one other touchy platform subject was the civil rights issue. Here the resolutions committee compromised by rejecting proposals for a federal fair employment practices act and by advancing a plank that was probably too weak to please the liberal elements of the party and too strong to please all Southern Republicans or Southern Democrats who might be "presidential Republicans." The civil rights plank was agreed to without serious trouble, however, and both groups—those who favored an FEPC and those who opposed it— agreed not to fight it on the floor of the convention.

As the hour for the presidential roll call finally arrived it was clear that the large lines of strategy for the leading candidates had changed little from the time the national committee began its hearings on the disputed contests July 1. Taft, with a slight edge in committed delegates, was counting heavily on these delegates' holding firm. So close was he to going over on the first ballot that a bold, confident attitude seemed all that would be necessary to swing the 70 or 80 additional delegates that he needed.

Eisenhower, with fewer committed delegates, needed an issue. In Ike's case an issue was necessary to do for him what many of his managers feared the seasoned professionals working for Taft could do on the final infighting for delegates. For Ike, the issue of the Texas "steal" seemed heaven-sent. And his managers made the most of it, for they kept beating their tom-toms until the Taft leaders finally yielded completely. One change in the Taft strategy was perceptible when Taft offered to compromise the Texas struggle on a 22-16 basis. The supposition, at least after this move, was that the Taft managers were at last beginning to be disturbed by the Texas catcalls in which a large part of the nation seemed to be joining.

Taft's chances of winning lay in capturing some 70 or 80 of approximately 120 delegates who were uncommitted at convention time. There was little chance that Taft could raid the delegates of either Warren or Stassen. Long an outspoken critic of Stassen, Taft nursed a tender sore from Stassen's invasions of the Ohio presidential primary in 1948 and 1952. Many Taft supporters, in fact, felt that Stassen had entered the 1952 campaign largely for the purpose of hurting Taft. There was also little likelihood that Taft could secure Warren's support and it was likewise doubtful whether Warren could have delivered his delegation to Taft even if he had wished to do so. Thus Taft had to seek to win by converting the uncommitted delegates. This chance began to appear lost.

Banging for order on Thursday evening, July 10—the convention's fourth day—chairman Joe Martin laid down the ground rules for nominating speeches. Nominating efforts were limited to fifteen minutes, with four seconding speeches of not more than five minutes each allowed to each candidate. It was to be a long evening.

Alabama, first alphabetically, yielded to Illinois, giving Senator Dirksen the privilege of placing Taft in nomination first. There-after Senator Knowland of California nominated Earl Warren, while General Eisenhower was presented to the convention by Theodore R. McKeldin, Maryland's governor.

In a departure from precedent, the person selected to place Harold Stassen in nomination was a woman, Mrs. C. Edward Howard of Minnesota. Finally the last name, that of General MacArthur, was placed in nomination by delegate Fred Coogan of Oklahoma.

Next morning chairman Joe Martin made a brief announcement as the delegates twisted into their narrow lanes of metal seats, show-ing obvious signs of weariness from the strains of the evening before. "The Chair wishes to state that he will pause for several minutes after the completion of the roll should any state desire to change its vote." Then the secretary began calling the roll. Midway through the roll call—after the vote of Montana, the twenty-fourth state—the vote stood: Eisenhower 256, Taft 228; Warren 71, Stassen 20, MacArthur 1. Moving further along the alphabet, with New York standing firm at 92-4 for Ike, and Pennsylvania splitting 53-15 for the general, it became apparent that Eisenhower would come very close to the 604 votes needed to win on the first ballot. On through the territories, with the last vote cast by the Virgin Islands (1 vote), the total at the end of the first presidential roll call was Eisenhower 595, Taft 500, Warren 81, Stassen 20, MacArthur 10.

It was at this point that the Minnesota standard began to bobble for the chairman's attention. Speaking for the Minnesota delegation, Senator Ed Thye put an end to any thought of a second ballot. "Mr. Chairman," said big Ed, "Minnesota wishes to change its vote to Eisenhower."

It was all over; all over, that is, except for the final rush of vari-ous state leaders to switch the votes of many delegates who were at last free of other commitments and wished to go on record for Eisen-hower. Previously Minnesota had voted 9 for Eisenhower, 19 for Stassen. Thus the Minnesota switch had put Eisenhower over by 614 to Taft's 500. The time was 12:45 P.M.

Almost an hour later chairman Martin was able to say: "Senator Knowland is entitled to make the motion that the vote be unanimous. He has agreed to share that honor with Senator Bricker of Ohio, representing Senator Taft." Bricker then announced that Taft and Eisenhower had already met (watched by an estimated 14,272,000 on television, Ike had walked from his headquarters in the Black-stone Hotel to visit Taft at the Conrad Hilton immediately after his nomination), and that Taft had "pledged his unlimited and active support to elect General Dwight Eisenhower."

What Bricker said, however, could hardly be expected to mollify the feelings of all Taft supporters. For many friends of the Ohio Senator took his defeat grimly. Typical was Judge Dawson, of Kentucky, who stormed out of the convention hall after the Minnesota switch with the remark: "These bandwagon fellows are going to wake up on election day and find that instead of jumping on a bandwagon, they've been taking a ride on a hearse. They're taking a hearse trip to a grave that can't be dug deep enough to cover up the corpses of malicious and even dishonest conduct which has characterized the Eisenhower campaign on the floor."

Even a year later visceral reactions of many die-hard Taft supporters were far from being entirely spent. Wrote Basil Brewer—a Taft leader in Massachusetts—for his New Bedford paper the day of Taft's death on August 1, 1953:

> Bob Taft is gone.
>
> And with him went something of the heart and soul of every true American.
>
> To say he died "in the saddle," as would be his wish, is an understatement.
>
> Bob Taft gave his life, every drop of his energy, his last breath to his beloved country—just as truly as did the last Marine killed in Korea last Saturday.
>
> It will be said it was well Bob Taft was not elected President last Nov. 4, in that event a Vice President would not be President.
>
> But this superficial reaction does not fit the story.
>
> There is medical testimony that Bob Taft's ailment can come from the emotional strain of supreme and lofty effort, followed by great disappointment.
>
> Taft did not grieve that he was defeated in his effort to achieve the Presidency. He told this writer his "chief disappointment" was for those millions of loyal supporters who must share his disappointment and defeat.
>
> Unspoken was his grief over the methods used by his opponents to procure his defeat, including attacks upon his personal character and honesty.
>
> I still can see the masked and hooded hoodlums bearing the banners in front of the Convention Hall at Chicago "stop thief."
>
> Yes Bob is gone and there is no one to take his place. This alone is a tragedy comparable to the passing of Lincoln.
>
> But with Bob Taft goes the Republican party.
>
> In its place is a faceless, slinking thing, bearing only the name Republican, a name indeed, which President Eisenhower hardly has mentioned since he was elected under its label.
>
> It was to save this country, and the party which to him symbolized

his country's greatness and security—that Bob Taft died, and as Stanton said at Lincoln's bier, "Now he belongs to the ages."

Bob Taft's name is secure in history.

May history, with equal justice, record the infamy of his detractors.

Particularly may history record the infamy of those who at Chicago broke the great man's heart by charging him with deceit and dishonesty.

Good-by, Bob. May God have you in his keeping.[4]

Like all parties that develop a deep fissure over the pre-convention campaigns, the Republican party needed time to close ranks. How much time and what concessions would have to be made were uncertain at the moment and did not become even relatively clear until September.

But in July, 1952, the extent of the feeling was indicated statistically in at least some degree by the pattern of an hour's vote-switching while the tally was being made final before the motion to make the vote unanimous. Votes were changed by 250 delegates, finally bringing the Eisenhower total up from 595 to 845. But 280 die-hard delegates, mostly from Middle-Western states, remained with Taft to the end, and 77 Warren delegates and 4 MacArthur delegates also stood fast, refusing to change their votes before the final motion.

Taking a short recess, an exhausted convention returned in late afternoon on Friday to go through the motions of selecting a vice-presidential nominee. Throughout the week a long parade of names for the Vice-Presidency had been the object of the usual speculation, with no single candidate appearing to have the inside track on either an Eisenhower or a Taft ticket. For Taft, there was talk of General MacArthur, Senator Dirksen, governors McKeldin and J. Bracken Lee of Utah (after the latter had recanted from the heresy of the Houston manifesto), with frequent mention also of Senator Knowland of California when the practicalities of ticket-balancing were considered. Prominently mentioned for an Eisenhower ticket were governors Thornton, Driscoll, Arn, and Langlie; Congressmen Halleck and Judd; and both California Senators, Knowland and Nixon. By Friday of the convention week, however, the name of Richard Nixon began to protrude more prominently.

Publicly, Nixon discredited all talk of the vice-presidential nomination for himself with such asides as: "Who dreamed that one up?" But those who watched Nixon closely, particularly his fellow Californians, were inclined to discount his protests. It was Senator Knowland of California who doggedly led the drive to keep Earl

Warren in the race. In any event, once Eisenhower was nominated, his managers lost no time in calling a conference led by Herbert Brownell, Jr., to discuss the vice-presidential nomination. At this meeting, which included Thomas E. Dewey, several other state chief executives, and state party leaders, the conferees quickly agreed upon Senator Nixon. Brownell then telephoned Eisenhower to inform him of their recommendation, which Ike quickly approved.

During the brief interval between the Eisenhower nomination and the reconvening of the convention to name a running mate rumors buzzed over the national television and radio networks that Senator Taft might be named for the Vice-Presidency. It was widely believed that in the interests of party harmony he might be willing to accept. But the Eisenhower managers had come too far on a winner-take-all basis to change the signals at the last moment. Actually there is no reason to believe that they gave any serious thought to the possibility of offering the Vice-Presidency to Taft. But the fact that the generous gesture was not made did much to enhance the bitterness of the Taft followers as they left the convention.

With the general's approval, Nixon's nomination was a routine procedure. Clare Boothe Luce, who was to have placed the first woman in nomination for the Vice-Presidency in the history of the party (Margaret Chase Smith), told the delegates that she was withholding the nomination at the request of her candidate, who did not wish to "create any division of loyalties." Thereafter Senator Knowland presented Nixon's name to the convention, and upon the motion of Governor Fine of Pennsylvania Nixon was nominated by acclamation.

At last, after five tumultuous convention days and several years of pre-convention campaigning, the 1952 Republican convention came to a close in a swirl of the usual last-minute resolutions of thanks.

Speeding homeward, delegates, alternates, and visitors could mull over many matters. They could think about what they might have missed by not seeing the many facets of the convention on television; they could reflect on where the Taft managers made their mistakes or rejoice over the way the Eisenhower leaders capitalized on the breaks. They could also indulge in that wonderful game of political prophecy that is open to all, and wonder if the twenty-fifth Republican nominee would make the grade. He did!

21

The Far Side of Politics

🐘

The seven voters of Millsfield, New Hampshire (total population 16), stayed up late November 3, 1952. It was nearing Tuesday after the first Monday in November. The place was the home of Mrs. Genevieve N. Annis, the town clerk, whose burly husband trapped beavers for fun. Promptly at the stroke of midnight, all seven voters cast their ballots by the light of a kerosene lamp and watched Mrs. Annis collect and count them quickly, then record one absentee ballot, reporting proudly at 12:02 A.M., Tuesday, the nation's first election returns in the contest to select the thirty-fourth President of the United States. Result: eight votes for Eisenhower.

It would be quite a few hours before the full force of the trend could definitely be established. But long before the electronic brain —"Univac"—began to register its cold calculations of election trends the signs were unmistakable. An Eisenhower landslide was beginning.

Two hours after the voting booths closed in Parker county, Texas, raindrops were felt—hardly more than a sprinkle, but for the Parker county farmers "it was the first heaven-sent moisture in weeks, promising an end to the summer-long drought that had withered the corn and burned pastures brown. Watching the rain fall, a filling-station operator exclaimed with prophetic jubilation, 'Democratic tears! Ike must be sweeping the country!' "

Soon voters would know the full weight of the landslide that would bring the first Republican President to the White House in twenty years. "From the Eisenhower electoral maps," commented Sam Lubell soon afterward, "the proverbial visitor from Mars would never know that Franklin D. Roosevelt had lived." [1] Eisenhower with 33,936,301 votes had outstripped his Democratic opponent by 6½ million votes (Stevenson received 27,311,354). In a deep dive into Dixie, Ike carried Texas, Florida, Tennessee, and Virginia, came close to carrying Kentucky and South Carolina. While the Republican ticket carried 146 Southern counties in 1944, and 149 in 1948, this time 498 Southern counties went Republican.[2]

With few exceptions the overturn was almost unbelievable. In Massachusetts Ike carried three counties that had not been in the Republican column since the Coolidge landslide of 1924, and ended up with a total of 13 out of the Bay state's 14 counties—winning all but the unregenerate Suffolk (Boston). Al Smith had carried nine populous counties in New England which had remained "religiously Democratic afterward"; now Eisenhower swept all but three, becoming the first Republican candidate since Coolidge to make simultaneous inroads among both Catholics and Yankees in New England. And in Illinois, Indiana, Maryland, and New Mexico he carried counties that never before voted for a Republican President.

In the popular vote, Eisenhower won 55.1 percent to his opponent's 44.4 percent. Ike carried 39 states, while the Democratic nominee won nine. (Eighteen states came into the Republican column which had been consistently Democratic for twenty years.) In a tremendous upsurge in popular interest, thirteen million more people voted in 1952 than in 1948. Across the nation generally, of some 670 Northern counties that piled up Democratic majorities in all of the Roosevelt-Truman elections, at least one-fourth shifted to Ike.

Impressive as it appeared, Eisenhower's landslide was bettered by several of his Republican predecessors—Roosevelt in 1904 (56.4 percent); Harding in 1920 (60.3 percent); Coolidge in 1924 (57.3 percent); and Hoover in 1928 (58.1 percent). Elsewhere the magnitude of the Eisenhower sweep following twenty years of non-rule for the Republicans tended to obscure certain facts of earlier elections. All in all, there was a gain for the Republicans in the South, but its significance called for a closer look.[3] In 1928, for example, Hoover's margin in Florida when the state last went Republican was 58.8 percent, compared with Ike's total of 54.6 percent in 1952. Moreover, in 1928 the Republican gubernatorial candidate in Florida won 40 percent of the two-party vote, while in 1952 the GOP nominee for governor took only 27 percent of the total vote. Vermont, a state with a long line of Republican consistency, gave Ike 71.5 percent of its vote in 1952—a figure that trails the 75.9 percent captured by both Harding and Coolidge.

As the roof caved in on Democratic hopes at 11:20 P.M. on election night, however, when Democratic national committeeman Jacob Arvey conceded Illinois, no one cared about the ebb and flow of individual performances in party history. At least no one in the GOP encampment cared, at party headquarters in New York's Commodore Hotel where 2,000 jammed the ballroom to congratulate Ike. With votes still spilling in, a Republican President was assured. And when the final precincts were in and all adjustments had been made in official tallies, Republicans would also control the House and Senate. But it would be a close control—47 to 46 in the Senate; 221 to 213 in the House. There would be far more at stake than the modest determination to hold tight that Ike expressed in his victory statement: "We can't afford to lose one recruit." For while the Republican party gained ground in every state of the Union in 1952, it lost ground in 45 states in the general elections of 1954. (In 1954 the GOP gained in just two states; held its own in one.)

But if Republicans were slightly sobered by the closeness of the result on the congressional side in 1952, and knew that the large lead of the presidential candidate over the congressional ticket was undoubtedly a factor in pulling some GOP candidates over the tape in the congressional races, again there were compensating factors to encourage a jaunty optimism. In Virginia the Republicans wound up with three congressional seats, they captured one in North Carolina, and across the nation twenty-eight state executives were Republican. Surely the comeback picture, with several promising patches for cultivation in the South, was encouraging for the future.

The campaign brought more than the usual glow of feverish excitement to the cities and farms of America. Sam Lubell reports that it was probably the "most emotional election" since McKinley defeated Bryan in 1896, commenting that many editors reported two levels of abusiveness in their campaign mail. He also discovered many voters in his post-election survey who told him that they "prayed not once but several times" before finally voting.

But whether the tone of the campaign was more abusive than a great many of our presidential canvasses is a debatable matter. The Democrats called Lincoln a "vulgar village politician" in 1860, while the Charleston *Mercury* suggested that he was "a cross between the nutmeg dealer, the horse-swapper, and the night man." Hoover was charged with having a Negro concubine, while Andrew Jackson was called "an adulterer, a gambler, and a murderer." And more recently, of course, some will remember that the hate hucksters claimed Franklin Roosevelt was a Jew, contending that he had changed his name from Rosenfeld. While there is little doubt that the campaign scraped some sore spots, generally it was not so intensely virulent in tone as many earlier ones had been. Truman's entry into the foray with another of his famous whistle-stop tours brought one sharp exchange between the President and presidential-nominee Eisenhower. Truman accused the general of endorsing Republican Senators who helped pass the McCarran act, which by reason of its quota limitations excluded many European Catholics and Jews. Truman then charged Ike with accepting "practices" identified with the "so-called 'master race' " theory. Ike countered this charge by snapping back hard at the President for injecting "bigotry" into the campaign.

Eisenhower's running mate Richard Nixon lit the firecracker that brought the loudest shouts from the Democratic high command. (With the possible exception of Senator Joseph McCarthy's telecast construed by many as an attempt to pin the label of Communist sympathizer on Stevenson. McCarthy's slip-of-the-tongue reference to ". . . Alger . . . I mean Adlai" drew quick cries of "foul" from Democrats as well as from some Republicans for what they considered a sly implication that Mr. Stevenson was somehow indistinguishable from a convicted perjurer.) Nixon opened up on Stevenson by linking him with the issue of Communism. And he did so by reference to the first trial of Alger Hiss, during which Stevenson submitted a deposition attesting to the "good character" of Hiss. This, said Nixon, was "poor judgment," and while Eisenhower maintained a complete silence Democrats angrily asked whether Nixon's attack had his endorsement or that of the Republican party strategists.

The campaign, in a sense, led off from the night of July 24, 1952, when Adlai E. Stevenson became the best-known reluctant Democratic presidential candidate since his predecessor Horatio Seymour in 1868. With John Sparkman as his running mate, Stevenson moved at once to get the campaign under way, for unlike his preconvention rival Kefauver he was without a nationally organized following—a handicap which he never did overcome.

Moving by train, plane, and motorcar cavalcade, the campaign built up an impressive mileage total. Eisenhower traveled 33,000 miles—22,000 by plane, 11,000 by train—visiting 44 states. (He missed only Nevada, Maine, Vermont, and Mississippi.) He also made 270 speeches, 40 of which were major ones. His rival Stevenson traveled 32,500 miles, of which 27,000 were by air and 5,500 by rail. Stevenson visited 32 states and made 200 speeches—21 of which were nationally televised. With both parties pledging peace and prosperity, promising aid to the farmer, laborer, and veteran, and extension of social security benefits, reduction of taxes, opposition to Communism and corruption, and to protect civil rights (the Republican platform also pledged to deliver the mail more promptly and efficiently), each candidate built his own bridges as to their meaning. Stevenson, surrounded by personal friends and many political amateurs, announced at the outset that he did not want to "alter the New Deal, but merely to "freshen" it. He also spoke of the "mess in Washington," a favorite phrase of the Republicans, and thereby irritated President Truman, who insisted that the Democrats must campaign on the cumulative record from 1933 through his own administration. Initially Stevenson said he had no intention of repealing the Taft-Hartley act—he only wanted to amend it. But this statement he would later regret, for further along in the campaign he shifted posture by saying that the law should be repealed, labeling it at the same time a tangle of "legal barbed wire."

Eisenhower followed the Dewey line by emphasizing his support of domestic welfare legislation, like social security, and the attention he gave to the charges of Stevenson and Truman that he was a candidate of the depression party suggests that he was much concerned over this line of attack. Time and again he pledged that "the depression must not return"; that "we are not going to turn the clock back—ever." Frequently hitting at "mismanagement in foreign affairs," Ike also banged away at "the wasters," "the bunglers," and at the whole "top to bottom mess" in the nation's capital. After Eisenhower's conciliation meeting with Robert A. Taft early in September, his attacks against administration tax and spending policies picked up in tempo. Stevenson then tried his best to create the impression that Eisenhower was now a captive of Taft and the Republican right wing. Eisenhower's "Great Crusade," he said, had become the "Great Surrender," and the Illinois governor gibed that Ike was sitting beside Taft on a love seat "matching pennies against principles." But Stevenson's quips and frequently lofty oratorical outbursts simply could not close the gap between himself and the man from Abilene. The need for a change—that sometimes ambiguous uprooter of political power—along with an immensely popular Republican candidate, was crunching down the coalition of forces that had brought five presidential victories to the Democrats.

As early as July, Walter Lippmann began giving reasons for a change in the governing party: the first, he said, was that if new decisions in foreign affairs called for both additional sacrifice and diplomatic flexibility, Eisenhower more than Truman would be able to carry the country with him, because he was less vulnerable than any Democrat to the charge "that if he uses diplomacy he is an appeaser." Second, the surest way to retire the "ensconced beneficiaries of twenty years of patronage, and to open up the offices of responsibility to the new political generation" would be to elect a Republican President. A Democratic President, even as independent as Stevenson might be, argued Lippman, would hardly be ruthless enough "to remove all the loyal and deserving Democrats who need to be removed." Third—admittedly an argument with little appeal to many Democrats, publicly at least—was the thesis that if, after the liberal elements of the Republican party succeeded in nominating

Eisenhower, the Republican party should meet its sixth successive defeat, the party then might well fall completely into the hands of its "most irreconcilable and ruthless factions." And these groups, having lost all prospect of attaining legitimate power and responsibility, might "become entirely reckless in their actions." [4]

But while Lippman joined the issue for the independents and "eggheads" seeking special reasons for voting Republican, the mounting Democratic defections that supplied the Eisenhower margin of victory—estimated at one out of every four of Truman's 1948 supporters—were attracted by simpler appeals: the personal confidence Eisenhower inspired, and the angers aroused by the Korean conflict. Eisenhower's name, now a household fixture for at least a decade, and constantly burnished by successive achievement, was formidable. The Korean fighting, moreover, had millions of people in a great state of agitation. From its outbreak to Election Day, more than one million youths were drafted, and approximately one million additional reservists and national guardsmen were called to active duty. Inevitably this aroused serious discontent. One reservist who was interviewed summed up the feeling by expressing resentment at "having my life upset for a war that isn't getting anywhere." And a San Francisco woman who was asked how she was voting replied: "They just called my husband back into service. Need I say more?" Out in the Middle West, the same sentiments echoed. "I am against this idea that we can go on trading hills in Korea indefinitely," observed one Truman voter who shifted to Eisenhower. "We've got to end it one way or the other. My boy is in the Air Force. Naturally I want peace, but if it's a war that we're in, then let's fight it with everything we've got. If it's not a war, then let's get out of there." [5]

And so in the national mind Eisenhower was pictured as a leader who stood ready to repudiate the insecurities of the national mood. His military experience, overlaid now with a reputation for profound interest in such civil affairs as education, was reassuring. It convinced people that here was a man whose skill would be useful in disengaging us from the Korean conflict with an honorable peace, and that here also was a military leader who could be trusted. At the same time Eisenhower also appeared to be a man who stood ready to repudiate the insincerities of modern politics. Having lived apart from politics, moreover, he escaped many liabilities of the traditional presidential candidate, whose career moves largely in the convoy of one major party or the other, and is accordingly handicapped by the mistakes of that party. When the Democrats tried to place Eisenhower on the defensive by saying he belonged to a depression party, this was an important factor in helping the general to throw off the criticism. Even so, there is impressive evidence that the principal issue favoring the Democrats was fear of another depression.[6]

With Korea taking the front center stage in the debate on foreign policy, and Europe actually receiving little attention from either Eisenhower or Stevenson, a device conceived late in the campaign had a dramatic impact. In a simple statement—"I shall go to Korea"—Eisenhower pledged that if elected he would personally visit the Korean front with a view to sizing up at first hand the alternatives available to us. Since Ike had accused the administration of having no plan to end the war, this appeared to suggest that here at last was a possible way to end a struggle that had disrupted millions of lives and promised to disrupt more. At once the Democrats countered this proposal with the charge that it was a cheap trick to win votes and "to play politics with peace." But again it is doubtful that these accusations affected the confidence of those who saw in Eisenhower a leader who could bring peace.

Only one real crisis turned up in the campaign, and this one threatened serious consequences. It involved the disclosure by a Los Angeles newspaper of a campaign fund of some $18,000 placed, by several of his campaign backers, at the disposal of Senator Richard Nixon for political expenses. So alarmed were some Republicans in their first reaction to this disclosure that even the staunchly Republican New York *Herald Tribune* declared editorially that Nixon should be dropped from the ticket and a new running mate selected. And at one point Eisenhower himself appeared ready to drop the vice-presidential nominee. But after several conferences he declared that Nixon would have to "come clean as a hound's tooth," and thereafter the nation settled back for a few days.

Then in a half-hour broadcast Nixon presented his case, claiming that he himself had experienced no personal gain from the fund set up for political expenses, and pledging that those who had subscribed the fund were the beneficiaries of no special favors. In the course of his telecast, which, judging by the response, found widespread sympathy and understanding, Nixon bounced himself and his party out of a difficult position through a masterful use of the TV medium. In detail he recounted his entire life—working as a boy with his four brothers in his father's grocery store, the difficult time that he and his wife had after they were married: "Pat doesn't have a mink coat, but she does have a respectable Republican cloth coat and I always tell her that she would look good in anything." And he wound up by reminding his audience: "It isn't easy to come before a nationwide audience to bare your life as I have done. . . ."

Reaction was instantaneous. Republican national headquarters received 400,000 telegrams and fan letters commending his performance. From California Nixon sped eastward, joining the Eisenhower train at Wheeling, West Virginia, where he was embraced by a misty-eyed presidential candidate, while other members of the entourage looked on, visibly moved, and all agreed that for emotional voltage this was the high point of the campaign.

Amazingly, the published polls gave few indications of the triumph that was in store for the GOP.[7] George Gallup, though indicating Eisenhower's strength in his American Institute of Public Opinion polls, was ever cautious. "Continuation or acceleration of the trend to Stevenson, reported in earlier surveys, would give him a majority of the popular vote. . . . [His chances] depend on winning a three-to-one ratio of the undecided or non-committed votes." Louis H. Bean declined to make a prediction on the ground that there were "too many factors involved for which there were no statistical analyses," and the New York *Times,* in its seventh and final pre-election survey based upon the combined judgments of its state correspondents, said the day before election that the outcome was "highly uncertain." No doubt because of the 1948 election, when the experts were so roundly wrong, caution became the byword of all those joining the quest for the inner mysteries of ballot behavior.

Later, no doubt, while listening, as Mr. Dooley says, for "th' thrillin' news fr'm th' first precinct iv th' foorth ward," the experts must have wondered why they had been so timid. For some of Eisenhower's most spectacular gains came from relatively low-income areas and territory that had been predominantly Democratic in the last five presidential elections. Among minority groups the most conspicuous place where the Republican candidate failed to make appreciable gains was in the Negro wards. And here Stevenson ran extremely well, capturing some 71 percent of the two-party vote in the Negro wards of major metropolitan areas, bettering even the record of Franklin Roosevelt.[8]

Well financed, the Republican campaign of 1952 was organized to move with two forward speeds, one operated by the Republican national committee and its subsidiary affiliates of the regular Republican state central committees and county organizations; the other by the National Citizens for Eisenhower, an organization formed to bring Ike the nomination and used after the convention to enlist the support of independents and Democrats.

With Arthur Summerfield of Michigan in charge of the pros (he became chairman of the national committee after Eisenhower's nomination), and Walter Williams, a mortgage banker of Seattle whom

Eisenhower privately called the "greatest salesman in the world," in charge of the amateurs (Citizens for Eisenhower), the "great crusade" did not lack organizational enthusiasm. As anticipated, conflicts did emerge, as they always do, between the regular team and the auxiliary shock troops. But noticeably after Robert A. Taft met with Eisenhower in New York in September, the two organizations began working better in harness, and while never functioning as one big happy family, the two succeeded better in this respect than their counterparts in the rival Democratic camp—the Democratic national committee and subsidiaries, and the Volunteers for Stevenson.

What the cost of the 1952 campaign eventually was is anyone's guess. Certainly it was high. Senator Paul Douglas, a Democrat, estimates that the two parties probably spent in the neighborhood of a hundred million dollars in the grand total of their election efforts, while others set the sum at around eighty million. Some idea of the costs involved can be had from the fact that Eisenhower delivered forty major addresses which were televised, and the prevailing price for a half-hour (full network of 65 stations) was $32,000. (Today's full network is 160 to 185 stations, and costs over $60,000.)[9]

Probably the bulk of even the most dejected followers of Taft, who vowed they would never vote for Eisenhower after Taft's defeat at the Republican convention, did so spiritedly on Election Day. But not all was forgiven the supporters of General Eisenhower, and this may have been costly in the GOP congressional races. Basil Brewer of Massachusetts, publisher of the New Bedford *Times,* and leader of the Taft forces in Massachusetts at the Republican convention, struck savagely at Henry Cabot Lodge, Eisenhower's pre-convention manager, when he ran for re-election to the United States Senate. Brewer not only supported the Democratic candidate John Kennedy, but also contributed to his campaign fund.[10] (Lodge lost to Kennedy by 70,000 out of two and a half million votes.) Elsewhere there were other Republican defections, but like frost boils in a pavement, most of them were easy to repair, at least for the current campaign, and did not crack open the party across the nation.

Whether another Republican would have won still stirs debate. The polls in the pre-convention period indicated that Taft would lose to Stevenson or Kefauver. Some, however, believe Taft would have driven to victory; they point to his win in Ohio in 1950 by a margin of 450,000 votes.[11] But Joe Martin adds his own epilogue on the slim congressional victory that went with Eisenhower's personal success: "I don't think we would have won if Eisenhower had not headed the ticket."[12]

All conjecture aside, it is apparent that Eisenhower's lack of strident partisanship was an important factor in his victory, and the way he wound up loping far ahead of his Republican ticket indicates something of the personal dimensions of the result. In only five states did Republican Senators run ahead of Eisenhower—Flanders in Vermont, Ives in New York, Thye in Minnesota, Williams in Delaware, and Knowland in California. (Knowland won both the Republican and Democratic nominations and was without major party opposition in the general election.)

To the personal factor, of course, must be added what has been called "the tide of revulsion" running against "Trumanism." This was surely helpful in upending the voters who still felt jittery about voting Republican.

One year away from its centennial anniversary, the Republican party was back in power. And now the eccentric orbits in which parties and politics travel would move again under Republican rule after an interruption of twenty years. Would it take just one Republican administration to make the New Deal secure, as Sam Lubell predicted? Or was there a Republican majority, as Louis Harris searchingly asked? [13] What were the Republican prospects?

The Republican party was out of power for nearly a quarter of a century, while the nation was undergoing profound changes. Both major parties also underwent severe change, along with the nature of the party system in our country. The decline in patronage has long been realized, but its secondary effects have probably not been fully appreciated. In New York, out of 82,000 state positions there are only 100 appointments the governor may make that lie outside the merit system; in Michigan the number is 107 out of 40,000; and out in California, where there are some eighty thousand state positions, there are only 64 appointments over which the governor of the state has a completely free hand. Obviously there are ways of increasing this number of appointments, by getting around merit system requirements through temporary appointments and other expedients. Yet patronage has steadily dried up. And an undoubted consequence of this is that it has conditioned candidates for public office to think in terms of personal machines, personal followings, individual campaigns, and less strongly in terms of party organization. Thus, while many an old-time Republican shakes his head at the candidacies of men like Warren, Dewey, Youngdahl, McKeldin, and others, and tends to regard the bipartisan appeal of these figures with a critical eye, the fact remains that changing conditions in political life have compelled candidates to build a majority out of broader beams than a party organization affords.

What is true of the states, of course, has been perhaps even more true of the patronage possibilities of the federal government. For after eighteen months in office following the victory of 1952, only 2,500 patronage jobs were found for deserving Republicans, and precious few after that. The number of patronage appointments stood at about 15,000 in May, 1956. And Senators and Congressmen were candidly acknowledging that the likelihood of a changed situation was very remote. (Even Joe Martin remarked that he had more patronage jobs to fill when he was minority leader than he had as Speaker of the House.) The sudden introduction to this stone wall of patronage resistance was a bitter pill for Republicans to swallow. But it was a condition building over a period of many years.

No one would contend that the merit system should be scrapped for a return of the spoilsmen. But both parties—Republican and Democratic—do have a stake in seeing that a reasonable number of public posts are available as incentives for strengthening political organization. Perhaps what is indicated is a tighter merit system that is really based upon merit for the great majority of federal, state, and local positions, but which leaves out a generous number of policy positions at the top, along with certain routine positions, where character is perhaps a more important requisite.

Again, no one would seriously claim that a return to wholesale political replacements in the public service is desirable. But far more than a few thoughtful people have questioned whether the indiscriminate extension of the merit system at some levels has produced enough improvement in the public service to compensate for the risk of further atrophy in the ranks of party organization. The problem would seem to be acute for the Republican party.

For some time now it has been apparent that, in place of the little personal-power relationships of party leaders mustered among precincts and wards, there seems to be growing a power structure based upon mass consent and support. Increasingly public-relations and advertising men have figured in political campaigns. And this is a circumstance that provokes many misgivings. The importance of the advertising or public-relations man to the party leaders cannot be underestimated, for these professionals have become expert in the use of mass media. As one figure puts it, "they must not only be able to think in multi-dimensional terms of radio, television, newsprint, minority group publications, labor publications, trade journals, foreign language papers, and the like, but additionally they must be able to determine how television, for example, may or may not be superior to the use of radio spot announcements in a particular situation." Is it likely, for example, that on a sunny summer Saturday or Sunday the radio will be a better way to reach the voter than television? The advertising man obviously must also know the ways and means to greater effectiveness in the use of direct mail, ads, posters, and the whole elaborate assortment of tools at his disposal.

Admittedly party leaders require technical assistance from the advertising profession. Leona Baxter, wife of Clem Whitaker, co-partner in the famous Whitaker and Baxter team that has functioned so skillfully for the American Medical Association, for Richard Nixon's 1950 senatorial campaign, and in several other California political campaigns, puts it this way:

> It's because the public relations profession and its allied professions know something about presenting abstract ideas in attractive form, to masses of people who are too occupied with their daily lives to think analytically on their own account, that the average man today is in a better position to know more about the trends of human affairs than ever in history.

No doubt from the standpoint of communicating effectively, this is a competent statement of the problem as the advertising expert sees it. But beyond the rim of this cozy explanation about how the average man is to be fed his pre-digested political pabulum, there are some treacherous traps.

Some years back—1946—a little volume called *How to Win in Politics* was published that well illustrates the pathway to these traps. Noting in orthodox fashion the commonplace idea that "advertising will sell a million tubes of toothpaste at 35 cents, while an unadvertised toothpaste twice as good, selling for 10 cents, will go out of business," the author argues that personality must be sold by advertising the same way. "Advertising tailored to the needs of politics," the author says, "can reshape the whole history of campaigning"; and somewhere a little further along, as if by way of apology, he adds: "Advertising, after all, is infinitely better in the long run than bribery or murder"! The overriding lesson presented here, and elsewhere by scores of others, is that the real secret of campaigning is to be as nonpolitical as possible. And so the real intention is to depoliticize a candidate—a method which, we are reminded constantly, "has been here for some time now, it only remains for candidates to use it." [14]

There are, of course, certain short-run strategic advantages in merchandising candidates by blurring partisanship, particularly when the party is numerically in the minority. But while most will agree that the national interest demands at times that all rise above party, a party must still have intellectual meat and muscle, and exaggerated emphasis upon personalities along with conspicuous blurring of the issues will not build a durable party. It may lead to the entrapment of votes in one or more campaigns, but the long-run consequence will mean enfeeblement of the party symbol.

If a party is to symbolize the hopes and aspirations of its followers, there are other sober misgivings that arise out of this trend that offers the advertising lair as successor to the politician's den. Certainly the increased reliance upon advertising and public-relations experts tends to heighten their role in campaign direction at the expense of party hierarchial leadership. Befogged by the arguments put up by public-relations men about the effectiveness of one appeal rather than another, the higher councils of political parties frequently give in completely. In California, for example, Whitaker and Baxter insist upon complete control of all campaign expenditures. Elsewhere, firm control of campaign policy direction by party leaders is becoming increasingly difficult.

Obviously it would be a mistake to argue that the capabilities of an advertising agent are less than or his judgments are not so sound as, those of a party leader. But the public-relations man does tend to discredit the party professionals as "buggy-whip" salesmen, insisting that the secret of party success lies in the methods of successful marketing research and that his guild has the answer. And inevitably the development of mass media has hastened this trend that has taken much of the former leadership from party leaders and placed it directly in the hands of those who follow an aerial route to communicate with the party rank and file. The danger here is that the development, training, and apprenticeship of the leadership process will shrink and the energy force that goes into the struggle for leadership succession at the precinct, ward, county, city, state, and national level will be seriously diminished. Patronage as a cartilage builder in political organization is already fading fast. Now the transfer of power from the party professionals to the advertising archers brings threats from a new direction. For it promises to dry up much of the heady enthusiasm that flows from decision-making and other responsibilities long exercised by the politician. And here we need to take a hard look at the Republican politician.

Many years ago David Lloyd George said that what America needed most was not more statesmen, but more politicians. Implicit in this statement is an uncommonly slippery matter to articulate. Somehow, despite many flat denials, a broad chasm grew up over the years between the business world and the rank-and-file Republican professionals—the Republican politicians. Many businessmen have a certain contempt for the party professionals, and have never shown that they really appreciate what the problems of running a campaign actually involve. A large body of the professionals, on the other hand, have no love for the businessman. Yet businessmen do hold a certain enchantment for them, though they may grumble about how unappreciative he is as they scurry about helping him win elections. In a sense, some of this gulf between businessmen and party professionals is probably symptomatic of the growing pains of a nation headed toward a classless middle-class society. But for a party of a conservative coloration, like the Republican party today, the political partnership of the businessman and the party professional is a relationship of a critical nature.

Many businessmen within the Republican party, of course, are the professionals—the party leaders. Yet in the ranks of the Republican professional organizations, particularly in the cities, there are large numbers of salaried employees, with no entrepreneurial status, whose allegiance to the Republican party has long been taken for granted. Standing somewhere in the pyramid of thirteen million white-collar workers are the bulk of the professional millwrights in the Republican party. And the ability of this group to recruit interested followers in sufficient depth is basic to the future success of the Republican party. For the white-collar groups have been the largest-growing body in our society. It is to this group that the party looks for the maintenance of contact with many workers in society in the lower middle-income group, who have either maintained some hereditary tie to the Republican party, are independent, or have rejected other political ties to come over to the GOP. And if the loyalties of this group should shift elsewhere politically, it would be a hard blow to Republican prospects.

Clearly the steady upthrust of the new middle class in American society has been our vigorous answer to the challenge of collectivists that our system is static and due to collapse. And the very climb from hard-pressed circumstances has taken many of these groups into the Republican party, where their continued loyalties will depend on the promise of the party to raise standards of living, create new occupational opportunities, and to utilize the abilities of an ever-increasing class of trained men. Elsewhere, many people making the transition from factory worker to white-collar status "could not be brought into the Republican party in one move . . . but they could be brought to take a stand 'above party' and to vote for a nonpartisan general." [15] And having been brought this far their future relationship with the Republican party can very well be affected by the professional leadership they encounter. It is precisely because the middle groups have become so formidable in our society that the Republican party should be concerned about the health of its politicians.

The politician is an important figure in stabilizing the power relationships of a community. And since our pressure groups in America are becoming more and more like European parties in their organizational structure, the health of the party politician should be of even greater concern to us.

Politicians, of course, may be the agents of pressure groups, but politicians with an active loyalty to party organizations can moderate the more strident power-thrusts of interest groups. And there is in this connection an implicit truth in the elder Lodge's remark that "the business man dealing with a large political question is really a painful sight." The same idea has been put forward more delicately yet more persuasively in a recent number of the *Harvard Business Review* by a lawyer and former Republican governor of Massachusetts, Robert Bradford. In his plea, "Politicians are Necessary Too," Bradford says:

> There are many instances in which a business has been damaged beyond repair when turned over to politicians. The consequences of turning over the government to executives intent on running it exclusively like a business may be less obvious, but equally disastrous. In one sense politics might be said to be the profession of compromise, and in this respect as well as by training and approach perhaps all agree that business executives and politicians are two different kinds of animal.[16]

In line with Bradford's observation, it may be noted that many modern business structures have lost part of the interpersonal character of business in an earlier era, and that the responsible politician perhaps should be used as the practitioner in the domain of politics more extensively than the businessman. Clearly, as James Pollock reminds us, "We cannot exalt and enthrone the citizen without at the same time utilizing the politician."

Both parties, of course, are subject to the forces that C. Wright Mills speaks of when he argues that politics and political life are becoming increasingly depersonalized. And in this environment it is easy to see why the advertising man has leaped ahead to serve as the political strategist for "those who know what they want, but don't know how to get it," as one spokesman of the profession puts it. But the depersonalizing of politics would seem to be a more serious matter at the moment for the Republican than for the Democratic party. For it further weakens leadership at the local level. Candidates come and go in a political party, but the politician stays on and he does develop an interest in holding the party together. And since he does not have the patronage of an earlier day to dispense and many pow-

ers he formerly held have now passed to other hands, the state of
health of the politician takes on a new significance.

Organizationally the strongest stroke for Republican fortunes today is manned by the new leaders of America's fast-rising suburbs.
Here the prodigious influx of white-collar groups has bulged the ballot box with sufficient Republican majorities to shrink the long leads
of the Democrats in the major metropolitan centers.

In the four heavily populous suburban counties surrounding
Philadelphia—Bucks, Chester, Montgomery, and Delaware—Professor Janosik finds not a single election district (there are a total of
608 election districts in Delaware, Montgomery, and Chester alone)
where the Republican party is unorganized. Here there is keen competition for any organizational vacancy no matter how minor, and "it
is not unusual to find as many as twenty Republican workers at the
polling place on election day." [17]

What the firepower can be from these suburban counties hits
home if we look at recent elections. Philadelphia produced the
brightest major metropolitan showing of Democratic presidential candidate Stevenson in 1952. The Friendly City gave him a majority of
more than 160,000 votes. But "the Democratic tide stopped at the
borders of the city." For when the suburban votes were thrown in
from the four surrounding counties, Stevenson left "the Philadelphia
region with a shrunken lead of 20,000." Statewide, 142,000 of the
269,000 Republican plurality came from the same suburban source,
and in 1950 the same four counties provided 51,000 of the 86,000
plurality received by the Republican gubernatorial candidate. Surely
the suburban rising has shaken the confidence of the Democratic high
command in their ability to carry the large industrial cities handily—
a fact confirmed by former Democratic chairman Stephen Mitchell,
who frequently commented on the tendency of Democrats to change
their registration, as well as party sympathies, when they roll out
into the suburbs.

But the growth of the suburbs, unfortunately, has tended to obscure the fact that in the older parts of cities there has been a tendency to neglect political leadership or to be unsympathetic to the
need for holding beachheads in all areas of the community. And an
unhappy consequence of this policy, if continued, would be to encourage the feelings that lead to charges that the Republican party
is a "class" party. Admittedly, a much larger proportion of the upper-
income groups are located in the Republican party. But it is not a
"class" party, nor should it be. Moreover, as Angus Campbell and
his associates reported in their painstaking survey of 1952: "There

is no group that belongs exclusively to one or the other party. Each may be said to represent the entire American public."

Taking stock of their position at mid-passage in the twentieth century, the Republicans can find comfort in the new role of the suburbs and in the fact that the white-collar workers who are overtaking labor groups in numbers seem destined to become the largest single social group. Because the great cities, long New Deal strongholds, have risen only slightly in population, while the suburbs have sprinted ahead with an astonishing growth, the promise of the suburbs as "a new center of political gravity" has stirred much conjecture. Three-fourths of the population increase in the New York-New Jersey-Connecticut metropolitan region between April 1, 1950, and January 1, 1954, occurred outside the twenty cities with more than 50,000 inhabitants. And while the same twenty largest cities held 81 percent of the region's population in 1920, their share by 1954 was only 68 percent. In Chicago proper there was a decrease of 76 precincts during 1953, brought about by slum clearance, construction of superhighways, and other factors, while the suburbs had an increase of 60 precincts.

In 1952 at least five of the nation's ten largest metropolitan centers yielded Republican suburban pluralities that were larger than Democratic pluralities in the cities. But this was hardly brought about, as Louis Harris suggests, by the fact that Mr. Eisenhower was a liberal internationalist. For in 1950 Senator Taft's thunderous re-election to the Senate scored as strikingly impressive margins in Ohio suburbs as Eisenhower did in 1952. Actually the Republican triumphs in the suburbs seem to have been inspired more by economic considerations than questions of foreign policy, though the latter may have been a factor among some independent voters in 1952.

Harris himself, though thoroughly persuaded of the tremendous power of the new suburban groups, answers the question "Is there a Republican majority?" with: "Not yet." But despite this commendable caution, it is still easy to err on the side of overoptimism in grading the potential Republican yield in our fast-climbing suburbs. While these areas embrace substantial numbers at the upper end of the middle-income group, it is well to note that they are also mixed areas and increasingly they have attracted workers—sometimes called "blue-collar workers" who live out and work in—workers who have left the older, more congested parts of metropolitan areas for new homes, but still work in factories located in cities. Initially, Republicans have made gains here.[18] This is confirmed by Democrats like Richard Moloney, the party boss of Louisville, Kentucky, who complains that when a worker moves out and gets a mortgage on his house, the Democrats can no longer count on his vote. Actually, the movement away from the older, more compact, congested areas of the cities out to the fringes and suburban areas has weakened the hold of the boss and has helped to unstring the old deliverable majorities of certain heavily Democratic areas of the cities. And the rising prosperity, particularly among skilled workers, has been more important in cutting some voters adrift from the Democrats.

But however promising the GOP yield from the suburban acreage, certain elements are not to be ignored. Both the mixed character of these areas and the fact that the more congested suburban patches may ultimately become urbanized should be fair enough warning that no suburban solidarity for Republican candidates can be casually assumed. Moreover, the vast majority of home owners in these areas will be quick to feel any ups and downs in the nation's economic health. In Pennsylvania an official of the Delaware county planning commission estimated that 99 percent of the houses purchased were mortgaged, and in a Montgomery county housing development with 143 single homes selling for between $13,000 and $15,000, 142 had been financed partially or entirely. Whether such indebtedness will make the suburban voter more sensitive to economic fluctuations, and in turn be quickly reflected in voting behavior, is a question not yet tested. But it is one that the Republican party cannot welcome as a test, and it is one that should spur the party toward policies designed to make the nation's economy as depression-proof as possible.

Today too many Republican leaders are still far from the uplands when it comes to adjusting to the new mass industrialism and liberal capitalism that the early organizers of the party helped lay the foundations for a century ago. And some will never make the grade. Soberly and prophetically, a native of Ann Arbor, Michigan (Washtenaw county, where the first Republican platform was framed and the first Republican ticket nominated), laid the truth of the matter on the line two months after the disastrous defeat of 1936. In a lead article for *Atlantic Monthly*, "As Michigan Goes," he said:

> If the Republican party loses Michigan for good, it has lost the nation for good. Because it leads in newer techniques, Michigan is worth watching. As Michigan goes economically, socially, politically —so goes the nation. The brand of conservatism with a chance of winning Michigan and the rest of the union back to the Republican party requires elements beyond wealth in the present and fear of the future. We Republicans rely too much on musty adjectives, socialistic and communistic. Out the window too should go the obsession for

high tariffs. But if the party tarries too long in not reexamining its foundations, the pillars of freedom set in the cement of indissoluble union eighty years ago, there will be more need for a wailing wall than a loudspeaker under the oaks at Jackson.

Twenty years away from this article, with a Republican in the White House but the national legislature in Democratic hands, Republicans would be well advised to take another long look at Michigan. Talking things over in 1955 after the sorriest showing in fifteen years, state political leaders were shaking their heads: "The party is at the lowest point in my memory," remarked one leader from Oakland County, while Edward Wilson, son of Defense Secretary Charles E. Wilson, said: "I suppose I should talk like a politician and say things aren't as bad as they really are, but what's the use. We're at a low ebb. . . ." In two discouraging elections that had seen the Democrats take the governorship for the fifth time, elect a United States Senator and two members to the state Board of Regents and make serious inroads in the township elections, Republicans were far from agreement as to what was the cause. One former state senator felt his party had made a serious mistake in distributing literature in the campaign to elect supreme court judges and state education officials which charged that "The CIO bosses are trying to brainwash our children." "When are we going to learn," wearily asked another Republican leader, "that Union members interpret our intemperate attacks on CIO officials as attacks on the Union as such?"

Others were not so sure: "It's time we stopped coddling the labor leader," snapped blunt-spoken Wilson. "He'll never support us anyway. We should bypass the labor leader and make a direct appeal to the worker." [19]

Meanwhile, as Michigan Republicans scrambled to scrub off the "party of wealth and privilege" label hung on them by the Democrats and the CIO, the rest of the GOP members across the nation could watch the struggle going on in this state with renewed interest. For the debate here is very similar to that of other political battlegrounds. And there is hard-headed realism in the statement, "As Michigan goes, so goes the nation," for if the Republican party does not wish to become a class party, it must show a willingness to adapt itself to the newer techniques of the industrial society that the party itself played such a dramatic role in creating.

Looking elsewhere, there are still other unerasable and unreassuring facts for the Grand Old Party. Leonard Hall called the shot on the gravest: "We crossed into the big cities just once [between 1940 and 1952], and that was in the 1946 congressional election when we won 246 seats in the House. We never deluded ourselves either. It was because of meat. . . . The size of the Republican majority was due primarily to the meat shortage which the Truman administration handled so badly. When housewives had to line up in major cities for two or three hours simply to buy meat, the results were bound to show at the polls and they did." [20]

Of 123 congressional districts that have been immovably Republican since 1940, only six are completely urban. And looking at the 1954 congressional elections where the winning candidates won by less than five percent of the two party vote, we find 63 Republican and only 31 Democratic marginal districts.

Significantly, while General Eisenhower was winning the Presidency with 55.4 percent of the popular vote in 1952, the Republican party could muster a majority of no more than three seats in the House, and a margin of one vote in the Senate, where the lineup was 48 Republicans, 47 Democrats, and Wayne Morse. Yet when Truman captured the Presidency with only 49.9 percent of the popular vote in 1948, becoming perhaps the only winning presidential candidate to run behind his congressional ticket, the nation gave the Democratic party a majority of 90 seats in the House and sent 54 Democrats to the Senate for a margin of six.

For other evidence of party preferences, there is little comfort in the public-opinion polls. George Gallup tells us that approximately 67 percent of the electorate identifies itself with the Democratic party. In their 1952 study the Michigan Survey Research Center found that 47 percent of those interviewed "thought of themselves as Democrats as compared to 27 percent who thought of themselves as Republicans." These figures are a bit deceptive when one recalls that the superiority of Democratic registration in areas like California has not prevented the Republican party from winning handily and freezing out the Democrats to the extent that they have had only one governor in fifty years. But the fact that three-fifths of the voters are inclined to identify themselves as sympathetic to the Democratic party does stand as a broad gauge of public sentiment—one disturbing to the analyst of Republican registrations. Nor is the immediate evidence of increases in GOP registration reassuring.

In Pennsylvania, the Republican registration lead dwindled from one million in 1953 to five hundred thousand at the end of 1955, the lowest ebb in registration since 1938. One year earlier, George M. Leader, a New York county chicken farmer and political unknown, captured the governor's office by 279,000 votes, a ten thousand larger majority than Eisenhower's 269,520 in 1952. In heavily Republican Bucks county, Pennsylvania, Democrats elected their first assemblyman in eighty years. And in Indiana county the Democrats won their first victory since 1833.

In Baltimore, where the Democrats have long held a three-and-a-half-to-one registration advantage over Republicans, the Democrats appeared to be holding this margin of superiority by showing an over-all increase of nine percent in a ten-month period between June 1954 and March, 1955, the Republicans gaining eight percent.

Too early to identify as a trend, and by no means identifiable as a possible development favoring one party or the other, is the rise of independent registration in some areas. In several Massachusetts counties there are more "decline to state" or "independent" registrations than Republican and Democratic registrants combined. And in the state as a whole, which is evenly divided—750,000 registered Republicans and 750,000 registered Democrats—there are approximately one million two hundred and fifty thousand registered voters who give no party designation. Mercer county, New Jersey, also has more independent registrations than combined Democratic and Republican registrants. Conceivably the rapidly growing white-collar groups could be accounting for part of this increase in independent registration. And it may well be that among such voters are many former Democrats who prefer faceless voting labels for the moment—but for how long, and how many Republicans are among them? And can either party take comfort in an increase in independent registrations which lowers participation in the primaries?

Like that of the independent voter, the role of women in Republican voting has been of increasing interest and has led to wide-swinging conjecture. George Gallup, in an unpublished study reported by the American Heritage Foundation, estimates that about seventeen million six hundred thousand women voted for Eisenhower, while twelve million seven hundred thousand supported Stevenson. And on this basis he concludes that of 30,900,000 men who voted in 1952, only 52.7 percent cast ballots for Eisenhower, while 58.1 percent of the 30,300,000 women who voted supported Ike. Some studies in localized areas also purport to show that women supported Eisenhower in greater proportions than did men in 1952.[21] But against this view and that of Louis Harris, who contends that women "reacted more sharply" than their husbands to all major issues in the 1952 elections, and that this was "what turned a close race into an Eisenhower runaway," there are some sharp dissents. Angus Campbell found no such dramatic difference between the sexes—a judgment in which Samuel Lubell concurs.

Just what the true measure of difference was between the sexes, if there really were variations, is difficult to assess. Moreover, any difference that might be revealed could also be more related to personality factors for a specific candidate rather than a preference for a political party. Thus, if we take polls indicating candidate preferences by sex over a period of several years, Thomas E. Dewey runs consistently behind with female voters in contrast to his support from male voters.

On party registration, the evidence is too scanty and local factors make generalizations on national trends quite impossible. In Baltimore, for example, it is interesting to note that female Republican registrations exceed male registrations for the first time (43,000 to 39,000), while in Minneapolis a Minnesota public-opinion poll suggests that women are more attracted to the Democratic Farmer-Labor party than are men, by approximately a ten percent margin.

All in all, the fact cannot be obscured that the Republican party nationally is a minority party, and very much in need of that added burst of speed—that magical fifteen-percent increase that Eisenhower said could hold the party in power forever. Despite the suburban shock troops that have aided the Republican cause mightily in recent elections, and the additional support that Sam Lubell identifies as "the temper of the country . . . so clearly in favor of moderation," the pathways to full Republican control of the national government are beset by many obstacles.

That Republicans can capture the Presidency has been demonstrated. But congressional control is quite another matter. And too often dismissed is the fact that legislative gerrymandering, long heavily discriminatory against cities, is likely to undergo Democratic surgery in the years ahead. Certainly if the steadily increasing Democratic registration in the farm-belt states over the past twenty years, and stepped-up political organization, brings legislative control to the Democrats in some of these states, the bulge that Republicans have long enjoyed because of congressional districting favorable to their interests is going to be dented.[22] And in Pennsylvania, for example, which lost three seats in the last congressional redistricting in 1951, and where the Republican legislature labored to make Democratic areas absorb as much of the loss as possible, it should not be forgotten that in 1954 the Democrats took control of the House at Harrisburg and came within 60 votes of gaining a tie in the State Senate.

While not a situation of alarmist dimensions, the reapportionment threat is sufficiently grave for Republican prospects in the House to speed far greater organizational efforts at local, county, and state levels. If a grim reminder is needed that the Democratic threat to Republican control of some state legislatures which hold the key to congressional redistricting is not an imagined fear, the

1954 general elections are painful examples. For that year the Democrats gained 500 legislative seats among the 48 states, more than at any time even during the high tide of the New Deal years (the Republicans gained just five seats in 1954 among state legislatures). In Connecticut alone the Democrats picked up 42 seats, and also added 20 each in Montana and Michigan.

Partly in disbelief, some Republicans look to the South in the hope that recent Democratic defections in Dixie will become chronic and that a two-party system, like prosperity, lies just around the corner. But as the Marines are fond of saying "the impossible takes a little longer." The South is being integrated with the rest of the nation, that we are agreed. But at what speed, and with what immediate impact on the party system we are not so sure.

In 1952, Eisenhower polled 48.9 percent of the major-party vote cast in the "Solid South," the highest popular vote of any Republican presidential candidate except Herbert Hoover's 52 percent over Al Smith in 1928. Encouraging also in 1952 were the Republican congressional victories in Virginia and North Carolina. But despite such a widely heralded event as the election of a Republican Congressman from Florida's First district in 1954 (the first since 1878), and the capture of one seat in Texas, or the unusual local success in Georgia, where two Republicans were elected as county commissioners in Muscogee county out of a field of sixteen aspirants, the Republican future in the South is still filled with obstacles.[23]

In Louisiana, the 300,000 Democrats who almost delivered the state to a Republican presidential candidate for the first time since 1876 have preferred to remain presidential Republicans and settle the course of public affairs in the Democratic primaries. Even after the Eisenhower showing, and under the energetic leadership of a highly capable national committeeman (John Minor Wisdom) there are fewer than 6,000 registered Republicans. Here candidates are very hard to find, legal barriers are troublesome, and all in all Mr. Wisdom finds the prospects unencouraging.[24]

On policy matters another factor impedes Republican growth in the South. Is the conservatism the Republican party appears to stand for similar to that represented by conservative Southern Democrats? asks Douglas Weeks. On the race question the answer seems to be no. Nor does the acceptance of much of the New Deal-Fair Deal philosophy by Dewey and other Eastern leaders of the Republican party appeal to Southern conservatives. Yet the latter reject isolationism, and here is part of their dilemma in an era of party realignment.[25]

But the story across the South is not one of all dark shadows for the GOP. Strong Republican enclaves are appearing in Florida (Republican registration increased 40 percent between November 1952 and November 1953, and the GOP had an all-time-high legislative representation of six in 1955), which seems closer to becoming a bona-fide two-party state than any of its Southern neighbors. And even in Arkansas, the vote of a Republican gubernatorial candidate served notice that some unaccustomed winds blow on Election Day. Broadly stated, all competent observers are agreed that a fairly reliable number of Republican patches will soon begin appearing in the South. But instead of a movement of any great bloc into the Republican party, the more plausible expectation would be what Key calls "a spotted kind of development."

Many changes are prodding this development. From 1930 to 1950 the population of Southern cities of 50,000 or more increased at a rate three times that for the nation as a whole. The implications of this growth, of course—particularly the effects of industrialization —are bound to be felt in the political arena. Certainly they were in 1952. Donald Strong found that few Northern cities could "boast the improvement in Republican fortunes found in Mobile, Richmond, Dallas, Houston, and Atlanta." And since he found that Eisenhower's strongest support invariably came from wards and precincts in the upper-income white residential areas, while those top-heavy for Stevenson were without exception principally housing Negroes, he concludes that the most "fertile field for Republican expansion" lies in Texas and Florida. Both these states have few Negroes, hold large urban populations, expanding industry, many prosperous urbanites, and have "less tradition to shake off. . . ." [26]

Clearly the Eisenhower success in the South, which was "an exaggerated form of Presidential Republicanism," was quite unrelated to any desire on the part of Democrats who supported Ike to run Republicans for sheriff or county commissioner. Nor is real Republicanism likely to explode out of Presidential Republicanism on short notice. Democratic state leaders who supported Eisenhower had no intention of menacing their future. And no doubt this is what prompted Governor Kennon's request that a Republican congressional nominee pull out of the race in Louisiana in 1952. Presidential Republicanism can bring GOP victories in competing for the Presidency, it is surely helpful in sweetening campaign finance, and it should embolden an increasing number of brave spirits to shake off tradition and register Republican. But the protracted hangover from the Civil War is still a formidable barrier to full-blown Republicanism in the South. "When all the obstacles to Southern Republican growth are viewed together . . ." writes Alexander Heard, "one wonders

how the party can become a serious force in any southern state."
And yet there is little doubt "that much of the South is moving
closer to competitive party politics." [27] The South still has a sectional
role to play before it takes on a closer resemblance to the political
pigmentations of the rest of the nation. But industrialization, the
decline in the Southern Negro population, and the promise of increased education in moderating ancient prejudices are all bringing
it closer—though we should not forget that while the South is changing, the rest of the country is changing too. Probable Republican
gains in the South, therefore, may be offset by Democratic gains in
some parts of the Middle West.

Amidst the exciting period of party readjustment, the Republican
party, like the federal government as well as the Democratic party
and some of our great pressure groups, has experienced some central-
izing tendencies and has not remained unaffected in bureaucratic
growth. The national staff, a modest four salaried employees in the
middle thirties, now hovers around a hundred. Thus the quartet that
John D. M. Hamilton started out with in the 1936 campaign (Hamilton became an exception among Republican party chairmen by
being the first to receive a salary)[28] is a far cry from the headquarters
staff that Leonard Hall took command of in 1953. And what has
happened on the national scene has also had some counterparts at
state levels. In Michigan, where the state central committee employs
six full-time workers, one of the complaints has been that this working force looks woefully weak when compared with the GOP
counterpart in its sister state of Ohio, where the state central chairman draws $20,000 a year, and is aided by a full-time year-round
staff of 29 persons.

Whether Leonard Hall would agree with the judgment of James
Reston that "no modern chairman with a President in the White
House ever had it better," because General Eisenhower co-operates
and "leaves the fiddling to Mr. Hall," while the last two Presidents
were professional politicians "who liked to fiddle with the mysteries
of political patronage," is a debatable matter.[29] For in the final analysis Hall, like any party chairman, is still in charge of a "ramshackle
alliance held together by prayers and promises." [30] Though he may
have 125 on the payroll (expanded to 300 during campaigns), and an
organizational command chart as elaborately styled as the Pentagon,
with young men and women running divisions for women, farmers,
veterans, youth, television, radio, minority groups, newspapers,
magazines, and other categories, the same frailties and frictions that
inevitably give life to intra-party conflicts have also badgered the

present chairman. While notable improvements have been made in the South, where heretofore many GOP leaders held back the advance of the Republican party locally, absentee ownership still complicates the scene. For example, Perry Howard, a seventy-eight-year-old Negro lawyer who has lived in Washington, D. C., since 1921, still continues as the GOP boss and national committeeman of Mississippi, a role he has held since 1924.

Some of the more notorious of the old leaders in the South have been ignored in distributing jobs. What little patronage there has been to spread has gone to newer, more spirited leaders of the GOP, and occasionally to Eisenhower Democrats, who then changed their party affiliation to Republican. And some old-timers were subtly drawn out of the play by appointments which placed them under the Hatch act—a device designed to bring control to pro-Eisenhower men. But "caretaker Republicanism" is still a problem of the national chairman and one not completely resolved.

Forty years ago Victor Rosewater, Republican national chairman and the only Jew ever to be national chairman in either major party, remarked that "in the early days of President choosing," the process was as simple "compared to modern methods as kindergarten exercises beside a course in four-dimensional mathematics." [31] And he longed for a national organization adequate to meet the demands of party responsibility. Could he view today the bustling national headquarters, which one observer comments looks more like "the head office of International Business Machines' organization than a political headquarters," he would be quite unprepared for what he would see. For the times have influenced a new kind of relationship between our parties and the social structure. The decline of local bosses—the bosses who could not compete and organize on a wide scale—has been one factor in increasing the size of the bureaucratic party structure at the national level. Another element, of course, has been the nationalization of pressure politics and the competition of these pressure groups in party politics. At the last count there were forty-six international union headquarters in Washington, with a grand total of 6,478,000 members in the United States. Also a factor in the drift toward greater national party organization is what one observer refers to as the extension of the area of competition—a result brought about by the gradual decline of sectionalism.[32]

Collectively all of these forces have tended to emphasize the fact that elections may be increasingly won and lost in the national dimension. And while local considerations will continue to be very important, the tendency of our national political party organizations to compete in the national dimension before a national audience is taking us into an era that will bring new demands upon the parties. It means, of course, that the stimulus for organization, particularly in the soft spots, must come from the national level as parties bite right down into the lowest level of precinct organization to bring out the votes that may keep a state in the Republican column by the shade of a shadow. Admittedly many benefits will flow from an increased role of the national staff headquarters, particularly as effective measures are undertaken to stimulate party activity in areas where only paper organizations have existed. But there are many traps on the path of activating local party organization. Local party chieftains were amused but not impressed by the receipt of a plan from national committee headquarters intended for use in Maryland's Fourth congressional district during the 1954 campaign: "How to Organize a Hayride." (Maryland's Fourth is a heavily populated metropolitan district lying wholly within the city limits, and many of its narrow streets might have quite a difficult time accommodating a hay wagon.) Yet quite apart from human errors that shake confidence in the ability of a national staff to step into local campaigns, there are more serious questions that ought to be asked. Does the mountain of expensive literature that flows from party headquarters get the most mileage out of the dollar in recruiting party membership and building organizations? Moreover, at what point does further enlargement of a national party staff run the risk of drawing on resources that might be put to more effective use at the local level?

In its manpower bank, the Republican party found symbols of a new era as it readied itself for the 1956 campaign. Meeting at Denver, where all 48 state central chairmen convened in September of 1955, to breakfast with President Eisenhower, were 23 state party executives under the age of fifty. Of this group four were thirty-seven, one thirty-nine, and two forty. The youngest of all was only thirty-five. In a roundup for the New York *Times* one correspondent concluded his estimate of the GOP chairmen by saying that "most were intelligent; nearly all were capable, informed, and aggressive," and "only a handful among them could have qualified for the old-guard stereotype that dominated the GOP during its two long decades in the political wilderness after the 1932 defeat." [33]

Another indication of a faster backfield for the GOP came from James Reston. "Something has happened to the old party. It is hunting night and day for new young congressional candidates. It is conducting more surveys than George Gallup, and believe it or not it is even getting together a stable of eggheads to help it with its pamphleteering in 1956." [34]

Serving notice that the Democrats were no longer to have a monopoly on intellectuals, Mr. Hall himself said: "No sir. We are out looking for people who can write. We still haven't made our position clear on some of the major issues of the campaign. We're going to mobilize the people in the universities and elsewhere who can do the job." What Mr. Hall chooses to emphasize, of course, is the desire to recruit persons skilled in the art of the engineering of consent—those particularly adept at communicating with mass media in marching ideas across the stage of American politics. What he does not make is a bid to the intellectual or the thinker in policy matters. Nor is there a generous gesture from the party itself, seeking this type of person. For the theorist there is still a tendency toward hostility. Yet thinking men were not feared in the formative period of the Republican party, and Lincoln or earlier figures like Jefferson and Hamilton, from whom the party took much of its inspiration, were conspicuously good at using their minds.

Perhaps this resistance to the intellectual is in the process of being gradually overcome, but there is more than a grain of truth in the assertion that a large part of the leadership of the Republican party is anti-intellectual to the point of keeping out of its councils valuable human resources of men and women not only dedicated to the Republican party but often in key positions to keep a dynamic interest in Republicanism alive in the nation's intellectual centers. The problem is nowhere more cogently expressed than in a confidential report to national chairman Leonard Hall, submitted by Val Bjornson, Republican nominee for the United States Senate, after his defeat by Senator Hubert Humphrey in the Minnesota general elections of 1954. "One thing I'd like to say in closing," wrote Bjornson, a Phi Beta Kappa with a major in political science, a publicly elected state treasurer, and an editorial writer for the St. Paul *Dispatch:*

> What I envy about our opposition . . . is the host of vigorous recruits it gets from the intelligent, aggressive, devoted, college-trained age bracket. The "supply" seems non-ending for our Minnesota Democratic-Farmer-Labor ranks. There are such people among the Republicans, to be sure. But for the most part, they have good jobs in industry and the professions. What we lack is a devoted group of really sharp, intellectual young folks. . . . Why is there that lack among Republicans? The answer is an easy one, in my opinion. We have a generation reared to the adult level, knowing nothing but Democratic administrations nationally. On the average college campus—and the Humphrey machine is a college campus product here in Minnesota at our University, and at such institutions as Macalester College, St. Thomas, and Hamline—it has been "smart" to be a Democrat. One can almost hear these youngsters saying during recent years: "You wouldn't want to be a staid, old, stodgy Re-

publican, would you?" We need to get closer to the people in every particular; but for the "sinews of war" . . . we need aggressive, intelligent, devoted educated youth. And we need a structure that brings such a group right in with older party leaders. . . .[35]

Quite apart from the organizational matters confronting the Republican party after its victory in 1952, there was one monumental problem deeply affecting the party's future. On the minds of many as the Eisenhower team planned its key movements from New York's Commodore Hotel before the inauguration in January of 1953 was the question: What kind of a balance would the new President strike in congressional-executive relations? Would the Republican party move forward on the operating principle of a supercharged stewardship in line with the tradition of Lincoln and Theodore Roosevelt? Would the President maintain an "organic connection with Congress," or would Republican policy revert to an emphasis upon congressional rather than executive leadership?

Feeling his way cautiously, the President gave no clear-cut answer to this question for the first two years. On November 1, 1953, a year after Ike was elected, James Reston noted that like a constitutional monarch the President "has reigned but he has not yet ruled." On occasion he stood out as "president of all the United States," as he himself described it. And there were times when he stood out as both the leader of the nation and leader of a whole coalition of nations. But there were also many days when he looked like a reluctant politician, not yet in consolidated control of his party and still surveying the congressional field cautiously.

Initially the movements of the President in his relationship with Congress and with his own party were understandably slow-gaited. For Dwight Eisenhower, like U. S. Grant, entered the Presidency with a profound respect for Congress. This tended to obscure the early hand he did take in gently plugging his legislative policies. After the "congressional taunts and demands that used to come from Truman and Roosevelt," Eisenhower's co-operative approach made him appear to be taking a back seat on policy and legislation.[36] With a little more than a year in office behind it, the Republican party's Congress was given an over-all mark of 74 percent by *Congressional Quarterly* on supporting the leader of their party. This mark, as one writer puts it, conforms to a grade of about C-minus—comparatively not too bad a mark, considering that Harry Truman during his seven years got less than half of what he requested from Congress. Truman, however, apparently asked for a lot more than he thought he could get, on "the assumption that Congress would cut his programs in half," and in view of the broad appeal of the Eisenhower program to the American electorate, the C-minus Republican congressional support for the President's legislative program was not an auspicious start. It led, moreover, to gibes from the Democratic sector of Congress: "We'll have to save him from the Republicans."

Later the Republican batting average for supporting the President fell lower. Voting in the 84th Congress through May 3, 1955, Republicans on the average chose to uphold the President 64 percent of the time—showing less enthusiasm than in 1954, when they scored 74 percent. And on matters of foreign policy during this period, the Democratic opposition helped the President more than his own party did. On the eighteen roll calls dealing with foreign policy, the Democrats voted with Eisenhower 69 percent of the time, the Republicans only 62 percent.

While he pondered the political pile-up of contradictory pressures from his White House and congressional associates, and sought to reconcile certain inner conflicts of his own as well, Eisenhower warmed up slowly to the task of becoming a party leader. In the 1952 campaign he had obviously found it distasteful to support certain Republicans, including William Jenner of Indiana and Joseph McCarthy of Wisconsin. Yet he did not strike out against McCarthy, nor did he make overt moves to consolidate his position as party leader in his first two years. And right on into the midterm congressional elections of 1954 it was self-evident that the President struggled uncomfortably in the role of party leader.

Then as the midterm elections approached many political leaders, perhaps with the old adage of Jim Watson in mind—"There comes a time when every man must rise above principle"—began beating on him. At first the President did not take kindly to their advice. And on October 21 he appeared to take the White House out of election campaigning on the ground that it would be unfitting to lend his high office to partisan purposes. Yet within a week he was maneuvered into a direct contradiction of this stand. On October 28 the President said that some measure of campaigning might not be out of the question after all, and that there were certain conditions under which a candidate might look for a presidential pat on the back. But the next day his withdrawal policy was completely reversed by an announcement from the White House (October 29) that President Eisenhower favored the election of Republican candidates everywhere in the nation. So the President found himself in the position of supporting those who had served as a wrecking crew in Congress for the plans of his administration. And the effect of his endorsement was to leave the considerable crowd of Republican obstructionists "free to raise the magic Eisenhower name for election purposes after sabotaging the Eisenhower program." [37]

Obviously the result was not what the President had really intended, for his own sympathies were in the direction of selective praise, spoken at appropriate moments, well in advance of the election, for such candidates as Christian Herter, running for re-election as governor of Massachusetts, and Leverett Saltonstall, striving to be re-elected to the United States Senate from the same state.

Some legislators who had opposed the President steadily—like George W. Malone of Nevada, who in eighteen months voted against the President 35 times, and voted for his policies 31 times— contend that votes against the President are not necessarily against his policy. "The fight on the Senate floor is not for or anti-President Eisenhower . . ." says Malone, "the fight is whether the legislative branch is going to be a satellite just like it's been for twenty years. . . . After all, the Congress has to make the policy for the Republican party." [38] (Senator Jenner of Indiana struck the same theme when he charged that a "bureaucratic elite" in the United States was trying "to make a monarch of the President" or transform him into a Roman emperor.[39] The more likely explanation, however, is that the opposition encountered by the President was inspired partly by the fatal fascination of many Republicans for a weak executive, as well as uncompromising opposition to the direction of his policies. In this kind of setting, where a Republican President has been compelled to contend with opposition that sometimes has been close to one-half the membership of the GOP congressional wing, what of the future for the Republican party and its leadership? "President Eisenhower's hold on the country," as Professor Holcombe reminds us, "is not contingent upon his leadership of the Republican party, but his hold on the country is contingent upon his retention of the actual power to govern." And Presidents who have tried to govern without benefit of any organized partisan support "have never succeeded very well." [40]

Eisenhower's hold on the country survived Republican defeat at the polls in November of 1954 because in the eyes of his countrymen Ike stood for something more than the leadership of a major party. And the personal popularity of the President has continued to soar incredibly. (The Gallup poll of December 18, 1955, showed the country voting 3 to 2—higher than in 1952—in favor of the President, while a poll of December 25—also conducted by Gallup—indicated 75 percent of the American people approved his handling of the Presidency.) But the President's popularity and that of his

party in the middle 1950's were admittedly something very different
—a difference spelled out very well by the fact that Ike carried 297
congressional districts in 1952, while his party's candidates for Congress won only 221. Vice-President Nixon states the problem somewhat differently, but equally free of any "comforting vagueness" for
GOP partisans: "The Republican party is not strong enough to elect
a President. We have to have a presidential candidate strong enough
to get the Republican party elected." [41]

Certainly the Republican party can compete effectively for the
Presidency under present national party alignments. But it seems unlikely that the GOP will achieve congressional victories that are commensurate with the striking presidential victory of Eisenhower until
party realignments substantially raise Republican registrations
throughout the North and South.[42]

The problem of party management under these conditions is to
recognize frankly that we are on the verge of a political era that
has brought extensive split-ticket voting, a steadily increasing number of "decline to state" voters, and a growing number of independent voters in national politics. Since Eisenhower ran well ahead
of most of his associates on the Republican ticket, his was a personal triumph rather than an indication of a firm victory for the
Republican party. Moreover, the party that Eisenhower led to victory is not only a party with insufficient numbers to win handily
without Eisenhower, but it is also a party raked by factionalism
that can give even a leader with the prestige of President Eisenhower some difficult moments. Of basic importance for the journey
ahead, therefore, is the ability of the party to organize some of the
principal factions throughout the country so that when the party does
come to power in future elections the policy-determining branches of
the government can devise a legislative program and "make effective use of the power to govern." If recent experience is prophetic,
the Republican party will continue, for an unpredictable time, to
have difficulty in building congressional majorities.

But the problems are far from insurmountable. A President with
high-caliber leadership and capacity for government does not have
to depend solely upon his own party for the success of his administration. He can utilize both parties under the American party system. "For, as the head of the state as well as the head of the government, he can stand above the parties, when it suits his purposes,
without forfeiting his right to stand by one of them in whatever
properly belongs to the party." [43] In this role President Eisenhower
has excelled. Amidst a sea of disconnected partialities he has made
superb use of his gift for leadership in utilizing members of the op-

position party to drive through policies he has set for his own party but has sometimes lacked sufficient partisan support to put across. Eisenhower's achievements as a factional co-ordinator within his own party have been limited. But his talent for mediation between different groups and sections of the country has been impressive. And as the head of a party that may be called upon to govern in the future after winning the Presidency but not control, or at best a slim control, over the congressional branch, he has blazed a significant new trail for a new era of American politics. And the lessons of the Eisenhower leadership are important for the American party system, quite apart from whether the Republican party soon catches up to the Democratic party in registration, or whether the period ahead brings us to the point of dwindling majorities for either party at the congressional level, and in turn a situation calling again for greater utilization of members outside one's own party.

If Eisenhower has only imperceptibly contained the factional fires within his party in his first term, it is none the less true that his methods may have produced more than meets the eye. Criticized for not squaring off against McCarthy, he left no doubt about his feelings when he struck back at the Senator by saying that the paramount issue in the 1954 congressional elections would not be "communism in government" but "a progressive and dynamic program" that he himself would formulate and make clear to the country in due course. And while Democrats grew violent and many members of his own party became restive and impatient at the conduct of Senator McCarthy (which finally drew a vote of censure against him in the Senate, by a vote of 67 to 23 on December 2, 1954), Eisenhower still preferred to deal with the problem in his own way. Even McCarthy's attack of December 7, 1954, in which he apologized for having supported the President in 1952 and accused Eisenhower of being soft on communists, was ignored by the President. Apparently the belief upon which the President acted follows the sentiment of André Siegfried's *American Mid-Century:* "In the American environment demagoguery does not lead to revolution; it rather acts as a vaccine."

Even so, saddle sores have continued to develop over the direction of Republican leadership in the last three years, and the groups who are far from satisfied have given every notice of continuing the struggle. With admiring ardor, the right-wing conservative organ, *Human Events,* recently published the "frankly abusive" document against Thomas E. Dewey, issued during the pre-convention campaign of 1952 by Robert Taft's campaign chairman David S. Ingalls, which closes with a statement: "Until and unless Dewey and

Deweyism are crushed, our party can never win and America [can] never [be] made safe from the insidious efforts of the New Dealers, whatever the party label, to take us down the road to socialism and dictatorship." [44] Elsewhere a right-wing meeting of Republicans at Chicago on Lincoln's birthday in 1955 brought these remarks from Robert E. Wood, co-chairman of the For America organization (a group strongly isolationist and nationalist in character):

> The trouble is that Eastern Republicans and Middlewestern Republicans don't talk alike, don't think alike and don't act alike.
> All of us here despise Dewey, and there aren't many leaders east of the Alleghenies we do like.[45]

Obviously many party leaders share the opinion (but even Wood thinks third-party action unlikely—at least for ten years) implied in this statement. A poll of Republican county chairmen, for example, before the 1952 convention, indicated that the 3,000 county chairmen favored Taft over Eisenhower by two to one. William S. White capsulates the meaning of this division skillfully. "For two decades," he writes, "it [*the Republican party*] has sustained within itself a fierce struggle between hostile internal forces seeking an ultimate control." The GOP, as he now sees it, is two bodies, and has been so through four presidential elections. And the lesser of the two bodies, the "Orthodox" party, "is in a sense the greater." For it is the "Orthodox" party, he says, that has the "decisive" Republicans in most of the county courthouses, state houses, and in Congress itself. Only at the very top of the pyramid does the Orthodox party fail to control.

Philosophically the orthodox faction believes more in the congressional than in the executive form of government, and is far less inclined to make accommodations with the "political movement of the times." In the language of the courthouse corridors, the Orthodox wing holds the "pros," the non-Orthodox side the amateurs, and in the struggle for power the "pros" have been dislodged by the amateurs in the domain of presidential politics. But the "pros," while losing national conventions, have resolutely held their ground between conventions. White sees the present "tactical truce" between the Orthodox Republicans and the non-Orthodox wing as "fairly sound for extraparty affairs, but quite sticky in the intra-party sense." And the reasons are not hard to discern. The "pros" believe grimly in the true English parliamentary tradition—the duty of the opposition is to oppose. Madison Avenue, familiar terrain to the amateurs, is untrod land for most of the "pros." Senator Knowland himself, the inheritor of the Taft mantle in the Senate, and leader of the "pros," has no press agent, "no 'public relations' and little or no talent for the techniques of the profession."

The "pros" believe in rigorous fiscal conservatism and the supremacy of business, though "big, big business" has now gone over mostly to the non-Orthodox side.

Where the battle will lead in the struggle for the mind of the party will take more than a little time to tell. But when we speak of the mind of the party it is well to ask, what mind and what body? For the general thought-stream of that great body of the citizenry making up the Republican party inclines to more progressive policies than the more vocal reactionary elements of the party indicate. The more conservative leanings of a large segment of Republican leadership have tended to obscure the progressive orientation of the great majority of Republican voters. One way of demonstrating this feeling is to comb through all of the public-opinion polls on Republican presidential possibilities between 1935 and 1946.[46] During this period 31 names were recorded by the polls of the American Institute of Public Opinion as being the choice of some discernible percentage of a national cross-section of Republican voters. Of these 31, only six were at one time or another sufficiently attractive to GOP voters to receive the support of 30 percent or more of the Republicans responding to a preferential poll. Interestingly, these leaders were Landon, Vandenberg, Dewey, Willkie, Stassen, and Eisenhower, all spokesmen in a general way for the more progressive forces within the party.

When Republicans were asked in 1937 if the Republican party should be more liberal, more conservative, or about the same as it was in the 1936 election campaign, 59 percent said it should be more liberal, 24 percent felt it should be about the same, and only 17 percent thought it should be more conservative. On the subject of winning or losing with a more liberal candidate, the Republicans responded even more decisively. Asked if they thought the Republican party had a better or worse chance of winning in 1940 if it nominated a liberal candidate and adopted a liberal program, 77 percent felt that chances would be better with a liberal candidate, and only 10 percent thought they would be worse, while 13 percent thought they would be about the same. No poll, of course, should be accepted uncritically, but if one runs through similarly designed polls over the years, the results all lean in the same direction.[47]

Amidst the gloomy fears about sneaking socialism, of which a favorite example is that low-cost public housing will lead us into a socialist economy, it is useful to be reassured by the judgment of a very distinguished Republican on this subject. He said:

It is no reflection on private industry to say it never has and probably never will meet the serious low-income problem in the housing
field. The general theory that the government has the duty to assist
the lowest income groups has been accepted . . . in every state in
the Union, and it does not involve any departure of principle from
that which we have pursued during the 150 years of the life of the
Republic.

That Republican was not a socialist, nor a leftist of any stripe. His
devotion to our system of private enterprise was as complete and unassailable as one might find in the breadth of the land. The speaker
was the late Senator Robert A. Taft of Ohio, an advocate of federal
public housing, and the words above were spoken at the last public appearance Taft made before his death in the summer of 1953.
Surely it is difficult to believe that Taft was either an advocate of socialism or a man to be deceived by a socialist technique.

It would be highly inaccurate to say that the disgruntled dino-
saurs on the extreme right of the Republican party are about to be
taken into camp by the more moderate progressive elements of the
party. The President's announcement of February 29, 1956, that
he would be available for another term dampened the hopes of some
right-wingers. But there is still a strong sediment of opinion in the
party that Representative Hugh Scott was speaking of on a cold November night in 1948 as he watched the election returns come in
from his command post as chairman of the national committee. The
surprise Truman victory he had suspected all along, for his pleas to
his partisans of the Eightieth Congress to set their sights on broader
social legislation were disregarded. Partly in bitterness and "partly
in frustration and partly also in hope," reported Joe Harsch of the
Christian Science Monitor, Hugh Scott turned to the little group of
reporters who were waiting with him until the end and said: "It's a
good thing. Those mastodons wouldn't listen to me. They had to learn
their lesson. Now maybe they'll go out and pass some good social
legislation." [48]

Granted the inevitable uncertainties of the political battlefield,
it is unquestionably true that the Republican party is deployed on a
broader front than it has presented to its opposition at any time
since Teddy Roosevelt held aloft his standard of the Square Deal.
"The really big story here," reported James Reston as Congress got
under way in January of 1956, "is that the Republicans are offering a program and a budget that are so New Dealish and internationalist that Bob Taft, if he were here, would feel betrayed." Moreover, he added, "There is probably not another capital in the world
today where the party in power has offered a program which meets

with such widespread approval from one end of the political spectrum to the other." [49] Stretching from right to left, the Republican party offered the promise of a balanced budget along with a record of substantial encouragement to big industry, while on the left-wing salient it was pressing for social security for more people, higher minimum wages, public health measures, farm aid, and a greater school-building program.

The difficulties of estimating the direction of our party system make it far from easy to be sure-footed in judgments. But surely the taunts from many Democrats during the past twenty years, stereotyping Republicans as persons mentally mildewed, turn out to be reckless. For the fact is, of course, as David Butler shows us in a stimulating piece—"American Myths About British Politics"—that "the public picture of government always lags behind reality." Too many people and too many textbooks, he tells us, still see the British party struggle in terms of the thirties, when actually it has changed profoundly. Since 1945, Butler reports that the British parties have never clashed fundamentally on the principles of the welfare state or on basic issues of foreign policy. Moreover, with the tacit consent of the Labor party, "nationalization has receded from the center of the political scene." [50] Judged by the extremists, there is an unbridgeable gap between the socialists and the orthodox conservatives in England. But judged by the responsible leaders in both parties, and evident still more in their performance in office, this gap is small.

Elsewhere, a related idea is expressed by Mr. Hugh Gaitskell, the new leader of the British Labor party, in explaining the reason for the Labor party's defeat in the summer of 1955. The defeat was brought about, he said, because the British working class has become "Americanized"; that is to say, it no longer seeks fundamental changes in society.[51] Actually there is encouraging evidence that our own unsystematic party system has transcended the pattern of European party conflicts, and we are evolving not *toward* socialism, but *past* socialism. And the observations of both Butler and Gaitskell hold an important object lesson for Republicans. For in the United States the steady climb of working groups has been tending to break down the underlying identity of interest between the prosperous and unprosperous groups. In a recent poll to determine opinions on which party can do the best job of keeping the country prosperous, George Gallup found that union members by a vote of four to three have more faith in the Democratic party. But he also found that skilled workers were about evenly divided, and that for the first time in a decade more people reported that good times in the immediate years ahead were more likely to be found under

Republican than under Democratic rule (38 percent thought that the GOP could best keep America prosperous, while 34 percent felt the Democrats most likely to bring about prosperity; 10 percent held there would be no difference, and 18 percent had no opinion).[52] In November of 1951 the same question found 29 percent of America's voters believing the Republican party could best keep the country prosperous, while 37 percent had more faith in the Democrats, with 19 percent feeling there was no difference and 15 percent having no opinion.

Clearly we are headed toward a society where there will be a reduction in the number of manual workers and an increase in administrative and clerical workers. This development, of course, is likely to produce a greater spread of party workers, and it may well bring new political alliances.

Where the party that is the more conservative of our two parties is to stand is not a matter to be resolved here, but a remark of one of the ablest party chairmen in recent Republican history, Will Hays, is not without relevance. In a famous comment to the motion-picture producers while head of the controversial Hays Office, he noted that in the presentation of a film the object should not be how high you can raise a hemline and get away with it, but rather how far you can lower it and still hold a man's attention.

In a sense here is the Republican party's challenge. Basically, as New York Attorney General Jacob Javits defines it for us, "the Republican party is committed to endeavoring to realize the ultimate in human satisfactions of which our economic system is capable through a competitive and private economy with government help and cooperation—but not domination." [53] It cannot outpromise the party of the New Deal-Fair Deal, yet it must hold the voter's attention.

Not all persons will agree with Senator Ralph Flanders that the strength of our two-party system lies in the fact that "they are administrative rivals rather than political rivals. Either is in a position to take over from the other without involving a complete and predestined change in the foreign and domestic policies of the nation." [54] But the fact is that these sentiments have broad currency throughout the land. And this is why the presidential office has become so prestige-laden in our system. For the chief executive is the fountainhead of administration. The real infighting these days is increasingly over the way our foreign and fiscal affairs, military establishment, farm policy, and protective and regulatory measures are handled.

Legislative measures, of course, generate heated contests that eventually condense into partisan differences in several areas. But the area of agreement is wider than meets the eye, particularly when the operations of Congress are examined at the committee level. As Walter Lippmann footed up these areas of agreement early in 1956 there seemed to be a national consensus among Eisenhower Republicans and the "main mass" of Democrats "on the principle of social security," acceptance of the idea that "consumers shall be protected against the unregulated impact of the open market," and acceptance by both parties of the principle—long regarded as heretical—of government intervention "with subsidies and controls into the free market for farm products." [55]

In other areas, such as power and resource development, housing, health, education, and highway construction, the Republicans who have generally followed the President have inclined toward subsidy measures designed to help and protect private enterprise, while the Democrats have less reluctance to use the government itself in such undertakings. But even here the lines are not always clear-cut between the parties, just as the tariff issue has again demonstrated. In the summer of 1955 at the Southern governors' conference, fourteen governors, all belonging to the party of Cordell Hull, "in something of a pet and panic," adopted a resolution protesting reductions in tariff rates on textiles and calling for limitations to be set on these products, particularly those from Japan. Only one governor—a Republican (McKeldin of Maryland)—remained faithful to the doctrine of unfettered trade.[56]

Essentially, of course, Republicans also argue that they stand for the welfare and protective measures of modern politics within the bounds of a balanced budget, whereas the Democrats stand more ready to apply government powers, and are not particularly worried about deficit spending. Yet both parties are basically committed to the Keynesian fiscal doctrine that calls for balancing the budget with a surplus in times of boom, a balanced budget without a surplus in reasonably good times, and an unbalanced budget without a surplus during a recession. The President's own administrative assistant for economic affairs, Gabriel Hauge, indicated administration acceptance of this principle in defining a dynamic conservative. Referring to an annually balanced budget, he noted that sometimes temporary "departure in the direction of a deficit may help increase purchasing power to offset contraction in the economy." [57]

Should the cloud of a recession appear in the midst of an industrial boom and unemployment climb, who can doubt that a Republican administration "will reverse the engines in order to have the Federal Government spend more money than it takes in"? [58] These are unusual times and they have thrown new challenges upon the adaptability of our party system. World War II brought us bipartisan or, more accurately described, "unpartisan" approach to foreign policy. The great depression, and demobilization fears from World War II, made us worry about making the economy depression-proof. Now for three years at the helm of the President's Council of Economic Advisers, the nerve center for feeling the pulse of the economy and making recommendations to head off recessions, we have had a man outside the President's own party—the distinguished economist, Arthur Burns, a Democrat who enjoys the complete confidence of the President. It is highly doubtful that this situation could have existed thirty years ago, or that it would have been conceivable to place such a post in the hands of a person not in the President's party.

Whatever the estimate of the bends and turns ahead, the real renaissance of the Republican party will not flow from the building of abstractions about conservatism. Policy is not found by sitting down, heads swathed in towels, and thinking. Political policy is not so much an intellectual concept as it is an element that grows out of the needs of groups of people. And essentially policy is the response to these demands, and a party's policy is its response to the demands made by the people it represents. The real work cut out for it, therefore, is with the building blocks of the political process rather than with the airy abstractions that are either obscure or intent on eulogizing concepts long since inoperative.

In a complex political order the Republican party may still claim that it is best equipped to champion the idea that in any society based upon majority rule there must be an abundance of energetic and gifted people who achieve eminence and power. And its aim, therefore, is not to hold down such persons to the level of those less talented and active, but to insure that each member of society shall have "an equal place at the starting line" to develop such faculties as he may possess. Positions of eminence and distinction, moreover, as secured by free competition, should carry with them certain overt rewards. And close to the heart of all Republicanism should be the conspicuous desire to articulate the case against mediocrity in an elaborately planned society. In the academic world, the academic man cries out against conformity, and lionizes the nonconformist. But in the business world, there is often a presumption that the nonconformist is a callow conniver. Obviously conformity is imperative in many areas of business, for straightening matters out in the public interest. But the ten million centers of initiative with strong regenerative powers in the United States are potentially creative mills, and here there is need for reaffirming a willingness to protect the nonconformist, just as this insistence is rightfully maintained within generous limits in the academic world.

At the very heart of orthodox Republicanism is a faith in the ability of citizens to comport themselves with a decent regard for the truth. We are, of course, not rid of the hate hucksters in either party, but there are signs that we may have entered an era of moderation and that our illogical party system has once more managed to curb the extremists within the major parties. "To blur and compromise conflicts before they become irreconcilable, and to deposit power in the hands of moderates" is the genius of our system. In this context the record of the Republican party is one of no mean achievement. In this setting the Republican party will continue to accommodate itself in new situations and changes as it labors to win over that additional fifteen percent Mr. Eisenhower spoke of when he said that if this could be mastered the Republican party could stay in power forever. And the Republican party faithfully reminds us, in the words of one of its sons: "Where people are the government they do not get rid of their burdens by attempting to unload them on the government."

Notes

CHAPTER 1

1 Several accounts refer to a call issued on February 28 and 29, but these dates are erroneous. It actually appeared in the Ripon *Herald* on March 1.

2 Ripon *Herald,* March 1, 1854. It has been suggested by S. M. Pedrick that a paid advertisement might have been the only way notice of the meeting could be given in a Democratic paper. See his article, "The Republican Party's Origin," in the Ripon *Press,* November 25, 1915.

3 A. J. Turner: "Genesis of the Republican Party," a newspaper article appearing in the Wisconsin *State Register,* Portage, Wisconsin (March, 1898).

4 See Minneapolis *Journal,* June 10, 1904; St. Paul *Pioneer Press,* June 7, 1912; and Los Angeles *Times,* April 20, 1914. See also *Leslie's Weekly,* June 18, 1896; *Evening Wisconsin* (Milwaukee), November 11, 1899; *Chautauquan,* November, 1897; and *Metropolitan Magazine,* August, 1900.

5 Andrew Wallace Crandall: *The Early History of the Republican Party, 1854-1856,* p. 21. (A doctoral dissertation of the University of Pennsylvania, published by the Gorham Press, Boston, 1930.)

6 New York *Tribune.*

7 William Harlan Hale: *Horace Greeley: Voice of the People* (New York, 1950), pp. 164-5.

8 The subsequent career of Bovay, incidentally, ran through into the next century. He was twice elected to the Wisconsin legislature as a Republican. "After serving in the Civil War as a major and as provost marshal of Norfolk and Portsmouth, Va., he returned to Ripon, where he remained for many years a political force. After 1880, he spent most of his time developing new communities along the North Dakota frontier, and returned to Ripon only at rare intervals; there are a few who still remember him—'a tall, spare figure, with stooping shoulders, long legs and flowing beard . . . walking with long steps and vigorous stride.'

"Toward the end of the century, Bovay returned to New York, a 'stately, dignified old gentleman,' and lived for several years in a quiet corner of Brooklyn. . . . In 1901, in search of health, Bovay crossed the continent to California, and on January 29, 1903, he died in Santa Monica at the age of 85." See Henry Christman, *Tin Horns and Calico* (New York, 1945), p. 316.

9 Furnished to the writer by his friend and collaborator, Wilfred E. Binkley, who was told of this experience by Mayor Mumaugh.

10 March 17, 1954.

11 Peter Allen Isley: *Horace Greeley and the Republican Party, 1853-1861: A Study of the New York Tribune* (Princeton University Press, 1947), pp. 52-3.

12 "Horace Greeley and the Working Class Origins of the Republican Party," *Political Science Quarterly,* 24 (1909), p. 469.

13 See P. Orman Ray: "Repeal of the Missouri Compromise"; and F. H. Hodder: "Genesis of the Kansas-Nebraska Act," in *Wisconsin State Historical Society Proceedings,* 1912.

[14] Detroit *Free Press,* July 7, 1854. Some time later (July 13), it might be remarked, the same paper derisively noted that the names for the petition to hold the Jackson convention were taken in part "from tombstones," in substantiation of which it noted a dispatch from the Grand Rapids *Inquirer* to the effect that "not a single name [is on the lists] which we recognize as a citizen of this county; our Postmaster says the same."

[15] July 19, 1854.

[16] We are indebted to Charles Deland for an account of the Jackson convention which was run in the *American Citizen* on July 12, 1854.

[17] According to the *American Citizen* (July 5, 1855) it was Dr. McNaughton who called the convention to order at Bronson Hall before Judge Baxter was made chairman *pro tempore.* This account must have been written in anticipation of what was expected to happen, however, since it appears in the July 5 *American Citizen,* the day before the convention actually met. The same anticipatory story has the hour of the meeting at Bronson Hall as 1 P.M., which obviously does not square with other accounts.

[18] *American Citizen,* November 8, 1854.

[19] July 7, 1854.

[20] Carrington: "Early History of the Republican Party in Ohio," *Ohio Archeological and Historical Quarterly,* 2 (1888), pp. 327-31.

[21] Isely: *Horace Greeley and the Republican Party,* p. 88.

[22] Herbert Agar: *The Price of Union* (Boston, 1950), p. 376.

[23] Crandall: "The Early History of the Republican Party," p. 21.

[24] William W. Doherty: "The Republican Party in Massachusetts," *New England Magazine,* 48 (1913), pp. 505-15. (It was Senator George Hoar who was asked by a newspaper reporter as he stepped off a train in Boston: "Have you heard of the death of William Lloyd Garrison, Mr. Hoar, and do you expect to attend his funeral?" "No, I do not, but I approve of it," snapped Hoar.)

[25] Quoted in *National Intelligencer,* November 20, 1854; and in *American Political Parties,* p. 207. Douglas thought it was a Know-Nothing rather than an anti-Nebraska victory.

[26] See Crandall: "The Early History of the Republican Party," p. 25.

[27] See Benjamin P. Thomas: *Abraham Lincoln* (New York, 1953), p. 146.

[28] See his "Abraham Lincoln Becomes a Republican," in *Political Science Quarterly,* 59 (1944), pp. 420-38.

[29] Arthur Bestor, David C. Mearns, Jonathan Daniels: *Three Presidents and Their Books* (University of Illinois Press, Urbana, 1955).

[30] See *The Collected Works of Abraham Lincoln,* II, edited by Roy P. Basler (Rutgers University Press, New Brunswick, 1953), p. 255.

[31] Binkley: *American Political Parties.*

[32] Binkley: *American Political Parties.*

[33] Binkley: *American Political Parties,* p. 155.

[34] *The American Party Battle* (New York, 1928), p. 68.

[35] "Our Two Great Parties: Their Origin and Tasks," *Political Quarterly,* 7 (1892), p. 523.

[36] *American Political Parties,* p. 186.

[37] Binkley: *American Political Parties,* p. 143.

[38] William G. Carleton: "Political Aspects of the Van Buren Era," *South Atlantic Quarterly,* 50 (1951), pp. 165-85.

[39] Carleton: "Political Aspects of the Van Buren Era," p. 184.

[40] *American Political Parties,* p. 213; "Horace Greeley and the Working Class Origins of the Republican Party," p. 588.

[41] New York *Weekly Tribune,* November 29, 1845, p. 5.

[42] "Horace Greeley and the Working Class Origins of the Republican Party," p. 474.

[43] A. N. Holcombe: *The Middle Classes in American Politics* (New York, 1940), p. 192.

44 Binkley: *American Political Parties,* p. 214.

45 November 8, 1854.

46 *The Disruption of American Democracy* (New York, 1948), p. 216.

CHAPTER 2

1 Quoted in Crandall: *The Early History of the Republican Party,* p. 49.

2 George W. Julian: "The First Republican National Convention," *American Historical Review,* 4 (1898), p. 315.

3 "The First Republican National Convention," p. 318.

4 New York *Tribune,* June 17, 1856.

5 Ruhl Jacob Bartlett: *John C. Frémont and the Republican Party* (Ohio State University Press: Columbus, 1930), p. 12.

6 *John C. Frémont and the Republican Party,* p. 2.

7 "Frémont," *Atlantic Monthly,* 66 (1890), p. 548.

8 See Fred Harvey Harrington: "Frémont and the North Americans," *American Historical Review,* 44 (1939), pp. 842-8.

9 Crandall: *The Early History of the Republican Party,* p. 153.

10 Crandall: *The Early History of the Republican Party,* p. 215.

11 See Roy Franklin Nichols: "Some Problems of the First Republican Campaign," *American Historical Review,* 28 (1922), pp. 492-6.

12 Quoted in Bartlett: *John C. Frémont and the Republican Party,* p. 67.

13 Carl B. Swisher: *American Constitutional Development* (Boston, 1943), p. 251.

14 Robinson: *The Evolution of American Political Parties,* p. 152.

15 Thomas, *Abraham Lincoln,* p. 178.

16 Quoted in Harlan Hoyt Horner: *Lincoln and Greeley* (University of Illinois Press, 1953), p. 138.

17 Horner, *Lincoln and Greeley,* p. 138.

18 *The Disruption of American Democracy,* pp. 202, 203.

19 Thomas: *Abraham Lincoln,* p. 198.

CHAPTER 3

1 Murat Halstead: *Caucuses of 1860: A History of the National Conventions of the Current Presidential Campaigns* (Columbus, Ohio, 1860), p. 149.

2 *The Convention That Nominated Lincoln* (Chicago, 1916). This was a lecture delivered by Professor Ray before the Chicago Historical Society on May 18, 1916, the 56th anniversary of Lincoln's nomination for the Presidency.

3 See Victor Rosewater's illuminating article: "Republican Convention Reappointment," *Political Science Quarterly,* 28 (1913), pp. 610-26.

4 For a careful and illuminating account of the jockeying for position at the convention, see Reinhard H. Luthin: *The First Lincoln Campaign* (Cambridge, 1944), Chapter 9.

5 See the account of delegate-at-large Thomas H. Dudley in his open letter to *Century Magazine:* "The Inside Facts on Lincoln's Nomination," 40 (1890), pp. 477-85.

6 Tracey E. Strevey: "Joseph Medill and the Chicago *Tribune,*" from "The Nomination and Election of Lincoln" in Paul M. Angle (ed.): *Papers in Illinois History* (1938), pp 58-9.

7 Later Joseph Medill claimed that he whispered to Cartter to swing to Lincoln and that Ohio would be handsomely cared for. Cartter in the aftermath said he had been promised the governorship of the Nebraska Territory. Whatever the incentives, however, Lincoln worked the situation out by appointing Cartter minister to Bolivia. See Reinhard Luthin: *The First Lincoln Campaign* (Harvard University Press: Cambridge, Mass., 1944), p. 166.

8 See Glyndon G. Van Deusen: "Thurlow Weed's Analysis of William H.

Seward's Defeat in the Republican Convention of 1860," *Mississippi Valley Historical Review*, 34 (1947), pp. 101-4. (Greeley was "malignant," complained Weed to Seward in a letter of May 20, 1860.)

[9] See Francis Curtis: *The Republican Party* (New York, 1904), 1, p. 360.

[10] Emerson David Fite: *The Presidential Campaign of 1860* (New York), p. 118.

[11] *Proceedings of the National Republican Convention, 1860*, p. 39.

[12] Lincoln to Judge Davis, October 27, 1860, quoted in Luthin: *The First Lincoln Campaign*, p. 170.

[13] Emanuel Hertz: *Abraham Lincoln: A New Portrait* (New York, 1931), p. 779.

[14] Quoted in Morison and Commager: *The Growth of the American Republic*, p. 637.

[15] Thurlow Weed Barnes: *Memoirs of Thurlow Weed*, p. 300.

[16] Albany *Evening Journal*, November 5, 1860.

[17] William E. Baringer: "Campaign Techniques in Illinois, 1860," *Transactions of the Illinois State Historical Society* (1932), 52, p. 276.

[18] Jane Grey Swisshelm: *Half a Century*, p. 172.

CHAPTER 4

[1] A. H. Bullock to Samuel Bowles (editor of the *Springfield* [Massachusetts] *Republican*), October 6, 1859. Banks Papers, Illinois State Historical Library.

[2] James A. Rawley: *Edwin D. Morgan: 1811-1883, Merchant in Politics* (New York: Columbia University Press, 1955), p. 110.

[3] Ralph M. Goldman: *Party Chairmen and Party Faction, 1789-1900: A Theory of Executive Responsibility and Conflict Resolution* (Doctoral dissertation, University of Chicago, 1951), p. 272. This admirable study is now being expanded for publication by Dr. Goldman of the Brookings Institution.

[4] Quoted in Harry J. Carman and Reinhard H. Luthin: *Lincoln and the Patronage* (New York: Columbia University Press, 1943), p. 3.

[5] J. Lothrop Motley to Grinnell, Nov. 2, 1860, quoted in *Lincoln and the Patronage*, p. 4.

[6] L. A. Warren: "Lincoln and the Patronage," *Lincoln Lore*, No. 290 (Oct. 29, 1934), quoted in Carman and Luthen, p. 5.

[7] See Winifred Audis Harbison: *The Opposition to President Lincoln Within the Republican Party* (Doctoral dissertation, University of Illinois, Urbana, 1930).

[8] Volume 24, November, 1879, p. 919.

[9] Burton J. Hendrick: *Lincoln's War Cabinet* (Boston, 1946), pp. 268-77.

[10] South Carolina's convention to consider secession convened December 17, 1860.

[11] See David Potter: *Lincoln and His Party in the Secession Crisis* (New Haven: Yale University Press, 1942), p. 47.

[12] Binkley: *American Political Parties*, p. 237.

[13] See Carman and Luthin, *Lincoln and the Patronage*, p. 12.

[14] Lincoln to W. Jayne, February 26, 1864.

[15] Quoted in E. Hertz: *The Hidden Lincoln* (New York, 1940), p. 299.

[16] See *Lincoln the President: Springfield to Gettysburg* (New York, 1945), Vol. 1, Ch. 14.

[17] See Goldman: *Party Chairmen and Party Faction*, p. 283.

[18] Theodore Roosevelt: *An Autobiography* (New York, 1913), p. 389.

[19] Carman and Luthin, p. 134.

[20] Salmon P. Chase: *Inside Lincoln's Cabinet: The Civil War Diaries of Salmon P. Chase*, edited by David Donald (New York, 1954), pp. 150-1.

[21] See William A. Dunning: "The Second Birth of the Republican Party," *American Historical Review,* 16 (October, 1910), pp. 56-63.

[22] "Lincoln and the Republicans," a review of Randall's *Lincoln the President,* in *The American Mercury,* 62 (1946), p. 375.

[23] Frederick W. Seward: *Seward at Washington as Senator and Secretary of State,* III (New York, 1891), p. 196.

[24] William Frank Zornow: *Lincoln and the Party Divided* (Oklahoma University Press, Norman, 1955), p. 3.

[25] Quoted in *Inside Lincoln's Cabinet,* pp. 260-1.

[26] The powerful group that formed against the President has been characterized by a multitude of labels. "Radicals" is the term most frequently applied, although Professor James G. Randall preferred to call them "Vindictives." Some historians have objected that the term "Radical" is a misnomer for this group, and that more appropriate nicknames would be "Reactionaries" or "Bourbons." John Hay, Lincoln's secretary, influenced by the French Revolution, called them "Jacobins."

[27] Chicago *Tribune,* December 17, 1863. Medill, however, never let up in his criticism of Seward, whom he blamed for keeping "a sponge saturated with chloroform to Uncle Abe's nose all the while. . . ." He also had a low opinion of Bates, whom he described as "a fossil of the Silurian era—red sandstone, at least—and should never have been quarried out of the rocks in which he was embedded." Joseph Medill to Schuyler Colfax, in O. J. Hollister: *Life of Schuyler Colfax* (Chicago, 1887), p. 200.

[28] Henry J. Raymond: *The Life and Public Services of Abraham Lincoln* (New York, 1865), p. 458.

[29] New York *Times,* February 23, 1864.

[30] See Zornow: *Lincoln and the Party Divided,* p. 51.

[31] It was Riddle, a member of the Radical group, who said when the 37th Congress adjourned in December, 1863, that Lincoln's support had come from only two men. See his *Life of Benjamin F. Wade* (Cleveland, 1888), p. 255.

[32] See Kenneth P. Williams: *Lincoln Finds a General,* Volume 2 (New York, 1949), p. 776. This study, while concentrating on military history, is very useful because it also sheds insight on the zones of leadership where the President's military and political problems converged.

[33] Zornow: *Lincoln and the Party Divided,* p. 88.

[34] Rawley: *Edwin D. Morgan,* p. 199.

[35] See the present writer's "New Light on the Nominating Process," in *Research Frontiers in Politics and Government* (Washington, D. C.: The Brookings Institution, 1955), p. 146.

[36] James H. Glonek: "Lincoln, Johnson and the Baltimore Ticket," *The Abraham Lincoln Quarterly,* VI (March, 1951), pp. 255-71.

[37] Zornow: *Lincoln and the Party Divided,* p. 100.

[38] Another on-the-scenes observer, however, was highly critical of the number of selfish interests represented. See Adam Gurowski: *Diary,* III, p. 253.

[39] Adam Gurowski: *Diary,* III (Washington, 1866), p. 329.

[40] New York *Sun,* June 30, 1889.

[41] Carl Sandburg: *Abraham Lincoln: The War Years,* Vol. 2 (New York, 1939), p. 591.

[42] Lincoln to Morton McMichael, August 5, 1864, in "Memorandum of an Interview with the Postmaster of Philadelphia," June 20, 1864, in *Complete Works of Abraham Lincoln,* X, p. 182.

[43] Zornow: *Lincoln and the Party Divided,* p. 160.

[44] Cited in Zornow: *Lincoln and the Party Divided,* p. 161.

[45] See Sidney Kaplan: "The Miscegenation Issue in the Election of 1864," *Journal of Negro History,* 34 (July, 1949), pp. 274-343.

[46] Zornow: *Lincoln and the Party Divided,* p. 210.

CHAPTER 5

[1] See David M. Dewitt: *The Impeachment and Trial of Andrew Johnson* (Macmillan, 1903), pp. 6-7.

[2] See Leslie H. Fishel: "Northern Prejudice and Negro Suffrage, 1865-1870," *Journal of Negro History,* 49 (January, 1954), p. 25.

[3] James G. Blaine: *Twenty Years of Congress* (Norwich: Henry Bill Publishing, 1886), pp. 118-21.

[4] This action was suggestive of the premature admission of Nevada in 1864 in response to Lincoln's need of Congressional support.

[5] See Gordon S. P. Kleeberg: *The Formation of the Republican Party as a National Political Organization* (New York, 1911), pp. 225-6.

[6] M. Ostrogorski: *Democracy and the Organization of Political Parties* (New York, 1902), Vol. 1, p. 374.

[7] Quoted by John F. Kennedy: "Ross of Kansas," *Harper's Magazine,* December, 1955, p. 43.

[8] See George S. Boutwell: "The Impeachment of Andrew Johnson," *McClure's Magazine,* Vol. 14 (1899), p. 175.

[9] See Olive Hall Shadgett: "A History of the Republican Party in Georgia," *The Georgia Review,* 7 (1953), p. 434.

[10] See Fishel: "Northern Prejudice and Negro Suffrage, 1865-70," p. 24.

[11] See Helen J. and T. Harry Williams: "Wisconsin Republicans in Reconstruction, 1865-70," *Wisconsin Magazine of History,* 23 (1939), pp. 17-39.

[12] August 13, 1868.

[13] May 13, 1867.

[14] See Fishel: "Northern Prejudice and Negro Suffrage, 1865-1870," p. 23.

[15] Others whose names were soaring about were: Ex-governor Andrew G. Curtin of Pennsylvania; Lincoln's first Vice-President, Hannibal Hamlin; two ousted members of Johnson's cabinet, James Speed of Kentucky and James Harlan of Iowa; ex-Senator John A. J. Creswell of Maryland; Senator Samuel C. Pomeroy of Kansas; and Congressman William D. "Pig Iron" Kelley of Pennsylvania.

[16] See William B. Hesseltine: *Ulysses S. Grant, Politician* (New York: Dodd, Mead & Co., 1935), p. 124.

[17] The expression stems from a speech by Ben Butler in the House of Representatives. Demanding stern measures with Southern terrorists, he brandished a nightshirt stained with the blood of a Mississippi carpetbagger.

[18] See Matthew Josephson: *The Politicos* (New York: Harcourt, Brace, 1939), p. 60.

[19] See Allan Nevins: *The Emergence of Modern America, 1865-1878* (New York: Macmillan, 1927), pp. 350-1.

[20] Quoted in Russel B. Nye: *Midwestern Progressive Politics* (East Lansing: Michigan State College Press, 1951), p. 44.

[21] See Wilfred E. Binkley: "West Pointers in the White House," *New Republic,* March 9, 1953.

[22] New York *World,* March 9, 1869.

[23] See Joe P. Smith: *The Republican Expansionists of the Early Reconstruction Era* (Chicago: University of Chicago Libraries, 1933).

[24] See Earle Dudley Ross: *The Liberal Republican Movement* (New York: Holt, 1919), pp. 17-20.

[25] July 11, 1872.

[26] See Irving Stone: *They Also Ran* (New York: Doubleday), pp. 8-10.

[27] New York *Tribune,* June 4, 1872.

[28] See Ross, pp. 147-9; Goldman, p. 349; McKee, pp. 147-8.

[29] See Ross, pp. 185-6, and Hesseltine, pp. 280-1. Their figures differ slightly. Other large contributors included the Philadelphia firm of Drexel and Childs;

the minister to Brussels, J. Russel Jones; a group of Indian traders; contractors; and the "whiskey rings" recruited by General McDonald in St. Louis.

[30] 1873, p. 78.

[31] Ross, pp. 198-239.

[32] See Ralph Korngold, *Thaddeus Stevens: A Being Darkly Wise and Rudely Great* (Harcourt, Brace: New York, 1955).

[33] See Hesseltine, pp. 169-79.

[34] See Albert B. Paine: *Thomas Nast* (New York: Macmillan, 1940), pp. 300-1.

[35] See Fred E. Haynes: *Third Party Movements Since the Civil War* (Iowa City, 1916), pp. 51-66.

[36] June 17, 1876.

[37] See David S. Muzzey: *James G. Blaine* (New York: Dodd, Mead, 1934), pp. 105-6.

[38] See E. Bruce Thompson: "The Bristow Presidential Boom of 1876," *Mississippi Valley Historical Review* (June, 1945), pp. 3-30.

[39] Quoted in Leon B. Richardson: *William E. Chandler, Republican* (New York, 1940), p. 179.

CHAPTER 6

[1] See C. Vann Woodward: *Reunion and Reaction.*

[2] See Harry Barnard: *Rutherford B. Hayes and His America* (Indianapolis: Bobbs-Merrill, 1954), pp. 414-19.

[3] John W. Burgess: *Administration of President Hayes* (New York, 1911), p. 65.

[4] Quoted in Schlesinger: pp. 17-18.

[5] See E. P. Cubberly: *Public Education in the United States* (Boston, 1920), p. 251.

[6] Quoted in Vincent P. De Santis: *Republican Efforts to Break Up the Democratic South, 1877-1892* (unpublished doctoral dissertation, The Johns Hopkins University, 1952), p. 6.

[7] See Barnard, pp. 474-5.

[8] See Muzzey, pp. 160-3. Also see James Ford Rhodes: "The National Republican Conventions of 1880 and 1884," *Scribners*, 50 (1911), pp. 297-306.

[9] See Robert G. Caldwell: *James A. Garfield* (New York: Dodd, Mead, 1931), pp. 283-92.

[10] July 17, 1880.

[11] Eugene V. Smalley: *A Brief History of the Republican Party: From Its Organization to the Presidential Campaign of 1888* (New York, 1888), p. 73.

[12] George F. Hoar: *James Abram Garfield* (Boston: Houghton, Mifflin, 1882), p. 36.

[13] See George F. Howe: *Chester A. Arthur* (New York: Dodd, Mead, 1934), pp. 135-7; also, De Santis, pp. 131-5.

[14] July 1, 1881.

[15] Before the railroads built branch lines, mail was delivered to rural areas by "Star routes." The carriers were under contract to transport the mails with "Certainty, celerity, and security," words which came to be represented in the contracts by asterisks, thus giving the service its name. Contracts were given at the discretion of the Second Assistant Postmaster General. Extensive frauds were revealed, and one of the prominent persons implicated was ex-Senator Stephen W. Dorsey of Arkansas, then secretary of the Republican national committee. See Howe, pp. 179-80.

[16] The Reapportionment Act of 1882 had increased the House from 293 to 325 members.

[17] Although there is little information about Donaldson, he is grouped with the others in the newspaper accounts.

18 See Howe, p. 261. Howe also mentions Elihu Root, whom the President had appointed United States Attorney at New York city, as among the Arthur managers. But Root's biographer denies that he took any substantial part in the campaign. See Phillip C. Jessup: *Elihu Root, 1845-1909* (Dodd, Mead, 1938), p. 163.

19 See Morrison (ed.): Theodore Roosevelt to Ann Roosevelt, June 8, 1884, *Letters of Theodore Roosevelt,* Vol. 1, p. 71.

20 See Herbert Croly: *Marcus Alonzo Hanna* (New York: Macmillan, 1923), pp. 122-3.

21 June 5, 1884.

22 Other candidates and their greatest votes: Joseph R. Hawley of Connecticut, 15; Robert T. Lincoln of Illinois, 8; William T. Sherman of Missouri, 2.

23 De Santis, pp. 183-4. On the fourth and final ballot Arthur received 149 of his 207 votes from the South.

24 Morrison, Vol. I, p. 71.

25 Francis Curtis claims that the first use of the term "Mugwump" was on June 20, 1884, in the New York *Evening Post:* "We have yet to see a Blaine organ which speaks of the Independent Republicans otherwise than as Pharisees, hypocrites, dudes, *Mugwumps,* transcendentalists, or something of that sort." And after the *Nation's* use of the term on July 24, 1884, it became commonly accepted. Curtis, Vol. II, pp. 146-7.

26 See David G. Farrelly: "Rum, Romanism and Rebellion Resurrected," *The Western Political Quarterly* (June, 1955), pp. 266-7.

27 Quoted in Odegard and Helms: *American Politics* (New York: Harper, 1938), p. 90.

28 Other candidates and their greatest votes: John J. Ingalls of Kansas, 28; Jeremiah M. Rusk of Wisconsin, 25; William W. Phelps of New Jersey, 25; E. H. Fitler of Pennsylvania, 24; William McKinley, Jr., of Ohio, 16; Joseph R. Hawley of Connecticut, 13; Robert T. Lincoln of Illinois, 3; Samuel F. Miller of Iowa, 2; Frederick Douglass of the District of Columbia, 1; Joseph B. Foraker of Ohio, 1; Frederick D. Grant of New York, 1; and Creed Haymond of California, 1.

29 The "do or die" position of Sherman reflected a growing bitterness in the Ohio delegation that would have important consequences in later years. It was rumored that the chairman of the delegation, Governor Foraker, was playing a double game and did not really have Sherman's interests at heart. On the other hand, both Hanna and McKinley were warm supporters of the Senator. One incident that helped to bring on the rupture between Hanna and Foraker, and was to bloom into a bitter rivalry years later when they were both in the Senate, was the criticism the governor made of Hanna for buying up the convention tickets of Negro delegates from the South—a widespread practice of the day. See Croly, pp. 136-7.

30 Quoted in Henry J. Sievers: *Benjamin Harrison, Hoosier Warrior* (Chicago: Henry Regnery, 1952), p. 9.

31 A popular Republican jingle of the campaign went:

> Yes, grandfather's hat fits Ben—Fits Ben;
> He wears it with dignified grace, Oh yes!
> So rally again and we'll put Uncle Ben
> Right back in his grandfather's place.

And the Democrats responded with: "Grandpa's pants won't fit Benny."

CHAPTER 7

1 *Forum,* 8 (1890), p. 676.

2 Edward Noyes: "The Ohio GAR in Politics from 1866 to 1900," *Ohio State Archeological and Historical Quarterly,* 55 (1946), pp. 79-105.

3 See George Gunton: "The Economic and Social Aspects of Trusts," *Political Science Quarterly,* 3 (1888), p. 387.

4 William G. Carleton: "Triumph of the Moderates," *Harper's,* 210 (1955), p. 32.

5 John D. Hicks: *The Populist Revolt: A History of the Farmers' Alliance in the People's Party* (Minneapolis: University of Minnesota Press, 1931), p. 406.

6 "How I got into politics was damn simple, young man. It was ten-cent flax!" A. C. Townley to the author, September 9, 1950.

7 Arthur M. Schlesinger: *The Rise of Modern America, 1865-1951* (New York, 1951), p. 150.

8 Russel Nye: *Midwestern Progressive Politics* (Michigan State University Press, 1951), p. 61.

9 For an admirable account of this episode see C. Vann Woodward: *Tom Watson: Agrarian Rebel* (New York, 1938), Chapter X.

10 See Kleeberg: *The Formation of the Republican Party as a National Organization,* p. 212.

11 See George Harmon Knoles: *The Presidential Campaign and Election of 1892* (Stanford: Stanford University Press, 1942), p. 52.

12 Detroit *Free Press,* March 27, 1955.

13 See George Harmon Knoles: *The Presidential Campaign and Election of 1892* (Stanford University Press, 1942), p. 54.

14 Quoted in James E. Watson: *As I Knew Them* (Indianapolis, 1936), p. 48.

15 See Hicks: *The Populist Revolt,* p. 253.

CHAPTER 8

1 Thomas H. Carter: "The Republican Prospects," *North American Review,* 158 (1894), pp. 421-2.

2 "A Theory of Critical Elections," *Journal of Politics,* 17 (February, 1955), p. 13.

3 See Nye: *Midwestern Progressive Politics,* p. 93.

4 *Autobiography,* p. 233.

5 See Belle C. La Follette and Fola La Follette: *Robert M. La Follette* (New York, 1954), Vol. 1, p. 117.

6 See *National Magazine,* 15 (1902), p. 405.

7 "The Party of Business," *Fortune* (January, 1949), p. 98.

8 See Herbert Croly: *Marcus Alonzo Hanna: His Life and Works* (New York, 1912), p. 94.

9 Marcus A. Hanna: "Industrial Conciliation and Arbitration," *Annals of the American Academy of Political and Social Science,* 20 (July, 1902), pp. 21-6.

10 *American Political Parties,* p. 329.

11 Nye: *Midwestern Progressive Politics,* p. 113.

12 To negate the power of minorities to exercise "constructive absence"; that is, to stop the practice of House members who refused to answer roll calls when present. On a quorum call Reed insisted on counting members who were present but not voting. This was vehemently opposed by the Democrats and led to Senator John T. Morgan's remark that Reed was a "White Czar"—an epithet which stuck.

13 See John Bemer Crosby: *Conditions and Events Whose Combination Forced the Nomination of William McKinley for President* (Chicago, 1896).

14 See Harold Gosnell: *Boss Platt and His New York Machine* (Chicago, University of Chicago Press, 1924), pp. 114-17.

15 See Elmer Ellis: "The Silver Republicans of the Election of 1896," *Mississippi Valley Historical Review,* 18 (March, 1932).

16 *Autobiography,* p. 276.

17 June 19, 1896.

[18] See New York *Times,* June 20, 1896.

[19] For an excellent account of the national committee factionalism between 1892 and 1896, see Goldman: *Party Chairman and Party Faction,* pp. 514-35.

[20] *Report of the Joint Committee of the Senate and Assembly of the State of New York Appointed to Investigate the Affairs of Life Insurance Companies,* 1905, p. 59. Hughes showed that the payments were not disclosed by satisfactory entries upon the companies' books, and that every effort was made to conceal them.

[21] "Myths of the Bryan Campaign," *Mississippi Valley Historical Review,* 34 (December, 1947), pp. 367-404.

[22] For further comment on Hanna as campaign manager, see Wilfred Binkley: "The Party of Business," *Fortune* (January, 1949), p. 102.

[23] *Politics, Parties, and Pressure Groups,* 3d ed., p. 187.

[24] V. O. Key: "A Theory of Critical Elections," p. 15.

[25] Key discounts the city-county tension theory advanced by William Diamond, in his "Urban and Rural Voting in 1896," *The American Historical Review,* Vol. 56 (January, 1941), pp. 281-305.

[26] Key: *A Theory of Critical Elections,* p. 16.

[27] *Masks in a Pageant* (New York, 1928), p. 306.

[28] *The Price of Union,* p. 615.

[29] Members of the original cabinet were John Sherman of Ohio, Secretary of State; Lyman J. Gage of Illinois, Secretary of the Treasury; Russell A. Alger of Michigan, Secretary of War; Joseph McKenna of California, Attorney General; James A. Gary of Maryland, Postmaster General; John D. Long of Massachusetts, Secretary of the Navy; Cornelius N. Bliss of New York, Secretary of the Interior; and James Wilson of Iowa, Secretary of Agriculture.

[30] March 2, 1898.

[31] Fred H. Harrington: "The Anti-Imperialist Movement in the United States: 1898-1900," *Mississippi Valley Historical Review,* 22 (1935), p. 218.

[32] *Congressional Elections: 1896-1944* (Oklahoma University Press, Norman, 1947), p. 24.

[33] These were Joseph R. Hawley of Connecticut; S. Woodward and George Snyder of Illinois; Jacob Russell of Maryland; D. F. Appleton of New York; Rush R. Sloan and D. C. Brinkerhof of Ohio; John Jacobs, Walter Laing, G. W. Holdstein, Edgar M. Levy, and Jacob Wyand of Pennsylvania; and George H. Bell of Rhode Island.

[34] Quay later said this effort served its purpose—meaning, of course, that he used it to bargain for votes from Southern delegates to support Roosevelt, his candidate for the vice-presidential nomination.

[35] John Morton Blum: *The Republican Roosevelt* (Harvard University Press, 1954), p. 16.

[36] Edward W. Townsend: "The National Republican Convention," *Harper's Weekly,* 44 (1900), p. 593. Italics added.

[37] Thomas Beer: *Hanna* (New York, 1929), p. 231.

CHAPTER 9

[1] Robert J. Donovan: "The Man Who Didn't Shake Hands," *The New Yorker,* Vol. 29 (November 28, 1953), pp. 88-110. This article, like Jim Bishop's book, *The Day Lincoln Was Shot,* is an exhaustive and exciting chronicle of an assassination.

[2] Czolgosz was sentenced to death and electrocuted in Auburn state prison 45 days after McKinley's death.

[3] See Kohlsaat: *From McKinley to Harding.*

[4] *The Price of Union,* p. 616.

[5] Goldman: *Rendezvous with Destiny,* p. 163.

6 *Our Times*, p. 71.

7 My father, then nineteen, was Governor Van Sant's executive secretary and was the embarrassed young man who mixed up the presidential and gubernatorial coats.

8 See J. Hampton Moore: *Roosevelt and the Old Guard*. Moore served in Congress and was also mayor of Philadelphia.

9 See Francis E. Luepp: "The Republican Convention," *The Outlook*, 77 (1904).

10 See James H. Eckels: "The Republican Convention at Chicago," *Review of Reviews*, Vol. 30 (1904), pp. 182-90.

11 *The Republican Roosevelt*, pp. 62-3.

12 Edward Lissner: "The Disruption of the Republican Party in the Middlewest," *North American Review*, 183 (1906), pp. 365-71.

13 *The Price of Union*, p. 646.

14 See "The Unsystematic American System," *Harper's*, 204 (1952), p. 22.

15 See Hermann Hagedorn: *The Roosevelt Family of Sagamore Hill* (Macmillan and Company, 1954).

CHAPTER 10

1 See Delman: "The Management of the Taft Campaign," *Review of Reviews* (1908), pp. 432-8.

2 Edgar E. Robinson: "Recent Men of the Stations of Sectionalism," *American Journal of Sociology*, Vol. 19 (1913-14), p. 446.

3 See Henry F. Pringle: *The Life and Times of William Howard Taft* (New York, 1939).

4 An excellent account of this entire period is in George E. Mowry: *Theodore Roosevelt and the Progressive Movement* (University of Wisconsin Press: Madison, 1946), p. 68.

5 See William Roscoe Thayer: "Chapters of Roosevelt's Life: Which Was the Republican Party?" *North American Review*, 210 (1919), pp. 222-34.

6 See George E. Mowry: "Theodore Roosevelt and the Election of 1910," *Mississippi Valley Historical Review*, 25 (1939), p. 524.

7 Arthur M. Schlesinger: "Tides in American Politics," *The Yale Review*, 29 (1939), p. 225.

8 Kohlsaat: *From McKinley to Harding*, pp. 161-2.

9 The regional character of this organization is suggested by its officers, who came from California, Oregon, Washington, Idaho, Montana, North Dakota, Nebraska, Kansas, Iowa, Wisconsin, Minnesota, Michigan, and Indiana.

10 Quoted in Victor Rosewater: *Backstage in 1912: The Inside Story of the Split Republican Convention* (Philadelphia, 1932), p. 33.

11 On this point, over which there is considerable controversy, see Belle and Fola La Follette: *Robert M. La Follette*, Vol. I, pp. 399-414. While La Follette's wife and daughter contend that accounts of his performance were distorted, many fair-minded witnesses, including William Allen White, have written that La Follette did himself irreparable damage by seeming to be incoherent and actually re-reading long sections of his speech.

12 The governors were Stubbs of Kansas, Osborn of Michigan, Aldrich of Nebraska, Hadley of Missouri, Bass of New Hampshire, Glasscock of West Virginia, Vessey of South Dakota, and Carey of Wyoming.

13 Borah estimated that 52 seats were stolen; a friend of La Follette fixed it at 50.

14 Quoted in Victor Rosewater: *Backstage in 1912*, pp. 182-3.

15 La Follette received 41 votes, Borah 21, Merriam 20, Cummins 17, Hadley 14, Beveridge 2, Hughes 2, and Gillette 1.

16 Bristow: *Fraud and Politics at the Turn of the Century*, p. 12.

CHAPTER 11

[1] See Harold Ickes: "Who Killed the Progressive Party?" *American Historical Review*, 46 (1940), p. 315. Italics added.

[2] Quoted in Pusey: *Charles Evans Hughes*, pp. 317-19.

[3] The details of Perkins's strategy to keep the Progressives from naming a presidential candidate until the Republicans had nominated, and then urging the Republican choice on the Progressives, is convincingly set forth in William Allen White's *Autobiography*, pp. 520-7; and in Harold Ickes's article, "Who Killed the Progressive Party?" *American Historical Review*, pp. 306-37.

[4] Quoted in Mark Sullivan: *Our Times*, p. 26.

[5] See Finley Peter Dunne: "Look at Harding from the Sidelines," *Saturday Evening Post*, 209 (1936), p. 25.

[6] See White: *Autobiography*, pp. 524-5.

[7] Quoted in Ickes: "Who Killed the Progressive Party?" pp. 325-6.

[8] Hughes himself, upon receiving news of the vote in Washington, told his wife: "That settles it. I shall not be nominated. I am going to bed." Pusey: *Charles Evans Hughes*, p. 327.

[9] The official canvass gave Hughes a 359-vote margin.

[10] *American Political Parties*, pp. 368-9.

[11] See letter in New York *Herald Tribune*, February 22, 1949.

[12] For careful narratives of this episode see Frederick M. Davenport: "Did Hughes Snub Johnson?—An Inside Story," *American Political Science Review*, 63 (1949), pp. 321-32; George E. Mowry: *The California Progressives*, Chapter X, "1916 and the Lost Election," pp. 247-77; and Pusey: *Charles Evans Hughes*, Chapter 22, "The California Incident," pp. 335-59. See also Davenport's article in *North American Review* (February, 1917), pp. 199-211.

[13] Davenport: "Did Hughes Snub Johnson?" p. 323.

[14] "Did Hughes Snub Johnson?" p. 326.

[15] See Josephus Daniels: *The Wilson Era: Years of Peace—1916-1917* (Chapel Hill, North Carolina, 1944), p. 466.

CHAPTER 12

[1] See W. A. White: *Autobiography*, p. 584.

[2] *Incredible Era, The Life and Times of Warren Gamaliel Harding* (Boston, 1939), p. 129.

[3] William Starr Myers felt the disclosure "especially fatal" to Lowden. See his *The Republican Party: A History* (Century, 1928), p. 443.

[4] See Bowers: *Beveridge and the Progressive Era*, pp. 516-17.

[5] H. F. Alderfer: *Personality and Politics of Warren G. Harding*.

[6] The closing time for filing was midnight, Friday. Harding's name was actually filed at 11:58 P.M., because in all the exciting movements of the evening no one remembered to change the signals for his representation in Columbus. It was withdrawn the next morning.

[7] See Daugherty's *The Inside Story of the Harding Tragedy* (New York, 1932), p. 36. "We'll form an alliance . . . first to beat Wood, for we can't allow Harding's vote to be too small, but we'll loan every vote we can until you [*Lowden*] pass Wood. The minute you do this, Wood is out of the race and all friendship on the floor of the Convention ceases between us—you understand that?" See also Mark Sullivan: *Our Times* (New York, 1935), p. 55.

[8] I am indebted for this information to my father, Charles J. Moos, who was present on the occasion and at the time was serving as Kellogg's proxy on the national committee.

[9] See the New York *Times*, January 9, 1932. One writer, however, insists that not until the Saturday afternoon recess of the convention, "was there evidence of intervention by Senator Penrose in behalf of Harding." See Wesley M.

Bagby: "The 'Smoke-Filled Room' and the Nomination of Warren G. Harding," *Mississippi Valley Historical Review,* 61 (1955), p. 669.

[10] Sullivan refers to it as "what politicians call a woman story." See *Our Times,* p. 64. Also see *Incredible Era,* p. 156.

[11] *The Future of American Politics* (Harper, 1952), p. 242.

[12] Bagby: "The 'Smoke-Filled Room' and the Nomination of Warren G. Harding," p. 572.

[13] June 13, 1920.

[14] E. E. Robinson: *The Presidential Vote: 1896-1932* (Stanford University Press, 1934), p. 21.

CHAPTER 13

[1] See Grant McConnell: *The Decline of Agrarian Democracy* (University of California Press: Berkeley, 1953), p. 55.

[2] See Jerry A. Neprash: *The Brookhardt Campaigns in Iowa, 1920-1926: A Study in the Motivation of Political Attitudes* (Columbia University Press: New York, 1932), p. 120.

[3] See *The Future of American Politics* (New York, 1952), p. 140.

[4] See William G. Carleton's comparison of the South with the farm belt states: "The Southern Politician," *Journal of Politics,* 13 (1951), pp. 215-31.

[5] See his *Statistics and Politics* (Memphis, 1919).

[6] Letter to the New York *Herald Tribune,* February 22, 1949.

[7] He shot himself on the evening of May 29, 1923, presumably because of his despondency upon hearing that Harding would no longer admit him to the White House and had suggested that Smith leave Washington for good.

[8] Mark Sullivan gives the Attorney General a sturdy word of support on this question. "Of one thing I am sure," he writes, "none of the money Jess Smith got to facilitate the American Metal case went into Daugherty's pocket. See note in *Our Times,* 7, p. 356.

[9] October 13, 1923.

[10] The phrase "back to normalcy" came about because Harding misread a speech prepared for him by Professor Jacob Hollander of the Johns Hopkins University. Dr. Hollander had written "back to normality." See Goldman: *Rendezvous with Destiny,* p. 285.

[11] For further comment on his attitude see George L. Grassmuck: *Sectional Bias in Congress on Foreign Policy* (Johns Hopkins Press, Baltimore, 1951), pp. 58-61.

[12] *Rendezvous with Destiny,* p. 286.

[13] See S. E. Morison and H. S. Commager: *The Growth of the American Republic* (Oxford University Press, 1942), II, p. 536.

[14] Quoted from an interview with Hugh Johnson, in Charles A. Beard: *Jefferson, Corporations, and the Constitution* (National Home Library Foundation: Washington, 1936), p. 79.

[15] See David Lilienthal: *Big Business: A New Era* (New York, 1953).

[16] Told by the President in a National Press Club speech. Quoted in Adams: *Incredible Era,* pp. 7-8.

[17] Adams: *Incredible Era,* p. 389.

[18] W. A. White: *Autobiography,* p. 623.

[19] *American Political Parties,* p. 351.

[20] See the present writer's *Politics, Presidents, and Coattails,* Chapters 2-5.

CHAPTER 14

[1] It was Coolidge's own idea that his father, a magistrate and notary public, administer the oath. Harry Daugherty, still Attorney General, had "grave doubts" about the legality of this oath, and so apparently did the Solicitor

General of the United States, James M. Beck. In any case Daugherty arranged to have Judge A. A. Hoehling, Justice of the Supreme Court of the District of Columbia, administer a second oath shortly after Coolidge moved into the White House. See Harry Daugherty: *The Inside Story of the Harding Tragedy* (New York, 1932), pp. 278-80.

[2] Quoted in Claude G. Bowers: *Beveridge and the Progressive Era* (Boston, 1932), p. 538.

[3] See William Allen White: *A Puritan in Babylon.*

[4] Merlo J. Pusey: *Charles Evans Hughes,* pp. 568-9.

[5] For a careful account of this movement see Kenneth C. MacKay: *The Progressive Movement of 1924* (Columbia University Press, 1948). On La Follette in the 1924 campaign see also Russel B. Nye: *Midwestern Progressive Politics* (Michigan State College Press, 1951), pp. 334-46.

[6] See Samuel J. Eldersveld: "The Influence of Metropolitan Party Pluralities in Presidential Elections since 1920," *American Political Science Review,* 43 (1949), p. 1196.

[7] See Reinhold Noyes: "The Restoration of the Republican Party," *North American Review,* 221 (1925), pp. 417-30.

[8] See William G. Carleton's excellent comparison of this region with the South in "The Southern Politician," *Journal of Politics,* 13 (1951), pp. 215-31.

CHAPTER 15

[1] *A Puritan in Babylon,* p. 294.

[2] See E. R. A. Seligman: *The Economics of Installment Selling* (New York, 1927), Vol. I, pp. 111, 117; Vol. II, p. 426.

[3] See "The Legend of Isolationism in the 1920's," in *Science and Society* (Winter, 1954), Vol. 18, p. 1. See also George L. Grassmuck: *Sectional Biases in Congress on Foreign Policy* (Baltimore: Johns Hopkins, 1951), pp. 32, 93, 162, 49.

[4] Statement of J. W. Good, Hoover's campaign manager, in New York *Times,* June 13, 1928.

[5] Baltimore *Sun,* June 12, 1928.

[6] Some unpleasantness developed in the convention because of the failure of Fess to mention the name of Theodore Roosevelt. Next day Fess said this was unintentional, then proceeded to deliver the presumably omitted passage.

[7] A full and discerning account of this convention and ensuing campaign appears in Roy V. Peel and Thomas C. Donnelly: *The 1928 Campaign: An Analysis* (Richard Smith: New York, 1931).

[8] See Herbert Hoover: *The Memoirs of Herbert Hoover: The Cabinet and the Presidency, 1920-1933* (New York, 1952), p. 199.

[9] "A Theory of Critical Elections," p. 4.

[10] See *The Memoirs of Herbert Hoover; The Great Depression, 1929-1941* (New York, 1952).

[11] *The Age of Reform* (Knopf: New York, 1955), p. 37.

[12] "A Reckoning of Twelve Years of Republican Rule," *Yale Review,* 21 (1931-32), pp. 647-60.

[13] New York *Times,* December 16, 1931.

[14] See Roy V. Peel and Thomas C. Donnelly: *The 1932 Campaign* (Farrar and Rinehart: New York, 1935).

[15] Senator Blaine of Wisconsin received 13 votes, Dawes 1, and James Wadsworth, Jr., 1. On the first roll call Curtis received 633¾ votes, MacNider 178¾, Harbord 161¾. A majority was 578.

[16] *The Decline of American Liberalism* (Longmans: New York, 1955), p. 269.

[17] David Haroid Kurtzman: *Methods of Controlling Votes in Philadelphia* (University of Pennsylvania Press, 1935).

18 November 25, 1932.

19 See Lawrence Sullivan: *Prelude to Panic* (Statesman Press: Washington, 1936), p. 112.

20 New York *Times,* July 1, 1955.

21 *A Puritan in Babylon* (New York, 1938), p. 296.

CHAPTER 16

1 A. N. Holcombe: *The Middle Classes in American Politics* (Cambridge, Mass., 1940), p. 67.

2 See V. O. Key: *Politics, Parties and Pressure Groups* (3rd ed., New York, 1952), pp. 203-4.

3 Arthur Pound: "As Michigan Goes," *Atlantic,* 159 (1937), p. 78.

4 See Harold R. Bruce: "Presidential Campaigns," *The American Political Scene,* edited by Edward B. Logan (New York, 1936), pp. 155-6.

5 *The Secret Diary of Harold L. Ickes: The First Thousand Days* (New York, 1953), pp. 645-6.

6 Baltimore *Sun,* September 11, 1936.

7 See Elbert Lee Tatum: *The Changed Political Thought of the Negro* (New York, 1951), pp. 139-40.

8 See C. A. H. Thomson: "Research and the Republican Party," *Public Opinion Quarterly,* 3 (1939), pp. 306-13.

9 See Ronald Bridges: "The Republican Program Committee," *Public Opinion Quarterly,* 3 (1939), p. 299.

10 See *Toward A More Responsible Two Party System* (New York, 1950), p. 38.

11 Baltimore *Evening Sun,* November 5, 1936.

12 For the best account of this dramatic episode, see Joseph Alsop and Turner Catledge: *The 168 Days* (New York, 1938).

CHAPTER 17

1 Quoted in Dillon: *Wendell Willkie,* pp. 126-7.

2 See Joseph Barnes: *Willkie* (New York, 1950), pp. 181-2.

3 See *The Economist,* July 6, 1940.

4 See William L. Langer and S. Everett Gleason: *The Challenge to Isolationism* (New York, 1952), p. 670. This is the judgment of Robert Sherwood, expressed in his *Roosevelt and Hopkins* (New York, 1948), p. 174.

5 Dillon: *Wendell Willkie,* p. 220.

6 See Dillon, p. 218.

7 Willkie made speeches in 32 states.

8 See Samuel Lubell: "Post Mortem: Who Elected Roosevelt?" *Saturday Evening Post,* 213 (January 25, 1941), p. 11.

9 *The Future of American Politics* (New York, 1952), p. 132.

10 Barnes, *Willkie,* p. 235.

11 *Autobiography,* p. 645.

12 Minneapolis *Star Journal,* March 28, 1944.

13 See Malcolm Moos and E. W. Kenworthy: "Dr. Shipstead Come to Judgment," *Harper's* (1946), 193, p. 24.

CHAPTER 18

1 See Holcombe: *Our More Perfect Union,* p. 129.

2 Minneapolis *Star Journal,* August 22, 1953.

3 New York *Herald Tribune,* May 24, 1948.

4 See Roy V. Peel: "The 1948 Pre-Convention Campaign," *The Annals* (1948), 259, p. 84.

5 New York *Herald Tribune,* May 24, 1948.
6 *Our More Perfect Union,* p. 125.
7 *The Future of American Politics,* p. 58.
8 Baltimore *Sun,* November 7, 1948.
9 *The American Political System* (Albany, New York, 1952), p. 6.

CHAPTER 19

1 Quoted in Edward N. Doan: *The La Follettes of Wisconsin* (New York, 1947), p. 195.
2 See Jack Steele: "How Stassen Did It," in the New York *Herald Tribune,* April 19, 1948.
3 (New York, 1952), pp. 9-11.
4 New York *Times,* June 2, 1950.
5 New York, New Jersey, Pennsylvania, Missouri, Oregon, Washington, Michigan, Kentucky, Pennsylvania, and Colorado.
6 See account by Murray Snyder in New York *Herald Tribune,* July 1, 1950.
7 New York *Herald Tribune,* July 5, 1950.
8 July 5, 1950.
9 July 5, 1950.
10 July 11, 1950.
11 Taft's vote of 1,642,537 exceeded Dewey's 1948 presidential vote in Ohio by 196,853.

CHAPTER 20

1 New York *Times,* July 3, 1952.
2 New York *Times,* July 4, 1952.
3 See *Official Proceedings,* pp. 27-8, for text.
4 New Bedford *Standard Times,* August 1, 1953.

CHAPTER 21

1 "Who Elected Eisenhower?" *Saturday Evening Post,* January 10, 1953, p. 26.
2 For a detailed and illuminating analysis of the Southern vote see Donald S. Strong: "The Presidential Election in the South, 1952," *Journal of Politics,* 17 (1955), 343-89.
3 See V. O. Key: "Solid South: Cracked or Broken," *The New Republic* (December 1, 1952), 9.
4 New York *Herald Tribune,* July 29, 1952.
5 See Lubell: "Who Elected Eisenhower?"
6 See Angus Campbell, Gerald Gurin, and Warren Miller: *The Voter Decides* (Evanston, Illinois, 1954), 51.
7 Privately the Survey Research Center of the University of Michigan came up with an accurate forecast of the popular-vote breakdown, but since forecasting was not a part of this agency's 1952 study, this was kept in strict confidence.
8 In Baltimore, for example, Stevenson carried the 72 Negro precincts (precincts with more than 50 percent of the population Negro) by slightly better than 72 percent of the two-party vote.
9 Speech of Carroll Newton of Batten, Barton, Durstine and Osborn, time buyer for the Republican national committee for the 1952 and 1954 campaigns, Washington, D.C., September 8, 1955.
10 See the *Standard Times,* September 26, 1952. Brewer denied that his opposition to Lodge was based upon the Senator's prominent role in depriving Taft of the nomination. He insisted that Lodge had "bolted" the party by "his vote for the Truman-Socialist New Deal."

[11] See Samuel Lubell, quoted in *Wall Street Journal,* October 25, 1955.

[12] St. Paul *Pioneer Press,* November 7, 1952.

[13] See his study: "Is There a Republican Majority?" *Political Trends, 1952-1956* (New York, 1954).

[14] Harold Gauer: *How to Win in Politics* (New York, 1946), p. 185. Interest in the methods has also produced a number of novels on the advertising profession and politics. See John G. Schneider: *The Golden Kazoo* (New York, 1956); and Frederick Pohl and C. M. Kornbluth: *The Space Merchants* (Boston, 1952).

[15] See David Riesman and Nathan Glazer: "Intellectuals and the Discontented Classes," *Partisan Review* (1955).

[16] Vol. 32, December, 1954, p. 41.

[17] See G. Edward Janosik: "Suburban Balance of Power," *The American Quarterly* (1955), pp. 132-4.

[18] Louis Harris: *Is There a Republican Majority?* (New York, Harper's, 1954), pp. 138-9. See also E. Gartly Jaco and Ivan Belknap: "Is a New Family Form Emerging in the Urban Fringe?" *American Sociological Review,* 18 (October, 1953), pp. 551-7.

[19] See article by Ed Winge in the Detroit *Free Press,* April 17, 1955.

[20] Address before the Republican national committee, January 17, 1953.

[21] See Earl Roger Kruschke: "The Woman Voter: An Analysis Based Upon Personal Interview" (Public Affairs Press: Washington, D.C., 1955).

[22] See Malcolm Moos: *Politics, Presidents, and Coattails,* pp. 79-81.

[23] See Olive Shadgett: "A History of the Republican Party in Georgia," *Georgia Review,* 7 (1953), p. 428.

[24] See article by Tom O'Neill, Baltimore *Evening Sun,* January 30, 1956.

[25] O. Douglas Weeks: "Republicanism and Conservatism in the South," *Southwestern Social Science Quarterly* (December, 1955), p. 254.

[26] "The Presidential Election in the South," *Journal of Politics,* pp. 384-9.

[27] *A Two-Party South* (University of North Carolina Press: Chapel Hill, 1952), p. 133. The obstacles to a real grass-roots two-party system in the South are extensively treated in this volume and are also laid out at considerable length in V. O. Key's *Southern Politics* (Alfred A. Knopf: New York, 1949). See particularly Chapter 13 for a discussion of the Republican party.

[28] See Marie Chatham: "The National Chairmen from Hanna to Farley" (unpublished doctoral dissertation, University of Maryland, College Park, 1952).

[29] New York *Times,* September 15, 1955.

[30] *The Price of Union,* pp. 342-3.

[31] *Backstage in 1912,* p. 211.

[32] E. E. Schattschneider, in an address before the American Political Science Association at Boulder, Colorado, September 7, 1955.

[33] New York *Times,* September 11, 1955.

[34] See Alan Drury, New York *Times,* September 15, 1955.

[35] Confidential Report on Minnesota Outcome, 1954 Elections, submitted by Val Bjornson to Leonard Hall, November 17, 1954.

[36] See James L. McConaughy, Jr.: "While Eisenhower Proposes, the Old Guard Disposes," *Life,* 36 (June 21, 1954), p. 125.

[37] See Thomas O'Neill, Baltimore *Evening Sun,* November 3, 1953.

[38] Quoted in *Life,* June 21, 1954, p. 133.

[39] Speech before the Abraham Lincoln National Republican Club, a right-wing group that describes itself as "conservative grass-root Republican." See Baltimore *Sun,* February 12, 1956.

[40] See Arthur N. Holcombe: "Presidential Leadership and the Party System," *The Yale Review,* 43 (1954), p. 325.

[41] Quoted in New York *Herald Tribune,* January 30, 1956.

[42] See Paul David: "Comparative State Politics and the Problem of Party

Realignment," in *Research Frontiers in Politics and Government,* The Brookings Institution (Washington, D.C., 1955), p. 191.

[43] Holcombe: "Presidential Leadership and the Party System," p. 335.

[44] *Human Events,* 13 (January 21, 1956), p. 3.

[45] See Russell Baker in New York *Times,* February 13, 1955.

[46] See Hadley Cantril: *Public Opinion, 1935-1946* (Princeton University Press, 1951).

[47] *Public Opinion, 1935-1946,* p. 631.

[48] Quoted in *Christian Science Monitor,* January 17, 1956.

[49] New York *Times,* January 15, 1956.

[50] *Virginia Quarterly,* 31 (1955), p. 48.

[51] Baltimore *Sun,* November 2, 1955.

[52] New York *Herald Tribune,* January 27, 1956.

[53] "Modernizing the Republican Party," New York *Herald Tribune,* June 28, 1951.

[54] "The Future of the Republican Party," *The Virginia Quarterly,* 28 (1952), p. 177.

[55] New York *Herald Tribune,* January 12, 1956.

[56] What the Southern governors were worried about was that allegedly the August, 1955, imports of Japanese textiles were at an annual rate that "represented sufficient cloth to provide jobs for an estimated 19,000 textile workers." Assuming this to be correct, the 19,000 workers would be a bare four percent of the average number (472,726) of textile mill workers in the South Atlantic states.

[57] Quoted by Arthur Krock in New York *Times,* October 20, 1955.

[58] Walter Lippmann in the New York *Herald Tribune,* January 12, 1956.

Index

ABOUT THE AUTHOR

MALCOLM MOOS was born in St. Paul, Minnesota, in 1916, of Scotch, German, and French ancestry. He is a graduate of the University of Minnesota, a Ph.D. from the University of California, and has taught at the universities of Alabama, Wyoming, and Michigan. At the age of thirty-six he attained a full professorship (of Political Science) on the faculty of Johns Hopkins University, where he now teaches. From 1953 to 1955 he was consultant to the Brookings Institution in Washington.

Author of *Politics, Presidents and Coattails*, and co-author of *A Grammar of American Politics* and *Power through Purpose*, he was co-editor of the five-volume study, *Presidential Nominating Politics in 1952*, and has been a contributor to *Harper's*, *The Yale Review*, *The American Scholar*, and various professional journals.

The son of a Midwest "Bull Moose" Republican who was executive secretary to a Minnesota governor at the age of nineteen, Malcolm Moos has been active in Republican politics since childhood, and has known every major-party presidential nominee from Calvin Coolidge to General Eisenhower. In Maryland he has been chairman of the Republican State Central Committee for Baltimore City since 1954, and he has been a steady delegate to Republican national conventions. He now lives, with his wife Tracy and their three small children, in a converted farmhouse overlooking a lake on the edge of Baltimore.